D1596831

BUSINESS AND GOVERNMENT IN AMERICA SINCE 1870

A *Twelve-Volume Anthology*
of Scholarly Articles

Series Editor
ROBERT F. HIMMELBERG
Fordham University

A GARLAND SERIES

131320

SERIES CONTENTS

VOLUME

10

EVOLUTION OF ANTITRUST POLICY FROM JOHNSON TO BUSH

Edited with introductions by

ROBERT F. HIMMELBERG

GARLAND PUBLISHING, Inc.
New York & London
1994

Library of Congress Cataloging-in-Publication Data

Evolution of antitrust policy from Johnson to Bush / edited with
introductions by Robert F. Himmelberg.
     p.   cm. — (Business and government in America since
1870 ; v. 10)
    Includes bibliographical references.
    ISBN 0–8153–1412–4 (alk. paper)
    1. Trusts, Industrial—Government policy—United States.
2. Consolidation and merger of corporations—Government
policy—United States.   3. Industry and state—United States.
4. Antitrust law—Economic aspects—United States.
I. Himmelberg, Robert F.   II. Series.
HD2795.E95   1994
338.8'0973'09045—dc20   93–47499
                                                  CIP

Printed on acid-free, 250-year-life paper
Manufactured in the United States of America

CONTENTS

Series Introduction

This compilation of articles provides a very broad and representative selection of the scholarly literature found in learned journals on the subject of government-business relations in the age of industry, the period since 1870. The scope of this collection is wide, covering all the arenas of business-government interaction. Sectorially, the focus is on manufacturing and transportation, upon whose rapid expansion after the Civil War the modern industrial economy was founded.

For the volumes covering the years from 1870 to 1965 (Volumes I through IX) it has been possible, while exercising selectivity, to include a very high proportion of everything published within the past thirty years. This literature is found largely in historical journals. More selectivity had to be employed for Volumes X through XII, which cover the period since 1965. Historians have not yet trodden much on the ground of the very recent past but social scientists and legal scholars have offered abundant materials, so abundant as to require a relatively severe selectivity. By choosing articles that appear to have a long-term analytical value and by excluding those too narrow in scope, too preoccupied with methodological questions or otherwise unsuitable for a non-specialized audience, an extensive and accessible body of writing has, however, been assembled for the post-1965 period, mainly from economics and legal periodicals.

The volumes are designed to contain articles relating to a particular period and to one or more topics within a period. The literature of business-government relations has four logically distinct major topics: antitrust, regulation, promotion, and cooperation. These topics define distinctive aspects of the relationship. Yet, the distinctions sometimes in practice blur, the ostensible, publicly proclaimed purposes of policy sometimes differing from the actually intended purposes or the actual outcomes.

Antitrust policy emerges in Volume I, which covers the era 1870–1900 when big business appeared, and figures prominently throughout the series. Several volumes are devoted entirely to it. Uniquely American, at least until relatively recently, antitrust policy has a complex history and much of what scholars have discovered about its origin and evolution is recorded only in the articles gathered in this collection. The literature reproduced here makes clear that the intent and impact of antitrust policy has varied enormously during its one-hundred-year history, which dates from the Sherman Act of 1890. Tension between competing objectives has existed from the outset. Should the "trusts" be broken up on the grounds that super-corporations inevitably conflict with democratic government and entrepreneurial opportunity? Or should only "bad trusts", those guilty of crushing competitors through unfair methods, suffer dissolution? Is cartelistic behavior always an illegal restraint of trade, or should it sometimes be tolerated if it helps small business to survive? Put most broadly, should the aim of antitrust policy be simply promoting competition, or should other conflicting social and economic values be recognized?

Business regulation also arose during the early stages of industrialization, appearing at the federal level with the enactment of the Interstate Commerce Act in 1887. The term "regulation" is used here to denote government policies intended, not to promote or restore competition, but to require specific behavior from business. The classic justification for regulation was the argument that in some situations the public interest could be served only through governmental prescription, that in some instances a remedy simply could not be obtained through the workings of the marketplace. Theoretically there are two such instances. The first occurs in the case of "natural monopoly," market situations in which competition would be wasteful and competing firms do not and should not exist. Railroads and public utilities were early identified as industries of this sort and were the first targets of government regulation. Would-be regulators early discovered a second justification for applying the regulatory approach, the situation in which competition fails to provide rival firms with incentives to avoid methods that may injure public health or well being. The argument found early expression in regulation of the meat-packing industry and has over the course of the twentieth century created a remarkable body of federal regulatory practices. The history of regulation, however, has not unfolded, any more than the history of antitrust, according to the logic of theory. It has been determined by the interplay between many factors, including the ideas of reformers, the complaints of those who have felt injured, policy rivalries among businessmen themselves, and the capacity or incapacity of government to execute planned reform. A major focus of recent literature on regulation, and to an extent on antitrust also, is the thesis of capture, the notion that regulatory efforts have often fallen captive to the interests they were intended to oppose.

The third theme of relations between government and business, promotion and encouragement, also emerged during the initial stages of the industrial era. Railroad subsidies abounded during the age of building the transcontinentals, of course, and protective tariffs were almost as old as the Republic itself. In the early twentieth century government support of trade expansion abroad enlarged and gradually became a major thread of government policy. Resembling promotion but logically distinct in many respects is the fourth category of business-government interaction, the area of cooperative relationships. Few scholars, even those who believe ongoing conflict has chiefly characterized business-government relations, would deny that cooperation has occurred at certain points, as during American participation in the major wars of the twentieth century. But in recent years many writers who conceive of business-government relations as taking place within a "corporatist" framework have perceived the scope and continuity of cooperative tendencies as very broad.

These four categories describe the subjects or topics around which scholarly investigation of business-government relations has revolved. There is, however, another approach to analyzing the literature of this relationship, one in which we ask about a writer's interpretive perspective, the conceptualizations the writer brings to the subject. All historians and social scientists, including those who created the literature collected here, adopt an interpretive standpoint from which to view society and its workings. An interpretive standpoint is a way of understanding the structure of society and the way those structural elements relate and interact; in other words, it is a "model" of society. Several rival models have competed for acceptance among scholars in recent times. Readers will be better equipped for informed reading of the literature assembled in these volumes if they are knowledgeable about these interpretive standpoints and the aim here therefore is to define the most important of these and give them appropriate labels.

Until the 1950s the prevailing interpretation of business-government relations—indeed, of American history generally— was the progressive viewpoint. The term progressive refers in the first place to the reform ideology and activity of the early twentieth century, the period before World War I. The perspective of the progressive generation continued for many years to dominate historical writing, not only on the period itself but on the whole of American history. According to the progressive perspective, the rise of big business during the late nineteenth and early twentieth

centuries created a radical shift in the balance of economic and
political power in America in favor of concentrated wealth. The
rise of the "trusts", the powerful firms that came to predominate in
many industries in the years after 1880, and the creation of cartels
and other arrangements for suppressing competition, threatened
independent capitalists and consumers with raw economic exploitation. This concentration of economic power threatened to utterly
suborn representative political institutions as well and reduce
American democracy to a plutocracy. In the progressive view the
predominating tone of business-government relations was therefore necessarily antagonistic and conflictual.

The progressive paradigm became deeply embedded in the
American consciousness. Reformist politicians have often reverted
to it in shaping their ideological and rhetorical appeals. Franklin
D. Roosevelt's attack in the campaign of 1936 upon "economic
royalists" and John Kennedy's denunciation in 1962 of Big Steel
during the controversy over price guidelines as "utterly contemp-
tuous of the public interest" are vivid examples. The progressive
outlook is evidently a persistent element in the popular historical
consciousness. The power of the progressive conception of American history is in fact readily confirmed by reference to the way
twentieth-century history is periodized, in textbooks and popular
histories, into epochs of reform (the Progressive, New Deal, Fair
Deal and Great Society periods) and of reaction (the Twenties, the
Eisenhower and Reagan eras).

But if the progressive interpretation of business government
relations retains some force among some historians and in the
consciousness of liberal opinion makers and the public, its hold on
much of the academic mind has long since weakened. A reaction
among historians and other academics against the progressive
paradigm emerged soon after the end of the Second World War and
gathered force during the 1950s. The reaction was especially sharp
among historians writing business history. Writing at a time when
a reinvigorated American economy appeared to have overcome the
doldrums of the 1930s and to be demonstrating the superiority of
capitalism over other systems, energetic business and economic
historians completely revised the progressive interpretation of the
founders of American big business. The revisionists interpreted
the founders not as greedy robber barons but as heroes of the
entrepreneurial spirit, the spirit of enterprise and productivity.
This revisionist interpretation proved too one-dimensional and
celebratory to be maintained without modification. Revisionism,
however, did succeed in thoroughly discrediting the progressive
point of view. This circumstance, together with the impact of
interpretive concepts emanating from post-war social science,

moved historians to replace the progressive paradigm with a new and more sophisticated framework for understanding American political economy, the pluralist framework.

Pluralism as the dominant interpretive mode replaced progressivism in the 1950s and 60s. Speaking broadly, the pluralist model understands public policy as the result of struggle between economic and social groups. A major by-product of industrialization is the sharpening of differences between groups playing distinctive economic roles and a heightened articulation of self-interested goals and purposes on the part of such groups. Thus, government-business relations, that is, the shape of government policies towards business, are the result of rivalries among the major interest groups, business, labor, consumers, and so on. But the nature of the struggle is complex because the major groups are themselves divided into more or less rivalrous sub-groups. Business itself is divided; both intra- and inter-industry rivalries exist, sometimes in acute forms. Government policy is not merely the result of nonbusiness groups seeking to shape that policy but also of some business interests seeking to impose their own wishes on others.

During the 1960s pluralist interpretation became more complex. One important source of this heightened complexity was what some commentators have called the "organizational" outlook. Again influenced by currents in American social science, this time sociology, practitioners employing the organizational perspective are struck by the ever-increasing importance of large bureaucratic organizations in American life since the onset of industrialization. Business has continuously evolved in terms of an ever larger role for the large corporation, but other spheres, including government and the professions, also are organized in terms of large hierarchical bureaucracies. Borrowing from Weberian sociological traditions, writers impressed by the organizational perspective have explored the thesis that large bureaucracies wherever situated have similar requirements and tend to develop in those who manage them similar values and expectations. Thus, this brand of pluralism stresses the extent to which group leaders, including the managers and technicians who run the large corporations, developed accommodative as well as merely self-seeking motives. Business leaders, many of them at least, came to share certain values, such as respect for stability in the overall economy, which leads them to seek harmonious and cooperative relationships between interest groups and between them and the government. Government is assigned the role, in this construct, of facilitating and stimulating cooperative modes of behavior and umpiring conflicts. In the literature on business and government, figures who have advocated this kind of polity are often dubbed "corporatists" or "corporate liberals." Broadly defined, corporatism is the practice of cooperation between government and the corporate world to resolve economic issues. The existence and the importance of corporatist relationships has been one of the major emphases of recent scholarship but there is much disagreement as to the intentions of its practitioners and its impact. Some scholars have interpreted corporatism in a more or less positive light, as an ideology and a practice entailing cooperation rather than conflict between government and business, as an alternative to an adversarial relationship, a way of obtaining desirable economic performance from business without resorting to governmental coercion.

But others, especially but not only those writing in the vein of the "New Left", have argued that members of the corporate elite have frequently pursued their own narrow interests under the cover of ostensibly cooperative endeavors. The New Leftists emerged in the 1960s, expounding a more radical criticism of business than the progressive-liberal historians had advanced. The New Leftists doubted or denied outright that the American system was pluralist at all in any meaningful sense. Control of public policy might appear as a contest between social groups, but in fact one group, or rather class, those who controlled big business, enjoyed such lopsided power that the contest was apparently not real. Behind the facade of political infighting over government policy toward business, the masters of the corporate world quietly steered events toward outcomes which cemented in place control of the economy by monopoly capital.

These four conceptualizations, the progressive, the pluralist, the corporatist, and the New Leftist, are essentially theories of the structure and process of American political economy. However, rarely are researchers slavishly devoted to a theoretical perspective. Thus, those who see, in the progressive vein, an ongoing conflictual relationship between the people and business sometimes argue against the reformers and in favor of the businessmen. Even more significant and widespread is the conclusion of many writers using the pluralist or corporatist modes of interpretation, that regulation has not fostered equity and economic progress but rather has hardened the economy's vital arteries. Pluralists initially assumed that policies arising from a political arena to which all organized interests have access will inevitably achieve benign results, that the policy outputs will construct a system of "countervailing power" among organized interest groups. The assumption of acceptable outcomes is still prevalent, but a skeptical version of the results of interest group rivalries became manifest in the late

1960s, holding that both in origin and ongoing impact, business regulation was too often subject to "capture." In this view, regulatory measures and agencies and other policies seeking to guide business behavior toward balanced and generally acceptable outcomes readily fall under the control of the very interests they were intended to regulate.

There has emerged in recent years still another approach to the origin and process of social-economic policy that has been applied to the business-government connection. In this interpretation of the connection, a few examples of which will be found in articles collected here, emphasis is placed on the relative autonomy of government administrators and regulators. Seen by the pluralists as merely the creatures of the organizational struggles that result in public policies, in this new view regulators are seen as possessing substantial room for independent action. Thus the state is not merely to be seen as a passive receptor and executor of outcomes that social forces determine but as having a partially autonomous role which the officers of the state presumably will use to extend their own interests rather than the interests articulated by social groups.

These categories, progressivism, pluralism, corporatism, Leftism and the "autonomous officialdom" viewpoint, represent the major schools of thought and interpretation that readers will discover in the literature reproduced in these volumes. Writers investigating specific historical incidents, trends or problems have, in most cases, written through the framework provided by one or another of these interpretive models. As an alert reader will discover, most writers do have certain assumptions about the structure and dynamics of social relationships, and these assumptions stem from one of the models that have been described.

Interpretation of the relationship between business and government in the age of industry has given rise to a literature that is large and complex. It presents a stimulating intellectual challenge and is certainly relevant for anyone seeking understanding of contemporary business-government relations and endeavoring to predict, or to shape, their future course.

INTRODUCTION

The final period in the story of business-government relations is the subject of Volumes X to XII. It is the preserve of economists and legal scholars. Historians have as yet contributed little perspective to this aspect of recent history. A survey of the literature in the social science and legal periodicals, however, provides abundant materials on what appear to be the major developments in business-government interaction over the past quarter century. Whether these evident developments will seem as important to future observers as they do now or will give place to underlying themes not yet in clear focus remains to be seen. Up to this point, those investigating the recent history of political economy have emphasized four major themes or lines of development. The first theme is the new direction antitrust policy took during the 1970s and 1980s. A second theme is the wave of deregulation of industries subject to traditional regulatory practices that swept through government during the same period. This theme is developed in Volume XI. A third theme is the coming of new kinds of regulation. Concomitantly with deregulation, and somewhat paradoxically, political pressures developed that persuaded government to extensively regulate business behavior with regard to consumerist, environmental and safety issues. This theme, the new regulation, together with a fourth theme, the growth of demands for an "industrial policy" to deal with the problems of lagging economic growth and severe foreign competition, are taken up in Volume XII.

This volume presents a substantial array of articles detailing the evolution of antitrust policy. Until the 1970s the Justice Department pursued the antitrust policy lines inherited from the postwar era, treating horizontal mergers and price-fixing severely. The doctrine that mergers should be judged by whether they increased concentration of an industry was, however, increasingly challenged by the "New Learning" of the Chicago School, which argued that merger activity should be judged solely by its impact on efficiency. The argument would have a profound effect on antitrust policy during the 1980s.

Antitrust liberalization was put forward as a remedy for the declining capacity of American industry to compete. During the 1950s and 1960s, the argument went, horizontal mergers (mergers between firms in the same line of business) routinely were prevented by antitrust doctrines predicated on the theory that a competitive market structure (one composed of many relatively equal firms) produced better economic results than an oligopolitic structure (one dominated by a handful of very large firms). Heavy academic guns pummelled this position in the 70s and sought to secure acceptance of antitrust guidelines that would judge mergers on the grounds of whether they promoted efficiency and technical progress, not merely whether they might create a more concentrated market structure. This attack on an antitrust policy guided by structural criteria was initiated by academic economists and legal theorists committed to the thesis that free markets nearly always produce economic results superior to markets shaped or modified by government interference. By the time of the Reagan Administration, the argument was achieving concrete results as antitrust guidelines were revised and strictures on merger activity were relaxed.

For more than four years the FCC has been considering a proposed rule to require the breakup of local newspaper-TV combinations. The proposal's fate has been instructive.

The FCC's nonbattle
against media monopoly

STEPHEN R. BARNETT

■ Consolidation of ownership is one of the dominant facts of mass media operations in this country. Newspaper chains now control more than 60 per cent of the nation's daily newspaper circulation [see "The Rush to Chain Ownership," Nov./Dec.] and are fast acquiring the rest. At the local level, daily newspaper monopoly prevails almost everywhere. And there are some ninety-three instances in some eighty-five American cities where the owner of the daily paper also owns a local TV station.

The existing anti-trust laws, even assuming the Department of Justice enforced them against the media, would have a limited effect in deterring concentration. They do not apply to newspaper chains, since newspapers in different cities are not in competition with one another, and they do not reach newspaper monopolies, unless the monopoly is created or maintained by improper means. Their impact on newspaper-TV combinations has never been tested; it would probably have to be fought out, in any event, through lengthy trials on a city-by-city basis.

The Federal Communications Commission,

Stephen R. Barnett is a law professor at the University of California at Berkeley.

however, almost certainly does have authority to decline to license TV stations to the owners of daily papers in the same city. In fact, for more than four years the FCC has been considering a proposed rule to require the breakup of these combinations. This is the most significant attempt to deal with media concentration in this country since 1941-44, when the FCC similarly examined newspaper ownership of radio stations (and ultimately declined to adopt a rule prohibiting such ownership, promising instead to deal with the problem on a case-by-case basis—which it generally has not done). The handling of the newspaper-TV issue by the FCC deserves attention, and so does the treatment of the story by the news media.

In the thirty years since the FCC last made a broad-scale inquiry into newspaper-broadcast combinations, two developments have transformed the media landscape. The rise of TV and the near-total development of newspaper monopoly have made it clear that any concern over media concentration must focus on newspaper-TV combinations. FCC Chairman Dean Burch, concurring in the FCC rule-making proposal (but without indicating how he would eventually vote), has put the problem succinctly: "There are only a few daily newspapers in each large city and their

January/February, 1973 □ 43

1

numbers are declining. There are only a few powerful VHF stations in these cities and their numbers cannot be increased. Equally important, the evidence shows that the very large majority of people get their news information from these two limited sources. Here then are the guts of the matter."

Concern over media concentration, and newspaper-TV combinations in particular, was not a bureaucratic figment of the FCC. Vice President Agnew, his political motivation notwithstanding, raised a real issue when he declared in November, 1969, "The American people should be made aware of the trend toward monopolization of the great public information vehicles and the concentration of more and more power over public opinion in fewer and fewer hands." He then went on to attack newspaper broadcast combinations in particular (albeit only those of the Washington *Post* and New York *Times*).

The President's Commission on Violence recommended in its 1969 report that "private and governmental institutions encourage the development of competing news media and discourage increased concentration of control over existing media." Hubert Humphrey—who, like Spiro Agnew, has since dropped the subject—wrote in a syndicated newspaper column in December, 1969, that "the really serious questions involving the media should be continually raised," and included among those questions, "Is there too much concentration of media ownership?" and "Should newspapers be prevented from owning broadcast stations in the same city?" Congress itself, in passing the Newspaper Preservation Act in 1970, espoused a policy designed to preserve separate ownership of the two newspapers in a city in order to provide "separate and independent voices"; that policy applies at least as strongly in favor of separate ownership of a newspaper and a TV station where there is no need to sacrifice economic competition through an anti-trust exemption.

The most potent expressions of concern have come from the Department of Justice and, in response, from the FCC. In August, 1968, the Department, in a filing with the FCC, pointed to "the existing concentration of media ownership in many . . . cities" and recommended that the

Commission do something about it, namely adopt a rule divorcing the ownership of daily newspapers and TV stations within the same city. The FCC entertained "comments" on the proposal for a prolonged period—four times extending the deadline at the request of the National Association of Broadcasters. Finally, in April, 1970, instead of making a decision, the Commission simply repeated the proposal, this time as its own, for more comments.

Specifically, the FCC proposed to adopt a rule requiring the owners of daily newspapers and TV stations in the same city—and also of daily newspapers and radio stations, of which there are some 230 instances—to sell either the station or the newspaper within five years. Citing a wide variety of surveys, the FCC declared: "In view of the primary position of the daily newspaper of general circulation and the television broadcast station as sources of news and other information, and discussion of public affairs, particularly with respect to local matters, it is not desirable that these two organs of mass communication should be under the same control in any community."

Far from being Draconian, the proposed rule would have a gentle, cushioned impact. By allowing divestiture in five years, it would "forfeit" no broadcast licenses. By banning only *local* combinations it would produce a trading process between combination owners in different cities. A special dispensation from the tax laws would waive the payment of capital-gains tax on sales or exchanges resulting from the rule. In addition, the rule would be subject to waiver in individual cases, specifically if it was shown that the newspaper or TV station as in the case of UHF could not survive without subsidies from its local cross-media affiliate. (Few if any of the affected newspapers, however, will need such subsidies; of the approximately ninety-three newspaper-TV combinations, some sixty-three involve the only daily newspaper publisher in town. In eight others, the TV licensee is one of two publishers who share a monopoly of the local newspaper market by virtue of a joint-operating agreement. In all the remaining cases except New York City—where the paper involved is the *Daily News*, which seems solvent—there are now only two competing pub-

2

lishers, each of which typically has the morning or evening market to himself, a situation in which the paper should be profitable if it even remotely deserves to be.)

Thus the rule would do little to bring new or independent owners into the mass media, but it would at least diversify the control of the dominant media outlets in each city. The result would be greater diversity and competition in local news coverage, in editorial points of view on local issues, in concepts of media service, and of course in the economic sphere. There would be a freer flow of news, commentary, and criticism on the many stories in which one of the local media outlets, or

"Legal badminton between the Commission and the courts . . ."

its owner, was interested or involved. One can see advantages on both ends, for example, if the Washington *Post* were to swap its TV station in Washington for the one in Chicago owned by the Chicago *Tribune*, or for one of the newspaper-owned stations in Dallas or Houston.

After reiterating in April, 1970, the proposal made by the Justice Department in 1968, the FCC started all over again with another protracted process of receiving comments. This included four more extensions of time granted at the request of the NAB and the American Newspaper Publishers Assn. before the process finally came to an end in August, 1971. It is now more than a year since then, more than two and a half years since the FCC proposed the rule, and more than four years since the original proposal by the Justice Department. Yet the FCC still has not acted. And according to a report in *Television Digest* in mid-September, 1972, the Commission has put the newspaper-broadcast proposal "on the back burner."

The reasons for the delay are not hard to find. The FCC's proposal has been the target of all-out opposition by the newspaper and broadcast

industries. The NAB alone has raised and spent more than $300,000 in the fight. It has hired Lee Loevinger, who resigned as an FCC commissioner in 1968 to represent broadcast interests, as special counsel to present its case to the FCC. "Studies" opposing the rule have been commissioned from the academic world and elsewhere, and scores of opposing comments prepared by Washington lawyers have descended on the FCC. (ANPA told the Commission that opposing comments have come from "more than 150 responsible and informed publishers, broadcasters, press associations, and other spokesmen for the nation's newspapers and broadcast stations" while the proposed rules "have been supported so far by a *total* of only five pleadings.") Meanwhile, the industries have lobbied extensively to arouse opposition to the proposal from Congress and the White House. And through it all the nation's news media, with only the barest exceptions, have somehow overlooked the story.

Under cover of the media blackout, the industry's lobbying campaign has paid off handsomely at the White House. The Administration's two chief spokesmen on media matters, communications director Herbert Klein and Clay T. Whitehead, director of the Office of Telecommunications Policy, have made the circuit of broadcasters' and publishers' conventions expressing White House opposition to the FCC's proposal. At an NAB convention in 1970, for example, Klein praised "newspaper ownership of stations." Whitehead told the ANPA convention last April that adoption of the proposal "would be a great mistake," adding: "We are much more concerned about performance than who gets to own what." President Nixon himself may have conveyed the same message during the private meeting he held with thirty broadcast executives at the White House on June 22. (In supporting the industry's position, the White House repudiates the public stance of its own Justice Department, which has continued to urge the FCC to adopt the proposed rule.)

The net result of all this has been to keep the issue of local media concentration in suspension—to preserve the status quo—by a game of legal badminton between the Commission and the courts. With the unique exception of the case of WHDH

3

in Boston [see "Did Boston's *Herald Traveler* Have to Die?" July/Aug.], the Commission and the courts have taken the position on challenges to renewal of broadcast licenses held by local daily newspapers that the issue of "undue concentration" should not be considered on a case-by-case basis since nonrenewal would mean "forfeiture of the license." Instead, they have said, concentration should be considered in the context of an across-the-board rule such as the FCC has proposed, since that would allow for sale or exchange of the licenses involved (or of the newspapers).

In February, 1970, for example, the Federal Court of Appeals in Washington upheld the FCC's renewal of one of the broadcast licenses held by the media empire of the Mormon Church in Salt Lake City, but only because the FCC in the rule-making proceeding "is seriously engaged in a sweeping policy review" of local media concentration. Judge Edward Tamm, concurring in the decision, pointed to the "disheartening statistics describing the marked trend toward concentration of media ownership," warned that "the risk inherent in allowing these accretions of power to persist unchecked is clear," and emphasized that he was voting to sustain the renewal "solely because" of the "single, crucial fact" that the FCC was considering the issue in rule-making proceedings—proceedings which he thought "offer some hope that the Commission will finally come to grips with the grave problems inherent in the rising concentration of ownership in the mass media. . . ."

Last June—more than two years later—another panel of the same court similarly upheld the FCC's action in renewing, without a hearing on the concentration issue, the TV license held by the *Evening Star* in Washington. Again the court relied on the fact that "the FCC is currently investigating—in the context of the rule-making proceeding—whether it should adopt rules which would require divestiture by newspapers or other multiple owners in a given market." But the FCC, after more than four years, continues to stall the proceeding.

The objective of those who oppose the rule, both within and outside the Commission, is apparently to keep the proceeding on ice at least until next summer. By then the FCC will have lost Commissioner Nicholas Johnson, who strongly favors the rule (his term ends in June).

Meanwhile, opponents of the proposed rule urge the FCC to reject it primarily on the ground that the subject should be handled by a case-by-case approach. Until recently, this was easy because that approach had never been tried. The approach may now be examined, however, in light of one application of it. This is the case of KRON-TV, the San Francisco TV station owned by the Chronicle Publishing Co., publisher of the city's only morning newspaper (and partner, since 1965, in a joint-operating agreement with the city's only evening newspaper, the Hearst-owned *Examiner*). The case involves charges of distortion of news on the TV station to promote the owner's newspaper interests; of distortion of the newspaper's contents to promote the owner's TV interests; and of distortion of TV news to promote the owner's interest in obtaining cable-TV franchises in the San Francisco area.

Ordinarily, allegations that a broadcast licensee

"To extend the license regardless of challenges . . ."

has engaged in self-interested news distortion will not be given a hearing by the FCC. This is not because the Commission condones such conduct; on the contrary, it has declared that "slanting of the news amounts to a fraud upon the public and is patently inconsistent with the licensee's obligation to operate his facilities in the public interest." The reason lies, rather, in the FCC's declaration that it will "eschew a censor's role, including efforts to establish news distortion in situations where Government intervention would constitute a worse danger than the possible rigging itself." The FCC therefore will not inquire into alleged news distortion unless presented with a

4

special sort of evidence. Nor will it hold up renewal of a broadcast license on this ground unless there is "substantial extrinsic evidence of motives inconsistent with the public interest," and "unless the extrinsic evidence of possible deliberate distortion or staging of the news which is brought to our attention involves the licensee, including its principals, top management, or news management."

To illustrate the kind of "substantial extrinsic evidence" that would meet this test, the FCC has regularly offered one example: "testimony of a station employee concerning his instructions from management," or documentary evidence of such instructions—"For example, if it is asserted by a newsman that he was directed by the licensee to slant the news, that would raise serious questions as to the character qualifications of the licensee. . . ." Not many newsmen will be willing to blow the whistle on their employers by presenting the FCC with the required evidence of news-distortion directives from the station's management, an act that must be done publicly and is very likely to ruin the career of the newsman who does it.

The KRON case is uniquely significant because that is what happened. Albert Kihn, a news cameraman who worked for KRON for eight years, became disenchanted with events in the newsroom, kept a diary and collected evidence, and in the fall of 1968, when the station's license was up for renewal, told his story to the FCC. (Kihn has not since been regularly employed in broadcast journalism.) On the basis of Kihn's allegations, the FCC held up renewal of the license and ordered a hearing to determine whether "the licensee has attempted to slant news and public affairs programs to serve its business interests."

The hearing was held in San Francisco for thirty-seven days in 1970. On March 1, 1971, the FCC's hearing examiner, Chester F. Naumowicz, Jr., resolved all the issues in favor of the KRON management and recommended renewal of the license. The FCC must review this recommendation and make the final decision (subject to court appeal), but as yet has not done so. Meanwhile, KRON continues to operate on the license issued in 1965 and not renewed in 1968.

The facts in the KRON case, as determined by the hearing examiner, have a good deal of relevance to the FCC's proposed rule on newspaper-broadcast combinations. Notwithstanding his conclusion in favor of the station owner, the examiner's report demonstrates two things: 1) common ownership of more than one media outlet in the same city, and of a daily newspaper and TV station in particular, does have harmful effects; and 2) the case-by-case approach is ill-suited to dealing with them.

The hearing examiner, even while exonerating the KRON management of any "abuse" resulting from common ownership of the newspaper and TV station, determined that the public had been harmed in one important instance. This occurred in September, 1965, when the *Chronicle* and Hearst were about to put into effect the joint-operating agreement between their San Francisco newspapers. The agreement, signed in October, 1964, but kept secret, provided not only for joint publication of the *Chronicle* in the morning and Hearst's *Examiner* in the afternoon (with a 50-50 split of all profits from either paper), but also for elimination of what was then San Francisco's third daily, the *News-Call Bulletin,* also published by Hearst.

As the hearing examiner found, the story of the upcoming "merger" began to break in the week before the eventual announcement by the two publishers on Sept. 10, 1965. During this period two San Francisco TV stations and various radio stations covered the story, reporting "such things as meetings of unions which might be affected, and alterations on the physical plants of the newspapers involved." But there was no coverage in any of San Francisco's three newspapers prior to the Sept. 10 announcement, except that on Sept. 5 "the *Chronicle* published a reference to it based on a story from the New York *Times* wire service." Meanwhile, "no mention of the matter was made on KRON-TV" before the publishers' announcement.

The examiner found, as indeed was admitted, that KRON's lack of coverage resulted from orders by the station's chief executive. He found that when the story began to break on the other stations, KRON newsmen had "importuned their superiors for permission to cover the story," but were denied such permission. The station's chief

5

executive, although a vice president of Chronicle Publishing Co., was unaware of the joint-operating agreement and telephoned the publisher of the *Chronicle* "to ascertain the validity of the rumors." But the publisher "refused to comment," whereupon the station chief "issued the instructions which blocked the KRON newsmen from broadcasting the story until the newspapers issued a statement on the matter."

The examiner concluded this was a "reasonable reaction to a unique and delicate situation, rather than an attempt to suppress news"; while "obviously a local newspaper merger was highly newsworthy," any coverage by KRON "would be publicly regarded as based on 'inside' information," and since the station actually had no inside information, the public would have been misled. It

---

"Four more extensions of time . . ."

---

was a situation "where neither course was free of hazards," and therefore "a decision to say nothing was not unreasonable."

Accepting this, it follows that the newspaper-broadcast tie was harmful to the public's interest in the news. Whichever course the station took, the public would suffer—either through not hearing of a "highly newsworthy" story, or through being misled into thinking it was getting inside information when it was not. Such a situation, moreover, was not in fact unique to the 1965 merger in San Francisco. While that story was especially newsworthy, a similar problem arises whenever a broadcast station is confronted with a potential news story involving a commonly owned newspaper, or vice versa—occasions by no means rare in these days of heightened public awareness of the mass media and frequent controversies involving them. It is inherent in common ownership of more than one significant media outlet in a city.

Another incident involved the municipality of South San Francisco at a time when the *Chronicle* was competing for the CATV franchise there. KRON newsmen were told, in a memo from the news director dated Dec. 20, 1966:

> Between now and the first of February, let us concentrate a little heavier on SOUTH San Francisco—if warranted. HPS would like to make those people happy. . . . ["HPS" was Harold P. See, president of KRON-TV and also of the *Chronicle*-owned cable-TV company.]

A second memo from the news director, dated Feb. 6, 1967, ordered coverage of a library dedication in South San Francisco and added:

> HPS wants to make sure that the mayor of South SF is prominent in any film we do!

KRON covered the dedication, but most of the film it took was ruined by the laboratory—a fact that led See to write a letter of explanation to the mayor of South San Francisco. See admitted the letter "was motivated by CATV considerations," but denied that "the dedication coverage was related to a CATV interest."

Weighing this evidence, the examiner found that it demonstrated "an unusual interest in a political figure" on See's part, but did not prove that his motives in ordering the coverage arose from the CATV interest. See denied such a motive, and there was "no direct evidence in contradiction" the examiner said. "While such an intention might be inferred from . . . [the] Feb. 6 memo, the inference could only be based on a conjectural choice of possible motives for See's interest in South San Francisco. If KRON is to be convicted on circumstantial evidence, the circumstances should be considerably less ambiguous."

As this incident and a number of others indicate, necessary proof of improper motive in questions of abuse of media power is very difficult to come by. Even after the initial hurdle is surmounted by employee testimony of questionable news orders from management the case turns on the subjective motive for those orders. The executive who gave the orders will deny that his motive was improper, and proving him a liar may well be impossible—even assuming the FCC may be conducting such an inquiry in the first place.

6

Still another example involved alleged distortion of *Chronicle* editorial material to promote the owner's interest in the TV station. The FCC, in its hearing order, had cited an allegation that a *Chronicle* column by Charles McCabe "had been censored because the article urged 'citizens to contact the FCC about violence on television'." At the hearing, McCabe testified that in his ten years of writing a daily column for the *Chronicle*, "perhaps a total of less than 100 words has ever been censored from the content of my column, with one exception": a column on TV violence, written upon the death of Robert Kennedy, which urged readers to complain to the FCC and which the newspaper had "killed outright." McCabe's entire testimony was stricken from the record by the hearing examiner—notwithstanding inclusion of the item in the FCC's hearing order—on the ground that inquiry into what a newspaper prints would be inconsistent with the First Amendment.

If this ruling was correct, it may be asked how the FCC, using the case-by-case approach, can ever protect the public against the various possible abuses of newspaper-broadcast cross-ownership that may affect the content of the newspaper. The FCC has not hesitated to denounce in principle the slanting of content to promote an owner's ancillary interests, and has considered newspaper content in a number of such cases. For instance, it

---

"What we have, then, is a shell game . . ."

---

has frequently considered (but never found proven) charges that a newspaper discriminates in favor of its own broadcast stations in TV and radio listings and related material.

Yet in refusing to hear such testimony, the examiner had a point. Even though a newspaper's right to publish does not include the right to hold a broadcast license, and even though the FCC correctly insists that distortion by a newspaper to promote the interests of the station would be improper action by the licensee, and even though the FCC will nonetheless refuse to hold a hearing except in the rare case presenting "extrinsic evidence" of such an abuse, a governmental inquiry into a newspaper's motive for what it prints or fails to print must cause discomfort. Whether or not it would be unconstitutional, such an inquiry should not be undertaken unless there is no alternative way of protecting the public's interest in an undistorted flow of news (an interest sharpened, of course, by the absence of competing newspapers in the city).

The objection to such a proceeding is not limited, however, to issues involving the content of the newspaper. If it is undesirable for the FCC to probe the news decisions and underlying motives of a newspaper, it is no less undesirable in principle for it to be doing the same thing with respect to a broadcast station. Yet that is what the KRON hearing mainly consisted of. Whatever one thinks of the facts of the KRON case or of the hearing examiner's decision, this kind of inquiry into alleged abuses of media ownership is at best awkward and very possibly unconstitutional. Yet this is the case-by-case approach so strongly touted by opponents of the FCC's proposed rule. Under it, hearings of this kind are the only protection the public has against the most flagrant abuses of power by the owners of dominant media outlets in cities throughout the country.

What we have, then, is a shell game. Outraged by the WHDH case, where the FCC lifted a TV license from a newspaper through a case-by-case approach to media concentration, broadcasters and publishers have persuaded the FCC to renounce the case-by-case approach in favor of rule-making. Accordingly, the Commission and the Court of Appeals have refused, in view of the pending rule-making proceedings, to consider the concentration issue when licenses come up for renewal—and this has now gone on for more than four years, with no rule-making decision yet in sight.

One may wonder whether the Court of Appeals, which has tolerated the FCC's inaction in renewal cases out of deference to the rule-making proposal, will continue to do so indefinitely. But the industry has a solution to this danger, too. It is pushing for Congressional passage of a license-renewal bill—for which NAB already claims the support of forty-nine Senators and 256 Congressmen—that would extend the license period from three to five years and require renewal, regardless of any challenges or competing applications, as long as the incumbent licensee has made a "good faith effort" to serve the public. The bill would prevent the FCC from considering media concentration in such circumstances and would thus knock out permanently the case-by-case approach. It would leave a compliant FCC free to abandon the rule-making proceeding and walk away from the problem of local media concentration.

While waiting for the bill to pass, the industry can comfortably support keeping the rule-making proceeding alive to preserve its shield against case-by-case action, and the FCC can be expected to accommodate this desire. And the odds are that the bill will pass. Few lobbies are more powerful than broadcasters and publishers united. And there are *no* other lobbies that can back up their efforts to get what they want in Washington with an information blackout in the nation's newspapers and TV media.

8

USE OF ANTITRUST TO SUBVERT COMPETITION*

WILLIAM J. BAUMOL   *and*   *JANUSZ A. ORDOVER*
Princeton and New York Universities   *New York University*

> The day after Congress passed the changes in the clean air legislation which substantially tightened emissions standards the Japanese automakers called an emergency meeting of their engineers. On the same day the carmakers in Detroit called an emergency meeting of their lawyers. [JOKE CIRCULATING AT THE TIME]

THERE is a specter that haunts our antitrust institutions. Its threat is that, far from serving as the bulwark of competition, these institutions will become the most powerful instrument in the hands of those who wish to subvert it. More than that, it threatens to draw great quantities of resources into the struggle to prevent effective competition, thereby more than offsetting the contributions to economic efficiency promised by antitrust activities. This is a specter that may well dwarf any other source of concern about the antitrust processes. We ignore it at our peril and would do well to take steps to exorcise it.

The problem is not an easy one. In a sense it is inherent in the very nature of the antitrust process. There is no doubt, for example, that mergers can sometimes inhibit or undermine competition and that predatory pricing can sometimes serve as an instrument of monopolization. But then, because of that, a merger that promises to introduce efficiencies that make it necessary for other firms in the industry to try harder is vulnerable to challenge by those rivals, who will claim that it is anticompetitive. Similarly, a firm that by virtue of superior efficiency or economies of scale or scope is able to offer prices low enough to make its competitors uncomfortable is all too likely to find itself accused of predation. Such attempts

* We thank the C. V. Starr Center for Applied Economics at New York University for assistance in the preparation of this paper. Professor Ordover's research has been financed in part by the National Science Foundation. We also thank W. Baxter, J. Miller, and the other participants at the Conference for helpful comments. E. F. Glynn of the FTC vastly improved our discussion of antitrust in Japan and in the EEC Member States.

[*Journal of Law & Economics*, vol. XXVIII (May 1985)]

247

9

to use the law as an instrument for the subversion of competition do not confine themselves to private lawsuits. All too often the enterprise seeking to erect a protective umbrella about itself will be tempted to try to subvert the antitrust authorities, Congress, and even the president's office as partners in its purpose. One suspects that the costs in terms of the efficiency of the firm and the economy that is subject to this sort of attack are high. One knows that the costs in terms of the time of management, lawyers, economists, and others absorbed in the litigation process itself are enormous. And it is almost all economic waste.

I. Protectionism as Rent Seeking

Few observers will deny that some firms succumb to the temptation to seek governmental protection from the unpleasantness of effective competition. The blatant attempts by some steel and auto firms to have foreign imports restricted, the transparent purpose underlying a number of private antitrust suits, among other examples, can leave little doubt that the phenomenon is a reality. Yet, at least in some discussions, the volume of such protectionist activity is viewed as fortuitous, explainable largely in terms of cultural characteristics, political climate, and other influences beyond the purview of economic analysis. For example, American litigiousness is sometimes contrasted with Japanese distaste for direct confrontation as an explanation of the differences in the volume of private suits in the two countries.

Economic theory nonetheless has a good deal to say about the matter. The theory of rent seeking contributed by James Buchanan and extended to a variety of legal issues by Richard Posner tells us just how much protectionist effort one can expect in any particular set of circumstances. To summarize the argument very briefly, rent is defined by economists as any earnings by the supplier of an activity that exceed the minimum amount necessary to elicit the services of that supplier. Any supercompetitive (monopoly) profits of a firm are a rent. The theory of rent seeking tells us that where entrepreneurs are free to spend money in an attempt to gain control of such a source of rent, that is, when entry into a rent-seeking activity is completely free, when rent seeking is perfectly competitive or at least perfectly contestable, the resources devoted to the attempt will reach just the amount necessary to consume the entire rent. Rent seekers suing one another to gain control of a source of monopoly profit will spend so much on lawyers, consultants, and so on, that they will dissipate the entire expected monopoly profit in the process. That is just a corollary of the theorem that under perfect competition (excess) profits must be zero. In the circumstances posited, the struggle for the monopoly profits is a perfectly competitive process (or, at least, one that is perfectly contestable).

The result may seem to constitute a mere transfer of wealth from the monopolist to lawyers and economists, but it is much worse than that. In the process the latter are led to devote considerable (and valuable) time in a way that yields no socially valuable product. In other words, here rent seeking transforms into pure waste a quantity of resources equal in value to the rent that is sought.

The search for protection, which is the subject of this paper, is rent seeking (or rent preserving), as we now show. But it is not necessarily competitive, and so the analysis requires some modification. Envision the following scenario. Firm A offers generous salaries to its management, and firm B, with a leaner compensation package, undercuts A's prices, thereby eliminating the rents constituted by the overcompetitive salaries. A can hope to force B to cease and desist and perhaps even to collect treble damages from B by suing it for predatory pricing. What quantity of resources will A devote to this purpose?

First we note that even if other firms in the industry are hurt by A's pricing behavior, there is no competitive pressure driving A to use up its entire expected gain in its rent-preserving outlays. To see what will occur, let us first assume that A is the only firm affected by B's prices and then consider the case where several enterprises have their rents threatened.

Where A alone is involved, and assuming that its chances of achieving its protectionist goal increase monotonically with the quantity of resources it devotes to the purpose, then, as usual, profit maximization requires it to spend on its litigation effort up to the point where an additional dollar in outlay increases the expected rent yield by no more than $1.00. This may well leave firm A with a considerable expected gain from the undertaking. But it is also likely to involve a very substantial total outlay, that is, a very large amount of waste.

Where several other firms C, D, and E will benefit along with A if B is forced to end its "unfair competition," each of them will find it profitable to spend some money to increase the probability of victory. The joint profit-maximizing outlay will be greater, in general, than when only A's rents are at stake, since the marginal expected yield to the group as a whole must be at least as great as the marginal yield to A alone. However, in the absence of effective collusion, the behavior of the group may well not be (joint) profit maximizing, and it may involve outlays by the group lower than those that maximize their joint profits. This is so because an externality (free-rider) issue is involved. Any increment in probability of success against B achieved by an increase in A's expenditure will also benefit firms C, D, and E. As a result, when the marginal net benefit of such outlays to firm A reaches zero, its marginal benefit to the group of firms will still be positive. It follows that the total rent-seeking expenditure of the group can be expected to be less than that which maximizes their combined expected rent return.[1] The group's outlay will almost certainly be at least as large as the largest of the outlays of any one of the four rent-seeking firms would have been had it been the only competitor of B. To see this, it would have paid, say, firm C to spend X dollars in litigation if A and D were not spending anything for the purpose. If C finds that A and D together are spending only $X - \Delta$ for the purpose, then surely it will pay C to obtain the same probability of success as it would have in isolation since now it only costs him $\Delta < X$ dollars to do so. The Slutsky theorem for the firm not subject to a budget constraint tells us that this must be so because what is involved is a reduction in the price of increased probability of success in the rent-seeking undertaking.

We conclude from all this that while protectionist activity is a form of rent seeking, its expected benefits to the rent seeker are not likely to be dissipated completely in wasteful litigation expenditure. But the theory suggests nevertheless that the expenditures may typically be very substantial and that the social costs stemming from such direct waste may well prove very high.[2]

This is by no means the only type of social cost of protectionism. There are at least two other sorts of cost: monopolistic resource misallocation, and disincentives for internal operating efficiency for the individual firms, which may prove far more serious. The nature of the first of these is obvious to anyone familiar with welfare economics. After all, the immediate purpose of the protectionist activity is to subvert the forces of competition, and if the effort succeeds, it will lead to pricing and other decisions that are different, perhaps very different, from those that would emerge under competition. It follows that resources can be expected to be misallocated, as is always true under unregulated monopoly in a market that is not contestable.

---

[1] We cannot be certain of this since it depends on the concavity-convexity properties of the pertinent relationships. The presence of externalities themselves is likely to cause problems on that score. On this see William J. Baumol & David F. Bradford, Detrimental Externalities and Non-Convexity of the Production Set, 40 Economica 160 (n.s. 1972); or William J. Baumol & Wallace E. Oates, The Theory of Environmental Policy (1975), at ch. 8.

[2] The astonishing outlays by major firms on the antitrust litigations in which they have been involved confirms that these expenditures can indeed be substantial. For example, Alan A. Fisher & Robert H. Lande, Efficiency Considerations in Merger Enforcement, 71 Calif. L. Rev. 1580, 1673 (1983) estimate that Du Pont, Seagram, and Mobil spent about $13.5 million in private legal fees to acquire Conoco. In addition, they estimate at 1673 n.308 that an average merger antitrust case costs anywhere between $700,000 and $1.4 million. To this one must add costs incurred by the DOJ, or the FCC, and the courts.

The second social cost takes the form of inefficiency in the protected firm. First, if a company is insulated from competition, the pressures that would otherwise force it to operate with maximal efficiency are simply removed.[3] It is freer than it otherwise would be to engage in nepotism and sloppy supervision, to display excessive caution in risky decisions, and to avoid innovations that require management to exert itself. In short, protectionist activity frees the firm to engage in the degree of inefficiency that suits the proclivities and abilities of its management.

The third social cost of protectionism is its effect on the immediate objectives, and hence the organization, of the firm. If such rent seeking is the easier way to increase its profits or to achieve other managerial objectives, the firm's energies will be directed toward preparation for its litigative ventures, which will receive priority over efforts to increase productivity or to improve the product line. Engineers will become relatively less numerous in the ranks of top management, and lawyers will assume a correspondingly larger share.[4]

In sum, the social costs of rent-seeking protectionism can be very high (though we have no estimate of their magnitude). Indeed, if it is true that productivity growth in the United States is suffering from a serious longer-term malaise, it is not implausible that the incentives for firms to undertake the sort of rent seeking we are discussing has played a role that is not negligible.

We repeat that the antitrust and regulatory institutions have shown

---

[3] Some sense of magnitude of the expenditures that insulation from competition can elicit is suggested by the surprising size of the cut in wage and salary outlays in aviation that followed airline deregulation.

[4] A simple model making use of the Slutsky theorem readily confirms that if the antitrust laws increase the expected returns to litigation, they will also increase the firm's outlays on lawyers and other inputs that contribute to the probability of success in such litigation. A very elementary model for the purpose maximizes the profit function.

$$\Pi^*(\mathbf{Z}, x) = \Pi(Z) + vr - x \tag{1}$$

subject to

$$r = f(x), f'(x) > 0, \tag{2}$$

where $\mathbf{Z}$ = the vector of the firm's inputs and outputs, x = its litigation-related expenditure, r = its probability of victory in litigation, v = its expected increase in profit as a result of victory, $f(x)$ = probability of litigative success as a function of the firm's expenditure on litigation, and $\Pi(Z)$ = the firm's profit from its normal production activities in the absence of litigation.

We may regard r, the probability of success, as an additional output of the firm and v as the per unit return to an increase in the value of r. Then, if the sufficient conditions for the Slutsky theorem are satisfied, we know that we must have $\partial r/\partial v > 0$. That is, if the availability of the antitrust rules increases the payoff to litigative rent-seeking activity, the profit-maximizing firm will act to increase the probability of success in this arena. But by (2), in order to do so it must increase x, so that we have our result, $\partial x/\partial v > 0$.

themselves to be sources of substantial incentives and opportunities for such rent-seeking activity. Whenever a competitor becomes too successful or too efficient, whenever his competition threatens to become sufficiently effective to disturb the quiet and easy life his rival is leading, the latter will be tempted to sue on the grounds that the competition is "unfair." Every successful enterprise comes to expect almost as a routine phenomenon that it will sooner or later find itself the defendant in a multiplicity of cases. It is an enchanted topsy-turvy world in which vigorous competition is made to seem anticompetitive and in which "fair competition" comes to mean no competition at all.

The runners-up, the firms that despair of succeeding through superior efficiency or more attractive products, use different instruments in seeking protection from rivals. The antitrust laws are not always useful as means to handicap competition from abroad, but they are apparently a prime instrument for the creation of impediments to effective competition by American rivals. The reason the antitrust laws can be used in this way is clear. The borderline between measures that are legitimate competitive moves and those that are destructive instruments of monopolization is often difficult to define even in principle (witness, for example, the intricacies of the concept of predatory innovation). Moreover, whatever the criteria adopted, in practice they rarely lend themselves to clear-cut evidence and unambiguous conclusions. The runner-up firm then finds itself with the opportunity to claim that almost any successful program by a rival is "anticompetitive" and that it constitutes monopolization. Antitrust, whose objective is the preservation of competition, by its very nature lends itself to use as a means to undermine effective competition. This is not merely ironic. It is very dangerous for the workings of our economy.

II. ANTITRUST PROVISIONS THAT ENCOURAGE PROTECTIONISM

We cannot hope to provide an exhaustive list of the antitrust institutions that lend themselves to the purposes of the protectionist. We simply offer several illustrations. We discuss the treble-damages provisions, vagueness of criteria of predation and other types of unfairness of competition, and excessive severity of tests of anticompetitiveness.

Treble Damages[5]

The availability of trebled damages payments to the plaintiff has several arguments in its favor. First, there is evidence that in antitrust suits pri-

[5] See Kenneth G. Elzinga and William Breit, Private Antitrust Enforcement: The New Learning, in this issue, and Frank H. Easterbrook, Detrebling Antitrust Damages, in this issue, for an extensive discussion of the social costs and benefits of the trebling of damages.

vate plaintiffs have a relatively low probability of winning their cases.[6] If private antitrust suits are considered desirable in at least some cases, the plaintiffs must be offered an expected return at least equal to the heavy litigation costs they are likely to incur. While treble damages do not generally increase the probability of victory (and may well decrease it by forcing the defendant to expend larger resources to protect his interests), they almost certainly increase the expected award to a plaintiff. Second, in some cases (such as successful price fixing), in addition to the culprit's ill-gotten gains, his victims suffer a deadweight loss in the form of distorted relative purchase quantities which the courts do not recognize in their damage calculations. A multiplied damage payment then serves as very rough compensation for such deadweight losses, though any resemblance between the two magnitudes is certain to be purely coincidental. Third, no doubt some violators of the antitrust laws escape unscathed and sometimes are not even brought to trial, let alone convicted and punished. Optimal deterrence requires such firms to face ex ante a probable punishment that does fit the crime. This means that the higher the probability that any particular violator of the law will get away with it, the higher must be the fine exacted from those who are brought to justice.

All of these arguments are legitimate so far as they go, but they neglect the other side of the matter. From the point of view of society, escalated damages awards also increase the probable payoff to protectionist activity. The runner-up who hopes to impose legal obstacles on the vigorous competitive efforts of his all-too-successful rival is offered the prospect of also acquiring a substantial amount of funding in the process. It has even been charged that runners-up have been known to start such suits in the hope of acquiring the funding that the capital market denied them.

Trebled damages also increase the amounts it pays both defendant and plaintiff to expend in combating the case, for such damages increase the pool of rents to be disputed. And, as usual, the waste of economic resources elicited can be expected to be proportional to the size of the available rents. It is noteworthy that, as in the case of rivalrous advertising, such enhanced outlays on a legal battle will tend to cancel one another, at least in part. They will benefit neither the plaintiff nor the defendant, while raising the cost to society.

All in all, the case against trebled damages is far from clear-cut. Yet the fact that they provide a direct incentive for protectionist activity suggests that the issue requires reconsideration. We will return to this subject

---

[6] See Richard A. Posner, A Statistical Study of Antitrust Enforcement, 13 J. Law & Econ. 365 (1970); National Economic Research Associates, Statistical Analysis of Private Antitrust Enforcement, Final Report (1979).

15

later, when we discuss policy appropriate for the phenomenon of protectionist misuse of antitrust institutions.

Vagueness of Antitrust Criteria

Knowledgeable students of antitrust issues often are impressed with the difficulty of determining and defining in a manner that is universally applicable the borderline between acceptable and unacceptable behavior. Scherer's attack on the famous Areeda-Turner article is a classic illustration, carefully cataloguing a variety of circumstances under which almost any reasonable but explicitly defined standard of predatory pricing can be expected to condone activities that are anticompetitive or to condemn activities that are innocent or even benign.[7] No categorical rule can fully encompass intentions, antecedent and subsequent circumstances and developments, interdependence with actions other than those under immediate consideration, and the host of other pertinent considerations. Such a point of view would seem to lead toward heavy reliance on the good judgment of the courts, toward a universal reign of some form of rule of reason. It leaves matters subject to vague and general guidelines derived from the obscure admonitions of the pertinent law and the available precedents, and beyond that it gives the courts the duty of deciding matters case by case, on the basis of individual judgment and in light of attendant circumstances.

Here is not the place to examine all the likely consequences of such a procedure or to consider the implications of wide range in capability and economic sophistication that one encounters among judges. Rather, our concern here is that obscurity and ambiguity are convenient tools for those enterprises on the prowl for opportunities to hobble competition. As we know, it is not always necessary to win cases in order to blunt a rival's competitive weapons. Harassment by lawsuit or even the threat of harassment can be a marvelous stimulus to timidity on the part of competitors. The potential defendant who cannot judge in advance with any reasonable degree of certainty whether its behavior will afterward be deemed illegal is particularly vulnerable to guerrilla warfare and intimidation into the sort of gentlemanly competitive behavior that is the antithesis of true competition.

Thus, to continue with our example, whatever one may think of the Areeda-Turner test (and we do consider it to constitute a major infusion of

---

[7] F. M. Scherer, Comment on Areeda and Turner, 89 Harv. L. Rev. 869 (1976). Phillip Areeda and Donald F. Turner, Predatory Pricing and Related Practices under Section 2 of the Sherman Act, 88 Harv. L. Rev. 697 (1975).

logic into the arena), it seems to us certainly to have made a critical and beneficial contribution simply by reducing vagueness in the criterion of predation in pricing. This makes protectionist misuse of the antitrust laws much less easy.

Severity of the Tests of Anticompetitiveness

A third phenomenon that facilitates protectionist efforts is reliance on rules increasing the range of private activities subject to condemnation as "anticompetitive." Here, too, the Areeda-Turner contribution provides an excellent illustration. The long debate between advocates of fully distributed cost tests of anticompetitiveness in pricing and advocates of incremental or marginal costs for this purpose has a straightforward interpretation in terms of our discussion. Though we are not disinterested observers of this debate, we are reasonably confident that it is not bias alone that leads us to interpret advocacy of the fully distributed cost approach as a systematic protectionist onslaught. We believe the evidence strongly supports the thesis that it is a standard put forward almost exclusively by firms that were unlikely to compete successfully on the merits of their performance alone. They advocate their costing approach as a device to limit the price-cutting opportunities of rivals rendered more efficient by economies of scale or scope, by superior management, or by other legitimate sources of superiority. This is surely attested to by the frequency of cases in which full distribution has been used to argue that some prices are unacceptably low, when the pricing behavior that should most be feared by guardians of the public interest in the presence of market power is overcharging, not underpricing.

Thus, rules that make vigorous competition dangerous clearly foster protectionism. That point is obvious enough. What is perhaps only a bit less obvious is that protectionists are not prone to wait passively for such overrestrictive rules to fall into their laps. Rather, a central element in their strategy is persistent expenditure of money and effort to change the rules in ways that favor their cause, and resistance to any attempt to reduce impediments to effective competition. When an agency such as the FTC proposes to hold hearings on the advisability of revision of one of its rules that may be suspected of discouraging competition, those who stand to bear the brunt of any enhanced competitive pressures can be expected to resist energetically.

In sum, it seems plausible that rules defining unacceptable competitive practices that lean toward potential plaintiffs are a major source of encouragement to protectionist efforts. The presence of such rules is not happenstance. They are often attributable to the deliberate efforts of those who stand to gain by using the antitrust mechanism to emasculate competition.

The preceding paragraphs are intended to suggest that the search for protection from competition by runner-up firms, and the use of antitrust institutions for the purpose, is encouraged by a number of attributes of those institutions themselves. We do not mean to apportion blame or even to claim that any one group can be said to be at fault. Our purpose is to look for strategic points that lend themselves to modification and that are therefore appropriate foci for ameliorative policy—a subject to which we will return presently.

It must, however, be pointed out that even if antitrust rules were modified to make them less susceptible to rent-seeking activities described here, such activities might not disappear or even decline materially. More likely, firms might merely divert their rent-seeking resources to other political and legal arenas.

III.   Case Examples of Strategic Uses of Antitrust

The purpose of this section is to illustrate by means of a few actual cases the protectionist uses of antitrust and associated forms of government intervention such as regulation. Our examples involve mergers and joint ventures, as well as monopolization cases.

A.   The GM-Toyota Joint Venture

The GM-Toyota joint venture illustrates clearly the strategic role of antitrust litigation. Here, it is Chrysler and Ford, the horizontal competitors of the joint venturers, that have pressed the Federal Trade Commission to reject the joint venture on the ground that it will restrain competition in the automobile market in general and in the subcompact segment of the market in particular. Recently the FTC approved the joint venture. Undeterred, Chrysler has been pressing a private antitrust action in an attempt to accomplish what it failed to do at the FTC.

This sort of opposition is predictable, and in a manner that is rather ironic it can signal clearly the likely effects of the joint venture. If the enterprise were in fact likely to acquire monopoly power and charge excessive prices, other U.S. auto firms undoubtedly would benefit from the resulting protective umbrella, which would enable them to raise their prices as well. If this is the probable outcome, then those rivals can be expected to view the joint venture with equanimity and silent acquiescence. But if the joint venture really is likely to introduce economies or improve product quality, it is sure to make life harder for the domestic rivals of the participants who will then have to run correspondingly faster in order to stand still.[8] Paradoxically, then and only then, when the joint venture is really beneficial, can those rivals be relied on to denounce the undertaking as "anticompetitive."[9] That is exactly the response of Chrysler and Ford, who have presented themselves here as defenders of consumers' interests even though before other forums they have not hesitated to argue for blatantly protectionist measures such as higher trade barriers. Once again, consistency has given way to expediency.

B.   MCI v. AT & T: The Economics of Price Inflexibility[10]

MCI was perhaps the first firm to challenge AT & T's monopoly in the long-distance telecommunications market. Beginning in 1963, MCI embarked on an extensive investment program in microwave transmission facilities. Because of its (and the FCC's) policy of "universal service" or "nationwide averaging," AT & T's relative rates along different routes did not correspond closely to relative costs, with service along sparsely used routes comparatively underpriced. This was a clear invitation for "cream skimming" entry. Understandably, MCI at least initially attempted to specialize in serving the high-density routes in which AT & T earned more substantial profit margins.

MCI's moves to enter these routes predictably led to an attempt by AT & T to adjust its relative rates to correspond more closely to costs. MCI alleged that these responses were anticompetitive. Litigation ensued.[11] Of course, MCI's initial entry primarily into AT & T's more profitable routes is unobjectionable. The benefits of competition depend on the willingness of entrants to seek out profitable opportunities. What is far more questionable is MCI's attempt to use antitrust litigation as a means to restrain AT & T's ability to respond to competitive incursions. It was charged that by adjusting its prices on different routes to correspond more closely to

[8] Admittedly, it is possible that the joint venture will make GM a more formidable competitor not because of any gains in economic efficiency but merely because it will make it easier for GM to satisfy the asinine Company Average Fuel Efficiency (CAFE) regulations.

[9] Steven Salop suggested to one of us that a merger of joint venture may be a part of a strategy employed by the merging partners, or co-venturers, to elevate the rivals' costs and thereby harm competition. We doubt that "predatory" mergers or joint ventures are a frequent occurrence. In such a rare instance, the rival would have to assume the standard of proof of a potential anticompetitive effect that is appropriate for monopolization cases, rather than that which is appropriate for a merger case.

[10] We are not disinterested discussants of this case. Both of us have carried out work for AT & T. One of us not only served as a witness for AT & T in the MCI case but also recommended the type of price response to MCI's entry that AT & T later adopted.

[11] MCI Communications Corp. v. AT & T, 369 F. Supp. 1004 (E. D. Pa. 1973) vacated and remanded, 496 F.2d 214 (3d Cir. 1974); MCI Communications Corp. v. AT & T, 462 F. Supp. 1072 (N. D. Ill. 1978), rev'd, 708 F.2d 1081 (7th Cir. 1983).

costs, even on routes where competition had not yet appeared, AT & T was launching "preemptive strikes." One can imagine what would have been said if instead AT & T had reduced prices *only* on the routes where MCI had opened for business.

MCI insisted during the trial and in its appellate brief that a "full-cost" approach should be used to calculate AT & T's costs and to perform the tests of predatoriness.[12] Indeed, according to MCI, citing Dr. William Melody's testimony, many "economists advocate the use of fully distributed costs as the proper test for below-cost predatory pricing in the telecommunications industry."[13]

There is no need to dwell here on the inefficiencies that result from the use of fully allocated costs as constraints on the price responses of regulated and unregulated firms. It suffices to note that insistence that such costs are the appropriate price floors invites socially inefficient entry that is elicited not by genuine cost advantages and productive efficiencies but by false profitability signals. There is no doubt that potential and actual entrants (such as MCI) have a strong incentive to rigidify the price responses open to an incumbent who is confronted with newly emerging competition. It seems clear that the staunchest advocates of full-cost pricing have been firms anxious to hobble their disquietingly effective rivals.

C. Strategic Uses of Antitrust in Takeover Cases

The targets of tender offers frequently initiate antitrust suits against their unwanted suitors. The critical issues are whether the targets should be allowed to institute injunction proceedings or whether instead the enforcement of merger statutes should be left to the government and to customers who are likely to be injured if the merger brings competition to an end, elevates prices, and causes resource misallocation. The issue is not straightforward. While the incentive for management to bring an antitrust case need not coincide with the interests of the consumers,[14] it is nevertheless true that the management of the target is probably better informed than any other group about the likely consequences of the acquisition for future competition.

There is no question that a target's management, bent on derailing the tender offer, has a potent weapon in the antitrust laws. The two most

[12] Brief of Appellees, MCI Communications Corp. and MCI Telecommunications Corp. (March 5, 1981), at 112.

[13] *Id.* at 113–14. The court of appeals disagreed and decided against MCI on most points.

[14] This point is made in Frank H. Easterbrook & Daniel R. Fischel, Antitrust Suits by Targets of Tender Offers, 80 Michigan L. Rev. 1155 (1982).

recent instances in which highly lucrative offers were defeated with the aid of the antitrust laws were *Grumman Corp. v. LTV Corp.*[15] and *Marathon Oil Co. v. Mobil Corp.*[16] The latter case illustrates the problem clearly. Marathon's management possessed extensive, firsthand information about the scope of its geographic operations and about the marketing of gasoline to independents, which was at issue in the antitrust proceedings. On the other hand, Marathon's management hardly shared the interests of the automobile owners in cheap and plentiful gasoline.[17] Indeed, if the target's management were truly guided by shareholders' interests, it ought to sell the company to the bidder likely to obtain the highest profit from the transaction.[18] But when such enhanced profits result from the elevation of market power in the postmerger market, the interests of the consumers and of the target's stockholders clash directly.

IV. ALTERNATIVE ENFORCEMENT PROCEDURES: JAPAN AND THE EEC

In this section we briefly compare antitrust procedures in the United States with those of our major trading partners: Japan and the EEC. We do not claim any expertise on the antitrust laws of other countries. However, expertise is not required in light of our limited objective—to explore how other countries have held in check the use of antitrust litigation as a strategic weapon in the hands of competitors. (Of course, none of the discussion is meant to imply that the antitrust policies in other countries constitute ideal models for the United States that should recommend themselves to American scholars and policymakers.)

A. Japan[19]

Japan has dealt with the problem of strategic use or abuse of the antitrust laws by largely consolidating enforcement in its Fair Trade Commission (JFTC). In Japan a person injured by acts in violation of the antimonopoly laws has a right to sue for damages under Section 709 of the Civil Code. And any person injured by conduct found illegal by the JFTC has a right, under Section 25 of the Antimonopoly Act, to recover dam-

---

[15] 665 F.2d 10 (2d Cir. 1981).

[16] 669 F.2d 378 (6th Cir. 1982).

[17] In fact, if the management had wanted to trigger an auction for Marathon by impeding Mobil's actions, it might have been implying that it was expecting another oil company as the next suitor.

[18] That is, if the target's managers can somehow share in these incremental profits.

[19] Information in this section is culled from notes by Matsushita; see M. Matsushita, Informal Notes for the Conference on Japan's Antimonopoly Legislation and Doing Business with Japan, Japan Society (January 5, 1978).

ages.[20] Yet as of 1983 only five damage suits had been filed under Section 25. The reasons for the reluctance of private Japanese plaintiffs to seek damages in court are not easy to determine. We think that the national distaste for litigation cannot explain it fully. In particular, the fact that damages are not readily awarded in Japan and that plaintiffs can sue under Section 25 only if the JFTC has found the conduct complained of to be illegal surely discourages private actions for damages.[21]

Japan's FTC is basically an administrative agency with some quasi-judicial powers. Its judicial powers are exercised only rarely. According to the Japanese antitrust expert M. Matsushita of Sophia University, only four antitrust criminal cases have occurred in the past thirty years of antitrust enforcement. The main channel through which the JFTC shapes competition is informal. The JFTC may issue "warnings" that are usually respected. In addition, the JFTC provides "guidance" that helps the companies to avoid conflict with the antitrust laws, especially in international contracts.

When the JFTC brings a formal action, it usually ends with the company (or companies) accepting the JFTC's recommendation decision. Available estimates indicate that some 90 percent of these recommendations are accepted. Those that are not accepted usually are resolved during trial through consent decisions that embody the proposals of the respondent.

Private complaints are filed with the JFTC. The JFTC must then investigate but need not take an enforcement action. However, according to the Japanese experts, frequently investigation alone suffices to induce the investigated firm (or firms) to stop the activity that has been challenged.

---

[20] Hiroshi Iyori & Akinori Uesugi, The Antimonopoly Laws of Japan 127 (2d ed. 1983). We are grateful to Edward Glynn of the FTC for correcting our earlier discussion of private enforcement in Japan.

[21] Economists are usually loath to seek explanations in alleged differences in "national character" to explain the Japanese record. Arguments based on national character are difficult to test and are, in any event, treacherous, as the following illustrative story suggests: "An Australian expert, invited by the Japanese government, had this to say in his Report, as excerpted in the *Japan Times* of August 18th 1915: 'Japan commercially, I regret to say, does not bear the best reputation for executing business. Inferior goods, irregularity and indifferent shipments have caused no end of worry . . . My impression as to your cheap labour was soon disillusioned when I saw your people at work. No doubt they are lowly paid, but the return is equally so; to see your men at work made me feel that you are a very satisfied easy-going race who reckon time is no object. When I spoke to some managers they informed me that it was impossible to change the habits of national heritage . . . First class managers . . . are required to wake things up and get out of the go-as-you-please style that seems universal at present.' " Cited in J. N. Bhagwati, Development Economics: What Have We Learnt (mimeographed, Columbia Univ. 1984), at 27.

Thus, here there does remain some scope for strategic use of the JFTC investigatory powers.

Yet the incentives for the allegedly harmed petitioners to use this process are limited. They receive no financial recompense for any harm they have suffered. Their only benefit derives from the JFTC's ability to require cessation of the allegedly anticompetitive activity. The incentive to use the JFTC for protection from competition is thereby weakened, especially if the cost of filing the complaint is high.

It is noteworthy that in a few cases complaining parties have attempted to sue the JFTC for the failure to act on their complaints. However, appellate authorities have ruled that only respondents can appeal a JFTC decision and have thereby severely restricted the complainants' standing to sue.

In sum, in Japan antitrust enforcement is placed almost exclusively in the hands of its JFTC, which relies heavily on informal mechanisms such as warnings and reviews. The strategic use of the antitrust mechanism is circumscribed because the parties who claim they were harmed must first convince the JFTC to act and cannot appeal from the JFTC decisions.

One may well feel that this arrangement goes too far and that its protection of anticompetitive activities is excessive. However, it does certainly help to check the litigiousness of business firms and their use of antitrust as a means to restrain effective competition.

B.   The EEC Member States

It would add unduly to the length of this paper, and strain the information at our disposal, to analyze the vulnerability to strategic abuse of the national laws on competition where they exist in the EEC countries. It is safe to say, however, that the incentives for abuse probably are significantly weaker in the EEC member states than they are in the United States, at least for the following reasons. First, in the EEC member states the plaintiff who wins a case is not entitled to treble damages. Second, in the EEC member states contingent fee arrangements with lawyers do not exist in antitrust cases. Third, discovery procedures are less developed in Europe than they are in the United States, which may make it more difficult for a plaintiff to obtain the "incriminating" evidence with which to fuel rent-seeking anticompetitive activities.[22] Fourth, in the EEC mem-

---

[22] However, as Edward Glynn has noted, extensive "discovery" available under American law can at times also be used to "bludgeon" a financially weak plaintiff into dropping his case.

ber states the right to trial by jury in money damage cases is not available. Fifth, in Britain especially an unsuccessful plaintiff must bear the defendant's costs.[23] And, finally, in Europe some aspects of the competition law, for example merger statutes, fall only within the purview of governmental bodies. This greatly reduces the opportunity for strategic use of these laws.

Having said all this, we must emphasize one important continuing development in the EEC member states that bears directly on the issues raised in this paper. It has by now become fairly well established through judicial authority that "actions for injunctions and for compensation may be brought in national courts by plaintiffs claiming to suffer loss as a result of infringements of Articles 85–86 and 90 EEC Treaty. . . . This confirms that Articles 85–86 are laws for the protection of individual interests and *not* merely laws for the protection of the public interest or the community."[24] Thus, for example, rivals now can avail themselves of EEC statutes on competition if they can claim to have been affected in their intracommunity business activities by allegedly anticompetitive actions of a dominant firm.

This extension of the enforcement of the EEC competition statutes in general, and of Article 86 in particular, opens an opportunity for strategic use of the statutes. The leading United Kingdom case that has established that plaintiffs can, in fact, sue shows that the EEC competition statutes can be used to retard rather than promote allocative efficiency.[25] In that case, the plaintiff was purchasing most of its "bulk butter" from the Milk Marketing Board (which apparently had a dominant position in the relevant market) for resale to a single purchaser in the Netherlands. At some point the defendant changed its marketing strategy and decided to sell its bulk butter to four distributors in England and Wales. The plaintiff was instructed to purchase its butter requirements from the designated distributors. Allegedly, this would have rendered its resale activities unprofitable. The plaintiff sued and asked for injunctive relief. The relief was not granted. Nevertheless, the case set a precedent for future suits.

The preceding sequence will be familiar to the American students of

---

[23] We note, however, that the effects of fee shifting on litigation incentives are not as clear as one might expect. See Steven Shavell, Suit, Settlement and Trial: A Theoretical Analysis under Alternative Methods for the Allocation of Legal Costs, 11 J. Legal Stud. 55 (1982); and Janusz A. Ordover & Ariel Rubinstein, A Sequential Concession Game with Asymmetric Information (mimeographed, C. V. Starr Center for Applied Economics, New York Univ., July 1984).

[24] John Temple Lang, Enforcement in National Courts of Community Competition Rules on Enterprises, Notes for Lecture, Brussels (March 1983).

[25] Garden Cottage Foods, Ltd. v. Milk Marketing Board (1983) 2 ALL ER 770.

antitrust. Vertical relations between a manufacturer and his dealers have been a subject of frequent litigation, often of doubtful merit. It appears that now, by involving Article 86, dealers in the EEC may have acquired an important weapon with which to attack the distribution arrangements of their suppliers.[26] This has occurred at a time when, in the United States, various commentators have suggested that per se legality be granted to such arrangements. Time will tell whether competitors in the EEC will use the statute against one another.

V.   WHAT IS TO BE DONE?

There are no easy and costless remedies for the abuse of antitrust by those who use it for protection from competition. The difficulty is inherent in the problem, for anything that is done to make it harder for plaintiffs to use our antitrust institutions anticompetitively automatically also makes it easier for others to get away with acts of monopolization. This trade-off is apparently unavoidable, because anything that makes conviction of the defendant more likely necessarily makes suits more attractive to plaintiffs in pursuit of protection from effective competition. The Japanese, as we have seen, have largely solved the problem of protectionism, but only by virtual prohibition of initiatives by the victims of monopolistic behavior. In dealing with the shortcomings of our antitrust institutions that are the subject of this paper, we must be careful not to undermine the antitrust laws themselves.

The most obvious remedial change is a restriction of the sort of circumstances to which treble damages apply. One should consider both the use of a multiple smaller than three, at least in those types of cases, such as predatory pricing, in which rent-seeking protectionist activity seems to abound, and in some types of cases one might even consider restriction of the amount of the award to the magnitude of the damage actually shown to have been sustained.

Such proposals are not new, but we do have a new wrinkle to suggest. The choice of multiplicand in damages payments faces at least two conflicting goals. Given the possibly low probability of discovery of an antitrust violation and of conviction on the charge, optimal deterrence clearly calls for a multiplicand greater than unity, and on that score trebling of damages may perhaps not be too bad an approximation to the optimum.

---

[26] In the United Kingdom, such practices are also examined in the Restrictive Practices Court in which there is "a great deal of wasted time particularly with economists swearing against each other—canceling each other out!" As was observed extrajudicially by Advocate-General Warner of the Court of Justice of the European Communities, in Enterprise Law of the 80's 235 (F. M. Rowe, F. G. Jacobs, & M. R. Joelson eds. 1980).

On the other hand, if this encourages rent seeking we may want, on this score, a much smaller damages award.

Environmental economics has shown how an analogous problem can be dealt with. There, deterrence policy can use the polluter pays principle as an effective instrument. But if that payment is used to compensate the polluter's victims on the basis of the amount of damage they suffer, a moral hazard problem arises—for it undermines the incentive for potential victims to seek pollution-avoiding locations or to take other measures to protect themselves from damages. Indeed, it can be proved that *any* such compensation to utility-maximizing victims will reduce their pollution-deterrent resource outlays below the socially optimal level. The solution implicitly advocated by economists for pollution policy is simple. The polluter should indeed pay, but the payments should be collected by government, at least in part, and should not go to the victims. In that way the payment scheme is provided with two parameter values—the price the polluter is charged, and the amount that victims are compensated. These parameter values can then be chosen so as to elicit both the optimal reduction of polluter emissions and the optimal self-defensive effort by the victim.

In private antitrust suits a similar solution is at least worth considering. That is, the defendant who is found guilty might continue to pay three times (or some other multiple of) the estimated damages. But the plaintiff can be made eligible to a smaller multiple (and perhaps even a multiple less than unity) of that damages figure. The difference would then go into the public treasury as a tax on violators of the antitrust laws. Once again, this provides two distinct parameters (the defendant's multiple and the plaintiff's multiple) to the designers of public policy who can select their values separately so as to provide the proper incentive for deterrence of violations while at the same time offering an appropriate disincentive for rent-seeking protectionism.

One may want to take a further step in this direction. Mere accusation and trial subjects the defendant firm to enormous expenses and even greater ex ante risks of an expensive adverse decision, even if it transpires ex post on the basis of convincing evidence that it is completely innocent. The possibility of required compensation to the defendant for these damages caused by the plaintiff might well discourage frivolous and mischievous suits, including those undertaken in the hope that an out-of-court settlement will prevent the latter from having to reveal the weakness of his case. Thus, the third remedy we propose for consideration is liability of the plaintiff for costs incurred by the defendant in the event of acquittal.

A fourth line of defense against protectionism is the adoption of clearer criteria of unacceptable behavior, such as the predation tests proposed by Areeda and Turner or those we have suggested.[27] For reasons already discussed, vagueness in the standards of unacceptable behavior plays into the hands of those who would use the antitrust laws as anticompetitive weapons.

Fifth, one may well consider it desirable, for similar reasons, to inhibit, if not necessarily prohibit, the ability of the management of a company that is a takeover target to bring an antitrust suit against the unwanted acquirer.[28]

Here it should be emphasized that we do not want to immunize mergers or acquisitions from the antitrust laws. Rather, we suggest the possibility that (only) those most likely to misuse the process for protectionist purposes be limited in their ability to bring private suits against the transaction on antitrust grounds. Others, including the pertinent government agencies, should clearly remain free to do so.

All of these suggestions are offered very tentatively and with great hesitation. They are mostly untried, and our lack of competence in the law surely raises questions about their workability, their consistency with other legal rules, and perhaps even (in some cases) their constitutionality.

We end by repeating an earlier caveat. It is not by accident that every one of our very tentative proposals incurs some social cost in that it reduces to some degree the available deterrents to monopolistic behavior. This is unavoidable, because any measure that offers some promise of dealing effectively with the problem discussed in this paper must necessarily involve some reduction in the incentive to bring litigation and hence must weaken to a degree the position of the potential plaintiff. It seems clear to us that *some* move in this direction is urgent if antitrust and regulation are to be prevented from becoming major impediments to competitiveness, efficiency, and productivity growth in the U.S. economy. The question is not whether some such moves are justified. The issue, rather, is how substantial those moves should be—how great a modification constitutes a social optimum in the trade-off between the two competing perils to true competition—excessive weakening of the deterrents to monopolization and excessive facilitation of attempts to subvert effective competition through protectionist misuse of our antitrust institutions.

---

[27] William J. Baumol, Quasi Permanence of Price Reduction, 89 Yale L. J. 1 (1979); Janusz A. Ordover & Robert D. Willig, An Economic Definition of Predation: Pricing and Product Innovation, 91 Yale L. J. 8 (1981).

[28] In a recent case, the U.S. District Court for the Central District of California ruled that the target of a tender offer lacks standing to seek a preliminary injunction to halt the acquisition as a violation of the Clayton Act. Carter Hawley Hale Stores, Inc. v. The Limited, Inc., 587 F. Supp. 246 (C. D. Cal. 1984).

INTEREST GROUPS AND THE ANTITRUST PARADOX

Bruce L. Benson, M. L. Greenhut, and Randall G. Holcombe

Economists have generally assumed that the intention of the antitrust laws is to increase economic efficiency. Many observers, however, have noted that the antitrust laws are applied inconsistently and often do not use economic analysis to promote economic efficiency. Judge Robert Bork (1979) referred to this failure of the antitrust laws to promote economic efficiency as the "antitrust paradox," and Peter Asch (1970) called it the "antitrust dilemma." The special interest theory of regulation developed by Stigler (1971) and others assists in understanding the antitrust paradox, because pursuant to it one must not expect antitrust to be applied to benefit the general public.[1]

The special interest view of economic regulation has found its way into evaluations of the antitrust laws.[2] For example, Judge Richard Posner (1969, p. 87) claimed that Federal Trade Commission (FTC) investigations are seldom in the public interest and are undertaken "at the behest of corporations, trade associations, and trade unions whose motivation is at best to shift the costs of their private litigation

---

Cato Journal, Vol. 6, No. 3 (Winter 1987). Copyright © Cato Institute. All rights reserved.

Bruce L. Benson is Associate Professor of Economics at Florida State University, M. L. Greenhut is Alumni Distinguished Professor of Economics at Texas A&M University, and Randall G. Holcombe is Professor of Economics at Auburn University.

[1]Stigler (1985) does not see the special interest theory as completely convincing in the case of antitrust. Some extensions of the special interest theory of government are found in Posner (1974), Peltzman (1976), McCormick and Tollison (1981), Becker (1983), and Holcombe (1985). Some of the many empirical examinations of the theory include Abrams and Settle (1978), Jarrell (1978), Kau and Rubin (1978), McCormick and Tollison (1981), Smith (1982), and Ross (1984). A parallel development to the literature on interest group regulation is the rapidly growing literature on rent seeking. See Tollison (1982) and Benson (1984) for a discussion of the relationship between the two developments and reviews of the relevant literature.

[2]See, for example, Posner (1969), Faith et al. (1982), Weingast and Moran (1983), Benson (1983b), Benson and Greenhut (1986), and High (1984–85).

to the taxpayer and at worst to harass competitors." The special interest theory of regulation goes a long way toward explaining the antitrust paradox, but there are important differences between antitrust and most other regulatory constraints on business. Moreover, there are many facets of antitrust that are not readily explained by that theory.

Several aspects of antitrust law differentiate it from the types of regulation that are normally considered within the special interest framework. Regulation is normally concerned with one or a few industries, but the antitrust laws are considerably broader in scope. In addition, the courts play a much more visible role in antitrust than they do in regulation. One can legitimately question how laws as broad in scope as the antitrust laws can be the product of special interests. One can further question how special interests could hope to benefit from court decisions that normally are considered to be outside the influence of narrow special interests.[3] These basic issues are evaluated throughout the paper.

Our thesis is that the antitrust laws are a result of a special interest struggle between small and large economic entities seeking changes in the general economic environment rather than the specific favors usually associated with special interest legislation. We explain why a rather general approach was sought for antitrust laws, not the typical goal of many narrowly focused special interests. We also explain Judge Bork's antitrust paradox, both in origin and application, and account for enforcement by both courts and governmental bureaus of the property rights assigned under the antitrust laws.

The Antitrust Process

There are three main participants in the antitrust process: special interests; legislators; and the commissioners, bureaucrats, and judges who interpret and enforce the statutes. These groups are not mutually exclusive. In particular, bureaucrats and commissioners may also act as interest groups and possess considerable political power that often is used to further their own interests. Stigler (1971) observed that the object of special interest groups is the transfer of wealth, but this is rarely accomplished by a simple transfer of funds from the public treasury, especially in the antitrust arena. Rather, as Benson (1984) noted, wealth transfers are provided through governmental assignments of or transfers of property rights.

---

[3]Posner (1972), Rubin (1977), Priest (1977), and Holcombe (1983, chap. 9) all suggest a type of invisible hand mechanism leading the courts to reach efficient decisions.

30

The process of assigning or transferring property rights can be divided into two distinct stages: first, the assignment of property rights; second, the enforcement of the resulting property rights assignment. The first stage is a legislative function; for the assignment to be worth anything, an enforcement mechanism must also be established. These two stages can be thought of as a single object demanded by interest groups because different enforcement levels are possible given any assignment of rights. Thus, one goal of interest groups is to obtain and defend favorable property rights.

When examining antitrust issues there is particular reason for distinguishing between the assignment and the enforcement of rights, because legislators assign antitrust rights but do not enforce them, even though in theory they could. Legislators delegate the enforcement function to agencies (commissions) and to the courts, and the legislature's delegates wield considerable power and independence.[4]

The Basic Model

Legislators favor special interest groups but never to the extent that the favored group would prefer. They favor the group up to the point where the marginal political benefit received in exchange for the favor equals the marginal cost in terms of lost support from other groups (Peltzman 1976, p. 217). Of course, the favored group would most prefer to receive greater benefits, that is, up to the point where the marginal benefit is zero. Stigler (1971, p. 4), Posner (1974, p. 350), Peltzman (1976), and Becker (1983) concluded that the political exchange in the United States results in an efficient transfer of wealth from a political perspective. There should be no excessive waste or unnecessary inefficiencies caused by such exchange. As Tullock (1965), Eckert (1973), Hilton (1972), Benson (1983b), and Benson and Greenhut (1986) observed, however, the bureaucrats and commissioners to whom the antitrust enforcement power is delegated do not have incentives to behave efficiently. Why the delegation? The answer is because the legislature has a time constraint, and time spent enforcing the rights it has granted reduces the new rights assignments that the legislature can make (Benson 1983b). In addition, the legislature requires the agreement of a large number of people for it to take

---

[4]In many cases, enforcement agencies have the ability to assign rights, bypassing the legislature. This opens the possibility that an agency might favor an interest group the legislature does not wish to support and tend to corrupt public officials (see Benson and Baden 1985). One would expect that any deviation between legislatively supported interest groups and agency-supported interest groups to be a short-run phenomenon, however, because ultimately the legislature can control the agency through its budget.

action, so it will be an inefficient organization for accomplishing the enforcement of rights (Erlich and Posner 1974). For these reasons, the legislature delegates the enforcement of the rights it assigns.

The favored interest groups will also want the enforcement function delegated. The theory of bureaucracy suggests that a bureau will produce more output than would be most preferred by the legislature (Tullock 1965; Niskanen 1968, 1971, 1975); and when enforcement of a rights assignment is the output, the result will be over-enforcement (Benson and Greenhut 1986). Because the favored interest will prefer a rights assignment larger than the legislature will grant, over-enforcement by the enforcing agency will benefit the special interest. This explanation applies not only to all types of regulation but to antitrust as well. Special interests will prefer that the enforcement of rights be delegated because the rights will be over-enforced, increasing the special interest's benefits. As Niskanen (1975) observed, agency managers' incentives are closely linked to the size of the agency's budget; and although his model was applied generally to bureaucracy, it fits antitrust as well.[5]

The antitrust model examined in this paper is a straightforward use of Niskanen's bureaucracy model applied to the regulatory environment characterized by Peltzman and others. In general, special interests approach the legislature with demands for favorable property rights assignments. And rights are assigned in a way that establishes a majority for the legislator. After assignment, enforcement is delegated to an agency that over-enforces. If one then considers the agency to be an interest group, one can even support the Stigler-Peltzman predictions of political efficiency. The initial assignment was made due to a political exchange with an interest group; but once the enforcement mechanism is in place, the enforcer becomes another interest group, thus increasing the demand for enforcement. The supposed conflict between the Stigler-Peltzman interest group approach and the Niskanen bureaucracy approach raised by Weingast and Moran (1983) may not exist at all if bureaucrats play an interest group role.

Several vital aspects of the antitrust laws warrant specification at this point. First, the laws are economy-wide rather than focused on just one or a few industries. Second, the laws are couched in very vague language, so that what constitutes a violation is largely a matter of interpretation. Third, the laws involve a commission. Fourth, they involve the courts. The importance of these features distinguishes

---

[5]Niskanen's early model (1968, 1971) has been subjected to a number of criticisms, several of which were dealt with by Niskanen (1975). See also Benson (1981, 1983a).

our antitrust model from the bureaucracy model and from Stigler's model of special interest legislation.

In essence, the antitrust laws represent a transfer of rights from large economic entities to small ones, the response of the legislator having been tuned to the times. This is why the laws are economy-wide in scope, rather than being centered on a few industries.

The advantage of having a vague statute is that it could be enforced, not only against those viewed as a present threat to small entities but also against any future threats. In addition, the special interest vagueness allows paradigms to be applied, such as the incipiency doctrine, in which substance can completely disregard the realities of existing competition and economic theory (Greenhut and Ohta 1979; Greenhut et al. 1985). It also explains away (and contradicts) the idea that the antitrust statutes were designed to improve the country's markets and to yield more efficient economic relationships.

What about antitrust enforcement being effected by commissions and courts? Are not appointed commissions less aggressive than the classical bureaucracy model would suggest? Hilton (1972), Eckert (1973), and others have proposed different outputs by commission regulators than by civil service regulators. Essentially, Hilton considered commissioners to be maximizing support, in effect seeking future employment.[6] But maximizing support is certainly consistent with favoring powerful political interest groups. Eckert viewed their salaries as being fixed and not tied to budget size; thus, he characterized commissioners as effort minimizers. It may appear to follow, then, that commissions have no real impact, as Stigler and Friedland (1965) suggested with respect to electric utilities. But commissions enforcing rights that are in the best interest of the regulated industry, as Stigler (1971) suggested is likely, could easily appear to be doing nothing if by doing "something" observers mean "restricting the industry." Furthermore, non-salary perquisites of the office are tied to the size of a commission's operator and level of enforcement. Thus, while the incentives for excessive enforcement may be relatively weak for a commissioner, they still exist, and the general conclusions of Niskanen's view of enforcers hold.

The courts also offer a basic difference vis-à-vis civil servants in the bureaucracy model. One difference is they are less subject to capture than are bureaus. A second difference is that they will be the final authority, because vague legislation fails to identify specific actions that violate the assigned rights. It is our objective to apply

---

[6]See also Mitnick and Weiss (1974), Russell and Shelton (1974), and Joskow (1974) for arguments similar to Hilton's.

the bureaucracy model to a set of laws, the antitrust laws, that are economy-wide in scope, vague, and enforced by commissioners and the courts.

Completing the Theory: Ambiguity and the Courts

The Sherman Act was basically inspired by and lobbied for by interest groups made up of small economic entities, particularly from the agricultural sector. Rather than a specific act aimed against, say, machinery companies, the general law could also protect small farmers from large banks or other present or future entities that might threaten them.[7] This same principle applies today with regard to civil rights legislation. Rather than specific laws, a general law to protect civil rights can be enforced by the courts against any present or future violators. The point is that if the special interest group has a large enough constituency and a distinct identity (for example, small economic entity, minority race), a general regulation enforced by the courts can provide more benefits to the interest group than a specific regulation.

While it is true that a series of specific regulations could accomplish the same thing, this would require the special interest to continue returning to the legislature for additional legislation whenever it appeared that a transfer of rights would be beneficial. A general transfer of rights from large economic entities to small ones will continue to benefit the small entities in specific instances that the small entities could not foresee. Because the characteristics of the recipient of the transfer are relatively well defined, this type of transfer will provide more benefits than would a specific regulation. With a general transfer of this type, however, it is not always clear when the law has been violated, so the courts enter as an interpreter of the intent that underlies the law. As long as the courts interpret the intent as being the protection of small economic entities from large ones, the small entities that compose the special interest will benefit from the transfer.

The ambiguity of a general transfer of this type also benefits the recipient, because one can never be certain when the line has been crossed that constitutes a violation. In the case of antitrust, this could cause large economic entities to wield their power carefully, lest they be accused of a violation. Again, this is to the benefit of the small economic units that made up the special interest.

[7]Note, however, that the Interstate Commerce Commission (ICC) act was passed at about the same time to regulate rail rates, in part because of pressure from farmers (and, of course, from the railroads themselves).

Another factor is that the courts are likely to be less influenced by special interests than by a governmental agency. In many circumstances a special interest would prefer enforcement by an agency as a means of increasing the effective transfer of rights, but this may not always be so. When rights are transferred from large economic entities to small ones, there is always the threat that once an enforcing agency is established, the large entities will use their economic power to influence the agency, resulting in a transfer of rights back to them.[8] When rights are being transferred from large entities to small ones, there is good reason for the special interest to prefer the enforcement of rights to take place through the courts. A court enforcer may prevent the large economic entities from capturing the enforcing agency.

In summary, antitrust laws tend to transfer rights from large entities to small ones. There are two reasons for special interests to prefer court enforcement. First, the general transfer can apply to cases not specifically mentioned in the law; court interpretation is required to identify these particular cases. Second, court enforcement will prevent the large economic entities from whom rights were transferred from capturing the enforcing agency to reverse the transfer.

Interest Groups and Antitrust

The demand for antitrust legislation began building during the 1870s and 1880s (Areeda 1974, p. 44). It involved the formation of many organizations "with revealing names like the National Anti-Monopoly Cheap Freight Railway League" (Neale 1970, p. 12). The primary source of pressure was from farm groups that faced what they perceived to be excessively high rail rates as well as high prices of farm equipment and other manufactured goods. They believed that the high prices were caused by monopoly power exercised in the market and by import tariffs. There was also a general belief among farmers that eastern financiers controlled the credit market and charged them unfairly high interest rates. "Dissatisfaction with manufacturers of farm machinery and other goods, railroads, and eastern financiers became the cry against monopoly" (Areeda 1974, p. 43), and because "the farmers were better endowed with political influence than economic strength, . . . organizations like the National Grange and the National Farmers Alliance insistently demanded

---

[8]This can be observed today in the Department of Energy. Originally established to control large oil companies, much of its early effects amounted to a transfer from large oil companies to small ones and to the general public. The department's recent programs, however, primarily benefit large energy producers.

some control of the railways and of monopolies in general" (Neale 1970, p. 12). Neale concluded that "the paramount aim of politicians" in passing the Sherman Act was to meet this demand for action by such organizations.[9]

The business interests that farmers opposed were not without political power themselves, and Congress did not choose full-scale regulation or nationalization of these enterprises due to the political pressure from business (Areeda 1974, p. 44). Thus, the Sherman Act represents congressional attempts to balance the interests of various interest groups, as described by Peltzman (1976). Interest group pressure rather than a desire for economic efficiency led to the passage of the Sherman Act, and Neale (1970, p. 473) noted that the courts have consistently refused to consider economic efficiency issues in judging whether an antitrust violation has taken place, although many Department of Justice and Federal Trade Commission economists stress such issues in their analyses.

The passage of the Sherman Act fits well into the model of special interest legislation. It was clearly understood at the time that farmers demanded some antitrust action and that the passage of the Sherman Act was a response to that demand (see Gordon 1963). It was never intended to produce efficiency; even the name gives away the fact that the law was intended as a transfer of property rights away from trusts. What else could antitrust mean?

The form of the Sherman Act can also be understood within the context of the model. The act was passed to benefit the farmers as a special interest group, but the businesses the act opposed also had considerable political power. In balancing the interests of both groups, Congress could hardly legislate away the businesses. Viewed in this light, the vague nature of the statute and the delegation of its enforcement to the Department of Justice and to the courts make good sense from the standpoint of the farmers for whom the act was passed. Because the act generally declares combinations, contracts, or conspiracies in restraint of trade to be illegal, it is simply a vague piece of legislation that endorsed the common law and was designed to protect small economic entities from being harmed by large ones. Because the farmers were small entities and the railroads, banks, and manufacturers were large entities, the act appears to be a one-way transfer of property rights to the farmers (and any other small businesses that might feel harmed).

[9]Baxter (1979) and Katzman (1980) have argued that there is no strong evidence that one group is being favored by the antitrust laws; but Williamson (1979), commenting on Baxter's argument, found room for disagreement.

The structure of the act benefited the farmers in several ways. First, because the act did not name offenders ahead of time (it was not aimed at railroads or banks specifically but at anyone acting to restrain trade), action could be taken not only against present offenders but also against future ones. Because individual farmers could always foresee being economically small entities in relation to the other businesses with whom they dealt, the umbrella of the act protected farmers from a wide variety of economic threats.

Second, because of the act's vagueness, it enabled small economic entities to bring complaints under the act in a wide variety of circumstances. That vagueness would also ensure that there was always the possibility of a violation, having the corollary effect of making larger businesses behave cautiously even before any enforcement proceedings began, simply because of the threat of action.

Third, because victims could bring complaints, the Sherman Act could be over-enforced, even though an agency does not have the direct power of enforcement.[10] As a result, the act ended up providing more benefits to the special interests that the act favored than Congress had originally intended. The act was an example of special interest legislation and was recognized as such at the time of its passage.

The next major development in antitrust was the passage of the Federal Trade Commission Act and the Clayton Act in 1914. The establishment of the FTC was the result of many sources of political pressure, including the big businesses that found themselves constrained by the vagueness of the Sherman Act. There was considerable pressure from business organizations for more clearly articulated standards, and some observers have concluded that the establishment of the FTC was a victory for those businesses that wanted to ensure their political power and protect themselves from competition (Areeda 1974, pp. 47–48; Kolko 1963). In this view, the FTC was created to advise businessmen, to approve of their collusive organizations, and to create order in markets. As in the model above, large businesses could not effectively capture the courts, but the FTC gave them an agency through which they could use their economic power and influence.

Clearly, the FTC is not solely a pro-business agency, but was developed through compromise. The *Ralph Nader Study Group*

---

[10]Neale (1970, pp. 374, 385) noted that both the Federal Trade Commission and the Department of Justice rely almost exclusively on complaints to determine when the antitrust laws should be enforced, and that complaints predictably come from those who believe they are being injured.

809

Report on Antitrust recognized that "in 1914 both sides—those advocating a kind of business advisor and those seeking more energetic trustbusting—compromised to produce the Federal Trade Commission" (Green et al. 1972). And Areeda (1974, p. 48) noted that "similar differences of opinion were reflected in the Clayton Act, passed in the same year. . . . These differences were compromised in the ultimate enactment." As Peltzman's theory of regulation would predict, the favored group will not receive the maximum possible benefit. The FTC and Clayton acts, however, can clearly be seen as a transfer of rights to big business in response to the larger-than-intended transfer away from big business that had been the result of the Sherman Act.

It is interesting that the 1914 rights transfer was reversed somewhat as the FTC and the courts began to rule against incipient violations. In *Triangle Conduit and Cable Company v. FTC* (168 F.2d 175, 7th Cir. [1948]), for example, the court held that manufacturers utilizing a basing-point pricing system in order to stabilize competition among themselves were in violation of the Sherman Act. In itself, this decision seems unremarkable.[11] But the court proposed that unilateral adoption of a basing-point pricing scheme by an individual firm could also be prohibited, as long as other firms might adopt similar schemes. Even if unilateral at the start, the court saw this as the first step toward a conspiracy (see Greenhut [1970] 1974, chaps. 7, 14). In *Fashion Originators Guild v. FTC* (381 U.S. 357, 367 [1965]), the Supreme Court held that it was an object "of the Federal Trade Commission Act to reach not merely in their fruition but also in their incipiency," and in *E. B. Muller and Co. v. FTC* (142 F.2d 511, 517 6th Cir. [1944]) the Sixth Circuit Court ruled that "the purpose of the Federal Trade Commission Act is to prevent potential injury by stopping unfair methods of competition in their incipiency." Clearly in antitrust cases this represents a transfer of rights from large economic entities to small ones. The party bringing the complaint has to show neither actual nor present harms; it must only show that some harm can be predicted as a result of the offending policy.[12]

Exemptions and Interest Groups

Perhaps the strongest evidence of the influence of interest groups on antitrust legislation lies in their success in gaining immunity to

---

[11]See Greenhut ([1956] 1983) for a concurrence with the decision.

[12]The incipiency doctrine reflects the public's distrust of oligopolies as well as the general failure (including that of economists) to distinguish between organized (collusive) and competitive oligopolies, the market prices and factor incomes of which are

the antitrust laws (Adams 1965). Agricultural interests comprised the major pressure group pushing for the early antitrust laws, so it is not surprising that agricultural organizations were able to obtain specific exemptions from coverage under the antitrust laws. Section 6 of the Clayton Act partially exempts agricultural organizations, allowing farmers to form cooperative associations without violating the law. The Capper-Volstead Act of 1922 extends the Clayton Act to exempt capital stock agricultural cooperatives that were not exempted under the Clayton Act.

The courts have interpreted the Clayton Act as allowing farm organizations to "set association policy, fix prices at which their cooperative will sell their produce, and otherwise carry on like a business corporation without thereby violating the antitrust laws."[13] Thus, agricultural interest groups—who were instrumental in having the antitrust laws passed as a transfer of property rights to them—also had the political power to see that the laws were not applied to them, even when their actions represented combinations or contracts in a restraint of trade that clearly would have been considered a violation if committed by another business entity. A similar exemption was given to fishermen's organizations in the Fisheries Cooperative Marketing Act of 1934. In some cases, the courts ruled in favor of the special interests; in others the interests were able to get additional acts passed that specifically exempted them.

In 1908, the Supreme Court ruled in *Lowe v. Lawlor* (208 U.S. 274) that a nationwide boycott organized by a union to persuade wholesalers and retailers not to buy a particular firm's product was an interference with the interstate shipment of goods and, therefore, a restraint of trade. The Court awarded treble damages and ordered the union and individual union members to pay shares of the award. Following the decision, labor union officials "immediately commenced pressure for exemption of labor from the antitrust laws." The drive resulted in the Clayton Act's declaration that labor organizations are exempt from the antitrust laws (Northrup and Bloom 1965, p. 313). Section 6 of the act reads: "[N]othing contained in the antitrust laws shall be construed to forbid the existence and operation of labor . . . organizations, instituted for the purposes of mutual help,

---

of opposite order (Greenhut [1970] 1974). This doctrine and its increasing use, reflected even in Judge Learned Hand's *Alcoa* decision, are based on the failure to recognize that conscious parallelism of action by oligopolists can derive from competitive behavior and in turn generate market-efficient results. The vested interests of those who identify with the small entities must condemn any form of Loschian conjectural variations behavior (Greenhut et al. 1975) and thus relegate the antitrust laws to a set of restrictions with no roots at all in any quest for economic efficiency.

[13] Maryland and Virginia Milk Producers v. United States, 362 U.S. 458, 466 (1970).

and not having capital stock or conducted for profits, or to forbid or restrain individual members of such organizations from lawfully carrying out the legitimate objects thereof, be held or construed to be illegal combinations or conspiracies in restraint of trade under the antitrust laws." Section 20 of the act prevents the use of federal injunctions against strikes, boycotts, picketing, and similar activities "in any case between an employer and employees, or between persons employed and persons seeking employment, involving or growing out of, a dispute concerning terms or conditions of employment."

Despite the Clayton Act's exemption of labor from the antitrust laws, the Supreme Court ruled in 1921 in *Duplex Printing Company v. Deering* (254 U.S. 433) that labor unions could be held accountable under the antitrust laws for some of their actions. In this case, a union that was trying to organize the Duplex plant had succeeded in getting members of other unions to refuse to handle the firm's products. The Court held that Section 20 protected a union only when its members were employed by the company they were acting against. The American Federation of Labor turned to Congress; after continual pressure, the Norris-La Guardia Act was passed in 1932, which deprived the federal courts of antitrust jurisdiction in almost all labor disputes.

The labor case parallels the agricultural case. Though labor interests were not actively seeking passage of the antitrust laws, this powerful lobbying group nevertheless managed to remain exempt from the laws' influence. If the courts did not rule in favor of a special interest, then the special interest was able to turn to Congress to have exemptions to the antitrust laws legislated for it.

Other exemptions could be mentioned. For example, if regulated industries are the beneficiaries of regulation, as Stigler (1971) argued, then the regulated firms should be able to protect their benefits from potential challenges through the antitrust laws. As Areeda (1974, pp. 105–14) and Adams (1965, pp. 277–84) noted, regulated industries are largely exempt from the antitrust laws. Similarly, the Miller-Tydings Act (1937) and the McGuire-Keough Act (1952) were results of a movement among small retailers that had successfully obtained passage of "fair trade" laws in 45 states prior to 1937. This legislation exempted firms from antitrust laws in states with legalized minimum resale prices. The "fair trade" laws, which are widely viewed as protecting small shopkeepers from the more efficient larger retail chains (in a clearly collusive manner in restraint of trade), caused Neale (1970, p. 276) to note that "many political groups which would yield to none in zeal for trust busting are to be found in the van of the so-called fair trade movement. . . ." The Robinson-Patman Act preventing price discrimination is yet another example of an antitrust law designed to protect a special interest, that interest once again being small retailers who could not buy in large enough quantities to receive quantity discounts often given to chains.[14] The exemptions to the antitrust laws are all easily recognized as the result of special interest pressure on the legislature.

The Antitrust Laws over Time

Neale (1970, p. 11) observed that "there is evidence that the aims and scope of antitrust policy have changed a good deal since the passage of the Sherman Act, and may easily change some more in the future." Following the interest group theory of regulation, this is precisely what one would expect if the relative strengths of interest groups change over time (Benson 1984; Weingast and Moran 1983). For example, Clarkson and Muris (1982) noted that prior to 1969 the bulk of the FTC antitrust enforcement was aimed at discouraging price competition under Robinson-Patman when it threatened the well-being of small firms. After significant criticism, the FTC in 1969 suddenly closed about 600 of its investigations, reorganized the commission's work to deemphasize Robinson-Patman, and began several large-scale industry investigations. Similarly, the settling of the AT&T case and the closing of the IBM case within months of each other can be seen as a response to a change in the political climate during the Reagan era.

Posner's (1969, p. 83) study of the FTC emphasizes that a congressman must support the demands of interest groups in his district, noting that "the welfare of his constituents may depend disproportionately on a few key industries. The promotion of the industries becomes one of his most important duties as a representative of the district." One might well expect cases to be biased in favor of the firms in the districts of legislators serving on committees that have oversight over the FTC; this is exactly what Faith et al. (1982) found. Weingast and Moran (1983, p. 775) reached a similar conclusion with regard to oversight committees, noting that "markedly different preferences on the committee lead to major shifts in agency policy." Because oversight committees are merely a reflection of interest group demands, Weingast and Moran and Faith et al. conclude that the FTC's output is best explained by the interest group theory.

[14]See Ross (1984) for a discussion of the interest groups who were influential in obtaining passage of the Robinson-Patman Act and for empirical estimates of the benefits obtained and the costs incurred by various groups as a result of the enforcement of the act.

813

41

This discussion places a different light on the general vagueness of the antitrust laws. Earlier, the vagueness of the laws was seen as a means to transfer rights to one well-defined group (for example, small economic entities) from other unspecified groups. Small farmers could obtain transfers from railroads, banks, manufacturers, and any other future economic threats without the threats being spelled out in the law. But the laws' vagueness also benefits the legislature; due to its oversight capacity, the legislature will be able to influence the type of enforcement in response to the changing power and demands of interest groups, all without writing a new law.

In light of the fairly obvious political nature of the passage and enforcement of antitrust laws, we might wonder why such widespread acceptance of the efficiency-enhancing goals of antitrust appears to characterize the economics profession. This view appears to be an after-the-fact rationalization, however, because economists were not advocates for or even concerned with passage of the earliest statutes. As Scherer (1970, p. 424) reported:

> About the only group in America other than big businessmen outspokenly unconcerned about the trust problem were the professional economists. Many were captivated by Darwin's theory of biological selection. They saw the growth of big business as a natural evolutionary response consistent with economies of scale, or when economics were patently absent from mergers, as a step necessary to eliminate cut-throat competition. But in that unenlightened era, the views of unenlightened economists concerning big business had little influence on public policy.

Clearly, Scherer holds with the efficiency-enhancing perception of antitrust, and he reflects the view that came to dominate the profession early in the 20th century.

Summary and Conclusion

This paper has fit the antitrust laws into the special interest theory of regulation, stressing the influence of special interests on antitrust. The paper also spotlighted the significant differences between antitrust and other forms of regulation, emphasizing the vagueness of the antitrust statutes, their broad focus, and the fact that the laws are generally subject to interpretation and enforcement by the FTC and the courts rather than by a narrowly focused agency. It is clear that the effects of antitrust diverge from those of other forms of regulation. For example, the interaction of vagueness and use of the courts sometimes requires legislators to pass new statutes in order to protect the favored special interest. On the other hand, to the extent that the

FTC serves as the final authority, the legislators' interest in reelection is being protected by insulating the legislature from direct responsibility for specific actions. Most generally, we propose that antitrust in the United States centers on special interest effects and the legislators' quests for reelection. The real antitrust paradox is to have expected legislatures to be concerned with the general welfare.

References

Abrams, Burton A., and Settle, Russell F. "The Economic Theory of Regulation and Public Financing of Presidential Elections." *Journal of Political Economy* 86 (April 1978): 245–57.

Adams, Walter. "Exemptions from Antitrust: Their Extent and Rationale." In *Perspective on Antitrust Policy*, pp. 273–311. Edited by Almarin Phillips. Princeton, N.J.: Princeton University Press, 1965.

Areeda, Phillip. *Antitrust Analysis*. Boston: Little, Brown and Co., 1974.

Asch, Peter. *Economic Theory and the Antitrust Dilemma*. New York: John Wiley and Sons, 1970.

Baxter, William F. "The Political Economy of Antitrust." In *The Political Economy of Antitrust: Principal Paper by William Baxter*, pp. 3–50. Edited by Robert O. Tollison. Lexington, Mass.: Lexington Books, 1979.

Becker, Gary S. "A Theory of Competition among Pressure Groups for Political Influence." *Quarterly Journal of Economics* 98 (August 1983): 371–400.

Benson, Bruce L. "Why Are Congressional Committees Dominated by 'High Demand' Legislators?" *Southern Economic Journal* 48 (July 1981): 68–77.

Benson, Bruce L. "High Demand Legislative Committees and Bureaucratic Output." *Public Finance Quarterly* 11 (July 1983a): 259–81.

Benson, Bruce L. "The Economic Theory of Regulation as an Explanation of Politics Toward Bank Mergers and Holding Company Acquisitions." *Antitrust Bulletin* 28 (Winter 1983b): 839–62.

Benson, Bruce L. "Rent Seeking from a Property Rights Perspective." *Southern Economic Journal* 51 (October 1984): 388–400.

Benson, Bruce L., and Baden, John. "The Political Economy of Government Corruption: The Logic of Underground Government." *Journal of Legal Studies* 14 (June 1985): 391–410.

Benson, Bruce L., and Greenhut, M. L. "Special Interest, Bureaucrats, and Antitrust: An Explanation of the Antitrust Paradox." In *Antitrust and Regulation*, pp. 53–90. Edited by Ronald E. Grieson. Lexington, Mass.: Lexington Books, 1986.

Bork, Robert H. *The Antitrust Paradox: A Policy at War with Itself*. New York: Basic Books, 1978.

Clarkson, Kenneth, and Muris, Timothy J. "Letting Competition Serve Consumers." In *Instead of Regulation: Alternatives to Federal Regulatory Agencies*, pp. 135–68. Edited by Robert W. Poole. Lexington, Mass.: Lexington Books, 1982.

Eckert, Ross. "On the Incentives of Regulators: The Case of Taxicabs." *Public Choice* 14 (Spring 1973): 83–99.

Erlich, Isaac, and Posner, Richard. "An Economic Analysis of Legal Rule-Making." *Journal of Legal Studies* 3 (January 1974): 257–86.

Faith, Roger L.; Leavens, Donald R.; and Tollison, Robert D. "Antitrust Pork Barrel." *Journal of Law and Economics* 25 (October 1982): 329–42.

Gordon, Sanford D., "Attitudes Towards Trusts Prior to the Sherman Act." *Southern Economic Journal* 30 (October 1963): 156–67.

Green, Mark J.; Moore, Beverly C.; and Wasserstein, Bruce. *The Closed Enterprise System: Ralph Nader's Study Group Report on Antitrust Enforcement.* New York: Grossman Publishers, 1972.

Greenhut, M. L. *Plant Location in Theory and Practice* [1956]. Westport, Conn.: Greenwood Publishing Co., 1983.

Greenhut, M. L. *A Theory of the Firm in Economic Space* [1970]. Austin, Texas: Lone Star Publishers, 1974.

Greenhut, M. L., and Ohta, H. "Vertical Integration of Successive Oligopolists." *American Economic Review* 69 (March 1979): 137–41.

Greenhut, M. L.; Hwang, C. S.; Norman, G.; and Smithson, C. "An Anomaly in the Service Industry: The Effect of Entry on Fees." *The Economic Journal* 95 (March 1985): 169–77.

Greenhut, M. L.; Hwang, C. S.; and Ohta, H. "Observations on the Shape and Relevance of the Spatial Demand Function." *Econometrica* 63 (July 1975): 669–82.

High, Jack. "Bork's Paradox: Static versus Dynamic Efficiency in Antitrust Analysis." *Contemporary Policy Issues* 3 (Winter 1984–85): 21–34.

Hilton, George. "The Basic Behavior of Regulatory Commissions." *American Economic Review* 62 (May 1972): 47–54.

Holcombe, Randall G. *Public Finance and the Political Process.* Carbondale: Southern Illinois University Press, 1983.

Holcombe, Randall G. *An Economic Analysis of Democracy.* Carbondale: Southern Illinois University Press, 1985.

Jarrell, G. "The Demand for State Regulation of the Electric Utility Industry." *Journal of Law and Economics* 21 (October 1978): 269–95.

Joskow, P. "Inflation and Environmental Concern: Structure Change in the Process of Public Utility Price Regulation." *Journal of Law and Economics* 17 (October 1974): 291–327.

Kau, James B., and Rubin, Paul H. "Voting on Minimum Wages: A Time Series Analysis." *Journal of Political Economy* 82 (April 1978): 337–42.

Katzman, Robert A. *Regulatory Bureaucracy: The Federal Trade Commission and Antitrust Policy.* Cambridge, Mass.: MIT Press, 1980.

Kolko, Gabriel. *The Triumph of Conservatism: A Re-Interpretation of American History, 1900–1916.* New York: Free Press, 1963.

McCormick, Robert E., and Tollison, Robert D. *Politicians, Legislation, and the Economy: An Inquiry into the Interest Group Theory of Government.* Boston: Martinus Nijhoff Publishing, 1981.

Mitnick, B., and Weiss, C. "The Siting Impasse and a Rational Choice Model of Regulatory Behavior: An Agency for Power Plant Siting." *Journal of Environmental Economics and Management* 1 (August 1974): 150–71.

Neale, A. D. *The Antitrust Laws of the U.S.A.* Cambridge: Cambridge University Press, 1970.

Niskanen, William A. "The Peculiar Economics of Bureaucracy." *American Economic Review* 58 (May 1968): 293–305.

Niskanen, William A. *Bureaucracy and Representative Government.* Chicago: Aldine-Atherton, 1971.

Niskanen, William A. "Bureaucrats and Politicians." *Journal of Law and Economics* 18 (December 1975): 617–43.

Northrup, Herbert R., and Bloom, Gordon F. "Labor Unions and Antitrust Laws: Past, Present, and Proposals." In *Perspectives in Antitrust Policy,* pp. 312–54. Edited by Almarin Phillips. Princeton: Princeton University Press, 1965.

Peltzman, Sam. "Toward a More General Theory of Regulation." *Journal of Law and Economics* 19 (August 1976): 211–40.

Posner, Richard. "The Federal Trade Commission." *University of Chicago Law Review* 37 (1969): 47–89.

Posner, Richard. *Economic Analysis of Law.* Boston: Little, Brown, 1972.

Posner, Richard. "Theories of Economic Regulation." *Bell Journal of Economics and Management Science* 5 (Autumn 1974): 335–58.

Priest, George L. "The Common Law Process and the Selection of Efficient Rules." *Journal of Legal Studies* 6 (January 1977): 65–82.

Ross, Thomas W. "Winners and Losers under the Robinson-Patman Act." *Journal of Law and Economics* 27 (October 1984): 243–71.

Rubin, Paul H. "Why Is the Common Law Efficient?" *Journal of Legal Studies* 6 (January 1977): 51–63.

Russell, Milton, and Shelton, Robert. "A Model of Regulatory Agency Behavior." *Public Choice* 20 (Winter 1974): 47–62.

Scherer, F. M. *Industrial Market Structure and Economic Performance.* Chicago: Rand McNally, 1970.

Smith, Janet K. "Production of Licensing Legislation: An Economic Analysis of Interstate Differences." *Journal of Legal Studies* 11 (January 1982): 117–37.

Stigler, George J. "The Theory of Economic Regulation." *Bell Journal of Economics and Management Science* 2 (Spring 1971): 3–21.

Stigler, George J. "The Origin of the Sherman Act." *Journal of Legal Studies* 14 (January 1985): 1–12.

Stigler, George J., and Friedland, Claire. "What Can Regulators Regulate? The Case of Electricity." *Journal of Law and Economics* 5 (October 1965): 1–16.

Tollison, Robert D. "Rent Seeking: A Survey." *Kyklos* (1982): 575–602.

Tullock, Gordon. *The Politics of Bureaucracy.* Washington, D.C.: Public Affairs Press, 1965.

Weingast, Barry R., and Moran, Mark J. "Bureaucratic Discretion or Congressional Control? Regulatory Policymaking by the Federal Trade Commission." *Journal of Political Economy* 91 (October 1983): 765–800.

Williamson, Oliver. "Commentary." In *The Political Economy of Antitrust: Principal Paper by William Baxter,* pp. 77–93. Edited by Robert D. Tollison. Lexington, Mass.: Lexington Books, 1979.

EMPIRICAL EVIDENCE ON FTC ENFORCEMENT OF THE MERGER GUIDELINES

MALCOLM B. COATE and FRED S. MCCHESNEY*

The Justice Department's 1982/1984 merger guidelines identify various factors—concentration, entry barriers, ease of collusion, efficiency—that would thereafter determine whether the government will challenge a merger. Analysts have criticized enforcement agencies, however, for not following the guidelines, and criticize the guidelines themselves for not identifying the weights attached to the factors. Using a 1982-86 sample of seventy horizontal mergers, we examine which factors influenced Federal Trade Commission decisions to challenge mergers. The relative importance of the guidelines and other factors in merger challenges is measured, and related empirical issues are also explored.

I. INTRODUCTION

The 1982/1984 "merger guidelines" adopted by the Antitrust Division of the Department of Justice (DOJ) and followed by the Federal Trade Commission (FTC) marked important antitrust policy changes by the Reagan administration. The Herfindahl index replaced the four-firm ratios used in the old (1968) guidelines as the measure of concentration. Other non-concentration factors (barriers to entry, ease of collusion) were elevated in importance. In the 1984 revision of the 1982 guidelines, efficiency considerations were for the first time generally included as a relevant factor.

* Bureau of Economics, Federal Trade Commission; and Professor of Economics and Robert T. Thompson Professor of Law and Business, Emory University. Richard Higgins helped shape several points analyzed here while co-authoring an earlier paper with us (Coate et al. [1990]). He, George Bittlingmayer, Thomas DiLorenzo, David Haddock, James Langenfeld, William Shughart, and Robert Tollison provided helpful comments. This article is based on nonpublic data obtained from Federal Trade Commission internal files. The Commission's General Counsel has authorized publication of such data in aggregated form under commission Rule 5.12(c), 16 C.F.R. 5.12(c). The analysis and conclusions presented herein are those of the authors and do not purport to represent the view of the Commission, or of any individual commissioner, or the official position of any commission bureau.

However, commentators who applauded the newer guidelines have complained subsequently that the Reagan administration did not apply them. The objections of two veteran academic antitrusters, Krattenmaker and Pitofsky [1988, 232], are typical:

> Certainly, in many respects, the announced merger guidelines are a substantial accomplishment....This accomplishment, however, has been almost completely undercut by the Administration's behavior in ignoring those guidelines in practice and instead enforcing, without any public explanation, a merger policy that was not only exceptionally lenient but substantially at odds with professed standards.

In an earlier paper (Coate et al. [1990]), we, along with coauthor Richard Higgins, tested one hypothesis why merger policy (at least at the FTC in 1982-86) has departed from mere enforcement of the guidelines: politics. We showed how external pressures imposed on the Commission by Congress to block mergers, independent of the factors identified in the guidelines as meriting a merger challenge, are a statistically significant factor in the FTC's decision whether to challenge a merger.

47

In the present paper, we use the same data—seventy horizontal mergers from 1982 to 1986—to examine in greater detail the charges that the FTC has not followed the guidelines, plus several related issues not considered in our earlier article. These include the extent to which various guidelines factors are either necessary or sufficient for the Commission to vote to challenge a merger, and the role of the new efficiency criterion in merger evaluation. An econometric model is presented as one approach to determine how the FTC balances the various guidelines factors. This allows an estimate of the relative importance and influence of lawyers and economists in the evaluation process. Finally, the data also permit an appraisal of the extent to which a structuralist or Chicago approach to competition issues dominated merger votes at the FTC during the relevant period.

Section II discusses briefly the factors identified in the merger guidelines and the process by which the Commission determines whether to oppose a proposed merger. That section also identifies several testable hypotheses concerning the Commission's reliance on the guidelines variables. Section III then explains the data to be used for testing. Section IV, the bulk of the paper, presents empirical evidence concerning the FTC's use of the guidelines and related issues.

II. EVALUATING MERGERS AT THE FEDERAL TRADE COMMISSION

The Merger Guidelines

The Federal Trade Commission enforces (along with the Justice Department) the federal antitrust laws, including those applicable to mergers. The Commission takes formal action through a majority vote of the sitting (ordinarily five) commissioners. Commissioners vote whether to challenge a merger on the basis of formal staff memoranda that the lawyers of the Bureau of Competition (BC) and the

economists of the Bureau of Economics (BE) prepare and submit separately. The memoranda are based in turn on data submitted to the Commission by would-be merging partners as required by the Hart-Scott-Rodino Act, and on information developed independently by FTC staff lawyers and economists. Mergers that raise greater anticompetitive concerns usually elicit a supplemental FTC demand for more information, known as a Hart-Scott-Rodino "second request." The parties to the merger also may present their own analyses to the staff, and thus may influence either the Bureau of Competition or Bureau of Economics evaluation.

In analyzing a prospective merger, the FTC claims that its own process follows the Department of Justice merger guidelines.[1] The current guidelines were promulgated in June 1982 (and fine-tuned somewhat in 1984), replacing the guidelines issued in 1968. They focus on preventing a price increase from enhanced market power due to a merger, particularly when no countervailing efficiencies are present. To determine whether such a price increase is likely, the guidelines call for examination of several factors: concentration (including definition of relevant markets), entry barriers, ease of collusion, efficiency, and failing-firm status.[2]

Concentration analysis, based on the Herfindahl-Hirschman index (HHI), is probably the guidelines' best known aspect. The 1984 version establishes three index classifications:

1. The FTC's "Statement Concerning Horizontal Mergers" of June 14, 1982 noted that the 1982 guidelines had been a joint effort of the DOJ and the Commission staffs, and that the guidelines "will be given considerable weight" in FTC merger evaluations.

2. Of course, antitrust lawyers and economists differ considerably about the relevance, measure and even definition of such things as concentration, efficiency and entry barriers. See for example Demsetz [1982]. In this article, we take as given the definitions and measures provided in the merger guidelines and the relevance of the variables included therein. Our interest is solely in the positive issue whether the guidelines are followed in government merger enforcement.

1. Where the post-merger Herfindahl index is under 1000, the merger will be challenged only "in extraordinary circumstances." Thus, a Herfindahl index of 1000 is a safe harbor; mergers falling below that level will rarely be challenged.

2. If the post-merger Herfindahl index is between 1000 and 1800 and the merger increases the Herfindahl by 100 points, the government is "likely" to challenge these transactions unless other factors suggest "the merger is not likely substantially to lessen competition."

3. Finally, for a post-merger index value over 1800, a challenge is "likely" if the merger increases the index by over 50 points, unless other factors suggest "the merger is not likely substantially to lessen competition." However, there will be a challenge in all but "extraordinary circumstances" if the merger raises the Herfindahl index by over 100 points to a level substantially above 1800.

The remaining (non-concentration) factors in the guidelines influence the decision within each Herfindahl index class. Ease of entry will prevent current rivals from raising price for any extended period, and so lowers the likelihood of a merger challenge. Entry is considered easy if a new firm can break into the market within two years of a merger, and difficult if entry would take longer. The guidelines note that likelihood of entry is a function of sunk assets, industry growth rate, economies of scale, and the specific capital needed to compete. But no quantitative measures of these entry determinants are provided, leaving one with the practical two-year standard.

The guidelines analyze ease of collusion or dominant-firm pricing (for reasons other than entry barriers) through proxies: product homogeneity, spatial similarities of merging firms, information available in the market, ease of fringe expansion, market conduct, and past performance. No weights for those proxies are given. Al-though consideration of collusion would appear necessary in all cases to tell an economically-plausible anticompetitive story, the guidelines state that the collusion factors will be most important when the merger decision is a close call. (For simplicity, we refer to these other factors under the heading "collusion," although they may sometimes refer to dominant-firm behavior.)

Greater efficiency (scale economies or lower transportation costs, for example) was generally excluded from consideration in the 1968 guidelines. But the 1984 guidelines listed efficiency gains as a factor that may save a merger that otherwise would be challenged. Efficiencies must be shown by "clear and convincing" evidence, a higher standard than that for anticompetitive factors (high concentration, entry barriers and ease of collusion).[3]

The final guidelines factor discussed is merger with a failing firm. If one merging firm will soon exit the market anyway, fewer competitive concerns arise. Since the Supreme Court has accepted this argument as a legal defense, antitrust regulators are unlikely to challenge a merger with a failing firm.

Empirical Issues

The merger guidelines are supposed to structure merger regulation to make enforcement decisions consistent, increasing predictability and lowering private transaction costs. Subsequent application of the guidelines, however, has resulted in two general types of complaint.

---

3. This higher standard may betray an institutional bias against case-by-case efficiencies. Policy makers argue, however, that the other guidelines factors are themselves designed to tolerate some chance of anticompetitive effects in mergers, to insure that efficiency-enhancing mergers are allowed without the need to prove efficiencies explicitly. If efficiencies are already incorporated in other factors, one would expect the case-specific efficiency defense would succeed less often.

Failure to Follow Stated Guidelines. Many commentators complain that antitrust enforcers do not follow their own guidelines. Some, such as Leddy [1986] and White [1987], claim that the Justice Department and the FTC have ignored mergers in the concentration ranges that the guidelines label as likely to elicit challenge and have targeted only those with greater Herfindahl index numbers.[4] Similarly, Krattenmaker and Pitofsky state [1988, 226], "What is clear, but is very difficult to document by people who lack access to the confidential H-S-R [Hart-Scott-Rodino] reports and DOJ and FTC internal memoranda, is that the agencies have...not enforced the guidelines." As described below, access to the documents Krattenmaker and Pitofsky refer to permits us to evaluate their claims.

Likewise, questions have been raised about whether some finding of important barriers to entry is required before a merger will be challenged. Almost all economists would deem the existence of significant entry barriers a necessary condition for mergers to reduce welfare appreciably. But the guidelines leave it unclear whether barriers are necessary for a merger challenge, stating that "[t]he more difficult entry into the market is, the more likely the Department is to challenge the merger." Indeed, because the guidelines state that significant mergers in concentrated markets will be challenged in all but extraordinary circumstances, enforcers presumably believe entry to be almost impossible in those cases.

The role of the other (non-entry) collusion factors also merits attention. The guidelines state that these factors "are most likely to be important where the

Department's decision to challenge a merger is otherwise close." This suggests that these factors would affect the occasional case, but would not be a systematic consideration in decisions to challenge mergers. The role of both entry barriers and perceived ease of collusion can both be evaluated using the internal FTC data at our disposal.

Use of the new efficiency criterion has also drawn criticism. Some (e.g., Lande [1988]) claim that efficiency has been elevated to a favored position in merger analysis, dominating the more traditional concentration and non-concentration criteria. The data permit an evaluation of this claim as well.

The Relative Importance of Different Factors. A second set of questions concerns the trade-offs among the different guideline factors. The guidelines leave to the discretion of antitrust enforcers how to weigh the different concentration and non-concentration factors. This is another feature that has been criticized: "Where everything is relevant, nothing is determinative" (Krattenmaker and Pitofsky [1988, 220]). If one factor (high concentration, for example) is a necessary but not sufficient condition for a merger challenge, how are high Herfindahl numbers traded off against other factors, such as entry barriers and perceived ease of collusion?

A related issue concerns the different agency roles of lawyers and economists. One feature frequently noted about antitrust in the Reagan years was that "staff economists at the Commission and the DOJ have gained considerable influence" (Salop [1987, 3]). Their antitrust assessments are said to differ from those of lawyers, particularly because lawyers have greater incentives to litigate in order to increase their human capital for subsequent careers in private practice (Posner [1969, 86]; Clarkson and Muris [1981, 300]). If so, the ultimate trade-off made by the Commission among guideline factors

---

4. Just the opposite complaint was raised about enforcement under the 1968 guidelines. Rogowsky [1984], for example, finds empirically that prior to 1982 the Justice Department brought many cases involving such small levels of concentration that under the applicable (1968) guidelines the mergers should have been allowed to proceed.

would depend on the differing evaluations by the two groups and their relative influence in Commission votes. Both issues can be examined with the available FTC data.

A final issue concerning FTC application of the different guidelines factors can be addressed with the data. The intellectual battles in antitrust for the past generation have pitted more traditional structuralists against partisans of the Chicago school of antitrust. In some areas of antitrust law, Chicago-school learning has gained ascendency among academicians and even in the courts. It is not clear, however, to what extent antitrust enforcers themselves have adopted a Chicago-style approach. The differences between the two models, however, are registered largely in terms of the relative importance of the variables (concentration, entry barriers, collusion) identified by the guidelines, meaning that our data can be used to determine which model better predicts Commission decisions.

III. DATA

To explore the empirical issues noted above, we used a data set of seventy merger investigations at the FTC from June 14, 1982 (the date of the new merger guidelines) to January 1, 1987. The sample includes every important horizontal merger that came to the FTC at that time, as indicated by the fact that it merited a "second request" for data under the Hart-Scott-Rodino Act.[5] In forty-three of the cases, the Commission allowed the merger, while in twenty-seven the Commission voted to challenge the merger.[6]

For each proposed merger in the sample, we reviewed the separate lawyers' and economists' memorandum-evaluations of the different guidelines factors. Markets were defined and concentration data were available in all proposed mergers, and we noted the various estimates of the Herfindahl index and the change in the index for both the lawyers in the Bureau of Competition and the economists in the Bureau of Economics. Entry barrier data were available in most of the memos, with sixty-five observations for the Bureau of Economics and sixty-six for the Bureau of Competition. We follow the general interpretation of the guidelines, treating evidence that entry would require at least two years as indicating that important barriers exist, and evidence that entry could occur within two years as evidence that entry was easy. Evidence on the perceived ease of collusion was sparser. We found analysis of an anticompetitive effect in thirty-seven of the Bureau of Economics memos and in a somewhat different group of thirty-seven Bureau of Competition memos; information was obtained from at least one bureau in forty-six cases. We required the memo explicitly to explain how the collusion-based factors did or did not produce an anticompetitive effect before counting the analysis as information sent to the Commission. Efficiency and failing-firm factors were even more rarely considered or discussed. The Bureau of Economics addressed efficiencies in twenty-eight memos and the Bureau of

---

5. The seventy-case sample includes all the 109 second requests made by the FTC during the relevant period, except those for vertical mergers (ten cases), joint ventures (four cases), and cases where the post-merger Herfindahl Index was below 1000 (five cases). (The FTC blocked no mergers with Herfindahls under 1000.) Also excluded are cases where the FTC files contained insufficient information for our evaluation, such as when the attempted merger was abandoned when the second request was issued (eight cases), the merger was given early approval following the second request (nine cases), or the case was closed prior to completion of the Hart-Scott-Rodino filing (three cases).

6. There is a growing literature (e.g., Priest and Klein [1984], Cooter and Rubinfeld [1989]) modeling disputants' decisions to settle or litigate. One prediction of the basic model is that, under certain plausible assumptions, plaintiffs would win about half the cases litigated. In that respect, it is of interest that the FTC, as plaintiff in challenging mergers, won all twenty-seven of the challenges it brought. (Three victories in litigation are still on appeal or undergoing other review.) Thus the FTC's litigation record is surprising.

Competition in twenty-three. Finally, the Bureau of Competition raised the failing firm defense in four of the reports.

Before these data are used to answer the questions about FTC merger enforcement presented above, one issue must be addressed. Guidelines factors could conceivably not be evaluated on their merits, but might instead be manipulated to push a result that the FTC staff has decided (for whatever reason) it wishes the Commission to take. If so, the guidelines themselves would afford no predictability in evaluating mergers. It is important to determine, therefore, whether the individual guidelines factors are analyzed on their own merits.

One way to check is to look at the correlations between each pair of guidelines factors. If the factors are not independently evaluated, there should be high correlation among them.[7] We calculated the simple correlations among the concentration, entry barriers and ease of collusion variables, and found no significant correlation between any pair of variables, as they were evaluated by either lawyers or economists. Apparently, then, variables are evaluated independently and pressure to make or close a case does not generally lead to "cooking" the data.[8]

IV. EMPIRICAL EVIDENCE

Role of Individual Guidelines Factors

Concentration. The internal FTC evidence allows one to determine if the Commission is actually following the guidelines with respect to concentration. Table I presents a classification for the Bureau of Competition estimates of the Herfindahl indices and changes in index values for the seventy cases. (The Bureau of Economics data is distributed similarly.) As the table shows, in twenty-two of the twenty-seven cases filed the Herfindahl index was over 1800; twelve had index numbers over 3000. There were no complaints when the Herfindahl index increased less than 100 points, and only five when it increased less than 200. In eleven complaints, the increase exceeded 500 points. There is, however, a surprisingly similar pattern for the forty-three closed cases. Twenty-nine cases were not brought even when the Herfindahl index exceeded 1800; in eleven of those cases, the index increased by more than 500 points.

Thus, the FTC's practice from 1982-86 does not corroborate the guidelines' claim that a challenge will be made in all but the most "extraordinary circumstances" when the post-merger Herfindahl index is over 1800 and the change is greater than 100. There were eight cases in which the merger was abandoned when the second request was issued (and thus could not be included in the sample here). Even if all eight involved high concentration and would have resulted in merger challenges, this would mean thirty merger challenges and twenty-seven closed cases in highly concentrated industries with changes of over 100 points. It is hard to believe that truly "extraordinary circumstances" could exist in almost half the cases.[9] Thus, it

---

7. It might be argued that if one wanted to manipulate a result, one would do so for the single variable most likely to be believed. But as shown below, a merger is unlikely to be challenged if only a single guidelines variable is thought worrisome.

8. In a similar vein, we tested (Coate et al. [1990, 478]) for political influence on Bureau of Competition staff in making recommendations to the Commission about particular mergers. While the commission itself is demonstrably influenced by politics in its votes, the evidence indicates that Bureau of Competition staff recommendations to the Commission do not reflect political pressure.

9. We interpret the "extraordinary circumstances" language as applying to the set of mergers reviewed by the enforcement agencies. Firms would attempt mergers in highly concentrated industries when they believed (1) they could substantiate a broad market, so the Herfindahls would be low; (2) the competitive concern would be only a small part of the transaction and hence subject to a divestiture (as happened in eleven of our twenty-seven complaints); or (3) extraordinary circumstances existed. Thus we believe that the data should reflect the extraordinary nature of closing a high-concentration merger if the language was actually enforced.

TABLE I

Herfindahl Indices and Change in Herfindahls for FTC
Decisions to Challenge/Not Challenge Merger
(Bureau of Competition Evaluations)

Post-Merger Herfindahl	Change in Herfindahl					
	0–99	100–199	200–499	500–999	1000	TOTAL
1000–1400	0/0	1/3	0/2	0/0	0/0	1/5
1401–1800	0/1	1/1	3/7	0/0	0/0	4/9
1801–2400	0/0	1/2	4/4	2/2	0/0	7/8
2401–3000	0/1	2/2	1/4	0/1	0/0	3/8
3001+	0/1	0/1	3/3	3/1	6/7	12/13
TOTAL	0/3	5/9	11/20	5/4	6/7	27/43

Note: Figures refer to mergers challenged/not challenged by the FTC following a Hart-Scott-Rodino second-request filing.

would appear that the guidelines have been implicitly revised, with the term "challenge" replaced by "investigate."

By comparison, the data indicate that the Commission has not implicitly raised the lower bound for an investigation from the Herfindahl index level of 1000 stated in the guidelines. Five complaints were filed when the Herfindahl index did not exceed 1800. Fourteen cases with index numbers below 1800 were investigated, although closed upon further analysis. Of these, five involved Herfindahls under 1400; five had changes in the index of less than 200 points.

By itself, the table suggests that levels and changes in the Herfindahl numbers may not matter in the FTC vote. Cases were brought in all the Herfindahl classifications, from between 1000 and 1400 to over 3000. Moreover, cases were closed in all these classifications. The relatively small number of cases in most of the cells of Table I makes statistical testing difficult. However, index data can be aggregated into three cells (under 1800, 1800-3000, over 3000) and separated into complaints and closings. In a test of the hypothesis that the decision on a merger is independent of the Herfindahl level, the chi-square statistic is 2.14, well below the critical level necessary to reject the hypothesis of independence. The same test for Herfindahl change yields the same inference, with a chi-square of 1.97. These results should be interpreted with care, given the aggregation necessary to run the test.

The data are also useful for evaluating the guidelines' assertion that the government is "more likely than not" to challenge a merger when the Herfindahl index is under 1800 but "other factors" support issuance of a complaint. If the other factors are taken to mean both entry barriers and ease of collusion, there were six cases (using the Bureau of Competition's evaluations) in which a challenge should have been "more likely than not." In fact, the Commission challenged four of those mergers.

Barriers to Entry. The evidence suggests that entry barriers are virtually a necessary condition for a merger challenge. In the Commission's twenty-seven complaints, the Bureau of Competition claimed barriers would block entry for at least two years in twenty-six cases and the Bureau of Economics agreed in twenty-

53

two of them. The evidence also suggests, however, that entry barriers were not a sufficient condition. There were sixteen cases in which the Bureau of Competition found both low Herfindahl index numbers and difficult entry. The Commission issued complaints in only five of these cases. Moreover, in the forty-three cases where the FTC voted not to challenge, the Bureau of Competition noted high barriers for thirty-one mergers; the Bureau of Economics claimed barriers were high for twenty. Evidently, the FTC has required evidence beyond entry barriers to vote a complaint.

Nor does the Herfindahl statistic interact predictably with entry barriers to generate a complaint. The Bureau of Competition reported entry barriers for twenty of the twenty-eight (71 percent) closed cases with Herfindahls over 1800 and changes of over 50, and for eleven of the fifteen (73 percent) closed cases where the Herfindahl index was below 1800 (or change was less than 50). Figures for Bureau of Economics findings of high barriers were also similar: eleven of twenty-one (52 percent) for high-Herfindahl closed cases and nine of twenty-two (41 percent) for low-Herfindahl mergers.

Ease of Collusion. The guidelines indicate that ease of collusion will be particularly important in marginal cases. In marginal cases, difficulty of collusion should result in case closings, and ease of collusion should cause complaints to be filed. To evaluate this assertion, one must define marginal cases. For example, a marginal case could be a merger with an Herfindahl index under 1800 or a change in the index of under 200.

The evidence indicates that collusion has not played the role indicated in the guidelines. For marginal cases resulting in complaints, the Bureau of Competition presented evidence of feasible collusion in five of eight mergers. The Bureau of Economics staff found collusion plausible in

just two of ten marginal cases ending as complaints; the Bureau of Economics even thought collusion difficult in three of the ten. In the marginal cases ultimately closed, the Bureau of Competition found collusion difficult in only four of nineteen cases, but collusion easy in five. The Bureau of Economics found collusion difficult in ten of twenty-one marginal cases that closed, and collusion allegedly easy in only two.

The evidence thus contradicts the claim that perceived ease of collusion is a tie-breaker in marginal cases. For the Bureau of Competition, collusion seems to explain some complaints, but it cannot explain the numerous closings of marginal cases. Conversely, the Bureau of Economics collusion evaluations help explain closings but not complaints. Overall, no predictive pattern emerges from the data on collusion.

Efficiency. The internal FTC data also permit evaluation of the claim that the new efficiency criterion has come to dominate other considerations in merger policy. If efficiency considerations have really affected merger policy, one would expect to see otherwise anticompetitive transactions excused because of expected resource savings. In particular, one would expect in numerous closed cases to find efficiency explanations and evidence suggesting complaints would be favored but for the efficiency argument.

The Bureau of Economics and Bureau of Competition claims of efficiencies can be contrasted with the Commission's final decision on the merger. Perhaps surprisingly, efficiency claims were made more frequently in challenged cases, with the Bureau of Economics claiming efficiencies existed in 33 percent of the complaints filed and the Bureau of Competition in 26 percent. But the Bureau of Economics found efficiencies in only 21 percent and the Bureau of Competition in 7 percent of the closed cases. Obviously, this evidence suggests that the legal and economic staff's efficiency defenses are not generally successful.[10]

One can further explore the efficiency issue by comparing the number of factors (Herfindahl index, barriers or collusion) either favoring or disfavoring complaints in the closed cases where efficiencies were found to those where no efficiencies were claimed. For the Bureau of Economics, in the nine closed cases where efficiencies were claimed, the staff found an average of 1.44 factors indicating the merger would otherwise not have an anticompetitive effect. This is not significantly different (t = .25) from the average number of 1.38 factors deemed not anticompetitive by the Bureau of Economics in the other closed cases. Thus, a Bureau of Economics efficiency claim apparently did not substitute for other guidelines factors that the Bureau of Economics said supported letting a merger proceed, when the Commission decided to close the case. For the Bureau of Competition, the inference is the same. In the three closed cases for which the lawyers claimed efficiencies existed, they found an average of 1.33 other factors suggesting a problem could exist, as compared to the average of 1.68 factors thought to be at anticompetitive levels for the other cases. This difference is also insignificant (t = .76). Again, at the margin the efficiency factor seems unimportant in explaining FTC merger challenges.

Multivariate Analysis

Analyzing the role of a single guidelines factor without controlling for other factors is potentially misleading. Multivariate techniques may be more appropriate. Multivariate analysis is also useful for investigating two issues in merger enforcement of interest to many: the relative importance of the different guidelines factors, and the differences between lawyers

and economists in influencing Commission votes.

Weights of Different Guidelines Factors. Using the internal FTC data, we defined a probit model for the Commission's decisions on merger challenges (Coate et al. [1990]). The dependent variable (*VOTE*) equalled one if the Commission approved a complaint (including cases in which the parties negotiated a settlement) and zero if the investigation was closed with no action. We explained the merger vote as a function of both the Bureau of Competition and Bureau of Economics analysis of the Herfindahl, barriers to entry, and ease of collusion. To avoid extreme multicollinearity problems, we transformed the Bureau of Competition and Bureau of Economics concentration estimates into two dummy variables.[11] For the Bureau of Competition, the concentration variable (*BCHERFHI*) takes on the value of 1 if the Herfindahl is over 1800 and the change is more than 50, and a value of 0 otherwise. The Bureau of Economics dummy variable (*BEHERFLO*) was defined as a mirror image of the Bureau of Competition variable, with a value of 1 if the Herfindahl was below 1800 or the change was less than 50 and 0 in all other cases.[12]

For the first non-concentration factor, entry barriers, we constructed two dummy variables, the first (*BCBARHI*)

11. The correlation coefficient between the continuous measures of the Bureau of Competition and Bureau of Economics Herfindahl index is .95. For the binary variables used here (*BCHERFHI* and *BEHERFLO*), the coefficient is -.67.

12. Reversing the coding on the Bureau of Competition and Bureau of Economics variables is done for ease of interpreting coefficients. It reflects the fact (explained further below) that in more than half the second-request cases lawyers support a merger challenge, while economists oppose a challenge in most cases. In the typical case, the regression analysis here shows, the Bureau of Competition evaluated the guidelines factors in such a way as to increase the likelihood of a merger challenge, while the typical Bureau of Economics analysis decreased that likelihood. The coding of course has no effect on the significance of the results or inferences therefrom, other than to change the intercept term.

10. This result is compatible with the hypothesis that merger partners present efficiency defenses for troublesome mergers.

with the value 1 if the Bureau of Competition evaluated barriers to entry as high, and the other (BEBARLO) equalling 1 if the Bureau of Economics thought serious barriers did not exist. For the next non-concentration factor, ease of collusion, again we constructed two variables, one (BCCOLHI) with the value 1 when the Bureau of Competition found collusion likely and the other (BECOLLO) with the value 1 when Bureau of Economics found collusion was unlikely. Finally, the legal failing-firm defense was included by a variable (FAILFIRM) equal to 1 in those four cases in which the Bureau of Competition claimed the defense applied.

Two political pressure variables are also included. The first (CITES) is the number of Wall Street Journal articles about the merger prior to the FTC's decision and is designed to measure the pressure to block high-profile transactions. The second (HEARINGS) is a twelve-month moving average of the number of times Congress summoned FTC commissioners or politically-appointed staff to hearings to defend their antitrust records.

The probit parameter estimates are shown as regression 1 ("base model") in Table II. As expected, Bureau of Competition analysis that concentration, entry barriers and collusion possibilities are at worrisome levels significantly enhances the probability of a complaint; Bureau of Economics evaluation that none of the guidelines factors are worrisome significantly lowers the likelihood of a challenge. The political, the Bureau of Competition and the Bureau of Economics variables all pass independent chi-square tests, indicating that each type of variable affects the Commission's decision making.

As a test of the role of efficiencies, a variable not included in the first model, we now insert a dummy variable (EFFCY) equal to 1 for any case in which either the Bureau of Competition or Bureau of Economics claimed that efficiencies were present. As shown in regression 2 ("efficiency model") of Table II, efficiencies themselves are an insignificant factor in FTC votes, and their inclusion in the model has only trivial effects on the size and significance of the other variables. With other guidelines factors controlled for, staff efficiency claims have no apparent influence on a Commission merger decision.

The model is robust with respect to other specifications. One important issue concerns the missing values for the independent variables. As noted above, for example, out of the seventy total cases, the Bureau of Competition discussed collusion in only thirty-seven and the Bureau of Economics in a somewhat different set of thirty-seven mergers. Regressions 1 and 2 are based on a default coding of zero for the Bureau of Competition and Bureau of Economics independent variables when the bureau failed to mention a particular factor. But the results are not sensitive to this coding option, as regression 3 ("recoded model") in Table II indicates. Reversing the coding of the Bureau of Economics variables to match the Bureau of Competition variables, so the missing values would be treated identically, results in only minor differences from the prior estimates. Finally, if the concentration dummies for the Bureau of Competition and Bureau of Economics are multiplied by the Herfindahl index estimated by each bureau so as to create a truncated continuous variable, the estimated coefficients are insignificant, as shown in regression 4 of Table II. This may suggest that the FTC responds less to continuous Herfindahl changes than to discrete changes in classification (e.g., a post-merger HHI above 1800).[13]

13. We also tested whether Commission decisions respond to cost or benefit variables similar to those included in models of private litigation decisions (see note 6). None of the variables proved significant. For example, larger firms might more easily bear the fixed costs of litigating to achieve a merger, meaning that the FTC would itself have to expect higher litigation costs if it voted to challenge. However, firm size (measured by sales) was not a significant determinant of the FTC decision whether to litigate, ceteris paribus.

TABLE II
Parameter Estimates for the Probit Model
(absolute value of t-statistics in parentheses)

	1. Base Model	2. Efficiency Model	3. Recoded Model	4. Continuous Model
BCHERFHI	1.11* (1.53)	1.11* (1.52)	1.12* (1.55)	.144 (1.21)
BCBARHI	1.84** (1.85)	1.84** (1.84)	1.79** (1.78)	1.50* (1.64)
BCCOLHI	1.65*** (3.16)	1.65*** (3.11)	1.16*** (2.47)	1.60*** (3.26)
BEHERFLO	-.962* (1.65)	-.962* (1.63)	.857* (1.53)	-.556 (1.29)
BEBARLO	-.880* (1.58)	-.880* (1.58)	5.86 (1.13)	-.777* (1.39)
BECOLLO	-.880** (1.83)	-.880** (1.81)	1.08* (1.31)	-.635* (1.39)
FAILFIRM	-4.33 (.01)	-4.33 (.01)	-3.04 (.03)	-4.43 (.002)
CITES	.169** (1.82)	.169** (1.82)	.190** (2.19)	.159** (1.84)
HEARINGS	.151** (1.71)	.151** (1.70)	1.81** (2.00)	.098 (1.29)
EFFCY	—	-.0002 (.0005)	—	—
Constant	-4.01 (2.47)	-4.01 (2.47)	-5.89 (3.38)	-3.04 (2.38)
Adj. R^2	.493	.493	.458	.467
Likelihood	46.3	46.3	43.1	43.9

*significant at .10 level
**significant at .05 level
***significant at .01 level

Using the first probit equation (regression 1) and holding the political variables constant at their means, one can investigate the relative importance of the merger guidelines factors in a Commission decision to challenge a merger. If lawyers and economists agree that the Herfindahl index, entry barriers and ease of collusion are all at levels deemed worrisome under the guidelines, the probability of a merger challenge is 97 percent. Suppose, next, that both the Bureau of Competition and Bureau of Economics agree that one of the factors is not a concern. If both bureaus find that the Herfindahl level is low, the probability of an FTC challenge falls from 97 to 43 percent, a statistically significant decline. Since every merger in the 1982–86 FTC sample had an Herfindahl index above 1000 and all but three increased the index by at least 100 points, it is interesting that the Commission would challenge only 43 percent of those mergers, even when both entry barriers and an ability to collude allegedly were present.

The Herfindahl index was apparently of less importance to the Commission during this time than other guideline measures. Although there is still a 43-percent chance the Commission will challenge a merger when lawyers and economists agree that the Herfindahl is low (and the two other factors are high), bureaucratic agreement that either of the other guideline factors is low reduces the probability of a merger challenge even more. When both bureaus agree that the Herfindahl is high and collusion likely, but also that entry barriers are low, there is only a 21 percent probability of a merger challenge. Likewise, when concentration and barriers are judged high, but collusion is thought unlikely, the probability of a complaint is only 27 percent. Ceteris paribus, satisfying the FTC staff that the Herfindahl is under 1800 (or its change is less than 50) appears less likely to shield a merger from challenge than a bureaucratic finding that entry barriers or the likelihood of collusion are low. (Of course, the best way to prevent a merger challenge under the guidelines is to show that the Herfindahl index is below 1000.)

These results are consistent with the conclusion above that, despite the guidelines, the Commission was not "likely to challenge" but rather "likely to investigate" mergers pushing the Herfindahl index over 1800. Even if the Herfindahl is assumed to be high, the decision whether the merger will be challenged depends heavily on the evaluation of the other guidelines factors. Indeed, the regression model shows, if concentration alone were judged high but barriers judged low and collusion difficult, a complaint would have no measurable chance of success.

Bureau of Competition and Bureau of Economics Agreement on Guidelines Factors. Table III notes the positions taken by both the Bureau of Economics and Bureau of Competition with respect to the Herfindahl index , barriers, ease of collusion and effi-

ciencies. There was considerable agreement among lawyers and economists concerning the facts presented to the Commission, ranging from 83 percent on the Herfindahl index to 61 percent on the ease of collusion. Disagreements occurred almost exclusively when the Bureau of Competition thought a variable indicated anticompetitive problems, but the Bureau of Economics did not.

However, the data mask some disagreements, such as differences in market definition or market share. Only 59 percent of the Herfindahl statistics were absolutely identical. Moreover, missing values indicated large potential for further disagreement between the Bureau of Economics and Bureau of Competition. Counting as disagreements any situation where one bureau ventured an opinion and the other did not lowers the agreement rate to 73 percent for barriers, 37 percent for ease of collusion, and 52 percent for efficiencies.

The table indicates that when presented with the same facts, attorneys are more likely than economists to claim that a merger raises issues of antitrust concern. This finding is consistent with the hypothesis that different career incentives induce lawyers to support cases more often than economists. This hypothesis can be tested directly. The internal files reveal that the Bureau of Competition staff supported a complaint in 54.3 percent of the sample cases, while the Bureau of Economics staff supported a complaint in only 30.0 percent. This difference is statistically significant at the 1-percent level.

The effects of bureaucratic disagreement tend to indicate that lawyers have greater influence over the ultimate Commission vote. Table IV (estimated from regression model 1 of Table II with political variables held constant at their means) presents the effects of bureau disagreements over the Herfindahl index, entry barriers and ease of collusion under alternative assumptions concerning evaluation of each of these factors. Suppose hypothet-

TABLE III

Evaluation of Guideline Variables by Bureaus of Competition and Economics

Number of Cases in which BE Claims the Variable Is:		Number of Cases in which BC Claims the Variable Is:	
		HIGH	LOW
H	HHI	39	1
I	Barriers	40	0
G	Collusion	12	0
H	Efficiencies (i.e., no efficiencies present)	9	0
L	HHI	11	19
O	Barriers	15	9
W	Collusion	11	5
	Efficiencies (i.e., efficiencies present)	4	7

ically that both groups at first agree that one variable—the Herfindahl, barriers to entry, or likelihood of collusion—is low while the other two are high. Then let the lawyers change their opinion and also evaluate the first variable as high. As shown in line 1 of Table IV, the probability of a challenge rises by 40 to 64 percent, depending on the variable. Suppose alternatively that both the Bureau of Competition and Bureau of Economics initially find that all merger guidelines factors are high, but that the economists then re-evaluate one of these factors as low. Line 2 of Table IV indicates that the probability of a challenge falls by 12 to 14 percent.[14]

In short, under our econometric model of Commission decision making the lawyers' evaluation of the merger guide-

lines variables apparently have had a greater impact than those made by economists. Moreover, all the predicted probability changes for lawyers are statistically significant at the .05 and .10 levels. The estimated effects for economists are not significant.[15]

Structuralist vs. Chicago Approaches at the FTC

The probability models above use econometric techniques to determine the simultaneous impact of particular variables on FTC merger decisions. That approach is usually the only one available, because economic theory itself does not specify a priori the exact relationship between the dependent and explanatory variables. In this case, theory suggests two deterministic models that can be constructed with data on Herfindahls, entry barriers and ease of collusion to model FTC merger decisions.

14. The hypothetical cases used here reflect the fact that the Bureau of Competition is more likely to support cases than the Bureau of Economics. Thus, the most likely scenarios involve either the Bureau of Competition changing their evaluations of a particular guidelines factor from low to high while the Bureau of Economics continues to evaluate the factor as low, or the Bureau of Economics changing from high to low while the Bureau of Competition continues to evaluate the factor as high. These are the two cases presented in Table IV.

15. Our model fails to capture any influence that the Bureau of Economics has on the Bureau of Competition's factual analysis, and therefore may understate the influence of economists at the FTC.

59

TABLE IV

Impact of Bureau Disagreement on Probability of Merger Challenge

	HHI	Barriers	Collusion
BC changes from LOW to HIGH (BE remains LOW):	+40**	+64*	+58*
BE changes from HIGH to LOW (BC remains HIGH):	-14	-12	-12

* significant at the .05 level

** significant at the .10 level

Note: The change in probabilities of an FTC merger challenge accompanying a change by one bureau in its evaluation of the factor stated is based on the assumption that the other two factors are already evaluated as being high.

Economists differ on those conditions necessary for a merger to be anticompetitive, although entry barriers would probably be given by all as a necessary condition. If barriers are present, evaluation of a merger hinges on how easily one believes firms could coordinate their actions. So-called "Chicago school" economists typically maintain that something other than mere concentration is necessary for successful, long-term collusion. "Structuralists," on the other hand, tend to hold that once entry barriers have been shown, high concentration can substitute for evidence of the ease of collusion as a sufficient predictor of anticompetitive effect.

The debate is a long-running one. It is interesting, therefore, to use the FTC data on merger challenges to see whether the Chicago-school or structuralist model better predicts FTC merger challenges. We used two definitions that fit the competing theories. A Chicago-school approach would require evidence of all three of the principal guidelines factors: high Herfindahl index, entry barriers and ease of collusion. If any of these factors was missing, a Chicagoan would likely infer that the merger could not be anticompetitive. But a structuralist approach would deem a merger anticompetitive if, in addition to entry barriers, either the Herfindahl index was high or collusion

was perceived to be easy. Neither of these approaches is the same as the probit model set out in the regressions above. In that third model, the bureaucracy's evaluation of mergers under its own guidelines is treated as making no one factor either necessary or sufficient; external pressure variables are included as significant predictors as well.[16]

The issue thus is which model better predicts Commission decisions, the Chicago or structuralist model. We used each model to predict the anticompetitive effect of a merger for both the Bureau of Competition and Bureau of Economics data.[17] Under the Chicago model, a challenge would be predicted whenever (under the Bureau of Competition and Bureau of Economics data, alternatively) all three factors were deemed worrisome: concentration, entry barriers and ease of collusion. Under the structuralist model, a challenge is predicted when barriers and either high concentration or ease of collusion is posited.

It is useful to separate the sample into three periods. The first, from the an-

16. Both the Chicago-school and structuralist models treat antitrust as a "public interest" form of regulation, and thus would treat political variables as irrelevant. See McChesney [1991].

17. The predictions were adjusted for the few failing-firm defenses in the sample.

nouncement of the 1982 merger guidelines to the 1984 revision, contains sixteen cases. The second period (with twenty-seven cases) runs from the revision to the resignation of FTC Chairman James C. Miller III. A question naturally of interest to economists is whether the FTC evaluated mergers differently during the tenure of Miller, the only professional economist ever to chair the Commission. The third period (also twenty-seven cases) runs from Miller's resignation to the end of the sample.

Table V compares, for all three subperiods, the predictive success of each model. The structuralist model with the Bureau of Competition data predicts Commission merger decisions 67 percent of the time, while the Chicago model is correct 74 percent of the time. Similar results are found by using the Bureau of Economics data with either model. Thus, the deterministic models of Commission decision making do not show that lawyers have more influence than economists on enforcement decisions.

Among the three subperiods,[18] one finds that the Chicago model seemingly outperformed the structuralist model while the 1982 guidelines were in effect, but again there was no significant difference. When the 1982 guidelines were revised, the Chicago model's predictive success fell for both the Bureau of Competition and Bureau of Economics data, with the Bureau of Economics decline being statistically significantly ($t = 1.90$). However, the opposite result occurred following Chairman Miller's departure, with the

increase in the Bureau of Economics's predictive ability again significant ($t = 3.53$).[19]

The predictions of the Chicago and structuralist models can be compared to the results obtained from the bureaucratic-political probit model (regression 1 of Table II). Assuming a fitted probability from the regression of over (under) 50 percent predicts a complaint (closing), the probit model correctly forecasted the Commission's decision with 84 percent accuracy. Figures for the three subperiods are 88, 81 and 85 percent, respectively. The probit model generally outperforms the Chicago and structuralist models, not a surprising result since the probit model incorporates significant political variables.

V. CONCLUSION

As the merger wave of the 1980s rolled on, commentators alleged that antitrust agencies had tacitly revised the merger guidelines, challenging only extreme increases in concentration. Also, efficiencies supposedly had been elevated above the other guidelines factors. Moreover, there were rumors that economists were actually taking part in antitrust enforcement decisions.

It is useful to look back and separate fact from fiction. Our data on Federal Trade Commission merger challenges from the mid-1980s provide evidence that for the most part the merger guidelines have not been applied as written. The use of concentration measures is perhaps the

18. For the subperiods, there is a risk of bias if the results of one cell are driven by the type of case (closing or complaint) considered disproportionately during the period. To check for this problem we used the sample weights of 38.5 percent complaints and 61.5 percent closings to weight the predictions of complaints and closings to determine the sample prediction rates. The results were comparable to those in Table V, indicating no bias problem.

19. Table V's Bureau of Economics figures do not depend critically on the Bureau of Economics's position on collusion in those cases when the economists did not mention collusion explicitly in their memoranda. As noted above, we treated failure to mention collusion as indicating that economists believed it plausible. If the opposite inference is drawn, the predictability of the Chicago model using Bureau of Economics data declines from 93 percent in the post-Miller years to 74 percent. However, treating failure to discuss collusion as an indication that economists thought it unlikely increases the predicative power of the Chicago model for the Miller years, and so has little impact on the model's power overall.

TABLE V
Success of Structuralist and Chicago Models in Predicting FTC Merger Challenges

	Time Period			
	June 1982– May 1984	June 1984– August 1985	August 1985– December 1986	TOTAL
1. Using BC Evaluation of Guidelines Factors				
– Structuralist Model	63	63	74	67
– Chicago Model	81	74	70	74
2. Using BE Evaluation of Guidelines Factors				
– Structuralist Model	69	63	78	70
– Chicago Model	81	55	93	76

Note: Figures are the percentages of FTC decisions correctly predicted by the alternative models, using BC and BE evaluations of the merger guidelines variables.

best example. However, the data do not reveal an increase in the critical Herfindahl levels. Instead, the evidence suggests simply that concentration has not been used to establish a presumption of guilt. Rather, it has served to determine which cases should be investigated. The cases appear to be examined on their merits and some proof of anticompetitive effect—beyond mere concentration numbers—often required before a complaint is issued. In that respect, the FTC's approach thus has been consistent with economic theory: concentration has been a necessary but not sufficient condition for a merger challenge.

As for non-concentration factors, there is considerable evidence that a finding of barriers to entry was a necessary but not sufficient condition for a merger challenge. On the other hand, there is no evidence (despite critics' claims to the contrary) that explicit inclusion of efficiencies in the guidelines has made any difference. Closed cases where efficiencies were allegedly present in 1982-86 presented competitive concerns similar to those in which no efficiency claims were made.

Moreover, both economist and attorney evaluations of guidelines factors appear to have an impact. At the margin, attorneys seem to have more influence at the Commission if one accepts the econometric model. Finally, both the structuralist and Chicago models predict the Commission's decisions reasonably well over the sample period. But both are inferior to the probability model, shown to be rather robust here, that includes political variables as predictors of FTC merger decisions.

REFERENCES

Clarkson, Kenneth W., and Timothy J. Muris. "Commission Performance, Incentives, and Behavior," in *The Federal Trade Commission Since 1970: Economic Regulation and Bureaucratic Behavior*, edited by Kenneth W. Clarkson and Timothy J. Muris. Cambridge: Cambridge University Press, 1981, 280–306.

Coate, Malcolm B., Richard S. Higgins, and Fred S. McChesney. "Bureaucracy and Politics in FTC Merger Enforcement." *Journal of Law and Economics*, October 1990, 463–82.

Cooter, Robert D., and Daniel L. Rubinfeld. "Economic Analysis of Legal Disputes and Their Resolution." *Journal of Economic Literature*, September 1989, 1067–97.

Demsetz, Harold. "Barriers to Entry." *American Economic Review*, March 1982, 47–57.

Krattenmaker, Thomas G. and Robert Pitofsky. "Antitrust Merger Policy and the Reagan Administration." *Antitrust Bulletin*, Summer 1988, 211–32.

Lande, Robert H. "The Rise and (Coming) Fall of Efficiency as the Ruler of Antitrust." *Antitrust Bulletin*, Fall 1988, 429–65.

Leddy, Mark. "Recent Merger Cases Reflect Revolution in Antitrust Policy." *Legal Times*, 3 November, 1986, p. 2.

McChesney, Fred S. "Be True to Your School: Conflicting Chicago Approaches to Antitrust and Regulation," *Cato Journal*, Winter 1991, 775–98.

Posner, Richard A. "The Federal Trade Commission." *University of Chicago Law Review* 37(1), 1969, 47–89.

Priest, George L., and Benjamin Klein. "The Selection of Disputes for Litigation." *Journal of Legal Studies*, January 1984, 1–55.

Rogowsky, Robert A. "The Justice Department's Merger Guidelines: A Study in the Application of the Rule." *Research in Law and Economics*, 6, 1984, 135–66.

Salop, Steven C. "Symposium on Mergers and Antitrust." *Journal of Economic Perspectives*, Fall 1987, 3–12.

U.S. Department of Justice. "Merger Guidelines" (1968, 1982 and 1984 versions), in *Horizontal Mergers: Law and Policy*, Section of Antitrust Law, American Bar Association, 1986, 264–336.

White, Lawrence J. "Antitrust and Merger Policy: A Review and Critique." *Journal of Economic Perspectives*, Fall 1987, 13–22.

INDUSTRY STRUCTURE, MARKET RIVALRY, AND PUBLIC POLICY*

HAROLD DEMSETZ

University of California, Los Angeles and the Hoover Institution

I. INTRODUCTION

QUANTITATIVE work in industrial organization has been directed mainly to the task of searching for monopoly even though a vast number of other interesting topics have been available to the student of economic organization. The motives for this preoccupation with monopoly are numerous, but important among them are the desire to be policy-relevant and the ease with which industrial concentration data can be secured. This paper takes a critical view of contemporary doctrine in this area and presents data which suggest that this doctrine offers a dangerous base upon which to build a public policy toward business.

II. CONCENTRATION THROUGH COMPETITION

Under the pressure of competitive rivalry, and in the apparent absence of effective barriers to entry, it would seem that the concentration of an industry's output in a few firms could only derive from their superiority in producing and marketing products or in the superiority of a structure of industry in which there are only a few firms. In a world in which information and resource mobility can be secured only at a cost, an industry will become more concentrated under competitive conditions only if a differential advantage in expanding output develops in some firms. Such expansion will increase the degree of concentration at the same time that it increases the rate of return that these firms earn. The cost advantage that gives rise to increased concentration may be reflected in scale economies or in downward shifts in positively sloped marginal cost curves, or it may be reflected in better products which satisfy demand at a lower cost. New efficiencies can, of course, arise in other ways. Some firms might discover ways of lowering cost that require that firms become smaller, so that spinoffs might be in order.

* The author wishes to thank the Research Program in Competition and Public Policy at U.C.L.A. for assisting in the preparation of this article.

1

In such cases, smaller firms will tend to earn relatively high rates of return. Which type of new efficiency arises most frequently is a question of fact.

Such profits need not be eliminated soon by competition. It may well be that superior competitive performance is unique to the firm, viewed as a team, and unobtainable to others except by purchasing the firm itself. In this case the return to superior performance is in the nature of a gain that is completely captured by the owner of the firm itself, not by its inputs.[1] Here, although the industry structure may change because the superior firm grows, the resulting increase in profit cannot easily serve to guide competitors to similar success. The firm may have established a reputation or goodwill that is difficult to separate from the firm itself and which should be carried at higher value on its books. Or it may be that the members of the employee team derive their higher productivity from the knowledge they possess about each other in the environment of the particular firm in which they work, a source of productivity that may be difficult to transfer piecemeal. It should be remembered that we are discussing complex, large enterprises, many larger (and more productive) than entire nations. One such enterprise happens to "click" for some time while others do not. It may be very difficult for these firms to understand the reasons for this difference in performance or to know to which inputs to attribute the performance of the successful firm. It is not easy to ascertain just why G.M. and I.B.M. perform better than their competitors. The complexity of these organizations defies easy analysis, so that the inputs responsible for success may be undervalued by the market for some time. By the same token, inputs owned by complex, unsuccessful firms may be overvalued for some time. The success of firms will be reflected in higher returns and stock prices, not higher input prices, and lack of success will be recorded in lower returns and stock prices, not lower input prices.

Moreover, inputs are acquired at historic cost, but the use made of these inputs, including the managerial inputs, yields only uncertain outcomes. Because the outcomes of managerial decisions are surrounded by uncertainty and are specific to a particular firm at a particular point in its history, the acquisition cost of inputs may fail to reflect their value to the firm at some subsequent time. By the time their value to the firm is recognized, they are beyond acquisition by other firms at the same historic cost, and, in the interim, shareholders of the successful or lucky firm will have enjoyed higher profit rates. When nature cooperates to make such decisions correct, they can give rise to high accounting returns for several years or to a once and for

---

[1] A detailed discussion of the implicit notion of team production that underlies these arguments can be found in Armen A. Alchian & Harold Demsetz, Production, Information Costs, and Economic Organization, 62 Amer. Econ. Rev. 777 (1972).

all capital gain if accountants could value *a priori* decisions that turn out to be correct *ex post*. During the period when such decisions determine the course of events, output will tend to be concentrated in those firms fortunate enough to have made the correct decisions.

None of this is necessarily monopolistic (although monopoly may play some role). Profit does not arise because the firm creates "artificial scarcity" through a reduction in its output. Nor does it arise because of collusion. Superior performance can be attributed to the combination of great uncertainty plus luck or atypical insight by the management of a firm. It is not until the experiments are actually tried that we learn which succeed and which fail. By the time the results are in, it is the shareholder that has captured (some of) the value, positive or negative, of past decisions. Even though the profits that arise from a firm's activities may be eroded by competitive imitation, since information is costly to obtain and techniques are difficult to duplicate, the firm may enjoy growth and a superior rate of return for some time.

Superior ability also may be interpreted as a competitive basis for acquiring a measure of monopoly power. In a world in which information is costly and the future is uncertain, a firm that seizes an opportunity to better serve customers does so because it expects to enjoy some protection from rivals because of their ignorance of this opportunity or because of their inability to imitate quickly. One possible source of some monopoly power is superior entrepreneurship. Our patent, copyright, and trademark laws explicitly provide as a reward for uncovering new methods (and for revealing these methods), legal protection against free imitation, and it may be true in some cases that an astute rival acquires the exclusive rights to some resource that *later* becomes valuable. There is no reason to suppose that competitive behavior never yields monopoly power, although in many cases such power may be exercised not by creating entry barriers, but through the natural frictions and ignorance that characterize any real economy. If rivals seek better ways to satisfy buyers or to produce a product, and if one or a few succeed in such endeavors, then the reward for their entrepreneurial efforts is likely to be some (short term) monopoly power and this may be associated with increased industrial concentration. To destroy such power when it arises may very well remove the incentive for progress. This is to be contrasted with a situation in which a high rate of return is obtained through a successful *collusion* to restrict output; here there is less danger to progress if the collusive agreement is penalized. Evidence presented below suggests that there are definite dangers of decreasing efficiency through the use of deconcentration or anti-merger policies.

III. Inefficiency Through Anti-concentration Public Policy

The discussion in part II noted that concentration may be brought about because a workable system of incentives implies that firms which better serve buyers will tend to grow relative to other firms. One way in which a firm could better serve buyers is by seizing opportunities to exploit scale economies, although if scale economies are the main cause of concentration, it is difficult to understand why there is no significant trend toward one-firm industries; the lack of such a trend seems to suggest that superiority results in lower but *positively* sloped cost curves in the relevant range of large firm operations. This would set limits to the size of even the successful firms. Successful firms thus would seem to be more closely related to the "superior land" of classical economic rent analysis than to the single firm of natural monopoly theory. Whether or not superiority is reflected in scale economies, deconcentration may have the total effect of promoting inefficiency even though it also may reduce some monopoly-caused inefficiencies.[2]

The classic portrayal of the inefficiency produced by concentration through the exercise of monopoly power is that of a group of firms cooperating somehow to restrict entry and prevent rivalrous price behavior. Successfully pursued, this policy results in a product price and rate of return in excess of that which would have prevailed in the absence of collusion. However, if all firms are able to produce at the same cost, then the rate of return to successfully colluding firms should be independent of the particular sizes adopted by these firms to achieve low cost production. One firm may require a small scale, and hence have a smaller investment, while another may require a large scale, and corresponding large investment. At any given collusive price, the absolute amounts of monopoly profits will be proportional to output, but capital investment also will be proportionate to output, so we can expect the rate of return to be invariant with respect to size of firm.

If one size of firm earns a higher rate of return than another size, given any collusive price, then there must exist differences in the cost of production which favor the firm that earns the higher rate of return. Alternatively, if there is no single price upon which the industry agrees, but, rather a range of prices, then one firm can earn a higher rate of return if it produces a superior product and sells it at a higher price without thereby incurring proportionately higher costs; here, also, the firm that earns the higher rate of return can be judged to be more efficient because it delivers more value per dollar of cost incurred.

[2] For a discussion of the social costs that might be incurred by deconcentration, especially in the context of scale economies, see John S. McGee, In Defense of Industrial Concentration 159 (1971).

A deconcentration or antimerger policy is more likely to have benign results if small firms in concentrated industries earn the same or higher rates of return than large firms, for, then, deconcentration may reduce collusion,[3] if it is present, while simultaneously allocating larger shares of industry output to smaller firms which are no less efficient than larger firms. But if increased concentration has come about because of the superior efficiency of those firms that have become large, then a deconcentration policy, while it may reduce the ease of colluding, courts the danger of reducing efficiency either by the penalties that it places on innovative success or by the shift in output to smaller, higher cost firms that it brings about. This would seem to be a distinct possibility if large firms in concentrated industries earn higher rates of return than small firms.

The problem posed is how to organize data to shed light on the probability that deconcentration will promote inefficiency. Correlating industry rate of return with concentration will not be enlightening for this problem, for even if concentrated industries exhibit higher rates of return, it is difficult to determine whether it is efficiency or monopoly power that is at work. Similarly, large firms would tend to earn high profit rates in concentrated industries either because they are efficient or because they are colluding. However, partitioning industry data by size of firm does suggest that there exists a real danger from a deconcentration or anti-merger public policy, for the rates of return earned by small firms give no support to the doctrine relating collusion to concentration. A successful collusion is very likely to benefit the smaller firms, and this suggests that there should be a positive correlation between the rate of return earned by small firms and the degree to which the industry is concentrated. By the same token, if efficiency is associated with concentration, there should be a positive correlation between concentration and the difference between the rate of return earned by large firms and that earned by small firms; that is, large firms have become large because they are more efficient than other firms and are able to earn a higher rate of return than other firms.

Tables 1 and 2 show 1963 rates of return based on internal revenue data partitioned by size of firm and industry concentration for 95 three digit industries. In these tables, C_{63} designates the four firm concentration ratio measured on industry sales; R_1, R_2, R_3, and R_4, respectively, measure accounting rates of return (profit plus interest)/total assets, for firms with asset value less than \$500,000, \$500,000 to \$5,000,000, \$5,000,000 to \$50,000,000 and over \$50,000,000. Table 1 is calculated by assigning equal weight to all in-

---

[3] This statement is incorrect if a deconcentration or anti-merger policy causes firms to adopt socially less efficient methods of colluding than would be adopted in the absence of such a policy.

TABLE 1

RATES OF RETURN BY SIZE AND CONCENTRATION (UNWEIGHTED)

C_{63}	Number of Industries	R_1	R_2	R_3	R_4	$\overline{R}$
10-20%	14	6.7%	9.0%	10.8%	10.3%	9.2%
20-30	22	4.5	9.1	9.7	10.4	8.4
30-40	24	5.2	8.7	9.9	11.0	8.7
40-50	21	5.8	9.0	9.5	9.0	8.3
50-60	11	6.7	9.8	10.5	13.4	10.1
over 60	3	5.3	10.1	11.5	23.1	12.5

TABLE 2

RATES OF RETURN BY SIZE AND CONCENTRATION (WEIGHTED BY ASSETS)

C_{63}	Number of Industries	R_1	R_2	R_3	R_4	$\overline{R}$
10-20%	14	7.3%	9.5%	10.6%	8.0%	8.8%
20-30	22	4.4	8.6	9.9	10.6	8.4
30-40	24	5.1	9.0	9.4	11.7	8.8
40-50	21	4.8	9.5	11.2	9.4	8.7
50-60	11	0.9	9.6	10.8	12.2	8.4
over 60	3	5.0	8.6	10.3	21.6	11.3

dustries. It is based, therefore, on the assumption that each industry, regardless of size, offers an equally good observational unit for comparing the efficiency and monopolistic aspects of industry structure. Table 2 presents the same basic data with accounting rates of return weighted by asset value. Hence, an industry with many assets owned by small firms receives a larger weight in calculating the small firm rate of return for a given interval of concentration ratios.

Both tables fail to reveal the beneficial effects to small firms that we would expect from an association of collusion and industry concentration. The rate of return earned by firms in the smallest asset size does not increase with concentration. This seems to be true for the next two larger asset size classifications also, although in Table 1 the 11.5 per cent earned by R_3 firms in industries with concentration ratios higher than 60 per cent offers some indication of a larger rate of return than in less concentrated industries.[4] The data do not seem to support the notion that concentration and collusion are closely related, and, therefore, it is difficult to remain optimistic about the beneficial efficiency effects of a deconcentration or anti-merger public policy.

[4] Since firms are segregated by absolute size, for some industries the R_3 firms will be relatively large. A better test could be secured by contrasting the rates of return for the 1—% largest and 10% smallest firms in each industry. But the data do not allow such a comparison. However, see footnote 6 for the result of a similar type of adjustment.

On the contrary, the data suggest that such policies will reduce efficiency by impairing the survival of large firms in concentrated industries, for these firms do seem better able to produce at lower cost than their competitors.[5] Both tables indicate that R_4 size firms in industries with concentration ratios greater than 50 per cent produce at lower average cost.

Since a larger fraction of industry output is produced by larger firms in the more concentrated industries, these industries may exhibit higher rates of return than other industries. That this is so can be seen from the unweighted row averages given by column $\bar{R}$. Industries with $C_{63} > 50$ per cent seem to have earned higher rates of return than less concentrated industries. But this result, which is consistent with some earlier studies, may be attributed to the superior performance of the larger firms and not to collusive practices. Table 2 reveals this pattern even more clearly. Because the rates of return of smaller firms receive a larger weight (by total assets) in Table 2, industry rates of return are reduced even for concentrated industries in which large firms continue to perform well.

The general pattern of these data can be seen in Table 3. The results of regressing differences in profit rates on concentration ratios are shown in this table.

TABLE 3

$R_4 - R_1 = -1.4 + .21^*C_{63}$ (.07)	$r^2 = .09$
$R_4 - R_2 = -2.6 + .12^{**}C_{63}$ (.06)	$r^2 = .04$
$R_4 - R_3 = -3.1 + .10^{**}C_{63}$ (.05)	$r^2 = .04$

*, **, significant at the 1% and 5% levels respectively.
Standard errors are shown in parenthesis.

These regressions reveal a significant positive relationship between concentration and differences in rates of return, especially when comparing the largest and smallest firms in an industry.[6] The three regressions taken to-

[5] On the margin of output, however, these large firms need not have an advantage over small firms, just as fertile land has no advantage over poor land for producing marginal units. The failure of the large firms to become more dominant in these industries suggests the absence of such advantage.

[6] Three adjustments in procedure and in variables were undertaken to analyze certain problems in the data and the theory.

(1) It is believed by some that the profits of firms, and especially of small firms, are hidden in administrative wages. To check on the possibility that this phenomenon might have accounted for the data relationships shown above, the data were recalculated after adding back to profits all administrative salaries of firms in the R_1 asset size class. Although this

gether indicate a nonlinear, decreasing impact of concentration on relative rates of return as the size of the smaller firms is increased from R_1 to R_3.

The competitive view of industry structure suggests that rapid changes in concentration are brought about by changed cost conditions and not by alterations in the height of entry barriers. Industries experiencing rapid increases in concentration should exhibit greater disparities between large and small rates of return because of the more significant cost differences which are the root cause of rapid alternations in industry structure. The monopoly view of concentration does not imply such a relationship, for if an industry is rapidly achieving workable collusive practices there is no reason to suppose that the difference between large and small firm profit rates should increase. At the time of writing, matching data on concentration were available for both 1963 and 1967. This time span is too short to reveal much variation in concentration ratios, and so we cannot be very confident about evidence gained by regressing differences in profit rates on changes in concentration ratios. However, the persistently positive coefficient of the variable $C_{67}-C_{63}$

---

increased very slightly the rates of return for this asset size class, as, of course, must be the case, no correlation between concentration and rate of return was produced. In fact, rates of return so calculated were virtually perfectly correlated with the rates of return shown above for this asset size.

(2) The asset size categories used to calculate the above data are uniform over all industries. Some industries, however, had no firms in the largest asset size category, and these were dropped from the sample. An alternative method was used to check on the impact of this procedure. For each industry, the largest asset size class was redefined so as to include some firms in every industry. The mechanics of the procedure was to categorize asset sizes more finely and choose the largest three size categories containing some observations for each industry. These were then counted as the larger firms in each industry, and the rate of return for these firms was then compared to those firms contained in the three smaller asset size categories containing some observations. The unweighted average difference between large firm rate of return, R_L, and small firm rate of return, R_S, compared with industry concentration is shown below. This table is consistent with the text tables.

C_{63}	$R_L - R_S$
0 — 20%	6.4%
20 — 30	9.4
30 — 40	7.0
40 — 50	7.0
50 — 60	12.8
over 60	14.0

(3) The efficiency argument suggests that for a given degree of industry concentration, measured by the four firm concentration ratio, the greater the difference between the sizes of the largest firms and the sizes of the smallest firms, the larger will be the disparity between R_4 and R_1. A linear regression of $R_4 - R_1$ on C_{63} and the average size of firms in the R_4 class yields a positive but not highly significant coefficient for the variable "average asset size of firms in the R_4 class." Also, there was a small reduction in the significance of the coefficient of C_{63}.

TABLE 4

$$R_4 - R_1 = \quad 1.5 + .21^*C_{63} \quad + .21(C_{67} - C_{63}) \qquad r^2 = .09$$
$$\qquad\qquad\qquad (.07) \qquad (.42)$$

$$R_4 - R_2 = -2.9 + .12^{**}C_{63} + .37(C_{67} - C_{63}) \qquad r^2 = .06$$
$$\qquad\qquad\qquad (.06) \qquad (.28)$$

$$R_4 - R_3 = -3.4 + .10^{**}C_{63} + .29(C_{67} - C_{63}) \qquad r^2 = .05$$
$$\qquad\qquad\qquad (.05) \qquad (.24)$$

*, **, respectively, 1% and 5% confidence levels.

in Table 4 is consistent with the competitive viewpoint, and must increase our doubts, however slightly, about the beneficial effects of an active deconcentration or anti-merger policy.

I have presented an explanation of industry structure and profitability based on competitive superiority. The problem faced by a deconcentration or anti-merger policy was posed on the basis of this explanation. Is there a danger that such a policy will produce more inefficiency than it eliminates? The date presented suggest that this danger should be taken seriously.

Presidential Control versus Bureaucratic Power: Explaining the Reagan Revolution in Antitrust*

Marc Allen Eisner, *Wesleyan University*
Kenneth J. Meier, *University of Wisconsin-Milwaukee*

This analysis assesses the impact of the Reagan presidency on the antitrust policy of the Department of Justice. Explanations of policy change generated by the principal-agent and bureaucratic politics perspectives are tested using an interrupted time series model. The analysis reveals that the enforcement record of the 1980s did not reflect presidential or congressional politics but was the product of changes within the bureaucracy initiated well before the advent of the 1980 elections.

The relationship between elected officials and the bureaucracy is a key question in modern political science. With the decline of the politics-administration dichotomy (Wilson 1887; Goodnow 1900), scholars of public policy recognized that effective public policies could not be made without vesting discretion in nonelected bureaucrats (Rourke 1984). Such transfers of authority, however, create practical and normative problems. The magnitude of these problems depends on the limits of political control and the bureaucracy's ability to act as an independent policymaking force. The Reagan administration provides a perfect natural experiment to examine political control and bureaucratic discretion. President Reagan's conservative policy agenda directly collided with the federal bureaucracy's reputation for favoring liberal policy options (Aberbach and Rockman 1976).

This research examines the relative impacts of presidential control and bureaucratic discretion on antitrust policy actions over the past 25 years. On the surface such an analysis appears biased in favor of presidential control. A number of scholars including Anderson (1986) and Mueller (1986) have attributed massive changes in antitrust policy to the Reagan revolution: major monopoly cases such as AT&T and IBM were abandoned; multibillion-dollar mergers in oil, transportation, and other industries were permitted; and price-fixing conspiracies became the major concern of the antitrust agencies. Our analysis challenges this view; it shows that the policies of the Reagan administration were nothing more than an extension of earlier policies originating in the antitrust bureaucracy.

The analysis proceeds in several stages. First, two competing perspectives on policy change—the principal-agent model and the bureaucratic politics model—are presented. Second, recent changes in antitrust policy are framed in

*The authors would like to thank the Antitrust Division for staffing figures. Interviews were conducted at the Antitrust Division in January and August 1988. Many of the insights regarding the history and expansion of the Economic Policy Office were gained at this time.

American Journal of Political Science, Vol. 34, No. 1, February 1990, Pp. 269–87
© 1990 by the University of Texas Press, P.O. Box 7819, Austin, TX 78713

terms of general antitrust goals. Third, a principal-agent perspective is used to show how such changes fit within the political control literature. Fourth, an alternative explanation of policy change is derived from the bureaucratic politics literature and the history of the Antitrust Division. Fifth, the competing perspectives are subjected to an empirical test using an interrupted time series model.

Competing Perspectives on Policy Change

Bureaucracies are not unbiased organizations that neutrally implement policy decisions made elsewhere. The vagueness of legislative mandates, the policy goals of bureaucrats, the constituent ties of bureaucracies, the values incorporated into expertise, and bureaucratic incentive mechanisms promote the redefinition of policy at the implementation stage (Rourke 1984; Downs 1967; Niskanen 1971; Aberbach and Rockman 1976). The growth of bureaucratic discretion and the consequent reduction of presidential and congressional control are seen as highly problematic in a democratic polity (Finer 1941; Friedrich 1940; Lowi 1979). In fact, some argue that greater political control has been eschewed because the expansion of bureaucratic discretion reinforces the goals of elected officials. By transferring power to administrators, politicians minimize personal responsibility while retaining the ability to claim credit and meet the demands of special constituencies (Fiorina 1977, 1984).

Advocates of greater political control have recently adopted the principal-agent perspective to argue that far more accountability exists than is often recognized (Moe 1985; Wood 1988). The preferences of representative institutions (principals) are imposed on bureaucracies (agents) through numerous relationships of dependency (Mitnik 1980). The president has appointment powers, formal hierarchical powers, and centralized budget and legislative clearance powers (see Stewart and Cromartie 1982; Stewart, Anderson, and Taylor 1982). Congress can exert control through legislation, appropriations, and oversight (Ogul 1976; Key 1959). Principals, therefore, can create incentives for bureaucrats to be responsive to political demands. Despite substantial bureaucratic discretion, the principal-agent perspective predicts that bureaucratic outputs will generally conform with the ideological positions and/or agendas of presidents and members of relevant congressional committees (Moe 1984).[1]

The insights of the principal-agent perspective are not new. Indeed, the perspective is, in many ways, a return to a more traditional view of the political-

---

[1] Recent analyses of bureaucratic control (see Wood 1988; Weingast and Moran 1983) have created a caricature of the principal-agent perspective. As Moe (1984, 768–72) correctly argued, the principal-agent problem is interesting because politicians seek control and bureaucrats have discretion. The position that politicians dominate bureaucrats is an extreme and not particularly useful view of principal-agent relationships. We are indebted to an anonymous reviewer for pointing out the subtleties of Moe's original argument.

bureaucratic relationship that Emmette Redford (1969) describes as overhead democracy. What is new, however, is the methodological sophistication that has accompanied these studies. Numerous quantitative analyses have provided evidence that bureaucratic power may, indeed, be constrained by and accountable to representative institutions (see Moe 1982, 1985; Wood 1988; Weingast and Moran 1983).

In contrast to the principal-agent perspective, the bureaucratic politics perspective[2] emphasizes the limits of external controls on bureaucracy. The fragmentation of political power in the United States leads to a diffusion of political authority to subunits of government (Freeman 1965). In this fragmented political environment, bureaucracies can develop and nurture sources of power independent from the institutions of accountability (Long 1952). The sources of the bureaucracy's power and autonomy are its ability to extract resources from the environment and its discretion in the use of these resources. This ability is a function of the bureaucracies' political support, expertise, leadership, and cohesion (Rourke 1984).

Although the bureaucratic politics perspective emphasizes the role of organizational factors in structuring the policy process (see March and Olsen 1984), explanatory power is not gained through the sacrifice of human agency. Political executives remain important forces in the determination of policy. They must work, however, within the constraints imposed by organizational legacies, existing administrative capacities, and the input of other actors in the policy process. The differences between the bureaucratic politics and principal-agent perspectives, therefore, are differences of degree rather than differences in kind.

Law, Economics, and Antitrust Policy

Antitrust policy finds its legislative foundations in the Sherman Act of 1890, the Clayton Act of 1914, and a few major amendments. Policies are enforced by lawsuits filed by the Justice Department, the Federal Trade Commission, and private citizens.[3] Unfortunately, the legislative debates and the history of court decisions have shown that antitrust laws reflect a host of competing economic, political, and social goals. A cursory listing of policy goals would include maintaining unconcentrated economic power, preserving small business and local ownership, promoting economic justice, and forcing corporations to be accountable to public authority (Meier 1985). As a solution to the problem of conflicting goals, many antitrust policymakers and analysts have looked to eco-

---

[2]The term bureaucratic politics is often attributed to Allison (1971). We are not using the term as Allison does. Rather we are using the term to emphasize that bureaucracies are political institutions that exercise discretion in the policy process. Our use follows that of Rourke (1984).

[3]Historically, the Justice Department's Antitrust Division rather than the Federal Trade Commission has been the major policymaker. Accordingly, our analysis focuses on the Antitrust Division.

nomics. Economics supports a single goal for antitrust—efficiency (see Bork 1978). As economic theory entered the debate over antitrust goals, it also came to play a central role in defining optimal enforcement strategies.

For many decades industrial organization economics (the branch most relevant to antitrust) was dominated by the structure-conduct-performance (SCP) paradigm. Structuralists argued that industrial structure had a direct impact on the conduct of constituent firms. In concentrated industries with barriers to entry (e.g., oligopolies), major firms possessed the capacity to form and maintain collusive arrangements. They could adopt a variety of pricing, output, and promotional policies to realize supracompetitive profits and to limit the ability of other firms to enter the market. Through its impact on conduct, structure also affects performance. A host of market studies have associated oligopolistic markets with inflation, unemployment, a misallocation of wealth, and a drag on innovation (see Weiss 1974, 1979).

The SCP framework was adopted by members of the antitrust policy community for a number of reasons. It met the practical needs of bureaucrats, legislators, and judges by providing simple decision rules. Because concentration was causally related to the existence and abuse of market power, an arithmetic representation of market structure (e.g., market concentration figures) could identify probable violations and define the limits of legality. Undoubtedly, the acceptance of the framework was also tied to its populist implications. Through its focus on concentrated economic power, its assumption that this power promoted abusive forms of conduct, and its reaffirmation of open markets with multiple small actors, it provided technical justification for the anti–big business goals advocated by prominent Democrats such as Phillip Hart, Emmanuel Celler, and Wright Patman (Baker and Blumenthal 1984; Rowe 1984).[4]

Although the SCP framework acknowledged the validity of most antitrust prohibitions, it suggested that the most effective antitrust policy would stress structural (i.e., monopoly) and merger cases because excessive concentration provided the foundation for collusion. By the 1960s, economic structuralism played such a central role in the policy debates that it informed Congress's assessment of agency performance. In recessionary and inflationary periods, congressional committees often advocated that the Justice Department file cases that reflected structuralist priorities. The most striking displays of Congress's adherence to the SCP framework came in the late 1960s and early 1970s when national deconcentration programs were considered. These policy proposals would have

---

[4]Antitrust was not a partisan issue before 1980. Democrats might well have been attracted to SCP arguments for populist reasons. Ralph Nader, in the late 1960s, was a strenuous supporter of structural antitrust. Republicans of this era, on the other hand, were more likely to be attracted to the efficiency aspects of the SCP framework. Structuralist actions implied industrial deconcentration and a more competitive market.

required that major firms in concentrated industries divest certain holdings to achieve acceptable concentration levels.

In the 1970s the political dominance of the SCP framework was challenged by the Chicago school approach. The Chicago school presented existing markets as self-sufficient and at all times efficiency promoting. According to the Chicago school, concentration is not the structural basis for collusion but an expression of efficiency and the technical demands of producing in a given market. Firms became large and profitable because they were efficient. When the Chicago school considered the industrial structures that concerned SCP analysts, it viewed them as efficient or of little long-term concern, given the power of market forces. This was particularly the case with the vertical arrangements (e.g., relationships with suppliers or distributors) identified by the structuralists as means of monopolizing markets (see Demsetz 1974; Bork 1978).

Once markets were presented as self-sufficient and the relationships central to the SCP framework were discounted, the structuralist antitrust agenda could not be justified by economics. Since vertical restraints and the vast majority of mergers were efficiency promoting, cases brought against these activities were without economic merit. Although the Chicago school was critical of antitrust enforcement, its representatives did not advocate its complete elimination. They recognized the need for price-fixing cases because price-fixing entailed significant short-term welfare losses. Similarly, horizontal mergers in highly concentrated markets and vertical mergers that resulted in the monopolization of primary inputs were considered problematic. Such mergers, however, would be exceedingly rare (Posner 1976, 1979).

The Chicago school position quickly came to define the academic consensus in industrial organization economics because it was more closely tied to neoclassical microeconomic theory. Since economic theory structured the antitrust policy debates, the Chicago school's policy influence was equally pronounced. With its limited justification for state intervention, the Chicago school could be used to bolster calls for the relaxation of the antitrust laws. The Chicago school perspective provided the technical justification for the Reagan administration's policy agenda in antitrust.

The Reagan Revolution in Antitrust

The common perception of the Reagan administration's antitrust policies is consistent with the principal-agent perspective (Anderson 1986). President Reagan appointed individuals who shared his conservative views on antitrust policy. Using the principles of the Chicago school, the administration's political appointees rejected most of the traditional goals of antitrust enforcement. Assistant Attorney General William Baxter stated, "Economic efficiency provides the only workable standard from which to derive operational rules and by which the effectiveness of such rules can be judged. . . . the same cannot be said for social and political standards. . . . There is no objective manner for valuing social and political costs and values" (Baxter 1985, 308).

The enforcement record for the Reagan administration provides clear evidence that these policy proclamations were more than just rhetoric. Many traditional antitrust violations were considered as being without economic merit and thus no longer subject to prosecution. The Antitrust Division presented specific guidelines with respect to mergers and vertical restraints, treating them as competitively benign if not efficiency promoting. As a result, few horizontal merger cases were filed, and no vertical or conglomerate mergers were challenged from 1981 to 1984. The vast majority of cases were brought against price-fixing arrangements, one of the few antitrust areas supported by the Chicago school. Despite the investment of considerable financial resources, a number of cases pending from previous administrations were dismissed. Perhaps the most striking example was dismissing the highly publicized case against IBM. Other cases, such as that brought against AT&T, ended in negotiated settlements on terms quite favorable to the firms in question (Mueller 1986; Bickel 1982; Cohodas 1986).

The principal-agent perspective generates three hypotheses regarding the sources of policy change in general, and policy change during the Reagan administration, in particular. First, presidents can influence the direction of antitrust policy (Stewart and Cromartie 1982; Lewis-Beck 1979, 180). They appoint key policymakers and seek to realize their policy goals by placing loyalists in charge of the antitrust agencies. Agency executives, in turn, can structure the organization and its incentives to bring agency output into conformity with predefined priorities. Policy priorities, in turn, should be affected by partisanship. Because Democratic presidents have a populist orientation toward big business, they should favor outputs consistent with the structure-conduct-performance framework. Republican presidents—Ronald Reagan in particular—should favor Chicago school priorities.

The principal-agent perspective is not limited to the relationship between the president and the bureaucracy (see Moe 1985). A second hypothesis concerns the role of Congress in defining bureaucratic outputs. Weingast and Moran (1983) use the principal-agent perspective to examine Federal Trade Commission actions. They find a correlation between the changing ideology of oversight committee members and FTC policies. In antitrust policy, one could hypothesize that as ideological positions of subcommittee members shift to the left, the Antitrust Division will pursue a more interventionist enforcement program along the lines of the SCP framework. Conversely, as subcommittee members become more conservative, one should witness a movement toward Chicago school priorities.

We are skeptical, however, that Congress exerts a great deal of control over the policies of the Antitrust Division (see Lewis-Beck 1979, 181). The Justice Department as an executive agency is more insulated from congressional pressures than the independent regulatory agencies often linked to Congress through the principal-agent perspective (e.g., the NLRB, the FTC, and the ICC; see Cohen 1985; Weingast and Moran 1983). In addition, an examination of the Antitrust Division's oversight hearings rarely reveals discussions about substantive policy content. Congressional concerns focus on the size of the caseload rather than policy priorities. Nonetheless, we shall provide an empirical test of this hypothesis.

A third hypothesis is somewhat more complex, yet easily reconciled with the basic tenets of the principal-agent perspective. While acknowledging that presidents and congressional committees exert influence over agency activity, the intensity of this influence may be affected by the performance of the economy. The political business cycle literature suggests that higher salience for economic issues (particularly inflation and unemployment) leads electorally vulnerable officials to seek changes in policy (see Tufte 1978; Alt and Chrystal 1983). Although antitrust is a microeconomic policy, the violations it addresses have macroeconomic ramifications. As inflation and/or unemployment increase, we hypothesize that the number of cases filed will also increase. In this case, economic fluctuations act as an exogenous variable with the principal responding to changing macroeconomic indicators with demands for adjustments in policy. Before testing these hypotheses, it is necessary to address the explanations suggested by the bureaucratic politics perspective.

Bureaucratic Evolution and Agency Professionalization

Unlike the principal-agent perspective, the bureaucratic politics perspective focuses primarily on internal changes in the organization. Bureaucracies exercise discretion in the implementation of public policies. Discretion can produce public policies more consistent with the values of bureaucrats than the goals of elected officials. Policy change, therefore, should be closely tied to changes in administrative values and administrative capacities.

A prime source of bureaucratic values is the professional orientation of individual bureaucrats (see Janowitz 1960; Kaufman 1960). The Antitrust Division is a litigation agency staffed primarily with attorneys. Attorneys approach antitrust on a case-by-case basis, often with little recognition that antitrust is anything more than pure law enforcement. As a result, the Antitrust Division has been characterized by a certain prosecutorial dynamic. New attorneys come to the division seeking litigation experience to enhance their market value to private sector employers. To gain this experience, they often pursue cases that can be litigated to a successful conclusion in a relatively short period of time (Hamilton and Till 1941; Weaver 1977; Katzmann 1980). Although the division has been dominated by attorneys, staff economists have played a role of increasing importance over the agency's history. While an economics section was created in the late 1930s to aid in the evaluation of cases, it was never truly given a role in managing the caseload. The section was staffed by underqualified economists who served a support function, working at the pleasure of the attorneys. They were relatively insignificant in either setting policy or establishing goals/values for the organization.[5]

In 1972 Assistant Attorney General Thomas Kauper initiated a professionalization process that would bring a large number of Ph.D. economists into the Antitrust Division as part of an Economic Policy Office (EPO). The goal was to create a staff of sufficient size and quality that an economist could be assigned to each potential case at an early stage. Rather than serving as a support staff, the economists were to function as independent analysts. The distinction was important. Although economics had been used to support cases in the past, cases were generally selected in accordance with legal rather than economic criteria. As independent analysts, Kauper hoped, economists would be able to promote economic analysis as a basis for case selection (Kauper 1984).

Given the dominance of the legal staff, Kauper realized that the EPO would affect policy only if the economists could convince the attorneys that economic analysis had a positive role to play in Antitrust Division affairs. Using the logic of economics, economists simplified the lawyers' case selection process by focusing on precise goals and enforcement strategies. Because economists were able to simplify the attorneys' complex problem of case selection, economists were soon working directly with attorneys to identify antitrust violations. The convergence of the legal and economic staffs can be attributed to a number of factors including the greater role of economics in the policy debates, a series of court cases in which the Supreme Court based its decisions on detailed economic analysis, and the practical advantages associated with using economics to discover and build promising cases. By the end of the decade, economists had been fully integrated into each stage of investigation and case development. Economic expertise had been given a central role in decision making (Kauper 1984; Hay 1988; U.S. Department of Justice 1978).

The role of economists in the Antitrust Division continued to expand in the 1980s. First, it became established policy that no case would be brought unless it was supported by economic analysis. At that point the EPO exercised what amounted to a veto power over all cases.[6] Second, the organizational presence of the economists was enhanced when the Reagan administration's staff reductions fell disproportionately on the legal staff. Third, the EPO was charged with training the legal staff in economic analysis. Mandatory courses in microeconomics and industrial organization were conducted as part of what was referred

[5]A detailed presentation of the role of economics in the history of the Antitrust Division and the Federal Trade Commission can be found in Eisner (1989).

[6]This conclusion is based on personal interviews with several high-ranking officials in the Reagan Antitrust Division.

to as EPO-U. As a final expression of the new status of the division's economists, the EPO's chief economist was elevated to the position of deputy assistant attorney general for economic analysis in 1984. In a decade economists went from a secondary position as members of a support staff to being equal partners in the policy process.

The significance of this bureaucratic evolution was enhanced by changes taking place in the economics discipline during the same period. The EPO was created when the SCP paradigm was the dominant antitrust theory. As noted above, in the 1970s the dominance of the SCP framework was successfully challenged by the Chicago school.[7] By hiring young economists from the best graduate schools, the Antitrust Division provided an institutional basis for Chicago school values. Although the initial intent may have been to incorporate economic analysis that reflected structural values, in practice the analysis embodied Chicago school values.

The bureaucratic politics perspective generates a hypothesis that challenges those presented by the principal-agent perspective. The bureaucratic politics perspective identifies change at the level of the organization as the significant independent variable in explaining policy change. More to the point, the creation of the EPO and the increasing presence of economists in the Antitrust Division should be positively associated with specific changes in antitrust policy. Because the EPO was created long before Reagan became president, the bureaucratic politics perspective holds that policy change should have its origins before the Reagan presidency. The Reagan revolution in antitrust should be nothing more than a continuation of a trend established earlier.

Data and Methods

The method of analysis used to contrast the impacts of the principal-agent relationships and internal bureaucratic forces on antitrust policy will be interrupted time series analysis (Lewis-Beck 1986). The method treats political impacts as deviations from trends determined by historical and economic forces. The analysis covers the years 1959 to 1984.[8]

The SCP framework and the Chicago school present divergent visions of an optimal composition of the antitrust caseload. Structuralists, because they believe that structure affects conduct which affects performance, emphasize monopoly and merger cases. Chicago school economists downplay the importance of monopoly and merger cases, advocating greater reliance on price-fixing cases

---

[7]The triumph of the Chicago school was not related to empirical evidence. The Chicago school, in fact, declared a variety of empirical tests irrelevant and argued that its position was closer to the heart of the microeconomic price theory (see Posner 1979). The Chicago school victory was a political victory not an empirical one.

[8]The method is described at length by Lewis-Beck (1986). For applications of the technique, see Lewis-Beck and Alford (1980) and Copeland and Meier (1987).

to combat collusion. The dependent variable measures are fairly straightforward. We use the percentage of antitrust cases that are filed in each year in three areas: monopoly, mergers, and price fixing. The impact of the Chicago school should be revealed by declines in merger and monopoly cases and corresponding increases in price-fixing cases.

The independent variables in this analysis fall into three general clusters: exogenous economic forces, external political forces, and internal bureaucratic forces. Many public policies follow secular trends as agencies become more adept at handling policy problems or as government and economic forces reach an equilibrium. To prevent the secular trend from confounding the impact of the various independent variables, a countervariable was used to filter out any trend in the dependent and independent variables.[9]

The two exogenous economic forces, the consumer price index and the national unemployment rate, are likely to affect antitrust policy actions. The consumer price index is our measure of inflation. As inflation rises, antitrust actions should increase to counter the inflationary effects of monopolistic behavior. Unemployment, while only rarely linked to antitrust policy, is a major electoral force. Efforts to reduce unemployment might translate into a greater willingness to file antitrust actions, especially during Democratic presidential administrations.[10]

Two external political actors are hypothesized to affect antitrust policy, Congress and the president. An extensive body of research has linked the policy liberalism of congressional committees to the antitrust outputs of the Federal Trade Commission (see Weingast and Moran 1983; Faith, Leavens, and Tollison 1982). While we are skeptical that Congress has similar impacts on the Department of Justice, two measures of congressional liberalism were included. These are the average liberalism scores assigned by the Americans for Democratic Action to the members of the House and Senate antitrust subcommittees.[11]

The impact of the president is one of our major concerns. This potential impact is assessed in two ways. First, since Democratic presidents are more likely to share the populist bias of the structure-conduct-performance school,

[9]The countervariable is coded one in year 1959 and increased by one for each year thereafter. See Lewis-Beck (1986) for a discussion of the need for a countervariable.
[10]An exception to this generalization is the work of Amacher et al. (1985).
[11]Both committees are subcommittees of the respective Judiciary Committees. Two coding problems were faced. First, when Emmanuel Celler was chair of the Judiciary Committee, subcommittees were designated by number rather than by substantive area of legislation. Examination of the dockets reveals that Celler assigned antitrust legislation to subcommittee 5; this subcommittee was used in the analysis. In 1981 with the Republican majority in the Senate, Strom Thurmond, the Judiciary chair, abolished the subcommittee on antitrust (reportedly to avoid having Charles Mathias serve as chair). For the Senate after 1981, therefore, ADA averages for the entire Judiciary Committee were used. The results of the analysis do not differ if the averages for the entire committee or the score of the subcommittee chair is used rather than the subcommittee average.

they should favor structural antitrust caseloads. A dummy variable was used for Democratic presidential administrations. Second, because our specific concern is the impact of the Reagan administration, a second dummy variable is used that is coded as one for the Reagan administration and zero otherwise.[12]

To test the institutional hypothesis, internal bureaucratic factors are reduced to a single force, that of the Economic Policy Office. Two impacts are possible: a single, one-time impact that changes the level of antitrust cases and a long-term impact that changes the trend of antitrust cases over time. The first potential impact is measured by the ratio of economists to lawyers in the Antitrust Division after the creation of the EPO. The second potential impact is measured by a change in slope variable coded one in the first year of the EPO and increasing by one each year thereafter. The means and standard deviations of the variables used in the analysis are listed in Table 1.[13]

Two statistical problems must be considered in any interrupted time series model. First, autocorrelation is often a problem that results in ordinary least squares regression coefficients that are not efficient (Lewis-Beck 1986). The practical impact of this problem is that relationships will appear to be significant when they really are not. Whenever autocorrelation is a significant problem, the

---

[12] We also considered using dummy variables for each president. Some might argue that since Carter, Ford, and Nixon were advocates of deregulation, they would also favor reductions in antitrust enforcement. This argument is difficult to support. All three presidents saw antitrust as distinct from regulation. The Nixon administration saw the filing of major structural cases by both the Justice Department and the FTC. The Ford studies of deregulation frequently argued that vigorous use of structural antitrust could take the place of industrial regulation (see MacAvoy 1979). President Ford (1976, 349) himself endorsed a structuralist agenda: "It seems to me that through [antitrust enforcement] we can make certain, in the business world at least, that there will be a proper governmental role in making an environment where free enterprise can operate without a monopolistic development. . . . The strength of our free enterprise system depends on competition. We can't have big business, big labor—or big government, I might add—dominating our economy." Carter also supported structural antitrust. Alfred Kahn, Carter's architect of airline deregulation, for example, has made clear that he supported airline deregulation in part because he felt that antitrust would be used to prevent concentration in the industry (see Kahn 1988).

An empirical test also failed. When dummy variables for Nixon, Ford, and Carter were added to the equations in Tables 3, 4, and 5 not a single presidential dummy variable was statistically significant. The residuals of the significant equations reveal that Nixon and Ford were by far the most structuralist presidents. Even Carter was slightly more structuralist than Eisenhower. This version of the principal-agent argument, therefore, fails for two reasons. First, the presidential actions and statements of Nixon, Ford, and Carter reflect structural not Chicago school ideas. Second, the empirical analysis shows no significant impact for the individual presidents.

[13] The ratio of economists per 10 attorneys was 1.0 at the time that the EPO was created. By the end of the 1970s, it had reached 1.5. Although the Reagan budget reductions forced dramatic reductions in the Antitrust Division staff, the reductions were not borne equally by the attorneys and economists. Accordingly, by 1987 there were 2.9 economists for every 10 attorneys, almost twice the number as before the reductions began. Figures provided by Frederick Warren-Boulton, Deputy Assistant Attorney General for Economic Analysis.

TABLE 1

Means and Standard Deviations for Variables Used

Variable	Mean	Standard Deviation
Consumer Price Index	213.48	99.29
Unemployment rate	5.95	1.70
Economists to lawyers ratio	.76	.81
House subcommittee ADA score	55.61	9.69
Senate subcommittee ADA score	45.99	8.22
Price-fixing percentages	68.74	18.11
Monopoly percentages	10.78	7.81
Merger case percentages	20.48	13.25

regression equation will be estimated with generalized least squares (Hanushek and Jackson 1977, 146).

The second problem is collinearity. Time series data often contain high levels of collinearity as a result of common secular trends or impacts from other variables excluded from the analysis. Collinearity produces unstable regression coefficients. In order to reduce this problem, each model is reestimated deleting the insignificant variables from the model and testing the remaining model for collinearity problems. The final models included are not appreciably affected by collinearity.

Findings

Our main goal is to assess the power of external political and internal bu-reaucratic forces in explaining policy change, particularly during the Reagan administration. While we are interested in the relationships between all the in-dependent variables and antitrust policy, our major concern is the impact of the Reagan presidency and the Economic Policy Office. If the Reagan presidency is associated with policy change, then any changes should occur in 1981 or after-ward. This impact should produce a significant slope for the Reagan presidency variable. If the creation of the EPO is associated with changes in antitrust, then any changes should occur shortly after 1972. This impact should produce a sig-nificant impact for either the economists to lawyers ratio (short-term impact) or the slope change variable (long-term impacts).

The policy change equation for price-fixing cases is presented in Table 2. A significant trend exists: price-fixing cases have dropped in frequency at the rate of 2.67% per year. The proportion of price-fixing cases is unaffected by the president, Congress, and external economic events. The influx of economists with the creation of the Economic Policy Office had a significant impact on the proportion of price-fixing cases. The creation of the EPO resulted in a short-term

13.55% increase in price-fixing cases. In addition, the EPO appears to have a long-term impact on price-fixing cases. The creation of the EPO results in an annual 5.16% increase in price-fixing cases.

Table 3 presents the equations for monopoly cases. The political variables are once again noticeable in their lack of impact. Neither Congress nor the president has a significant impact on the proportion of monopoly cases over time. The major influence on monopoly cases are exogenous economic factors and the creation of the Economic Policy Office. Again, monopoly cases follow a trend with an increase of .75% per year in the proportion of monopoly cases. The unemployment rate also has a significant impact. A 1% increase in unemployment is associated with a 2.7% increase in monopoly cases, a relationship consistent with the notion that monopoly restricts production and thus affects employment. The largest impact is once again that for the EPO. The creation of the EPO produces a long-term decrease of 3.2% per year in monopoly cases filed for each year after the EPO was created. Given the values of this variable, this relationship predicts that the number of monopoly cases would be reduced to zero during the 1980s—a prediction that is consistent with reality.

Table 4 reveals the results of our model for merger cases. The pattern is completely consistent with the results for monopoly and price-fixing cases. As with the other components of the caseload, the president and the Congress do not have a significant impact on the proportion of merger cases. The impacts are either exogenous economic forces or internal bureaucratic forces. The proportion

TABLE 2

Determinants of Department of Justice Price-Fixing Cases

Independent Variable	Dependent Variable = Percentage of Price-Fixing Cases	
	Slope	Slope**
Consumer Price Index	−.45	—
Unemployment rate	1.08	—
Counter	−.29	−2.67*
Reagan presidency	17.20	—
Democratic administrations	−.62	—
House subcommittee ADA scores	.09	—
Senate subcommittee ADA scores	.25	—
Economists in Antitrust Division	8.48	13.55*
Slope change for economists	10.60	5.16*
R^2	.81	.81
Adjusted R^2	.70	.78

*$p < .05$

**Estimated with generalized least squares.

TABLE 3

Determinants of Department of Justice Monopoly Cases

Dependent Variable = Percentage of Monopolization Cases		
Independent Variable	Slope	Slope**
Consumer Price Index	.30	—
Unemployment rate	2.07	2.70*
Counter	.79	.75*
Reagan presidency	7.66	—
Democratic administrations	2.93	—
House subcommittee ADA scores	−.10	—
Senate subcommittee ADA scores	−.21	—
Economists in Antitrust Division	−2.35	—
Slope change for economists	−6.97	−3.20*
R^2	.76	.72
Adjusted R^2	.49	.66

*$p < .05$

**Estimated with generalized least squares.

of merger cases follows a secular trend, increasing by 1.77% a year. The filing of merger cases is affected by the unemployment rate. A 1% increase in unemployment is associated with a 2.77% decline in merger cases. The most interesting relationships are again those for the Economic Policy Office. The creation of the office results in a short-term reduction of approximately 11% and a long-term annual decrease of 2.11% in merger cases filed for every year after the creation of the EPO.

In combination, the tables provide strong support for the hypothesis that changes in antitrust policy reflect the evolution of the Antitrust Division rather than the changing demands of external political actors. In no case is the Reagan administration associated with a significant change in antitrust policy. The significant changes in antitrust that were noticed in the Reagan administration were nothing more than the extension of trends that predate the advent of the Reagan presidency. Such visible actions as the AT&T settlement or the IBM dismissal might have drawn greater attention to antitrust, but they did not change nor accelerate the underlying trend in composition of the caseload. Policy change found its origins in the bureaucracy—in the influx of economists into policy-making positions.

Conclusion

This article contrasts two perspectives on policy change, the principal-agent perspective and the bureaucratic politics perspective. While the principal-agent

TABLE 4

Determinants of Department of Justice Merger Cases

Independent Variable	Dependent Variable = Percentage of Merger Cases Slope	Slope**
Consumer Price Index	.15	—
Unemployment rate	−3.14	−2.77*
Counter	1.08	1.27*
Reagan presidency	−9.54	—
Democratic administrations	−2.30	—
House subcommittee ADA scores	.01	—
Senate subcommittee ADA scores	−.04	—
Economists in Antitrust Division	−10.43	−11.06*
Slope change for economists	−3.63	−2.11*
R^2	.70	.73
Adjusted R^2	.54	.67

*$p < .05$

**Estimated with generalized least squares.

perspective appeared to provide an intuitively correct explanation of recent changes in antitrust policy, the interrupted time series analysis revealed that policy changes originated well before the Reagan presidency. The source of change was not found in the policy agendas of presidential administrations nor in the composition of congressional committees but in the bureaucracy of the Antitrust Division. Our analysis revealed that the redefinition of policy priorities was driven by a professionalization process; economists were brought into the division and provided with a crucial position in the policy process. The economists' professional norms and values (as embodied by the dominant school of economic thought) came to play a central role in the definition of policy. The interplay of bureaucratic evolution and critical shifts in the economics discipline provided the basis for change in antitrust.

While our analysis addresses the limited case of antitrust, two points require emphasis. First, although the bureaucracy is often presented as being little more than a source of resistance, in the case of antitrust the bureaucracy pursued a positive and coherent enforcement program. Undoubtedly, individual political executives encountered resistance when seeking to realize policies that countered the organizational biases of the Antitrust Division. When the division functioned as a pure litigating agency, attempts to impose economic reasoning were largely rejected. Similarly, after the creation of the EPO, attempts to pursue structuralist enforcement programs were unrealized. Because economists had been given an institutional presence at each stage of the policy process, the agency generated cases that were compatible with Chicago school theory. The bureaucracy imposed a coherent and consistent set of priorities on the caseload. In short, it set policy.

Our analysis suggests a second conclusion regarding the status of expertise in bureaucratic organizations. Expertise is often identified as an internal source of bureaucratic strength (Rourke 1984). Specialized knowledge is necessary for making, implementing, and evaluating technically complex policies. And yet, as the case of antitrust reveals, greater reliance on economics was a source of vulnerability. Economics was brought into the Antitrust Division to meet the practical demands of administering antitrust and rationalizing policy. Because economics had become central to the administration of policy, changes in the body of economic knowledge were transmitted into the policy process. The agency, as a result, was vulnerable to changes in economics that it could neither control nor foresee. The agency accepted a role for economists when structuralism was the dominant economic belief. With the emergence of the Chicago school, the agency was forced to rely on a form of knowledge that denied the justification for much of antitrust. In this manner, the Antitrust Division came to harbor a bias against its own mission. Given the critical functions performed by expertise in the policy process, the lesson presented by the case of antitrust should be taken quite seriously (see Noble 1987).

Our analysis has shown that the Reagan antitrust record is little more than an extension of well-established trends which predated the elections of 1980. The substantial changes that found an expression in the 1980s were a product of bureaucratic evolution. Whether these findings can be extended to other policy areas affected by the Reagan presidency is open to question. Scholars are only beginning to assess the significance of policy change during the 1980s. While it may be attractive and convenient to speak in terms of executive-led policy revolutions, our analysis calls attention to an observation that is as old as the study of politics, namely, that institutions matter. When analyzing the extent of change under the Reagan administration, scholars would be wise to consider the impact of bureaucratic politics.

Manuscript submitted 15 October 1988
Final manuscript received 13 June 1989

REFERENCES

Aberbach, Joel D., and Bert A. Rockman. 1976. "Clashing Beliefs within the Executive Branch: The Nixon Administration Bureaucracy." *American Political Science Review* 70:456–68.
Allison, Graham. 1971. *Essence of Decision*. Boston: Little, Brown.
Alt, James E., and K. Alec Chrystal. 1983. *Political Economics*. Berkeley: University of California Press.
Amacher, Ryan C., Richard S. Higgens, William F. Shughart II, and Robert D. Tollison. 1985.

"The Behavior of Regulatory Activity over the Business Cycle: An Empirical Test." *Economic Inquiry* 7–20.

Anderson, James E. 1986. "The Reagan Administration, Antitrust Action, and Policy Change." Presented at the annual meeting of the Midwest Political Science Association, Chicago.

Baker, Donald I., and William Blumenthal. 1986. "Ideological Cycles and Unstable Antitrust Rules." *Antitrust Bulletin* 31.2:323–39.

Baxter, William. 1982. "Separation of Powers, Prosecutorial Discretion, and the 'Common Law' Nature of Antitrust Law." *Texas Law Review* 60:661–704.

————. 1985. "Responding to the Reaction: The Draftsman's View." In *Antitrust Policy in Transition: The Convergence of Law and Economics,* ed. Eleanor M. Fox and James T. Halverson. Chicago: American Bar Association.

Bickel, David R. 1982. "The Antitrust Division's Adoption of a Chicago School Program Calls for Some Reorganization. But Is the Division's New Policy Here to Stay?" *Houston Law Review* 20:1083–1127.

Bork, Robert H. 1978. *The Antitrust Paradox: A Policy at War with Itself.* New York: Basic Books.

Cohen, Jeffrey. 1985. "Congressional Oversight: A Test of Two Theories." Presented at the annual meeting of the American Political Science Association, New Orleans.

Cohodas, Nadine. 1986. "Reagan Seeks Relaxation of Antitrust Laws." *Congressional Quarterly Weekly Report* 44:187–92.

Copeland, Gary W., and Kenneth J. Meier. 1987. "Gaining Ground: The Impact of Medicaid and WIC on Infant Mortality." *American Politics Quarterly* 15:254–73.

Demsetz, Harold. 1974. "Two Systems of Belief about Monopoly." In *Industrial Concentration: The New Learning,* ed. Harvey J. Goldschmid, H. Michael Mann, and H. Fred Weston. Boston: Little, Brown.

Downs, Anthony. 1967. *Inside Bureaucracy.* Boston: Little, Brown.

Eisner, Marc Allen. 1989. "Antitrust and the Triumph of Economics: Institutions, Expertise, Policy Change." Ph.D. diss., University of Wisconsin-Madison.

Faith, Roger L., Donald R. Leavens, and Robert D. Tollison. 1982. "Antitrust Pork Barrel." *Journal of Law and Economics* 15:329–42.

Finer, Herman. 1941. "Administrative Responsibility in Democratic Government." *Public Administration Review* 1:335–50.

Fiorina, Morris P. 1977. *Congress: Keystone of the Washington Establishment.* New Haven: Yale University Press.

————. 1985. "Group Concentration and the Delegation of Authority." In *Regulatory Policy and the Social Sciences,* ed. Robert Noll. Berkeley: University of California Press.

Ford, Gerald R. 1976. *Public Papers of the Presidents of the United States.* Washington, DC: Government Printing Office.

Freeman, J. Leiper. 1985. *The Political Process.* New York: Random House.

Friedrich, Carl J. 1940. "Public Policy and the Nature of Administrative Responsibility." *Public Policy* 1:3–24.

Goodnow, Frank J. 1900. *Politics and Administration.* New York: Macmillan.

Hamilton, Walton, and Irene Till. 1941. *Antitrust in Action.* Temporary National Economic Committee Monograph No. 16. Washington, DC: Government Printing Office.

Hanushek, Eric A., and John E. Jackson. 1977. *Statistical Methods for Social Scientists.* New York: Academic Press.

Hay, George A. 1988. Correspondence with Marc Eisner, April 1, 1988.

Janowitz, Morris. 1960. *The Professional Soldier.* Glencoe, IL: Free Press of Glencoe.

Kahn, Alfred E. 1988. "I Would Do It Again." *Regulation* 12.2:22–28.

Katzmann, Robert. 1980. *Regulatory Bureaucracy.* Cambridge: MIT Press.

Kaufman, Herbert. 1960. *The Forest Ranger.* Baltimore: Johns Hopkins University Press.

Kauper, Thomas E. 1984. "The Role of Economic Analysis in the Antitrust Division before and after the Establishment of the Economic Policy Office: A Lawyer's View." *Antitrust Bulletin* 29:111–32.

Key, V. O. 1959. "Legislative Control." In *Elements of Public Administration,* ed. Fritz Morstein Marx. Englewood Cliffs, NJ: Prentice-Hall.

Lewis-Beck, Michael S. 1979. "Maintaining Economic Competition: The Causes and Consequences of Antitrust." *Journal of Politics* 41:169–91.

———. 1986. "Interrupted Time Series." In *New Tools for Social Scientists,* ed. William D. Berry and Michael S. Lewis-Beck. Beverly Hills: Sage.

Lewis-Beck, Michael S., and John R. Alford. 1980. "Can Government Regulate Safety?" *American Political Science Review* 74:745–56.

Long, Norton E. 1952. "Bureaucracy and Constitutionalism." *American Political Science Review* 46:808–18.

Lowi, Theodore J. 1979. *The End of Liberalism: The Second Republic of the United States.* 2d ed. New York: Norton.

MacAvoy, Paul W. 1979. *The Regulated Industries and the Economy.* New York: Norton.

March, James G., and Johan P. Olsen. 1984. "The New Institutionalism: Organizational Factors in Political Life." *American Political Science Review* 78:734–49.

Meier, Kenneth J. 1985. *Regulation: Politics, Bureaucracy, and Economics.* New York: St. Martin's.

Mitnick, Barry M. 1980. *The Political Economy of Regulation.* New York: Columbia University Press.

Moe, Terry M. 1982. "Regulatory Performance and Presidential Administration." *American Journal of Political Science* 26:197–224.

———. 1984. "The New Economics of Organization." *American Journal of Political Science* 28:739–77.

———. 1985. "Control and Feedback in Economic Regulation: The Case of the NLRB." *American Political Science Review* 79:1094–1116.

Mueller, Willard F. 1986. "A New Attack on Antitrust: The Chicago Case." *Antitrust Law and Economics Review* 18:29–66.

Niskanen, William A. 1971. *Bureaucracy and Representative Government.* Chicago: Aldine-Atherton.

Noble, Charles. 1987. "Economic Theory in Practice: White House Oversight of OSHA Health Standards." In *Confronting Values in Policy Analysis: The Politics of Criteria,* ed. Frank Fischer and John Forester. Beverly Hills: Sage.

Ogul, Morris. 1976. *Congress Oversees the Bureaucracy.* Pittsburgh: University of Pittsburgh Press.

Posner, Richard A. 1976. *Antitrust Law: An Economic Perspective.* Chicago: University of Chicago Press.

———. 1979. "The Chicago School of Antitrust Analysis." *University of Pennsylvania Law Review* 127:925–48.

Redford, Emmette S. 1969. *Democracy in the Administrative State.* New York: Oxford University Press.

Rourke, Francis E. 1984. *Bureaucracy, Politics, and Public Policy.* 3d ed. Boston: Little, Brown.

Rowe, Frederick M. 1984. "The Decline of Antitrust and the Delusion of Models: The Faustian Pact of Law and Economics." *Georgetown Law Review* 72:1511–71.

Stewart, Joseph, Jr., James E. Anderson, and Zona Taylor. 1982. "Presidential and Congressional Support for 'Independent' Regulatory Commissions: Implications of the Budgetary Process." *Western Political Quarterly* 35:318–26.

Stewart, Joseph, Jr., and Jane S. Cromartie. 1982. "Partisan Presidential Change and Regulatory Policy: The Case of the FTC and Deceptive Practices Enforcement, 1938–1974." *Presidential Studies Quarterly* 12:568–73.

Tufte, Edward R. 1978. *Political Control of the Economy.* Princeton: Princeton University Press.

U.S. Department of Justice. 1978. *Annual Report of the Attorney General of the United States.* Washington, DC: Government Printing Office.

Weaver, Suzanne. 1977. *Decision to Prosecute: Organization and Public Policy in the Antitrust Division.* Cambridge: MIT Press.

Weingast, Barry R., and Mark J. Moran. 1983. "Bureaucratic Discretion or Congressional Control? Regulatory Policymaking by the Federal Trade Commission." *Journal of Political Economy* 91:765–800.

Weiss, Leonard W. 1974. "The Concentration-Profits Relationship and Antitrust." In *Industrial Concentration: The New Learning,* ed. Harvey Goldschmid, H. Michael Mann, and J. Fred Weston. Boston: Brown, Little.

————. 1979. "The Structure-Conduct-Performance Paradigm and Antitrust." *University of Pennsylvania Law Review* 127:1104–40.

Wilson, Woodrow. 1887. "The Study of Administration." *Political Science Quarterly* 2:197–222.

Wood, B. Dan. 1988. "Principals, Bureaucrats, and Responsiveness in Clean Air Enforcement." *American Political Science Review* 82:213–34.

GUESS WHO CAME TO DINNER

An Empirical Study of Federal Antitrust Enforcement
for the Period 1963–1984

JOSEPH C. GALLO*
JOSEPH L. CRAYCRAFT*
STEVEN C. BUSH*

Abstract

This paper highlights the trends in antitrust
enforcement for 1963–84. It is based upon an update by the
author's of Posner's study and follows his methodology,
format, and operational definitions. The specific data
examined include number of antitrust cases instituted, the
duration of cases, DOJ and FTC won-loss records, nature of
cases, fines and imprisonment and violations alleged.

Since 1890, the number of multiple cases instituted by
the DOJ resulting from the investigation of a single
conspiracy has increased. Consolidating cases to reflect
this pattern shows the apparent increase in DOJ cases
represent fewer conspiracies of more limited nature that
are being prosecuted under the Reagan administration. It
is an intense cultivation of a well-known terrain rather
than exploration of new frontiers in antitrust.

The Antitrust Penalties and Procedures Act of 1974 has
increased the size of fines and the use of jail sentences.
Structural relief is less frequent.

Although a study of Federal antitrust cases is as dull and messy
as a stack of dirty dishes, the height of the stack, how dirty it is
and how long the dishes remain dirty gives us some insight into the
housekeeping habits of the Federal antitrust enforcement agencies.
Who the Department of Justice (DOJ) and Federal Trade Commission
(FTC) invited to dinner, the menu they served (the violation alleged)
and whether their guests left happy (cases dismissed) says something
about the quality of their hospitality. Posner's pioneering study of
Federal antitrust enforcement provides an analysis of the
housekeeping habits and the hospitality of these agencies for the
period 1890-1963.(1) This paper highlights trends in antitrust
enforcement for the period 1963-1984 and is based upon our update of
Posner's article.(2) The methodology, format, and operational
definitions used by Posner have been followed closely to facilitate
direct comparisons of the two works.

The CCH Transfers Binders for the DOJ and the FTC are the social
registers providing information about the guest lists (who was
indicted), the number of parties (cases), their length, who had a
good time (cases dismissed), the choice of menu (the violations
alleged) and whether there were any paying guests (convictions).

The underlying rationale for a statistical analysis of DOJ and

FTC cases is the attempt to measure antitrust enforcement effort and effectiveness. The simple enumeration of cases may be deceptive as such a measure. This is a common problem of output measurement in economic analysis. Is a case, a case a la Gertrude Stein or is there significant heterogeneity among cases? It would seem that antitrust enforcement, for purpose of economic analysis, ought to have some relation to the number of conspiracies involved. Does a state-wide conspiracy in highway construction resulting in twenty cases indicate twenty times the enforcement effort of a single case against a national conspiracy? During the period of Posner's study, a strong one-to-one relation between a case and a conspiracy exists; therefore, Posner's measurement of cases also measured conspiracies. In more recent years, however, this relationship is no longer holds. A simple count of cases would overstate enforcement effort where the attack on a single conspiracy results in numerous indictments. Rather than counting each CCH number, all numbers evolving from a single investigation or conspiracy have been consolidated and counted as one case regardless of the year the case was reported. This inter-year consolidation was not a significant factor in Posner's analysis. Each consolidated case was treated as if it originated at the same time as the case first reported. The influence of the consolidation can be seen in Figure 1.(3) The solid line represents the number of cases without consolidation. The dotted lines represents the consolidated cases as reported in Figure 1. In order to stress the continuity with Posner's study, the term "case" has been retained; however, it is more appropriate to treat the data reported, particulary in recent years, as referring to "conspiracies" or single investigation.

Consistent with an attempt to measure enforcement effort or activity, criminal contempt cases are not included in the data. Such cases reflect behavior of convicted defendants rather than new enforcement activity by the DOJ.

I. THE NUMBER OF DINNER PARTIES
(The Number of Cases)

Over the past twenty-two years the DOJ has been very social. It had almost half as many dinner parties in the last 22 years as it did in the first 73 years of its existence (918 cases out of a total of 2,197)(4).

Figure 1 and Table I show a steady upward trend in the number of DOJ cases, reaching a peak in 1972. The average of 38 cases per year during 1963-1969 rose to 52.4 for the five-year period 1970-1974 and returned to the original level over the last ten years. Although the last ten years represent levels of enforcement lower than those of the 1970-1974 period, they remain high by historical standards. Only the two prior decades, 1955-1965 and 1965-1975, show greater number of cases.

Contrary to popular belief, examination of Table I indicates the Reagan-Baxter-McGrath DOJ has maintained a historically high level of hospitality, especially during the last two years. Subsequent examination will review the nature of these cases.

The Posner data reveal similar upward trends with abberations associated, in particular, with the Great Depression and World War II.(6)

FTC activity shows a slight increase in cases brought through

Bush, Craycraft and Gallo   107

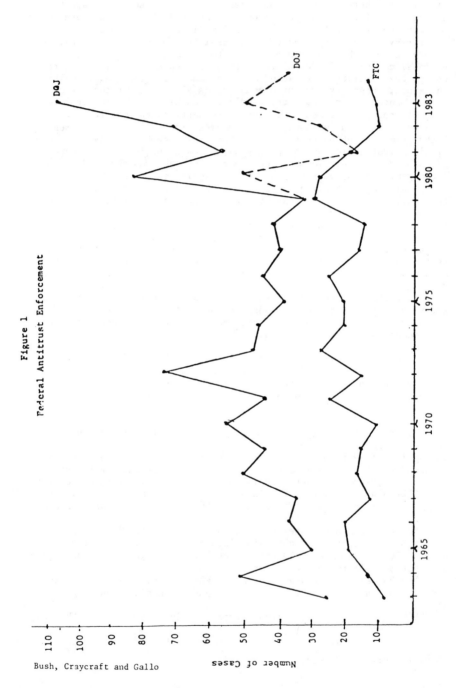

Figure 1

Federal Antitrust Enforcement

Bush, Craycraft and Gallo

Number of Cases

Source: Joseph C. Gallo and Steven C. Bush, "A Statistical Analysis of Antitrust Enforcement for the
Period (1963-1983),unpublished manuscript, University of Cincinnati, 1983.

TABLE I

ANTITRUST CASES INSTITUTED BY THE FEDERAL ANTITRUST
ENFORCEMENT AGENCIES AND PRIVATE ANTITRUST CASES

(1) Year In Which The Case Was Instituted	(2) Number of DOJ Cases	(3) Number of FTC Cases	(4) Private* Antitrust Cases
1963	26	9	380
1964	51	12	363
1965	29	18	472
1966	36	19	722
1967	34	12	543
1968	47	15	659
1969	43	14	740
1965-1969	189	78	3,136
1970	54	11	877
1971	43	25	1,445
1972	72	16	1,299
1973	47	26	1,152
1974	46	20	1,230
1970-1974	262	98	6,003
1975	39	20	1,375
1976	45	24	1,504
1977	40	16	1,611
1978	43	14	1,435
1979	33	30	1,234
1975-1979	200	104	7,159
1980	50	28	1,457
1981	18	19	1,292
1982	30	10	1,037
1983	52	11	1,213
1984	40	15	—
1980-1984	190	83	4,999**
TOTAL	918	384	22,040

Source: Joseph C. Gallo and Steven C. Bush, "A Statistical Analysis of
         Antitrust Enforcement for the Period 1963-1983", unpublished
         manuscript, University of Cincinnati, 1983.

*Based on fiscal year.

**Total for fiscal years 1980-1983

TABLE II

FEDERAL ANTITRUST CASES CLASSIFIED
BY DURATION*

Percentage of Cases Settled by

(1)	(2)	(3)	(4)	(5)
	DOJ**		FTC***	
Year Case Instituted	Within Six Months	In Excess of Six Months	Within Six Months	In Excess of Six Months
1963	42	58	0	100
1964	12	88	25	75
1965	21	79	0	100
1966	28	72	20	80
1967	38	62	0	100
1968	26	74	0	100
1969	30	70	0	100
1965-1969	29	71	6	94
1970	33	67	0	100
1971	26	74	0	100
1972	40	60	0	100
1973	28	72	0	100
1974	15	85	0	100
1970-1974	30	70	0	100
1975	18	82	0	100
1976	22	78	9	91
1977	18	83	29	71
1978	37	63	14	86
1979	21	79	0	100
1975-1979	23	77	10	90
1980	22	78	0	100
1981	29	71	0	100
1982	41	59	0	100
1983	92	8	33	67
1984*	94	6	-	-
1980-1984	56	44	4	96

Source: Joseph C. Gallo and Steven C. Bush, "A Statistical Study of
Federal Antitrust Enforcement for the Period 1963-1983," a
unpublished manuscript, University of Cincinnati, 1983.

*Excludes ongoing cases. All 1984 FTC cases are ongoing.

**Calculation based on 838 completed DOJ cases.

***Calculation based on 166 contested FTC cases.

Bush, Craycraft and Gallo

110

98

most of the 1963-1984 period, although this agency has been less sociable during the Reagan administration. Measured by this statistic, the level of FTC antitrust activity is little less than one-third that of the DOJ. The number of FTC cases brought during each five year period of the study increased, from 78 in 1965-1969, to 98 in 1970-1974 and to 104 in 1975-1979. The pattern since 1980 indicates a decrease in activity. The FTC averaged 17.7 cases per year during the 17 years before 1890, and 16.6 since then, with only 12 per year for the last three years.

Examining the FTC from a long term perspective, the agency was very social during the early years of its existence. During the period 1916-1962 the FTC brought 524 restraint-of-trade cases, of which 443 were initiated by 1929.(6) Posner has proposed three hypotheses to explain this trend. First, the poor won-lost record of the FTC in its early years strongly suggests that the agency was not very selective in its screening procedures and adjudicative procedures were much more casual than in the later periods. Second, since the enactment of the Robinson-Patman Act in 1936, the large number of Robinson-Patman cases brought by the FTC (which are not classified as restraint-of-trade cases) suggests an attenuation of antitrust enforcement by the FTC in favor of small business protection. Third, the FTC has become more concerned with nonadjudicative enforcement methods such a Trade Practice Conferences and advisory opinions than with adjudication.(7) During the period 1963-1984 the FTC brought 384 cases. Although the number of FTC cases brought in the last twenty-two years is smaller than in the earlier period, there appears to be slight increase in FTC enforcement and an improvement in its selection procedures during the latter part of the period. This seems plausible since the dinner guests frequently left happier during the earlier period 1915-1919, when 73% of FTC cases were dismissed as compared to 59% for the period 1920-1962 and only 10% for the period 1963-1983 (see Table IV).

Adding DOJ and FTC parties to obtain an index of sociability for both agencies, the average number of cases initiated annually in the period 1981-1984 is 49, compared with 62 annually for the period 1963-1980. This represents a 21% decrease. There is some evidence that the index of sociability for both agencies rose in the last two years, although, it is still not as high as it was for the period 1963-1980.

Private actions rose steadily each year from 1963 through 1977, and then declined somewhat. The largest increase came during the period 1972-1977, which followed a period of significant increase in DOJ activity, this may have been due to the bandwagon effect on private plaintiffs. It is also possible that, even with treble damages, the cost of such litigation has produced disappointing results for plaintiffs.

II. HOW LONG DID THEY STAY FOR DINNER?
(The length of Antitrust Proceedings)

There are some difficulties associated with measuring the length of the dinner parties (the duration of the antitrust proceedings) since so many ended abruptly (with consent judgements or nolo contendere pleas). Inclusion of these cases in the statistics would

Bush, Craycraft and Gallo   111

underestimate the length of the average litigated case. Following Posner, we employed a test which designated a case as "litigated" if it lasted more than six months. This methodology is imperfect, but will suffice in lieu of a better test.

Thirty-two percent of all cases brought by the DOJ in the period 1963-1984 were settled within 6 months compared with 51% for the 1890-1962 period.(8) It is interesting to note the wide range of values; as low as 12% in 1964 and 18% in 1975 and 1977 to as high as 94% in 1984. The extremely high percentage for 1983 and 1984 may suggest a tendency for the agency to entertain less elaborately. It may also reflect the exclusion of ongoing 1983 and 1984 cases; by definition they are longer than those settled in 1983 and 1984. The statistic is, therefore, biased downward. The DOJ may be bringing less complicated cases or cases where the legal rules or facts are clearer than they were during the middle '70's, while downplaying or actively avoiding "pioneering" cases. Certain aspects of its success record and the violations alleged lend some credibility to this hypothesis.

During the period 1963-1984, 68% of cases lasted more than six months, as noted above. This is in contrast to 43% for the period 1890-1964. Cases lasting more than six years are rare; (4.49%) of litigated cases, and there have been none since 1976. Since that time, the duration of DOJ has declined steadily.(9)

The lower proportion of contested cases may also be explained by a reallocation of DOJ effort from civil to criminal cases. Table VII indicates that in most years before 1974, the number of civil actions exceeded the number of criminal. Since 1974 the trend has reversed. This reversal reflects the Antitrust Division's current policy to bring criminal cases only where the facts and law do not involve any substantial legal questions and the allegations are well-established under the Sherman Act. Price fixing, bid-rigging, market allocation and certain predatory monopoly practices fall into that category. Price fixing is the most common of these offenses and is the focus of the Antitrust Division's "Guidelines For Sentencing Recommendations in Felony Cases Under the Sherman Act." These cases tend to be simple, shorter in duration and do not involve any "pioneering" issues.

The pattern of FTC enforcement differs from that of the DOJ. The percentage of FTC cases lasting more than six months is higher than the DOJ (in excess of 90%) and remained fairly constant for most of the period. The percentage of cases lasting more than six years is also higher; 14% for the FTC as compared to 4.6% for the DOJ. The number of FTC cases settled within one year fell in the mid-1970's, but has risen since then (though this pattern is not as dramatic as in the cases of the DOJ).(10)

The length of antitrust proceedings provides evidence to support the hypothesis that antitrust enforcement may have been pioneering new areas in the 1970's but has since concentrated on cases which require less litigation. Though we hear a great deal about our slow process of justice, there is no evidence to show that most antitrust cases tend to be extremely protracted. This last observation agrees with trends noted by Posner for 1890-1969.(11)

III. DO THE GUESTS LEAVE HAPPY?
(The Success Record of the Antitrust Claimant)

The findings indicate the Federal agencies' guests leave dinner much less happy now than they did previously. Table III indicates the DOJ raised its success record to 86% during 1963-1984 compared to 74% during the previous 73 years.(12) The Department won 88% of its cases in 1965-1969, but its success fell to 84% during the 1970's. Since 1980, it has won 89% of its cases, and since 1979 has won all its civil cases by consent decree. There is some evidence that guests who stay overnight for an extended time are given a more elaborate meal and generally leave. The DOJ has had a poor success record in highly protracted cases. Of 13 cases lasting more than 97 months, the government has won only twice.(13) The figures noted so far in this section suggest that the DOJ may be increasingly selective about its cases, especially its civil cases, with a view toward quick uncomplicated success.

The recent record of the FTC is just as impressive in terms of percentage of success and represents a improvement over its earlier record. Before 1963, the FTC won 51% of its cases. Since then, it has been successful however, 90% of the time. As suggested earlier, this may reflect a more cautious screening policy.

Both agencies have had good success in persuading the Supreme Court to hear their appeals. The FTC record is nearly perfect (Tables V and VI). Both have won a high percentage of cases heard in the high court, although the DOJ has not done as well here as it has overall; 71% vs. 86% overall while the FTC's supreme Court record is virtually the same as its overall record. This difference in success rates may stem from legal differences in the types of cases each agency brings before the Court. Supreme Court reviews of FTC cases often deals with matters of the agency's statutory authority. It is interesting to note the DOJ and FTC each have been involved in a Supreme Court cases only three times since 1975. This may be the result of the length of time needed for a case to wind its way through lower courts or more likely the result of conservative screening. It does not necessarily reflect lack of interest in antitrust on the part of the court since numerous private cases were heard during the same period. The only cases that go to the Supreme Court are those with controversial legal question.

The success record of both agencies indicates they have assumed a more conservative role since the mid 1970's. Even in view of this conservative stance, their success records before the Supreme Court have been remarkable.

IV. COSTUMES AND THE DOOR PRIZE
(The Nature of the Case and Choice of Remedies)

Part of the explanation for the pattern of door prizes given at these parties lies in the choice of costume worn by the DOJ guests. The most popular costume is a black and white striped suit with a ball and chain attached to the guest's ankle. It is common for these guests to win an extended stay in the local lodge at the expense of the taxpayer. The ratio of criminal to total DOJ cases varies from 2 to 85% in various years during the period (see Table VII). The DOJ has placed greater emphasis on criminal prosecution more in recent years. The proportion of criminal cases has increased form 46% for the entire period 1890-1984 to 61% in 1975-1984. Once again, 1974

Bush, Craycraft and Gallo   113

TABLE III

THE DEPARTMENT OF JUSTICE WON-LOST RECORD*

(1) Year In Which The Case Was Instituted	(2) Number of Cases Won*	(3) Number of Cases Lost*	(4) Total Number of Cases*	(5) % Won by The Dept. of Justice*
1963	20	6	26	77
1964	43	8	51	84
1965	25	4	29	86
1966	35	1	36	97
1967	29	5	34	85
1968	38	9	47	81
1969	40	3	43	93
1965-1969	167	22	189	88
1970	43	11	54	80
1971	34	9	43	79
1972	60	12	72	83
1973	37	10	47	79
1974	41	5	46	89
1970-1974	215	47	262	82
1975	33	6	39	85
1976	39	6	45	87
1977	34	6	40	85
1978	38	3	41	93
1979	28	5	33	85
1975-1979	172	26	198	87
1980	34	4	38	89
1981	14	2	16	88
1982	17	3	20	85
1983	21	4	25	84
1984	17	0	17	100
1980-1984	103	13	116	89
TOTAL	720	122	842	86

Source: Joseph C. Gallo and Steven C. Bush, "A Statistical Analysis of
         Antitrust Enforcement for the Period 1963-1983," unpublished
         manuscript, University of Cincinnati, 1983.

*Excludes ongoing cases

TABLE IV

THE FTC'S WON-LOST ANTITRUST RECORD
RESTRAINT OF TRADE CASES*

(1) Year Case Instituted	(2) Order Entered (#)	(%)	(3) Case Dismissed (#)	(%)	(4) Total
1963	8		1		9
1964	12		0		12
1965	16		2		18
1966	18		1		19
1967	12		0		12
1968	15		0		15
1969	14		0		14
1965-1969	75	(96)	3	(4)	78
1970	10		1		11
1971	21		4		25
1972	12		4		16
1973	24		2		26
1974	16		4		20
1970-1974	83	(85)	15	(15)	98
1975	20		0		20
1976	19		4		23
1977	14		2		16
1978	10		4		14
1979	27		2		29
1975-1979	90	(88)	12	(12)	102
1980	25		3		28
1981	17		2		19
1982	9		0		9
1983	8		2		10
1984*	–		–		–
1980-1984	59	(89)	7	(11)	66
TOTAL	327	(90)	38	(10)	365

Source: Joseph C. Gallo and Steven C. Bush, "A Statistical Analysis of
         Antitrust Enforcement for the Period 1963-1983," unpublished
         manuscript, University of Cincinnati, 1983.

*Excludes ongoing cases. At the time of these calculations there were 19
ongoing FTC cases and 365 completed FTC cases. All 1984 FTC cases are
ongoing.

Bush, Craycraft and Gallo

115

103

TABLE V

THE DEPARTMENT OF JUSTICE WON-LOST RECORD
IN THE SUPREME COURT

(1) Year Case Instituted	(2) Total DOJ Cases*	(3) DOJ Lost	(4) DOJ Won**	(5) % Won By DOJ
1963	2	0	2	100
1964	4	1	3	75
1965	3	1	2	67
1966	4	1	3	75
1967	2	1	1	50
1968	3	0	3	100
1969	5	0	5	100
1965-1969	17	3	14	82
1970	1	1	0	0
1971	2	1	1	50
1972	2	1	1	50
1973	4	2	2	50
1974	0	0	0	−
1970-1974	9	5	4	44
1975	0	0	0	−
1976	1	0	1	100
1977	0	0	0	−
1978	0	0	0	−
1979	0	0	0	−
1975-1979	1	0	1	100
1980	0	0	0	−
1981	0	0	0	−
1982	0	0	0	−
1983	2	1	1***	50
1984	0	0	0	−
1980-1984	2	1	1	50
TOTAL	35	10	25	71

Source: Joseph C. Gallo and Steven C. Bush, "A Statistical Analysis of
Antitrust Enforcement for the Period 1963-1983," unpublished
manuscript, University of Cincinnati, 1983.

*Excludes ongoing cases.

**Includes pre-decree and post-decree cases.

***In 1983, State of California challenged the Antitrust Division break-up
AT&T. The U.S. Supreme Court ruled against the State of California and
summarily affirmed the reorganization plan.

TABLE VI

WON-LOSS RECORD OF THE FTC RESTRAINT-OF-TRADE
CASES REVIEWED BY THE SUPREME COURT

(1) Year When Supreme Court Decided Case	(2) Total	(3) FTC Lost	(4) FTC Won	(5) % Won by FTC
1963	0	0	0	–
1964	0	0	0	–
1965	2	0	2	100
1966	2	0	2	100
1967	3	0	3	100
1968	2	0	2	100
1969	0	0	0	–
1965-1969	9	0	9	100
1970	0	0	0	–
1971	0	0	0	–
1972	1	0	1	100
1973	0	0	0	–
1974	1	0	1	100
1970-1974	2	0	2	100
1975	0	0	0	–
1976	0	0	0	–
1977	0	0	0	–
1978	0	0	0	–
1979	1	1	0	0
1975-1979	1	1	0	0
1980	1	0	1	100
1981	0	0	0	–
1982	1	0	1	100
1983	0	0	0	–
1984	0	0	0	–
1980-1984	2	0	2	100
TOTAL	14	1	13	93

Source: Joseph C. Gallo and Steven C. Bush, "A Statistical Analysis of
Antitrust Enforcement for the Period 1963-1983," unpublished
manuscript, University of Cincinnati, 1983.

Bush, Craycraft and Gallo   117

TABLE VII

BREAKDOWN BETWEEN CRIMINAL AND CIVIL CASES
BROUGHT BY THE DEPARTMENT OF JUSTICE

(1) Year Case Instituted	(2) Total of Cases	(3) Criminal	(4) Civil	(5) % Criminal	(6) % Civil
1963	26	10	16	38	62
1964	51	17	34	33	67
1965	29	8	21	28	72
1966	36	17	19	47	53
1967	34	13	21	38	62
1968	47	16	31	34	66
1969	43	1	42	2	98
1965-1969	189	55	134	29	71
1970	54	10	44	19	81
1971	43	9	34	21	79
1972	72	20	52	28	72
1973	47	19	28	40	60
1974	46	26	20	57	43
1970-1974	262	84	178	32	68
1975	39	25	14	64	36
1976	45	24	21	53	47
1977	40	25	15	62	38
1978	43	30	13	70	30
1979	33	17	16	52	48
1975-1979	200	121	79	60	40
1980	50	23	27	46	54
1981	18	7	11	39	61
1982	30	15	15	50	50
1983	52	44	8	85	15
1984	40	27	13	68	32
1980-1984	190	116	74	61	39
TOTAL	918	403	515	44	56

Source: Joseph C. Gallo and Steven C. Bush, "A Statistical Analysis of
Antitrust Enforcement for the Period 1963-1983," unpublished
manuscript, University of Cincinnati, 1983.

TABLE VIII

CRIMINAL CONVICTIONS*
DEPARTMENT OF JUSTICE

(1) Year Case Instituted	(2) Nolo Contendere Plea	(3) Other Conviction	(4) Total Convictions	(5) Acquitals or Dismissal	(6) Percentage of Convictions
1963	7	1	8	2	80
1964	14	0	14	3	82
1965	7	0	7	1	88
1966	16	0	16	1	94
1967	12	1	13	0	100
1968	13	2	15	1	94
1969	0	1	1	0	100
1965-1969	48	4	52	3	95
1970	8	1	9	1	90
1971	8	0	8	1	89
1972	19	0	19	1	95
1973	16	1	17	2	89
1974	19	6	25	1	96
1970-1974	70	8	78	6	93
1975	20	3	23	2	92
1976	21	0	21	3	88
1977	21	3	24	1	96
1978	26	2	28	1	97
1979	14	2	16	1	94
1975-1979	102	10	112	8	93
1980	10	4	14	2	88
1981	3	3	6	0	100
1982	2	4	6	2	75
1983	4	14	18	3	86
1984	0	12	12	0	100
1980-1984	19	37	56	7	89
TOTAL	260	60	320	29	92**

Source: Joseph C. Gallo and Steven C. Bush, "A Statistical Analysis of
Antitrust Enforcement for the Period 1963-1983," an unpublished
manuscript, University of Cincinnati, 1983.

*Exclude ongoing cases.

**Calculation based upon 349 completed criminal cases.

TABLE IX

DEPARTMENT OF JUSTICE CASES
CRIMINAL SANCTIONS - FINES

(1)	(2)	(3)	(4)	(5)	(6)	(7)
	Total Criminal Cases		Aggregate	Average Fine Per Case	Aggregate Fines*	Avera; Fines
Year Case Instituted	Convictions (#)	Fine Imposed (#)	Fines ($)	(4) / (3) ($)	(1972 Dollars)	(1972 Dolla
1963	8	8	690,500	86,313	963,444	120,431
1964	14	14	1,333,450	95,246	1,832,417	130,866
1965	7	7	1,408,150	201,164	1,893,693	270,527
1966	16	16	2,047,650	127,978	2,667,600	166,725
1967	13	11	1,064,707	96,792	1,346,708	122,429
1968	15	15	1,172,750	78,183	1,420,826	94,721
1969	1	1	130,000	130,000	149,787	149,787
1965-1969	52	50	5,823,257	116,465	7,478,614	149,572
1970	9	9	761,800	84,644	833,024	92,558
1971	8	8	577,500	72,188	601,500	75,188
1972	19	17	1,480,500	87,058	1,480,500	87,058
1973	17	17	2,164,700	127,335	2,048,160	120,478
1974	25	25	3,164,500	126,580	2,753,655	110,146
1970-1974	78	76	8,149,000	107,224	7,716,839	101,537
1975	23	23	2,121,600	92,244	1,689,710	73,408
1976	21	20	5,313,130	265,657	4,021,747	201,088
1977	24	23	8,700,750	378,294	6,222,377	270,539
1978	28	27	11,832,375	438,236	7,885,622	292,060
1979	16	14	12,380,500	884,321	7,605,824	541,133
1975-1979	112	107	40,348,355	377,087	27,425,280	256,311
1980	14	13	15,570,000	1,197,692	8,726,000	671,277
1981	6	6	5,316,000	866,000	2,724,198	454,033
1982	6	5	3,514,200	702,840	1,698,666	339,733
1983	18	16	6,010,000	375,625	2,786,665	174,166
1984	12	12	2,318,500	193,208	1,042,116	86,843
1980-1984	56	52	32,728,700	629,398	16,977,645	326,493
TOTAL	320	307	89,073,262	290,141	62,394,239	203,239

Source: Joseph C. Gallo and Steven C. Bush, "A Statistical Analysis of
          Antitrust Enforcement for the Period 1963-1983," unpublished
          manuscript, University of Cincinnati, 1983.

*Calculated using annual GNP Deflators (1972 = 100)

represents the watershed of the recent period. Most 1963-74 cases are civil cases; after 1974 with exception of 1980 and 1981, most cases are criminal cases. In criminal cases, 81% of the Department's wins from 1963-34 result form nolo contendere pleas (see Table VIII). This may be due to the types of cases pursued and/or to the fact that such a plea is cheaper for all parties. The government is spared the cost of an extended trial, although such a plea cannot be used as prima facie evidence in a subsequent civil suit. The DOJ has won 92% of its criminal cases compared to 86% overall. As the percentage of criminal cases won shows no upward trend it is evident the improvement in the DOJ success record over the period is the result of a reallocation of efforts from civil to criminal cases.

Depending on the type of action brought, courts may choose between jail terms, fines, and structural sanctions in cases where the agency is successful. Some imaginative judges occasionally prescribe non-traditional remedies as well. During the period of the study, a change in the legal environment was brought about by the 1974 Antitrust Procedures and Penalties Act (APPA)(15), which authorized stiffer fines and jail terms for law breakers. The average level of both remedies has increased since APPA went into effect, although the increases are less than proportionate to the increases in the maximum allowable penalties (see Table IX). The effect of the Act on fines can be seen in the fact that average fines have increased by approximately 325% from the period 1963-1974 to the period 1975-1984. The increase in real terms is 130%. While significant, these increases are far less than the twenty-fold increase in maximum fines provided for in APPA. It is interesting to note that the level of real fines has fallen significantly since 1980.

The use of imprisonment (Table X) increased for the period of this study compared with the years prior to 1963 when it was extremely infrequent. In those years prison sentences were imposed in 24 of the 463 criminal convictions. (16) During 1963-1973, 4.8% of convictions resulted in jail terms. Since the passage of the APPA, 20% of criminal convictions have drawn jail terms. The APPA seems to have had a significant effect in this area although the maximum term was seldom imposed.

On rare occasions did the guests leave thinner than they arrived. The use of structural options, specifically significant divestiture, was extremely uncommon involving only 2.6% of those cases where monopolization was alleged.(17) This reflects a significant drop from Posner's years when 8.6% of such cases resulted in divestiture.(18) This may indicate acceptance of the view that dissolution and divestiture are inefficient and ineffective remedies.

It appears that the FTC and DOJ make little use of the courts to ensure that remedies are carried out. Of 1,667 wins since 1890, the DOJ has filed only 42 contempt actions accusing defendants of violating the decrees issued.(19) This may indicate that defendants comply with court orders or the DOJ allocates few resources to monitoring compliance. Strikingly, however, the average fine levied in a contempt proceeding skyrocketed from under $50,000 during 1890-1974 to $530,000 during 1974-1979.(20)

Much of the distribution in remedies imposed can be explained by the DOJ's choice of civil or criminal proceedings. The APPA of 1974 also had a significant effect on the severity of penalties although

TABLE X

CRIMINAL SANCTIONS - IMPRISONMENT*

(1)	(2)	(3)	(4)		(5)	(6)
	Total	Total	Number of Imprisonments Imposed			
Year Case Instituted	Number of Criminal Cases	Number of Convictions	Cases	Persons	Length of Sentence	Characteristic of Case
1963	10	8	0			
1964	17	14	1	(2)	30 days	Price Fixing
				(1)	90 days	Bid Rigging
1965	8	7	0			
1966	17	16	1	(2)	1 day	Price Fixing
				(1)	15 days	
				(1)	50 days	
				(1)	60 days	
1967	13	13	0			
1968	16	14	0			
1969	1	1	1	(1)	6 months	Monopolizatio Violence Labor Racketeering
1965-1969	55	51	2	(6)		
1970	10	9	0			
1971	9	8	0			
1972	20	18	1	(6)	30 days	Bid Rigging
				(1)	9 months	Price Fixing Customer Allocation
1973	19	17	2	(1)	30 days	Monopolizatic
				(2)	30 days	Price Fixing
1974	26	25	3	(2)	30 days	Price Fixing Bid Rigging
				(3)	6 months	Price Fixing
				(3)	30 days	Customer Allocation

Bush, Craycraft and Gallo   122

110

Year Case Instituted	Total Number of Criminal Cases	Total Number of Convictions	Number of Imprisonments Imposed		Length of Sentence	Characteristics of Case
			Cases	Persons		
1970-1974	84	77	6	(18)		
1975	25	23	2	(1)	45 days	Price Fixing
				(1)	30 days	Bid Rigging
1976	24	21	4	(1)	1-15 days Work Release	Price Fixing
				(2)	30 days	Price Fixing
				(1)	30 days	Customer and
				(1)	45 days	Territory Allocation
				(2)	4 months	Price Fixing
1977	25	24	8	(2)	1 year	Bid Rigging
				(1)	18 months	Bid Rigging
				(1)	2 years	Bid Rigging
				(1)	30 months	
				(1)	30 days	Price Fixing
				(1)	60 days	Price Fixing
				(2)	30 days	Price Fixing
				(2)	20 days	
				(1)	60 days	Bid Rigging
				(1)	45 days	Customer Allocation
				(5)	30 days	Price Fixing
				(5)	90 days	
1978	30	28	4	(1)	15 days	Customer Allocation Bid Rigging
				(4)	90 days	Bid Rigging
				(1)	1 year & 1 day	
				(2)	30 days	Bid Rigging
				(1)	3 years	

Bush, Craycraft and Gallo   123

111

Year Case Instituted	Total Number of Criminal Cases	Total Number of Convictions	Number of Imprisonments Imposed		Length of Sentence	Characteristics of Case
			Cases	Persons		
				(1)	45 days	Price Fixing
				(3)	30 days	
				(2)	60 days	
1979	17	16	2	(2)	90 days	Price Fixing
				(2)	10 days	Bid Rigging Customer Allocation
1975-1979	121	112	20	(51)		
1980	23	14	6	(1)	2 months	Bid Rigging
				(4)	2 months	Bid Rigging
				(9)	1 month	
				(1)	71 days	
				(1)	45 days	
				(1)	75 days	
				(1)	24 months	Bid Rigging
				(2)	1 month	
				(3)	2 months	
				(2)	2 months	Bid Rigging
				(3)	1 month	Price Fixing
				(3)	45 days	Price Fixing Customer Allocation
1981	7	6	0			
1982	15	6	3	(1)	120 days	Bid Rigging
				(1)	2 months	Bid Rigging
				(1)	90 days	Bid Rigging
				(1)	60 days	
1983	44	18	5	(1)	1 month	Bid Rigging
				(1)	45 days	Bid Rigging
				(1)	200 days	Bid Rigging

Bush, Craycraft and Gallo   124

112

Year Case Instituted	Total Number of Criminal Cases	Total Number of Convictions	Number of Imprisonments Imposed		Length of Sentence	Characteristics of Case
			Cases	Persons		
				(1)	6.5 months	Price Fixing Bid Rigging
				(1)	14 days	Bid Rigging
1984	27	12	2	(1)	30 days	Price Fixing
				(1)	75 days	Bid Rigging
1980-1984	116	56	16	(42)		
TOTAL	403	318	45	(120)		

Source: Joseph C. Gallo and Steven L. Bush, "A Statistical Analysis of Antitrust Enforcement For the Period 1963-1983," unpublished manuscript, University of Cincinnati, 1983.

*Suspended and remitted prison sentences and probation are excluded.

judges have tended not to impose the maximum sanctions it allows.

V. THE MENU SERVED
(The Violation Alleged)

The DOJ is becoming more limited in its choice of menu. In fact, if it continues to serve the same meal, it may be more difficult to find individuals who will accept their invitation. Most violations alleged by the DOJ involve horizontal conspiracies, acquisitions short of monopoly, or territorial or customer restrictions (see Table XI). The first category, which includes price fixing and bid rigging, predominates. These horizontal conspiracies tend to involve ancillary arrangements which make the conspiracy possible but increase the threat of detection. Trade associations were very common when the number of conspirators involved was larger than the average of five for the period.

Interestingly, a large number of dinner guests have fat friends. Most of the horizontal conspiracies involve sales to the government rather than to private parties. This is especially true in 1981-1984 when bid rigging cases account for almost all cases brought.(21) These facts are a significant departure from Posner's earlier findings that government and private buyers were involved in about equal numbers of cases.(22) Such observations are consistent with a hypothesis that price fixing when the government is the buyer may be more common since the purchasing agent has less incentive to obtain the lowest price than does a competitive private business.(23)

There appears to have been a reduction of horizontal merger cases in recent years as the emphasis has switched to bid rigging. What effect the 1982 Merger guidelines will have on this activity remains to be seen, but 1983 and 1984 findings indicate the trend is continuing.

Recently the FTC has changed its menu (see Table XII). The FTC has switched from primarily price fixing to acquisition short of monopoly as compared with 1915-1963.(24) Since most Federal activity during 1963-1984 is in horizontal cases, this is consistent with the earlier observation there may have been a reallocation of antitrust effort to the DOJ.

The examination of the pattern of violations alleged has shown that the government recently has been interested in horizontal activity. While this agrees with Posner's data, the emphasis is much stronger during the recent period. The near total concentration of the DOJ on bid rigging in the last years of the study lends support to the idea that the DOJ may be avoiding pioneering cases and sticking to the area where economic theory is most clearcut in its indication that social welfare is impaired - namely price fixing. By emphasizing cases where the government is the buyer, it may be protecting the government's interests, or it may be that these cases are attractive for prosecution because the sealed bid mechanism makes proof easier.

VI. SUMMARY

The data in this paper indicate there are significant trends in antitrust enforcement during the period 1963-1983 and provides the bases for future investigation of these trends.

Bush, Craycraft and Gallo   126

114

Although the number of cases brought by the DOJ under the Reagan-Baxter-McGrath administration appears to have increased, when cases are consolidated fewer conspiracies are being prosecuted. The DOJ's activity is maintained only through a large number of bid-rigging cases, primarily against highway contractors. This shift in emphasis away from non-horizontal concerns explains also the increase in the criminal proportion. Since the charges are clearcut if conduct is established, the stronger criminal approach is adopted in contrast to the situation in vertical cases.

It is questionable whether the increased tempo of DOJ price fixing prosecutions will deter the price fixer more effectively than previous policies, at least apart from the DOJ target industries. Since the remaining antitrust areas are getting less attention, it is possible that the net effect is a considerably less stringent antitrust policy. This is further substantiated by the decline in FTC's activity. The 1970's were devoted to pushing back the frontiers of antitrust policy. The exploration of the unknown areas of frontiers is time-consuming and expensive. Many of these explorations failed. Antitrust enforcement under the Reagan administration is an intense cultivation of well-known terrain. It is efficient, cost-effective, and limited. Camelot was more interesting but the question of socially optimal antitrust policy is still open.

The passage of the Antitrust Penalties and Procedures Act in 1974 had some influences. There seems to be an increased judical propensity to use jail terms. At the same time the application of structural relief is less frequent.

It is sad to note Posner's program for improved antitrust statistics has not been implemented. Our efforts to update the Posner study has found the sources of information little improved over the situation which confronted Posner. We hope to leave the situation better than we found it through continuous updating of our data base. We return, however, to where we started with the observation that the study of antitrust cases may be dull as a stack of dirty dishes and just as messy, but knowing the guest list, the menu they served and whether the guests left happy said something about the quality of Federal antitrust enforcement.

Bush, Craycraft and Gallo   127

TABLE XI

TOPICAL CLASSIFICATION OF DEPARTMENT OF JUSTICE
ANTITRUST CHARGES*

(#)	Nature of Charge	1963	1964	1965 1969	1970 1974	1975 1979	1980 1984	Total (#)	(%)
1.	Horizontal Conspiracy	11	22	65	100	115	446	759	(50
2.	Monopolization	5	5	17	42	4	10	83	(5.5
3.	Acquisition Short of Monopoly	6	12	78	75	30	34	235	(15
4.	Boycott	2	4	13	12	2	3	36	(2.4
5.	Resale Price Maintenance	2	7	9	11	2	2	33	(2.2
6.	Vertical Integration	1	2	9	6	9	2	29	(2
7.	Tying Arrangements	0	0	3	27	4	0	34	(2.2
8.	Exclusive Dealings	1	0	9	8	7	2	27	(2
9.	Territorial and Customer Limitations	7	10	28	38	33	69	185	(12.2
10.	Violence	0	0	2	1	1	0	4	(.26
11.	Price Discrimination	3	1	2	4	2	0	12	(.78
12.	Other Predatory or Unfair Conduct	3	2	11	11	9	14	50	(3.3
13.	Interlocking Directorates	0	0	0	2	4	0	6	(.3
14.	Clayton Act Sec. 10	1	1	0	0	0	0	2	(.1
15.	Labor Cases	0	0	1	1	1	0	3	(.1
16.	Patent and Copy Right Cases	0	1	12	7	4	0	24	(1.
	TOTAL	42	67	259	345	227	582	1,522	

Source: Joseph C. Gallo and Steven C. Bush, "A Statistical Analysis of
         Antitrust Enforcement for the Period 1963-1983," unpublished
         manuscript, University of Cincinnati, 1983.

*Table shows distribution of allegations not of cases.

Bush, Craycraft and Gallo

12

TABLE XII

VIOLATIONS ALLEGED IN FTC RESTRAINT OF TRADE CASES*

(#)	Nature of Offense	1963	1964	1965 1969	1970 1974	1975 1979	1980 1984	Total (#)	Total (%)
1.	Horizontal Price Fixing	0	3	2	5	18	8	36	(9)
2.	Monopolization	0	0	5	5	6	10	26	(6)
3.	Acquisition Short of Monopoly	4	4	50	39	32	49	178	(42)
4.	Resale Price Maintenance	0	0	7	15	23	10	55	(13)
5.	Tying	0	1	1	4	6	0	12	(3)
6.	Exclusive Dealing	0	1	7	13	3	2	26	(6)
7.	Price Discrimination	1	0	5	5	6	4	21	(5)
8.	Patents	0	0	1	1	1	1	4	(1)
9.	Labor	0	0	0	1	1	0	2	(.5)
10.	Interlocking Directorates	0	0	0	3	8	2	13	(3)
11.	Boycott	0	2	7	0	0	1	10	(2)
12.	Reciprocity	0	0	0	2	0	1	3	(.7)
13.	Restrictive Leasing	0	0	1	4	6	0	11	(3)
	Other	4	1	2	5	5	5	22	(5)
	TOTAL	9	12	88	102	115	93	419	

Source: Joseph C. Gallo and Steven L. Bush, "A Statistical Analysis of Antitrust Enforcement For the Period 1963-1983," unpublished manuscript, University of Cincinnati, 1983.

*Excludes Robinson-Patman Cases except those charging predatory price discrimination.

117

FOOTNOTES

* The authors are Associate Professors of Economics, University of Cincinnati and a graduate student, University of Chicago, respectively. This study has benefited from comments from Howard Marvel, Charles J. Parker, an anonymous reviewer, and a DOJ Antitrust Division Research in 1983. Special thanks to Paul Laux who encouraged us to tell this story and the Antitrust and Public Policy class at the University of Cincinnati which assisted in the calculation of the 1983 and 1984 statistics.

(1) Richard Posner, "A Statistical Study of Antitrust Enforcement," The Journal of Law and Economics, Vol. 13, (2) October 1970.
(2) Joseph C. Gallo and Steven C. Bush, "A Statistical Study of Federal Antitrust Enforcement for the Period 1963-1983," unpublished manuscript, University of Cincinnati. Copies of the study can be obtained from the authors.
(3) The numbers of cases without consolidation are 82 in 1980, 55 in 1981, 69 in 1982, 108 in 1983 and 68 in 1984.
(4) For the period 1890-1969, Posner calculated 1,551 DOJ antitrust cases. In an overlapped year, 1965, we were only able to identify 29 cases instead of the 35 cases reported by Posner. The 6 cases difference is not included in to total of 2,197 DOJ antitrust cases, Richard Posner, p. 366.
(5) Ibid.
(6) Ibid., p. 369.
(7) Ibid., p. 370.
(8) Calculated from Ibid., Table 6, P. 376.
(9) Gallo and Bush, p. 16.
(10) Gallo and Bush, p. 17.
(11) Ibid., pp. 374-381.
(12) Ibid., pp. 381, 382.
(13) Gallo and Bush, p. 20.
(14) Calculated from Posner, Table 12, p. 382.
(15) Public Law 93-528, 88 Stat 1706.
(16) Calculated from Posner, Table 19, p. 391.
(17) Gallo and Bush, p. 55.
(18) Posner, Tables 23 and 29, pp. 398 and 406.
(19) Posner, Table 16, p. 387; Gallo and Bush, p. 34 and 35.
(20) Ibid.
(21) Gallo and Bush, p. 34.
(22) Posner, Table 25, p. 401.
(23) Armen A. Alchian, "Electrical Equipment Collusion: Why and How," Economic Forces at Work, Indianapolis: Liberty Press, 1977, pp. 259-269.
(24) Posner, Table 31, p. 408.

Climbing the antitrust staircase

BY ERNEST GELLHORN*

Introduction

In the space of about 15 years, antitrust has moved from a time when the guiding principle seemed to be that the government always wins[1] to a situation where critics frequently charge that the government never sues.[2] While both comments are obviously overstatements, there is more than a kernel of truth in each. The question arises, therefore, whether recent differences in the direction of antitrust policy are solely ones of philosophy and political power. Are the antitrust policies and judgments under President Reagan, as compared with antitrust rulings while Jimmy Carter or Gerald Ford was president, explained simply by the fact that we now have a conservative, business-oriented regime in power unwilling to enforce antitrust with the same vigor as prior administrations? Or is something more significant taking place?

I believe that a careful examination of antitrust trends and current practices reveals substantial shifts in the center of antitrust analysis and economic understanding. And this redirection is likely to continue regardless of which party controls the

---

*   Attorney, Jones, Day, Reavis & Pogue; formerly, Dean and Galen J. Roush Professor of Law, Case Western Reserve University.

1   United States v. Von's Grocery Co., 384 U.S. 270, 301 (1966) (Stewart, J.) ("The sole consistency that I can find is that in litigation under Section 7, the Government always wins").

2   *See* Seiberling, *Congress Makes the Laws: The Executive Should Enforce Them*, 53 ANTITRUST L.J. 175 (1984).

executive branch. This conclusion is supported by the fact that many recent changes have been confirmed by courts even though only about one-third of all federal judges have been appointed by Mr. Reagan, including only one member of the Supreme Court. It seems, in other words, that something more than naked power is operating to refocus antitrust enforcement.

In determining what other, perhaps more rational factors are deciding the course of antitrust, I propose first to examine earlier shifts in antitrust doctrine and then to explore some of the forces that have forged these changes. They are, I believe, instructive in seeking an understanding of the likely future direction of antitrust. This is not to suggest, however, that politics and normative values should be discounted. Rather, the thesis of this article is that the future of antitrust is profoundly affected by developing insights into market operations as well as by the state of the economy and the political process. Each has a place and each plays a role in the shaping of antitrust policy.

Four phases of antitrust

The primary operative terms of the major antitrust statutes are extraordinarily brief yet equally vague. The Sherman Act simply prohibits "every contract . . . in restraint of trade" and makes "every person who shall monopolize" subject to liability.[3] The Clayton Act completes this picture by condemning mergers whose effect "may be substantially to lessen competition."[4] These broad, Constitution-like delegations of interpretative authority to the courts have led to a kaleidoscope of reactions over the years, including confusion, hostility, expansive application, and skepticism.

Contractual (1890–1910)

The formative years of antitrust, from the adoption of the Sherman Act in 1890 until the establishment of the "Rule of

---

[3]   15 U.S.C. §§ 1-2.

[4]   15 U.S.C. § 17.

Reason" at the time of the statute's majority,[5] were an important if confusing period. When first confronted with this broad responsibility to regulate trade, the courts lacked a sense of direction and often retreated to literalist interpretations of the statutory language. For example, the first antitrust case to reach the Supreme Court held that the manufacture of sugar was not "commerce," and the Court's initial substantive rulings held that agreements to fix prices for all shipments by rail carriers were illegal because the statutory language barred "every contract" in restraint of trade.[6] Similarly, a merger of competing railroads was condemned because it (necessarily) eliminated all competition between the merged lines.[7]

While the results in these cases were often more reasonable than their rationales, the operative tests they created were troublesome. Read as literally as the tests themselves read the Sherman Act, they appeared to mean that almost every contract which supported trade—contracts to sell goods or services, contracts to create a partnership or corporation, or contracts that otherwise intensified competition—could be readily condemned. This obviously went beyond the Court's intentions, so exceptions were quickly created and limiting rules were developed. Nonetheless, the law seemed unduly oppressive, confusing, and rigid. There was no connecting thread for identifying the line between dangerous, undue exercises of private market power and competitive activities that should be promoted or allowed to go unchecked. As one would expect, there was strong pressure for change.

Analytical (1911–1940)

Responding to some of these criticisms, the Court shifted its approach and began to analyze more carefully the practical effects of the challenged business activity. The Congress, it said in

---

5   *See* Standard Oil of N.J. v. United States, 221 U.S. 1 (1911).

6   United States v. Trans-Missouri Freight Ass'n, 166 U.S. 290 (1897).

7   Northern Securities Co. v. United States, 193 U.S. 197 (1904).

Standard Oil of N.J., had meant only to condemn unreasonable restraints of trade.[8] Thus, before finding a practice illegal under the "Rule of Reason," the purpose and likely effect of the practice were to be examined; this could include a close examination of market operations, an industry's history, the scope of competition, and related factors.

This analytical approach to antitrust proved easier to state than apply. Trials became lengthy affairs filled with speculation about the effect of particular practices, as courts were asked to base their conclusions on unknown future market trends. Business success is often as intuitive as it is rigorous; close market analysis may be only the first step. In any case, judges were trained to read legal doctrines rather than make successful business decisions. Recognizing this limitation, they tended to defer to business judgments and the rule of reason became synonymous with antitrust immunity. The principal exception was the Court's prohibition of price-fixing, although even this exception was abandoned temporarily during the Depression of the 1930s.[9] This period was marked by antitrust's continuing search for a unifying theory.

Structural (1940–1970)

Antitrust was restored as a policy tool when the New Deal abandoned its cartel approach to business revival in the late 1930s. Concerned with the time, cost, and results of rule of reason trials, antitrust doctrine increasingly relied on per se rules and structural tests to challenge boycotts, market allocations, vertical restraints, mergers, and monopolies.[10] Oligopoly theory

---

8   221 U.S. at 1.

9   *See* Appalachian Coals, Inc. v. United States, 288 U.S. 344 (1983).

10   *See* Fashion Originators' Guild of America, Inc. v. FTC, 312 U.S. 457 (1941) (boycott); United States v. Topco Associates, Inc., 405 U.S. 596 (1972) (market allocation); United States v. Arnold, Schwinn & Co., 388 U.S. 365 (1967) (vertical restraint); United States v. Von's Grocery Co., 384 U.S. 270 (1966) (merger); United States v. Aluminum Co. of America, 148 F.2d 416 (2d Cir. 1945) (monopolization).

captured the imagination of policy makers and courts. It supplied a seemingly coherent, market-based framework for testing the potential dangers of various arrangements that expanded private economic power.[11]

During this period, the focus of antitrust theory and its rules was on possible misuses of business arrangements. The advantages of monopoly/oligopoly power to producers (and dangers to consumers) were so great—of increased prices and profits from controlled output and entry—that it seemed likely that most restraints served some malign purpose. The difficulties of detecting cartels and oligopolies as well as the inherent problems associated with unwinding complex transactions also favored immediate challenges to practices posing only incipient dangers.

These expansive applications of antitrust were not without their difficulties. Many case results seemed unreasonable and inconsistent with the underlying theory.[12] Trials took as long as ever, since litigants felt compelled to introduce rule of reason–type evidence to answer questions of characterization, *i.e.*, whether a practice fit within a per se category. The process proved awkward since these covert methods misdirected the decision maker's attention and sacrificed the likely accuracy of the outcome.

Economic (1970–

The structuralist view of antitrust began to fade even as it was reaching widespread acceptance.[13] The major challenge came from those associated with the "Chicago school," who viewed

---

11 *See* J. Bain, Barriers to New Competition (1956); C. Kaysen & D. Turner, Antitrust Policy: An Economic and Legal Analysis (1959).

12 *See, e.g.*, FTC v. Brown Shoe Co., 384 U.S. 316 (1966); United States v. Aluminum Co. of America, 377 U.S. 271 (1966) (Alcoa–Rome merger). *See generally*, R. Bork, The Antitrust Paradox (1978).

13 *See* Industrial Concentration: The New Learning (H. Goldschmid, H. Mann & J. Weston eds. 1974).

antitrust primarily through the lens of price theory.[14] In addition
to questioning the empirical and theoretical foundations of oligopoly theory, they outlined numerous possible benefits from
various restraints. These ideas spread from the law reviews to the
enforcement agencies and the courts, and there has been a steady
retreat in recent years from the once dominant per se approach.[15]
Even when the per se rule has not been abandoned, its application
has been constrained.[16]

This increasing reliance on economic theory, which began
(albeit with a different understanding) under the structuralists,
but was now based on the concept of efficiency, has often been
controversial. The scope and meaning of various rules—including, for example, the tests for monopolization—are far from
clear, as often only part of the "new learning" has been understood or accepted.[17] Moreover, the jury's continuing role in
private antitrust litigation has furthered this uncertainty as recent
cases have frequently involved nongovernment suits.[18]

Within these limitations, however, it now seems clear that
antitrust is generally limited to considering arrangements involv-

---

[14]   *See* Posner, *The Chicago School of Antitrust Analysis*, 127 U.
PA. L. REV. 925 (1979); R. BORK, *supra* note 12.

[15]   *See, e.g.*, Continental T.V., Inc. v. GTE Sylvania Inc., 433 U.S.
36 (1977); Broadcast Music, Inc. v. CBS, 441 U.S. 1 (1979). *See also*
National Soc'y of Professional Engineers v. United States, 435 U.S. 679
(1978); NCAA v. Board of Regents of the Univ. of Okla., 104 S. Ct.
2984 (1984).

[16]   *See* Jefferson Parish Hospital Dist. No. 2 v. Hyde, 104 S. Ct.
1551 (1984); Northwest Wholesale Stationers, Inc. v. Pacific Stationery
& Printing Co., 105 S. Ct. 2613 (1985).

[17]   A particularly apt illustration is Justice Stevens' recent opinion in
Aspen Skiing Co. v. Aspen Highlands Skiing Corp., 105 S. Ct. 2847
(1985), which emphasized the Sherman Act's focus on efficiency while
nonetheless holding that a firm with monopoly power could not alter its
joint venture arrangement with a competitor without first giving a
business reason for the change.

[18]   *See* Monsanto Co. v. Spray-Rite Service Corp., 104 S. Ct. 1464
(1984); *Aspen Skiing*, 105 S. Ct. at 2847.

ing firms with substantial market power. In most situations an examination of the likely adverse effects must demonstrate substantial impairment of competition before an antitrust court will intervene.

Climbing the antitrust staircase

These shifts in antitrust policy and doctrine may be seen as nothing more than mindless oscillations reflecting political or personal agendas of those currently in power. Indeed, political scientists have often viewed antitrust as a reflection of the continuous struggle between capitalism and populism, with the outcome determined principally by the fortunes of the economy. There is obvious force to this contention as both history and logic suggest that when the economy is strong there is a greater tendency to worry about the misuse of economic power, whereas pressures are often overwhelming to abandon competition theory and accept (and even encourage) cartels during periods of economic dislocation.[19]

If this health-of-the-economy/political-power picture were a complete analysis, antitrust enforcement would simply reflect the swings of a pendulum between various polar and intermediate positions. During periods of economic prosperity antitrust would be expansive and widely used, and vice versa. That has not been the case, however. The prosperity of the 1920s and the recovery of the 1980s were not accompanied by a similar growth in antitrust enforcement. Consider also the reaction to the abandonment of the per se rule for vertical restraints in the *Sylvania* decision.[20] A major shift in antitrust enforcement, it reflected intensive economically based criticism of the prior per se rule. While aspects of *Sylvania* remain controversial, there is widespread agreement that the rule of reason standard adopted by the Court is the appropriate measure for evaluating territorial and

---

19 *See generally*, E. HAWLEY, THE NEW DEAL AND THE PROBLEM OF MONOPOLY 12-34 (1966).

20 *Sylvania*, 433 U.S. at 36.

similar restrictions. This decision has caused a reexamination of numerous doctrines, as its approach of examining the likely justifications and effects of a restraint has now been applied to tie-ins, boycotts, and even price-fixing.[21]

It is particularly significant that the four phases of antitrust have cut across partisan lines and differing economic trends. Antitrust has only generally paralleled the state of the economy. The development of antitrust has been more like the climb of a zigzagging staircase than the swings of a pendulum, with numerous landings at odd intervals and varying degrees of steepness in the steps. The one constant over time has been the incremental development of doctrine and the increasing sophistication of policy. Reflecting its common-law origins, new insights have been added to old ones. The specific lines drawn in the 1982 and 1984 Merger Guidelines might change under a more liberal administration, but the likelihood is that the changes would be modest and the basic framework would be left intact.[22] The general dismissal of the leverage theory that once dominated antitrust is another illustration of the intellectual growth of antitrust.[23]

This is not to deny the political nature of antitrust or its role as a catalyst in the ongoing debate over distribution of society's resources. Similarly, not all cases can be fit into this analysis, and many decisions reflect conflicting views. But the dominant development over the past two phases of antitrust has been the central

---

21   *See* cases cited *supra* noted 16; *Broadcast Music*, 441 U.S. at 1.

22   *See* Alpert & Kitt, *Is Structure All?*, 53 ANTITRUST L.J. 255 (1984) ("As a practical matter, remarkably little has changed: . . . . the primary emphasis continues to be upon structural considerations and, in particular, upon individual firm market shares and industry concentration measures"); Gellhorn, *Government Merger Policy and Practice— 1983*, 52 ANTITRUST L.J. 419 (1983). *See also* John H. Shenefield, Address to New England Antitrust Conference, Cambridge, Mass. (Nov. 14, 1981).

23   *See* H. HOVENKAMP, ECONOMICS AND FEDERAL ANTITRUST LAW 222-24 (1985); Posner, *supra* note 14, at 926, 929, 934-38. *But see* Kaplow, *Extension of Monopoly Power Through Leverage*, 85 COLUM. L. REV. 515 (1985).

role that economic analysis has played and the increasing understanding of policy makers and courts in the operation of markets
and business incentives. This understanding has led to a greater
skepticism of the benefits of antitrust intervention and a new
caution in applying antitrust to disrupt potentially beneficial
market practices. In lawyer's terms, the burden of persuasion has
shifted to those who would prohibit a vertical restraint or stop a
merger, except where the transaction demonstrably increases the
market power of firms with a large share of a concentrated
market.[24]

In large measure, this new antitrust doctrine is more favorable
to business and competitive experimentation. The predisposition
of antitrust enforcers and advisers is to identify permissible
methods for a business to achieve specific ends. To some degree,
of course, this has always been the rule. What has changed in the
past decade is that fewer devices are foreclosed from consideration. For example, a manufacturer who wants to encourage
dealer promotion and servicing can rely on exclusive territories,
customer allocations, and tie-ins more readily than in the past;
less desired methods such a areas of primary responsibility,
reserved accounts, profit pass-overs, etc. are no longer avenues of
first resort. Whether a practice will be approved will depend on
the market power of the participants and the likelihood that it
could enhance competition by increasing efficiency.

On the other hand, increased reliance on the rule of reason
standard has also introduced greater uncertainty and, in some
situations, raised business costs for complying with antitrust
requirements. It is no longer true that a trial under the rule of
reason standard will result in approval of the challenged business
practice. The process of transition from the per se standard to the
rule of reason measure is also far from complete—indeed, it is
unclear whether the courts will ever completely abandon the per
se rule for price-fixing, boycotts, tie-ins, or resale price main-

---

24   *See* U.S. Department of Justice Merger Guidelines (1982; rev'd
1984); U.S. Department of Justice Vertical Restraints Guidelines (1985).
See generally, Easterbrook, *The Limits of Antitrust*, 63 TEX. L. REV. 1
(1984).

tenance—and this heightens the costs of uncertainty. The Department of Justice guidelines and advice on mergers, vertical restraints, joint ventures, patents, etc. may prove helpful in reducing these costs. But the Antitrust Division's use of guidelines to press for change as well as to provide guidance means that they are less important as precedent.

Antitrust is, in other words, in a state of ferment. We are still in the midst of the economic phase and considerable doctrinal development has yet to occur.

Future directions

Analyzing past movements in antitrust is difficult enough without hazarding a guess as to its future direction. I have no reason to suppose that my crystal ball is clearer than anyone else's. Rather than attempting to divine the meanings of a necessarily clouded crystal ball, I thought it would be more helpful to identify some of the factors likely to influence the direction that antitrust may take and to discuss some of the major issues that will determine the slope and direction of the antitrust staircase.

First and perhaps foremost is that fact that the primary ingredients determining the direction of antitrust policy are probably unrelated to antitrust itself. The state of the economy—at least at the extremes—will probably decide the major questions. If the imbalance of trade continues or worsens, efforts to narrow antitrust enforcement in the merger and export areas will not only continue but possibly succeed. Similarly, if the economic downturn often predicted for the late 1980s occurs, and especially if it is steeper than currently envisioned, political pressures to curtail antitrust will intensify. As this suggests, the most favorable climate for the development of an independent, rational antitrust policy seems to be a period of modest economic growth when there is widespread recognition of the need to compete.[25]

[25] Paradoxically, the "need to compete" is probably the greatest when the economy is not performing well and the pressures are the greatest to avoid the rigors of competition.

Similarly, politics and ideology count for something. Two recent leaders of the Antitrust Division, Sanford Litvak and William Baxter, held very different antitrust philosophies. And I cannot conceive of either serving under the other's president. While there were undoubtedly many decisions made by each that the other would also have made, their decisions at the critical margin were very different. Indeed, their differences were often basic and fundamental—as illustrated by their positions on the virtues of resale price-fixing—and undoubtedly had much to do with the changing atmosphere of antitrust since 1980. The point should not be overplayed, however. Messrs. Baxter and Litvak are somewhat unusual cases, at least in their rhetoric, and they probably are not representative of most appointees to lead antitrust.

Of greater significance to the future of antitrust is the accident of Supreme Court appointments. Only one appointment has been made in the past decade, a record unlikely to be matched in the next 10 years. While not a basis for selecting justices, the philosophy of the new appointees and their knowledge of antitrust economics will undoubtedly have much to do with controlling the future direction of antitrust.[26]

It is important for antitrust followers to recall that the economy and politics probably have a greater effect on determining the direction of antitrust enforcement than anything else. To a substantial degree, antitrust is not in control of its own destiny. Nonetheless, there are substantial areas of agreement among most participants in antitrust policy development and this agreement is likely to be reflected in future actions regardless of who wins elections or is appointed to the Supreme Court. These areas of policy agreement tend to set the framework for political maneuver and probably to limit political choices.[27]

---

26 However, the current list of frequently mentioned possible Supreme Court appointees—Bork, Easterbrook, and Posner—includes an unusually large number of antitrust experts.

27 This is not always the case, however. General agreement among antitrust observers that the Robinson–Patman Act's prohibition of price discrimination as written is counterproductive has not seemed to have had much impact on Congress.

One such area is the acknowledged relevance of economic analysis to determining antitrust outcomes. The parsing of case precedent or applying simplistic notions of the leveraging of monopoly power is no longer an acceptable basis for developing policy. The focus of antitrust is on consumer welfare and more specifically on whether the challenged activity was aimed at increasing output. The classical perfect-competition paradigm is now firmly established in the antitrust hierarchy; it is the measure against which particular policies and actions are first tested. Increasingly, this also requires sophisticated determinations of the relevant market, the time frame during which a practice or action is to be viewed, and the market power and concentration of those competing in the market. With the development of theories of strategic and opportunistic behavior, contestable markets, etc., it is also clear that the economic data set will not necessarily point policy in only one direction. There will continue to be large areas of judgment where the predisposition of the decider is the single most important element determining the outcome.

The primary effect of this agreement on basic economic analysis will continue to be the identification of a wide branch of cases not suitable for antitrust intervention—even though they were formerly the staple of government as well as private activity. These will include non-price vertical restraints, most conglomerate and many horizontal mergers, and most price discrimination matters (even those that may be technical violations of the Robinson–Patman Act). Antitrust economics will continue to be used most widely to create filters and to identify safe harbors free from antitrust challenge.[28] The reason is not that antitrust is being unduly cut back or made ineffective. Rather, economic analysis demonstrates that the challenged practice cannot impair competition—because of limited market power—and that it serves a likely useful purpose.

Similarly, once prevalent populist notions are unlikely to make a comeback, having been purged from serious antitrust review. These include proposals to establish "no-fault" or indus-

---

[28]   *See* sources cited, *supra* note 24.

trial deconcentration laws for attacking persistent monopolies or concentrated markets, conglomerate merger bills usually aimed at particular industries, and so forth. They have been replaced in recent years by equally implausible (at least from a political standpoint) proposals to eliminate juries from private antitrust cases, to limit treble damages, to modify the merger law, and to repeal the price discrimination law. At this point there is no economic or political consensus on either set of proposals and, unless underlying economic and political forces change radically, it seems unlikely that we will witness major substantive change in the antitrust laws in this century.

Much harder, of course, is to identify future issues in antitrust and how they will be resolved. Despite the absence of any persuasive case justifying the treble-damage jury system for private antitrust actions, I see little likelihood of serious reform. The system has been in place for so long that the burden of persuasion seems to have shifted to those proposing any changes. As the Georgetown Private Damage Project illustrates, the evidence is so difficult to collect and evaluate that one must despair of ever establishing a persuasive case. More easily challenged, although seemingly still impregnable against change, is the current multilayered antitrust enforcement scheme involving three government agencies—state attorney generals, the Federal Trade Commission, and the Antitrust Division. Here the case for consolidation, at least of the FTC and Division's enforcement authority, is particularly powerful.[29]

On a substantive note, there remains considerable room for movement regarding the rules applicable to price-fixing, boycotts, horizontal mergers, and vertical restraints. In particular, numerous Supreme Court decisions are simply irreconcilable or irrational. Both tie-ins and boycotts are subject to per se condemnation "in some cases," but when is unclear.[30] The test for measuring permissible activities of a monopolist was further

---

[29]   *See* Gellhorn, *Regulatory Reform and the Federal Trade Commission's Antitrust Jurisdiction*, 49 TENN. L. REV. 471 (1982).

[30]   *See* cases cited *supra* note 16.

confused by the Court's recent *Aspen Skiing* decision, which seems to be a sport in law as well as fact.[31] And the current rules allowing manufacturers to establish exclusive territories but not fix resale prices—yet enforce other non-price restraints with their dealers—cry out for clarification.[32]

However, if the recent past is any indication of the future, observers 10 and 20 years from now will repeat this lament. The genius of the common-law system of antitrust is that a court decides only the case before it and avoids the errors of broad rules encompassing unknown situations. The cost is that inconsistent and sometimes incoherent rules result, intensifying the law's uncertainty. This leads me to suggest (rather than predict) that substantive antitrust doctrine focus on three central issues in the years ahead. One issue is whether we should abandon the per se test in antitrust. The concept began with price-fixing and spread over the years to include both horizontal (boycotts, market allocations) and vertical (tie-ins, exclusive territories) restraints. But as recent cases have shown, even the "hard-core" areas such as price-fixing (*ASCAP*) and boycotts (*Northwest Wholesale*) may involve practices deserving rule of reason analysis.[33] The result is that the per se rule no longer eases antitrust administration or provides business with sound guidance.[34] Its primary effect is to distract antitrust trials into arguments over character-

---

[31] *See Aspen Skiing*, 105 S. Ct. at 2847; Malina, *Supreme Court Update—1985*, 54 ANTITRUST L.J. 289, 293-95 (1985).

[32] *See, e.g.*, Easterbrook, *Vertical Arrangements and the Rule of Reason,* 53 ANTITRUST L.J. 135 (1984); Liebler, *1983 Economic Review of Antitrust Developments: The Distinction Between Price and Non-price Distribution Restrictions*, 31 UCLA L. REV. 384 (1983) (vertical restraints, price or non-price, have similar effects and cannot be distinguished on economic or other analytical grounds).

[33] *See Broadcast Music*, 441 U.S. at 1; *Northwest Wholesale*, 105 S. Ct. at 2613. *See also NCAA*, 104 S. Ct. at 2984.

[34] *See* Note, *Fixing the Price Fixing Confusion: A Rule of Reason Approach*, 92 YALE L.J. 706 (1983). *See also* Haddock, *Basing-Point Pricing: Competitive vs. Collusive Theories*, 72 AM. ECON. REV. 289 (1982); Liebler, *supra* note 32.

ization that confuse judges and juries and waste substantial societal resources. Courts should instead focus on the likely effects of the questioned activity to determine if it will impair or improve consumer welfare—as is the case under the rule of reason.

A second and related recommendation is that antitrust should focus its attention on fleshing out the meaning of the rule of reason.[35] The much maligned soft drink and beer bills—that provide that a producer's exclusive territorial licenses for wholesalers in these industries cannot be challenged if "substantial and effective competition" exists in the distribution market—may prove to be important steps in this direction.[36] The Vertical Restraints Guidelines reflect a different and, I think, less persuasive approach.[37] Whatever the approach, however, my point is

---

[35]   *See, e.g.*, Easterbrook, *supra* note 32, at 153 ("The Emptiness of the Rule of Reason"); H. HOVENKAMP, *supra*, note 23, at 271 ("Courts are simply incapable of dealing with the kind of nondescript, open-ended 'rule of reason' articulated in *Sylvania*").

For a personal effort, *see* Gellhorn & Tatham, *Making Sense Out of the Rule of Reason*, 35 CASE WES. RES. L. REV. 155 (1984–85).

[36]   *See* Soft Drink Interbrand Competition Act, 15 U.S.C. §§ 3501-03; S. 412, Malt Beverage Interbrand Competition Act, 99th Cong., 1st Sess. (1985). I should note that I have contributed to the drafting of these legislative items and testified on their behalf.

These statutes adopt the filter design of the Merger and Vertical Restraints Guidelines also urged in a somewhat different way by Judge Easterbrook (see sources cited *supra* note 24). However, rather than rely initially on market shares and market structures to distinguish between benign and possibly dangerous restraints—increasingly questionable measures in light of the theory of contestable markets (see Baumol, *Contestable Markets: An Uprising in the Theory of Industry Structure*, 72 AM. ECON. REV. 1 (1982)—the soft drink act and beer bill rely on evidence of intense competition to limit antitrust coverage to those practices that might injure consumer welfare. That is, where there is substantial and effective competition, the non-price vertical restraint poses no threat and should be immune from antitrust challenge.

[37]   As already noted (see *supra* note 36), the problem of the guidelines is that they automatically equate market structure with the benefits or absence of competition. Increasingly, however, the economic evidence is to the contrary. *See, e.g.*, Alpert & Kitt, *supra* note 22.

that further attention needs to be given to clarifying the application of the reasonableness standard. If it is to play an important role on the center stage of antitrust—as seems to be the direction of Supreme Court cases—its content and approach must be defined.

On the other hand, if the per se rule is to retain validity a third recommendation is that the Court (or, alternatively, the Division) spell out with greater clarity the distinction between suspect horizontal activity and benign vertical arrangements. The problem is particularly acute when a manufacturer of a branded article presses his dealers to promote his product or otherwise seeks to market his product aggressively, particularly against discounters. The current case law is unpredictable and inconsistent. Cases such as *Klor's*,[38] *General Motors*,[39] *Monsanto*,[40] *Sealy*,[41] and *Topco*[42] demonstrate the depth of the current confusion. All involve essentially similar free-rider fact situations, yet their results turn on whether the practice is characterized as horizontal or vertical. Of course, as long as different standards (per se or rule of reason) apply to similar conduct, the horizontal/vertical distinction will not be dispositive. But at least an understandable method for distinguishing horizontal from vertical arrangements would lead to similar cases being decided in the same way.[43]

* * * *

---

[38] Klor's Inc. v. Broadway-Hale Stores, Inc., 359 U.S. 207 (1959).

[39] United States v. General Motors Corp., 384 U.S. 127 (1966); *see* Baker, *Interconnected Problems of Doctrine and Economics in the Section One Labyrinth: Is Sylvania a Way Out?*, 67 VA. L. REV. 1457 (1981).

[40] *Monsanto*, 104 S. Ct. at 1464.

[41] United States v. Sealy, Inc., 388 U.S. 350 (1967).

[42] *Topco*, 405 U.S. at 596.

[43] See, for example, the thoughtful analysis by Professor Liebler suggesting a focus on whether the restraint could directly restrict output as a method for distinguishing horizontal from vertical arrangements. Liebler, *Intrabrand "Cartels" Under GTE-Sylvania*, 30 UCLA L. REV. 1 (1982). *See also* Liebler, Book Review, 66 CALIF. L. REV. 1317, 1334-39 (1978).

The agenda for antitrust has not been shortened by the emphasis on economic analysis in recent years or the introduction of courts and policy makers to price theory. Indeed, it seems likely that only the easiest questions have been answered where there is general agreement among economists. Concepts such as contestable markets or opportunistic behavior may be relatively simple to grasp; yet their application in particular markets to guide antitrust policy makers seems another matter. Even if more sophisticated economic analysis is within the general antitrust lawyer's grasp, it is far from certain that these insights will provide clear answers to basic policies or particular cases.

Antitrust at its core involves values and normative judgments. After close to 100 years of antitrust it is still unclear whether antitrust enforcement significantly contributes to consumer welfare. To some this suggests that those who would intervene in the market must bear a heavy burden, or at least that intervention should be limited to those markets where the likelihood of collusion and injury to consumer welfare is relatively high. Where competitive and monopolistic behavior are basically indistinguishable, the costs of intervention—including the cost to consumer welfare when antitrust is used to restrain competition—must be calculated carefully.

Perhaps the principal lesson from antitrust history for the future is to realize how little we really understand about markets and how they operate.

Policy Studies Review, Vol. 2, No. 4, May, 1983

GOVERNMENT STRUCTURAL POLICIES AND
THE AUTOMOBILE INDUSTRY
George R. Heaton, Jr.

INTRODUCTION

Structural policy is the set of government actions that are intended
to affect the composition of a nation's economy and the nature of competition among actors within it. Two sub-categories encompass the variety
of government actions that fall within this broad rubric:
  — policies that establish legal rules of competition and/or concen-
    tration in particular markets
  — policies that actively encourage the formation of particular types
    of industrial organizations.
The first category includes the legislation and regulatory frame-
works that comprise an antitrust or competition policy. Typically, these
rules govern both trade practices—pricing, marketing, competitor colla-
boration, etc.—and the degree of structural concentration in a particular
market. The government's role is to establish the rules and enforce them
through the judicial system in an essentially ad hoc fashion.
The second category of structural policy casts the government in
a more activist role. Here, government typically conceives and facilitates
the achievement of industrial structures thought to be desirable. A wide
variety of programs and policies fall within this category. In the automobile industry, for example, governments have frequently tried to
rationalize the sector. In extreme cases, direct aid to troubled firms has
been mounted. These activities all imply that the government actively
conceive and carry out programmatic responsibilities over a long period.
In Europe and Japan, governments without exception have been
concerned with the relationship between structural policy and international competitiveness. Particularly in the automobile sector, deliberate
attempts have been made to promote the development of domestic firms
that are internationally competitive. Where necessary, exceptions have
been made to the rules of competition in the domestic market in order
to achieve this goal. A relatively clear national consensus has supported
these decisions. In contrast, structural policy in the United States has
been concerned with preserving competition in the domestic market
and has operated through a highly decentralized regulatory regime. Antitrust regulation of the U.S automobile industry has only sometimes been
successful in achieving its stated goals, and ambivalence and disagreements have often pervaded national policy. From such comparisons of
structural policies, one can infer fundamentally differing national perceptions of international competition and the appropriate role of government in affecting it. To a significant extent, the European countries and
Japan appear to share a common viewpoint: the belief that nations are
in competition and that the private and the public sectors should work
together to promote a discernible national interest. In the U.S., the economic model of competition among private actors is presumed to apply

both domestically and internationally, and the avowed purpose of government is to correct imperfections in these markets.

THE U.S. EXPERIENCE

The U.S. has a vigorous and wide-ranging structural policy. Detailed rules of competition and concentration—antitrust policy—have been in existence for about a century. More recently, the government has promoted small businesses through many programmatic initiatives. Beyond this, the government does not deliberately structure the economy or particular sectors within it, nor has it been concerned with how the structure of the domestic economy relates to the international context.

For the automobile industry, only one kind of structural policy has been important: antitrust. Until recently almost wholly absorbed with domestic competition issues, antitrust policy toward the automobile industry—and other U.S. industries—must now reconsider some of its long-held postulates in light of new international realities.

Antitrust Policy: Underlying Concepts

The structure and specific provisions of the U.S. antitrust laws bespeak fundamental and uniquely American attitudes about economics, the role of government, and the structure of society. Broad, ambiguous, and essentially idealistic, this body of law is constantly redefined and modified by judicial precedent. These decisions almost always represent a compromise among the many and often-conflicting societal goals at issue. Nevertheless, there has been a fairly strong historical continuity in this policy area, which can be expected to continue.

The economic underpinning of the antitrust statutes is a belief in free competition as the guarantor of economic efficiency and consumer well-being. If this is not specifically stated in the statutes, it has become clear from both interpretive case and commentary (*Standard Oil*. . ., 1911; *Northern Pacific*. . . , 1958; Antitrust Policies. . ., 1982; Klein, 1977). Thus, the preservation of competition in the relevant market and the achievement of economic efficiency are the economic issues that absorb antitrust analysis. As an important corollary, free competition implies not only that monopolies and other restraints of trade be prevented, but also that the economy not be subject to government direction: impersonal market forces are presumed to work better. Thus, the government role is simply to enforce the laws, not to plan or direct the economy.

Antitrust policy must also be seen in social-political-historical context. As an outgrowth of the populist movement during the late nineteenth century, antitrust has always contained elements of a crusade. Its targets have consistently been big businesses and great wealth, and thus, antitrust has sometimes been a means of garnering political support from the less affluent, rural sectors of society. In addition, however, antitrust can be seen as a way of decentralizing economic, and by extension, political power. Socially, it contains a preference for mobility,

763

137

George R. Heaton, Jr.

entrepreneurship, and small enterprise. In fact, from time to time legislative proposals have been advanced to make size alone an antitrust violation (Asch, 1977, p. 129). An appreciation of these political/social purposes can help explain some of the actions that might be hard to justify economically (Sullivan, 1977).

A last purpose of antitrust is to establish ethical standards governing business conduct. The Federal Trade Commission Act's proscription of "unfair" methods of competition is the broadest of several such standards. These laws protect both competitors and consumers and have tended to be strictly enforced against both individuals and corporations, especially when an intentional violation can be shown.

The institutional structure of the antitrust regulatory system mirrors the legal/economic/political concepts that underlie it. Most importantly, decision-making is decentralized. In the Executive Branch of the government, the Department of Justice and the Federal Trade Commission share concurrent jurisdiction. The Congress has continuously concerned itself with antitrust issues via legislation, committee hearings, investigations, and special commissions. The statutes can also be enforced by private individuals, who collect treble damages for violations; whereas about 50 antitrust actions are begun by the government each year, many more private suits arise—about 1500 in the year ending June 30, 1980. Because antitrust decisions are mostly made by the judiciary, the development of the law has been complex and somewhat unpredictable. While some people bemoan the lack of certainty (Ginsburg, 1980), the argument can also be made that the threat inherent in this uncertainty is precisely what makes U.S. antitrust policy effective.

These basic principles have been enacted into several statutes whose most important provisions are the following: (1) the Sherman Act's proscriptions on combinations "in restraint of trade"; (2) the Clayton Act's prohibitions against discriminatory behavior and combinations that "substantially lessen competition"; (3) the Federal Trade Commission Act's proscription of "unfair or deceptive" acts or practices.

Given the ambiguity and breadth of these statutory mandates, a long history of judicial precedent has been necessary to apply and explain them. From these, a distinction has been developed between per se violations—infractions of the law for which there is no excuse—and others, which the surrounding circumstances may excuse under a "rule of reason." The rule of reason approach requires that the courts consider the factors that contributed to the creation of the situation in question. Judicial analysis must also define a "relevant market" and the nature of competition within it. To date, courts have tended to focus almost exclusively on the domestic market. Moreover, competition tends to be measured by tests such as numbers of firms and market shares at a particular point in time. Rarely do concepts of dynamic, technologically-based rivalry over time or competitiveness in international markets enter the analysis.

While the antitrust laws have enjoyed a century of strong popular support in principle, a clear national consensus has never emerged as to

764

138

their purposes, interpretation, or application. Thus, many antitrust initiatives have been mounted in one era only to be discarded in another. While these changes in direction can sometimes be accounted for by differences in the political coloration of antitrust administrators, they also bespeak the diversity in American attitudes about competition, big business, and the role of the state, and thus about the merits of any particular antitrust initiative.

Antitrust Actions Against the Automobile Industry

For about 50 years, the U.S. automobile industry has been the almost-continuous target of antitrust activity. Some of the more important actions are listed in Table 1. These actions have been of various types—civil law suits, criminal indictments, investigations, hearings, legislation—and have involved many different actors. One aspect the table does not capture is the large number of private antitrust actions brought against automobile manufacturers, either by dealers or consumers. These number in the many hundreds.

A few periods of intense activity stand out: the late 1930s, when the first important cases were brought concerning financing and dealership arrangements; the middle 1950s, when legislative hearings were held about the need for structural change; and the late 1970s and early 1980s, when traditional antitrust concepts began to be re-evaluated.

Given the extent of the activity, it is surprising that so little occurred in the way of definitive results. Many cases proposed by agency staff were never brought. Of those that were, relatively few proceeded through the judicial system to a clear decision; many, instead, were abandoned or compromised in a consent decree. Legislative hearings and investigations, an almost constant phenomenon, frequently produced reports, some legislative proposals, but almost no legislation. Thus, although the antitrust threat to the industry has been ever-present, its realization has been far from complete. The relative failure of antitrust regulators to achieve what they intended can be ascribed to three factors:

(1)	the lack of viable legal and economic theories on which to attack some aspects of industry structure and practice—most notably, the law's inability to deal with oligopolies and non-intentional concentration;

(2)	the automobile industry's enormous resources—political and legal—by which to resist;

(3)	the ambivalence about whether strong antitrust action against the automobile industry was desirable—reflected in changing regulatory postures, Congressional lack of support for structural change, and judicial reluctance to impose drastic remedies.

The various initiatives that arose had four different foci: (1) the structure of automobile manufacturing, (2) the structure of closely related industries (components, finance companies, trucks), (3) the relationship of the automobile industry to the transportation sector more generally, and (4) anticompetitive conduct cases.

George R. Heaton, Jr.

Table 1

Chronology of Selected Antitrust Actions Against the U.S. Automobile Industry

Time Period	Actors	Type of Action	Focus	Outcome
1937-42	FTC/GM	FTC/Clayton Act Suit	exclusive dealerships	changes in dealer relationships*
1933-39	FTC	Study	concentration and conduct	principal findings: no price fixing: active competition: unfair dealership arrangements
1933-53	DOJ/GM	Sherman Act litigation	financing	GM retained GMAC: coercive practices barred**
	DOJ/Ford/ Chrysler	Sherman Act Indictment	financing	consent decrees** barred finance company affiliation
1939-53	FTC/GM/ AC Spark	Clayton/FTC Act Suit	exclusive dealing. price fixing	cease and desist ordered: no structural relief
1947-55	DOJ/GM/Nat'l City Lines	criminal indictment. divestiture action	municipal bus transport	criminal conviction, divestiture suit dismissed
1949-61	DOJ/DuPont/GM	Clayton Act Suit	monopolization of fabrics and finishes	divestiture GM holdings
1963	DOJ/Independent automakers	scrutiny	improvements in competition against big three	mergers approved
1955-55	Senate Antitrust Committee	study/hearings	GM	preliminary report criticising GM: Car Dealers Day in Court Act
1957	Senate Antitrust Committee	study/hearing	administered pricing, financing	report critical of GM; proposed legislation banning financing-manufacturing affiliations to DOJ
1958-59	DOJ/Ford	criminal indictment	price fixing	nolo contendere
1959-68	DOJ/GM/Euclid	Clayton Act	monopolization earth moving	divestiture of Euclid
1960-69	DOJ	task force	shared monopoly theory: case against GM	much analysis: many proposals: all abandoned
1961-63	DOJ/Chrysler	Sherman/Clayton Suit	exclusive dealerships	suit dropped with Chrysler notices freeing dealers
1961-71	DOJ/Ford/ Autolite	Clayton Act Suit	vertical integration	Autolite divestiture

766

140

Table 1 (Concluded)

Chronology of Selected Antitrust Actions Against the U.S. Automobile Industry

Time Period	Actors	Type of Action	Focus	Outcome
1964	DOJ/Chrysler/ Mack	Sherman/Clayton Suit	related industries	Chrysler/Mack merger dropped
1966	DOJ/GM	Sherman Act	"location clauses" barring discount sales	Supreme Court found to be per se violation
1967-68	Senate Antitrust Committee	hearings	auto industry market control	no report
1969-81	DOJ/Mfgrs. Assn.	Sherman Act Suit	joint development emissions technology	consent decree barred joint activities***
1974	Senate Antitrust Committee	hearings	industrial concentration/ground transportation	proposed legislation/no report
1974	DOJ/Chrysler/ GE	law suit	interlocking directorates	consent decree: boards disaffiliated
1976-81	FTC	investigation	monopolization in domestic and foreign industry: GM	issuance of subpoenas. investigation dropped, 1981
1980	DOJ	guidelines	joint R&D	clarification/more permissive
1981	FTC/Echlin/ Borg-Warner	Clayton/FTC Act Suit	reduced supplier competition	pending
1981	FTC/Tenneco/ Monroe	Clayton Act Suit	reduced potential competition	divestiture order pending

* The long history of these cases, and other related actions, makes the outcomes complicated. For example, *Standard Oil Company of California* v. *U.S.* 337 U.S. 288 (1949). Barring exclusive dealerships for oil companies, also had an important impact on the automobile industry.
** These consent decrees, along with all others outstanding, were under review by the Justice Department as of this writing. Justice may modify them "to lift improvements in auto financing."
*** In the last two years, this decree has been relitigated and modified, with the government currently proposing its termination.

767

In the first category, the table shows seven major investigations focusing on the need for structural change in passenger car manufacturing. In spite of these initiatives, the government never brought a civil or criminal suit alleging monopolization of car manufacturing, and no vote was ever taken on legislation to "break up" the automobile industry.

In the second category, a number of rather clear outcomes occurred. Integration forward, from manufacturing into financing the dealerships, was attacked quite vigorously. For example, Ford and Chrysler effectively were prevented for about ten years from affiliating with finance companies. GM, though the target of similar cases, never lost its affiliation with GMAC. Integration backward was also attacked, most notably in the Ford-Autolite and GM-DuPont cases. In these, Ford's control of Autolite and DuPont's control of GM were prevented. Chrysler, always less vertically integrated, was also eliminated from acquiring Mack Truck. The horizontal structure of the supplier industries has also been a major focus of concern. For example, in the GM-DuPont case, the principal issue was DuPont's ability to monopolize the fabrics and finishes sector. More recently, the Tenneco and Echlin cases, which prevented mergers among suppliers, show the continuing impetus to prevent concentration and preserve individual competitors in the supplier sector.

A number of cases addressed attempts by automobile companies to diversify into other transportation-related businesses. Most of these actions were brought against GM: to bar it from the business of local transportation and from the production of transit buses, earthmoving equipment, and locomotives. The Euclid case was terminated in the government's favor, as GM agreed in a consent judgment to sell the Euclid assets to White Motor Company and not to enter the earthmoving equipment business for ten years. A more equivocal result was reached in the Bus Monopoly consent decree, as GM agreed to "increase the possibilities for competition," by making available for license all new patents over a ten year period, but no divestiture remedy was reached. Similarly in the National City Lines litigation, although GM and other corporate defendants were convicted of conspiracy to control local transportation companies, the parallel attempt to force divestiture failed. The Locomotive Monopoly cases were ultimately dropped by the government. GM was also the target, along with Ford, of charges that it fixed prices in the automobile fleet market, but both were found not guilty. Lastly, as a result of a consent decree, Chrysler was prevented from affiliating with General Electric via interlocking directorates.

Actions in the fourth category, anticompetitive conduct, are by far the most numerous. Many suits were brought by automobile dealers against manufacturers, based on various objectionable practices, such as pressure to sell more cars, forced purchases of "genuine" parts, factory specification of dealer operating practices, and arbitrary termination of franchises. The government also brought several cases to reform dealer-manufacturer relationships. For example, the FTC sued GM in 1937, and the Justice Department moved against Chrysler in 1961 to ban exclusive dealership arrangements. Also, in 1966, the Supreme Court held that GM contracts that barred "discount house" selling were a classic per se violation. Although exclusive dealerships were thus declared illegal, allegations were routinely made by dealers well into the 1970s that informal practices continued to have the same effect.

A complicated history of conduct litigation has focused on joint or collaborative activities. For example, a number of actions were brought against several companies for price fixing. Most important, however, was the so-called "smog decree" litigation, brought in 1969 against the four domestic automakers and their trade association, charging them with conspiracy to delay and obstruct the development of emissions control technology. The resulting consent decree essentially barred joint activities and technology or information-sharing for ten years. It now appears that the decree will soon be formally modified and terminated in part, although the government will probably retain the right to scrutinize joint activity.

The Impacts of Antitrust Policy

Causal links between specific incidents of antitrust policy and changes in industry structure or company strategy are difficult to establish. Especially when only the threat, as opposed to the reality, of antitrust action is present, one is forced to hypothesize events that would have occurred "but for" the regulation in order to evaluate its impact. Thus, to assert that antitrust has had a negative impact on the U.S. industry's competitiveness is to suggest as well that the industry would have made better long-run strategic choices in its absence; and to argue antitrust's positive influence is to believe that the industry would have fared worse without it. The evaluation is complicated both by the fact that the impacts of antitrust have frequently fallen unevenly on different firms and by the realization that its outcome may appear diametrically opposite when viewed through either the industry's or the consumer's perspective.

Antitrust has relatively advantaged some firms and disadvantaged others. Ironically, GM, the most frequent target, has also emerged the relative winner. For example, Ford and Chrysler were prevented from affiliating with finance companies for a number of years; whereas GM never lost GMAC. This, as one Senate report noted, gave GM "the means, through its financial affiliates, of underwriting market expansion, a method not available to its competitors." Similarly, while Ford and Chrysler lost the opportunities to acquire Autolike and Mack Truck, respectively, GM kept AC Spark Plug and its truck manufacturing business. Indeed, the most important structural case that GM lost, the DuPont case, may actually have benefitted the company since the outcome released it from DuPont's control. On the other hand, GM's market strategy may have been substantially constrained by the threat of antitrust action. If, as many believe, GM had the ability to monopolize automobile production, its market share may have been deliberately kept around 50 percent in order to avoid further antitrust prosecution.

769

143

Foreign firms also have emerged as relative winners. Most of the antitrust actions against the U.S. industry occurred during the time when foreign competition was an irrelevance to the domestic manufacturers, and thus, the foreign industry has not been a target. Meanwhile, structural policy in Europe and Japan encouraged strategies—like intra-industry collaborative arrangements, domestic concentration, and inter-industry affiliations—that would have been legally suspect in this country. These practices, however, have not been attacked because of the difficulty of enforcing U.S. antitrust law against foreign companies and the new competitive situation in the automobile industry today.

It is not clear that, overall, the competitive position of U.S. manufacturers has been significantly hurt or helped as a result of antitrust policy. In simple terms, one can think of international competitiveness as being determined by three factors: scale, scope, and flexibility. (Since other aspects, like the cost of factor inputs, are not affected by structural policy, these can be excluded from consideration.) Certainly U.S. antitrust policy has not inhibited the formation of the scale in automobile production requisite to compete internationally. There have, however, been antitrust barriers to the creation of scope. Integration of automobile manufacturers, suppliers, finance companies, and dealerships has been resisted. There have also been constraints on affiliations outside of the industry. Lastly, it is likely that antitrust has in some respects inhibited the flexibility of U.S. companies. On the one hand, it has inhibited their diversification possibilities somewhat. On the other hand, to the extent that antitrust policy allowed a few, large companies to dominate the industry so completely for so long, it failed to create the conditions of rivalry necessary to promote company flexibility.

From the consumer's point of view, antitrust has also had both beneficial and negative impacts. The pricing and conduct cases have obviously helped to ensure a clear, though immeasurable, benefit to automobile purchasers. It might also be argued that the openness of the U.S. market—established in part by antitrust prohibitions on restrictive practices—aided the foreign companies in entering the U.S. market, to consumers' benefit. Nevertheless, the failure of antitrust to prevent oligopoly contributed to the preservation of a U.S. market that lacked diversity for many years.

Today, the antitrust climate has shifted dramatically, as a result of a changed economic and political climate. Short of conspiracy or price fixing, there are probably few restraints on joint activities, for either U.S. or foreign firms. Even intra-industry mergers might be approved under the perhaps-now-applicable "failing company" doctrine. Perhaps the most interesting, as yet unresolved, issues concern how, if at all, the U.S. antitrust laws might be applied to the conduct and structure of the new foreign entrants to the U.S. market.

770

144

STRUCTURAL POLICIES IN EUROPE AND JAPAN

Antitrust or competition policy, though less comprehensive than in the U.S., is fairly well developed in Europe and Japan. Its application to the automobile industry has been very sparing, while other structural policies have been vigorously pursued. (The information which follows in this section can be found condensed in Table 2.)

Antitrust or Competition Policy

Europe. In Europe, antitrust or competition policy exists at both the national and EEC levels. The EEC legislative framework is contained in Articles 85 and 86 of the Treaty of Rome. These prohibit agreements which may affect trade between Member States and which have as their object or effect the prevention, restriction or distortion of competition within the common market, and abuse of a dominant position within the common market.

The EEC system differs strikingly from U.S. law in that it only applies to trade between member states, not international trade. In addition, all cases are subject to a rule of reason approach, and there are no per se violations. Notification requirements apply to all transactions that might fall within the prohibitions. Proposed business transactions are then scrutinized by the Commission to determine whether they should be permitted. A broad exemption covers agreements which contribute to improving the production or distribution of goods or to promoting technical or economic progress, while allowing consumers a fair share of the resulting benefit.

Exemptions may be given either for a specific agreement or for a category of agreements. Typically, the exemptions will be for a limited time and may contain restrictive conditions. The breadth of the exemption gives the responsible administrative agencies great discretion to engage in a wide-ranging inquiry into many social and economic factors. Maintaining employment, protecting key industries, or strengthening the international competitiveness of European enterprises are, thus, important considerations. Most commentators agree that these exemptions make European antitrust law significantly less stringent than that in the U.S. (Grendell, 1980). Applications of EEC antitrust law to the automobile industry have been rare; one case has focused on the market conduct of BMW.

German and EEC law are similar, both being enacted in the same year. Monopolies or cartels are not illegal per se, only "abuses" by "market-dominating" businesses. Market domination can mean either that an enterprise is "without substantial competition" or "paramount" relative to competitors. Abuses are events that would not occur in a "fair bargaining" environment. A few antitrust actions have been brought against the German automobile industry. One, concluded in 1981, focused on VW's relationships with repair dealers. The German High Court ultimately allowed VW to maintain exclusive supply relationships, believing that VW had not exploited these and that they gave consumers better service. The most celebrated incident occurred during the mid-1970s when the

771

Table 2

Selected Government Influence on the Structure of The Autmobile Sector

Country	Time	Companies	Action	Government Role
France	1919	GM/Citroen	proposed acquisition	failed due to government opposition
	1946	Renault	nationalization	government ownership: various supports over time (lower interest loans, no dividend obligation): participation in acquisition plans
	1964	Ford/GM	proposed assembly plant	rejected by government
	1974	Peugeot/Citroen	acquisiton	government approval: the
	1978	Peugeot/Chrysler	acquisition	creation of a second "national champion"
	1972	Renault/Peugeot	joint ventures	government encouragement
	1978	Lucas-Ducellier-Ferodo	proposed acquisition	government blocks foreign control
	1979-1981	Renault	expansion abroad: Volvo, Mack Truck, AMC	government approval
Germany	1932	Auto Union	merger in response to GM acquisition of Opel	promotion of rationalization
	1937	VW	creation	state ownership
	1961	VW	partial denationalization	ownership reduced
		Borgward	failure	rescue efforts by Bremen Land
	1955	VW/Auto Union	merger to prevent GM takeover	government approval
	1974	VW	management changes	Federal Chancellor intervention
	1975	Daimler-Benz	ownership arrangements	Deutsche Bank action to ensure domestic control
	1978	GKN-Sachs	proposed acquisition	cartel office refused
U.K.	1915		high tariffs	tariff protection until mid-1950s.
	1954		partial	government scrutiny
	1967	Chrysler/Rootes	acquisition	
	1970		control	government approval
	1965	BMC/Pressed Steel	merger	government approval
	1968	Leyland/BMC	merger	government promotion: loan

Table 2 (Concluded)

Selected Government Influence on the Structure of The Automobile Sector

Country	Time	Companies	Action	Government Role
	1975	BLMC	failure	nationalization
	1978	Peugeot-Citroen/ Chrysler	takeover	government participation
	1979-1981	BLMC	deficits	government funding
Japan	1930s	Ford/GM Nissan/Isozu/ Toyota	expulsion of foregin companies: promotion of domestic	
	1947	Nissan/Toyota	resumed production	U.S. occupation
	1949	Toyota	financial assistance	Bank of Japan
	1953	domestic and foreign	technology imports	control of technology transfer: favoring few firms
	early 1960s		"people's car"	MITI concept, failed
	1961		plan	
	1966	Nissan/Prince	merger	MITI orchestration
	mid- 1960s	domestic	merger proposals	MITI plans, most unsuccessful
	1950s/60s	suppliers	consolidation	MITI plans, often unsuccessful

773

147

Federal Cartel Office successfully opposed the horizontal merger of GKN (U.K.) and Sachs, both manufacturers of automobile components. This case has been seen as retarding the progress of pan-European rationalization and the development of common European law, since the merger was not opposed at the EEC level.

The U.K. antitrust framework has two major components. On the one hand, the Monopolies and Mergers Commission is concerned with industry structure. It may challenge affiliations when issues are referred to it by the Secretary of State. During the 1960s, investigations of the automobile industry were mounted. These ultimately had little effect on the consolidation of the domestic industry. The British Office of Fair Trading is the second arm of antitrust enforcement and concerns itself with anticompetitive conduct.

Japan. Prior to World War II, antitrust law did not exist in Japan, and the economy was dominated by the *zaibatsu.* Cartels, quotas, divisions of the market, and price fixing were all legal. After the War (1947), the U.S. Occupation designed the Antimonopoly Law, modelled closely after U.S. statutes. Its rationale was probably more political than economic: the U.S. strongly desired a democratic, free-market society and believed that this could only occur if the *zaibatsu* were broken up (Hadley, 1970). Many Japanese resented the Act and believed that it could not work. Thus, post-Occupation amendments modified and weakened it considerably.

As it now exists, the Japanese statute prohibits forms of concerted conduct that cause a "substantial restraint of competition," and are "contrary to the public interest." This second criterion, interpreted narrowly in the immediate post-war years, has been substantially broadened since then. Japan has gone farther than any other country in fashioning a series of antitrust exemptions. Generic exemptions for "depression" and "rationalization" cartels pertain during economic downturns. Specific industry and commodity exemptions ease the restraints on companies competing in international trade, allowing export-oriented companies to be treated more leniently than those producing for the domestic market. About 40 special laws grant exemptions, including one for automobiles.

The administration of Japanese antitrust law is entrusted to the Fair Trade Commission, a small agency attached to the Prime Minister's Office. The FTC typically plays a negotiating role, guiding and suggesting corporate behavioral changes rather than compelling them. Although the FTC's powers seem weak by comparison with U.S. agencies, they were enlarged by statute in 1977. In addition, a 1980 conviction of twelve oil companies for price fixing and production limitations (during the 1973 oil embargo, apparently with tacit governmental approval) may indicate a resurgence of antitrust vigor in Japan.

Attempts to Structure the Automobile Sector

Europe. In France, two attitudes have dominated structural policies toward the automobile sector: the *dirigiste* tradition of state control over the direction of development, and strong nationalism in favor of domestic interests. The structure of the French industry today, dominated by Renault and Peugeot, may be seen as the logical result of a long series of consistent interventions. Although state-owned Renault enjoys considerable independence from government control, a number of specific government decisions have benefitted it: for example, the absence of a need to pay dividends, access to loan capital, and favorable treatment of tax and social security obligations.

Peugeot attained its current structure after it acquired Citroen in 1974 and Chrysler's European operations, including Simca, in 1978. Although Peugeot has always been a strongly private firm, clearly the government has smiled on its acquisitions and was involved to a significant extent in achieving the current industrial structure. For example, low-interest loans were extended to both Renault and Peugeot in the course of rationalization plans, which included the Renault takeover of Berliet and Talbot.

The French government has also helped restructure the supplier sector. For example, Ferodo was encouraged to take over SEV-Marchal after Boach was refused permission in 1971. Later, Ferodo became involved in legal battles with Lucas (U.K.) over the acquisition of Ducellier, in which the government showed a clear preference for Ferodo, the domestic company. Government support for French companies has been consistent; for example, GM and Ford's plans to build assembly plants were turned down, and the state prevented Fiat from acquiring more than 49 percent of Citroen.

German government policy toward the structure of the automobile industry has been characterized by a relative lack of involvement, punctuated by a few specific interventions. Public decision making authority toward the automobile industry is diffuse, resting in several different federal agencies, and the state governments. In fact, a government role has almost not been necessary, due to industry prosperity, the long-standing social contract between management and labor, and the consensual decision making framework that involves labor, government, and various private interests.

Before World War II, while GM and Ford were dominant, the government undertook to create a national champion. Although Volkswagen today is generally free from government control, its history of public ownership creates a unique situation. For example, VW's crisis during the early 1970s occasioned a major public debate, and although direct government intervention was minimal, the role played by Chancellor Schmidt in replacing old management and fostering a new consensus should not be underrated. Interventionist efforts by the Land (state) governments have also occurred. Bremen's 1961 attempt to save Borgward ultimately failed, but the 1967 effort to reconstitute BMW, accomplished with the aid of the Bavarian government, was successful.

Although the least protectionist European country, Germany has shown concern about foreign intrusions into the automobile industry.

Evidenced more by the actions of large banks than by those of the government, protectionism was apparent in the 1965 acquisition of Auto Union by Volkswagen so as to prevent a Chrysler take-over and in the 1975 maneuverings to prevent foreign control of Daimler-Benz.

British structural policies have to a great extent been rescue measures. Many mechanisms have been used, most of them unsuccessfully. Structural change began in the early 1950s when mergers, such as that between Austin and Morris, the two largest domestic companies occurred. Throughout this period the government was generally acquiescent. Policy began to change with the shift to Labour in 1964 and a worsening economy. The Industrial Reorganization Corporation was formed, with the mandate to improve efficiency and productivity. The implicit assumption behind its formation was that much of British industry consisted of units too small to compete in world markets. When in the late 1960s Leyland acquired Rover, and Chrysler took control of Rootes, the IRC participated. Then, in 1968 the government helped arrange the merger of Leyland and MBC, and the IRC provided loans for retooling.

This restructuring failed to rejuvenate the British industry: in 1975 BLMC was nationalized, and in 1976 Chrysler announced its inability to continue in operation. Government assistance buoyed Chrysler until 1978, when it was acquired by Peugeot-Citroen. Government funding was required for BLMC as efforts to rationalize the company's diverse facilities got underway. Restraints on foreign (i.e., Japanese) imports continued to be an important element favoring the domestic industry as well as attempts by the government to attract new investment from abroad.

Japan. Before World War II, the government expelled GM and Ford and encouraged a few companies—e.g., Nissan, Isuzu, Toyota—to serve the war effort. Afterwards, the U.S. Occupation forbade passenger car production. When in 1947 production resumed, for two years only small cars were permitted, a circumstance to which some partially credit Japan's emphasis on small vehicle production (Yakushiji, 1977). The Japanese automobile industry was then far from secure. Low consumer demand and the apparently more pressing need to develop heavy industry led some to oppose development of a Japanese automobile industry. After the Korean War boom, however, a consensus favored development, and MITI began to facilitate it. MITI's policy had four principal elements: protectionism, export development, technology imports, and rationalization.

MITI saw a highly concentrated domestic industry as necessary to international competitiveness, and it tried through various means to promote this. In 1953, for example, it rejected four of six companies' applications for technology transfer. Selective access to capital was another similar strategy. For example, Nissan was not given Japan Development Bank loans until it agreed to absorb Prince via merger. Perhaps MITI's most ambitious undertaking was its plan to standardize designs. A plan for one-company production of a "people's" car was never implemented, although it continued to influence the thinking of government policymakers. Later, another plan proposed three design types—regular cars, minicars, and specialty vehicles. The apparent objective was to force concentration and eliminate small producers. Opposed vigorously by some companies, the plan was eventually dropped (Magaziner & Hout, 1980). Meanwhile, mergers were encouraged. For example, the 1966 Nissan-Prince merger developed when Prince came close to bankruptcy. Within two years, six other affiliations occurred. Most were arranged by the companies and their banks with MITI's approval and/or contribution. Four of the six were ultimately unsuccessful, with only Toyota-Hino and Toyota-Daihatsu persisting.

Throughout this period, MITI also took a strong interest in the automotive suppliers, its apparent goal being to create a few large, export-oriented manufacturers. Horizontal combinations were encouraged by the availability of government financial assistance to facilitate mergers and underwrite joint R&D. Although the size of supplier firms did increase dramatically, their numbers never declined to anywhere near the MITI goal, nor did large horizontally integrated combines materialize to the extent hoped. Rather, the industry remained vertically integrated around relationships with primary manufacturers.

The relationships among automotive suppliers, primary manufacturers, and financial institutions illustrate one of the unique aspects of Japanese industrial structure: the *keiretsu* combinations. The *keiretsu* system has facilitated an enormous, albeit subtle, degree of integration in the automobile production and distribution systems (Anderson, 1981). This structure would not have been possible if the antitrust laws had been strictly enforced. Ironically, the *keiretsu* structure probably contradicted, to some extent, MITI's rationalization schemes. Competition among the *keiretsu* may have generated hostility to plans which would have decreased the numbers of firms, and the resources of the *keiretsu* may have given individual firms the ability to resist takeovers and/or government plans.

Whether MITI's structural policies toward the automobile and supplier industries were successful or not is open to question. A high degree of market dominance has indeed been achieved by the two largest groups— Toyota and Nissan—but the organization of the several medium-sized producers did not work as MITI had hoped. Some specific plans were accomplished (e.g., the Nissan-Prince merger) but others (e.g., a Japanese "people's car") were not. In addition, infusions of foreign capital, an event MITI feared, occurred in the links Mitsubishi, Toyo Kogyo, and Isuzu made with U.S. companies. It may even be that structural policies favoring concentration contradicted the protectionist measures that the government undertook simultaneously, since protectionism, which led to surplus profits, inevitably encouraged new entrants, especially in the rapidly growing market (Uneo & Muto, 1974).

CONCLUSIONS

Differing National Perceptions and Policies

Fundamentally different perceptions exist in the U.S., Europe, and

Japan about the nature of international competition, appropriate industrial structures, and the government's role in directing economic activity. Government policy in the U.S., especially antitrust, is based on the assumption that economic competition takes place primarily among private actors, each seeking its own best interests. A definable national economic interest has never been strongly in the American consciousness. This orientation can be seen in both the legal doctrines and structural features of the antitrust laws. Elsewhere, competition among societies may be perceived as more significant than internal competition among private actors. Thus, government structural policies are based on definite perceptions of a national economic interest, and free market dogmas can easily be discarded in favor of other goals. This orientation is obvious in antitrust law in Europe and Japan, which contains broad exemptions that overlay the basic regulatory scheme.

Different social attitudes pervade structural policy as well. In the U.S., antitrust arose as an element of the populist movement, and even today, large size is suspect. In Japan, large enterprises are highly respected, and in Europe as well the tradition of individual entrepreneurship has never enjoyed the mystique it has in the U.S. There are also fundamentally different attitudes about the role of government. For example, the tradition of state enterprises, common in Europe, is essentially non-existent in the U.S., where government's regulatory role has overshadowed partnership possibilities.

These differences in perceptions pervade and explain the differences in structural policies. Thus, in the U.S., structural policy has been almost entirely comprised of antitrust regulation. Measures to promote small and/or new ventures, though strong in general, have never been relevant to the automobile industry. Antitrust policy has been adversarial and strongly supportive of individual private interests. Some critics argue that U.S. antitrust policy has protected individual competitors and neglected competition (Stone, 1977). The purposes of the laws have always been diverse, consisting not only of economic efficiency but also of social/political values and a loosely formulated ethical code of business conduct.

Structural policy in Europe and Japan has always been dominated by policies other than antitrust, which may in fact sometimes be inimical to antitrust goals. The antitrust policies that have existed are basically non-doctrinaire, focusing primarily on abuses of market-dominant positions. The pattern of antitrust exemptions bespeaks a different set of social goals from those in the U.S. In both Europe and Japan the national economic interest is paramount, particularly as evidenced in the concern for international competition and "national champion" firms.

Structural Policies: Successes, Failures, and the Competitive Impacts

A coupling of the differences in policy patterns with disparities in economic performance offers some enlightening comparisons. In particular, Japan and the U.S. emerge as almost mirror images, and the European experience is similar to neither.

778

In the U.S. the long history of antitrust regulation has yielded little in the way of structural results. Efforts to "break up" the big three domestic automakers, GM in particular, were a perennial regulatory agenda that never materialized. Sometimes-successful efforts were made to limit vertical integration between the automakers and their suppliers or other affiliates, and horizontal combinations within the supplier sector were frequently prevented. The many "conduct" cases, relating to trade practices, were probably the element of antitrust litigation in which plaintiffs emerged the most successful. Thus, U.S. structural policy toward the automobile industry could be called a failure, if measured against its intention to change the industry structure. On the other hand, the threat of antitrust action has been real enough to prevent many actions that might have otherwise occurred, and to this extent the policy should be considered a success.

The situation in Japan has been almost exactly the reverse. Early on, the automobile industry was exempted from the anti-monopoly legislation. Moreover, the general tolerance of *keiretsu* permitted organizations of great scope to be developed. MITI's attempts to standardize automobile production and rationalize the industry, both suppliers and primary manufacturers, clearly failed to achieve the intended aims. At the same time, the Japanese government was pursuing other policies designed to nurture the industry, and in the aggregate these policies, although perhaps internally inconsistent, clearly contributed to the industry's success.

Ironically, Japanese policy tried to promote an industrial structure like that in the U.S.—something it failed to achieve. U.S. antitrust enforcers would have welcomed the rather large number of companies that existed in Japan—something they also did not achieve.

Structural policies in Europe have apparently been more successful in accomplishing their intended purposes. The French government goal of a domestic industry is a reality. In Germany, the laissex-faire approach persists even though it has been interrupted by successful efforts to rejuvenate ailing firms. Whether the British efforts to restructure and bolster the industry will succeed is open to question.

Whether structural policies have succeeded in creating internationally competitive national industries is another question entirely. Certainly that is not true in the U.S., but, of course, it was never an intended policy goal. Similarly, Japanese structural policy cannot be credited with the Japanese firms' success although other government policies clearly worked to their benefit. The European experience is equivocal in this regard. Overall, it is unlikely that explicit structural policies have made a great difference to the nature of international competition today. On the other hand, related policies—e.g., access to capital, the ability of foreign firms to form large combinations, the financial-industrial liaisons—may have benefitted the long-term strategic plans of foreign producers significantly.

U.S. automobile firms, as a result of the antitrust threat, have not had the same opportunity to develop similar strategies. U.S. society, however, has, by virtue of the antitrust laws, protected the openness and diversity—economic and political—that it prizes.

Policy Issues Today

The internationalization of the world automobile industry today calls into question the long-held structural policies of the U.S., Europe, and Japan. Past policies have ubiquitously been formulated from a narrow, domestic orientation. In the U.S., this has rooted antitrust law in an analysis of domestic competition and prevented the development of any national policy or significant analytical capability concerned with international trade. In Europe and Japan, the preoccupation with domestic producers' position in international trade has led to an over-emphasis on protectionist measures. Neither policy orientation is consistent with the internationalization of markets, companies, and production that will characterize the automobile industry in the future.

For the U.S., the new realities can be accommodated by a changed orientation in antitrust analysis. Greater cognizance should be taken of the trade practices and policies of other countries, as input to the formulation of U.S. policy. Similarly, the analysis of competition in relevant markets should be broadened into an international context. A particularly difficult issue is how to equalize antitrust policy toward U.S. and foreign firms when the latter achieve competitive advantages from practices that would be objectionable under U.S. law. In order to undertake any of these tasks, new analytical capabilities are needed, especially in government.

In Europe and Japan, the domestic orientation of structural policy has sometimes kept markets more closed than necessary and less rivalrous internally than might be desirable. The policy process may suffer because access to it is difficult, relatively centralized, and consensus relatively easy to achieve.

In all countries there is a need to reorient structural policy toward a longer-term, more dynamic view of international competitiveness. No policy can be prescient enough to accommodate all future developments, and thus flexible structures must be created—both in firms and governments. In no country have policies to promote industrial flexibility yet formed a sufficient aspect of structural policy.

REFERENCES

Anderson, M. *Japan's Strategic Umbrella,* 1981.

Antitrust policies affect not just corporate futures. *Sunday New York Times,* Jan 19, 1982.

Asch, P. Industrial concentration, efficiency and antitrust reform. *The Antitrust Bulletin,* 1977, *XXII,* p. 129.

Ginsburg, D. *Antitrust Uncertainty and Technological Innovation.* Washington, D.C.: National Academy of Sciences, 1980.

Grendell, T. The antitrust legislation of the United States, the European economic community, Germany, and Japan. *International and Comparative Law Quarterly,* 1980, *29,* 64.

Hadley, E.M. *Antitrust in Japan.* Princeton, New Jersey: Princeton University Press, 1970.

Klein, B. *Dynamic Economics.* Cambridge, Mass.: Harvard University Press, 1977.

Magaziner, I. & Hout, T. *Japanese Industrial Policy.* London: Policy Studies Institute, 1980.

Northern Pacific Railway v. *United States,* 356 U.S. 1 (1958).

Standard Oil Company of New Jersey v. *United States,* 221 U.S. 1 (1911).

Stone, A. *Economic Regulation and the Public Interest.* Ithaca, New York: Cornell University Press, 1977.

Sullivan, L. Economics and more humanistic disciplines: What are the sources of wisdom for antitrust? *University of Pennsylvania Law Review,* 1977, *125,* 1214.

Uneo, H. & Muto, H. The automobile industry of Japan. *Japanese Economic Studies,* 1974, *3*(2).

Yakushiji, T. *Dynamics of Policy Intervention: The Case of the Government and the Automobile Industry in Japan.* Ph.D. Thesis, MIT, 1977.

781

155

ANTITRUST POLICY AFTER CHICAGO

Herbert Hovenkamp*

The so-called "Chicago School" of analysis has achieved ascendancy within the fields of antitrust policymaking and scholarship. In this Article, Professor Hovenkamp predicts that flaws in the Chicago model's basic premises will one day cause it to be eclipsed, just as previously ascendant doctrines have been eclipsed. Professor Hovenkamp enumerates and expands upon a list of criticisms of the Chicago School's neoclassical efficiency model, grouping the arguments within two categories: criticisms from "outside" and "inside" the model. From "outside" the model, Professor Hovenkamp disputes the premises that policymakers can know enough about the real world to make truly efficient decisions, that antitrust law can pursue the single goal of efficiency and remain consistent with other legal policies, and that the antitrust laws' legislative history reflects an exclusive concern with efficiency. Furthermore, from "inside" the model, the author argues that even if it were appropriate for antitrust policy to take account only of efficiency concerns, the Chicago School's neoclassical efficiency model is not sophisticated enough to account for real world behavior. He demonstrates that Chicago scholars' erroneous characterization of markets as static leads them to underestimate the importance and severity of strategic behavior. Professor Hovenkamp reinforces his critique of the Chicago School model by describing two previously overlooked forms of strategic behavior and by showing how such behavior can and does undermine the model's reliance on the market.

I. INTRODUCTION

If one hundred years of federal antitrust policy have taught us anything, it is that antitrust is both political and cyclical. Almost every political generation has abandoned the policy of its predecessors in favor of something new. Antitrust policymakers have created the common law school,[1] the rule of reason school,[2] the monopolistic

---

* Professor of Law, University of California, Hastings College of the Law. — Ed.

The author admits a great admiration for Chicago School antitrust policy, and confesses that he has been a fellow traveler for some time. Nevertheless, he believes that the Chicago School generally did a much better job of defending its position when it was a tiny squad of embattled outsiders instead of a triumphant division. Those who no longer need to defend themselves, don't.

1. For example, see Judge Taft's opinion in United States v. Addyston Pipe & Steel Co., 85 F. 271, 279-83 (6th Cir. 1898), aff'd., 175 U.S. 211 (1899), applying common law principles to interpretation of "contract in restraint of trade" under the Sherman Act. Also, see Justice Holmes's opinion in Swift and Co. v. United States, 196 U.S. 375, 396 (1905), applying common law attempt principles to the Sherman Act. *See generally* Baxter, *Separation of Powers, Prosecutorial Discretion, and the "Common Law" Nature of Antitrust Law*, 60 TEXAS L. REV.

competition (New Deal) school,[3] the workable competition school,[4] the liberal school,[5] and the law and economics, or Chicago, school.[6]

Each of these schools left an impression that affected antitrust policy indefinitely, although some continue to have a far more visible influence than others. The common law may continue to guide antitrust decisionmaking, but in most cases the evidence is hard to find.[7] The rule of reason is very much with us, however, and continues to play a large and expanding role in antitrust adjudication.[8] The theory of monopolistic competition has frequent revivals, most recently in the ready-to-eat breakfast cereals case.[9] Both the workable competition thesis[10] and the liberal theory[11] are currently in disrepute among those

661 (1982); Easterbrook, *Vertical Arrangements and the Rule of Reason,* 53 ANTITRUST L.J. 135, 136-40 (1984).

2. See Chief Justice White's opinion in Standard Oil Co. v. United States, 221 U.S. 1, 63-67 (1911), adopting a rule of reason, apparently for all litigation under the Sherman Act. The historical development of the rule of reason is recounted in A. BICKEL & B. SCHMIDT, THE JUDICIARY AND RESPONSIBLE GOVERNMENT, 1910-21, at 86-199 (9 Oliver Wendell Holmes Devise History of the Supreme Court of the United States, 1984).

3. *See* E. CHAMBERLIN, THE THEORY OF MONOPOLISTIC COMPETITION (7th ed. 1956) (1st ed. 1933). For the relationship between the theory of monopolistic competition and Depression-era antitrust policy, see Rowe, *The Decline of Antitrust and the Delusions of Models: The Faustian Pact of Law and Economics,* 72 GEO. L.J. 1511, 1541-47 (1984). *See also* E. HAWLEY, THE NEW DEAL AND THE PROBLEM OF MONOPOLY: A STUDY IN ECONOMIC AMBIVALENCE 13, 35, 40-48, 297-99 (1966).

4. *See* REPORT OF THE ATTORNEY GENERAL'S NATIONAL COMMITTEE TO STUDY THE ANTITRUST LAWS 320-38 (1955) [hereinafter cited as 1955 COMMITTEE REPORT] (proposing that antitrust policy be guided by a theory of "workable competition"); *see also* Clark, *Toward a Concept of Workable Competition,* 30 AM. ECON. REV. 241 (1940). Clark's theory of "workable competition" was intended to be a rejection of Chamberlin's theory of monopolistic competition, under which public policy efforts to improve real-world competition by such devices as the antitrust laws were deemed to be ineffectual.

5. The "liberal school" here refers to the antitrust policy developed by the Warren Court during the 1950s and 1960s. *See* text at notes 28-37 *infra.*

6. *See* R. BORK, THE ANTITRUST PARADOX: A POLICY AT WAR WITH ITSELF (1978); Posner, *The Chicago School of Antitrust Analysis,* 127 U. PA. L. REV. 925 (1979).

7. *But see* United States v. American Airlines, 743 F.2d 1114, 1118-20 (5th Cir. 1984) (applying common law principles to the offense of attempt to monopolize), *cert. dismissed per stipulation,* 106 S. Ct. 420 (1985). Today, discussion about the "common law" nature of antitrust refers to the power of the courts to devise specific rules that interpret a broadly worded statute. The phrase is *not* generally used to suggest that federal antitrust law today follows the common law of restraints on trade. *See generally* Baxter, *supra* note 1; Easterbrook, *supra* note 1.

8. *See* National Collegiate Athletic Assn. v. Board of Regents, 104 S. Ct. 2948 (1984); Broadcast Music, Inc. v. Columbia Broadcasting Sys., 441 U.S. 1 (1979). *See generally* Blake, The Rule of Reason and Per Se Offenses in Antitrust Law (Columbia University Center for Law & Economics Studies, working paper No. 10, 1984).

However, some Chicago School writers argue that the dichotomy between per se and rule of reason analysis is wrongheaded and should be replaced by an analysis that develops through a series of presumptions. Easterbrook, *supra* note 1, at 153-68. *See generally* Easterbrook, *The Limits of Antitrust,* 63 TEXAS L. REV. 1 (1984) [hereinafter cited as Easterbrook, *Limits*].

9. *In re* Kellogg Co., 99 F.T.C. 8 (1982).

10. *See, e.g.,* G. STIGLER, THE ORGANIZATION OF INDUSTRY 12 (1968) (criticizing the "workable competition" thesis).

11. *See* R. BORK, *supra* note 6, at 198-216.

of the dominant (Chicago) school. Nevertheless, one can find any number of people who adhere to them, particularly to the liberal theory.[12]

The life of a school of antitrust policy is like the life of a scientific model.[13] First the model experiences a period when only one or a few people dare to propose it. These people may be treated as charlatans by those who work within the consensus model.[14] Later a breakthrough or discovery, or perhaps a series of discoveries, occurs that both discredits the accepted model and makes the new model seem far more palatable. Then the new model achieves consensus, and most people in the scholarly community try to jump on the wagon — to do research that will validate the model, or that is guided by the framework established by the model.[15]

The model determines "relevance."[16] Relevant evidence is that which is explained by or "fits into" the existing model. Irrelevant evidence is that which cannot be accounted for by the model. Within the neoclassical market efficiency model,[17] for example, evidence that a particular practice distributes wealth in a certain way or that a rule increases the opportunities for small business is generally irrelevant, because the model does not take such values into account. The model purports to distinguish only the efficient from the inefficient, without reference to distributional consequences. If "justice" has anything at all to do with the way wealth is distributed, then the model is unable to distinguish the just from the unjust.[18]

The Chicago School model of antitrust policy dictates that allocative efficiency as defined by the market should be the only goal of the antitrust laws.[19] Within that paradigm even evidence derived from the

---

12. *See* Fox, *The Modernization of Antitrust: A New Equilibrium,* 66 CORNELL L. REV. 1140 (1981); Pitofsky, *The Political Content of Antitrust,* 127 U. PA. L. REV. 1051 (1979); Schwartz, *"Justice" and Other Non-Economic Goals of Antitrust,* 127 U. PA. L. REV. 1076 (1979).

13. *See generally* T. KUHN, THE STRUCTURE OF SCIENTIFIC REVOLUTIONS (2d ed. 1970) (describing the process by which scientific thought evolves).

14. *Id.* at 10-34. For example, Posner notes that early Chicago School theorists were regarded by outsiders as a "lunatic fringe." Posner, *supra* note 6, at 931.

15. T. KUHN, *supra* note 13, at 10-34.

16. *Id.* at 15.

17. In this article the term "neoclassical market efficiency model" refers to the price theory of the Chicago School, which is the price theory that dominates American antitrust policy today. A good brief overview of the theory is R. BORK, *supra* note 6, at 90-133. *See also* H. HOVENKAMP, ECONOMICS AND FEDERAL ANTITRUST LAW 1-36 (1985).

18. *See* R. BORK, *supra* note 6, at 90 ("Antitrust . . . has nothing to say about the ways prosperity is distributed or used."); *see also* Hovenkamp, *Distributive Justice and the Antitrust Laws,* 51 GEO. WASH. L. REV. 1, 16-26 (1982). For criticism of this view, see text at notes 155-65 *infra.*

19. *See* R. BORK, *supra* note 6, at 91; R. POSNER, ANTITRUST LAW: AN ECONOMIC PERSPECTIVE 4 (1976).

legislative history of the antitrust laws is unimportant, unless to show that the legislative history supports or undermines the model. If the latter, the preservation of the model requires that the legislative history of the antitrust laws be deemed irrelevant to their current interpretation.[20]

The market efficiency model for antitrust policy is very powerful, and is as appealing intellectually as any of its predecessors. One of the strongest elements in its appeal has been its advocacy of expertise outside the legal profession. Today more than ever antitrust decisionmakers have been forced to submit their views to another group of specialists — economists — for evaluation.[21] Antitrust academia, the antitrust bar, and the federal judiciary are filled with people who have made serious efforts to learn about price theory and industrial organization.

This article begins with the premise that nothing — not even an intellectual structure as imposing as the Chicago School — lasts forever. In fact, a certain amount of stagnation is already apparent. Most of the creative intellectual work of the Chicago School has already been done — done very well, to be sure. The new work too often reveals the signs of excessive self-acceptance, particularly of quiet acquiescence in premises that ought to be controversial.[22]

Today the cutting edge of antitrust scholarship is coming, not from protagonists of the Chicago School, but rather from its critics.[23] The critics began as most critics of a model do, first by making refinements

---

20. *See* text at notes 167-97 *infra.*

21. For example, see ANTITRUST POLICY IN TRANSITION: THE CONVERGENCE OF LAW AND ECONOMICS (E. Fox & J. Halverson eds. 1984).

22. *See, e.g.,* Landes, *Optional Sanctions for Antitrust Violations,* 50 U. CHI. L. REV. 652 (1983) (assuming that economic efficiency should be the basis for damages measurement, notwithstanding that § 4 of the Clayton Act appears to mandate a compensatory basis for measurement — three times the damages "by him [the plaintiff] sustained"). *See also* Easterbrook, *The Limits of Antitrust, supra* note 8, at 2-3 (assuming without proof that overdeterrence is more socially costly than underdeterrence). For an alternative view, that overdeterrence is probably beneficial in highly concentrated markets, while underdeterrence is probably beneficial in competitive markets, see Joskow & Klevorick, *A Framework for Analyzing Predatory Pricing Policy,* 89 YALE L.J. 213, 222-39 (1979). Finally, see Baxter, *Reflections Upon Professor Williamson's Comments,* 27 ST. LOUIS U. L.J. 315 (1983) (acknowledging that industrial organization theory may have discerned ways in which strategic firm behavior is anticompetitive, but arguing that courts should not consider such questions).

23. *See* Dixit, *A Model of Duopoly Suggesting a Theory of Entry Barriers,* 10 BELL J. ECON. 20 (1979); Kaplow, *Extension of Monopoly Power Through Leverage,* 85 COLUM. L. REV. 515 (1985); Markovits, *The Limits to Simplifying Antitrust: A Reply to Professor Easterbrook,* 63 TEXAS L. REV. 41 (1984); Salop, *Strategic Entry Deterrence,* AM. ECON. REV., May 1979, at 335; Salop & Scheffman, *Raising Rivals' Costs,* AM. ECON. REV., May 1983, at 267; Scherer, *The Economics of Vertical Restraints,* 52 ANTITRUST L.J. 687 (1983); Wentz, *Mobility Factors in Antitrust Cases: Assessing Market Power in Light of Conditions Affecting Entry and Fringe Expansion,* 80 MICH. L. REV. 1545 (1982); Williamson, *Antitrust Enforcement: Where It's Been, Where It's Going,* 27 ST. LOUIS U. L.J. 289 (1983) [hereinafter cited as Williamson, *Antitrust*

in the given model, then by uncovering some major anomalies, and finally, in some cases, even by considering alternatives to the classical market efficiency model. This process is only barely underway, and this essay will do no more than carry it marginally toward its goal. However, the initial premise of this paper cannot easily be refuted: the Chicago School, just as its predecessors, is mortal.

II.   ON THE ROLE OF ECONOMICS IN FEDERAL ANTITRUST POLICY: 1890-1980

Chicago School antitrust advocates sometimes say that courts, the Federal Trade Commission, and the Department of Justice first developed an "economic approach" to antitrust in the early 1980s.[24] Critics of the Chicago School likewise suggest that "economists are kings" over antitrust policymaking in the 1980s in a way that they were not during earlier periods.[25] The impression created by these statements is that antitrust policymakers somehow discovered economics at the time of the Chicago School revolution in antitrust policy.

Such a conclusion must rest on one of two alternative premises. Either (1) economic theory had nothing useful to say about antitrust policy until the 1970s, or (2) although economists in earlier periods had something to say about antitrust policy, the policymakers paid little or no attention, but developed their policies in a vacuum that was free of theoretical economics. Only an extreme form of historical myopia will admit the first premise. While the second should perhaps be taken a little more seriously, its truth is far from clear.

Much of the criticism that American antitrust policy has historically been economically unsophisticated is really a criticism that the earlier policy employed a *different* economic model than the model that is currently in vogue. In that case the Chicago School "revolu-

Enforcement]; Williamson, *Predatory Pricing: A Strategic and Welfare Analysis*, 87 YALE L.J. 284 (1977) [hereinafter cited as Williamson, *Predatory Pricing*].
    The exchange in the *St. Louis University Law Journal* between Professor Baxter (then head of the Antitrust Division), *supra* note 22, and Professor Williamson, *supra*, is instructive. In it both Williamson, a critic of the Chicago School, and Baxter, a proponent, appear to agree that within the disciplines of price theory and industrial organization traditional Chicago School scholarship is giving way to more complex theories designed to account for strategic behavior. The two authors differ only on the question whether courts should accommodate the new scholarship. Courts ignored the Chicago School for thirty years. Mr. Baxter appears to believe that post-Chicago economic scholarship should be treated the same way.
    24. *See* Gerhart, *The Supreme Court and Antitrust Analysis: the (Near) Triumph of the Chicago School*, 1982 SUP. CT. REV. 319; Posner, *The Rule of Reason and the Economic Approach: Reflections on the* Sylvania *Decision*, 45 U. CHI. L. REV. 1, 5, 12-13 (1977).
    25. *See* Baker & Blumenthal, *The 1982 Guidelines and Preexisting Law*, 71 CALIF. L. REV. 311, 317-21 (1983); Fox, *Introduction, The 1982 Merger Guidelines: When Economists Are Kings?*, 71 CALIF. L. REV. 281, 281-83, 296-99 (1983).

tion" in antitrust policy is much less far-reaching than its supporters suggest, although its importance should not be understated. Antitrust policymakers did not first develop an "economic approach" in the late 1970s or early 1980s.[26] They simply changed economic models. This was hardly the first time that such a change occurred, and at least one earlier change was just as sudden and dramatic.[27]

The Chicago School has been particularly relentless in its criticism of the antitrust policy of the Warren Era, which has been presented as the antithesis of sound economic thinking in antitrust policy.[28] Yet despite all that has been said about the lack of sophistication or even the hostility toward economics manifested by Warren Court and Eisenhower administration antitrust policy, that policy was in fact very much informed by academic economists. The price theory and industrial organization that dominated the academic study of economics in the 1960s were simply quite different from the dominant economic ideology of the 1980s.

For example, Harvard economist Joe S. Bain, who exercised a strong influence on federal antitrust policy in the 1960s and 1970s, based his relatively prointerventionist theories on three important economic premises. The first was that economies of scale were not substantial in most markets and dictated truly anticompetitive concentration levels in only a small number of industries.[29] As a result, many industries contained larger firms and were more concentrated than necessary to achieve optimal productive efficiency.[30] The second was that barriers to entry by new firms were very large and

---

26. The date chosen for the adoption of an "economic approach" by antitrust policymakers is more or less arbitrary. The most plausible candidates are 1977, the year of the Supreme Court's decision in Continental T.V. v. GTE Sylvania, 433 U.S. 36 (1977) (adopting a rule of reason for vertical nonprice restraints), and 1981, when President Reagan took office and named William F. Baxter to head the Antitrust Division of the Department of Justice.

27. That change occurred in 1935 and 1936, and was in large part prompted by the Supreme Court's decision in Schechter Poultry Corp. v. United States, 295 U.S. 495 (1935), which struck down the National Industrial Recovery Act. Under the Act competing firms were strongly encouraged to "cooperate" with one another in the development of "codes of fair competition," and enforcement of the antitrust laws was nearly suspended. After the *Schechter* case, however, the Roosevelt administration suddenly shifted positions and adopted a policy of aggressive enforcement of the antitrust laws, based largely on 1930s theories of oligopoly performance in concentrated markets subject to substantial product differentiation. *See* E. HAWLEY, *supra* note 3, at 283-380.

28. *See, e.g.,* R. BORK, *supra* note 6, at 201-16.

29. *See* Bain, *Economies of Scale, Concentration, and the Condition of Entry in Twenty Manufacturing Industries,* 44 AM. ECON. REV. 15, 38 (1954).

30. J. BAIN, BARRIERS TO NEW COMPETITION: THEIR CHARACTER AND CONSEQUENCES IN MANUFACTURING INDUSTRIES 53-113 (1956); Bain, *Relation of Profit Rate to Industry Concentration: American Manufacturing, 1936-40,* 65 Q. J. ECON. 293 (1951); *see also* Stigler, *Monopoly and Oligopoly by Merger,* AM. ECON. REV., May 1950, at 23.

could easily be manipulated by dominant firms.[31] The third was that the noncompetitive performance (pricing above marginal cost) associated with oligopoly began to occur at relatively low concentration levels.[32]

The combination of these views created an antitrust policy that was quite concerned with deconcentrating oligopolistic markets and, to a degree, with protecting small firms from larger rivals, generally on the theory that a large number of small firms would yield lower prices than a relatively small number of larger firms.[33] To be sure, the Warren Court did not always follow this reasoning. For example, some of its merger decisions appear to identify low prices, rather than oligopoly or large firm dominance, as the primary "evil" at which the antitrust laws were targeted.[34] The Justice Department's enforcement policy manifested in the 1968 Merger Guidelines was not so careless, however.[35] Today no one can say that those guidelines reflect an approach that was any less "economic" than the approach taken by the 1984 Merger Guidelines.[36] The 1968 guidelines simply reflect the academic thinking of the 1960s, in which product differentiation, industrial concentration, barriers to entry, and large firm dominance rather than tacit collusion were the principal areas of economic concern for the competitive process.[37] All of these were explicitly "economic"

---

31. J. BAIN, *supra* note 30, at 1-42. Bain identified product differentiation as one of the most common ways that incumbent firms could manipulate the market to make entry more difficult. *Id.* at 114-43.

32. J. BAIN, *supra* note 30, at 1-42.

33. The best statement of the policy is C. KAYSEN & D. TURNER, ANTITRUST POLICY: AN ECONOMIC AND LEGAL ANALYSIS (1959), which relied heavily on Bain's work. *See also* Turner, *The Definition of Agreement Under the Sherman Act: Conscious Parallelism and Refusals to Deal,* 75 HARV. L. REV. 655 (1962).

34. *See, e.g.,* Brown Shoe Co. v. United States, 370 U.S. 294, 344 (1962) (holding that Congress wanted amended § 7 of the Clayton Act to be used "to promote competition through the protection of viable, small, locally owned businesses"). For that reason, a merger that lowered a firm's costs and thereby injured smaller competitors should be condemned. The Supreme Court applied similar analysis in United States v. Von's Grocery Co., 384 U.S. 270 (1966), and in FTC v. Procter & Gamble Co., 386 U.S. 568 (1967).

35. *See* 1968 Department of Justice Merger Guidelines, 2 TRADE REG. REP. (CCH) ¶ 4510 [hereinafter cited as 1968 Merger Guidelines].

36. 1984 Department of Justice Merger Guidelines, 49 Fed. Reg. 26,823, 26,837 [hereinafter cited as 1984 Merger Guidelines]; *see* R. POSNER & F. EASTERBROOK, ANTITRUST: CASES, ECONOMIC NOTES, AND OTHER MATERIALS 60 (2d ed. Supp. 1984) (suggesting that the 1984 Justice Department Merger Guidelines represent a "great advance in economic sophistication over the 1968 guidelines").

37. The most noteworthy difference between the Justice Department's 1968 Merger Guidelines and the 1984 Merger Guidelines is not that the former adopted the four-firm concentration ratio (CR4) as an index of market concentration, while the latter adopted the Hirfindahl-Hirschman Index (HHI). Both indexes have been around since before the 1968 guidelines were drafted and are simply alternative ways of measuring market concentration. *See, e.g.,* Hirschman, *The Paternity of an Index,* 54 AM. ECON. REV. 761 (1964); Stigler, *A Theory of Oligopoly,* 72 J. POL. ECON. 44, 55 (1964). A much more important distinction between the two sets of guidelines is

concerns — howbeit concerns that achieved prominence within a different economic model than the one that dominates antitrust policy today.

Even the 1950s and 1960s were not the first decades that economic models influenced antitrust policy.[38] Federal antitrust policy contained a strong economic element much earlier. In fact, one must go all the way back to the first thirty years of antitrust enforcement to find a policy that can reasonably be characterized as having little or no economic content.[39]

When the Sherman Act was first passed in 1890, most (but not all)[40] economists condemned it as at best irrelevant to the problem of the trusts and at worst as harmful to the economy because the statute would prohibit firms from combining to take advantage of economies of scale made possible by recent technological development.[41] During this period, roughly 1890-1930, American economists developed a set of theories that found consumer benefits in concentration and large firms probably to a greater extent than did any economic model until the rise of the Chicago School.[42]

---

the degree of danger that the Justice Department perceived in high market concentration. The 1968 Guidelines reflect the Justice Department's perception that concentrated markets discouraged vigorous price competition and encouraged other kinds of conduct, "such as use of inefficient methods of production or excessive promotional expenditures, of an economically undesirable nature." 1968 Merger Guidelines, *supra* note 35. On the other hand, virtually the only perceived danger under the 1984 guidelines is collusion. Another important difference between the two sets of guidelines is the concentration *level* at which mergers are considered to be dangerous. The 1968 guidelines, following Bain, regarded mergers as anticompetitive at generally lower concentration levels than do the 1984 guidelines.

38. For some insights into pre-1950s models, see Rowe, *supra* note 3.

39. Even in the early period the government may have followed prevailing economic theory. During that time the majority of economists believed that the antitrust laws were useless or perhaps even harmful, because they would deprive firms of the ability to take full advantage of scale economies. The government, for its part, brought very few antitrust cases during the first decade after the Sherman Act was passed. *See* W. LETWIN, LAW AND ECONOMIC POLICY IN AMERICA: THE EVOLUTION OF THE SHERMAN ANTITRUST ACT 106-42 (1965). Some Chicago School antitrust scholars have argued that the framers of the Sherman Act essentially had the market efficiency model in mind in 1890. *See* text at notes 179-80 *infra.*

40. One important economist who took exception to the consensus was Henry Carter Adams. *See* Adams, *Relation of the State to Industrial Action,* 1 PUBLICATIONS AM. ECON. A. 465 (1887). Adams argued for a certain amount of government intervention against monopolies; however, he believed it should be directed at monopoly conduct rather than market structure, which Adams believed was predetermined by economies of scale.

41. *See* Hatfield, *The Chicago Trust Conference,* 8 J. POL. ECON. 1, 6 (1899) (noting that a consensus of economists at this important meeting believed that the problems of high concentration and large firm size at which the Sherman Act was directed were the "outgrowth of natural industrial evolution," and were therefore efficient). The proceedings of this meeting were published as CHICAGO CONFERENCE ON TRUSTS: SPEECHES, DEBATES, RESOLUTIONS (1900).

42. In large part the free market bias of economists during this period may be attributed to the powerful influence of Alfred Marshall, whose *Principles of Economics* (1890) restored neoclassical price theory to its most eminent position since the publication of Adam Smith's *Wealth of Nations* (1776). For a summary of economists' typical attitudes toward the Sherman Act and

The First New Deal[43] saw substantial inroads of economic theory into antitrust policy[44] — but at that time the dominant economic theory was dedicated to the Progressive Era economic proposition that regulation, including self-regulation and creative cooperation, would be much more efficient than ruthless competition in increasing American wealth.[45] Only after the National Industrial Recovery Act was declared unconstitutional did the administration bring in a different group of economists who were much more aggressive in their antitrust enforcement goals.[46] Their work became the basis for the "workable competition" theory that dominated antitrust policy in the 1950s.

The workable competition theory was probably the first economic model expressly designed to be a tool of antitrust policy. Economist J.M. Clark, who first developed the theory,[47] accepted the most important premise of the far more academic monopolistic competition school:[48] that widespread product differentiation limits the degree to which firms in the same product market compete with one another and therefore permits them to raise price above marginal cost. However, from that point Clark attempted to define an amount of competition that could realistically be achieved by a real world enforcement policy.

Antitrust policymakers were happy to accept Clark's call for an antitrust policy that would respond to a complex economic model. The 1955 report of the Attorney General's National Committee to Study the Antitrust Laws relied heavily on Clark's workable competition thesis.[49] The Committee concluded that the theory of workable

---

existing antitrust enforcement during this period, see J.D. CLARK, THE FEDERAL TRUST POLICY 100-01 (1931); F. FETTER, MODERN ECONOMIC PROBLEMS 533 (2d ed. 1922); S. FINE, LAISSEZ FAIRE AND THE GENERAL-WELFARE STATE 139, 337 (1956).

Even liberal and progressive economists such as Richard T. Ely and Charles Van Hise were pessimistic about the federal antitrust laws. Both believed that economies of scale, particularly in innovation, necessitated the growth of monopoly in high technology markets. Antitrust would deprive firms in these markets from achieving optimal productive efficiency. Both Ely and Van Hise preferred a regime of broad federal price regulation rather than enforced "competition" along the lines of the neoclassical model. See R. ELY, MONOPOLIES AND TRUSTS (1900); C. VAN HISE, CONCENTRATION AND CONTROL: A SOLUTION TO THE TRUST PROBLEM IN THE UNITED STATES 76-87, 255-56 (1912).

43. I am referring to the period from the election of Franklin Roosevelt in 1932 until the National Industrial Recovery Act was struck down in Schechter Poultry Corp. v. United States, 295 U.S. 495 (1935).

44. See E. HAWLEY, *supra* note 3, at 41-46.

45. *Id.* For an analysis of the perceived dichotomy between "competition" and "cooperation" during this period, see Hovenkamp, *Evolutionary Models in Jurisprudence,* 64 TEXAS L. REV., in press.

46. *Id.* at 47-52, 283-303.

47. Clark, *supra* note 4.

48. E. CHAMBERLIN, *supra* note 3.

49. 1955 COMMITTEE REPORT, *supra* note 4, at 318-39. The report defined "workable com-

competition would operate as a kind of practical theory of "second best" that would permit antitrust enforcers to consider the differences between the economic model of perfect competition and the apparent degree of competition that existed in the real world.[50] The result was a state of affairs that was not capable of being precisely modeled, and this may explain the difficulties that some later economists had with the concept of workable competition.[51] In short, the concept of workable competition was an early attempt to create an economic model that took into account such real world market imperfections as economies of scale, information failures, and transaction costs. The goal of antitrust policy within this model was to discern areas in which legal rules or administrative controls could encourage a market to perform more similarly to the perfect competition model.[52]

Clearly, antitrust policymakers did not first discover economic the-

---

petition" as "the economists' attempt to identify the conditions which could provide appropriate leads for policy in assuring society the substance of the advantages which competition should provide." *Id.* at 320.

The Committee was chaired by Stanley N. Barnes and S. Chesterfield Oppenheim and included many economists and antitrust lawyers. The report is analyzed in T. KOVALEFF, BUSINESS AND GOVERNMENT DURING THE EISENHOWER ADMINISTRATION: A STUDY OF THE ANTITRUST POLICY OF THE ANTITRUST DIVISION OF THE JUSTICE DEPARTMENT 17-48 (1980). *See also* Hovenkamp, Book Review, 33 HASTINGS L.J. 755 (1982) (reviewing Kovaleff).

50. The theory of second-best suggests that in a world in which a certain amount of monopoly power (positive deviations from marginal cost pricing) is pervasive, an increase of competition in one area will not necessarily improve general welfare, for the increase may be more than offset by decreases elsewhere. Clark recognized already in 1940 that

[i]f there are, for example, five conditions, all of which are essential to perfect competition, and the first is lacking in a given case, then it no longer follows that we are necessarily better off for the presence of any one of the other four. In the absence of the first, it is *a priori* quite possible that the second and third may become positive detriments; and a workably satisfactory result may depend on achieving some degree of "imperfection" in these other two factors.

Clark, *supra* note 4, at 242. For further elaboration of the conditions that would facilitate the achievement of workable competition within Clark's model, see Sosnick, *A Critique of Concepts of Workable Competition*, 72 Q. J. ECON. 380 (1958).

For technical development of the theory of second-best, see Lipsey & Lancaster, *The General Theory of Second-Best*, 24 REV. ECON. STUD. 11 (1956). For less technical descriptions of the theory, see H. HOVENKAMP, *supra* note 17, at 37-39; F. SCHERER, INDUSTRIAL MARKET STRUCTURE AND ECONOMIC PERFORMANCE 24-29 (2d ed. 1980). Clark was perhaps the first economist to recognize the theory of second-best and deal with some of its ramifications. *See* C. FERGUSON, A MACROECONOMIC THEORY OF WORKABLE COMPETITION 27 (1964).

51. One example is George Stigler, who faulted the principle of workable competition for not containing any mechanism for quantifying *how much* competition is "workable." G. STIGLER, *supra* note 10, at 12; *see also* 1955 COMMITTEE REPORT, *supra* note 4, at 339 (noting that some members of the Attorney General's committee made a similar criticism).

52. *See* Markham, *An Alternative Approach to the Concept of Workable Competition,* 40 AM. ECON. REV. 49 (1950):

An industry may be judged to be workably competitive when, after the structural characteristics of its market and the dynamic forms that shaped them have been thoroughly examined, there is no clearly indicated change that can be effected through public policy measures that would result in greater social gains than social losses.

Id. at 361.

ory in the last decade. More accurately, they changed theories. However, the statement that recent antitrust policy was the first to develop an "economic approach" may mean that antitrust policymakers have only recently relied *exclusively* on economics. That is, earlier courts and enforcers may have recognized economic goals for antitrust policy, but they mixed these goals in some way with distributive goals. After the 1977 *Sylvania*[53] decision, or perhaps after the 1981 appointment of Mr. Baxter to head the Antitrust Division of the Justice Department,[54] however, antitrust policymakers may first have begun to consider efficiency goals exclusively. If that characterization is correct, one can say with some meaning that the rise of Chicago School antitrust policy represents the beginning of an "economic approach" — that is, an approach concerned exclusively with efficiency.

This view is subject to both an objection and a qualification, however. The objection is that it is probably untrue. Although the Justice Department may be going through a period in which it recognizes efficiency as the exclusive goal of the antitrust laws,[55] the Supreme Court has not adopted such a general antitrust policy, and some of its recent decisions seem inconsistent with such a policy.[56]

The qualification is much more fundamental and goes to the nature of the relationship between economic theory and public policymaking. Economists have long stated that theoretical economic models cannot evaluate a state of affairs on the basis of how its wealth is distributed. These models are capable only of distinguishing the efficient from the inefficient.[57] However, for just as long, economists — even free mar-

---

53. Continental T.V. v. GTE Sylvania, 433 U.S. 36 (1977).

54. *See* note 26 *supra.*

55. However, this author knows of no official policy statement of either the Department of Justice or the Federal Trade Commission stating that distributive concerns are irrelevant to antitrust policy. Furthermore, the Justice Department continues to recognize distributive concerns in antitrust law when those concerns are clearly expressed in congressional policy. For example, the Justice Department's 1984 Merger Guidelines continue to recognize the failing company defense in merger cases, even though the defense has traditionally been viewed as not based on efficiency but rather on distributive concerns. *See* 1984 Merger Guidelines, *supra* note 36, at 26,837; P. AREEDA & H. HOVENKAMP, ANTITRUST LAW ¶ 925.1 (Supp. 1986) (forthcoming). However, for a recent argument that even the failing company defense has a basis in efficiency, see Campbell, *The Efficiency of the Failing Company Defense,* 63 TEXAS L. REV. 251 (1984). For responses, see Friedman, *Untangling the Failing Company Doctrine,* 64 TEXAS L. REV., in press; McChesney, *Defending the Failing-Firm Defense,* 65 NEB. L. REV. 1 (1986).

56. *See, e.g.,* Monsanto Co. v. Spray-Rite Serv., 465 U.S. 752 (1984) (condemning vertical restraints by a nonmonopolist, in spite of a substantial Chicago School argument that the nonmonopolist cannot create market power by means of vertical restrictions); Easterbrook, *supra* note 1; Hovenkamp, *Vertical Restrictions and Monopoly Power,* 64 B.U. L. REV. 521 (1984); *see also* Arizona v. Maricopa County Medical Socy., 457 U.S. 332 (1982) (condemning a maximum price fixing agreement under the *per se* rule, in the face of substantial evidence that the arrangement was efficient).

57. However, the distinction between efficiency and distribution of wealth was not clearly established until the ordinalist revolution in the 1930s. The ordinalists generally attacked the

ket economists — have recognized an important difference between theoretical economics and public policymaking, particularly if the policies are being made in a democratic State.

The public purpose of theoretical economics is not to eliminate distributive justice as a public policy concern.[58] Rather, it is to enable policymakers to make some judgments about the cost or effectiveness of a particular policy. The relative weight to be given to efficiency concerns in policymaking varies with the ability of the relevant economic model to identify efficient policies in the real world. If the "efficient" solution to a policy problem is clear, and the degree to which alternative solutions deviate from the efficient solution is also quite clear, then policymakers are likely to weigh efficiency concerns heavily. These efficiency concerns will trump competing distributive concerns unless those concerns are very powerful.

On the other hand, if the application of the economic model to real world policymaking is not particularly clear, or if the model is very complex, then the "efficient" solution to a real world problem will not always emerge as obvious. In that case, distributive or political concerns, which are always more or less obvious, will weigh much more heavily.[59] For example, if the relevant economic model does not reveal unambiguously that big business is more efficient than small business, but the small business lobby is very powerful, a legislature is likely to be influenced very strongly by the lobby.

One important difference between the neoclassical market efficiency model and earlier economic models is that the neoclassical model claims a much greater ability to distinguish between efficient and inefficient policies. In this respect, the neoclassical model's largest virtue is its simplicity. The monopolistic competition model that was created by Chamberlin, and which influenced antitrust policy during the New Deal, was far more complicated and made it far more difficult to examine a particular business practice and proclaim it efficient or

---

notion that one could evaluate wealth distributions on the basis of interpersonal comparisons of utilities. *See* text at notes 113-22 *infra.*

58. *See* W. SHEPHERD, PUBLIC POLICIES TOWARD BUSINESS 5-6 (7th ed. 1985). However, some members of the Chicago School might disagree. *See* Posner, *Economics, Politics, and the Reading of Statutes and the Constitution,* 49 U. CHI. L. REV. 263 (1982) [hereinafter cited as Posner, *The Reading of Statutes*] (arguing that "public interest" statutes are efficient); Posner, *The Ethical and Political Basis of the Efficiency Norm in Common Law Adjudication,* 8 HOFSTRA L. REV. 487 (1980) [hereinafter cited as Posner, *The Efficiency Norm*] (arguing that the common law ought to pursue efficiency as a goal).

59. The point is made forcefully in M. HORWITZ, THE TRANSFORMATION OF AMERICAN LAW, 1780-1860, 99-101 (1977). *See also* Hovenkamp, *Technology, Politics, and Regulated Monopoly: An American Historical Perspective,* 62 TEXAS L. REV. 1263, 1279 (1984); Kainen, *Nineteenth Century Interpretations of the Federal Contract Clause: The Transformation from Vested to Substantive Rights Against the State,* 31 BUFFALO L. REV. 381, 396 (1982).

inefficient.[60] For example, within that model product differentiation could increase consumer choice or encourage innovation; however, it could also be a mechanism by which large firms in concentrated industries avoided price competition with one another.[61] Likewise, Joe Bain's complicated notion of "conditions of entry" appeared simultaneously to praise and condemn economies of scale in the production process. On the one hand, economies of scale reduced costs and facilitated lower consumer prices. On the other, they made it more difficult for new firms to enter the market and, at least in concentrated industries, facilitated oligopoly behavior.[62]

Within the Chicago School model, on the other hand, both of these problems have unambiguous solutions. Product differentiation is almost always a blessing for consumers. When it is not, the firms participating in the differentiation will be injured rather than benefitted, for customers will refuse to buy.[63] Likewise, economies of scale are an unmixed blessing in all but extremely concentrated markets.[64] In any case, the welfare of the small business in such markets should be ignored.

Today, however, antitrust policy is coming increasingly under the influence of a "post-Chicago" economics that is both more complex and more ambiguous than the Chicago School model. For example, within the "strategic behavior" models championed by such people as Oliver Williamson and Steven C. Salop, certain phenomena such as economies of scale are not necessarily an unmixed blessing. Often scale economies can be manipulated by firms in such a way as to permit monopoly pricing while discouraging competitive entry.[65]

This new complexity makes it much more difficult for enforcement agencies and particularly for courts to make judgments about whether a particular practice, such as the creation of a very large plant in a market subject to substantial economies of scale,[66] is competitive or anticompetitive. The likely effect of such complexity will be to make

---

60. E. CHAMBERLIN, *supra* note 3.

61. *Id.* at 56-57.

62. *See* J. BAIN, *supra* note 30, at 53-113.

63. *See* R. BORK, *supra* note 6, at 312-13.

64. *Id.* at 312-29.

65. *See* Salop, *supra* note 23; Williamson, *Predatory Pricing, supra* note 23; *see also* Scherer, *supra* note 23, at 697-704 (arguing that frequently vertical price restraints can be inefficient and anticompetitive).

66. *See In re* E. I. du Pont de Nemours & Co., 96 F.T.C. 653 (1980) (refusing to find an illegal attempt to monopolize in du Pont's development of a new, lost-cost process for manufacturing a chemical, its refusal to license the process to anyone else, and its construction of a plant large enough to handle all anticipated demand for the chemical).

more room once again for distributive concerns.[67]

III.   CHICAGO SCHOOL ANTITRUST AND THE NEOCLASSICAL MARKET EFFICIENCY MODEL

Orthodox Chicago School antitrust policy is predicated on two assumptions about the goals of the federal antitrust laws: (1) the best policy tool currently available for maximizing economic efficiency in the real world is the neoclassical price theory model; and (2) the pursuit of economic efficiency should be the exclusive goal of antitrust enforcement policy.

Both of these statements are controversial. The first one raises several economic questions about the internal integrity of the neoclassical price theory model, as well as questions about the ability of *any* economic model to identify efficient policies in the real world. The second statement is probably contrary to the intent of the Congresses that drafted the various antitrust laws. These criticisms are addressed in subsequent sections of this article.[68]

No attempt is made here to describe the content of the neoclassical market efficiency model. That has been done many times elsewhere.[69] However, the following discussion summarizes a few of the model's basic assumptions and principles that have been particularly important in Chicago School antitrust scholarship.

(1) Economic efficiency, the pursuit of which should be the exclusive goal of the antitrust laws, consists of two relevant parts: allocative efficiency and productive efficiency.[70] Occasionally practices that increase a firm's productive efficiency reduce the market's allocative efficiency. For example, construction of a large plant and acquisition of a large market share may increase a firm's productive efficiency by enabling it to achieve economies of scale; however, these actions may simultaneously reduce allocative efficiency by facilitating monopoly pricing. A properly defined antitrust policy will attempt to maximize *net* efficiency gains.[71]

---

67. There is a different possible response to such complexity: in cases of ambiguity assume that a practice is efficient and leave it alone; or alternatively, assume that the effect of an error of underdeterrence will be self-correcting, while one of overdeterrence will not be. Under either assumption the practice in question should not be condemned. *See* Easterbrook, *Limits, supra* note 8, at 2-3. The effect of Professor Easterbrook's argument is to say not merely that efficiency concerns should always trump distributive concerns in antitrust policy, but that distributive concerns are irrelevant even when efficiency consequences are unknown.

68. *See* text at notes 167-97 & 199-318 *infra.*

69. *See, e.g.,* R. BORK, *supra* note 6, at 90-160; R. POSNER, *supra* note 19.

70. The two are distinguished in the discussion at notes 123-42 *infra.*

71. In Bork's words, "[t]he whole task of antitrust can be summed up as the effort to improve

(2) Most markets are competitive, even if they contain a relatively small number of sellers. Furthermore, product differentiation tends to undermine competition far less than was formerly presumed. As a result, neither high market concentration nor product differentiation are the anticompetitive problems earlier oligopoly theorists believed them to be.[72]

(3) Monopoly, when it exists, tends to be self-correcting; that is, the monopolist's higher profits generally attract new entry into the monopolist's market, with the result that the monopolist's position is quickly eroded. About the best that the judicial process can do is hasten the correction process.[73]

(4) "Natural" barriers to entry are more imagined than real. As a general rule investment will flow into any market where the rate of return is high. The one significant exception consists of barriers to entry that are not natural — that is, barriers that are created by government itself. In most markets the government would be best off if it left entry and exit unregulated.[74]

(5) Economies of scale are far more pervasive than economists

---

allocative efficiency without impairing productive efficiency so greatly as to produce either no gain or a net loss in consumer welfare." R. BORK, *supra* note 6, at 91.

72. The modern Chicago School argument that even highly concentrated markets can perform competitively is made in R. BORK, *supra* note 6, at 179-91; Y. BROZEN, CONCENTRATION, MERGERS AND PUBLIC POLICY (1982); J. MCGEE, IN DEFENSE OF INDUSTRIAL CONCENTRATION (1971). *See also* Peltzman, *The Gains and Losses from Industrial Concentration*, 20 J. L. & ECON. 229 (1977).

Judge Posner, whose own antitrust policy is distinctively Chicago School, represents the "new" Chicago approach which is much more cautious about oligopoly than the approach of Brozen, Bork, or McGee. *See* R. POSNER, *supra* note 19, at 42-50 (arguing that oligopoly pricing, or tacit collusion, can be a significant problem in concentrated markets).

The more traditional argument about the danger of oligopoly pricing in concentrated markets can be found in C. KAYSEN & D. TURNER, *supra* note 33, at 25-43, which finds a dangerous propensity to oligopoly in markets with an eight-firm concentration level (CR8) of 50% — that is, a market in which the eight largest firms collectively occupy 50% of the market. Such a market could have a largest firm with a market share of as little as 7% and a Hirfandahl-Hirschman Index (HHI) reading as low as 500 or 600.

The Justice Department's 1984 Merger Guidelines do not follow the extreme Chicago School theory, but rather reflect a position between the "diehard" Chicago position and the Kaysen-Turner position. The guidelines perceive a real danger of oligopoly performance in markets with an HHI in excess of 1800. 1984 Merger Guidelines, *supra* note 36, at 26,823.

The traditional argument that product differentiation is an important mechanism by which oligopoly firms facilitate monopoly pricing can be found in J. BAIN, *supra* note 30, at 114-43. However, within the tacit collusion model developed by the Chicago School and written into the 1984 Merger Guidelines, product differentiation is regarded as making markets *more* competitive by making collusion more difficult. Thus the Justice Department is *less* likely to challenge a merger in a market in which product differentiation is substantial. 1984 Merger Guidelines, *supra* note 36, at 26,833.

73. *See* Easterbrook, *Limits, supra* note 8, at 2 (arguing that in the long run monopolies correct themselves; the goal of antitrust is merely to "speed up the arrival of the long run").

74. *See* R. BORK, *supra* note 6, at 310-29; *see also* Demsetz, *Barriers to Entry*, 72 AM. ECON. REV. 47 (1982); Weizsacker, *A Welfare Analysis of Barriers to Entry*, 11 BELL J. ECON. 399 (1980).

once believed, largely because earlier economists looked only at intra-plant or production economies, and neglected economies of distribution. As a result, many more industries than were formerly thought may operate most economically only at fairly high concentration levels.[75]

(6) Business firms are profit-maximizers. That is, their managers generally make decisions that they anticipate will make the firm more profitable than any alternative decision would. The model would not be undermined, however, if it should turn out that many firms are not profit maximizers, but are motivated by some alternative goal, such as revenue maximization, sales maximization, or "satisficing."[76] The integrity of the market efficiency model requires only that a few firms be profit-maximizers. In that case, the profits and market shares of these firms will grow at the expense of other firms in the market.[77]

---

75. The relevant issues are presented in the debate between John S. McGee, representing the Chicago position, and Frederic M. Scherer, representing a more traditional position, in INDUSTRIAL CONCENTRATION: THE NEW LEARNING 15-113 (H. Goldschmid, H. Mann & J. Weston eds. 1974).

76. The term "satisficing" refers to a theory of firm behavior that is contrary to the theory of profit maximization adopted by the Chicago School today. A firm "satisfices" when its management adopts a certain goal for profits, sales, or market share and then tries to meet the goal but not necessarily to exceed it. The theory posits that initially the firm's management will not be inclined to set an extremely high goal, because if they later fail to achieve it they will appear to the stockholders to be failures. Furthermore, once the goal is established the stockholders will demand an even higher goal in the future, and that higher goal will then be more difficult to achieve.

The theory of satisficing is part of a more general theory of the firm, which hypothesizes that the owners of capital (stockholders) and the managers of capital may have different motives, and that this circumstance makes the firm less efficient than the Chicago School would have us believe.

77. See R. POSNER & F. EASTERBROOK, ANTITRUST: CASES, ECONOMIC NOTES AND OTHER MATERIALS 855-57 (2d ed. 1981). A good discussion of some of the alternatives to profit-maximization is contained in P. ASCH, ECONOMIC THEORY AND THE ANTITRUST DILEMMA 90-101 (1970).

The classic book arguing that the separation of ownership and management in the large business corporation has encouraged firms to pursue goals other than profit maximization is A. BERLE, JR. & G. MEANS, THE MODERN CORPORATION AND PRIVATE PROPERTY (1932). See the symposium on the Berle and Means study, much of it written from a Chicago School perspective, in 26 J. L. & ECON. 235 (1983).

Those who believe that most firms are not profit-maximizers have the additional obligation of demonstrating why that fact should be relevant to antitrust policy. For one valiant but ultimately inconclusive attempt to demonstrate such relevance, see Kaplow, *supra* note 23, at 550-52. One possibility, of course, is that the antitrust laws should protect firms from the consequences of their own inefficient behavior. More plausibly, perhaps the antitrust laws should protect outsiders from non-profit-maximizing behavior which injures the actor, but also injures those with whom the actor deals.

The theory that firms are not rational profit-maximizers can be used to provide explanations for why firms do certain things that seem irrational. For example, see R. LAFFERTY, R. LANDE, & J. KIRKWOOD, IMPACT EVALUATIONS OF FEDERAL TRADE COMMISSION VERTICAL RESTRAINTS CASES 11-13 (1984), a recent Federal Trade Commission study of vertical restraints finding that at least one firm used vertical restrictions such as resale price maintenance in order to gain access to the market — that is, in order to purchase shelf space from retailers who would be unwilling to display new merchandise unless they could be guaranteed a high profit. The

(7) Antitrust enforcement should be designed in such a way as to penalize conduct precisely to the point that it is inefficient, but to tolerate or encourage it when it is efficient.[78] During the Warren Court era, antitrust enforcement was excessive, and often penalized efficient conduct.[79]

(8) The decision to make the neoclassical market efficiency model the exclusive guide for antitrust policy is nonpolitical.

The "neoclassical" nature of the Chicago School model is well illustrated by the list. The classical model originated before the rise of Big Government during the New Deal, and therefore before the State had become explicitly involved in the redistribution of social wealth. In the eighteenth century the redistribution of wealth was not perceived to be an important state function.[80] Within the market efficiency model, wealth distribution is not an "economic" concern at all.[81]

The Chicago School market efficiency model represents an explicit rejection of several revisionist economic theories which themselves had rejected various elements of the classical model. For example, the theory that firms in highly concentrated markets fail to perform competitively was a qualification of the naive classical model, which treated all firms as absolute price takers.[82] Orthodox Chicagoans such as Robert

---

study found, however, that the restrictions often persisted after the firm imposing them had become well-established and the restrictions actually reduced the firm's profits. *Id.* at 13. They were preserved largely as a result of managerial nonresponsiveness to the changed situation. In such a case it appears that the restrictions may have been procompetitive when they were first employed by a struggling new entrant, but were inefficient when the firm later became established. *See also* Kaplow, *supra* note 23, at 551-52 (arguing that firms may employ tying arrangements in order to increase revenues, rather than profits).

Whether "self-deterring" inefficient conduct should be condemned by the antitrust laws is a matter of some controversy. *See* Easterbrook, *Predatory Strategies and Counterstrategies,* 48 U. CHI. L. REV. 263, 331-32 (1981) (arguing that predatory pricing should not be condemned until after it has succeeded); Williamson, *Antitrust Enforcement, supra* note 23, at 312 (suggesting that certain instances of failed attempts at predatory pricing could be condemned).

78. *See* Landes, *Optimal Sanctions for Antitrust Violations,* 50 U. CHI. L. REV. 652 (1983); Schwartz, *An Overview of the Economics of Antitrust Enforcement,* 68 GEO. L.J. 1075 (1980); *see also* K. ELZINGA & W. BREIT, THE ANTITRUST PENALTIES: A STUDY IN LAW AND ECONOMICS (1976); H. HOVENKAMP, *supra* note 17, at 379-407.

79. *See* Easterbrook, *Is There a Ratchet in Antitrust Law?,* 60 TEXAS L. REV. 705, 714 n.42 (1982).

80. The State may, however, have redistributed wealth through court decisions rather than by means of taxation and social programs. *See* M. HORWITZ, *supra* note 59, at 99-101.

81. *See* text at notes 95-105 *infra.*

82. For example, there is no well-developed theory of oligopoly in A. SMITH, *supra* note 42, or in A. MARSHALL, *supra* note 42. With the exception of Cournot's simple oligopoly theory developed in 1838, modern economic theories of oligopoly are a product of the 1890s and the first three decades of the twentieth century. *See* A. COURNOT, RESEARCHES INTO THE MATHEMATICAL PRINCIPLES OF THE THEORY OF WEALTH (N. Bacon trans. 1897) (1st ed. Paris 1838). In chronological order, the major historical contributions to the theory of oligopoly through the 1930s were Bertrand, *Theorie Mathematique de la Richesse Sociale,* 1883 JOURNAL DES SA-

Bork have come close to rejecting the theory of oligopoly outright.[83]

Likewise, the classical model never seriously questioned that the firm's principal economic goal is the maximization of its profits. The arguments of Berle and Means,[84] who believed that firms do not maximize profits, were a product of the social science movement and Legal Realism of the 1930s and their attendant injection of sociological and psychological principles into theories about firm behavior.[85] Within the Chicago School model humankind's economic motives "trump" any noneconomic motives or else these noneconomic motives are irrelevant to the working of the model.[86]

Classical price theory was not heavily concerned with the "conditions of entry" that might permit incumbent firms to earn monopoly profits while outsiders were deterred from coming in.[87] To the extent entry barriers were considered in antitrust economics before the 1950s, they were generally "barriers" created by the firms themselves — such as covenants not to compete contained in monopolists' purchase and sale contracts, lease-only policies and maintenance clauses that allegedly reduced the entry opportunities of independent competitors,[88] or entry deterrence through predatory pricing.[89] The notion that the market might contain "natural" barriers to entry — that is, barriers inherent in the technology or economic structure of the market, and not products of the dominant firm's strategic decisionmaking — was first elaborated in the 1940s and 1950s.[90] One of the significant accomplishments of the Chicago School has been its debunking of the notion

---

VANTS 499; F. EDGEWORTH, *The Pure Theory of Monopoly*, in PAPERS RELATING TO POLITICAL ECONOMY 111 (1925; originally published in French in 1897); Hotelling, *Stability in Competition*, 39 ECON. J. 41 (1929); E. CHAMBERLIN, *supra* note 3.

83. R. BORK, *supra* note 6, at 92.

84. *See* note 77 *supra*.

85. *See* E. PURCELL, THE CRISIS OF DEMOCRATIC THEORY: SCIENTIFIC NATURALISM & THE PROBLEM OF VALUE 86-87 (1973); Kirkendall, *A.A. Berle, Jr.: Student of the Corporation, 1917-1932*, 35 BUS. HIST. REV. 43 (1961).

86. That is, the Chicago School model may allow that occasionally firms or actors in them make decisions not motivated by profit-maximization. However, these decisions are either random and incapable of being fit into the profit-maximization model, or else they are of no consequence to antitrust policy because they are self-deterring. A firm that does not make profit-maximizing decisions will, other things being equal, lose market share to one that does.

87. Likewise, Alfred Marshall's *Principles of Economics* generally assumes that entry is free, although he did acknowledge that entry takes time and that monopoly profits could be earned during the interval. A. MARSHALL, *supra* note 42, at 411.

88. For example, see the consideration of entry barriers in United States v. United Shoe Mach., 110 F. Supp. 295, 312-20, 323-25 (D. Mass. 1953), *affd. per curiam*, 347 U.S. 521 (1954).

89. *See* McGee, *Predatory Price Cutting: the Standard Oil (N.J.) Case*, 1 J. L. & ECON. 137 (1958).

90. Principally in J. BAIN, *supra* note 30.

that the world is filled with such "natural" entry barriers.[91] Barriers, when they exist, are generally artificial, created by either the government or else by the dominant, incumbent firms. The Chicago School has been quick to recognize the role of the State in the creation of entry barriers.[92] This paper later argues, however, that Chicagoans have often been slow to recognize the strategic creation of entry barriers by incumbent firms.[93]

Perhaps most significantly, Chicago School price theory adheres closely to the classical school's strong preference for a "free" market — that is, a market left alone by the State and its agencies unless a powerful reason exists for interfering.[94] Each of the "deviations" from the classical model described above — the oligopoly theory, the rejection of the profit-maximization theory, the entry barrier theory, and most importantly, the theory that the State should actively redistribute wealth — suggested increasing amounts of government intervention in the market process. In rejecting these theories, the Chicago School has restored the State to the position of neutral umpire, which it held in the classical model.

Finally, a word must be said about the eighth premise in the above list — the suggestion that Chicago School antitrust policy is "nonpolitical."[95] The classical market economist's notion of efficiency purports to evaluate states of affairs on the basis of criteria that have nothing to do with the way wealth is distributed.[96] The principle of potential Pareto efficiency or wealth maximization,[97] which guides Chicago School antitrust analysis, identifies a policy as "efficient" if total gains experienced by all those who gain from the policy are greater than the total losses experienced by all those who lose. The *identity* of the gainers and losers is irrelevant. If a policy produces bigger gains to businesses than it does losses to consumers, the Chicago School would approve the policy as efficient. However, it would also approve a policy that produced larger gains to consumers than losses to businesses. For this reason the Chicago School ideologist can

---

91. The strongest statement of the Chicago School position on entry barriers is probably R. BORK, *supra* note 6, at 310-29. *See also* Demsetz, *supra* note 74; R. POSNER, *supra* note 19, at 59; G. STIGLER, *supra* note 10, at 67-70.

92. *See* R. BORK, *supra* note 6, at 310-29.

93. *See* text at notes 247-55 *infra.*

94. A good statement of the position is Easterbrook, *Limits, supra* note 8, especially at 2-3, 5-7, 9.

95. *See* R. BORK, *supra* note 6, at 418-25; R. POSNER, THE ECONOMICS OF JUSTICE 92-94 (1981); Bork, *The Rule of Reason and the Per Se Concept: Price Fixing and Market Division,* 74 YALE L.J. 775, 831-32 (1965). *See generally* Pitofsky, *supra* note 12, at 1051.

96. *See generally* Hovenkamp, *supra* note 18.

97. *See* text at notes 135-42 *infra.*

argue that he is not taking sides in any political dispute about how wealth or entitlements from the State ought to be distributed to conflicting interest groups. Such things should always go where they will do the most *net* good.[98]

Outsiders regard this Chicago School claim of freedom from political interest with a good deal of skepticism, and some believe it to be simple hogwash, or perhaps even a cover for a very strong, probusiness political bias that works to the benefit of the rich.[99]

The claim that a particular policy has managed to transcend politics is both appealing and dangerous. Its appeal is that it permits the creation of a stable policy that will not change with every substantial change in political leadership.[100] Antitrust policy has been particularly susceptible to such changes. The danger, on the other hand, is that the assertion takes a particular policy out of the political process — which means, in the case of a democracy, that it is taken out of the democratic process. At the extreme, as is argued below, Chicago School policy does exactly that and permits the antitrust policymaker to ignore the legislative history of the antitrust laws.[101]

To be sure, within the American constitutional system we *do* attempt to exempt certain claims from democratic control — for example, claims involving the right to speak or the right to be free of discrimination based on one's race or gender.[102] At one time Americans came very close to having a constitutional right to a free market, governed pretty much by the neoclassical market efficiency model.[103] Today, however, a large literature argues that the constitutional doctrine of "liberty of contract" was anything but nonpolitical; on the contrary, it was a shrewd and calculated use of the political process to protect an established set of political interests from being displaced by

---

98. *See* note 58 *supra.*

99. Good examples of this kind of criticism are Horwitz, *Law and Economics: Science or Politics?,* 8 HOFSTRA L. REV. 905 (1980); Kennedy, *Cost-Benefit Analysis of Entitlement Problems: A Critique,* 33 STAN. L. REV. 387 (1981). For a critique of Kennedy's argument, see Markovits, *Duncan's Do Nots: Cost-Benefit Analysis and the Determination of Legal Entitlements,* 36 STAN. L. REV. 1169 (1984).

100. Bork, *supra* note 95, at 832.

101. *See* text at notes 167-98 *infra.*

102. *See* J. ELY, DEMOCRACY AND DISTRUST: A THEORY OF JUDICIAL REVIEW 73-104 (1980). *See generally* R. DWORKIN, TAKING RIGHTS SERIOUSLY (1977).

103. *See* Murphy v. Sardell, 269 U.S. 530 (1925) (striking down a state minimum wage statute under the fourteenth amendment); Adkins v. Children's Hosp., 261 U.S. 525 (1923) (striking down a District of Columbia minimum wage statute under the fifth amendment); Lochner v. New York, 198 U.S. 45 (1905) (striking down under the fourteenth amendment due process clause a New York statute that prohibited bakers from working more than ten hours per day or sixty hours per week).

new political interests.[104]

Within the liberal tradition, policy claims have often been defended with an argument that they are nonpolitical — that is, that they are somehow "best" for everyone, and not merely for the interest groups making the claims.[105] The problem with all such arguments is that they can be neither verified nor falsified in any general way. That is equally true of the claim that the market efficiency model is nonpolitical. Furthermore, it is easy to identify the beneficiaries of Chicago School antitrust policy — probably big business, certainly vertically integrated firms, perhaps some consumers. Likewise, one can predict that small businesses, less efficient firms, and perhaps some other consumers will be losers. However, we do not have the tools to quantify these gains and losses and net them out over all of society except in very easy cases. That leaves us with only the *claim* to political transcendence. Historically, many ideologies have made that claim, but none have been able to convince the rest of the world.

IV.   CHICAGO SCHOOL ANTITRUST POLICY: CRITICISM FROM
OUTSIDE THE MODEL

The neoclassical market efficiency model is designed to identify the prerequisites for efficient market performance, and to explain how deviations from perfect competition affect market efficiency. Given certain assumptions, the model can identify the efficiency consequences of certain behavior. For example, given an assumption of zero transaction costs, it predicts that vertical restrictions do not increase a firm's ability to earn monopoly profits.[106]

The application of the market efficiency model to federal antitrust

---

104. *See, e.g.*, L. FRIEDMAN, A HISTORY OF AMERICAN LAW 358-62 (2d ed. 1985); M. HORWITZ, *supra* note 59, at 259-66; P. MURPHY, THE CONSTITUTION IN CRISIS TIMES 1918-1969, at 41-67 (1972); A. PAUL, CONSERVATIVE CRISIS AND THE RULE OF LAW: ATTITUDES OF BAR AND BENCH, 1887-1895, at 1-81 (1960). Holmes, a contemporary observer, agreed:
When socialism first began to be talked about, the comfortable classes of the community were a good deal frightened. I suspect that this fear has influenced judicial action both here and in England . . . . I think that something similar has led people who no longer hope to control the legislatures to look to the courts as expounders of the Constitutions, and that in some courts new principles have been discovered outside the bodies of those instruments, which may be generalized into acceptance of the economic doctrines which prevailed about fifty years ago . . . .
Holmes, *The Path of the Law*, 10 HARV. L. REV. 457, 467-68 (1897).

105. *See, e.g.*, R. DWORKIN, *supra* note 102; J. ELY, *supra* note 102; J. RAWLS, A THEORY OF JUSTICE (1971); Wechsler, *Toward Neutral Principles of Constitutional Law*, 73 HARV. L. REV. 1 (1959).

106. *See* R. BORK, *supra* note 6, at 280-98, 365-81; Posner, *The Next Step in Antitrust Treatment of Restricted Distribution: Per Se Legality*, 48 U. CHI. L. REV. 6 (1981). The only likely exception to the statement in the text is that vertical restrictions may enable a firm to engage in price discrimination. *See* Scherer, *supra* note 23; Hovenkamp, *supra* note 56, at 548-59.

policy can be faulted for reasons that have nothing to do with the internal logic or completeness of the model itself, but rather with the premises upon which the model is based and the conclusions that flow from it. The model may solve its own problems very well, but nevertheless not be a very useful guide to antitrust policymaking. Such criticisms can generally be grouped into two types: (1) criticisms that, although the model's definition of "efficiency" serves the model's own purposes very well, it is different from any concept of "efficiency" that realistically can be applied to policymaking in the real world — more particularly, in a real world democracy;[107] and (2) criticisms that "efficiency" cannot be the only relevant factor in real world policymaking; or alternatively, that any argument to that effect rests on premises that can be neither verified nor falsified. These are criticisms from "outside" the model.

Any critique of Chicago School antitrust policy that begins from these premises must proceed very carefully if antitrust is not to become a meaningless hodge-podge of conflicting, inconsistent, and politicized mini-policies. One of the great achievements of Chicago School antitrust policy based on the market efficiency model is a claim to consistency that cannot be made by any alternative approach that requires the "balancing" of competing interests, such as consumer welfare and small business welfare.[108] At the same time, the Chicago School's claim of a unified, internally consistent, and nonpolitical antitrust policy rests on premises whose soundness and application to the real world are not self-evident.

Some of these criticisms are addressed in a substantial economic literature, although most have not been developed at any length in antitrust scholarship. Economists continue to debate many of these issues, however, largely because they involve premises that can be neither proven nor disproven, at least not to everyone's satisfaction. In short, these issues involve the "statements of faith" made by economists — statements which often reflect, in Lindley Fraser's words, the "individual temperaments" of the people who make them.[109] Every economist, including the Chicago School economist, whose commitment to positivist methodology is probably exceeded by no one,[110] ultimately rests his case on such statements of faith. Even the Chicago

107. *See* text at notes 133-54 *infra*.

108. For an attempt at such balancing, see Fox, *supra* note 12.

109. L. FRASER, ECONOMIC THOUGHT AND LANGUAGE 36 (1937).

110. Simply, a positivist scientific methodology is one that attempts to avoid metaphysical speculation by restricting scientific inquiry to those things that can be either verified or falsified from sensory experience. *See generally* K. POPPER, THE LOGIC OF SCIENTIFIC DISCOVERY (1959).

School policymaker assumes *some* things that could be assumed the other way by equally rational minds. Importantly, if these premises are given up, the Chicago School model falls apart.

Scientific models — and economic models are no exception — rest ultimately on unprovable premises. For example, every model that purports to explain the external world rests on the essential premise that our senses provide us with accurate information.[111] The researcher doing "normal science" — science within the confines of the model — generally accepts such premises as given and forgets about them.[112] Verifying them or disproving them is not a part of her research agenda.

The public policymaker, however, cannot always make such facile assumptions. As a general rule the policymaker assumes the less controversial premises — such as that our senses give us reliable information — but is forced by the political process continually to question the controversial ones. They are capable of being questioned, people question them daily, and because contrary assumptions give very different political results, someone is always around to assert them.

For example, the Chicago School assumes that welfare can be measured in constant dollars, so that a transfer of a dollar from a consumer to a monopolist has no welfare implications.[113] This (unprovable) assumption performs many essential functions in the Chicago School framework. Intellectually, it helps the academic employing the market efficiency model to distinguish between the "deadweight loss" and the "wealth transfer" caused by the existence of monopoly in the market system.[114] Secondly, it permits the Chicago School antitrust policymaker to justify a "nonpolitical" approach to antitrust, which distinguishes between politically neutral efficiency gains, and politicized wealth transfers.[115] Finally, and most important, the "constant dollar" welfare assumption forms the chief basis for the notion that antitrust should be concerned with the deadweight loss caused by monopoly or the costs that the monopolist incurs in attaining or maintaining its monopoly position, but should disregard the wealth transferred from consumers, suppliers or rivals to the monopolizing firm.[116] These principles are absolutely essential to Chi-

111. This concern dominates A.J. Ayer's recent book *Philosophy in the Twentieth Century* (1982).

112. *See* T. KUHN, *supra* note 13, at 10-42.

113. The assumption is defended in R. POSNER, *supra* note 95, at 48-87.

114. *See* H. HOVENKAMP, *supra* note 17, at 19-24.

115. *See* text at notes 95-105 *supra.*

116. For example, see R. BORK, *supra* note 6, at 111-12. *See generally* Posner, *The Social Cost of Monopoly and Regulation,* 83 J. POL. ECON. 807 (1975).

cago School antitrust analysis. In fact, Chicago School antitrust policy would lose its identity without them.

However, the constant dollar welfare assumption is both unprovable and quite controversial. One of the most significant debates in welfare economics this century has raged between the marginalist, or material welfare, school[117] and the ordinalist school. The former believed that measurement of utility across individuals was both possible and essential to policymaking, while the latter believed that such "interpersonal comparisons" of utility were impossible. Chicago School welfare economics, which substitutes "wealth maximization" for utility and measures welfare in constant dollars, rests on the ordinalist premise that no one can compare the amount of welfare, or satisfaction, that is created by giving a dollar to a poor person, with the amount that is created by giving the same dollar to someone who is wealthy. Chicago School economic policymaking responds by making the assumption (just as unprovable as the ordinalist principle itself) that a dollar given to one person must be treated for policy purposes as creating the same amount of welfare as a dollar given to someone else.[118]

Recent scholarship has argued, however, that the ordinalist critique of the material welfare school missed the point of that school by substituting a different notion of utility.[119] To be sure, interpersonal comparisons of utility are impossible if one must compare the *subjective* pleasure that one person receives from receiving, say, a dollar or a pair of opera tickets, with the pleasure that someone else might receive from the same gifts. However, the material welfare school measured utility *objectively* rather than subjectively. Furthermore, the objective criteria that it used were closely tied with such empirically measurable factors as productivity, which are the kind of data upon which the

---

117. The term "material welfare" school used here comes from Cooter & Rappoport, *Were the Ordinalists Wrong About Welfare Economics?*, 22 J. ECON. LIT. 507, 512 n.14 (1984).

118. *See* Markovits, *A Basic Structure for Microeconomic Policy Analysis in Our Worse-than-Second-Best World: A Proposal and Related Critique of the Chicago Approach to the Study of Law and Economics*, 1975 WIS. L. REV. 950, 984. Markovits notes that the basis for many economists' profession of indifference toward wealth transfers is the assumption that utility cannot be compared across persons. The conclusions to be drawn from such an assumption vary; however, the Chicago School appears to conclude that, since no assumption can be made that a dollar is worth more to one person than to another, they are entitled to assume that a dollar is worth the same to everyone. Markovits characterizes this assumption as "heroic." *Id.* at 987.

A large literature supporting the thesis that mere wealth transfers cannot effect a welfare improvement rests on the premise that utility cannot be quantified and compared across individuals. *See* L. ROBBINS, AN ESSAY ON THE NATURE & SIGNIFICANCE OF ECONOMIC SCIENCE (2d ed. 1935); Hicks & Allen, *A Reconsideration of the Theory of Value* (pts. 1 & 2), 1 ECONOMICA 52, 196 (1934). The literature, as well as the relevant economic issues, are summarized in Cooter & Rappoport, *supra* note 117, at 520-26.

119. *See generally* Cooter & Rappoport, *supra* note 117.

public policymaker must rely.[120] For example, the policymaker might make the empirical observation that a sum of money given to a poor person might enable the poor person to educate herself or buy an automobile, while the same sum given to a wealthy person would have no measurable effect on the wealthy person's behavior.[121]

This critique of ordinalist assumptions undermines any notion that the policymaker *must* regard wealth transfers as welfare neutral. The policymaker might just as easily assume that a dollar paid in wages to a consumer creates more welfare than a dollar paid in dividends to the shareholders of a monopoly corporation or in bonuses to its managers.[122] Perhaps more important for antitrust purposes, he might also assume that the profits earned by a small family business contribute more to total welfare than an equal amount of profits earned by a very large firm. If "welfare" is defined objectively in such cases, by measured changes in behavior that result from a particular allocation of resources, the policymaker could quite easily produce empirical data that would support the claim.

In short, the fact that within the ordinalist model "efficiency," or welfare, is distinct from wealth distribution, does not require the policymaker to regard distributional concerns as irrelevant to antitrust policy. The market efficiency model in this case rests on an unverified assumption that the policymaker may find uncompelling and inappropriate. As a result, a *value* decision must still be made about whether wealth transfers are to be ignored in antitrust policymaking. If the policymaker decided that monopoly wealth transfers *do* affect welfare and that the antitrust laws are as good a legislative mechanism as any to deal with this problem, he would find plenty of economic argument — also supported by unprovable premises — to back him up.

A. *Efficiency: Inside and Outside the Model*

Economists use the word "efficiency" in several ways.[123] They may mean productive efficiency, which is a ratio between the amount of a

---

120. *Id.* at 509.

121. *See generally id.* at 515 n.21 (noting that the validity of objective interpersonal comparisons is "a theme of current philosophical inquiry").

122. Cooter and Rappoport argue very convincingly that the great debate in welfare economics between the cardinalists, who assumed that interpersonal comparisons of utility are possible, and ordinalists, who denied such a possibility, was really semantic. In fact, interpersonal comparisons of utility are possible if utility is measured objectively, in terms of what the "average" or "typical" person or class of persons desires, or alternatively, in terms of the effect of particular wealth transfer on *observed* behavior. However, such comparisons are impossible if utility is measured subjectively, in terms of what individual people actually want. *Id.* at 526-28.

123. *See, e.g.,* F. SCHERER, *supra* note 50, at 13-20 ("allocative" efficiency), 302-03 ("productive" efficiency), 20-21, 464-66 ("X-inefficiency").

firm's inputs and the amount of its outputs. The firm that can produce a widget worth one dollar with inputs costing ninety cents is more efficient in this sense than the firm that requires inputs costing one dollar to produce the same widget.

The classical price theory model has many things to say about productive efficiency. For example, it says that in a competitive market price will be established by the costs of the "marginal" firm, or the least efficient firm capable of sustaining production and selling at a price equal to or greater than its costs.[124] That firm will make roughly zero economic profits, while any firm in the market whose productive efficiency is greater will earn some economic profits. The model also tells us that practices such as vertical integration or mergers that increase a firm's productive efficiency will permit the firm to cut its price and increase its market share, or else make higher profits at the same price. Once the practice that creates productive efficiency is copied by competitors, the price will be driven down to a new marginal cost lower than the marginal cost before the efficiency-creating practice came into existence.[125]

Even within the Chicago School paradigm, productive efficiency is not perceived to be a dominant concern of the antitrust laws, except in a negative sense.[126] Chicago School antitrust policy encourages productive efficiency merely by refusing to make increases in productive efficiency a reason for condemning certain practices[127] and by approving practices that are unlikely to increase a firm's market power and are likely to increase productive efficiency.[128] Under the Chicago School theory the market itself, not the antitrust laws, punishes productive *in*efficiency by loss of profits, loss of market share, or in extreme cases, forced exit from the market.[129] If a firm engages in a practice that raises its own costs above those of its competitors, that should be of no general concern to the antitrust laws, unless the prac-

---

124. This will generally be true only if the low-cost inputs enjoyed by the more efficient firms are incapable of being duplicated. If the low-cost inputs can be duplicated competition will force other firms to duplicate the low-cost input as well and the price will decrease. *See* H. HOVENKAMP, *supra* note 17, at 81.

125. *See generally* Bork, *Vertical Integration and the Sherman Act: the Legal History of an Economic Misconception,* 22 U. CHI. L. REV. 157 (1954).

126. For example, even Chicago School scholars are skeptical about the creation of an "efficiency defense" in merger cases, because the judicial task of measurement would be too complicated. *See* Hovenkamp, *Merger Actions for Damages,* 35 HASTINGS L.J. 937, 946-47 (1984).

127. The Supreme Court violated this rule in some Warren era cases such as Brown Shoe Co. v. United States, 370 U.S. 294 (1962), where it condemned a merger *because* the postmerger firm was able to take advantage of efficiencies that enabled it to undersell smaller rivals. *See* 370 U.S. at 344.

128. *See* R. BORK, *supra* note 6, at 91.

129. *See* Easterbrook, *Limits, supra* note 8, at 24.

tice also increases the firm's market power or raises the overall price level in the market.[130]

The Chicago School theory that antitrust policy generally ought to permit firms to maximize their own productive efficiency[131] is not particularly controversial today. The more serious difficulty with Chicago School policy concerning efficiency is its insistence that the *exclusive* goals of the antitrust laws should be to maximize net *allocative* efficiency, and that the classical price theory model can define the circumstances under which this will occur.[132]

Allocative efficiency is a much more global kind of efficiency than is productive efficiency. Allocative efficiency refers to the welfare of society as a whole. Situation *A* is more allocatively efficient than situation *B* if affected people as a group are somehow better off under *A* than they are under *B*.

The classic definition of allocative efficiency was provided by Vilfredo Pareto in 1909.[133] Under the Pareto definition, a situation is efficient, or "Pareto optimal," if no change from that situation could make someone better off without also making at least one other person worse off. Likewise, a given situation *A* is "Pareto superior" to situation *B* if the move from *B* to *A* does in fact make at least one person better off without making another person worse off.

The Pareto definition of allocative efficiency imposes such a strict requirement on efficiency-based policymaking that its conditions can virtually never be fulfilled. Nearly all policy changes fail to be allocatively efficient under the Pareto test. For example, the adoption of a rule condemning bank robbery is not a Pareto superior move from a situation in which bank robbery is tolerated, because people who profit from robbing banks are made worse off by the rule change. Nonetheless, most people would probably agree that society as a whole is somehow better off if bank robbery is forbidden.[134]

Because of this severe practical limitation in the Pareto efficiency criterion, efficiency-based policymaking must generally be guided by some notion of efficiency other than orthodox Pareto efficiency. The most common alternative, generally advocated by the Chicago School, is "potential" Pareto efficiency, sometimes called Kaldor-Hicks effi-

130. Productive inefficiency might become an antitrust concern if a firm does something that raises its own costs, but that raises rivals' costs even more. *See* text at notes 289-307 *infra.*

131. *See* R. BORK, *supra* note 6, at 91.

132. *See id.*; R. POSNER, *supra* note 19, at 8-22.

133. V. PARETO, MANUEL D' ECONOMIE POLITIQUE (1909).

134. *See* Hovenkamp, *supra* note 18, at 9.

ciency.[135] A change is efficient in the potential Pareto sense if the gains experienced by those who gain from the change are larger than the losses experienced by those who lose due to the change. Such a change is said to be "potential" Pareto efficient because it could be turned into a pure Pareto efficient move if the gainers would compensate the losers out of their gains. If that occurred, then the losers would be no worse off, because they would have been fully compensated. However, the gainers would still be better off, because they have something left over after they have paid the compensation. Importantly, the potential Pareto criterion does not require the gainers actually to compensate the losers. That would be a distributive concern. The move is "potential" Pareto superior if the gainers could compensate the losers fully and still have some gains left over.[136]

Unfortunately, the move from orthodox Pareto efficiency to potential Pareto efficiency as an efficiency norm for policymakers comes with a very large cost. The rigor of the orthodox Pareto criterion meant that real world changes seldom or never fulfilled its conditions; however, it also made a true Pareto improvement — or, more realistically, a change that was not a true Pareto improvement — relatively easy to identify. A change was a Pareto improvement if no one objected to it. On the other hand, if at least one person objected, then the change was presumptively *not* Pareto superior.[137]

The potential Pareto criterion, however, requires the policymaker not only to *identify* all those who gain and lose from a particular change, but also to *quantify* their individual gains and losses, sum them, and net them out against each other in order to determine whether the net effect is a social gain or a social loss. Even if welfare can be measured in constant dollars,[138] it is by no means clear that the policymaker is up to this task.

To be sure, perhaps in extreme cases it may be fairly clear that a certain policy change is efficient or inefficient under the potential Pareto criterion. For example, the adoption of a rule condemning child molesting is probably efficient, while the adoption of a rule condemning singing in the shower is probably inefficient. However, in the vast middle range of cases — the "controversial" cases where political interests line up on both sides of the question — the identification of the "efficient" rule under the potential Pareto criterion is unclear.[139]

---

135. R. POSNER, *supra* note 95, at 91.

136. *Id.* at 91-92.

137. *Id.* at 88.

138. *See* text at notes 116-22 *supra*.

139. For example, see Stigler, *The Origin of the Sherman Act,* 14 J. LEGAL STUD. 1 (1985), in

The market efficiency model provides considerable *conceptual* guidance in identifying efficient rule changes, provided that one accepts the limitations imposed by the model itself. For example, it can easily be shown that the move from competition to monopoly in a particular market is inefficient by the potential Pareto criterion. Although the amount of lost consumers' surplus is offset in part by a gain in producers' surplus, over and above this is a "deadweight loss" which entails that the net losses caused by monopoly are larger than net gains.[140]

However, the ease with which allocative efficiency can be quantified within the confines of the market efficiency model belies the many complexities of measurement in the real world.[141] For one thing, in a market economy every change imposed on one market affects dozens of other markets as well. Furthermore, the allocative effects of monopoly in multiple markets may tend to cancel each other out. In that case it is not at all clear that the elimination of monopoly in a single market will be Pareto efficient. Although the *existence* of such problems of "second-best" is widely accepted, the degree to which the problem frustrates the pursuit of allocative efficiency in the real world is quite controversial.[142]

Problems of second-best may be so overwhelming and so hypothetical that the antitrust policymaker is well off to avoid them.[143] Other external problems of the market efficiency model are not so easy to ignore, however. The model fails to account for preferences that peo-

---

which a leading Chicago School economist attempted to measure the support and opposition to the Sherman Act but was able to produce only very ambiguous conclusions, even though the Sherman Act was one of the least controversial statutes ever passed by Congress. *See also* Markovits, *supra* note 23, at 45.

140. *See* R. POSNER, *supra* note 95, at 91-92. Once again, however, the illustration assumes that welfare can be measured in constant dollars.

141. Some of the problems are summarized in Markovits, *supra* note 23, at 45-49; Markovits, *Monopolistic Competition, Second Best, and The Antitrust Paradox: A Review Article,* 77 MICH. L. REV. 567, 570 (1979) (reviewing R. BORK, THE ANTITRUST PARADOX: A POLICY AT WAR WITH ITSELF (1978)).

142. The literature on problems of second-best is extensive, and economists differ widely about the degree to which second-best problems frustrate any real-world policy of improving allocative efficiency. For an argument that second-best problems are substantial and generally make it impossible for the policymaker to know that an efficiency gain in one market will yield an overall efficiency gain, see Markovits, *supra* note 118, at 967-77. For arguments that second-best problems should be ignored, unless it is quite obvious that increased competition in one market is causing greater efficiency losses in a second market, see Baumol, *Informed Judgment, Rigorous Theory and Public Policy,* 32 S. ECON. J. 137, 144 (1965); Williamson, *Assessing Vertical Market Restrictions: Antitrust Ramifications of the Transaction Cost Approach,* 127 U. PA. L. REV. 953, 987 (1979). However, all these arguments are not "proofs" at all; rather, they should appropriately be regarded as "statements of faith" that an efficiency improvement in one market must, as a general rule, make all of society better off.

143. For a truly pessimistic conclusion, suggesting that second-best problems might be so substantial that they would undermine any policy search for allocative efficiency, see F. SCHERER, *supra* note 50, at 28.

ple do not express with their dollars — for example, a distrust of large concentrations of economic or political power in private hands, or perhaps even a preference for more expansive opportunities for small business.[144] As a general rule, these preferences have been considered even by supporters to be "noneconomic" — that is, as goals that have nothing to do with the public welfare.[145] Likewise, Chicago School scholars who advocate an exclusively "economic" approach to antitrust policy exclude such goals as being "noneconomic" or as somehow inconsistent with the notion that the antitrust laws ought to maximize allocative efficiency.[146]

Such reasoning is based on the irrational assumption that people do not place a value on these asserted "noneconomic" goals. The reasoning is irrational because the fact that people are willing to assert such goals, and that political dialogue in the United States is heavily loaded with references to them,[147] indicates that people do indeed value such things as the diffusion of privately held economic or political power or the preservation of small business opportunity. That these goals are so prominent in the legislative history of the antitrust laws[148] as well as in the more general American democratic and egalitarian ideology[149] illustrates clearly enough that some people value them greatly. The concept of allocative efficiency or wealth maximization must include *everything* to which people assign a value. If a regime of small businesses is worth anything to anybody, then it deserves to be calculated into the equation offsetting the costs and benefits of a given antitrust policy. In that case, the antitrust policy of protecting small business is very much an "economic" goal.

Why are goals such as the preservation of small business or the diffusion of power, which some Americans clearly value, not even entitled to inclusion in the Chicago School cost-benefit calculus? The answer, it appears, is that Americans, no matter how strongly they might state those preferences in other contexts, fail to vote them with their dollars. People may prefer small business or resent political power in the abstract, and they may make or applaud political speeches to the same effect, but when the time comes to make purchase decisions, they

144. Such concerns are summarized in Pitofsky, *supra* note 12; Schwartz, *supra* note 12.

145. *See* Schwartz, *supra* note 12.

146. *See, e.g.,* R. BORK, *supra* note 6, at 50-56; R. POSNER, *supra* note 19, at 19-20.

147. *See* Berthoff, *Independence and Enterprise: Small Business in the American Dream,* in SMALL BUSINESS IN AMERICAN LIFE 28-48 (S. Bruchey ed. 1980). See Schwartz, *supra* note 12, for citation of a substantial list of federal statutes concerned with the welfare of small business.

148. *See* H. HOVENKAMP, *supra* note 17, at 50-54; *see also* text at notes 167-76, *infra.*

149. *See* note 147 *supra.*

invariably look for the best product at the lowest price, even if the offeror is a very large and politically powerful corporation.

The explanation for such consumer behavior should be obvious to anyone familiar with the large literature on free riding, most of it written by Chicago School scholars.[150] Both a regime in which businesses have little political and economic power and expansive opportunity for small business are public goods — things that many people may want but believe they can avoid paying for.[151] Although Chicago School economists developed the free riding model to explain why certain vertical restrictions are really efficient, they have neglected to apply the free riding model to the manifold situations in which free riding is a common occurrence.

It seems clear from the literature and mystique surrounding the small business in America that many people and the legislatures they elect place a high value on the so-called "mom and pop" store. Likewise, many people appear to be quite uncomfortable about the large amount of political and economic power wielded by large firms.[152] Many members of society value a regime in which businesses do not have so much influence. However, such a regime can be paid for only if each consumer individually agrees to do business with smaller stores, stores with lower productive efficiency (and higher prices) and no such power. If each consumer prefers to save the money now, trusting others or the government to support the small firm, a substantial free rider problem exists. This is borne out by the fact that consumer statements frequently seem to be inconsistent with consumer exercises of preferences in the marketplace. The individual consumer buys where prices are low — not because he is not wary of economic concentration, but because his own unilateral purchase decision is not enough to change the economic structure of society. The Chicago School view that consumer preferences should dominate any "efficiency" analysis applies only to markets in which consumers are forced to pay for everything they receive. In most real world markets this is simply not the case.

One problem with this argument is that there is no way of stopping it. If people really prefer small shops but take a free ride by buying from larger stores with lower costs, then the world containing the

---

150. Bork, *Resale Price Maintenance and Consumer Welfare*, 77 YALE L.J. 950 (1968); Bork, *The Rule of Reason and the Per Se Concept: Price Fixing and Market Division* (pt. 2), 75 YALE L.J. 373 (1966); Telser, *Why Should Manufacturers Want Fair Trade?*, 3 J. L. & ECON. 86 (1960).

151. For an analysis of the economics of public goods, see E. MANSFIELD, MICROECONOMICS: THEORY AND APPLICATIONS 466-90 (4th ed. 1982).

152. *See* note 147 *supra.*

small shops can be more "efficient" than the world without them, and an antitrust policy that protects them would be "efficient" as well.

In short, the presumption made by the market efficiency model that consumer behavior is the best guide to allocative efficiency works only when consumers can be forced to pay for everything they receive. It fails to consider values that are not reflected in consumer choices in the marketplace. Today we know that externalities are pervasive in almost every market transaction. For example, we cannot rely on individual consumer behavior to control air and water pollution — even though the great majority of consumers presumably prefer unpolluted air and water. Firms that do not clean their emissions into the air and water have lower costs and correspondingly lower prices; however, they would quickly go out of business if each consumer unilaterally decided to buy instead from a higher-cost firm that was more protective of the environment.[153] Consumers are not likely to do that on their own, however, because each one individually knows that her own purchase decision will have little impact on the behavior of the firm; she shifts the burden elsewhere. If such consumer free riding is widespread in society, then the neoclassical market efficiency model's reliance on consumer *behavior* [154] as a measure of allocative efficiency is too naive to be a useful policymaking tool for the real world.

B. *Is Efficiency the Only Thing That Counts?*

The broadest statement of the Chicago School position on efficiency and public policy is that *all* policymaking by the State should be concerned exclusively with allocative efficiency. Some Chicago School scholars adopt this position, or at least one that is very close.[155] A narrower rule is that *antitrust* policy should be concerned exclusively with efficiency.[156] Certain parts of the federal government, including some federal judges, may follow the narrower version;[157] however, the government is not close to following the broader version. The Reagan administration's efforts to destroy the New Deal notwithstanding, distributive justice is still very much a part of *general* federal policymaking.

The arguments for both the broad and the narrow versions of the

---

153. *See* E. MANSFIELD, *supra* note 151, at 472-73.

154. *See* R. BORK, *supra* note 6, at 91.

155. *See* R. POSNER, *supra* note 95; Posner, *The Efficiency Norm, supra* note 58.

156. *See* R. BORK, *supra* note 6, at 81.

157. *See* Gerhart, *supra* note 24; *see also* 1984 Merger Guidelines, *supra* note 36; Schwartz, *The New Merger Guidelines: Guide to Governmental Discretion and Private Counseling or Propaganda for Revision of the Antitrust Laws?*, 71 CALIF. L. REV. 575 (1983).

Chicago School position on policymaking appear to rest on four premises: (1) A society in which allocative efficiency, or welfare, is maxi-
mized is better than one in which it is not; or alternatively, more
welfare is better than less. (2) Policymakers are capable of creating
and implementing a policy of maximizing total social wealth without
regard to the way in which wealth is distributed.[158] (3) Policy concerns about wealth distribution, on the other hand, reflect purely political conflicts between interest groups and cannot be justified in any
rigorous, scientific manner. (4) Efficiency goals and distributional
goals or, alternatively, efficiency effects and distributional effects can
be segregated from each other.

Analysis of the soundness of these premises is beyond the scope of
this paper.[159] Nevertheless, it is worthwhile to consider briefly the
fourth premise, that efficiency concerns and distributive concerns can
be separated from one another. If that premise is false, any notion
that allocative efficiency can be the exclusive goal of the antitrust laws
becomes unsupportable.

No one denies that wealth transfer policies can have a substantial
effect on efficiency, particularly if people know about the policies in
advance and plan their affairs around them. High tax rates on the
wealthy may reduce the incentive to invest or work. On the other side,
welfare payments may reduce the incentive to work or, alternatively,
they may provide needed support such as education or child care that
make the recipient a more productive member of society.

Likewise, no one doubts that a policy of maximizing wealth, which
is expressly concerned only with efficiency, nevertheless has important
effects on the way wealth is distributed.[160] An antimonopoly law may
have the effect of transferring wealth away from the monopolist and
toward consumers. An "efficiency defense" in merger cases may make
consumers and larger firms, or firms in a position to merge, better off
at the expense of other firms.[161]

It seems that the vast majority of policies simultaneously affect society's total wealth as well as the way that wealth is distributed. As a
result, the fourth premise above needs to be modified. In the real
world, efficiency and distributional *effects* generally cannot be separated from one another. It would probably be impossible to imple-

---

158. *See* text at notes 137-46 *supra.*

159. However, all four are discussed in somewhat different form in Markovits, *supra* note
118, at 38; Markovits, *supra* note 141, at 48.

160. *See* Hovenkamp, *supra* note 18, at 4.

161. *See* Williamson, *Economies as an Antitrust Defense: The Welfare Trade-Offs*, 58 AM.
ECON. REV. 18 (1968).

ment a policy that increased social wealth without affecting the way wealth is distributed. Alternatively, although perhaps less clearly, it may be impossible to transfer wealth without affecting total social wealth.[162] The correct premise must be that efficiency *goals* and distributive *goals* can be separated from one another, and that this fact, combined with the other three premises, justifies an antitrust policy of exclusive concern with efficiency.

If efficiency goals and distributive goals can really be separated, then it would appear that the duty of the Chicago School antitrust policymaker is to look only at the efficiency effects of a policy and ignore any distributional effects. Unpopular distributional effects can be corrected later by a different policy. For example, if a rigorous antitrust policy concerned exclusively with efficiency ends up transferring too much wealth away from small businesses, Congress can compensate by giving them low interest loans or other transfer payments.[163]

Unfortunately, the low interest loans will undermine the antitrust policy of encouraging efficiency. To use an efficiency-based antitrust policy that permits firms to become very large and injures those that remain inefficiently small, but then to "compensate" the small businesses by low cost loans or other transfer payments, diminishes the efficiency advantage of being big. For example, suppose that a small firm produces widgets at a cost of ten cents each, while a large firm produces them at nine cents each. An antitrust policy of promoting efficiency would at least passively encourage firms to become large, perhaps by permitting mergers or internal growth that achieved production economies or by refusing to condemn the lower prices of larger firms as "predatory." However, if the smaller firms became the beneficiaries of low interest loans or tax incentives unavailable to the larger firms, the incentive to become large would be diminished and the antitrust policy frustrated.

It appears that an antitrust policy of maximizing efficiency cannot

---

162. There might be some exceptions here. For example, if the government conducted a secret lottery and suddenly announced that everyone whose birthday is May 29 must pay $100 to someone whose birthday is August 27, the result might be a wealth transfer with no efficiency effects. In this case, however, the idiosyncratic nature of the exception probably proves the rule. Most real world wealth transfers invite people to alter their behavior, either so as to receive the benefit of the transfer or to avoid having to pay it. For an argument that the purpose of the just compensation clause of the fifth amendment is to force the state to pass efficient legislation that leaves the distribution of wealth untouched, see R. EPSTEIN, TAKINGS: PRIVATE PROPERTY AND THE POWER OF EMINENT DOMAIN (1985), especially at 3-6.

163. In fact, Congress has done that. For example, see the Small Business Act, 15 U.S.C. § 631-47 (1982); Small Business Emergency Relief Act, 41 U.S.C. § 252 (1982); Small Business Investment Act, 15 U.S.C. § 661-96 (1982).

be pursued with anything resembling consistency unless the government is willing to adopt a much more *general* policy of maximizing efficiency — or, to put the matter bluntly, unless the government abandons its concern with how wealth is distributed, at least with respect to business firms.[164] However, any argument in favor of a more general policy of maximizing efficiency while ignoring distributive concerns must meet one objection that no one has answered. The "efficient" allocation of resources in any particular society is substantially a function of the way that society's wealth is distributed initially.[165] For example, if members of a society of one hundred people are all given equal amounts of wealth and then commence a process of exchange that will yield an efficient outcome, the outcome will be different than it would be if one person in that society had been given ninety percent of the wealth, while the other ninety-nine divided the remaining ten percent. This is so because the amount of wealth that someone has affects his or her wealth priorities. The wealthy may place high values on expensive jewelry or exotic vacations, for example. On the other hand, the working poor may place a very high value on bologna and actually bid it away from the wealthy, who show little interest.

The principle that the "efficient" outcome depends on the initial distribution of wealth is not particularly controversial. However, the principle plays havoc with any notion that a public policy can be concerned exclusively with efficiency in all areas of life. The problem might not be great if society could plausibly have an *antitrust* policy concerned exclusively with efficiency, and then freely use other policies based on notions of fairness to redistribute wealth in ways that society finds appropriate. However, as we saw above, such an antitrust policy based exclusively on efficiency will not work unless other policies are based on efficiency as well.

The principle that the efficient outcome is a function of the initial distribution of wealth deprives the efficiency goal of a great deal of its intellectual appeal. Its proponents talk about the "initial distribution" of wealth and the "efficient outcome" as if both existed at some finite moment in time — as if there were a single starting distribution of wealth and a single concluding efficient outcome. In fact, in a dynamic world the problem is far more complex. The distribution of

---

164. A program of redistributing wealth might have no effect on an efficiency-only antitrust policy if the redistribution were completely random as to business firms. However, many government economic policies *do* favor smaller firms. See the statutes cited in note 163 *supra*. Furthermore, it would be impossible to devise a redistribution policy whose effects did not favor any particular class of business firm.

165. *See* Sen, *Rational Fools: A Critique of the Behavioral Foundations of Economic Theory,* 6 PHIL. & PUB. AFF. 317, 331 (1977).

wealth in society shifts daily, and the market itself never arrives at an efficient "outcome." It only approaches such an outcome through a never ending series of exchanges.

Monopoly distributes wealth to the monopolist and away from consumers. To the extent that the world contains monopolists, the efficient "outcome" at any particular time is a function of a starting distribution of wealth that already reflects the existence of monopoly. What, then, does it mean to say that the market is "efficient," or generates efficient solutions? It means simply that people's preferences are a function of the position in which they find themselves. People with wealth, including wealth caused by monopoly, express different preferences than people who are poor. As far as allocative efficiency is concerned, however, one initial distribution is as good as another.

To date, no compelling argument has been made for a policy of maximizing satisfaction from a given starting point that says nothing about the location of the starting point. Until such an argument is made, the notion of "allocative efficiency" is, at best, a trivial guide to policymaking.[166]

On the other hand, it seems clear that the market is a very powerful device by which people maximize their satisfactions *given* the existing distribution of wealth. Furthermore, absent legal restraints on alienation, the market functions *whether or not* the State is involved in the involuntary redistribution of wealth. People are very good at "inventing around" constraints imposed by the State, and they will use the market to pursue wealth maximizing, or "efficient" outcomes, no matter what the "starting" distribution of wealth is. As a result, from the point of view of allocative efficiency, one starting distribution is as good as another. From the viewpoint of justice, however, one starting distribution may be much more desirable than another. For this reason the State may as well pursue a just distribution of wealth as permit

---

166. That the efficient outcome is a function of the initial distribution of wealth weakens the argument for efficiency even more under the Chicago School concept of "wealth maximization" than under the more traditional utilitarian notion that welfare is reflected by people's preferences. Wealth maximization measures welfare *only* by what people actually buy, not by what they would like to have. As a result, the purchase "vote" of the wealthy person who does not care to have, say, a new house and that of a poor person who would like to have one very much but cannot afford one receive the same weight in the wealth maximization welfare calculation: zero. *See* Leff, *Economic Analysis of Law: Some Realism About Nominalism,* 60 VA. L. REV. 451, 478-79 (1974); *see also* Tribe, *Constitutional Calculus: Equal Justice or Economic Efficiency?,* 98 HARV. L. REV. 592, 595 (1985). On one hand, the theory of wealth maximization, which weights actual purchases rather than preferences, solves the empirical problem that no policymaker could ever measure stated preferences but can measure actual purchases. On the other hand, the result is that wealth maximization appears not to measure "welfare" at all, unless the ability to purchase is an essential ingredient in welfare. It seems clear, for example, that gifts of a new house to the wealthy person and the poor person described above would not produce identical amounts of satisfaction.

an unjust one. The market can always be trusted to maximize people's welfare, given any particular starting point.

C. *The Problem of Legislative History*

A democratic sovereign must pay more than lip service to the proposition that the voters are entitled to have what they want, even if they want something irrational or inconsistent with the dominant model for policy. This creates a problem for the economic policymaker different from any encountered by the academic economist or other scientist. The people who collect empirical data and "apply" a particular natural science model in, say, physics, have a certain sensitivity to the scientific model and its limitations. However, the participants in the democratic process usually exhibit no such sensitivity. This is certainly true of voters, special interest groups, and lobbyists, but it may also describe elected members of the legislative, executive, and even the judicial branches. To be sure, the economist employed by the Department of Justice "makes" economic policy, and may be very sensitive to the demands of a particular economic theory. But the Justice Department economist is hired and directed by an appointed antitrust chief, who answers to an appointed Attorney General who in turn responds to the policies of an elected president. As a result the Justice Department economist is likely to be pulled as hard by political necessity as by scientific integrity. Which of these should prevail in a democratic country? More appropriately, to what degree can an appointed policymaker take advantage of "market failures" in the *legislative* process[167] to create enforcement policy that is inconsistent with the legislative history of the statute being enforced?

The legislative histories of the various antitrust laws fail to exhibit anything resembling a dominant concern for economic efficiency. Dozens of scholars have scrutinized these legislative histories in order to determine what Congress had in mind.[168] Their efforts will not be

---

167. *I.e.*, instances when the legislative process fails to provide the efficient solution to the problem.

168. On the Sherman Act, see Bork, *Legislative Intent and the Policy of the Sherman Act*, 9 J. L. & ECON. 7 (1966) (arguing that the legislative history of the Sherman Act reveals a dominant concern for efficiency); Lande, *Wealth Transfers as the Original and Primary Concern of Antitrust: The Efficiency Interpretation Challenged*, 34 HASTINGS L.J. 65 (1982) (arguing that the framers of the Sherman Act were concerned about protecting consumers from unfair distributions of wealth away from them and toward monopolists). On the Clayton Act, see Bok, *Section 7 of the Clayton Act and the Merging of Law and Economics*, 74 HARV. L. REV. 226, 233-38 (1960) (arguing that Congress was excessively concerned with protecting small business, particularly in the 1950 amendments). On the Robinson-Patman Act, see Hansen, *Robinson-Patman Law: A Review and Analysis*, 51 FORDHAM L. REV. 1113 (1983) (concluding that Congress was concerned chiefly with protecting small businesses from the buying practices of larger firms). *See also* H. HOVENKAMP, *supra* note 17, at 50-54.

repeated here. No one, it appears, has even attempted to argue that Congress had "efficiency" in mind when it passed the Robinson-Patman Act in 1936, or the Celler-Kefauver amendments to Section 7 of the Clayton Act in 1950. Those statutes were designed to protect a particular constituency, small business, that had managed to make its case to Congress.[169] Likewise, no compelling case has been made that efficiency considerations dominated in the passage of the Clayton Act itself.[170] The strongest argument that Congress was motivated by concerns of efficiency when it passed an antitrust law has been made by Professor (now Judge) Bork, and is concerned largely with the Sherman Act.[171] However, Bork's work has been called into question by subsequent scholarship showing that in 1980 Congress had no real concept of efficiency and was really concerned with protecting consumers from unfavorable wealth transfers.[172]

Of course, Congress could rewrite the antitrust laws and make concerns for efficiency express, but it has not done so. In fact, the widely proclaimed Chicago School "revolution" has pretty much passed Congress by. Historically, liberals[173] have been fairly successful in getting Congress to write liability-expanding antitrust statutes.[174] However, with only a few trivial exceptions, free marketers have had no such luck.[175] Leaders in conservative administrations have asked for legislation weakening the merger laws or abolishing

---

169. See Hansen, *supra* note 168.

170. On the legislative history of the original Clayton Act, see W. LETWIN, *supra* note 39, at 273-76; D. MARTIN, MERGERS AND THE CLAYTON ACT 20-43 (1959).

171. See Bork, *supra* note 168.

172. See Lande, *supra* note 168.

173. That is, welfare liberals, not classical liberals.

174. For example, the Clayton Act, ch. 323, 38 Stat. 730 (1914) (codified as amended in scattered sections of 15 U.S.C. and 29 U.S.C. (1982)), passed in 1914 during the Wilson administration; the Robinson-Patman Act, ch. 592, 49 Stat. 1526-28 (1936) (codified at 15 U.S.C. §§ 13-13b, 21a (1982)), passed during the Franklin D. Roosevelt administration; the Celler-Kefauver amendments to § 7 (relating to mergers) of the Clayton Act, ch. 1184, 64 Stat. 1125 (1950) (codified at 15 U.S.C. § 18 (1982)), passed during the Truman administration.

Perhaps the one notable exception is the Consumer Goods Pricing Act of 1975, Pub. L. 94-145, 89 Stat. 801 (amending 15 U.S.C. §§ 1, 45a (1968)), which abolished "fair trade" and arguably restored the per se rule for resale price maintenance. That statute was passed during the Nixon administration. However, given the controversial nature of resale price maintenance, it is difficult to characterize the statute as either liberal or conservative.

175. The liability-restricting statutes that have been passed are generally either jurisdictional, or else nibble away at economic areas that cover a relatively small percentage of antitrust activity. Examples are the Local Government Antitrust Act of 1984, 15 U.S.C. §§ 35, 36 (Supp. II 1984), which abolished treble damages for antitrust violations by municipalities; the Export Trading Company Act of 1982, 15 U.S.C. §§ 4001-4021 (1982), which gives a limited antitrust exemption to qualified export trade associations and companies; and the National Cooperative Research Act of 1984, 15 U.S.C. §§ 4301-05 (Supp. II 1984), which gives an exemption from the per se rule to qualified research joint ventures. All three of these statutes were passed during the Reagan administration.

treble damages, but Congress has generally resisted these requests.[176]

To be sure, there may be a very good explanation for this: no one lobbies Congress for allocative efficiency. A statute is "efficient" if it produces more gains than losses, regardless of where the gains and losses appear. However, the interest groups that reach Congress are concerned not with maximizing the *amount* of wealth that is produced, but rather with making sure that a particular group gets its fair share. To be sure, the farmers' lobbyist may *argue* that price supports will make America as a whole wealthier — but what he really wants is to make farmers wealthier.[177]

Of course, this fact does not distinguish the antitrust laws from any other kind of legislation. Whether any legislation is "efficient" and enlarges social wealth, or merely reflects the desires of one or more interest groups, depends on the ability of Congress to listen to the arguments from all sides, "net them out," and then pass a statute that, on balance, does more good than harm to all affected interests. The more successful Congress is at this, the more frequently its statutes will be efficient. On the other hand, the more successful a particular interest group is in making its case to Congress, the more frequently that group will obtain legislation that shifts wealth in its direction, whether or not such legislation is efficient.[178]

Initially, Chicago School antitrust scholars expressed sensitivity to the relationship between economic policymaking and the democratic legislative process. At least they once felt obliged to demonstrate congressional approval of the view that efficiency should be the exclusive goal of antitrust enforcement. For example, Robert Bork attempted at various times to find a mandate for Chicago School antitrust policy in the legislative history of the federal antitrust laws.[179] Bork's argument may have strained credulity,[180] but that is not the point. The point is

---

176. For example, see Commerce Secretary Malcolm Baldridge's proposal to repeal § 7 of the Clayton Act, 48 ANTITRUST & TRADE REG. REP. (BNA) 385 (Feb. 28, 1985); and see the Reagan administration proposal to abolish treble damages for rule of reason violations, *Draft Reagan Administration Legislation on Antitrust, Patents, and Joint Research and Development Ventures*, 44 ANTITRUST & TRADE REG. REP. (BNA) No. 1121, at 1272 (June 30, 1983). The latter proposal is discussed in H. HOVENKAMP, *supra* note 17, at 405 n.4. See also the comprehensive administration package of antitrust proposals, intended to reduce damages, narrow the coverage of § 7 of the Clayton Act, and reduce the extraterritorial jurisdiction of the antitrust laws. *Administration's Antitrust Law Package*, [Current] TRADE REG. REP. (CCH) No. 744, pt. 2 (Feb. 24, 1986).

177. Professor Easterbrook uses the term "rent-seeking" statutes. Easterbrook, *Forward: The Court and the Economic System*, 98 HARV. L. REV. 4, 15-17 (1984).

178. *See* Posner, *The Reading of Statutes, supra* note 58, at 264-72; *see generally* Stigler, *The Theory of Economic Regulation*, 2 BELL J. ECON. & MGMT. SCI. 3 (1971); Peltzman, *Toward a More General Theory of Regulation*, 19 J. L. & ECON. 211 (1976).

179. *See* R. BORK, *supra* note 6, at 50-71; Bork, *supra* note 168.

180. *See* Hovenkamp, *supra* note 18, at 7-24; *see generally* Lande, *supra* note 168.

that Bork deemed it important to show that Congress had maximization of consumer welfare in mind. From that premise Bork developed the argument that this congressionally mandated consumer welfare principle necessitated the adoption of the market efficiency model for antitrust.

More recently, however, some Chicago School scholars have apparently abandoned as hopeless the attempt to find support for their position in the legislative history of the antitrust laws. Instead, they have adopted a different approach — developing arguments for the proposition that statutes should be interpreted relatively broadly or relatively narrowly depending on their nature. Efficient, or "public interest," legislation should be interpreted broadly, and courts should not hesitate to interpolate Congress' meaning when the language of such statutes contains ambiguities or gaps. On the other hand, rent-seeking, or "interest group," legislation should be interpreted narrowly, and no remedy should be provided unless Congress was very explicit about creating it.[181]

Within this paradigm the Sherman Act appears to qualify as public interest legislation.[182] The Sherman Act condemns "contracts in restraint of trade" and "monopolies." As a general rule, condemnation of both of those things is efficient, provided that they are properly de-

---

181. See Baxter, *supra* note 1, at 661 (written when Professor Baxter was head of the Antitrust Division of the Department of Justice). At various places in his discussion Baxter concludes: (1) Because the Robinson-Patman Act "recognizes as unlawful conduct that injures competitors, regardless of its effects on competition," the statute "is not regarded as a true 'antitrust' law." This justifies the Justice Department decision not to enforce that Act. *Id.* at 662 n.6. (2) The antitrust laws are really "enabling legislation that has permitted a common-law refinement of antitrust law through an evolution guided by only the most general statutory discretions." *Id.* at 663. (3) Although the framers of the Sherman Act probably intended to federalize the common law of trade restraints, they probably misunderstood that law as protecting competition rather than competitors; as a result, courts need not look to this common law in making federal antitrust policy. *Id.* at 664 n.12.

As for the first point above, Mr. Baxter's conclusion is inconsistent, not merely with the legislative history of the antitrust laws, but with its clearly expressed language. Section 1 of the Clayton Act, 15 U.S.C. § 12 (1982), defines the phrase "antitrust laws" to include the Clayton Act itself, § 2 of which is the Robinson-Patman Act. 15 U.S.C. § 13 (1982). Congress has amended the Clayton Act at least a half dozen times; however, it has never changed the definition of "antitrust laws" in such a way as to exclude § 2 of the Clayton Act.

The Chicago School literature on statutory interpretation is growing rapidly. In general, that literature argues that "public interest" statutes — i.e., statutes that are "efficient," or that create more social gains than losses — should be interpreted relatively broadly and courts should be willing to fill in statutory "gaps" by inferring the legislature's intent. See Posner, *The Reading of Statutes, supra* note 58, at 269. On the other hand, private interest statutes, in which an interest group "buys" favorable legislation from Congress, should be strictly interpreted, as a contract would be. See Easterbrook, *supra* note 177, at 15. For a view of executive policymaking and inefficient legislation that is much more sensitive to the democratic process, see Sunstein, *Cost-Benefit Analysis and the Separation of Powers,* 23 ARIZ. L. REV. 1267 (1981).

182. Easterbrook, *supra* note 177, at 15. *But see* Stigler, *supra* note 139, at 7 (finding "modest support" for the conclusion that support for the Sherman Act came from small business).

fined. Although various interest groups (such as farmers, who purchased from monopolists and cartels) may have supported the legislation,[183] the legislation itself was in the public interest — or, more precisely, was designed to produce total gains larger than total costs.

On the other hand, an antitrust law such as the Robinson-Patman Act[184] would probably have to be considered special interest legislation.[185] The Robinson-Patman Act does not articulate any goal of economic efficiency. On the contrary, it was designed to protect small, inefficient retail grocers from large chain stores, which had lower costs and would drive the small grocers out of business in a competitive market. In this instance the small grocers had managed successfully to make their case before Congress, which forced the rest of American society to pay the bill.[186] The same thing can be said for the 1950 Celler-Kefauver amendments to the antimerger statute,[187] which were designed primarily to protect small business from horizontal and vertical mergers that produced more efficient rivals.[188]

Even within the Chicago School there appears to be disagreement about the ease with which courts can distinguish between public interest, or efficient, legislation and interest group, or special interest, legislation.[189] Perhaps more important, this distinction between types of statutes inserts into political theory a definition of efficiency that can be applied only ambiguously, if at all, to real world policy problems. To permit judges to weigh statutes on the basis of presumed efficiency and to give the interpretive edge to parties invoking efficient statutes is little more than to attempt to force a particular concept of efficiency into the democratic process. The argument means, quite simply, that "efficient" statutes are to be given more weight than "inefficient" ones. In the case of the latter, enforcement should be no broader than is clearly mandated by the language of the statute.

The argument can too easily be used to deny remedies that Congress anticipated but did not write into the statutory language. For example, Congress clearly had the protection of small business from

---

183. *See* Stigler, *supra* note 139, at 7.

184. 15 U.S.C. §§ 13-13b, 21a (1982).

185. *See* Baxter, *supra* note 1, at 662 n.6 (asserting that the Robinson-Patman Act is not "a true 'antitrust' act").

186. *See generally* Hansen, *supra* note 168.

187. Celler-Kefauver Act, ch. 1184, 64 Stat. 1125 (1950) (codified as amended at 15 U.S.C. §§ 18, 21 (1982 & Supp. II 1984)).

188. *See generally* Bok, *supra* note 168.

189. *Compare* Easterbrook, *supra* note 177, at 16-17 (suggesting that it is difficult or impossible to draw the line between public interest and special interest statutes); *with* Posner, *The Reading of Statutes, supra* note 58, at 270-71 (creating a four-type classification scheme for statutes).

larger competitors in mind when it passed *both* the Robinson-Patman Act[190] and the Celler-Kefauver amendments[191] to the antimerger statute. However, that intent is not readily apparent in the language of either statute. For example, all of the dirty work done by the Celler-Kefauver amendments and castigated by the Chicago School was accomplished by the statute's legislative history, not by its language.[192] That language, which condemns mergers the effect of which "may be substantially to lessen competition, or to tend to create a monopoly," is pernicious by Chicago School measurement not because of what it says, but because of what it means.[193] "Competition" within the meaning of the statute does not refer to a state of affairs in which prices are driven to marginal cost and firms are encouraged to pursue all economies in production and distribution. Rather it refers to a regime in which small businesses have a chance to compete against larger, more efficient rivals. There is no question that Congress had precisely that in mind; however, one will reach this conclusion only by examining the *Congressional Record* and the reports, not by reading the statutory language.[194]

The Chicago School's classification scheme for statutes is troublesome not only for what it does to statutory interpretation, but also for its self-serving compromise of the Chicago School model itself. The argument shows the nation's leading advocates of the free market dealing with troublesome legislation by suggesting numerous "market failures" of truly gargantuan proportions. Nearly all the world's other markets, including the common law,[195] work quite well within the

---

190. *See* Hansen, *supra* note 168. Chicago School scholars acknowledge as much. *See* R. BORK, *supra* note 6, at 382-84; R. POSNER, THE ROBINSON-PATMAN ACT: FEDERAL REGULATION OF PRICE DIFFERENCES 25-26 (1976).

191. *See generally* Bok, *supra* note 168. At least one Chicago School scholar agrees. *See* R. POSNER, *supra* note 19, at 99-100.

192. See the Supreme Court's analysis of the legislative history of the Celler-Kefauver amendments in Brown Shoe Co. v. United States, 370 U.S. 294, 311-23 (1962).

193. This language is criticized by at least one member of the Chicago School for the "incipiency" test which it creates. That is, it is designed to nip anticompetitive mergers in the bud by condemning mergers whose effect "may be" to lessen competition or which may "tend to" create a monopoly. *See* R. BORK, *supra* note 6, at 47-49. However, it seems that the real problem is not the "incipiency" test itself, but rather the definition of "competition" implicit in both the Celler-Kefauver amendments and the Supreme Court cases such as *Brown Shoe,* which interpreted them.

194. The legislative history is quite clear. *See* notes 191-92 *supra.*

195. On the common law as an efficient market, see Priest, *The Common Law Process and the Selection of Efficient Rules,* 6 J. LEGAL STUD. 65 (1977); Rubin, *Why is the Common Law Efficient?,* 6 J. LEGAL STUD. 51 (1982) (suggesting that both common law and legislation have become increasingly efficient in recent years). For good critiques of the notion that the common law is efficient, written from somewhat different perspectives, see Epstein, *The Social Consequences of Common Law Rules,* 95 HARV. L. REV. 1717 (1982); Friedman, *Two Faces of Law,*

Chicago School paradigm.[196] As a result, the State's reliance on the market should be very broad and the need for price regulation, artificial restrictions on entry, or other forms of state intervention are minimal. However, for some reason one market that seems not to work is the political market. The Chicago School literature on legislation is full of detailed explanations of why the legislative process consistently fails to produce "efficient" statutes.[197]

If a statute is truly efficient — that is, if the gains enjoyed by the interest groups that profit from the statute truly outweigh the losses suffered by those who lose — then any good Chicagoan should expect the political process to generate passage of the statute. The lobbying and other political resources contributed by the potential gainers should exceed those contributed by the potential losers, because the former should be willing to pay more to purchase passage of the statute than the latter are willing to pay to purchase its nonpassage.

On the other hand, the Chicagoan ought to expect "special interest" legislation not to be passed at all. In order for special interest legislation to be enacted, the special interest group that supports the statute must succeed in having its will with Congress even though it stands to gain less from the passage of the statute than the losers stand to lose. To be sure, it seems clear to this author that this happens, and that it happens often. That is not the point here. Rather, the point is that the Chicago School's distinction between special interest and efficient legislation is manifestly inconsistent with the general Chicago theory that when a market speaks — even a political market — the presumption is very strong that it should be listened to.[198]

V. CHICAGO SCHOOL ANTITRUST POLICY: CRITICISMS FROM INSIDE THE MODEL

Criticisms from "inside" the model assume that the model ad-

1984 WIS. L. REV. 13; Kennedy & Michelman, *Are Property and Contract Efficient?*, 8 HOFSTRA L. REV. 711 (1980).

196. Within the Chicago School model even "natural monopoly" public utilities might be better left to competitive bidding rather than price regulation. *See* Demsetz, *Why Regulate Utilities?*, 11 J. L. & ECON. 55 (1968). The theory is criticized in Shepherd, *"Contestability" vs. Competition,* 74 AM. ECON. REV. 572 (1984).

197. For an atypical — in fact, almost out of character — explanation of why the legislative "market" does not work, see Posner, *The Reading of Statutes, supra* note 58. *See generally* Becker, *A Theory of Competition Among Pressure Groups for Political Influence,* 98 Q. J. ECON. 371 (1983).

198. In fact, the political market has many characteristics that suggest it should work quite well — rather low entry barriers (anyone who wants has a constitutionally protected right to petition the government), a large number of competing participants, and easy access to market information.

dresses all relevant values that the policymaker must consider. Furthermore, such criticisms generally do not fault the Chicago School
premise that allocative efficiency should be the exclusive goal of antitrust enforcement.[199] The general nature of such critiques is that, even
though efficiency should be the exclusive goal of antitrust enforcement, the neoclassical market efficiency model is not sophisticated
enough to describe or predict the consequences of real world behavior.

This discussion is too brief to consider all critiques from inside the
model.[200] Rather, it focuses on two prominent weaknesses in the neoclassical market efficiency model that render the model too naive to be
the exclusive tool of antitrust policymakers: (1) an excessive reliance
on static concepts of the market in empirical situations where only
dynamic concepts will explain behavior or results; and (2) a failure to
appreciate fully the extent and welfare consequences of strategic behavior. The second weakness is in large part a consequence of the first.

A. *The Static Market Fallacy*

The neoclassical price theory model is static.[201] This means that it
measures the effects of certain practices on price or output *given* a
premise that the market being examined is unaffected by external
events. Unfortunately, antitrust policy must deal with real world markets, and real world markets are always affected by a complex array of
external influences. Application of a static model to a real world market often causes a court to ignore the obvious. To be sure, the assumption of a static market is a highly useful explanation device. The
premise that the economic analyst can "freeze" a market often yields a
clearer understanding of how a particular practice or phenomenon,
ceteris paribus, will affect price, output, or competition.[202]

To illustrate, the neoclassical market efficiency model shows quite
clearly that the monopolist will reduce output below the competitive

---

199. Criticism internal to the Chicago School model *may* disagree with the premise that
allocative efficiency should be the exclusive goal of the antitrust laws if they conclude that no
model for economic efficiency is capable of assessing the efficiency consequences of real world
behavior. In that case, admission of factors other than efficiency may be essential to
policymaking.

200. In fact, a great deal of both welfare economics and price theory — particularly the
theories first developed in the 1930s — was devoted to criticizing the market efficiency model as
developed by such neoclassical economists as Alfred Marshall. *See* text at notes 81-86 *supra.*

201. *See* Posner, *supra* note 6, at 939-40; Williamson, *Antitrust Enforcement, supra* note 23,
at 299-300; *see also* Kaplow, *supra* note 23, at 529-30 (criticizing Professor, now Judge, Easterbrook for relying too heavily on a static model).

202. The point is that *ceteris paribus* is an imaginary island that no real explorer will ever
find.

level.[203] The Standard Oil of New Jersey trust became a monopolist in the 1860s and 1870s.[204] No one has ever contended, however, that petroleum output was less in 1900, when Standard was a monopolist, than in 1860, when the market was structured more competitively. When we say that a monopolist "reduces output" we ordinarily do not examine a real world market before and after monopolization occurred and conclude that output was greater before than after. Rather, we compare the output that occurs under the existing monopoly with the *hypothetical* output that would occur in a market that was identical in all respects but for the existence of the monopoly. Importantly, that alternative market does not exist, never did exist, and never will exist. Only in the most extreme situations, such as where a dominant firm buys the plant of its only rival and shuts it down, can we engage with some confidence in before-and-after comparisons of empirical situations and conclude that monopoly reduces output. Many monopolists acquire their initial dominant position as a result of patents. As a result, total pre-monopoly output may have been far lower than output during the monopoly period.[205]

Consider, for example, the case of *Kartell v. Blue Shield*,[206] recently decided by the First Circuit. Judge Breyer, who authored the opinion, is not only a good federal judge, but also a good economist.[207] The opinion exonerated Blue Shield from charges that its ban on "balance billing" violated the Sherman Act. Blue Shield, a large health insurer with a market share approaching monopoly levels, had created a system under which participating doctors agreed to accept Blue Shield's published reimbursement rates as their total payment for a specified medical procedure.[208] The result was that a patient who went to a participating physician (from a list provided by Blue Shield) knew that his or her insurance policy would provide full coverage.

In addressing the question whether the Blue Shield plan amounted to illegal monopolization, Judge Breyer concluded — quite correctly,

---

203. *See* R. BORK, *supra* note 6, at 101; H. HOVENKAMP, *supra* note 17, at 14-24; Harberger, *Monopoly and Resource Allocation,* AM. ECON. REV., May 1954, at 77.

204. *See* B. BRINGHURST, ANTITRUST AND THE OIL MONOPOLY: THE STANDARD OIL CASES, 1890-1911, at 10-16 (1979).

205. Examples of monopolies that almost certainly produced far more than was produced before the monopoly came into existence are the monopolies at issue in United States v. Aluminum Co. of America, 148 F.2d 416 (2d Cir. 1945) (aluminum); United States v. E.I. du Pont de Nemours & Co., 351 U.S. 377 (1956) (cellophane); and E.I. du Pont de Nemours & Co., 96 F.T.C. 653 (1980) (titanium dioxide).

206. 749 F.2d 922 (1st Cir. 1984), *cert. denied,* 105 S. Ct. 2040 (1985).

207. *See* S. BREYER, REGULATION AND ITS REFORM (1982).

208. 749 F.2d at 923. For example, if Blue Shield paid $100 for a covered procedure, a doctor participating in the Plan could not charge $120 and force the patient to pay the difference.

it seems — that Blue Shield was a purchaser of physicians' services on behalf of its insureds.[209] This raised the possibility that Blue Shield's ban on balance billing might be an exercise of monopsony power. That is, Blue Shield may have been using its buying power in the market for health care services to force the price below the price that would prevail in an unrestrained, competitive market. The result of such an exercise of monopsony power would be that the supply of physicians' services would be reduced below the competitive equilibrium level. Judge Breyer suggested that the plaintiff's argument of monopsony was not well founded, citing with apparent approval the district court's finding that the supply of doctors in the market area had "increased steadily" during the period covered by the litigation.[210]

It can easily be shown geometrically or algebraically that when a monopsony buyer reduces its outlay to the profit-maximizing level, the result will be reduced output of the monopsonized product.[211] This only means, however, that the absolute supply of the monopsonized product will decrease if all other elements of the market remain unaffected during the period in which the market becomes monopsonized. As a result, the *backwards* reasoning — from the premise that supply did not decrease to the conclusion that the market was not monopsonized — works only if we can assume that a market was completely static during the relevant time period, but for the alleged violation.[212]

Not only is that assumption of a perfectly static market unwarranted, but it is impossible for a court to identify and measure the degree to which the market changed — that is, the degree to which all factors external to the market caused the supply of doctors to increase or decrease.[213] For example, during the relevant time period, Blue Shield's monopsony may have tended to reduce the supply of doctors or of medical services offered. However, hundreds of other factors

---

209. *Kartell,* 749 F.2d at 925-26.

210. 749 F.2d at 927.

211. For a geometric illustration, see G. STIGLER, THE THEORY OF PRICE 205 (3d ed. 1966); for an algebraic illustration, see J. HENDERSON & R. QUANDT, MICROECONOMIC THEORY: A MATHEMATICAL APPROACH 190-91 (1980).

212. *I.e.,* the premise works if we can either assume that the market was static, or we can identify and quantify all other changes in the market.

213. Professor Easterbrook is quite sanguine about a court's ability to identify and quantify all such changes. He suggests in a recent article that courts should assess the competitive effect on output. As to the practicability of such an approach, he concludes that "[t]here are statistical tools for doing this, if the data are available." Easterbrook, *supra* note 1, at 163-64. In fact, sufficient data are never available, and if they were, no agency would be large enough or powerful enough to deal with them. For a discussion of some of the random determinants of output, and the problems of predicting firm size or market share, see F. SCHERER, *supra* note 50, at 145-50. For some interesting observations concerning the current inability of econometricians to make accurate predictions concerning market or firm growth, see Blatt, *How Economists Misuse Mathematics,* in WHY ECONOMICS IS NOT YET A SCIENCE (A. Eichner ed. 1983).

might have encouraged the supply of doctors to increase during the same period. These might have included: (1) higher income by medical patients in the relevant market area; (2) a high rate of medical school graduation, perhaps caused by increasing funding for such education; (3) a high rate of illness in the relevant market area; (4) increased federal or state subsidies for health care; (5) a reduction in state taxes in the relevant market area, which induced professionals to move into that area; (6) a population increase; or (7) a change in immigration policy which admitted more foreign doctors into the area. The list is merely illustrative, but the point should be clear: to conclude that Blue Shield was not monopsonizing the market because the amount of the monopsonized product increased rather than decreased is not a legitimate use of the theoretical observation — which is quite true as far as it goes — that the exercise of monopsony power reduces market supply.[214]

The same thing can be said of vertical restrictions, such as those analyzed by the Supreme Court in *Continental T.V., Inc. v. GTE Sylvania, Inc.*[215] The Court noted that after Sylvania imposed territorial restrictions its overall market share increased from roughly two percent to roughly five percent.[216] It has been suggested by members of the Chicago School that the fact that a firm's market share or output *increased* after it began to employ vertical restrictions is strong evidence that a practice is competitive rather than anticompetitive.[217] In most cases, however, such evidence is irrelevant, for the court is incapable of assessing its meaning.

---

214. Actually, even the "output" question that Judge Breyer addressed in *Kartell* was the wrong one. He cited evidence that the *total* supply of physicians in Massachusetts had increased during the alleged monopolization period. *Kartell,* 749 F.2d at 927. A more appropriate question, however — and one that is at least theoretically easier to measure empirically — is not whether the absolute number of doctors in the entire market decreased as a result of monopsonization, but rather whether Blue Shield's *market share* decreased. When Blue Shield exercised monopsony power, total supply in the market would, *ceteris paribus,* decline. More importantly, Blue Shield's market share within that market would decline to the extent that the doctors looked for more profitable alternatives than dealing with Blue Shield under its medical cost reduction plan. Evidence that a firm's market share within a market changed is somewhat more convincing than evidence about output in the market as a whole, because the first kind of evidence segregates out all exogenous factors that affected the market as a whole. Nevertheless, even change in market share is extremely difficult to measure empirically, for the fortunes of individual firms in markets can vary enormously. *See* F. SCHERER, *supra* note 50, at 145-50.

215. 433 U.S. 36 (1977).

216. 433 U.S. at 38.

217. *See* Easterbrook, *supra* note 1, at 163-64 (footnote omitted). Professor Easterbrook suggests that a court analyzing vertical restrictions hold other factors such as demand constant. Then, if "the manufacturer's sales rise, the practice confers benefits exceeding its costs. If they fall, that suggests (although it does not prove) that there are no benefits." *Id.*; *see also* Posner, *supra* note 24, at 18. Posner would place on the government the burden of showing, "perhaps utilizing econometric methods," that the effect of the vertical restraint was to reduce the defendant's output. *Id.*

Why would a television manufacturer's market share roughly double in the space of a few years? Some obvious explanations come to mind: (1) perhaps it developed a superior television, where formerly it had struggled along with sets that were inferior; (2) perhaps it had been able to lower its relative costs, maybe because larger competitors had entered into unfavorable labor contracts, or perhaps because it was able to negotiate for low-cost production from abroad; or (3) perhaps a dominant firm in the industry had exited from the market or fallen on hard times.

In fact, any one of these market changes could have had a much more substantial impact on Sylvania's market share than its adoption of a restricted distribution scheme.[218] The lesson to be learned here is not that restricted distribution is monopolistic or inefficient. It is probably efficient in most situations in which it is employed.[219] However, a court cannot profitably engage in the simple device of comparing market share before and after the restrictions took effect in order to determine the effects of the practice on competition or welfare — not, at least, unless it can isolate and quantify all other variables that may have affected the defendant's market share. No court is likely to be capable of doing this.[220]

B.   *The Problem of Strategic Behavior*

Strategic behavior is conduct designed by the actor to reduce the attractiveness of the offers against which it must compete.[221] Not all

---

218. In fact, the adoption of restricted distribution may be quite risky. Output fell after Arnold, Schwinn & Co. imposed vertical nonprice restraints. United States v. Arnold, Schwinn & Co., 388 U.S. 365, 368-69 (1967). The restraints in *Schwinn* were declared illegal per se, but that case was overruled by Continental T.V., Inc. v. G.T.E. Sylvania, Inc., 433 U.S. 36 (1977). Presumably, the loss of output in *Schwinn* was not a result of the restraints, but of Schwinn's changing competitive position in the market. In this case an aggressive rival, Murray Ohio Manufacturing Co., surpassed Schwinn in sales.

219. See H. HOVENKAMP, *supra* note 17, at 248-58; Hovenkamp, *supra* note 56.

220. See note 214 *supra*. This is not to say that the static market fallacy is the exclusive prerogative of the Chicago School. On the contrary, very liberal United States Supreme Court Justices have been guilty as well. See, e.g., United States v. Container Corp., 393 U.S. 333, 337 (1969), in which Justice Douglas wrote for the Court that a price information exchange between competitors is illegal under § 1 of the Sherman Act if the information exchange affects the market price. To be sure, within the neoclassical market efficiency model a price information exchange could "affect" an equilibrium price either by facilitating collusion, or else by improving market information and causing price to stabilize. See Posner, *Information and Antitrust: Reflections on the* Gypsum *and* Engineers *Decisions,* 67 GEO. L.J. 1187 (1979). However, a rule that requires a court to *begin* with price data and determine the degree to which those prices were affected by a price information exchange is hopelessly unrealistic, except in the most extreme cases.

221. The definition, used in a different context, comes from Markovits, *supra* note 23, at 44. See also Markovits, *Some Preliminary Notes on the American Antitrust Laws' Economic Tests of Legality,* 27 STAN. L. REV. 841 (1975).

strategic behavior is socially harmful, and much of it is competitive.[222] In general, however, strategic behavior is harmful and raises antitrust concerns when it reduces the attractiveness of the offers against which the strategizing firm must compete *without* producing substantial gains in productive efficiency to the strategizing firm.[223] When socially harmful strategic behavior is successful, the firm engaging in the behavior earns monopoly profits, and competitors (or potential competitors) and customers pay the bill.

The static market fallacy[224] and the failure of orthodox Chicago School antitrust policy to take strategic behavior seriously[225] are closely related weaknesses in the market efficiency model. Both errors result from the model's failure to appreciate time and change, and the havoc these factors play with the economist's idea of competitive equilibrium, which exists nowhere in the real world, or at least not for long.[226]

The fact that strategic behavior exists and that it can be anticompetitive is not particularly controversial.[227] Far more controversial is the question whether antitrust policy should do something about harmful strategic behavior and, if so, what it is capable of doing given the limitations of the judicial process. One position, perhaps not irrational, is to acknowledge that anticompetitive strategic behavior exists but to conclude that the issues are too complex to be dealt with in antitrust litigation.[228] However, there certainly is no consensus among the courts that strategic behavior should be ignored.[229]

Although anticompetitive strategic behavior can take a wide variety of forms, these forms may be roughly grouped into two different

---

222. An example is product-improving research and development, which reduces the relative attractiveness of the offers against which the innovating firm must compete.

223. *See, e.g.,* Aspen Skiing Co. v. Aspen Highlands Skiing Corp., 105 S. Ct. 2847 (1985), discussed at notes 308-18 *infra.*

224. *See* text at notes 201-20 *supra.*

225. *See, e.g.,* McGee, *Predatory Pricing Revisited,* 23 J. L. & ECON. 289 (1980); *see also* Baxter, *supra* note 22, at 315 (acknowledging that harmful strategic behavior may occur, but arguing that, at least for now, courts cannot do much about it).

226. For some insights into the difficulties of measuring market power in markets that are not in equilibrium, see Pindyck, *The Measurement of Monopoly Power in Dynamic Markets,* 28 J. L. & ECON. 193 (1985).

227. *See* Baxter, *supra* note 22, at 316 (a Chicago School proponent acknowleding that strategic behavior occurs).

228. *See, e.g.,* Barry Wright Corp. v. ITT Grinnell Corp., 724 F.2d 227, 230-36 (1st Cir. 1983) (acknowledging that a price above average total cost might be "predatory" and thus anticompetitive, but declaring such prices lawful in part because the judicial process is not capable of undertaking the relevant economic analysis).

229. Though not explicitly identifying the targeted evil as "strategic behavior," courts have proscribed predatory pricing, which is a variant of such behavior. *See* 3 P. AREEDA & D. TURNER, ANTITRUST LAW ¶ 711 (1978).

categories. First, strategic behavior may include conduct that forces both the rival and the victims to sustain immediate losses. The conduct is profitable to the strategizing firm, however, because the strategist anticipates that the victim will be driven out of the market or into submission, and that the strategist will then be able to reap monopoly profits. Such strategic conduct is necessarily temporary, for even the well-financed strategist will not maximize its profits by sustaining losses indefinitely. The large traditional literature and case law on predatory pricing is concerned with this kind of strategic behavior.[230] Most Chicagoans believe that true predatory pricing is at least rare; they are divided on the question whether it occurs at all.[231]

The other kind of strategic behavior is immediately profitable to the dominant, strategizing firm. This behavior is generally initiated by the dominant firm or group of firms and is directed against smaller firms or, in some cases, potential entrants. The behavior is generally designed for one of two purposes. First, it may take advantage of irreversible investments made by fringe firms already in the market.[232] Second, it may force upon the smaller firms higher costs than the behavior imposes on the strategizing firm, although the behavior may be costly to the strategizing firm as well.[233] In both cases the strategizer earns monopoly profits *during* the period in which such strategic behavior occurs. As a result, such behavior is profitable even if it lasts for an indefinite time.[234]

Traditionally, antitrust policy has not only recognized strategic behavior, it has imagined a great deal of it that either did not exist or was in fact beneficial to the competitive process.[235] In general, antitrust case law has classified illegal strategic behavior as either "predatory" — that is, directed at small firms already in the market[236] — or else as

---

230. The literature is summarized in H. HOVENKAMP, *supra* note 17, at 172-81.

231. Those arguing that predatory pricing virtually never occurs include R. BORK, *supra* note 6, at 144-60; Easterbrook, *supra* note 77; McGee, *supra* note 225. A Chicago scholar who believes that predatory pricing may sometimes occur is Richard Posner. *See* R. POSNER, *supra* note 19, at 184-96.

232. *See* text at notes 247-88 *infra*.

233. *See* text at notes 289-307 *infra*.

234. "Predatory" pricing at prices above average total cost — often accompanied by the strategic carrying of excess capacity — also fits into this category. *See* Baumol, *Quasi-Permanence of Price Reductions: A Policy for Prevention of Predatory Pricing,* 89 YALE L.J. 1 (1979); Williamson, *Predatory Pricing, supra* note 23.

235. The classic example is Utah Pie Co. v. Continental Baking Co., 386 U.S. 685 (1967). *See* Hovenkamp & Silver-Westrick, *Predatory Pricing and the Ninth Circuit,* 1983 ARIZ. ST. L.J. 443, 462-63.

236. *See* William Inglis & Sons Baking Co. v. ITT Continental Baking Co., 668 F.2d 1014 (1981), *cert. denied,* 459 U.S. 825 (1982).

raising "barriers to entry" — that is, directed at potential rivals.[237]

Some economists reject the distinction between strategic behavior directed at incumbents and that directed at potential entrants as not useful analytically.[238] In one sense they are correct. When strategic behavior raises rivals' costs, it makes little difference whether these are costs of production or costs of entry.[239] The effect in both instances is to shelter the strategist from competition. Nevertheless, the distinction is important for antitrust policy for a number of reasons. One reason has to do with the way that the antitrust laws are enforced. Although strategic behavior is often directed at potential entrants rather than actual competitors, and although the potential entrant is a much easier target for cost-raising strategies than the incumbent firm is, the courts have been extremely skeptical about claims brought by "precluded plaintiffs."[240] Such plaintiffs allege they *would* have gone into business but for the inefficient exclusionary practices of an established rival.[241]

Likewise, within traditional antitrust case law the well-developed but perhaps misguided[242] concept of "barriers to entry" serves to distinguish the fringe firm already in the market from the firm seeking to enter. A properly defined barrier to entry generally protects *all* firms already in the market at the expense of the firm seeking entry. For example, a dominant firm that lobbies hard for a government-imposed cap on new entry (such as a maximum number of taxicab medallions) generally protects both itself and smaller competitors from new entry by outsiders. On the other hand, a dominant firm that employs an aggressive pricing strategy generally injures *both* established rivals and firms seeking entry.

Much of the literature on strategic behavior has been concerned with predatory pricing[243] and certain nonprice practices, such as product innovation,[244] which are sometimes alleged to be predatory. This writing is not surveyed here. Rather the discussion analyzes two kinds

---

237. *See* United States v. United Shoe Mach. Corp., 110 F. Supp. 295 (D. Mass. 1953), *affd. per curiam,* 347 U.S. 521 (1954).

238. *See* Demsetz, *supra* note 74.

239. A firm with no rivals at all, however, is still better off than a firm with high cost rivals. *See* Note, *Standing at the Fringe: Antitrust Damages and the Fringe Producer,* 35 STAN. L. REV. 763, 769-73 (1983).

240. *See* H. HOVENKAMP, *supra* note 17, at 461-63.

241. *See, e.g.,* Neumann v. Vidal, 710 F.2d 856 (D.C. Cir. 1983); Hayes v. Solomon, 597 F.2d 958 (5th Cir. 1979), *cert. denied,* 444 U.S. 1078 (1980).

242. *See* Demsetz, *supra* note 74.

243. *See* note 230 *supra.*

244. *See* Ordover & Willig, *An Economic Definition of Predation: Pricing and Product Innovation,* 91 YALE L.J. 8, 22-53 (1981).

of strategic behavior that are not yet well developed in the legal literature on antitrust policy. The two forms of strategic behavior have to do with the relationship between the credibility of threats and the sunk costs of either the dominant firm or the victim,[245] and the strategy of raising rivals' costs.[246] Although analysis of these strategies has not often appeared in the antitrust case law, both appear to be more susceptible to intelligent judicial analysis than predatory pricing is. Furthermore, it is quite plausible that these strategies are commonly used. If that is the case, then the two strategies should play a much more dominant role in the antitrust litigation of the future, provided the litigation system is capable of handling their complexities.

1. *Sunk Costs and Credible Threats*

The neoclassical market efficiency model concentrates on (1) long-run behavior, and (2) markets in which assets are freely transferable from one firm to another. In the real world, however, firms are often committed to short run investments in assets the costs of which cannot be fully recovered. This facilitates a great deal of monopoly pricing.[247]

The market efficiency model tends to look at markets over the long run, over which they generally appear to behave competitively. The "long run" refers to a period that is sufficiently long that a firm can make the optimal choice about such questions as what size plant to build and where to build it.[248] Over the long run, firms will tend to build plants of optimal size which are efficiently distributed throughout the market. As a result, over the long run firms will be forced either to operate efficiently or to exit from the market. Likewise, over the long run, new firms will enter a monopolized market and bring it into competitive equilibrium.[249]

In many markets, however, the long run is indeed very long. A steel mill or chemical plant can easily have a life expectancy of forty years, and may last much longer. In the real world, firms frequently do not have the luxury of dwelling exclusively on the long run. They

---

245. *See* text at notes 247-88 *infra.*

246. *See* text at notes 289-307 *infra.*

247. Perhaps the best statement of this position is Klein, Crawford & Alchian, *Vertical Integration, Appropriable Rents, and the Competitive Contracting Process,* 21 J. L. & ECON. 297 (1978). *See also* Williamson, *Credible Commitments: Using Hostages to Support Exchange,* 73 AM. ECON. REV. 519 (1983).

248. *See* E. MANSFIELD, *supra* note 151, at 194-201.

249. *Id.* Professor Easterbrook suggests that the goal of the antitrust laws is to "speed up the arrival of the long run." Easterbrook, *Limits, supra* note 8, at 2. That language is largely rhetorical, since the long run never "arrives." Perhaps more accurately, the economic goal of antitrust policy is to make short-run market behavior approximate long-run behavior as accurately as possible.

must deal with a previously made decision about plant size and location. Often it is cheaper to operate the existing plant, in spite of possible inefficiencies, than to get rid of the plant and build one of a better size, or one that is located in a better place.

Likewise, in the real world many fixed cost assets are not freely transferable from one firm to another. Firms must constantly deal with the problem of "sunk" costs — that is, costs that simply cannot be recovered if a firm exits from the market. Sunk costs should be distinguished from "fixed" costs or capital costs, which a firm must spend in entering a new market but which it will be able to recover when it decides to exit. Although sunk costs are usually fixed costs, many fixed costs are not sunk costs. Every entry into a new market entails a certain amount of sunk costs, although the extent of sunk costs varies greatly from one market to the next.[250]

The extent of sunk costs depends on whether the firm exiting the market will be able to sell everything, including its good will, to a successor firm or whether it must take its productive capacity out of use entirely. For example, the restaurant owner who goes out of business may be able to transfer everything to a successor, including his built-up investment in name recognition, if the successor assumes the previous firm's name, method of doing business, etc. If liquor licenses are not transferable, however, the old firm's expense in obtaining its initial liquor license will be sunk — that is, it will have to be borne by the original firm. At the other extreme, a firm that goes out of business because it is poorly situated in a market with excess capacity may find that even its plant must be dismantled and sold for its salvage value. In that case, sunk costs may be substantial.[251]

Although the impact of sunk costs is felt most strongly when the firm exits from a certain market, a rational firm will consider the extent of these costs when it makes a decision to enter. In short, the cost of *exit* from a market operates as a barrier to *entry*.[252] In a market in which capital flows freely into profitable areas, the fact that it costs $10,000,000 to enter a certain market is not nearly as important as the

---

250. The economic literature on sunk costs, fixed costs, and strategic behavior is growing, although much of it is very technical. *See* W. BAUMOL, J. PANZAR & R. WILLIG, CONTESTABLE MARKETS AND THE THEORY OF INDUSTRY STRUCTURE 280-82, 482-83 (1982); Baumol & Willig, *Fixed Costs, Sunk Costs, Entry Barriers and Sustainability of Monopoly,* 96 Q. J. ECON. 405 (1981).

251. In this case sunk costs equal the unamortized cost of the plant, less the salvage value.

252. *See* Dixit, *The Role of Investment in Entry-Deterrence,* 90 ECON. J. 95 (1980); Eaton & Lipsey, *Exit Barriers Are Entry Barriers: the Durability of Capital as a Barrier to Entry,* 11 BELL J. ECON. 721 (1980).

fact that only ten percent of those costs can be recovered if the investment proves unprofitable and exit becomes necessary.

Likewise, the extent of sunk costs will influence a firm's decision about when to exit. For example, it is often said that a firm will continue to produce as long as it is covering its average variable costs, even if it is losing money because its earnings do not cover its fixed costs. The statement is true, however, only if the firm's fixed costs are also sunk costs.[253] If the firm can exit the market by selling out to another firm willing to assume its entire capital commitment, then exit will be the best alternative any time business becomes unprofitable.[254]

Dominant firms can make strategic use of sunk costs in two different ways: (1) the dominant firm might take advantage of the sunk costs of smaller firms in order to obtain monopoly profits at their expense; or (2) the dominant firm might make sunk cost investments of its own in order to make its threats credible.[255] Both strategies can result in extended periods of monopoly pricing.

a. Strategy, vertical integration and sunk costs. As a basic premise, vertical integration is efficient and should not be of concern to the antitrust laws. However, occasionally vertical integration, or in some cases the absence of integration, may permit a firm to take strategic advantage of a vertically related firm's sunk costs. The result of such advantage taking can be a deadweight efficiency loss similar to the loss that results from exercises of monopoly power.[256]

Certain vertical integration strategies, such as tying arrangements and exclusive dealing, permit firms to make the best use of or to minimize the risk of sunk cost investments. For example, the firm planning to build a large plant may use exclusive dealing arrangements to guarantee a market for itself once its investment in a certain amount of productive capacity has been made. Such use of market-based vertical integration strategies is generally efficient insofar as it prevents other

---

253. Sometimes fixed costs that are not sunk are referred to as "avoidable fixed costs." *See* D. McCLOSKEY, THE APPLIED THEORY OF PRICE 282-83 (1982).

254. For example, suppose that a firm's only capital asset is a general purpose delivery truck, whose fixed costs are amortized at $500 per month. Variable costs are $10 per hour. A firm operating the truck 100 hours per month with revenues of $12 per hour is covering its variable costs and contributing $200 to fixed costs. Continued operation in this case is "loss minimizing" — i.e., less costly than no operation at all. However, the firm is still losing $300 per month. If the firm can sell the truck to a different firm which is willing to assume the *entire* fixed cost liability, it will be even better off.

If an asset is highly specialized, its owner is less likely to be able to sell it for its entire fixed cost. Thus, in general, the more specialized an asset is, the higher will be the percentage of sunk investment in it.

255. *See* Williamson, *Predatory Pricing, supra* note 23.

256. *See* text at notes 123-41 *supra.*

firms from taking advantage of the investor's sunk costs.[257] However, the coin has another side. A firm may strategically take advantage of a vertically related firm's failure to guarantee its market by means of exclusive dealing arrangements or some alternative. One example of this is *Great Atlantic & Pacific Tea Co. v. FTC,*[258] which is known to antitrust lawyers as a case that substantially emasculated section 2(f) of the Robinson-Patman Act.[259] A&P was able to solicit a very low bid from Borden, one of its suppliers of dairy products, because Borden had recently built a new plant nearby and would not be able to produce at capacity if it lost the very large A&P contract. In short, once the Borden plant was built, Borden inadvertently made itself a "captive" to A&P, which was able to take advantage of the situation by forcing a very low bid from Borden.[260]

The best solution in such cases may be to permit the market to discipline Borden for its short-sightedness. Next time it will guarantee its market, perhaps by exclusive dealing arrangements, *before* it makes a large commitment to a new plant. The market solution will not always work, however, because not every situation conducive to taking advantage of sunk cost commitments can be foreseen. Perhaps more importantly, if every one that could be foreseen had to be covered before investment would occur, there would be much less investment.[261] In such circumstances the antitrust laws can encourage effi-

---

257. *See* Marvel, *Exclusive Dealing,* 25 J. L. & ECON. 1 (1982); Williamson, *Credible Commitments,* 29 ANTITRUST BULL. 33, 52-54 (1984). Firms may sometimes use tying arrangements in order to protect sunk cost investments. For example, see Northern Pac. Ry. v. United States, 356 U.S. 1 (1958), in which the Supreme Court condemned under the Sherman Act an arrangement by which Northern Pacific sold land close to its tracks using deeds containing covenants under which the grantee promised to ship over Northern Pacific's lines, provided that Northern Pacific's freight rates were competitive with those of other railroads. In this case Northern Pacific had made a large sunk investment in a natural monopoly market (railroad lines). In general, multifirm competition in natural monopoly markets will drive prices down to a level that is insufficient to enable each firm to make a profit. The covenants effectively guaranteed that Northern Pacific could retain 100% of the freight business simply by matching the price of any new entrant. The result was to create a very powerful entry deterrence mechanism. No firm would want to be second entrant into a natural monopoly market if it knew that it always had to undersell a rival in order to obtain any business at all.

258. 440 U.S. 69 (1979).

259. The case held that a buyer could not violate the Robinson-Patman Act unless the seller had also violated it. Thus, if the seller could avail itself of the good faith "meeting competition" defense, the buyer could not be in violation of the statute, even if the differential pricing ("price discrimination," within the meaning of the statute) was caused by the buyer's misrepresentation. 440 U.S. at 75-85. *See* H. HOVENKAMP, *supra* note 17, at 350.

260. 440 U.S. at 73. For an analogous situation involving contractual agreements between General Motors Corp. and Fisher Body Co., see Klein, Crawford & Alchian, *supra* note 247, at 308-10.

261. Arguably, such a rule would require complete vertical integration of all firms having sunk cost investments. Since all firms probably have at least *some* sunk costs, this could mean that virtually all of the enterprise would have to be organized into a single firm.

cient investment by protecting firms from strategic, inefficient advantage taking by others.

Within the Chicago School model, vertical integration is virtually always efficient; it is harmful only if it facilitates collusion or perhaps price discrimination.[262] Since the laws against collusion can be used against the first of these, and since the second is very difficult for courts to analyze, many Chicago School writers have argued that all vertical integration should be legal.[263]

For example, the Chicago School has been extremely critical of Judge Hand's analysis in *Alcoa*[264] of the price and supply "squeeze" by which Alcoa supposedly monopolized the market for aluminum.[265] The "squeeze," which was recently revived in *Bonjorno v. Kaiser Aluminum & Chemical Corp.,*[266] was described by Judge Hand as a mechanism by which a vertically integrated monopolist might leverage additional monopoly profits by squeezing independent firms between high costs and low output prices.[267]

The allegation in both *Alcoa* and *Bonjorno* was that the vertically integrated monopolist produced raw aluminum ingot, some of which it fabricated itself and some of which it sold to independent fabricators. The monopolist allegedly sold the raw aluminum to the independent fabricators at a high price, but charged a low output price through its subsidiary fabricators for the fabricated product. As a result the independents were caught between the high price they had to pay for the raw aluminum and the low price they were able to collect for fabricated aluminum.

The Chicago School critique of the price squeeze rests on a number of observations. First, why would a firm that presumably has the right to deal or refuse to deal as it pleases bother to use a price squeeze to injure independent fabricators? It could quite easily refuse to deal with independents and fabricate all of its aluminum itself. Second, the notion that the squeeze is profitable is simply another instance of the overused leverage theory that a monopolist can use its monopoly power in one market to obtain additional monopoly profits in a second market.[268] However, as has been demonstrated many times, the mo-

---

262. *See* Bork, *supra* note 125; Easterbrook, *supra* note 1; Posner, *supra* note 106.

263. *See* Bork, *supra* note 125; Easterbrook, *supra* note 1; Posner, *supra* note 106.

264. United States v. Aluminum Co., 148 F.2d 416, 436-37 (2d Cir. 1945).

265. *Cf.* Bork, *supra* note 125, at 163-65 (criticizing Hand's "squeeze" doctrine as applied in United States v. Corn Prods. Ref. Co., 234 F. 964 (S.D.N.Y. 1916)).

266. Bonjorno v. Kaiser Aluminum & Chem. Corp., 752 F.2d 802, 808-10 (3d Cir. 1984), *petition for cert. filed*, 53 U.S.L.W. 3883 (U.S. June 6, 1985) (No. 84-1907).

267. 148 F.2d at 436-37.

268. *See* R. BORK, *supra* note 6, at 243-44.

nopolist of a single stage in a distribution system can obtain its full monopoly markup in that stage alone and will not enlarge its profits by adding another stage. This criticism applies equally to tying arrangements and reciprocity, exclusive dealing, vertical mergers and the price squeeze, as well as other forms of vertical integration by the monopolist.[269]

Posner and Easterbrook argue that the price squeeze can reflect three different circumstances. The first is the existence of efficiencies on the part of the vertically integrated relationship: to the extent the market transaction between the aluminum manufacturer and the independent fabricator costs money, the fully integrated fabricators will be able to undersell the independent fabricators, which will have higher costs. Secondly, the squeeze may reflect Alcoa's efforts to break up a cartel of independent fabricators by vertically integrating into fabrication itself. Finally, the dual fabrication system may be a mechanism by which Alcoa engages in price discrimination. Posner and Easterbrook conclude that only the third of these phenomena raises any antitrust concerns.[270]

Their analysis is based on the assumption that the assets of the independent fabricators are costlessly transferable.[271] In fact, the price squeeze may often be a mechanism by which a monopolist takes advantage of a vertically related firm's sunk investment in order to force an infracompetitive rate of return on the firm — at the extreme, a rate of return sufficient to cover only the firm's average variable costs.[272] In that case the monopolist will effectively transfer to itself the smaller firm's return on the fixed-cost part of its investment. The independent fabricator will not go out of business because production in this case produces fewer losses than shutdown would.[273]

---

269. *See* H. HOVENKAMP, *supra* note 17, at 199 (vertical integration in general); *id.* at 222-224 (tying arrangements and exclusive dealing).

270. R. POSNER & F. EASTERBROOK, *supra* note 77, at 874-75.

271. Alternatively, this analysis may be based on the even more implausible assumption that the independent fabricators have no fixed costs.

272. Plus the annualized salvage value of its fixed cost assets. *See* text at notes 250-51 *supra.*

273. That is, assuming the firm is not forced into bankruptcy and shutdown. By pursuing this strategy, the monopolist will make more money than it would make by vertically integrating into fabrication itself. If it did that, it would have to recover its fixed as well as its variable costs. Effectively, the monopolist is transferring to itself that part of the independent fabricator's return that reflects the fixed cost investment.

Suppose that a firm invests in land and a plant capable of producing 1,000,000 units of fabricated aluminum per year. Retirement of the fixed cost investment over the life of the plant requires an annual payment of $1,000,000 per year. The costs of the raw material, energy, labor and other variable cost items total $1.25 per unit. When the plant is operating at capacity it will be marginally profitable at a market price of $2.25 per unit — $1.00 per unit to cover fixed costs and $1.25 to cover variable costs. However, the firm will not shut down unless the market price drops below $1.25 per unit. The fixed costs must be paid whether or not the firm produces. If

In the long run, when the plant wears out, the independent fabricator faced with this dilemma will exit the market or relocate where the supply of raw material is more competitive. At that time the monopolist may vertically integrate into the market from which the independent exits. For the time being, however, the monopolist profits by taking strategic advantage of the independent's sunk costs.

b. The Bonjorno *case.* The facts of the Third Circuit's recent decision in *Bonjorno v. Kaiser Aluminum & Chemical Corp.*[274] suggest that the defendant took anticompetitive advantage of a buyer's sunk costs in order to facilitate collusion at the buyer's expense, while simultaneously forcing the buyer to accept infracompetitive returns.

It is well known that various kinds of vertical integration can facilitate horizontal collusion at either the manufacturer (supplier) or the retailer (distributor) level.[275] Most of the literature on the use of vertical integration to facilitate collusion has focused on the conspirator's use of vertical new entry, mergers, territorial division and resale price maintenance. However, exclusive dealing probably facilitates horizontal upstream collusion more effectively than resale price maintenance and perhaps more effectively than vertical nonprice restraints such as territorial division.[276]

Collusion at the manufacturer level, whether express or tacit, can be frustrated if large, well-informed buyers force the colluders to compete against each other by making various concessions.[277] For example, the OPEC cartel has been nearly undermined by the fact that most of its buyers are large and well informed and have been able to strategize their buying so as to keep individual OPEC members unin-

---

the market price drops to $1.50 the firm will still contribute twenty-five cents per unit to fixed costs and will "lose" $750,000 per year. However, if it ceases production it will be obligated to pay $1,000,000 per year.

The strategizing firm, which operates in similar markets, can quite easily guess the amount of the victim's sunk costs. Furthermore, it does not need to rob the victim of all return on fixed costs. Any amount that it takes will be profitable.

274. 752 F.2d 802 (3d Cir. 1984), *petition for cert. filed,* 53 U.S.L.W. 3883 (U.S. June 6, 1985) (No. 84-1907).

275. *See* Hovenkamp, *supra* note 56; Liebeler, *Intrabrand "Cartels" under* GTE Sylvania, 30 UCLA L. REV. 1 (1982).

276. The concern that vertical restraints, including exclusive dealing, can facilitate collusion is addressed in the Department of Justice Vertical Restraints Guidelines, 48 ANTITRUST & TRADE REG. REP. (BNA) special supp. 3, 6 (Jan. 23, 1985). However, the guidelines do not distinguish the ways in which exclusive dealing might facilitate collusion from the ways in which vertical territorial division or resale price maintenance might accomplish the same end. *See generally* Marvel, *supra* note 257.

277. *See* E.I. du Pont de Nemours & Co. v. FTC, 729 F.2d 128, 141 (2d Cir. 1984) (citing this as a reason for not condemning alleged tacit collusion); H. HOVENKAMP, *supra* note 17, at 107-09.

formed about what competitors are doing.[278]

The cartel faced with disruptive buyers has a choice of strategic responses.[279] First, it can eliminate the buyers by integrating vertically into the buyers' production level. Such a strategy is expensive, however, and places the cartel members under the antitrust law of vertical mergers, unless they integrate by new entry into the market where the disruptions are occurring. Integration by new entry can be disruptive of existing capacity, however, calling unnecessary attention to the cartel members' activities.

The cartel members can eliminate the disruptive buyer problem by exclusive dealing with the established downstream firms. Under an exclusive dealing arrangement, each buyer has a requirements contract with a particular seller and will not be permitted to purchase from one of the other cartel members. The buyer obligated by the exclusive dealing arrangement is effectively prevented from forcing the members of the sellers' cartel to compete with one another.

Such exclusive dealing will work, however, only if the buyer is agreeable to exclusive dealing. The buyer who knows that the exclusive dealing is being used to facilitate collusion at the upstream level is not likely to be agreeable, because the upstream collusion will cut into its own profits. In that case, a certain amount of strategic behavior on the part of the upstream firm may be necessary. Such strategic behavior will be possible if the buyer has substantial sunk costs in its own position in the product and geographic markets.

The facts of the *Bonjorno* case were as follows: The aluminum industry was an oligopoly, with only a few major producers.[280] These producers had facilitated tacit collusion by developing a scheme under which all of them manufactured raw aluminum, but each became the dominant firm with respect to a particular intermediate level aluminum product from which finished products were fabricated. In short, they engaged in tacit product market division. The defendant Kaiser was the dominant firm in the manufacture of aluminum coil and sheet, which is used to make aluminum pipe. The plaintiff was an independent fabricator which purchased coil and sheet from the defendant and turned it into pipe. Because of the product division scheme, the

---

278. *See generally* J. MARQUEZ, OIL PRICE EFFECTS AND OPEC'S PRICING POLICY: AN OPTIMAL CONTROL APPROACH (1984).

279. The theory that a disruptive buyer can frustrate cartelization is developed in the context of vertical merger policy in 4 P. AREEDA & D. TURNER, *supra* note 229, at ¶ 1006. *See also* Justice Department's 1984 Merger Guidelines, *supra* note 36, at 26,836; P. AREEDA & H. HOVENKAMP, *supra* note 55, at ¶ 1000.1b.

280. Bonjorno v. Kaiser Aluminum & Chem. Corp., 752 F.2d 802, 809 (3d Cir. 1984).

plaintiff was effectively dealing with a monopolist.[281]

Defendant Kaiser also competed with the plaintiff in the fabrication of pipe by its wholly owned fabricators. The plaintiff alleged that Kaiser had imposed a classical price squeeze on the plaintiff by selling coil and sheet at a price so near the market price for finished pipe that profitable independent fabrication was impossible.[282] Secondly, the plaintiff alleged that the defendant continually ordered the plaintiff to buy coil and sheet only from the defendant and threatened to build its own fabrication plant near the plaintiff's plant if the plaintiff should ever attempt to buy coil and pipe from one of the defendant's competitors.[283] Finally, when the plaintiff purchased aluminum from a competitor, the defendant carried out its threat and built a plant forty miles from the plaintiff's plant.[284]

This strategy is quite plausible if the manufacturer is "best placed" vis-à-vis the buyer — that is, if the buyer in an industry with high transportation costs is closer to the manufacturer than any other buyer is, thus giving the two firms a transportation cost advantage with respect to one another. The strategy will work even better if the buyer has a specialized plant dedicated to the processing of the manufacturer's product. Because of the plant's specialized character, its salvage value if taken out of that particular market is much less than its cost. The difference between the unamortized cost of the buyer's plant and its salvage value is a sunk cost which the manufacturer can use to its advantage. At the extreme, the monopoly manufacturer could force the buyer's margin down to a level sufficient to cover average variable costs plus the salvage value of the plant, without enough left over to cover fixed costs. In that case the monopolist will have developed a captive purchaser, who cannot move, cannot find an alternative supplier, and would lose even more money if it shut down.[285]

Suppose, for example, that the plant has a cost of $1,000,000 per year and a salvage value of $200,000 per year. The average variable cost of fabricating the aluminum is $1500 per unit plus the price that the fabricator pays for the aluminum. The plant has a capacity of 1000 units of aluminum per year. In order to be profitable when it is operating at capacity, the fabricator must obtain $2500 more than the wholesale price for the final product — $1500 to cover average variable costs and $1000 to cover fixed costs.

---

281. 752 F.2d at 809.
282. 752 F.2d at 810.
283. 752 F.2d at 808.
284. 752 F.2d at 808.
285. *See* text at notes 271-73 *supra*.

However, the plant will not shut down unless its margin (the difference between the wholesale price and its output price) falls to an amount insufficient to cover the average variable costs plus the salvage value. Suppose that the monopolist manufacturer raises the wholesale price of ingot to the independent fabricator, while continuing to sell fabricated aluminum through its own fabricators at its profit-maximizing price. As a result the margin between the independent fabricator's wholesale price and its output price falls to $1800. In that case the fabricator will be losing money because the margin is insufficient to cover its total costs. Nevertheless, it will stay in production because the margin yields an annual amount equal to average variable costs plus $300,000, which is $100,000 more than the fabricator could obtain by shutting down and salvaging the plant.

The strategizing monopolist who knows that the independent firm's fabrication plant has a useful remaining life of, say, ten years, would engage in this price squeeze for ten years. Presumably at that time the independent fabricator would exit the market since it cannot make a profit, and the monopolist could build its own fabrication plant to serve that market. During the ten-year interval, the monopolist would pocket a substantial amount of the fabricator's annualized sunk costs.[286]

The view that a monopolist can make strategic, inefficient use of a vertically related firm's sunk costs does nothing to undermine the traditional Chicago School notion that vertical integration is efficient and generally should not raise antitrust concerns. On the contrary, vertical integration generally eliminates such advantage taking, and this is one of the principal reasons that firms engage in vertical integration.[287] In this case the antitrust concern is caused, not by vertical integration, but by its absence.

The manufacturer like that in the *Bonjorno* case, faced with fabricators unwilling to participate in exclusive dealing, might have to advance various credible threats in order to make the fabricators believe that de facto exclusive dealing was in their best interests. Since the fabricator's plants are already built, the threat to refuse to deal with a fabricator who bought from a competitor, and then to build a manufacturer-owned fabrication plant nearby, plus the well-publicized

---

286. The evidence in *Bonjorno* indicated that the defendant used a pricing formula for independent fabricators tagged to the costs of its wholly owned fabricators. The formula generated a markup sufficient to cover "direct costs" of production, but insufficient to cover "corporate overhead." *Bonjorno*, 752 F.2d at 809-10. That language, while somewhat ambiguous about the economic costs at issue, suggests that the formula gave the plaintiff enough revenue to cover variable costs, but not enough to cover fixed costs as well.

287. *See* Klein, Crawford & Alchian, *supra* note 247.

termination of one fabricator who failed to get the message, could certainly be effective.[288] This would be particularly true if the supplying manufacturer were better placed to supply the independent fabricator than other manufacturers were. For example, if Kaiser is closer to Bonjorno's fabrication plant than any other aluminum manufacturer, Bonjorno should know that its own costs will go up if it can no longer purchase aluminum sheet and coil from Kaiser. More to the point, Bonjorno could not compete with a Kaiser-owned fabricator close by if the Kaiser-owned fabricator had the advantages of both any economies created by manufacturer ownership *and* a better-placed supplier (Kaiser) than Bonjorno had. Moreover, once Kaiser had built its own plant nearby, Bonjorno would be unable to recover the costs of its plant, except for the salvage value. Bonjorno would realize that its own interests required taking Kaiser's threat seriously and deal only with Kaiser.

2. *Raising Rivals' Costs*

An important kind of strategic behavior generally overlooked in antitrust literature, although recently addressed in economic writing, has been most aptly described as "raising rivals' costs."[289] This behavior is generally initiated by the dominant firm or group of firms and directed against smaller firms. It is designed to force upon the smaller firms higher costs than it imposes on the strategizing firm, although the behavior may raise the costs of the strategizing firm as well. The result is that the profit-maximizing output of the victims is decreased, and the strategizer can reap the benefit in higher prices or enlarged output. Importantly, the strategizer can earn monopoly profits *during* the period in which such strategic behavior occurs — in fact, often it will earn them only during the period in which the strategic behavior occurs. As a result, such behavior is profitable even if it lasts indefinitely.

Since a relatively small amount of scholarship and virtually no litigation has been devoted expressly to the problem of raising rivals' costs, it is difficult to say how often the strategy is pursued by dominant firms or groups of firms, or what its welfare effects are. It is quite plausible, however, that the strategy is both common and quite harmful to consumer welfare.[290] In that case it should be an antitrust

---

288. Kaiser might also build its own fabricating plant if Bonjorno's plant became obsolete or was nearing the end of its useful life.

289. *See* Salop & Scheffman, *supra* note 23.

290. That is, the strategy results in reduced output and higher prices. Salop and Scheffman offer a few generalizations about the welfare effects. *Id.* at 270.

concern.

There is an intuitive reason for thinking that strategic raising of rivals' costs is more common than predatory pricing. As a strategy, raising rivals' costs can be both more profitable and less risky than predation, and it can occur in a wider variety of markets.[291] Under traditional theories of predatory pricing[292] a dominant firm attempts to dispatch a rival from the market by undergoing an indefinite period of below-cost selling in the hope that the victim will leave the market before the predator's resources are exhausted. Not only is this strategy very expensive at the onset, but it is also seldom likely to be successful. Even if the victim is forced into bankruptcy by the predatory pricing, it will sell its assets at a low price to a new firm who will maintain the victim's productive capacity on the market.

Raising rivals' costs, on the other hand, does not involve an initial term of loss selling to be followed by the mere likelihood of monopoly profits. The monopoly profits may flow in immediately. Furthermore, the strategy need not involve any event as cataclysmic (and therefore calculated to invite antitrust litigation) as the exit of a firm from the market. The market may look quite "normal," with relatively stable market shares and competitive profits earned by smaller firms, although dominant firms will earn more.[293] In fact, one of the greatest advantages of pursuing a strategy of raising rivals' costs is its subtlety. For all these reasons, but particularly because they are more likely to be successful, threats to raise rivals' costs may be more credible than threats to engage in predatory pricing.[294]

Finally, in many cases a strategy of raising rivals' costs will be profitable even if the market is not monopolized or not particularly conducive to monopolization or tacit price collusion. Tacit collusion with respect to activities that raise rivals' costs may be easier to

---

291. There is general agreement that predatory pricing will work only in concentrated markets containing high barriers to entry and in which the predator is a dominant firm. *See* H. HOVENKAMP, *supra* note 17, at 179-84.

292. It should be noted, however, that a substantial "predatory pricing" literature deals with nontraditional forms of predatory pricing — such as the strategic construction of excess capacity in industries subject to economies of scale, which facilitates so-called "limit pricing." In such cases the victims of the predatory pricing are generally firms that would like to enter the predator's market, but have not yet done so. *See* Salop, *supra* note 23; Williamson, *Predatory Pricing, supra* note 23. Other scholarship is summarized in H. HOVENKAMP, *supra* note 17, at 175-79.

293. Evidence that dominant firms are earning higher profits than fringe firms can be found in a variety of markets. Such evidence may imply no more than that the market is subject to economies of scale, although it generally suggests a certain amount of collusion, whether express or tacit, on the part of the dominant firms. *See* Weiss, *The Structure-Conduct-Performance Paridigm and Antitrust,* 127 U. PA. L. REV. 1104, 1115-19 (1979).

294. *See* Salop & Scheffman, *supra* note 23, at 267.

achieve than tacit collusion respecting price or output. Furthermore, such tacit collusion may work quite well in markets that do not have natural entry barriers that make them conducive to tacit collusion. In fact, one effect of raising rivals' costs may be to create artificial entry barriers.

For example, an industry dominated by three or four firms and containing a competitive fringe might be in a position either to engage in self-regulation or to petition the government for certain forms of regulation.[295] In that case the dominant firms might easily reach a tacit understanding regarding their support for a regulation, compliance with which is subject to economies of scale. Each dominant firm acting alone will know that the effect of the regulation will be to leave its position unchanged vis-à-vis the other larger firms but will disproportionately raise the costs of fringe firms and perhaps the entry costs for potential rivals.

The notion that dominant firms can strategically manipulate the costs of rivals may change some of our ideas about price behavior in concentrated markets.[296] Within the classical theory of oligopoly the "price leader" is generally a dominant firm in the market. A fringe firm would not make a good price leader because it would be unable to make credible threats against other fringe firms who cut price. Such threats are unnecessary, however, if no fringe firms are likely to cut price because their own costs are higher than those of the dominant firm. In that case it may work to the advantage of a dominant firm to permit one or more fringe firms to be the price leader(s). The high cost fringe firms will set a price sufficient to cover their costs, and the low cost dominant firm can earn monopoly profits and retain its market share simply by matching the fringe firm's pricing.

Consider the following strategies:

(1) The dominant firm files litigation against a nondominant competitor. This could be patent or other intellectual property litigation, regulatory litigation, or litigation of virtually any other kind. The litigation forces the two firms to spend roughly equal amounts, but it is much more costly to the smaller firm, for the costs are distributed over a smaller output.[297]

(2) The dominant firm or group of firms petitions the government

---

295. *See* text at notes 298-302 *infra*.

296. For the traditional Chicago School theory, see R. BORK, *supra* note 6, at 179-96; R. POSNER, *supra* note 19, at 42-47.

297. *See, e.g.,* MCI Communications v. American Tel. & Tel. Co., 708 F.2d 1081 (7th Cir.), *cert. denied*, 464 U.S. 891 (1983); National Cash Register Corp. v. Arnett, 554 F. Supp. 1176 (D. Colo. 1983). Other cases are discussed in Annot., 71 A.L.R. FED. 723 (1985).

or a regulatory agency for a procedure or fee that will cost both dominant and nondominant firms the same absolute amount to implement. The effect is that the compliance cost per unit is higher for the nondominant firm. Importantly, the petition need not be for a requirement that will have an impact only on the nondominant firm (as when a railroad petitions the government for stricter regulations for truckers).[298] A large trucker might petition the government for stricter regulations for all truckers, including itself. It might profit from the adoption of such a rule if compliance is cheaper per unit of output for large firms than it is for small firms. Today it is well established that substantial economies of scale obtain for compliance with certain types of regulation.[299] A dominant firm would do well to campaign for such regulation, for the result would be to impose disproportionately higher costs on smaller firms.

(3) Alternatively, a trade association that engages in self-regulation or self-evaluation of products and that is dominated by a few large firms might adopt a product standard compliance with which is subject to substantial economies of scale. The result is that the smaller firms' costs rise disproportionately to those of the larger firms. Once again, such a standard need not be "discriminatory."[300] The standard will raise the costs of smaller firms disproportionately even though it is applied uniformly to all members of the trade association. This activity, unlike the petitioning activity described above, is not sheltered by an antitrust "exemption" for strategic use of governmental processes.[301] Such discrimination against smaller firms may be com-

---

298. *See* Eastern R.R. Presidents Conference v. Noerr Motor Freight, Inc., 365 U.S. 127 (1961); Session Tank Liners, Inc. v. Joor Mfg., [Current] ANTITRUST & TRADE REG. REP. (BNA) No. 1250, at 185 (C.D. Cal. Jan. 17, 1986); *see also* Reaemco, Inc. v. Allegheny Airlines, 496 F. Supp. 546 (S.D.N.Y. 1980) (dismissing a complaint that the defendant airline had petitioned Congress to deny favorable federal loans to the plaintiff competitor).

299. The literature on the relationship between firm or plant size and the costs of regulatory compliance is quite extensive. *See* Curtis, *Trade Policy to Promote Entry with Scale Economies, Product Variety, and Export Potential,* 16 CANADIAN J. ECON. 109 (1983); Hovenkamp & Mackerron, *Municipal Regulation and Federal Antitrust Policy,* 32 UCLA L. REV. 719 (1985); Maloney & McCormick, *A Positive Theory of Environmental Quality Regulation,* 25 J. L. & ECON. 99 (1982); Neumann & Nelson, *Safety Regulation and Firm Size: Effects of the Coal Mine Health and Safety Act of 1969,* 25 J. L. & ECON. 183 (1982); Pashigian, *The Effect of Environmental Regulation on Optimal Plant Size and Factor Shares,* 27 J. L. & ECON. 1 (1984); *see also* Bartel & Thomas, *Direct and Indirect Effects of Regulation: A New Look at OSHA's Impact,* 28 J. L. & ECON. 1 (1985) (finding economies of scale in OSHA compliance).

300. Many complaints involving alleged refusals to deal or boycotts by trade associations engaged in standard setting have charged that the association discriminated against the plaintiff in the creation or application of the standards. *See, e.g.,* Radiant Burners, Inc. v. Peoples Gas Light & Coke Co., 364 U.S. 656 (1961). Likewise, most courts have identified the absence of such discrimination as a basis for dismissing the complaint. *See, e.g.,* Eliason Corp. v. National Sanitation Found., 614 F.2d 126 (6th Cir.), *cert. denied,* 449 U.S. 826 (1980).

301. *See* United Mine Workers v. Pennington, 381 U.S. 657, 669-72 (1965) (even anticompetitive petitioning of the government is exempt from antitrust scrutiny); Eastern R.R.

mon within trade associations. Several cases, some quite recent, suggest that precisely this has been occurring.[302]

(4) The dominant firm engages in a form of advertising that must be met by the smaller firms. In order to preserve their market shares each of the smaller firms must engage in a similar amount of advertising, which will give each of them the same amount of advertising expense as the large firm. However, for the smaller firms the expenses will be distributed over a much smaller amount of output.[303]

(5) A dominant firm researching a new product and knowing that it will be the first entrant, intentionally selects a technology in which economies of scale are substantial, knowing that the fringe firms will have to follow along.[304]

At this time someone — particularly someone from the Chicago School — might object that many if not all of the illustrations given above show nothing more than economies of scale. Furthermore, economies of scale are efficient — they result in higher output and lower prices.

As a general rule economies of scale *are* efficient and ought to be encouraged; however, it is now well established that scale economies can be used strategically for inefficient purposes. In fact, a large part of the strategic entry deterrence/predatory pricing literature is dedi-

---

Presidents Conference v. Noerr Motor Freight, 365 U.S. 127 (1961) (same). *See generally* P. AREEDA & H. HOVENKAMP, *supra* note 55, at ch. 2; Annot., 71 A.L.R. FED. 723 (1985) (discussing cases dealing with the so-called "sham" exception to the *Noerr-Pennington* doctrine).

302. The existence of economies of scale in compliance with the rules of a trade association has not been an issue in such antitrust cases. As a result, reported opinions do not generally provide information concerning such economies. Nevertheless, it is possible to infer such discrimination against smaller firms in Structural Laminates, Inc. v. Douglas Fir Plywood Assn., 261 F. Supp. 154 (D. Ore. 1966), *affd.,* 399 F.2d 155 (9th Cir. 1968), *cert. denied,* 393 U.S. 1024 (1969). Other possible examples include Moore v. Boating Indus. Assns., 754 F.2d 698 (7th Cir.), *vacated,* 106 S. Ct. 218 (1985), where the administrative "runaround" given a small firm in the association seemed calculated to injure smaller firms; and United States v. Realty Multi-List, Inc., 629 F.2d 1351 (5th Cir. 1980), which involved a real estate multiple listing service operated for member realtors. *See also* American Socy. of Mechanical Engrs. v. Hydrolevel Corp., 456 U.S. 556 (1982) (involving a firm that had brought suit against its competitors and against a 90,000-member professional society).

A related instance of strategic raising of the costs of rivals is discussed in Williamson, *Wage Rates as a Barrier to Entry: The Pennington Case in Perspective,* 82 Q. J. ECON. 85 (1968), concerning the litigation in United Mine Workers v. Pennington, 381 U.S. 657 (1965). Williamson argues that in this case dominant, capital-intensive firms sought or approved a wage contract calling for higher wages, knowing that the competitive fringe was more labor intensive and would feel the consequences of such a contract much more sharply.

303. Salop & Scheffman, *supra* note 23, at 268.

304. This may have happened in E.I. du Pont de Nemours & Co., 96 F.T.C. 653 (1980).

Salop & Scheffman, *supra* note 23, at 268, also argue that the vertical price "squeeze" discussed at notes 265-88 *supra* could be used by a vertically integrated firm to raise the costs of an unintegrated rival, although they do not specify precisely how this might occur. However, such a squeeze could be used to decrease the unintegrated rival's price/cost margin, at least where the rival's sunk costs are substantial.

cated to this phenomenon.[305]

Furthermore, to concentrate on economies of scale in the above examples misses the point. A cost is a cost, no matter how efficient the firm that pays it. In the above cases the market would be more competitive if the cost at issue did not have to be encountered *at all*. That is, the relevant issue is not who is the most efficient payer of these particular costs, but whether the costs would exist at all in a competitive market.

For example, the creation by trade associations of regulations, compliance with which is subject to economies of scale, is inefficient not because of the existence of the scale economies, but because the regulation itself is inefficient. It has been adopted by the dominant firms in the association because although it will raise *everyone's* costs, it will raise the unit costs of smaller rivals more than it raises their own.[306]

An antitrust policy effective against strategic raising of rivals' costs has yet to be designed. Certain barriers, such as the constitutional protection given to firms to petition the government for inefficient regulation,[307] appear to be insurmountable in some areas. However, in most areas conduct alleged to raise rivals' costs in order to facilitate supracompetitive pricing should be subject to traditional rule-of-reason analysis. There are some problems, however, particularly if a court is asked to determine whether an ambiguous act is efficient. For example, if a trade association is charged with intentionally adopting a regulation subject to compliance economies of scale in order to raise rivals' costs, the obvious defense in marginal cases (i.e., where the regulation is not clearly unreasonable) is that the regulation itself is efficient. The court would then need to determine whether the regulatory goal could be achieved in a less anticompetitive way. If the answer to that question is no, the court still may have to determine whether any efficiencies obtained from the regulation are greater than the offsetting

---

305. *See, e.g.,* Baumol, *supra* note 234; Salop, *supra* note 23; Williamson, *Predatory Pricing, supra* note 23.

306. The Chicago School position that all truthful advertising is efficient misses this point as well. *See* R. BORK, *supra* note 6, at 314-20. Advertising is subject to substantial economies of scale, because the costs of reaching a given number of potential consumers in a given media are fairly constant, and therefore must be divided over the output of the firm doing the advertising. (For example, a thirty-second prime time television commercial costs General Motors and American Motors the same amount, even though General Motors' output is five times higher.) As a result, if a large firm faces a smaller rival and the smaller firm must meet the larger firm's advertising in order to maintain its own market share, the larger firm will choose a rate of advertising larger than it would if its rival were the same size. The result will be to give the rival higher per unit costs. Robert Bork's argument, *id.* at 315, considers only excessive advertising that he regards as "predatory" — that is, as imposing immediate losses on the firm engaged in it.

307. *See* note 301 *supra* and accompanying text.

losses. Judicial analysis of such allegations may require resort to evidence of the defendants' intent.

3. *Strategic Manipulation of Shared Markets: The* Aspen *Case*

Aspen Skiing Co. v. Aspen Highlands Skiing Corp.[308] illustrates a variation of the problem of strategic behavior by a monopolist, calculated to raise its rival's costs. The plaintiff (Highlands) and the defendant (Ski Company) operated skiing facilities at the four skiing mountains in Aspen, Colorado, a popular ski resort. The defendant operated three of the mountains and the plaintiff operated the fourth. For many years the defendant and plaintiff had engaged in a joint venture under which they marketed a lift ticket that a purchaser could use at all four of Aspen's mountains. Initially, revenue from the joint tickets was divided on the basis of actual use of the slopes, with the plaintiff's share of the revenues averaging about sixteen percent.[309] Later, the defendant refused to participate in the joint scheme unless the plaintiff agreed to accept a fixed percentage of ticket revenues that was lower than the percentage reflecting actual use of the plaintiff's mountain. After a few years of controversy over how revenues should be divided, the defendant refused to participate any longer in the joint scheme. After that, the plaintiff attempted to market its single-slope lift ticket separately, but its market share steadily declined.[310]

The plaintiff sued, alleging that the defendant had illegally monopolized the market for downhill skiing services at Aspen. The specific exclusionary practices alleged were that the defendant: (1) used its dominant market share to impose a fixed revenue percentage under the joint ticket scheme that was lower than the percentage of the market actually controlled by the plaintiff; (2) refused to participate further in the joint venture with the intent or knowledge that the plaintiff would be injured thereby; (3) subsequently marketed and advertised its own three slopes in such a way as to create the impression that the Aspen area contained only the defendant's three slopes; (4) agreed with various tour operators to sell its tickets to the exclusion of plaintiff's tickets; and (5) refused to accept the plaintiff's ticket coupons in exchange for customer access to the defendant's slopes.

In affirming a judgment against the defendant, the Supreme Court observed that entry into the market for skiing services at Aspen was

---

308. 105 S. Ct. 2847 (1985).

309. 105 S. Ct. at 2847.

310. 105 S. Ct. at 2851.

restricted by both geography and regulatory obstacles.[311] As a result, future growth in the Aspen market was unlikely. Second, most skiers strongly preferred a multi-slope lift ticket to a single-slope ticket. Furthermore, most preferred a four-slope ticket to a three-slope ticket.[312]

This latter fact is important, for it indicates that market demand under the joint venture was greater than it was when each firm was selling its ski lift tickets separately — i.e., *assuming that the relative market shares of the two firms remained constant,* both firms would have benefitted from the selling of a joint lift ticket covering all four slopes. The effect of Ski Company's refusal to participate in the joint venture was twofold: (1) *overall* demand in the market dropped, because the best deal available in the market was a three-slope ticket instead of a four-slope ticket; and (2) Ski Company's share of the market increased, because it offered a three-slope ticket, which was far more attractive to skiers than Highland's single-slope ticket.[313]

Since the total market for Aspen skiing would be larger under the joint venture, why did Ski Company refuse to participate? There are two likely answers.[314] First, Ski Company may have thought that demand for its three-slope ticket would be sufficiently greater than demand for the plaintiff's single-slope ticket that the plaintiff would be driven out of business. More likely, however, Ski Company believed it would make more money even though total market demand was declining, because its share of that market would increase substantially.

---

311. 105 S. Ct. at 2850. There is good reason to believe, however, that the market was defined too narrowly. *See* P. AREEDA & H. HOVENKAMP, *supra* note 55, at ¶ 534.1.

312. This is simply another way of saying that the demand curve for a four-slope ticket was to the right of the demand curve for a three-slope ticket, which was in turn to the right of the demand curve for a single-slope ticket. *See Aspen,* 105 S. Ct. at 2859-60.

The evidence in the *Aspen* case suggests, although it does not fully establish, that the market for Aspen skiing was a natural monopoly, assuming that it was a relevant market at all. A natural monopoly is a market in which costs decline as output increases all the way to the point that demand in the market is saturated when price equals marginal cost. As a result, a firm that controlled 100% of the market would encounter lower costs than any firm that controlled less than 100%. There is no evidence that the costs of administering the Aspen slopes declined as the number of slopes controlled by a single firm increased. However, the evidence does indicate that a firm that *marketed* the four slopes together faced lower marketing costs in proportion to the number of buyers than any firm that marketed fewer than four slopes. A natural monopoly controlled by a single firm will generally yield monopoly pricing unless it is regulated. The unattractiveness of those two alternatives — monopoly pricing or price regulation — suggests that the most efficient way to run the market for Aspen skiing would be to permit multiple firms to operate the slopes, but permit a joint venture that would market the four slopes together. However, the market would then have to be watched carefully because of its obvious potential for collusion.

313. 105 S. Ct. at 2853.

314. The defendant raised a third possibility: an antitrust action that had been filed against the two companies alleging that the joint venture was collusive. However, at the time of this litigation the companies had signed a consent decree which expressly permitted the joint venture. 105 S. Ct. at 2851 n.9.

This prediction turned out to be correct: Highland's share of the market declined substantially after the joint venture fell apart and the defendant's share increased.[315]

The *Aspen* case is an example of strategic behavior that both raised a rival's costs disproportionately to those of the defendant[316] and reduced the relative attractiveness of the rival's market offering while simultaneously producing no efficiency gains to the defendant. In fact, the defendant's offering also became less attractive than it was prior to the strategic behavior, but not by as wide a margin as the plaintiff's. The conduct was "predatory;" however, its success did not require the defendant to sustain short-term losses in order to receive long-term gains. The gains accrued almost immediately.

The difficult problem raised by the *Aspen* case is how a court is to determine when behavior that raises a rival's cost, or that reduces the relative attractiveness of a rival's market offering, is anticompetitive and worthy of condemnation under the antitrust laws. The Supreme Court cited two convincing pieces of objective evidence: (1) contrary to the defendant's representations, the joint venture scheme was relatively easy to administer;[317] and (2) participation in the joint venture *would* have been the more profitable alternative for the defendant,[318] *except* on the premise that refusal to participate would increase the defendant's relative market share at the expense of the plaintiff's.

The Supreme Court held that the jury was entitled to find from these facts that the defendant had intended to monopolize the market. In fact, one of the most significant features of the decision is the increased weight that the Supreme Court assigned to the jury's fact finding, particularly to the jury's ability to infer anticompetitive intent in monopolization cases.

Unfortunately, the facts of the *Aspen* case made the decision too easy, and probably exaggerate a court's ability to determine whether inefficient monopolizing conduct has occurred without using evidence of intent. In a monopolization case the plaintiff must show that the defendant had monopoly power and that it engaged in one or more

---

315. 105 S. Ct. at 2853.

316. More accurately, the defendant's actions reduced the spread between the plaintiff's costs and the demand curve that it faced. Its costs were undoubtedly raised absolutely as well — for example, Highlands probably had to engage in more advertising in order to keep its market share from falling even faster than it did. Strictly speaking, actions that raise a rival's costs move its average cost curve (or perhaps marginal cost curve) upward; in this case, the actions moved the rival's demand curve downward. The effect in any case is the same: reduced output by the rival.

317. 105 S. Ct. at 2860-61.

318. 105 S. Ct. at 2859.

inefficient "exclusionary practices."[319] Many of a monopolist's practices are exclusionary; however, they may also be efficient. For example, the monopolist's research and development that yields a new
product is exclusionary, because it injures the monopolist's rivals. At
the same time, such conduct is legal because it makes consumers better
off.[320]

An important difference between efficient and inefficient exclusionary practices in monopolization cases is that the former enlarge total
market output, while the latter reduce it.[321] Both, however, enlarge
the market share of the monopolist at the expense of its rivals. The
Aspen case is a rare instance in which the Supreme Court was able to
determine that the monopolist's conduct reduced overall market demand without committing the static market fallacy. In most cases the
conduct's effect on the market is likely to be ambiguous, and evidence
of intent may be essential.[322]

The strategic manipulation of the market that occurred in *Aspen,*
like strategic raising of rivals' costs and taking advantage of competitors' sunk costs, illustrates the inadequacy of Chicago School theory to
account for important real-world behavior. That firms can engage in
such behavior to extract monopoly profits undermines the reliance
placed on the market by Chicago School antitrust theory and suggests
that antitrust policy based on that theory will fail to achieve efficient
results.

CONCLUSION

The Chicago School of antitrust analysis has made an important
and lasting contribution to antitrust policy. The School has placed an
emphasis on economic analysis in antitrust jurisprudence that will
likely never disappear. At the same time, however, the Chicago

---

319. United States v. Grinnell Corp., 384 U.S. 563, 570-71 (1966); *see also Aspen,* 105 S. Ct.
at 2854 n.19.

320. *See, e.g.,* California Computer Prod. v. IBM Corp., 613 F.2d 727, 744 (9th Cir. 1979)
(refusing to condemn technological innovation by a monopolist); Berkey Photo, Inc. v. Eastman
Kodak Co., 603 F.2d 263 (2d Cir. 1979), *cert. denied,* 444 U.S. 1093 (1980) (same).

321. For example, efficient research and develpoment by the monopolist either improves a
product, thus shifting its demand curve to the right, or else reduces its costs. In both cases the
effect is higher total market output. However, all the increases in market output accrue to the
monopolist, in addition to sales that the monopolist steals from competitors. On the other hand,
*in*efficient exclusionary conduct — for example, obtaining a patent by means of fraud — neither
improves the product nor reduces its costs. The only result is that competitors are excluded.
Total market output declines when the monopolist increases price.

322. That is, in a real world market a court could not consider whether a monopolist's alleged exclusionary practice increased or decreased total market demand, for the relevant information would not be available. See the discussion of the static market fallacy at notes 201-20
supra.

School's approach to antitrust is defective for two important reasons. First of all, the notion that public policymaking should be guided exclusively by a notion of efficiency based on the neoclassical market efficiency model is naive. That notion both overstates the ability of the policymaker to apply such a model to real world affairs and understates the complexity of the process by which the policymaker must select among competing policy values.

Second, the neoclassical market efficiency model is itself too simple to account for or to predict business firm behavior in the real world. The model has proved to be particularly inept at identifying many forms of strategic behavior. In large part this is so because the market efficiency model is static and dwells too much on long-run effects. In the real world, short-run considerations are critical to business planning. Furthermore, the short run can be a very long time. In many industries a monopoly that lasts only for the short run can inflict great economic loss on society. By ignoring the short run, the market efficiency model fails to appreciate the social cost of many forms of monopolistic behavior.

The willingness to take short-run, strategic behavior seriously comes with a price, however. An economic theory that includes such behavior becomes far more complex than the neoclassical model. Under more complex models information becomes more ambiguous and more difficult to interpret. When that happens, the value of economic models begins to diminish in relative importance. In short, once the model becomes more complex, the policymaker necessarily relies on values that lie outside the model. The result is an antitrust policy that will always have a noneconomic, or political, content.

Failed Expectations: The Troubled Past and Uncertain Future of the Sherman Act as a Tool for Deconcentration

William E. Kovacic*

Trustbusting is the Sherman Act's[1] most alluring and enduring mirage. Since 1890 the deconcentration possibilities suggested by the statute's ban on monopolization[2] have enticed generations of distinguished antitrust scholars and government policymakers. Federal enforcement officials have mounted memorable campaigns to disassemble leviathans of American business, yet the tantalizing goal of improving the economic and political order by restructuring dominant firms frequently has eluded its pursuers.[3] To most students of antitrust, the history of Sherman Act deconcentration endeavors is largely a chronicle of costly defeats and inconsequential victories.[4] Even the lustre of the government's greatest

*Assistant Professor, George Mason University School of Law. A.B. 1974, Princeton University; J.D. 1978, Columbia University. The author thanks Kathryn M. Fenton, Herbert Hovenkamp, Theodore P. Kovaleff, Robert H. Lande, James May, Robert J. Michaels, and David Millon for many useful comments and discussions.

1. 26 Stat. 209 (1890) (codified as amended at 15 U.S.C. §§ 1-7 (1982)).

2. Section 2 of the Sherman Act states in part: "Every person who shall monopolize, or attempt to monopolize, or combine or conspire with any other person or persons, to monopolize any part of the trade or commerce among the several states, or with foreign nations, shall be deemed guilty of a felony . . . ." 15 U.S.C. § 2 (1982).

3. A representative assessment of the situation has stated that the "government has since 1890 attacked and defeated monopolies in courtrooms across the country. Yet despite some notable successes, American monopoly policy in practice has fallen short of its promise." W. ADAMS & J. BROCK, THE BIGNESS COMPLEX 198 (1987); *see also* Rowe, *The Decline of Antitrust and the Delusions of Models: The Faustian Pact of Law and Economics*, 72 GEO. L.J. 1511, 1537 (1984) ("Antitrust's Big Case is doomed to a tragic cycle: by the time the barbecue is fit for carving, the pig is gone.").

4. The antitrust literature is replete with negative assessments of the country's experience with the Sherman Act as a deconcentration tool. *See* W. ADAMS & J. BROCK, *supra* note 3, at 198-203; Rowe, *supra* note 3, at 1535-40; *see also* STAFF OF SENATE TEMPORARY NATIONAL ECONOMIC COMM., 76TH CONG., 3D SESS., INVESTIGATION OF CONCENTRATION OF ECONOMIC POWER: A STUDY OF THE CONSTRUCTION AND ENFORCEMENT OF THE FEDERAL ANTITRUST LAWS, MONOGRAPH NO. 38, at 84 (Comm. Print 1941) (written by M. Handler) [hereinafter TNEC MONOGRAPH NO. 38] ("It is common knowledge . . . that the [monopolization dissolution] decrees have rarely succeeded in restoring competition."); D. DEWEY, MONOPOLY IN ECONOMICS AND LAW 247 (1959) ("Taken together the so-called big cases fought by the antitrust agencies in the last twenty years reveal a pattern of 'legal victory-economic defeat.' "); K. ELZINGA & W. BREIT, THE ANTITRUST PENALTIES: A STUDY IN LAW AND ECONOMICS 47 (1976) ("the consensus so far is that structural relief has been attempted in only a few cases, and that it has been performed rather badly in those"); R. POSNER, ANTITRUST LAW—AN ECONOMIC PERSPECTIVE 85 (1976) ("The picture that emerges of what antitrust divestiture [in monopolization cases] has meant in practice is not an edifying one."); L. SULLIVAN, ANTITRUST 141 (1977) ("it is not an easy thing to point to significant remedial successes in Section 2 proceedings"); Adams, *Dissolution, Divorcement, Divestiture: The Pyrrhic Victories of Antitrust*, 27 IND. L.J. 1, 31 (1951) ("the relief obtained by the Government in Section 2 cases under the Sherman Act has generally been inadequate . . . the Government . . . has won many a law suit but lost many a cause"); O'Connor, *The Divestiture Remedy in Sherman Act Section 2*

229

triumphs—for example, the dissolution of Standard Oil in 1911[5] and the restructuring of AT&T in the 1980s[6]—often dims in the face of recurring criticism that the execution of admittedly sweeping relief was either counterproductive or essentially superfluous.[7]

As the Sherman Act's centennial approaches, it is tempting to conclude that this country's fascination with deconcentration has ceased. Recent experience provides abundant support for such an appraisal. From 1969 to 1982, the Department of Justice and the Federal Trade Commission (FTC)[8] undertook an ambitious agenda of monopolization and attempted monopolization initiatives in which structural remedies[9] were

---

Cases, 13 Harv. J. on Legis. 687, 692-93 (1976) (concluding that "primary deficiency of current antitrust policy" is "inability or unwillingness of courts" to apply significant structural remedies such as divestiture upon finding a violation of Sherman Act ban on monopolization); 1 Report to the President and the Attorney General of the National Commission for the Review of Antitrust Laws and Procedures 117 (1979) [hereinafter NCRALP Report] (noting that "structural relief has seldom been ordered in Section 2 cases"). For more sanguine appraisals, see D. Waldman, Antitrust Action and Market Structure 155-65 (1978) (concluding that filing of monopolization suits in which divestiture might be ordered has caused dominant firms to adjust behavior in ways that lowered entry barriers and increased competition in several concentrated industries); 2 S. Whitney, Antitrust Policies: American Experience in Twenty Industries 388-92 (1958) (concluding that dissolution actions have achieved valuable results in some instances when used to restructure single-firm monopolies); *see also* Baldwin, *The Feedback Effect of Business Conduct on Industry Structure*, 12 J. L. & Econ. 123, 128-37 (1969) (finding that imposition of conduct decrees in government monopolization suits occasionally served to erode market positions of dominant firms).

5. Standard Oil v. United States, 221 U.S. 1 (1911). Useful historical accounts of the dissolution of Standard Oil include G. Gibbs & E. Knowlton, History of Standard Oil Company (New Jersey): The Resurgent Years 1911-1927, at 7-10 (1956); P. Giddens, Standard Oil Company (Indiana): Oil Pioneer of the Middle West 126-37 (1955); G. White, Formative Years in the Far West: A History of Standard Oil Company of California and Predecessors Through 1919, at 378-85 (1962).

6. United States v. AT&T Co., 552 F. Supp. 131 (D.D.C. 1982), *aff'd sub nom.* Maryland v. United States, 460 U.S. 1001 (1983). The disassembly of the Bell System is described in S. Coll, The Deal of the Century: The Breakup of AT&T (1987); P. Temin, The Fall of the Bell System (1987).

7. Conservative and liberal observers alike have questioned the impact of the Standard Oil dissolution as a stimulant to competition in the petroleum industry. *See* R. Posner, *supra* note 4, at 85-86; Adams, *supra* note 4, at 2. The returns from the AT&T divestiture are far from complete, but the antitrust-inspired reorganization of the Bell System has drawn its share of critical or highly skeptical commentary. *See* A. Stone, Wrong Number 332-38 (1989); P. Temin, *supra* note 6, at 353-66; Easterbrook, *Breaking Up Is Hard to Do*, 5 Reg. 25, 30-31 (Nov.-Dec. 1981); MacAvoy & Robinson, *Losing by Judicial Policymaking: The First Year of the AT&T Divestiture*, 2 Yale J. on Reg. 225, 261-62 (1985).

8. The FTC enforces the Sherman Act ban on monopolization indirectly. The Commission's antitrust enforcement powers concerning monopolization flow from § 5 of the Federal Trade Commission Act, which authorizes the agency to proscribe "unfair methods of competition." 38 Stat. 719 (1938) (codified as amended at 15 U.S.C. § 45(a)(1) (1982)). Since at least 1948, it has been settled doctrine that § 5 allows the FTC to bar conduct that would constitute a violation of the Sherman Act. *See* FTC v. Cement Inst., 333 U.S. 683, 690-95 (1948); *see also* Averitt, *The Meaning of 'Unfair Methods of Competition' in Section 5 of the Federal Trade Commission Act*, 21 B.C.L. Rev. 227, 239-40 (1980) (describing application of *Cement Institute* principle to FTC group boycott and price-fixing cases brought under § 5 of the FTC Act).

9. The principal form of structural relief is divestiture. *See* Fraidin, *Dissolution and Reconstitution: A Structural Remedy, and Alternatives*, 33 Geo. Wash. L. Rev. 899, 901 (1965); Comment, *Aspects of Divestiture as an Antitrust Remedy*, 32 Fordham L. Rev. 135, 136 (1963). When ordered as a remedy in monopolization litigation, divestiture ordinarily entails the

proposed to erode the market positions of dominant firms. The targets encompassed a breathtaking swath of American commerce, including major firms in the computer,[10] telecommunications,[11] petroleum,[12] food,[13]

---

realignment of a single firm's assets into two or more competing entities. In some instances, this reorganization has involved the comparatively simpler process of what some courts and commentators have labelled "dissolution"— the liquidation of a stock holding company or the spinning-off of subsidiaries or divisions originally assimilated into the defendant's organization through merger. *See, e.g.*, United States v. Reading Co., 253 U.S 26, 27-28 (1920) (dissolving intercorporate relations existing among railway carriers and coal companies); United States v. Union P.R. Co., 226 U.S. 61, 79-81 (1912) (directing disposition of dominant stock interest acquired by railroad in competing railroad); Standard Oil Co. v. United States, 221 U.S. 1, 78-81 (1911) (ordering stock transfer to subsidiary corporations). In other cases, divestiture decrees have compelled more difficult realignments, including the establishment of new companies out of the highly integrated operations of a single firm. *See* United States v. American Tobacco Co., 221 U.S. 106, 187-88 (1911) (ordering creation of new entities following dissolution of American Tobacco Co.); *see also* Wickersham, *Recent Interpretation of the Sherman Act*, 10 MICH. L. REV. 1, 17-19 (1911) (describing relative complexity of the Standard Oil and American Tobacco divestitures).

A second form of remedy with structural implications in monopolization litigation is compulsory licensing of property rights such as patents, sometimes on a royalty-free basis. *See* Hartford-Empire Co. v. United States, 323 U.S. 386, 413-18 (1945) (enjoining product distribution unless company agreed to license patent usage at reasonable royalty); United States v. General Elec. Co., 115 F. Supp. 835, 843-46 (D.N.J. 1953) (ordering royalty-free licensing of patents); Eli Lilly & Co., 95 F.T.C. 538, 546-52 (1980) (consent order requiring virtually unlimited, nonexclusive, royalty-free licensing of patents); Xerox Corp., 86 F.T.C. 364, 373-83 (1975) (consent order compelling limited royalty-free licensing of patents); *see also* Timberg, *Equitable Relief Under the Sherman Act*, 1950 U. ILL. L.F. 629, 640-47 (describing use of compulsory licensing of patents and related know how as a remedy in monopolization suits). Most commentators have concluded that compulsory licensing decrees generally have contributed little to the accomplishment of deconcentration objectives. *See* F. SCHERER, INNOVATION AND GROWTH—SCHUMPETERIAN PERSPECTIVES 207, 220 (1984) ("compulsory [patent] licensing under antitrust decrees had no significant impact in reducing concentration relative to the changes that might have been expected in any event, given the initial market structure, subsequent market growth, and the panoply of public policies (including antitrust actions) affecting manufacturing industry structures").

10. United States v. IBM Corp., [1961-1970 Transfer Binder] Trade Reg. Rep. (CCH) ¶ 45,069 (S.D.N.Y. filed Jan. 17, 1969) (complaint alleging monopolization and attempted monopolization). The Department of Justice filed a stipulation of dismissal in 1982. *See In re* International Business Machs. Corp., 687 F.2d 591, 593 (2d Cir. 1982) (ordering the issue of writ of mandamus directing district court to dismiss complaint in accordance with stipulation).

11. United States v. AT&T Co., [1970-1979 Transfer Binder] Trade Reg. Rep. (CCH) ¶ 45,074 (D.D.C. filed Nov. 20, 1974) (complaint alleging monopolization, attempted monopolization, and conspiracy to monopolize), *consent decree entered*, 552 F. Supp. 131, 178-79, 225 (D.D.C. 1982), *aff'd sub nom.* Maryland v. United States, 460 U.S. 1001 (1983).

12. Exxon Corp., 98 F.T.C. 453, 456-59 (1981) (complaint alleging agreement to monopolize and maintenance of noncompetitive market structure).

13. *See* International Tel. & Tel. Corp., 104 F.T.C. 280, 284-85 (1984) (complaint alleging attempted monopolization); General Foods Corp., 103 F.T.C. 204, 206-08 (1984) (complaint alleging attempted monopolization); Kellogg Co., 99 F.T.C. 8, 11-16 (1982) (complaint alleging maintenance of highly concentrated, noncompetitive market structure and shared monopolization); Sunkist Growers, Inc., 97 F.T.C. 443, 445-49 (1981) (complaint alleging monopolization, attempted monopolization, and maintenance of noncompetitive market structure); Borden, Inc., 92 F.T.C. 669, 671-72 (1978) (complaint alleging monopolization and maintenance of noncompetitive market structure), *aff'd*, Borden, Inc. v. FTC, 674 F.2d 498, 517 (6th Cir. 1982), *modified*, 102 F.T.C. 1147, 1147 (1983).

photocopier,[14] chemical,[15] and rubber[16] industries. As a group, these cases seemed to offer a decisive response to critics who claimed that the federal enforcement agencies timidly had declined to seek necessary, broad based reductions in existing levels of concentration in major sectors of the economy.[17]

Never in antitrust history has so massive a litigation program yielded such disappointing results. Most of the government's deconcentration cases either collapsed before trial or failed to establish liability.[18] The most noteworthy of the government's few victories received a mixed reaction, as commentators sharply disputed the merits of the relief obtained.[19] While

---

14. Xerox Corp., 86 F.T.C. 364, 367-68 (1975) (complaint alleging monopolization, attempted monopolization, and maintenance of highly concentrated market structure).
15. E.I. du Pont de Nemours & Co., 96 F.T.C. 653, 654-55 (1980) (complaint alleging attempted monopolization).
16. United States v. Goodyear Tire & Rubber Co., and United States v. Firestone Tire & Rubber Co., [1970-1979 Transfer Binder] Trade Reg. Rep. (CCH) ¶ 45,073 (N.D. Ohio filed Aug. 9, 1973) (complaints alleging attempted monopolization).
17. For example, in 1972 a Ralph Nader sponsored evaluation of antitrust enforcement commented:

> the Antitrust Division remains soft on concentration. . . . The Division does sue some firms who bring you kosher hotdog rolls and chrysanthemums, but ignores opportunities to attack GM and Anaconda Copper. By focusing on the transgressions of the less powerful, the enforcement agencies aid and abet the real economic royalists.

M. Green, B. Moore Jr. & B. Wasserstein, The Closed Enterprise System 293-94 (1972).
18. The Justice Department lost in *United States v. IBM Corp. See In re* International Business Machs. Corp., 687 F.2d 591, 593 (2d Cir. 1982) (affirming dismissal) and United States v. Goodyear Tire & Rubber Co., and United States v. Firestone Tire & Rubber Co., [1970-1979 Transfer Binder] Trade Reg. Rep. (CCH) ¶ 45,073, at 53,542 (N.D. Ohio filed Mar. 2, 1976) (dismissing complaints). The FTC lost in International Tel. & Tel. Corp., 104 F.T.C. 280, 451 (1984) (dismissing complaint); General Foods Corp., 103 F.T.C. 204, 364-68 (1984) (dismissing complaint); Kellogg Co., 99 F.T.C. 8, 269 (1982) (dismissing complaint); Exxon Corp., 98 F.T.C. 453, 461 (1981) (dismissing complaint); E.I. du Pont de Nemours & Co., 96 F.T.C. 653, 751 (1980) (dismissing complaint). The list of failures also might include the FTC's challenge to Borden's pricing and promotion strategies for its ReaLemon reconstituted lemon juice. Borden, Inc., 92 F.T.C. 669, 808-09 (1978), *aff'd*, Borden, Inc. v. FTC, 674 F.2d 498, 517 (6th Cir. 1982), *modified*, 102 F.T.C. 1147, 1147 (1983). In *Borden* the FTC found liability but declined to order compulsory licensing of Borden's ReaLemon trademark and instead directed Borden to alter its pricing and promotion conduct. 92 F.T.C. at 802-09. The Sixth Circuit sustained the finding of liability, 674 F.2d at 516, but the Commission severely reduced the scope of its order, 102 F.T.C. at 1147-50, partly out of concern that the Justice Department might urge the Supreme Court to accept certiorari and reject the reasoning of the FTC and Sixth Circuit opinions. *See Recall*, FTC: Watch, Sept. 24, 1982, at 1 (A. Amolsch & M. Madden eds.).
19. Most commentary has focused on the *AT&T* divestiture and the *Xerox* consent agreement. On the merits of the *AT&T* divestiture consent agreement, compare Easterbrook, *supra* note 7, at 30-31 (criticizing AT&T divestiture) and MacAvoy & Robinson, *supra* note 7, at 261-62 (same) with P. Huber, The Geodesic Network—1987 Report on Competition in the Telephone Industry 1.20-.35 (Department of Justice Jan. 1987) (assessing the divestiture in generally favorable terms) and Crandall, *Telecommunications Policy in the Reagan Era*, Reg. 28, 33 (1988) (same). The FTC consent order in *Xerox* compelled limited royalty-free licensing of Xerox' dry paper copying patent portfolio. Xerox Corp., 86 F.T.C. 364, 374-75 (1975). *Compare* D. Ginsburg, Antitrust, Uncertainty and Technological Innovation 30-33 (1980) (criticizing consent order) and Goetz & Schwartz, *Industry Structure Investigations: Xerox's Multiple Patents and Competition*, in The Federal Trade Commission since 1970: Economic Regulation and Bureaucratic Behavior 121 (1981) (same) *with* Bresnahan, *Post-Entry Competition in the Plain Paper Copier Market*, 75 Am. Econ. Rev. 15 (May 1985) (finding favorable net effects from FTC consent order) and Scherer, *Antitrust, Efficiency, and Progress*, 62 N.Y.U. L. Rev. 998, 1016-17 (1987) (same).

the benefits of rare litigation successes such as the *AT&T* case seemed uncertain, the costs of the failures were unmistakable and substantial. Most notably, the government's attacks upon IBM and the nation's leading petroleum refiners fruitlessly consumed vast resources and became notorious symbols of prosecutorial ineptitude.[20] When it announced the conclusion of the *AT&T* and *IBM* lawsuits on the same day early in 1982, the Justice Department seemed to draw the curtain on a century-long cause. Ralph Nader soon afterward observed that the "era of the big antitrust case is over, leaving a legacy of frustration and defeat for the Government's antitrust lawyers. No longer will the courts have a chance to restructure highly concentrated industries or oligopolies for more efficiency, innovation, and competition in pricing."[21]

This Article examines the history of this country's efforts to use the Sherman Act to achieve its deconcentration goals at a time when it is reasonable to suggest that government deconcentration litigation has entered a state of lasting repose. The Article recounts the history of Sherman Act deconcentration cases in three parts. Part I describes the major historical cycles of deconcentration activity and identifies the conditions that generated these cycles.[22] Part II analyzes these cycles and their causes to assess the likelihood that deconcentration, despite its low standing

---

20. Donald Baker, who headed the Antitrust Division from 1976 to 1977, quoted Robert Bork as calling the IBM case "the Antitrust Division's Vietnam." Baker, *Government Enforcement of Section Two*, 61 NOTRE DAME L. REV. 898, 899 n.13 (1986). Baker pointed out that the lawsuit "spanned the terms of five Presidents, nine Attorney Generals, and seven Assistant Attorney Generals." *Id.* The numbing scope of the 13-year long *IBM* litigation also emerges in a study Dean Peter Gerhart prepared in January 1979 for the National Commission for the Review of Antitrust Laws and Procedures. Dean Gerhart reported that, through November 1978, the two parties had produced a total of approximately 91 million pages of documents in discovery and had taken more than 1300 depositions. The trial had consumed 568 calendar days of testimony and document presentation, and the trial transcript exceeded 84,000 pages. Gerhart, *Report on the Empirical Case Studies Project*, in 2 NCRALP REPORT, *supra* note 4, at 1, 22-23 (Jan. 22, 1979). By the time the case was dismissed in 1982, the number of trial days had reached 700, the trial transcript exceeded 104,000 pages, and the parties had introduced 17,000 exhibits. The Justice Department's cost of litigating the suit, excluding expert witness fees, approached $17 million. *See Post-Mortem on IBM Case Provides Forum For Conflicting Perspectives*, 42 Antitrust & Trade Reg. Rep. (BNA) 310-11 (1982). IBM's cost to defend against the government's case surely exceeded this amount severalfold. *See* J. STEWART, THE PARTNERS 53-113 (1983) (discussing the size of IBM's litigation effort).

The history of the FTC's *Exxon* case is even more discouraging. *Exxon* consumed eight years in discovery and other pretrial proceedings before it was dismissed. Even so, the Commission order dismissing the case noted that "both complaint counsel and respondents agree that completion of discovery is at least several years away." 98 F.T.C. at 460. Through early 1979, the FTC's cost to support the *Exxon* litigation surpassed $13 million. *See Departments of State, Justice, and Commerce, the Judiciary, and Related Agencies Appropriations for 1980: Hearings before a Subcomm. of the House Comm. on Appropriations*, 96th Cong., 1st Sess. 823 (1979) (testimony of Alfred Dougherty Jr., Director of the FTC's Bureau of Competition). An attorney who represented one of the *Exxon* respondents estimated that the total cost of the litigation, for the FTC and the respondents combined, approached $100 million. Porter, *The Federal Trade Commission v. the Oil Industry: An Autopsy on the Commission's Shared Monopoly Case Against the Nation's Eight Largest Oil Companies*, 27 ANTITRUST BULL. 753, 756 (1982).

21. Nader, *Ended: Big Antitrust*, N.Y. Times, Mar. 4, 1982, at A23, col. 1; *see also* Rowe, *Antitrust in Transition: A Policy in Search of Itself*, 54 ANTITRUST L. J. 5, 7 (1985) (stating that "the *AT&T* decree sounds deconcentration's last hurrah") (footnote omitted).

22. *See infra* notes 27-211 and accompanying text.

today as an antitrust objective, will reemerge as a focal point for antitrust policy.[23] Part III applies Sherman Act experience to suggest appropriate conditions for future use of the statute as a deconcentration device.[24] This part identifies theoretical and institutional obstacles that antitrust policy-making bodies must overcome if they are to choose sensible enforcement targets and devise appropriate structural remedies.[25] Despite the largely unsatisfactory results of the structural initiatives of the 1970s, Part IV concludes that deconcentration will reemerge as a significant policy concern in antitrust's second century.[26]

I.   CYCLES OF SHERMAN ACT DECONCENTRATION INITIATIVES

Since 1890 the federal government has initiated 136 lawsuits challenging single-firm monopolization.[27] In addition, federal enforcement agencies have alleged in nine other cases that two or more firms used collusive, parallel, or interdependent conduct to acquire or maintain monopoly power.[28] Collectively, this body of 145 single-and multi-firm monopolization initiatives constitutes the government's Sherman Act deconcentration experience.[29]

---

23. *See infra* notes 212-46 and accompanying text.

24. *See infra* notes 247-65 and accompanying text.

25. *See infra* notes 253-65 and accompanying text.

26. *See infra* notes 266-76 and accompanying text.

27. I used the following methodology to derive this total. To begin, I consulted Richard Posner's studies of antitrust enforcement statistics dealing with government monopolization suits. *See* R. POSNER, *supra* note 4, at 81-85; Posner, *A Statistical Study of Antitrust Enforcement*, 13 J. L. & ECON. 365, 404-08 (1970). For the period 1890-1974, Judge Posner found that the Justice Department filed 125 single-firm monopolization cases. R. POSNER, *supra* note 4, at 81. I then supplemented Judge Posner's total with (a) two single-firm monopolization cases the Justice Department has brought since 1974 and (b) nine FTC single-firm monopolization cases brought from 1914-1988. I added the Justice Department's post-1974 cases by reviewing the Commerce Clearing House looseleaf services that record and describe federal antitrust cases and consent agreements. *See* United States v. Kentucky Utils. Co., [1980-1988 Transfer Binder] Trade Reg. Rep. (CCH) ¶ 45,081 (D. Ky. filed Feb. 26, 1981); United States v. Hercules, Inc., [1980-1988 Transfer Binder] Trade Reg. Rep. (CCH) ¶ 45,080 (D.N.J. filed Jan. 11, 1980), *consent decree entered*, 1981-1 Trade Cas. (CCH) ¶ 63,968. To identify the nine FTC cases, I reviewed the Commission's annual reports and the official reports of the Commission's proceedings. As indicated below, most of the FTC single-firm monopolization matters occurred in the past 25 years. *See, e.g.*, L.G. Balfour Co., 74 F.T.C. 345, 348-50 (1968) (complaint alleging monopolization and attempted monopolization), *aff'd*, 442 F.2d 1 (7th Cir. 1971); *see also infra* note 108 and accompanying text.

28. *See, e.g.*, American Tobacco Co. v. United States, 328 U.S. 781, 798-808 (1946) (challenging tacit horizontal conspiracy to fix prices of tobacco and cigarettes); United States v. National Lead Co., 63 F. Supp. 513, 522-25 (S.D.N.Y. 1945), *aff'd*, 332 U.S. 319 (1947) (challenging horizontal allocation of territories and restrictive patent cross-licensing agreements); Kellogg Co., 99 F.T.C. 8, 12, 14-15 (1982) (challenging parallel adherence to common policies concerning introduction of new brands, allocation of grocery store shelf space, pricing, and sales promotions); Exxon Corp., 98 F.T.C. 453, 456-58 (1981) (challenging parallel adoption of crude oil production, refining, transportation, and marketing practices to exclude independent refining and marketing firms).

29. I treat FTC cases such as *Kellogg* and *Exxon* as part of the Sherman Act deconcentration experience, even though the FTC originally conceived them as efforts to establish new antitrust doctrine beyond the bounds of Sherman Act jurisprudence. When first filed, the complaints in the two "shared monopoly" cases rested heavily upon what might be called

When classified by outcomes, these deconcentration suits fall into three categories. The first category consists of thirty-four cases in which the government secured substantial divestiture.[30] This set contains such landmark decisions as *Standard Oil Co. v. United States*[31] and *United States v. American Tobacco Co.*[32] A second category of prosecutions consists of cases such as *United States v. Aluminum Co. of America*,[33] in which the government prevailed on liability but failed to gain significant divestiture.[34] The final

---

purely structural theories of liability. *See Kellogg Co.*, 99 F.T.C. at 15 (complaint alleging that respondents "maintained . . . a highly concentrated, noncompetitive market structure in the production and sale of [ready-to-eat] cereal, in violation of Section 5 of the Federal Trade Commission Act"); *Exxon Corp.*, 98 F.T.C. at 459 (complaint alleging respondents "restrained trade and maintained a noncompetitive market structure in the refining of crude oil into petroleum products . . . in violation of Section 5 of the Federal Trade Commission Act"). As the Commission initially depicted these lawsuits, proof of conspiratorial conduct probably would play, at most, only a subordinate role in establishing the respondents' liability. *See Kellogg Co.*, 98 F.T.C. at 18-20. Facing a growing conservatism in appellate monopolization decisions and increasing congressional opposition to its "novel" shared monopolization theories, the FTC later recast its theory of liability in more conventional doctrinal terms. *See* Hurwitz & Kovacic, *Judicial Analysis of Predation: The Emerging Trends*, 35 Vand. L. Rev. 63, 139-50 (1982) (describing trend toward judicial acceptance of permissive conduct standards for dominant firms); Kovacic, *The Federal Trade Commission and Congressional Oversight of Antitrust Enforcement: A Historical Perspective*, in Public Choice and Regulation: A View from Inside the Federal Trade Commission 63, 92, 94 (1987) (discussing congressional reaction in the late 1970s to the *Exxon* suit and FTC efforts to gain structural relief in nonmerger cases). Thus, collusion, rather than mere structural interdependence, became the overriding focus. *See Kellogg Co.*, 99 F.T.C. at 21; Federal Trade Commission, Complaint Counsel's First Statement of Issues, Factual Contentions and Proof at 353-56, Exxon Corp., 98 F.T.C. 453 (Oct. 31, 1980 Docket No. 8934) (alleging respondents collusively maintained and reinforced noncompetitive market structure and restrained trade in oil refining industry) (document on file with the author). By the time the Commission dismissed the *Kellogg* and *Exxon* complaints in the early 1980s, the FTC's litigation strategy essentially had abandoned the largely structural causes of action that initially distinguished the two cases.

30. Judge Posner's 1970 study counted 32 Justice Department monopolization cases that resulted in significant divestiture or dissolution. Posner, *supra* note 27, at 406; *see also* Report of the Att'y Gen.'s Nat'l Comm. to Study the Antitrust Laws 352 (1955) [hereinafter Attorney General's Report] (reporting 24 instances of divestiture ordered in Sherman Act cases from 1890 through 1955). In his 1976 book, Judge Posner identified 24 instances in which the government had obtained "substantial divestiture" in the 118 Justice Department suits litigated to a decision or resolved by consent through 1974. R. Posner, *supra* note 4, at 84. The 1976 volume did not reconcile explicitly its apparent departure from the results in the 1970 article, although it appears that the 1976 study may have applied a more stringent criterion in defining "substantial divestiture." *See id.* at 84 n.9. For this Article, I have erred on the side of a more encompassing definition and used the count from Judge Posner's original study (32) and added the *AT&T* divestiture consent agreement and the FTC's *Sunkist* consent order to reach a total of 34.

To these matters one might add a handful of monopolization cases such as *Xerox* in which the government did not secure divestiture, but the remedy required compulsory patent licensing that served to reshape the affected industry's structure. Xerox Corp., 86 F.T.C. 364, 373-86 (1975); *see also* Bresnahan, *supra* note 19, at 16-18 (describing role of FTC consent decree in stimulating entry into copier market); Scherer, *supra* note 19, at 1016-17 (arguing that FTC-Xerox settlement did not weaken investors' confidence and resulted in greater innovation in copier market).

31. 221 U.S. 1 (1911).

32. 221 U.S. 106 (1911). For other cases involving orders mandating divestiture or other structural relief, see Attorney General's Report, *supra* note 30, at 354 n.13; O'Connor, *supra* note 4, at 711-13 & nn.81-83.

33. 148 F.2d 416 (2d Cir. 1945) [hereinafter *Alcoa*].

34. In addition to *Alcoa*, other Sherman Act cases frequently cited as "Pyrrhic victories" in

category includes cases such as *United States v. United States Steel Corp.* (U.S. Steel)[35] in which the government failed to establish the defendant's liability under the Sherman Act. This section identifies and analyzes the historical patterns in which these deconcentration measures have emerged. It begins with a review of the historical trends[36] and ends by attempting to explain their causes.[37]

A. *Three Eras of Deconcentration Initiatives*

Most Sherman Act deconcentration suits, successful and unsuccessful alike, have taken place during three discrete historical periods: 1904-1920, 1937-1956, and 1969-1982.[38] Each deconcentration period followed years of federal antitrust enforcement policies that either welcomed new concentration or largely declined to disturb established dominant firms. Government monopolization and attempted monopolization litigation has surged cyclically in response to perceived failures to curb new, and dismantle existing, positions of private industrial might. Nonetheless, federal enforcement agencies seldom have achieved fundamental structural change in concentrated industries.

1. *1904-1920:* Northern Securities *to* U.S. Steel

The earliest period of Sherman Act deconcentration activity was also the most prolific. Setting a pattern that later deconcentration eras would repeat, the first period of dissolution suits followed a wave of consolidation by acquisition and merger. A relative quiesence by public enforcement bodies also preceded this period of activism.

The Supreme Court's efforts to mold antitrust doctrine in the Sherman Act's first decade significantly influenced the process of consolidation that elicited a major round of deconcentration measures in the early twentieth century. The first formative influence was the Court's decision in *United States v. E.C. Knight Co.*[39] In *Knight,* the Court rejected the government's challenge to a series of acquisitions that afforded the Sugar Trust control over ninety-eight percent of the country's sugar refining capacity.

---

the deconcentration literature include Timken Roller Bearing Co. v. United States, 341 U.S. 593, 601-08 (1951) (finding Sherman Act violation, but refusing to order divestiture, therefore, doing little to alleviate monopolistic advantage) and United States v. National Lead Co., 332 U.S. 319, 348-52, 359-60 (1947) (same). *See* Adams, *supra* note 4, at 6-24 (criticizing unwillingness of courts in *Alcoa, National Lead,* and *Timken* to order divestiture).

35. 251 U.S. 417 (1920).
36. *See infra* notes 38-102 and accompanying text.
37. *See infra* notes 103-211 and accompanying text.
38. This grouping generally is consistent with the chronological framework often used in the antitrust and industrial organization literature to describe the history of efforts to apply the Sherman Act to attack concentrated market structures. *See* F. Scherer, Industrial Market Structure and Economic Performance 527-44 (1980); 1 S. Whitney, *supra* note 4, at 5-9; Flynn, *Monopolization Under the Sherman Act: The Third Wave and Beyond,* 26 Antitrust Bull. 1, 1-3 (1981); Rowe, *supra* note 3, at 1535-40; Shepherd, *The Economics: A Pep Talk,* 41 Antitrust L.J. 595, 598-99 (1972); Sullivan, *Monopolization: Corporate Strategy, the IBM Cases, and the Transformation of the Law,* 60 Tex. L. Rev. 587, 591-98 (1982).
39. 156 U.S. 1 (1895).

The Court rested its decision on the view that mere "manufacturing" failed to constitute "commerce" within the meaning of the new antitrust statute, thus leaving the consolidation of sugar refineries beyond the law's reach.[40] Commentators quickly perceived that the statute would tolerate horizontal consolidations yielding virtually absolute control of an industry's productive capacity.[41]

The Court further enhanced the attractiveness of the merger to attain market power two years later in *United States v. Trans-Missouri Freight Association*,[42] in which the Court outlawed a horizontal price-fixing agreement set by a cartel. To businessmen and their counselors, *Knight* and *Trans-Missouri* indicated that the Court would forbid price tampering and output limits adopted by "loose consolidations" such as cartels, but would tolerate sweeping integrations of ownership and control by acquisition or merger.[43] This realization helped trigger a wave of consolidations that saw many small and medium size companies combined into dominant or near dominant enterprises.[44] The era of "merger for monopoly," as characterized by George Stigler,[45] yielded such industrial titans as General Electric, International Harvester, Standard Oil, du Pont, Eastman Kodak, American Tobacco, and U.S. Steel, all of which became recurring targets for Sherman Act section two scrutiny by government enforcement agencies.[46]

40. Justice Fuller's opinion pointed out that "[c]ommerce succeeds to manufacture and is not a part of it." *Knight*, 156 U.S. at 12.
41. *See* A. CHANDLER JR., THE VISIBLE HAND 333 (1977); H. SEAGER & C. GULICK JR., TRUST AND CORPORATION PROBLEMS 58-59 (1929); Adams, *Federal Control of Trusts*, 18 POL. SCI. Q. 1, 3-5 (1903). High officials in President Cleveland's Justice Department welcomed the outcome in *Knight*. Soon after the release of *Knight*, Attorney General Richard Olney commented: "You will have observed that the government has been defeated in the Supreme Court on the trust question. I always supposed it would be and have taken the responsibility of not prosecuting under a law I believe to be no good . . . ." A. NEVINS, GROVER CLEVELAND: A STUDY IN COURAGE 671 (1932); *see also* H. THORELLI, THE FEDERAL ANTITRUST POLICY 383-89 (1954) (describing Olney's antipathy toward the Sherman Act).
42. 166 U.S. 290 (1897).
43. *See* A. CHANDLER JR., *supra* note 41, at 333. Despite its widespread acceptance, this interpretation of *Knight* and *Trans-Missouri* arguably misapprehends the holding of these and later cases such as United States v. Joint Traffic Ass'n, 171 U.S. 505 (1898), and United States v. Addyston Pipe & Steel Co., 85 F. 271 (6th Cir. 1898), *aff'd*, 175 U.S. 211 (1899). As Professor Sklar points out, *Trans-Missouri, Joint Traffic*, and *Addyston* could be read to indicate that *Knight* did not preclude successful Sherman Act assaults upon "tight combinations" accomplished through mergers or acquisitions. M. SKLAR, THE CORPORATE RECONSTRUCTION OF AMERICAN CAPITALISM, 1890-1916, at 161-63 (1988).
44. One leading study of merger movements in the United States identified approximately 3000 disappearances of individual manufacturing and mining firms through mergers from 1897 through 1904. *See* R. NELSON, MERGER MOVEMENTS IN AMERICAN HISTORY, 1895-1956, at 119-20 (1959); *see also* Markham, *Survey of the Evidence and Findings on Mergers*, in BUSINESS CONCENTRATION AND PRICE POLICY 141, 180 (1955) ("The conversion of approximately 71 important oligopolistic or near-competitive markets into near monopolies by merger between 1890 and 1904 left an imprint on the structure of the American economy that 50 years have not yet erased.").
45. Stigler, *Monopoly and Oligopoly by Merger*, 40 AM. ECON. REV. 23, 27 (1950).
46. *See* F. SCHERER, *supra* note 38, at 121. Two examples suggest the importance of these firms to future antitrust policy development. In this century, du Pont has been the subject of four significant government suits alleging monopolization, attempted monopolization, or conspiracy to monopolize. *See* United States v. E.I. du Pont de Nemours & Co., 351 U.S. 377, 378 (1956) (alleging monopolization of cellophane); United States v. National Lead Co., 332 U.S. 319, 325 (1947) (alleging conspiracy to monopolize titanium pigments); United States v.

The turn of the century merger movement ceased in 1904 with the Supreme Court's decision to invalidate the consolidation of the Northern Pacific and Great Northern railroads.[47] Contrary to the tenor of its ruling in *Knight*, the Court's opinion in *Northern Securities* indicated that the Sherman Act could bar mergers creating market dominance.[48] Along with the stock market crash of 1903, the *Northern Securities* decision stymied the establishment of new monopolies through horizontal acquisitions.[49] By then, however, the contours of American industry had been altered radically. As two prominent economists observed in 1912:

> The mere size of consolidations which have appeared recently is enough to startle those who saw them in the making. If the carboniferous age had returned and the earth repeopled itself with dinosaurs, the change made in animal life would have scarcely seemed greater than that which has been made in the business world by these monster like corporations.[50]

After *Northern Securities*, the foremost policy question facing the Justice Department and its newly formed Antitrust Division[51] became how to treat firms that, through merger or internal growth, already had achieved monopoly or near-monopoly positions. The Department addressed this problem by undertaking a series of lawsuits seeking to undo large concentrations of economic power that had been assembled in the late nineteenth and early twentieth centuries. From 1906 through 1917, the Department initiated monopolization suits against Standard Oil,[52] American Tobacco,[53]

E.I. du Pont de Nemours & Co., 188 F. 127, 130 (C.C. Del. 1911) (alleging monopolization of explosives); E.I. du Pont de Nemours & Co., 96 F.T.C. 653, 655 (1980) (alleging attempted monopolization of titanium dioxide). Du Pont also figured prominently in other government antitrust suits in which market structure concerns animated the government's decision to prosecute. *See* United States v. E.I. du Pont de Nemours & Co., 353 U.S. 586, 590 (1957) (vertical merger); E.I. du Pont de Nemours & Co. v. FTC, 729 F.2d 128, 140 (2d Cir. 1984) (use of facilitating practices in a tight oligopoly). In the same period Kodak faced three government suits claiming monopolization or attempted monopolization. *See* FTC v. Eastman Kodak Co., 274 U.S. 619, 625 (1927) (alleging monopolization of photographic equipment); United States v. Eastman Kodak Co., 226 F. 62, 64 (W.D.N.Y. 1915) (same), *decree entered*, 230 F. 522, 524 (W.D.N.Y. 1916), *appeal dismissed*, 255 U.S. 578 (1921); United States v. Eastman Kodak Co., 1954 Trade Cas. (CCH) ¶ 67,920 (W.D.N.Y. 1954) (alleging monopolization of film processing). In addition, both du Pont and Kodak encountered numerous private antitrust challenges in which their market power figured prominently. *See, e.g.*, Berkey Photo, Inc. v. Eastman Kodak Co., 603 F.2d 263, 267-68 (2d Cir. 1979) (alleging monopolization and attempted monopolization of cameras and photofinishing), *cert. denied*, 444 U.S. 1093 (1980); Argus Inc. v. Eastman Kodak Co., 552 F. Supp. 589, 593 (S.D.N.Y. 1982) (alleging monopolization of photographic equipment market and flashcube development); GAF Corp. v. Eastman Kodak Co., 519 F. Supp. 1203, 1209 (S.D.N.Y. 1981) (alleging monopolization of various aspects of amateur photography market).

47. Northern Securities Co. v. United States, 193 U.S. 197, 325, 360 (1904).
48. *Id.* at 325-54.
49. *See* A. CHANDLER JR., *supra* note 41, at 333-34.
50. J.B. CLARK & J.M. CLARK, THE CONTROL OF TRUSTS 14-15 (1912).
51. The Antitrust Division was created as a distinct unit in 1903. *See* STAFF OF SENATE TEMPORARY NATIONAL ECONOMIC COMM., 76TH CONG., 3D SESS., INVESTIGATION OF CONCENTRATION OF ECONOMIC POWER: ANTITRUST IN ACTION, MONOGRAPH NO. 16, at 23-26 (Comm. Print 1940) (written by W. Hamilton and I. Till) [hereinafter TNEC MONOGRAPH NO. 16]; H. THORELLI, *supra* note 41, at 536-37; 1 S. WHITNEY, *supra* note 4, at 6.
52. Standard Oil Co. v. United States, 221 U.S. 1 (1911).
53. United States v. American Tobacco Co., 221 U.S. 106 (1911).

Eastman Kodak,[54] International Harvester,[55] du Pont,[56] U.S. Steel,[57] United Shoe Machinery,[58] American Can,[59] Corn Products Refining,[60] and railroads that dominated anthracite coal production in the northeastern United States.[61] In all of these suits, the Department sought divestiture.[62] Although the government occasionally failed to establish a Sherman Act violation,[63] these cases usually resulted in a finding of liability and the entry of a decree for structural relief.[64]

In 1920 two developments ended this period of initiatives. The Supreme Court's decision to absolve U.S. Steel of liability for monopolization[65] discouraged further government assaults on corporate size and signaled the Court's unwillingness to approve additional measures to undo existing levels of concentration.[66] Judicial acceptance of a more tolerant legal standard anticipated a corresponding shift in executive branch enforcement philosophy as Warren Harding's election to the presidency began a reorientation of federal antitrust policy. For eight years

---

54. United States v. Eastman Kodak Co., 226 F. 62 (W.D.N.Y. 1915), *decree entered*, 230 F. 522 (W.D.N.Y. 1916), *cert. denied*, 255 U.S. 578 (1921).

55. United States v. International Harvester Co., 214 F. 987 (D. Minn. 1914), *petition for additional relief denied*, 10 F.2d 827 (D. Minn. 1926), *aff'd*, 274 U.S. 693 (1927).

56. United States v. E.I. du Pont de Nemours & Co., 188 F. 127 (C.C. Del. 1911).

57. United States v. United States Steel Corp., 251 U.S. 417 (1920).

58. United States v. United Shoe Mach. Co., 247 U.S. 32 (1918).

59. United States v. American Can Co., 230 F. 859 (D. Md.), *petition for dissolution decree denied*, 234 F. 1019 (D. Md. 1916).

60. United States v. Corn Prods. Ref. Co., 234 F. 964 (S.D.N.Y. 1916), *appeal dismissed*, 249 U.S. 621 (1919).

61. *See* United States v. Lehigh Valley R.R., 254 U.S. 255 (1920); United States v. Reading Co., 253 U.S. 26 (1920).

62. *See Lehigh Valley*, 254 U.S. at 257; *Reading*, 253 U.S. at 40-41; *U.S. Steel*, 251 U.S. at 436, 454-57; *United Shoe*, 247 U.S. at 46-47; *American Tobacco*, 221 U.S. at 149-50; *Standard Oil*, 221 U.S. at 43; *Corn Prods.*, 234 F. at 1015-18; *American Can*, 230 F. at 862, 902-04; *Eastman Kodak*, 226 F. at 64; *International Harvester*, 214 F. at 1001; *du Pont*, 188 F. at 154-55.

63. *See U.S. Steel*, 251 U.S. at 455-57 (absolving defendant of liability); *United Shoe*, 247 U.S. at 41, 66-67 (same).

64. *See, e.g., Lehigh Valley*, 254 U.S. at 270-71 (dissolution ordered); *American Tobacco*, 221 U.S. at 187-88 (parties ordered to provide trial court with "plan or method of dissolving the combination and of recreating, out of the elements now composing it, a new condition which shall be honestly in harmony with and not repugnant to the law"); *Standard Oil*, 221 U.S. at 77-82 (dissolution ordered); *Corn Prods.*, 234 F. at 1015-18 (dissolution ordered, with parties to submit divestiture plan to FTC acting as master in chancery); *du Pont*, 188 F. at 154-56 (dissolution ordered, with parties to provide court with divestiture plan). *But see* United States v. American Can Co., 234 F. 1019, 1020-22 (D. Md. 1916) (despite finding of liability, dissolution decree denied).

65. *U.S. Steel*, 251 U.S. at 457 (1920).

66. *See* Keller, *The Pluralist State: American Economic Regulation in Comparative Perspective, 1900-1930*, in REGULATION IN PERSPECTIVE 56, 75-76 (T. McCraw ed. 1981) (noting judicial acceptance of large enterprise well-established by 1920s); Levi, *The Antitrust Laws and Monopoly*, 14 U. CHI. L. REV. 153, 159-60 (1947) (arguing Supreme Court did little to stem economic concentration). The permissive implications of *U.S. Steel* were underscored seven years later in United States v. International Harvester Co., 274 U.S. 693, 702 (1927). In *International Harvester*, the Court relied upon the *U.S. Steel* decision in affirming a lower court's refusal to grant the Justice Department's request that a 1918 consent decree be modified to require the separation of International Harvester into at least three corporations. *Id.* at 708-09; *see also* H. SEAGER & C. GULICK JR., *supra* note 41, at 270-80 (discussing remedial history of farm machinery litigation).

the scope of federal antitrust enforcement narrowed sharply as Harding and Calvin Coolidge showed extreme solicitude for business community preferences and respect for the accomplishments of large industrial concerns.[67] As one commentator declared in 1928, "[t]his is the day of big business. . . . The day of the blatant trust-buster is definitely over."[68]

2. *1937-1956:* Alcoa *to* AT&T

The economic crash in 1929 eliminated the aura of legitimacy and respect American business institutions enjoyed in the 1920s.[69] The Depression fostered a major public policy debate about the government's role in guiding business activity. To some, the collapse discredited the competitive model and demonstrated the need for more comprehensive public regulation.[70] Particularly in Franklin Roosevelt's first term as president, this impulse manifested itself in collective planning solutions such as the National Industrial Recovery Act[71] and the cartelization of specific indus-

---

67. *See* T. BLAISDELL JR., THE FEDERAL TRADE COMMISSION: AN EXPERIMENT IN THE CONTROL OF BUSINESS 75-78 (1932) (concluding transfer of presidency from Democrat to Republican in 1920 imbued FTC with more conservative policy preferences); P. HERRING, PUBLIC ADMINISTRATION AND THE PUBLIC INTEREST 125-38 (1936) (describing impact of conservative Coolidge appointees upon policies of FTC); J. HICKS, REPUBLICAN ASCENDANCY 1921-1933, at 64-66 (1960) (stating Harding and Coolidge appointees to federal regulatory bodies reflected view that business knew best course for country); W. LEUCHTENBURG, THE PERILS OF PROSPERITY 1914-1932, at 96-97 (1958) (noting Coolidge policy to give business free reign). The laissez faire proclivities of Harding and Coolidge were not the sole intellectual basis for antitrust's retreat in the 1920s. A second limiting force was the ascent of associationalism, which urged the displacement of competition-oriented policies with greater business-government cooperation to guide the nation toward preferred economic ends. Born in regulatory programs of the War Industries Board in World War I, associationalism promoted more extensive reliance upon industry self-regulation under government supervision. *See* Cuff, *Business, the State, and World War II: The American Experience,* in THE ORDEAL OF TWENTIETH-CENTURY AMERICA—INTERPRETIVE READINGS 48 (J. Schwartz ed. 1974) (analyzing formation of new business-government relationships through preparedness programs during World War I); Hawley, *Three Facets of Hoover Associationalism: Lumber, Aviation, and Movies, 1921-1930,* in REGULATION IN PERSPECTIVE 95 (T. McCraw ed. 1981) (analyzing corporate self regulation); Hawley, *Herbert Hoover, the Commerce Secretariat, and the Vision of an "Associative State," 1921-1928,* 61 J. AM. HIST. 116, 118 (1974) (analyzing Hoover's associational order that functioned through entities other than public enterprise); Himmelberg, *The War Industries Board and the Antitrust Question in November 1918,* 52 J. AM. HIST. 59, 61 (1965) (describing sentiment of some business leaders to extend wartime relaxation of antitrust enforcement beyond conclusion of World War I).

68. Marx, *New Interpretations of the Anti-trust Law as Applied to Business, Trade, Farm and Labor Associations,* 2 U. CIN. L. REV. 211, 222-23 (1928).

69. *See* A. SCHLESINGER, THE CRISIS OF THE OLD ORDER 1919-1933, at 156-204 (1956).

70. *See* Miller, Walton, Kovacic, & Rabkin, *Industrial Policy: Reindustrialization Through Competition or Coordinated Action?,* 2 YALE J. ON REG. 1, 14-15 (1984) (identifying former War Industries Board members and younger policymakers who laid foundation for government coordination of economic activity in Franklin Roosevelt's first Administration).

71. 48 Stat. 195 (1933) (codified at 15 U.S.C. §§ 702-02f (repealed 1966)). The statute created the National Recovery Administration (NRA), which established industry codes governing output, prices, wages, working conditions, and trade practices. The NRA and its code-making activities are described in E. HAWLEY, THE NEW DEAL AND THE PROBLEM OF MONOPOLY 19-71 (1966); L. LYON, P. HOMAN, C. TERBORGH, L. LORWIN, C. DEARING & L. MARSHALL, THE NATIONAL RECOVERY ADMINISTRATION 8 (1935); C. ROOS, NRA ECONOMIC PLANNING 39 (1937). Two years after the Act's enactment, the Supreme Court struck down the enabling statute as an unconstitutionally broad delegation of legislative power. A.L.A. Schechter Poultry Corp. v. United States, 295 U.S. 495, 541-42 (1935).

tries through measures such as the Motor Carrier Act of 1935[72] and the Civil Aeronautics Act of 1938.[73]

A second group of policymakers attributed the crash and the sluggish pace of economic recovery in the 1930s to the domination of American industry by a small number of large corporations.[74] They felt the solution to the vice of corporate gigantism was not additional planning or regulation, but rather the dismemberment of existing structures into smaller commercial entities. Legislative measures such as the Glass-Steagall Banking Act of 1933,[75] the McKellar-Black Air Mail Act of 1934,[76] and, most dramatically, the Public Utility Holding Company Act of 1935[77] relied on deconcentration to prevent the reappearance of the abuses that many saw as causes of the Depression.

Within the Justice Department, the deconcentration orientation began to exert a significant influence in the late 1930s. In 1937, at the end of Robert Jackson's tenure as Assistant Attorney General for Antitrust, the government sued Alcoa for monopolizing the manufacture of aluminum and sought extensive divestitures of the firm's production facilities.[78] Although the World War II mobilization slowed the aluminum case and blunted antitrust enforcement generally, the Second Circuit's *Alcoa* decision in 1945 rehabilitated section two enforcement possibilities that had remained dormant since *U.S. Steel* in 1920. The government never obtained a decree to restructure *Alcoa*,[79] but the court's treatment of liability issues

---

72. 49 Stat. 543 (1935) (codified as amended in scattered sections of 49 U.S.C. (1982)).

73. 52 Stat. 973 (1938) (codified as amended at 49 U.S.C. §§ 1301-1542 (1982)).

74. See E. HAWLEY, *supra* note 71, at 283-303 (identifying principal architects of expanded reliance on antitrust enforcement and competition-oriented initiatives during FDR's presidency).

75. 48 Stat. 162 (1933) (codified as amended at 12 U.S.C. §§ 377-78 (1982)). The Glass-Steagall Act required banks belonging to the Federal Reserve System to divorce themselves from their securities affiliates, forced private banks to choose between deposit and investment banking to the exclusion of the other, and limited the underwriting activities of commercial banks to general obligation bonds of federal, state, and municipal bodies or government corporations. See V. CAROSSO, INVESTMENT BANKING IN AMERICA: A HISTORY 368-75 (1970); Hawke, *The Glass-Steagall Legacy: A Historical Perspective*, 31 N.Y.L. SCH. L. REV. 255 (1986).

76. 48 Stat. 933 (1934) (codified as amended in scattered sections of 39 U.S.C. (1982)). The McKellar-Black statute required all air mail contract carriers to divest themselves of their manufacturing and other aviation interests, thus separating air carriage services from aircraft manufacturing. See F. SPENCER, AIR MAIL PAYMENT AND THE GOVERNMENT 76-100 (1941); Freudenthal, *The Aviation Business in the 1930's*, in THE HISTORY OF THE AMERICAN AIRCRAFT INDUSTRY 93-98 (G. Simonson ed. 1968).

77. 49 Stat. 803 (1935) (codified as amended at 15 U.S.C. §§ 79a-z (1982)). The Holding Company Act required the dissolution of certain gas and electric holding companies into simplified, integrated utility systems. See generally R. RITCHIE, INTEGRATION OF PUBLIC UTILITY HOLDING COMPANIES (1954) (analyzing Holding Company Act's dissolution requirements and their implementation); Blair-Smith & Helfenstein, *A Death Sentence or a New Lease on Life? A Survey of Corporate Adjustments Under the Public Utility Holding Company Act*, 94 U. PA. L. REV. 148 (1946) (same).

78. See United States v. Aluminum Co. of Am., 148 F.2d 416, 421 (describing procedural history of *Alcoa* litigation). The filing of *Alcoa* was one of several steps Jackson took in laying the foundation for Thurman Arnold's heralded revival of federal antitrust enforcement during his tenure as head of the Antitrust Division from 1938 through 1942. See E. HAWLEY, *supra* note 71, at 374-76.

79. See United States v. Aluminum Co. of Am., 91 F. Supp. 333, 416-19 (S.D.N.Y. 1950)

greatly diminished the burden of proof government prosecutors need bear to establish section two liability.[80]

Alcoa strengthened ongoing Sherman Act monopolization prosecutions and invigorated Justice Department efforts to expand section two enforcement.[81] In 1946 Attorney General Tom Clark told a Senate subcommittee that "the times require that where the elimination of competition is threatened or actual that it be restored by the seldom-used processes of divestiture, divorcement, and dissolution."[82] Through greater recourse to structural remedies, the government would "establish complete and independent units of enterprise which can and will in fact compete one with the other."[83] The future Supreme Court justice emphasized that "[t]his is

---

(denying government request for divestiture).

80. Judge Learned Hand's opinion stated that the possession of monopoly power, without more, did not constitute illegal monopolization. "A single producer may be the survivor out of a group of active competitors, merely by virtue of his superior skill, foresight and industry," Judge Hand wrote. "[T]he successful competitor, having been urged to compete, must not be turned upon when he wins." *Alcoa*, 148 F.2d at 430. The crucial feature of Hand's analysis, however, was its broad definition of conduct that rendered the acquisition or maintenance of monopoly power illegal. In the following passage, the court condemned Alcoa's efforts to expand its aluminum production capacity:

> It was not inevitable that [Alcoa] should always anticipate increases in the demand for ingot and be prepared to supply them. Nothing compelled it to keep doubling and redoubling its capacity before others entered the field. It insists that it never excluded competitors; but we can think of no more effective exclusion than progressively to embrace each new opportunity as it opened, and to face every newcomer with new capacity already geared into a great organization, having the advantage of experience, trade connections, and the elite of personnel. Only in the case we interpret "exclusion" as limited to manoeuvres not honestly industrial, but actuated solely by a desire to prevent competition, can such a course, indefatigably pursued, be deemed not "exclusionary." So to limit it would in our judgment emasculate the [Sherman] Act; would permit just such consolidations as it was designed to prevent.

Id. at 431. The court then concluded that this pattern of capacity expansion violated § 2 of the Sherman Act:

> In order to fall within § 2, the monopolist must have both the power to monopolize, and the intent to monopolize. To read the passage as demanding any "specific" intent, makes nonsense of it, for no monopolist monopolizes unconscious of what he is doing. So here, "Alcoa" meant to keep, and did keep, that complete and exclusive hold upon the ingot market with which it started. That was to "monopolize" that market, however innocently it otherwise proceeded.

Id. at 432. The Supreme Court endorsed *Alcoa*'s reasoning one year later in American Tobacco Co. v. United States, 328 U.S. 781, 811-14 (1946).

81. By one count, between December 1936 and August 1954, the government filed 44 civil lawsuits in which it sought divestiture. *See* D. Dewey, *supra* note 4, at 246. *Alcoa* bolstered ongoing § 2 cases and inspired new government monopolization proceedings by approving a liability standard that substantially increased the likelihood that the Justice Department could establish a violation of the Sherman Act. Frederick Rowe observed that the "postwar antitrust programs against concentration gained thrust from *Alcoa*'s synthesis of law and economics into antimonopoly norms. The fusion of Populist ideology with oligopoly learning's linkage of concentrated market structures and anticompetitive behavior propelled ambitious antitrust aims." Rowe, *supra* note 3, at 1535.

82. *Departments of State, Justice, Commerce, and the Judiciary Appropriation Bill for 1947: Hearings on H.R. 6056 Before the Subcomm. of the Senate Comm. on Appropriations,* 79th Cong., 2d Sess. 959, 960 (1946) (testimony of Attorney General Tom Clark).

83. *Id.*

---

the only way to maintain free enterprise."[84] From the beginning of World War II until the mid-1950s, subjects of Justice Department monopolization actions included the distribution and exhibition of motion pictures,[85] cellophane,[86] shoe machinery,[87] Pullman sleeping cars,[88] telephone equipment,[89] film processing,[90] and bananas.[91] To a considerable degree, *Alcoa* foreshadowed the outcome of other deconcentration initiatives in this period. Despite notable setbacks such as *du Pont*,[92] the government ordinarily prevailed on liability issues. As in *Alcoa*, however, the high remedial expectations that attended the government's post-war antimonopoly program went unfulfilled.[93]

3. *1969-1982:* IBM *to* AT&T

The third and most recent round of Sherman Act deconcentration initiatives took root in the recommendations of President Johnson's Task Force on Antitrust Policy.[94] Chaired by Dean Phil Neal of the University of Chicago Law School, the Task Force proposed a dramatic program to restructure large sectors of the American economy.[95] It deeply influenced the thinking of public enforcement officials and helped focus the energies of the Justice Department and the FTC on developing large structural cases to achieve deconcentration ends.

The first result of this reorientation was the Justice Department's challenge to IBM's position as the country's preeminent manufacturer of electronic computing equipment. Filed in 1969 on the final day of the Johnson Administration, the suit proposed that IBM be broken up into several independent companies.[96] The case proved to be more than a

---

84. *Id.* In his annual report for fiscal year 1946, Attorney General Clark observed: "In regard to monopolies, I have encouraged the application of the remedies of divestiture and divorcement in civil suits brought under Section 2 of the Sherman Act, as the most expeditious means of eradicating this economic evil." 1947 ATT'Y GEN. ANN. REP. 8.

85. United States v. Paramount Pictures, Inc., 334 U.S. 131 (1948); Schine Chain Theatres v. United States, 334 U.S. 110 (1948); United States v. Griffith Amusement Co., 334 U.S. 100 (1948); United States v. Crescent Amusement Co., 323 U.S. 173 (1944).

86. United States v. E.I. du Pont de Nemours & Co., 351 U.S. 377 (1956).

87. United States v. United Shoe Mach., 110 F. Supp. 295 (D. Mass. 1953), *aff'd per curiam*, 347 U.S. 521 (1954).

88. United States v. Pullman Co., 50 F. Supp. 123 (E.D. Pa. 1943), *aff'd per curiam*, 330 U.S. 806 (1947).

89. United States v. Western Elec. Co., 1956 Trade Cas. (CCH) ¶ 68,246 (D.N.J. 1956).

90. United States v. Eastman Kodak Co., 1954 Trade Cas. (CCH) ¶ 67,920 (W.D.N.Y. 1954).

91. United States v. United Fruit Co., 1958 Trade Cas. (CCH) ¶ 68,941 (E.D. La. 1958).

92. United States v. E.I. du Pont de Nemours & Co., 351 U.S. 377, 399-404 (1956) (concluding that du Pont lacked monopoly power necessary to establish liability for monopolization).

93. *See* D. DEWEY, *supra* note 4, at 247; Rowe, *supra* note 3, at 1534-36 (discussing uneven prosecution and application of laws and untimeliness of remedies); *see also* Flynn, *supra* note 38, at 10 (describing second deconcentration era as "doctrinally significant" but "economically insignificant").

94. *See* WHITE HOUSE TASK FORCE REPORT ON ANTITRUST POLICY, *reprinted in* 2 ANTITRUST L. & ECON. REV. 11 (1968-69) [hereinafter NEAL TASK FORCE REPORT].

95. *Id.* at 14-15, 65-76.

96. *See* United States v. IBM Corp., [1961-1970 Transfer Binder] Trade Reg. Rep. (CCH)

freakish political gesture by an outgoing administration. The prosecution
of IBM represented the first of an extraordinary round of deconcentration
initiatives begun by the Nixon and Ford Administrations.[97] During President Nixon's tenure, the FTC launched "shared monopoly" cases seeking
structural relief against the petroleum[98] and breakfast cereal industries.[99]
The Ford Justice Department brought suits to restructure AT&T[100] and
the nation's leading tire manufacturers.[101] With rare but important exceptions, such as the restructuring of AT&T, the deconcentration cases of the
third era failed to achieve their structural aims.[102]

B. Formative Conditions

The cycles of deconcentration initiatives described above share three
basic characteristics. First, each cycle followed a period of perceived
indifference or permissiveness on the part of enforcement officials and
judges toward the existence and conduct of large firms. Second, each cycle
coincided with events that discredited business institutions and created a
political climate amenable to attacks on large accumulations of economic
power. Finally, the emergence of an appealing intellectual framework for
dissolving dominant firms into smaller constituent parts served as a
powerful catalyst for each deconcentration era.

1. Response to Permissiveness

Policies that tolerate or welcome corporate size have played a major
role in seeding the clouds for deconcentration. The move to restructure
dominant firms can be explained as an effort to cure the excesses of a
period of permissiveness or indifference by antitrust enforcement agencies

---

¶ 45,069 (S.D.N.Y. filed Jan. 17, 1969). The government's original complaint and its amended
complaint, both of which requested divestiture, are reprinted in their entirety in F. Fisher, J.
McGowan & J. Greenwood, Folded, Spindled, and Mutilated—Economic Analysis and U.S. v. IBM
353-68 (1983).

97. *See supra* notes 8-21 and accompanying text. Perhaps the most notable early indication
of an emerging Nixon Administration campaign against concentration came in a widely
reported speech given by Attorney General John Mitchell in 1969 to the Georgia Bar
Association. Mitchell declared: "I believe that the future vitality of our free economy may be
in danger because of the increasing threat of economic concentration by corporate mergers.
. . . The danger that this super-concentration poses to our economic, political and social
structure cannot be overestimated." Address by John Mitchell, Georgia Bar Association (June
6, 1969), *reprinted in Economic Concentration: Hearings Before the Subcomm. on Antitrust and
Monopoly of the Senate Comm. on the Judiciary*, 91st Cong., 2d Sess. 5122-23 (1970).

98. Exxon Corp., 98 F.T.C. 453 (1981). The Exxon complaint is analyzed in Note,
Structural Shared Monopoly Under FTC 5: The Implications of the Exxon Complaint, 26 Case W. Res.
615 (1976); *see also supra* notes 12, 18, 20 and accompanying text.

99. Kellogg Co., 99 F.T.C. 8 (1982). The Kellogg complaint is analyzed in Note, *Oligopolies,
Cereals, and Section Five of the Federal Trade Commission Act*, 61 Geo. L.J. 1145 (1973); *see also
supra* notes 13, 18 and accompanying text.

100. United States v. AT&T Co., [1970-1979 Transfer Binder] Trade Reg. Rep. (CCH) ¶
45,074 (D.D.C. filed Nov. 20, 1974); *see also supra* notes 6, 11, 19 and accompanying text.

101. United States v. Goodyear Tire & Rubber Co., and United States v. Firestone Tire &
Rubber Co. [1970-1979 Transfer Binder] Trade Reg. Rep. (CCH) ¶ 45,073 (N.D. Ohio filed
Aug. 9, 1973); *see also supra* notes 16, 18 and accompanying text.

102. *See supra* notes 18-20 and accompanying text.

and the courts to the perceived problems of corporate size. As Morton Keller observed in his study of American economic regulation: "[A]ntitrust response follows consolidation challenge as night follows the day."[103]

This response pattern is most evident in the first two cycles of Sherman Act deconcentration measures. The 1904-1920 round of cases followed on the heels of a merger movement that yielded monopolies or near monopolies in numerous industries. The establishment of dominant firms received strong impetus from the Supreme Court's decision in *Knight*, which signaled the Court's receptivity to large consolidations.[104] The flood of large horizontal mergers that followed *Knight* faced few impediments from a Justice Department that, owing to scant resources and presidential indifference, was ill-positioned to stem the tide.[105]

The 1936-1956 deconcentration era similarly followed a period of permissiveness toward large firms. Judicial antitrust decisions in the 1920s -most notably, *U.S. Steel*[106]—suggested that courts would allow large firms considerable latitude in choosing business strategies and would leave all but the largest aggregations of capital undisturbed. Furthermore, the Supreme Court rejected efforts by the FTC to use section five of the FTC Act[107] to close the "assets loophole" created by the Clayton Act's antimerger provision, which forbade anticompetitive stock acquisitions.[108]

---

103. Keller, *supra* note 66, at 94.

104. United States v. E.C. Knight Co., 156 U.S. 1, 16-18 (1895); *see also supra* notes 39-41 and accompanying text.

105. *See* H. FAULKNER, POLITICS, REFORM AND EXPANSION 1890-1900, at 101-02 (1959) (discussing permissive executive branch enforcement attitudes); H. THORELLI, *supra* note 41, at 380-410 (same); TNEC MONOGRAPH NO. 16, *supra* note 51, at 23-26 (discussing paucity of antitrust enforcement resources); *see also* M. SKLAR, *supra* note 43, at 162-63 ("It was not the law as judicially construed that facilitated or encouraged corporate consolidation; it was, rather, business and political policy—the decisions of capitalists and their lawyers in the private sector, and the decisions of the executive branch . . . under presidents McKinley and Roosevelt, and up to a point under Taft, not to prosecute or to prosecute selectively.").

106. United States v. United States Steel Corp., 251 U.S. 417, 457 (1920); *see also supra* notes 65-66 and accompanying text.

107. 15 U.S.C. § 45 (1982).

108. As enacted in 1914, § 7 of the Clayton Act prohibited mergers achieved through the purchase of the target firm's stock. 38 Stat. 730 (1914) (codified as amended at 15 U.S.C. § 18 (1982)). Companies soon began using asset acquisitions to carry out consolidation strategies. *See* G. HENDERSON, THE FEDERAL TRADE COMMISSION: A STUDY IN ADMINISTRATIVE LAW 40, 321 (1924) (describing business awareness that asset acquisitions would avoid the Clayton Act's anti-merger prohibitions). In FTC v. Eastman Kodak Co., 274 U.S. 619 (1927), the FTC sought to fill this gap by using the § 5 ban on "unfair methods of competition" to force Kodak to divest three recently acquired film processing plants. *Id.* at 623. The Supreme Court ruled that the FTC lacked authority to order divestiture under § 5, thereby vitiating the provision's usefulness as an enforcement tool for undoing the effects of consummated asset acquisitions. *Id.* at 623-25; *see* Kovacic, *The Federal Trade Commission and Congressional Oversight of Antitrust Enforcement*, 17 TULSA L.J. 587, 614 (1982) (discussing *Kodak*'s limiting effect upon the Commission's use of § 5 as an antimerger enforcement tool). Nearly four decades later, the Court reversed its field, concluding that subsequent cases interpreting generic grants of authority to administrative agencies had "repudiated" *Kodak*. FTC v. Dean Foods Co., 384 U.S. 597, 606 & n.4 (1966) (dictum) (rejecting *Kodak*); *see also* Averitt, *Structural Remedies in Competition Cases Under the Federal Trade Commission Act*, 40 OHIO ST. L.J. 781, 788-92 (1979) (tracing erosion of *Kodak*). This adjustment in the Court's assessment of the Commission's remedial powers under § 5 provided a crucial basis for FTC efforts in the 1970s to use § 5 to attack "shared monopolies."

These decisions received strong reinforcement from Harding and Coolidge antitrust enforcement policies that disdained aggressive intervention and treated large firms as valued engines of economic and social progress. Together with favorable stock market conditions, the tolerant executive branch and judicial attitudes toward corporate size in the 1920s created a favorable climate for mergers.[109] From 1924 to 1928, this country witnessed a wave of acquisitions equal in intensity to the first merger movement at the turn of the century. Unlike the first wave, the second movement involved a smaller number of multi-firm consolidations and produced relatively few transactions yielding a single dominant enterprise.[110] The second wave's distinguishing characteristic was the creation of oligopolistic market structures through mergers that formed strong "number two" firms in industries formerly controlled by a single company and reinforced some existing, comparatively weak oligopolies. The second wave also consisted of more mergers in which vertical integration, geographic and product line extension, and conglomerate diversification were strong features.[111]

The most recent deconcentration era is explained less easily as a reaction to lax antitrust policy,[112] but some important elements of perceived permissiveness toward corporate size nonetheless can be identified. Despite the government's pursuit of an occasional monopolization divestiture suit in the late 1950s[113] and early 1960s,[114] antitrust policy in this period rarely attempted to deal with concentrated market structures that had taken shape earlier in the century. The government's failure to bring substantial resources to bear upon restructuring tight oligopolies and instances of single-firm market power was seen as evidence of a serious policy default.[115]

The increased frequency of conglomerate mergers in the 1960s also contributed to the sense that antitrust policy had lost its ability to limit corporate size. By the mid-1960s, the prevailing merger jurisprudence had established stringent limits upon horizontal and vertical acquisitions, leaving conglomerate transactions as the principal focus of corporate dealmaking.[116] From 1964 through 1968 this country witnessed a sharp increase in postwar merger activity, with conglomerate acquisitions accounting for the bulk of the acquired assets.[117] Although they added little to horizontal concentration, these transactions produced large conglomer-

---

109. See Marx, supra note 68, at 221 (explaining judicial and executive receptiveness to combinations promoting public interest).

110. Eis, The 1919-1930 Merger Movement in American History, 12 J. L. & Econ. 267, 279-80 (1969).

111. See F. Scherer, supra note 38, at 122.

112. See, e.g., T. Kovaleff, Business and Government During the Eisenhower Administration: A Study of the Antitrust Policy of the Antitrust Division of the Justice Department 155 (1980) (concluding that "[i]n the context of the mid-twentieth century, the Eisenhower Administration, incontrovertibly, oversaw a period of vigorous and innovative enforcement of the antitrust laws by the Justice Department's Antitrust Division.").

113. See, e.g., International Boxing Club v. United States, 358 U.S. 242 (1959).

114. See, e.g., United States v. Grinnell Corp., 384 U.S. 563 (1966).

115. See infra notes 199-203 and accompanying text.

116. See Rowe, supra note 3, at 1524-28.

117. See F. Scherer, supra note 38, at 123-24.

ate enterprises whose existence suggested that antitrust policy was seriously deficient in dealing with sheer corporate size.

2. *Political Sentiment Disfavoring Bigness*

Periods of Sherman Act deconcentration activism have paralleled peaks in public distrust toward large corporate enterprise.[118] Passage of the Sherman Act and the government's trailblazing deconcentration initiatives after the turn of the century occurred amid strong public antipathy toward the trusts.[119] Provocative government reports and popular exposés extensively recounted corporate misdeeds,[120] and the efforts of new industrial combines to attain greater economies of scale dislocated small businesses and farmers, thus creating a vocal antitrust constituency. The onset of the Depression discredited the business community and convinced many that the unconfined discretion of large companies triggered the economic collapse. And by the late 1960s, the efforts of a new generation of consumer advocates such as Ralph Nader generated formidable public support for expansive government intervention to curb perceived excesses of the business community.[121]

---

118. The importance of public perceptions about the business community to the scope and direction of antitrust enforcement and other regulatory policies is explored in L. GALAMBOS, THE PUBLIC IMAGE OF BIG BUSINESS IN AMERICA, 1880-1940, at 253-69 (1975) (empirical study demonstrating shifts in public opinion of corporations); R. HOFSTADTER, *What Happened to the Antitrust Movement?*, in THE PARANOID STYLE IN AMERICAN POLITICS AND OTHER ESSAYS 188-237 (1965) (discussing temporal coincidence of decline of popular antitrust movement and growing antitrust enforcement efforts); Hayes, *Political Choice in Regulatory Administration*, in REGULATION IN PERSPECTIVE 124 (T. McCraw ed. 1981) (explaining economic regulation as political choice); Baker & Blumenthal, *Ideological Cycles and Unstable Antitrust Rules*, 31 ANTITRUST BULL. 323, 337-38 (1986) (urging incremental change rather than ideologically driven reform).

119. *See* S. HAYS, THE RESPONSE TO INDUSTRIALISM 1885-1914, at 4-93 (1957) (explaining how different socio-economic groups' reactions to industrialization shaped government policy); R. HOFSTADTER, THE AGE OF REFORM 213-69 (1955) (describing public dependence on federal regulation to curb perceived evils of big business); H. THORELLI, *supra* note 41, at 54-163, 235-368 (discussing how political, social, and economic change caused public antipathy toward trusts and how that antipathy influenced federal antitrust policy); R. WEIBE, THE SEARCH FOR ORDER 1877-1920, at 1-163 (1967) (noting anxiety over growing industrialization that manifests itself through antimonopoly sentiment); Millon, *The Sherman Act and the Balance of Power*, 61 S. CAL. L. REV. 1219, 1224-28 (1988) (explaining that many Americans viewed growth of monopolies as threat to vitality of democracy itself).

120. *See* H. FAULKNER, THE DECLINE OF LAISSEZ FAIRE 1897-1917, at 177-78 (1951) (describing popular magazine articles from 1902-1907); R. HIGGS, CRISIS AND LEVIATHAN 111 (1987) (analyzing relationship between muckrakers' articles and subsequent antitrust statutes). Scrutiny of the petroleum industry provides a representative illustration. Standard Oil's climb to power was documented in two studies requested by Congress. *See* DEPARTMENT OF COMMERCE AND LABOR, REPORT OF THE COMMISSIONER OF CORPORATIONS ON THE TRANSPORTATION OF PETROLEUM (1906); DEPARTMENT OF COMMERCE AND LABOR, REPORT OF THE COMMISSIONER OF CORPORATIONS ON THE PETROLEUM INDUSTRY, PART I, POSITION OF THE STANDARD OIL COMPANY IN THE PETROLEUM INDUSTRY (May 20, 1907); DEPARTMENT OF COMMERCE AND LABOR, REPORT OF THE COMMISSIONER OF CORPORATIONS ON THE PETROLEUM INDUSTRY, PART II, PRICES AND PROFITS (Aug. 5, 1907). These studies followed publication of Ida Tarbell's muckraking attack upon John D. Rockefeller's petroleum empire. *See* I. TARBELL, THE HISTORY OF THE STANDARD OIL COMPANY (1904) (two volumes); *see also* B. DEWITT, THE PROGRESSIVE MOVEMENT 49-50 (1915) (describing impact of Tarbell's studies on Standard Oil).

121. The emergence of broad public support in the 1960s for more encompassing federal intervention in the affairs of business is recounted in M. PERTSCHUK, REVOLT AGAINST REGULA-

One way to gauge public attitudes toward dominant firms is to consider the level of deconcentration activity within Congress during a given period. Since passing the Sherman Act in 1890, Congress seriously has considered legislation dealing with economic concentration roughly every other decade.[122] These periods of congressional activism have paralleled the peak periods of deconcentration litigation. In 1914 Congress passed the Clayton Act[123] and the Federal Trade Commission Act[124] to cure, among other perceived deficiencies, the Sherman Act's apparent inability to prevent or dismantle monopoly power.[125] With its enumeration of specific forbidden commercial practices and its ban on certain stock acquisitions, the Clayton Act sought to thwart the attainment of dominant market positions achieved by Standard Oil, American Tobacco, and other defendants in the first series of deconcentration suits.[126] The FTC Act also contained several provisions designed to arrest and redress concentration. The Act gave the Commission broad information gathering and reporting powers in the hope that research would identify promising targets for

---

TION—THE RISE AND PAUSE OF THE CONSUMER MOVEMENT 5-45 (1982).

122. The decades of legislative activism were the 1890s, 1910s, 1930s, 1950s, and 1970s. This is not to suggest the complete absence of legislative enactments with deconcentration overtones in the other decades. Two examples come to mind. Among other requirements, the Hepburn Act of 1906 forbade railroads to haul goods, except timber for their own use, in which they had a direct or indirect interest. 34 Stat. 584, 585 (1906) (codified at 49 U.S.C. § 1 (repealed 1978)). Known as the "commodities clause," this provision sought to prevent the anthracite railroads from exploiting their dual positions as public carriers and private shippers to the detriment of independent coal operators by forcing the railroads to divest their ownership of coal producing properties. See G. KOLKO, RAILROADS AND REGULATION: 1877-1916, at 127-54 (1965).

A second example is the Surplus Property Act of 1944. 58 Stat. 765 (1944) (codified as amended at 40 U.S.C. §§ 471-511 (1982)). For the disposition of certain government-owned facilities, the statute required a ruling by the Attorney General that the contemplated sale would not violate the antitrust laws. *Id.* § 488(a). Pursuant to this measure, the War Assets Administration transferred a substantial part of government-owned aluminum capacity built during the war to Alcoa's rivals. See 2 S. WHITNEY, *supra* note 4, at 96-98. These moves significantly strengthened the competitive positions of the Reynolds and Kaiser aluminum interests, helping to erode Alcoa's prewar status as the country's sole producer of primary aluminum. See J. BLAIR, ECONOMIC CONCENTRATION—STRUCTURE, BEHAVIOR AND PUBLIC POLICY 384 (1972); M. PECK, COMPETITION IN THE ALUMINUM INDUSTRY, 1945-1958, at 11-19 (1961).

123. 38 Stat. 730 (1914) (codified as amended in scattered sections of 15 U.S.C. (1982)).

124. 38 Stat. 717 (1914) (codified as amended at 15 U.S.C. § 45 (1982)).

125. *See* M. THOMPSON, TRUST DISSOLUTION 131 (1919) ("The almost complete ineffectiveness of the merely legal dissolution of the Standard Oil Company is a striking example of the lack of adaptation on the part of the courts for the work of reorganizing complicated industries. . . . This dissolution, which largely overshadows the good accomplished in its policy of suppressing the trusts, has been a large factor in bringing into existence additional trust legislation and the Federal Trade Commission."); D. MARTIN, MERGERS AND THE CLAYTON ACT 43-46 (1959) (explaining underlying reasons for Clayton Act).

126. The background and aims of the Clayton Act are discussed in H. SEAGER & C. GULICK JR., *supra* note 41, at 413-45. Enactment of the statute's prohibition of specific practices fulfilled one objective Woodrow Wilson identified during the 1912 presidential campaign. Wilson proposed "to prevent private monopoly by law, to see to it that the methods by which monopolies have been built up are legally made impossible." W. WILSON, THE NEW FREEDOM 132 (1961). He explained that "[e]verybody who has even read the newspapers knows the means by which these men built up their power and created these monopolies. Any decently equipped lawyer can suggest to you statutes by which the whole business can be stopped." *Id.* at 105.

deconcentration, and that publicity would discourage recourse to predatory conduct and alert potential entrants to lines of commerce that had generated large profits.[127] Because Congress feared that limited expertise might disincline judges to devise and order effective divestiture remedies in monopolization suits, the FTC Act also provided that the federal district courts could ask the Commission for advice in crafting dissolution decrees.[128]

Congressional efforts to deconcentrate the American economy also intensified during the second period of deconcentration initiatives. Following a hiatus in legislative activity in the 1920s, Congress enacted several major pieces of deconcentration legislation in the 1930s. The dispersal of economic power animated the key operative features of the Glass-Steagall Act,[129] the Air Mail Act,[130] and the Public Utility Holding Company Act.[131] Following another lull in activity in the 1940s, Congress in 1950 passed the Celler-Kefauver Act,[132] whose strengthening of the Clayton Act's antimerger provision stemmed partly from congressional perceptions that the

---

127. 15 U.S.C. §§ 46, 49 (1982). The House report on the FTC Act, for example, anticipated that publication of business profits would attract entry into lucrative markets and depress prices. *See* H.R. Rep. No. 533, 63d Cong., 2d Sess. 4 (1914), *reprinted in* 5 The Legislative History of the Federal Antitrust Laws and Related Statutes 3900, 3902 (E. Kintner ed. 1982). *But see* Kovacic, *supra* note 108, at 615 (discussing judicial narrowing of FTC's investigative and reporting powers).

The enactment of provisions designed to collect and disseminate information occurred at a time when a number of leading economists such as Arthur Hadley and Alfred Marshall believed that publicity about the activities of dominant firms would curb abusive trade practices and promote competition. *See, e.g.,* G. Stigler, The Economist as Preacher and Other Essays 43 (1982) (describing Alfred Marshall's endorsement of information-gathering and publicity as regulatory tools); H. Thorelli, *supra* note 41, at 322-23, 575 (discussing confidence of Arthur Hadley and other economists in publicity as device for deterring exclusionary conduct).

128. 38 Stat. 722 (1914) (codified at 15 U.S.C. § 47 (1982)). The FTC Act states: "In any suit in equity brought by or under the direction of the Attorney General as provided in the antitrust Acts, the court may, upon the conclusion of the testimony therein, if it shall be then of the opinion that the complainant is entitled to relief, refer said suit to the Commission, as a master in chancery, to ascertain and report an appropriate form of decree therein." *Id.* § 7, at 722. The Senate Report recommending passage of the 1914 statute noted that dissolution decrees in previous monopolization cases

> have apparently failed in many instances in their accomplishment simply because the courts and the Department of Justice have lacked the expert knowledge and experience necessary to be applied to the dissolution of the combinations and the reassembling of the divided elements in harmony with the spirit of the law.

S. Rep. No. 597, 63d Cong., 2d Sess. 12 (1914), *reprinted in* 5 The Legislative History of the Federal Antitrust Laws and Related Statutes 3900, 3909 (E. Kintner ed. 1982). Since 1914 this provision has been invoked once to assist a court in devising structural relief. In 1916 Judge Learned Hand called upon the FTC to assist in framing relief in the *Corn Products* monopolization suit. *See* United States v. Corn Prods. Ref. Co., 234 F. 964, 1018 (S.D.N.Y. 1916).

129. 48 Stat. 188-89 (1933) (codified as amended 12 U.S.C. §§ 377-78 (1982)).

130. 48 Stat. 933 (1934) (codified as amended in scattered sections of 39 U.S.C. (1982)).

131. 49 Stat. 803 (1935) (codified as amended at 15 U.S.C. §§ 79a-z (1982)). One also might add the Robinson-Patman Act of 1936 as an antibigness measure. 49 Stat. 1526 (codified as amended at 15 U.S.C. § 13 (1982)). Congress passed the statute mainly to arrest the expansion of chain stores as the chief conduits for the distribution of consumer goods. *See* E. Hawley, *supra* note 71, at 249-54.

132. 64 Stat. 1125 (1950) (codified as amended at 15 U.S.C. § 18 (1982)).

country was undergoing a significant trend toward greater economic concentration.[133]

The pattern of alternating decades of congressional activity also dovetails with the final era of deconcentration litigation. Congress initiated no major deconcentration measures in the 1960s, but the 1970s marked another period of legislative activism. As it had done in 1950, Congress strengthened the government's antimerger enforcement tools to forestall increases in existing levels of concentration. Among other provisions, the Hart-Scott-Rodino Antitrust Improvements Act of 1976[134] required firms to notify the FTC and the Justice Department before carrying out mergers that exceeded certain size thresholds.[135] The 1976 statute also created a mandatory waiting period for firms attempting specified acquisitions and tender offers.[136]

During the 1970s, congressional oversight committees aggressively pressed the government enforcement agencies to bring cases to restructure dominant firms. Congressional attention focused on the FTC, whose elastic substantive mandate seemed best suited for attacking oligopolistic market structures.[137] Despite a steady flow of ambitious monopolization initiatives from the Antitrust Division and the FTC in the first half of the 1970s,[138] many legislators complained that traditional antitrust litigation would not suffice to achieve important deconcentration goals. As Senator Robert Packwood pronounced in 1975:

> The present antitrust laws . . . even if rigorously enforced, will not achieve what is necessary in this country: A breakup of the concentrations of power in the major industries in this country, oil and otherwise, so that we might return to the numerous, small- and medium-size competitive industries that made this country grow, and continue to be needed to make this country great.[139]

The sentiments of Senator Packwood and many other liberal and moderate legislators spawned several deconcentration bills that, though never enacted, commanded widespread attention in Congress. Most of these measures originated in the Senate Judiciary Subcommittee on Antitrust and Monopoly[140] under the Chairmanship of Senator Philip

---

133. *See* Lande, *Wealth Transfers as the Original and Primary Concern of Antitrust: The Efficiency Interpretation Challenged*, 34 Hastings L.J. 65, 130-31 (1982); *see also* Fisher & Lande, *Efficiency Considerations in Merger Enforcement*, 71 Calif. L. Rev. 1580, 1588-93 (1983) (discussing congressional endorsement of incipiency antimerger standard in 1950).

134. 90 Stat. 1390 (1976) (codified as amended at scattered sections of 15 U.S.C. (1982)).

135. 15 U.S.C. § 18a(a).

136. *Id.* § 18a(b).

137. Legislative guidance urging the FTC to attack concentrated industries and the Commission's response to that guidance are documented in Kovacic, *supra* note 108, at 635-39, 645-48.

138. *See supra* notes 8-21 and accompanying text.

139. *Hearings on S. 2387 and Related Bills Before the Subcomm. on Antitrust and Monopoly of the Senate Comm. on the Judiciary*, 94th Cong., 1st Sess. 50 (1975) (statement of Sen. Packwood).

140. From its formation in the mid-1950s through the 1970s, the Senate Antitrust and Monopoly Subcommittee served as the principal forum for congressional inquiry concerning deconcentration. Over a 25-year period, the Subcommittee conducted extensive hearings on economic concentration and provided an arena in which the nation's leading antitrust lawyers

Hart.[141] The most prominent of these bills was the Industrial Reorganization Act, which called for the restructuring of seven basic domestic industries, subject to limited defenses.[142] The Industrial Reorganization Act never came up for a vote in the Subcommittee, but it catalyzed debate within the antitrust community about the desirability of deconcentration.[143] In 1976 Senator Hart also introduced the Monopolization Reform Act of 1976, which proposed to eliminate consideration of the defendant's conduct in Sherman Act cases involving persistent monopoly power.[144] Senator Hart's "no-fault" monopolization bill received no hearings in Congress, but it focused attention within antitrust circles upon the possibility of dispensing with the conduct requirement in certain monopolization cases.[145]

In addition to deconcentration proposals of broad applicability, Congress in the 1970s seriously considered several proposals dealing with specific industries. In particular, public rancor over high gasoline, natural gas, and fuel oil prices created a fertile environment for legislation to restructure the petroleum industry.[146] In the fall of 1975 forty-five senators voted for a measure to require the vertical divestiture of this country's leading oil companies.[147] The following year the Senate Judiciary Committee endorsed a bill to force the twenty largest domestic petroleum firms to participate in one of three designated segments of the oil industry—production, transmission, or refining/marketing—to the exclusion of the others.[148] Proposals to bar large oil companies from owning substantial interests in competing energy sources also received close attention during this period.[149]

---

and industrial organization economists discussed the structure and operation of the economy. *See* J. BLAIR, *supra* note 122, at vii-viii, 709-13. The printed volumes from the Subcommittee's hearings constitute one of the richest sources of material on the modern intellectual and political history of deconcentration.

141. Hart headed the Antitrust Subcommittee from 1963 until his retirement from the Senate in 1976. He was the intellectual and spiritual leader of congressional deconcentration advocates, and the legislative proposals strongly bear the imprint of his work. *See infra* notes 142, 144 and accompanying text.

142. *See Hearings on S. 1167 Before the Subcomm. on Antitrust and Monopoly of the Senate Comm. on the Judiciary*, 93d Cong, 1st Sess. 3 (1973). The bill created a rebuttable presumption of monopoly power for seven industries—chemicals and drugs, electrical machinery and equipment, electronic computing and communications equipment, energy, iron and steel, motor vehicles, and nonferrous metals—when rates of return and four-firm concentration ratios exceeded specified levels. *See* Note, *A Legislative Approach to Market Concentration: The Industrial Reorganization Act*, 24 SYRACUSE L. REV. 1100 (1973); Note, *The Industrial Reorganization Act: An Antitrust Proposal to Restructure the American Economy*, 73 COLUM. L. REV. 635 (1973).

143. *See, e.g.*, INDUSTRIAL CONCENTRATION: THE NEW LEARNING 339-426 (1974) (including essays by Harlan Blake, Walter Adams, Phil Neal, Almarin Phillips, and Richard Posner) [hereinafter INDUSTRIAL CONCENTRATION].

144. S. 3429, 94th Cong., 2d Sess. § 3, 122 CONG. REC. 13,872 (1976).

145. *See infra* notes 209-11 and accompanying text.

146. *See* R. SHERRILL, THE OIL FOLLIES OF 1970-1980, at 69-278 (1983) (describing emergence of strong public antipathy toward oil industry from 1970-1975).

147. *See* 121 CONG. REC. 32,289-96 (1975); *see also* R. SHERRILL, *supra* note 146, at 276-78 (describing Senate consideration of oil industry divestiture measures in 1975).

148. *See* PETROLEUM INDUSTRY COMPETITION ACT OF 1976, S. REP. No. 1005, 94th Cong., 2d Sess. 161. The Senate Judiciary Committee approved the bill, S. 2387, by an eight to seven vote. One member of the majority, however, Senator Robert Byrd, stated he would oppose the measure during consideration by the full Senate. *Id.* at 179. The bill never reached the Senate floor.

149. *See, e.g.*, *Hearings on S. 489 Before the Subcomm. on Antitrust and Monopoly of the Senate Comm. on the Judiciary*, 94th Cong., 1st Sess. 6 (1975) (reprinting S. 489, the Interfuel Competition Act of 1975). S. 489 would have forced producers or refiners of petroleum or

The cyclical coincidence of deconcentration litigation and congressional consideration of deconcentration-related legislation suggests how enforcement agency actions correspond to the political mood of the time. High levels of public dissatisfaction with the business community and its largest firms create a climate that tolerates or even welcomes antitrust initiatives to reduce the power and influence of dominant enterprises. Conversely, when public sentiment toward large companies is favorable, government assaults on dominant firms are less likely.

3. Intellectual Foundation

Since 1890 the strength of deconcentration as an antitrust ideal has hinged substantially on the outcome of a contest of ideas.[150] Each deconcentration cycle derived significant force from the ascent of an intellectual vision that justified strong government efforts to restructure major firms. These visions have served as the foundations upon which academicians, antitrust practitioners, and politicians have built the case for deconcentration. Despite serious contemporaneous opposition, each vision has imparted crucial force to government efforts to divide dominant firms into smaller constituent parts.

The earliest turn of the century efforts to create and apply a federal antitrust regime occurred amid considerable intellectual ferment concerning public policy toward newly developing large firms.[151] A broadly accepted intellectual rationale for dissolving dominant firms emerged only gradually over the Sherman Act's first quarter century. Most professional economists and academicians expert in corporate law initially treated the passage of the Sherman Act and its early enforcement with indifference or outright disapproval.[152] The works of many contemporary economists

---

natural gas to divest their interests in other energy sources, including coal, nuclear power, geothermal steam, and solar power. This bill was the subject of limited hearings and never came up for a vote within committee. A similar proposal, however, received 39 votes on the Senate floor in October 1975 when submitted as an amendment to a pending piece of natural gas legislation. *See* 121 Cong. Rec. 33,635 (1975).

150. The debate over the desirability of deconcentration has focused upon essentially five issues:

   1) The sources of concentration: how much do efficiency considerations determine concentration levels?

   2) Economic performance: how does concentration affect profitability and innovation?

   3) Political implications: does concentration confer undue political power upon large firms?

   4) Merits of structural relief: are problems arising from concentrated market structures best resolved by structural relief, conduct remedies, or regulatory controls?

   5) Feasibility of implementing structural relief: how substantial are the transaction costs associated with carrying out structural remedies?

151. Passage of the Sherman Act paralleled the enactment of state antitrust laws, whose enforcement was the chief focus of antitrust activity in the United States until the 1910s. *See* May, *Antitrust Practice and Procedure in the Formative Era: The Constitutional and Conceptual Reach of State Antitrust Law, 1880-1918*, 135 U. Pa. L. Rev. 495, 497-502 (1987) (describing the contributions of state antitrust enforcement during the early years of the Sherman Act).

152. *See* J. Clark, The Federal Trust Policy 78-108 (1931) (noting Congress neglected

echoed the assessment of Richard T. Ely, who declared "[i]f there is any serious student of our economic life who believes that anything substantial has been gained by all the laws passed against trusts . . . this authority has yet to be heard from."[153]

Academic disapproval of antitrust intervention, however, was not universal during the Sherman Act's formative period.[154] A small number of academicians favored prohibiting discrete types of conduct, such as local price discrimination, that were believed to facilitate the attainment and maintenance of monopoly power.[155] This approach was grounded substantially in the view that most monopolies were "unnatural" phenomena and could be sustained only through "artificial" means such as publicly imposed tariffs or private contrivances such as predatory conduct.[156] If one removed the artificial buttresses, monopolies necessarily would collapse. By this logic, the solution to "unnatural" monopolies formed by merger would be a decree banning the continuation of the corporate union—*i.e.*, the dissolution of the combination.

The first widely recognized intellectual justification for trustbusting emerged in the 1910s. By 1912, intellectual discourse on the trust question had crystalized around two competing views of appropriate government policy toward corporate bigness. These positions emerged most sharply in the presidential debates between Theodore Roosevelt and Woodrow Wilson.[157] Roosevelt, the Progressive Party candidate, had built a reputa-

---

economists' advice in favor of public opinion); W. LETWIN, LAW AND ECONOMIC POLICY IN AMERICA 71-77 (1965) (explaining that while they differed in detail, most economists were convinced that attempts to prohibit trusts would be "either unnecessary or futile"); G. STIGLER, *supra* note 127, at 41-43 (stating that "skepticism was shared by probably a majority of economists of the period"); H. THORELLI, *supra* note 41, at 117-32, 311-29, 574-75 (finding economic authors of the time expressed opinions on antitrust laws ranging from "relative indifference" to "contempt"); May, *Antitrust in the Formative Era: Political and Economic Theory in Constitutional and Antitrust Analysis, 1880-1918*, 50 OHIO ST. L.J. 257, 258-59, 287 (1989) (recognizing scholars "generally disapproved of antitrust litigation, declaring it to be unnecessary, ineffectual, or counterproductive"); Phillips & Stevenson, *The Historical Development of Industrial Organization*, in 6 THE HISTORY OF POLITICAL ECONOMY 324, 330 (1974) (highlighting "veritable flood" of works published about antitrust before passage of Sherman Act).

153. R. ELY, MONOPOLIES AND TRUSTS 243 (1900). Ely went on to observe: "The writer does not hesitate to affirm it as his opinion that efforts along the lines which have been followed in the past will be equally fruitless in the future." *Id.* at 244. *See also* G. STIGLER, *supra* note 127, at 41 ("A careful student of the history of economics would have searched long and hard, on the unseasonably cool day of July 2, 1890, the day the Sherman Act was signed by President Harrison, for any economist who ever recommended the policy of actively combatting collusion or monopolization in the economy at large.").

154. *See* Scherer, *Efficiency, Fairness, and the Early Contributions of Economists to the Antitrust Debate*, 29 WASHBURN L.J. (forthcoming 1989) (discussing economists' views considered sympathetic to antitrust controls on business conduct).

155. *See id.* (identifying economists who favored antitrust intervention); *see also* Bullock, *Trust Literature: A Survey and a Criticism*, 15 Q.J. ECON. 168, 204-05 (1901) (calling for controls on local price discrimination).

156. *See* May, *supra* note 151, at 569-71; Millon, *supra* note 119, at 1264-69. As suggested above, antitrust solutions appealed to a minority of economists who favored public intervention to control abusive conduct by dominant firms. *See supra* notes 154-55 and accompanying text. Most of those who supported government intervention proposed public ownership or comprehensive public utility regulation. *See* Millon, *supra* note 119, at 1271-75.

157. *See* Miller, *Woodrow Wilson's Contribution to Antitrust Policy*, in THE PHILOSOPHY AND POLICIES OF WOODROW WILSON 132, 136-38 (1958); Kovacic, *supra* note 108, at 603-05.

tion as a trustbuster during his presidency.[158] After leaving office, however, he embraced the thinking of Charles Van Hise, Jeremiah Jenks, and others who regarded immense corporate size as a necessary, albeit foreboding, feature of the political economy.[159] The correct solution to the trust problem was not further efforts at atomization, but rather, more effective tools for regulatory control. Roosevelt promised to dissolve "bad trusts" whose position rested upon sharp practices,[160] but he advocated formation of a federal commission to oversee and regulate the conduct of "good trusts" whose size flowed from the imperative to realize the benefits of large scale enterprise.[161]

Wilson attacked the former president's proposal on two fronts. The first concerned the trusts' impact on the political process and their significance for the soundness of public administration. Addressing the plan for a national regulatory body, Wilson warned that Roosevelt's commission would foster a dangerous alliance between the government and business. Wilson predicted that within a short time Roosevelt's "avowed partnership" between government and the trusts would be turned to private advantage, as large business concerns corrupted and manipulated the regulatory process.[162]

---

158. Roosevelt's Justice Department prosecuted Northern Sec. Co. v. United States, 193 U.S. 197 (1904), and initiated the dissolution suits in Standard Oil Co. v. United States, 221 U.S. 1 (1911), United States v. American Tobacco Co., 221 U.S. 106 (1911), and United States v. E.I. du Pont de Nemours & Co., 188 F. 127 (C.C. Del. 1911).

159. Van Hise wrote:

Concentration and cooperation in industry in order to secure efficiency are a world-wide movement. The United States cannot resist it. If we isolate ourselves and insist upon the subdivision of industry below the highest economic efficiency and do not allow cooperation, we shall be defeated in the world's markets.

C. VAN HISE, CONCENTRATION AND CONTROL: A SOLUTION OF THE TRUST PROBLEM IN THE UNITED STATES 277 (1912). Van Hise noted that the country "must modify our present obsolete laws regarding concentration and cooperation" and replace them with comprehensive administrative controls. *Id.* at 278. "Concentration and cooperation are conditions imperatively essential for industrial advance," he explained, "but if we allow concentration and cooperation, there must be control in order to protect the people, and adequate control is only possible through the administrative commission." *Id.* Jenks likewise believed government regulation would enable society to gain the benefits of large corporate enterprise while suppressing abusive behavior. M. SKLAR, *supra* note 43, at 60-61. The influence of Van Hise on Roosevelt's thinking is described in A. SCHLESINGER, *supra* note 69, at 22. Jenks's role in shaping Roosevelt's policy views is stated in M. SKLAR, *supra* note 43, at 334-35.

160. T. ROOSEVELT, AUTOBIOGRAPHY 462-500 (1913).

161. Roosevelt presented the framework of his policy in Roosevelt, *The Trusts, the People, and the Square Deal*, 99 THE OUTLOOK 649 (1911).

162. W. WILSON, *supra* note 126, at 122-23. Wilson cautioned:

If the government is to tell big business men how to run their business, then don't you see that big business men have to get closer to the government even than they are now? Don't you see that they must capture the government, in order not to be restrained too much by it?

Id. at 122. Wilson was not the first to focus on the corruptibility of regulatory systems. Earlier in the century, economists concerned with the growth of the trusts had warned that the emergence of manufacturing monopolies would create pressure for the establishment of regulatory controls of doubtful effectiveness. *See, e.g.*, Bullock, *supra* note 155, at 214 ("Remedy there will be none, save public ownership or public regulation; and past experience raises uncomfortable doubts whether, under the second method, the government or the trusts would be the regulating power.").

Wilson's second line of opposition to comprehensive regulatory control was more fundamentally economic. Wilson half-heartedly accepted the notion that some firms grew and remained large principally through superior efficiency and pledged not to tamper with such enterprises.[163] It is doubtful, however, that Wilson thought that "good trusts" truly existed —perhaps his sharpest difference with Roosevelt. Unlike his opponent, Wilson apparently believed that massive corporate size had little to do with efficiency and could not be attained or sustained without resort to predatory behavior. Little would be lost, and much would be gained, through an antitrust policy that proscribed predatory conduct and systematically sought to disaggregate dominant firms whose preeminence stemmed from "unnaturally" exclusionary behavior.[164]

The architect of Wilson's position on the trust question was Louis Brandeis, whose views ultimately shaped the enactment of the Clayton and Federal Trade Commission Acts in 1914 and animated the government's continued efforts to attack dominant firms until the entry of the United States into World War I.[165] The Brandeisian perspective toward large corporate size exerted a powerful influence on future deconcentration cycles. Its chief tenets—size begets political corruption and superior performance never accounts for dominance, while predatory conduct invariably does[166]—gave deconcentration advocates robust confidence in the

163. W. WILSON, *supra* note 126, at 101-15.

164. Kovacic, *supra* note 108, at 603-05. These views subsequently gained broad acceptance in Congress as it considered new antitrust legislation during Wilson's first term in office. For example, the final report of the House Conference Committee on the FTC Act stated: "It is now generally recognized that the only effective means of establishing and maintaining monopoly, where there is no control of a natural resource as [sic] of transportation, is the use of unfair competition." H.R. CONF. REP. No. 1142, 63d Cong., 2d Sess. 18-19, 51 CONG. REC. 14,924 (1914).

165. Arthur Link wrote:

It was Brandeis who clarified Wilson's thought and led him to believe that the most vital question confronting the American people was preservation of economic freedom in the United States. Brandeis taught, and Wilson agreed and reiterated in his speeches, that the main task ahead was to provide the means by which business could be set free from the shackles of monopoly and special privilege.

A. LINK, WOODROW WILSON AND THE PROGRESSIVE ERA, 1910-17, at 20-21 (1954) (footnote omitted); *see also* A. LINK, WOODROW WILSON: THE NEW FREEDOM 423-42 (1956) (describing efforts to revamp Sherman Act under Brandeis's tutelage); A. MASON, BRANDEIS—A FREE MAN'S LIFE 399-408 (1946) (noting that Brandeis was a major force behind Wilson's antitrust policies); T. McCRAW, PROPHETS OF REGULATION 80-147 (1984) (discussing history of the FTC and Brandeis's antitrust efforts). Many of Brandeis's writings on the question of corporate size are collected in L. BRANDEIS, THE CURSE OF BIGNESS: MISCELLANEOUS PAPERS OF LOUIS D. BRANDEIS (O. Fraenkel ed. 1934) [hereinafter L. BRANDEIS, CURSE OF BIGNESS].

166. Brandeis wrote that "no monopoly in private industry in America has yet been attained by efficiency alone. No business has been so superior to its competitors in the process of manufacture or of distribution as to enable it to control the market solely by reason of its superiority." L. BRANDEIS, *Competition*, in CURSE OF BIGNESS, *supra* note 165, at 114. He went on to explain the rationale for dissolving dominant firms:

The attempt to dismember existing illegal trusts is not, therefore, an attempt to interfere in any way with the natural law of business. It is an endeavor to restore health by removing a cancer from the body industrial. It is not an attempt to create competition artificially, but it is the removing of the obstacle to competition.

Id. at 115-16.

advantages of proposals designed to restructure major segments of American industry.

The Brandeisian distrust of dominant firms played a major role in the antitrust revival of Franklin Roosevelt's second term and the beginning of the second major era of deconcentration. Brandeis's perspective shaped the thinking of important Roosevelt advisors such as Felix Frankfurter, Thomas Corcoran, and Benjamin Cohen.[167] Corcoran and Cohen helped craft the Administration's major deconcentration legislation of the mid-1930s and encouraged Roosevelt's retreat from the planning and coordination policies that characterized the recovery programs of the early New Deal.[168] These views gained additional force in the late 1930s from the work of the Temporary National Economic Commission (TNEC),[169] which produced a number of monographs concluding that monopoly and collusion deserved much of the blame for the sluggish pace of economic recovery. Several TNEC monograph authors decried the failure of past deconcentration efforts and called for more effective policies to redress and prevent monopoly.[170]

The wartime mobilization program interrupted, but did not end, the formation of an intellectual consensus favoring vigorous antitrust enforcement and a revival of deconcentration as a central element of national competition policy. Postwar intellectual support for deconcentration derived its strength from three sources. The first was *Alcoa*.[171] To many observers, *Alcoa* rehabilitated deconcentration possibilities the Supreme Court had foreclosed in 1920 in *U.S. Steel*.[172] Learned Hand's condemnation of Alcoa's capacity expansion strategy,[173] coupled with the Supreme Court's endorsement of Hand's analysis one year later in *American Tobacco*,[174] inspired an outpouring of legal scholarship advocating new government efforts to use "the new Sherman Act" as a deconcentration

---

167. *See* W. Leuchtenburg, Franklin D. Roosevelt and the New Deal 1932-1940, at 148-49, 154-56, 163 (1963).

168. *See* E. Hawley, *supra* note 71, at 325-43; J. Lash, From the Diaries of Felix Frankfurter 52-53 (1975); B. Murphy, The Brandeis/Frankfurter Connection 152-85 (1982).

169. The formation and operation of the Commission are recounted in E. Hawley, *supra* note 71, at 404-19.

170. *See* TNEC Monograph No. 38, *supra* note 4, at 84; Staff of Senate Temporary National Economic Comm., 76th Cong., 3d Sess., Investigation of Concentration of Economic Power: Competition and Monopoly in American Industry, Monograph No. 21, at 309 (Comm. Print 1940) (written by C. Wilcox) [hereinafter TNEC Monograph No. 21].

171. United States v. Aluminum Co. of Am., 148 F.2d 416 (2d Cir. 1945); *see also supra* notes 78-81 and accompanying text.

172. United States v. United States Steel Corp., 251 U.S. 417 (1920); *see also supra* notes 65-66 and accompanying text.

173. 148 F.2d at 431.

174. American Tobacco Co. v. United States, 328 U.S. 781 (1946). The Court's endorsement of the Hand opinion was important in light of *Alcoa*'s unusual procedural history. Following a trial that included 358 days of hearings and testimony, the district court in 1942 absolved Alcoa of liability on all counts. United States v. Aluminum Co. of Am., 44 F. Supp. 97 (S.D.N.Y. 1942). The government appealed, but four members of the Supreme Court recused themselves, denying the Court a quorum to hear the appeal. Congress enacted an emergency measure allowing the final appeal to be taken to the circuit court of appeals in which the trial took place. *See* 2 S. Whitney, *supra* note 4, at 89. By this mechanism, the *Alcoa* appeal was heard by a Second Circuit panel consisting of Learned Hand, Augustus Hand, and Thomas Swan.

device.[175] As its most important feature, *Alcoa*'s broad conception of conduct that would constitute monopolization[176] appeared to foreshadow reliance on essentially structural liability standards. This paved the way for the government to establish section two liability in many other industry settings.[177]

A second stimulus for renewed interest in deconcentration arose from experience with the Public Utility Holding Company Act of 1935.[178] To many commentators, efforts to implement the statute's dissolution commands demonstrated convincingly that it was possible to execute large-scale antitrust divestitures without dire economic consequences.[179] Positive assessments of the Act's divestitures meshed with the work of scholars such as George Hale, whose reinvestigation of the court-ordered structural remedies in the first era of deconcentration suits concluded that massive, antitrust-mandated reorganizations could be carried out without undue administrative costs or economic dislocation.[180]

---

175. In a representative reaction, Eugene Rostow declared that *Alcoa* and *American Tobacco* "mark the new birth of Section 2." Rostow, *The New Sherman Act: A Positive Instrument of Progress*, 14 U. CHI. L. REV. 567, 577 (1947); *see also* Levi, *supra* note 66, at 183 ("Today . . . as a result of an increased awareness of the monopoly problem, and as a result of the *Alcoa* and *American Tobacco* decisions we appear to have a new interpretation of the [Sherman] [A]ct, closer probably to its original intention, which can give the act strength against monopolies as such, and also against control by three, four or five corporations acting together."). Rostow's support for broader exploitation of the Sherman Act's deconcentration possibilities proved particularly influential. *See* Rowe, *supra* note 3, at 1522 & n.64.

176. *See supra* notes 79-80 and accompanying text.

177. Rostow's 1948 book on the petroleum industry said recent cases showed that "the Supreme Court is putting less and less emphasis on conduct which hurts individuals by driving them out of business, or restricting their opportunities, and more and more emphasis on arrangements which result in market control, however benevolently exercised." E. ROSTOW, A NATIONAL POLICY FOR THE OIL INDUSTRY 124 (1948). One year earlier Rostow wrote that:

> The old preoccupation of the judges with evidence of business tactics they regarded as ruthless, predatory, and immoral has all but disappeared. We have come a long way towards assimilating the legal to the economic conception of monopoly. We are close to the point of regarding as illegal the kind of economic power which the economist regards as monopolistic.

Rostow, *supra* note 175, at 575.

178. 49 Stat. 803 (1935) (codified as amended at 15 U.S.C. §§ 79a-z (1982)).

179. *See, e.g.*, E. ROSTOW, *supra* note 177, at 144; Trienens, *The Utility Act as a Solution to Sherman Act Problems*, 44 NW. U.L. REV. 331, 338-39 (1949) (noting that Utility Act set out standards of size and achieved results demonstrating program's wisdom to affirmatively reduce concentration of economic power). The career of Howard Trienens involved one of the many ironies of Sherman Act deconcentration experience. In the 1949 article, Trienens criticized the failure of antitrust policymaking institutions to exploit the full deconcentration potential inherent in the Sherman Act. He argued that the Public Utility Holding Company Act experience pointed the way toward more expansive applications of divestiture to achieve deconcentration goals. Decades later, Trienens became vice president and general counsel for AT&T and managed the company's legal defense against the Justice Department's ultimately successful effort to restructure the Bell System. *See* P. TEMIN, *supra* note 6, at 204, 217-76 (discussing Trienens's role in the AT&T litigation).

180. In 1940, Hale wrote that:

> whatever doubts may be entertained as to the efficacy of dissolutions of the past, it seems clear that the mechanics of separating monopolistic combinations, in the degree of "atomization" heretofore attained, has not presented insuparable problems. Thus it is difficult to prove that more vigorous dissolution would be disastrous from the point of view of the technique of separating productive assets.

The third source of support for a new round of deconcentration initiatives came from an emerging branch of economic scholarship in industrial organization.[181] Though other scholars made important contributions,[182] the economics faculty of the University of Chicago supplied the principal economic foundation for the new deconcentration movement.[183] From the 1930s through the early 1950s, Chicago academicians such as Frank Knight, Henry Simons, Jacob Viner, and George Stigler developed economic arguments for expanded attacks on bigness.[184] These economists influenced the thinking of young legal scholars such as Ward Bowman, who argued that modern economic learning justified a presumption of illegal monopoly power for firms with market shares as low as ten to fifteen percent.[185]

Taken as a whole, the revival of deconcentration thinking in the 1930s and 1940s strongly reflected elements of the Brandeisian view of economic

Hale, *Trust Dissolution: "Atomizing" Business Units of Monopolistic Size*, 40 COLUM. L. REV. 615, 631-32 (1940).

181. *See* E. HAWLEY, *supra* note 71, at 292.

182. *See generally* G. STOCKING & M. WATKINS, MONOPOLY AND FREE ENTERPRISE (1951) (encouraging more extensive antitrust enforcement to control dominant-firm conduct); Adams, *supra* note 4 (advocating greater use of monopolization suits to restructure dominant firms); *cf.* Oxenfeldt, *Monopoly Dissolution: A Proposal Outlined*, 36 AM. ECON. REV. 384 (1946) (disfavoring dissolution of production facilities and proposing creation of additional "independent" selling entities to sell output of concentrated producers).

183. It is one of the historical ironies of antitrust that the "Chicago School" today commonly is associated with the view that "competition is prevalent and market dominance is weak, short-lived and often beneficial." Shepherd, *Three 'Efficiency School' Hypotheses About Market Power*, 33 ANTITRUST BULL. 395, 396 (1988) (footnote omitted). The transition from the early Chicago trustbusting tradition—most closely associated with the work of Henry Simons—to its later, better known efficiency perspective—built substantially upon the thinking of Aaron Director—is traced in *The Fire of Truth: A Remembrance of Law and Economics at Chicago, 1932-1970*, 26 J. L. & ECON. 163 (1983) [hereinafter *Fire of Truth*] (panel discussion); *see also* G. STIGLER, *supra* note 127, at 166-70 (describing influence of Henry Simon and change in perspective fostered by Aaron Director and Milton Friedman); Posner, *The Chicago School of Antitrust Analysis*, 127 U. PA. L. REV. 925, 932-48 (1979) (describing content of modern Chicago School antitrust analysis).

184. Stigler observed in his memoirs that "Until the 1950s I accepted the prevailing view of my profession that monopoly was widespread. . . . I was an aggressive critic of big business." G. STIGLER, MEMOIRS OF AN UNREGULATED ECONOMIST 97 (1988). Stigler added that in 1950 he "believed monopoly posed a major problem in public policy . . . and that it should be dealt with boldly by breaking up dominant firms and severely punishing businesses that engaged in collusion." *Id.* at 99. In recounting his advocacy in the early 1950s for the dismantling of U.S. Steel, which held 30% of the market, Stigler explained: "Economists (including me) generally believed that this level of industry concentration [four-firm steel industry concentration ratio of 60%] allowed a substantial amount of noncompetitive behavior, but the belief rested more upon consensus than upon evidence." *Id.* at 99-100. The consensus to which Stigler referred built substantially upon the work of Simons, who proposed far-reaching programs of deconcentration. *See* H. SIMONS, ECONOMIC POLICY FOR A FREE SOCIETY 81-83, 246-49 (1948).

185. *See* Bowman, *Toward Less Monopoly*, 101 U. PA. L. REV. 577, 589, 641 (1953); *see also Fire of Truth*, *supra* note 183, at 182 (acknowledgment by Ward Bowman of how Henry Simons's views on deconcentration influenced Bowman's work). Bowman was a research associate at the University of Chicago Law School when his article appeared in 1953. As was the case of mentors such as Levi and Stigler, Bowman's views toward concentration changed dramatically in the late 1950s and early 1960s. *See* Bork & Bowman, *The Crisis in Antitrust*, 65 COLUM. L. REV. 363 (1965) (advocating retreat from antitrust doctrines and enforcement approaches that promote economic decentralization at expense of efficiency).

concentration.[186] In purely economic terms, a program to dismantle dominant firms and concentrated market structures promised substantial improvements in performance with little danger of destroying valuable efficiencies. Eugene Rostow wrote in 1947 that "[t]here is a great deal of evidence, in fact, that on the whole Big Business is less efficient, less progressive technically, and relatively less profitable than smaller business."[187] Deconcentration "would not in any sense represent a turning back to the horse and buggy days in technology and business organization," but rather would help "eliminate the wastes, the non-use of capacity, and the restrictionism of monopolistic industrial organization."[188]

Equally important were the political returns to a program to restore the primacy of smaller scale enterprise. As Rostow explained:

> One of the major problems requiring a social decision in our time is whether we achieve a wider dispersal of power and opportunity, and a broader base for the class structure of our society, by a more competitive organization of industry and trade, in smaller and more independent units.[189]

The National Recovery Administration's experience revealed the hazards of fostering alliances between big business and large regulatory entities. By contrast, Rostow argued that "it should be easier to achieve the values of democracy in a society where economic power and social status are more widely distributed, and less concentrated, than in the United States today."[190] In a similar vein, Henry Simons maintained that "the compelling

---

186. Deconcentration thinking in the 1930s and 1940s differed from that of Brandeis in an important respect. Brandeis placed great faith in the power of prohibitions upon specific types of exclusionary conduct to erode and prevent monopoly power. "Diagnosis shows monopoly to be an artificial, not a natural product," Brandeis wrote. "Competition, therefore, may be preserved by preventing that course of conduct by which in the past monopolies have been established." L. BRANDEIS, *Competition*, in CURSE OF BIGNESS, *supra* note 165, at 123-24. By contrast, in deconcentration's second era, authorities such as Rostow and Levi preached the futility of focusing antitrust analysis on searching for and prohibiting exclusionary conduct. *See supra* notes 171-77 and accompanying text; *see also* Dorsey, *Free Enterprise vs. The Entrepreneur: Redefining the Entities Subject to the Antitrust Laws*, 125 U. PA. L. REV. 1244, 1248 (1977) ("By 1945 it was no longer credible to assume that the centrifugal and centripetal forces of the market would inevitably prevent concentrations so long as the government prevented anticompetitive acts."). Thus, the chief purpose of Sherman Act monopolization litigation should be to identify the existence of monopoly power and to eliminate it directly with structural remedies such as divestiture.

187. Rostow, *supra* note 175, at 568; *see also* H. SIMONS, *supra* note 184, at 246 ("The efficiency of gigantic corporations is usually a vestigial reputation earned during early, rapid growth—a memory of youth rather than an attribute of maturity. Grown large, they become essentially political bodies, run by lawyers, bankers, and specialized politicians, and persisting mainly to preserve the power of control groups and to reward unnaturally an admittedly rare talent for holding together enterprise aggregations which ought to collapse from excessive size.").

188. Rostow, *supra* note 175, at 568.

189. *Id.* at 569.

190. *Id.* at 570. Other respected academicians such as Edward Levi warned that serious political misfortune would befall the nation if public enforcement agencies did not seize the opportunities *Alcoa* presented. Levi wrote in 1947:

> It is doubtful if a free and competitive society can be maintained if the direction of concentration is to continue. . . . If the concentration problem in this country is to be dealt with by measures themselves not incompatible with free enterprise, it is probable that the hope lies in the new interpretation of the Sherman Act and an increased awareness of the responsibility of the courts to give adequate relief.

reason for stamping out private monopoly" was the tendency for monopoly to generate "an accumulation of government regulation which yields, in many industries, all the afflictions of socialization and none of its possible benefits; an enterprise economy paralyzed by political control; the moral disintegration of representative government in the endless contest of innumerable pressure groups for special favors; and dictatorship."[191]

The third major period of deconcentration activity also rested heavily upon an intellectual consensus supporting efforts to restructure concentrated industries. Two specific events were instrumental in eliciting the mixture of deconcentration litigation and legislation of this period. The first was the 1959 publication of Carl Kaysen and Donald Turner's *Antitrust Policy*.[192] Recognized as the leading synthesis of legal and economic scholarship in antitrust of its time,[193] the Kaysen-Turner volume called for new legislation mandating the restructuring of concentrated industries.[194] The second major intellectual force of this period was the Neal Task Force,[195] which also recommended the enactment of far-reaching deconcentration legislation.[196] Both the Kaysen-Turner and Neal Task Force proposals rested upon a body of economic literature that suggested a strong positive relationship between concentration and profitability.[197] As debated in antitrust circles, both measures also heavily drew from subsequent studies indicating that a deconcentration program was unlikely to sacrifice significant scale economies or other efficiencies.[198]

Levi, *supra* note 66, at 183. Levi later became dean of the Chicago law faculty and headed the Department of Justice during Gerald Ford's presidency.

191. H. Simons, *supra* note 184, at 87-88.

192. C. Kaysen & D. Turner, Antitrust Policy: An Economic and Legal Analysis (1959). Kaysen and Turner were knowledgeable students of government efforts applying § 2 of the Sherman Act to redress monopoly. Kaysen was a distinguished industrial organization economist and a professor on the Harvard economics faculty. Among other accomplishments, he served as a neutral expert to Judge Charles Wyzanski in United States v. United Shoe Mach. Corp., 110 F. Supp. 295 (D. Mass. 1953), *aff'd per curiam*, 347 U.S. 521 (1954). His experiences formed the basis for a cogent analysis of the government's efforts to dismantle United Shoe's machine manufacturing monopoly. See C. Kaysen, United States v. United Shoe Machinery: An Economic Analysis of an Antitrust Case (1956). Turner held a law degree and a doctorate in economics and was a professor at Harvard Law School. His analysis of the Supreme Court's decision in United States v. E.I. du Pont de Nemours & Co., 351 U.S. 377 (1956) established him as an authority in the field of Sherman Act jurisprudence. See Turner, *Antitrust Policy and the Cellophane Case*, 70 Harv. L. Rev. 281 (1956). Turner later headed the Justice Department's Antitrust Division from 1965 to 1968.

193. See, e.g., M. Handler, H. Blake, R. Pitofsky & H. Goldschmid, Cases and Materials on Trade Regulation 92 (1st ed. 1975); L. Sullivan, *supra* note 4, at 15. For an essay on the history of antitrust law that places the contributions of Kaysen and Turner in their intellectual context, see Rowe, *supra* note 3, at 1520-40.

194. See C. Kaysen & D. Turner, *supra* note 192, at 110-19, 261-66. "The principal defect of present antitrust law is its inability to cope with market power created by jointly acting oligopolists." *Id.* at 110. Among other sources, Kaysen and Turner's structural policy proposals drew substantially from Joe Bain's influential analysis of entry conditions as determinants of industry performance. See J. Bain, Barriers to New Competition (1956).

195. See supra notes 94-95 and accompanying text.

196. Neal Task Force Report, *supra* note 94, at 14-15, 65-76.

197. The relevant literature is summarized in Weiss, *The Concentration—Profits Relationship and Antitrust*, in Industrial Concentration, *supra* note 143, at 184-272; Phillips, *Market Concentration and Performance: A Survey of the Evidence*, 61 Notre Dame L. Rev. 1099 (1986).

198. See F. Scherer, A. Beckenstein, E. Kaufer & R. Murphy, The Economics of Multi-Plant

In the late 1960s and throughout the 1970s, proposals for programs to deconcentrate American industry dominated debate over antitrust policy.[199] Broad, though not universal, intellectual support for deconcentration assured the preeminence of market structure issues in antitrust discourse. Although some individuals later abandoned or drastically modified such views, numerous prominent academicians at various times in this period endorsed generic deconcentration legislation. Proposals receiving approval included the Neal Task Force recommendations to restructure industries exceeding certain concentration thresholds;[200] measures to reshape specific industries;[201] the application of "no fault" theories of monopolization liability;[202] and more aggressive applications of conventional Sherman Act doctrine and structural remedies to eliminate substantial concentrations of market power.[203]

OPERATION: AN INTERNATIONAL COMPARISONS STUDY (1975); Sherman & Tollison, *Public Policy Toward Oligopoly: Dissolution and Scale Economies*, 4 ANTITRUST L. & ECON. REV. 77, 78 (Summer 1971).

199. In 1978 Robert Bork wrote:

Issues of industrial concentration—of monopoly and, more especially, oligopoly—hold center stage in current debates over antitrust policy. They seem likely to prove the main battleground of policy in the coming decade. There are two possible paths to that battleground: The continuing judicial transformation of basic Sherman Act doctrine, or the effort to adopt one of the increasingly serious proposals for new antitrust legislation.

R. BORK, THE ANTITRUST PARADOX 163 (1978).

200. Academicians on the Neal Task Force who supported the panel's Concentrated Industries Act recommendation were Phil Neal, William Baxter, William Jones, Paul Mac-Avoy, James McKie, Lee Preston, and James Rahl. Of the Task Force's representatives from academia, only Robert Bork opposed the deconcentration proposal. NEAL TASK FORCE REPORT, *supra* note 94, at 53. Other academicians who were not members of the Neal Task Force also supported the Neal proposal or similar legislation. *See, e.g.*, Blake, *Legislative Proposals for Industrial Concentration*, in INDUSTRIAL CONCENTRATION, *supra* note 143, at 340-60 (supporting deconcentration legislation).

201. *See, e.g.*, J. BLAIR, THE CONTROL OF OIL 381-95 (1976) (petroleum industry); L. WHITE, A PROPOSAL FOR RESTRUCTURING THE AUTOMOBILE INDUSTRY, in *Hearings on S. 1167 Before the Subcomm. on Antitrust and Monopoly of the Senate Comm. on the Judiciary*, 93d Cong., 2d Sess. 1950-57 (1974) (automobile industry).

202. *See* 3 P. AREEDA & D. TURNER, ANTITRUST LAW ¶¶ 614-23 (1978); Flynn, *Do the Proposals Make Any Sense from a Business Standpoint? Pro No-Conduct Monopoly: An Assessment for the Lawyer and the Businessman*, 49 ANTITRUST L.J. 1255 (1980); Fox, *Separate Views of Professor Fox*, in 1 NCRALP REPORT, *supra* note 4, at 339-47; Sullivan, *Separate Views of Commissioner Sullivan*, in 1 NCRALP REPORT, *supra* note 4, at 413-14; Turner, *The Scope of Antitrust and Other Economic Regulatory Policies*, 82 HARV. L. REV. 1207, 1217-21 (1969); Williamson, *Dominant Firms and the Monopoly Problem: Market Failure Considerations*, 85 HARV. L. REV. 1512, 1527-30 (1972); Pitofsky, In Defense of 'No-Fault Monopoly' Proposals, Speech before the 20th Annual Law Symposium of the Columbia University Law School (Mar. 31, 1979) (mimeo) (copy on file with the author). *See also* Dougherty Jr., Kirkwood & Hurwitz, *Elimination of the Conduct Requirement in Government Monopolization Cases*, 37 WASH. & LEE L. REV. 83, 84 n.3 (1980) (noting Professors Phillip Areeda, Walter Adams, Harvey Goldschmid, Louis Schwartz, and Oliver Williamson testified in favor of no-fault measures in 1978 before the National Commission for the Review of Antitrust Laws and Procedures).

203. *See, e.g.*, W. SHEPHERD, THE TREATMENT OF MARKET POWER: ANTITRUST, REGULATION, AND PUBLIC ENTERPRISE 215 (1975) (noting "with revised procedures and allied with tax incentives a 'new' Section 2 could be effective"); Baldwin, *supra* note 4, at 150-53 (endorsing mix of structural conduct remedies in Sherman Act litigation to reduce structural barriers to competition); Brodley, *Industrial Deconcentration and Legal Feasibility: The Efficiencies Defense*, 9 J. ECON. ISSUES 365, 370-72 (1975) (discussing treatment of efficiencies in antitrust divestiture

Although important in eliciting a major round of deconcentration measures, the intellectual consensus for intervention was neither stable nor lasting.[204] The starkest portent of its disintegration occurred in 1974 in what came to be known as the Airlie House Conference on "the new learning" about industrial concentration. The Airlie House meeting supplied a forum for opponents of structural antitrust analysis to synthesize and highlight a developing body of literature that challenged the underlying economic assumptions of deconcentration policies.[205] The results of the conference and related scholarship were seen by many as dictating caution in embracing an aggressive deconcentration agenda.[206] Among the most important themes of the "new learning" was that, contrary to the conventional Brandeisian view of bigness, superior performance could, and typically did, account for the attainment and maintenance of large market shares over time.[207] Erosion of the underlying theoretical and empirical economic support for deconcentration led many individuals who had supported structural solutions to withdraw their endorsement for expansive monopolization initiatives.[208]

The Airlie House conference and subsequent academic attacks on the structural model and its policy proposals severely attenuated the intellectual support underpinning the third deconcentration movement. Nonetheless, the deconcentration vision's continuing vitality was apparent as late as 1979 in the work of President Carter's National Commission for the Review of Antitrust Laws and Procedures (NCRALP). Headed by John Shenefield, Carter's Assistant Attorney General for Antitrust, the NCRALP panel proposed that Congress consider amending the Sherman Act to establish a "no-fault" monopolization cause of action to redress instances of persistent monopoly power not attributable to ongoing superior performance.[209] The Shenefield Commission also recommended greater recourse to divestiture as a remedy in monopolization suits.[210] Although many commentators vigorously attacked these recommendations,[211] the NCRALP proposals,

---

cases); Sherman & Tollison, *supra* note 198, at 90 (recommending efforts to restructure concentrated industries and concluding that, in the absence of scale economies, "there is no need for the public to endure the social and economic burdens associated with the inordinately high levels of industrial concentration found in an important group of American industries").

204. *See* Rowe, *supra* note 3, at 1540-47.

205. *See, e.g.*, Demsetz, *Two Systems of Belief About Monopoly*, in INDUSTRIAL CONCENTRATION, *supra* note 143, at 164-84 (criticizing antitrust's preoccupation with market concentration and private exclusionary conduct).

206. *See* F. Scherer, On the Current State of Knowledge in Industrial Economics 4-11 (Aug. 1984) (unpublished discussion paper) (on file with author) (addressing the crumbling of the structure-conduct-performance paradigm on which many deconcentration proposals of the late 1960s and early 1970s rested).

207. For a representative synthesis of this view, see R. BORK, *supra* note 199, at 163-97.

208. *See, e.g.*, Brozen, *The Concentration-Collusion Doctrine*, 46 ANTITRUST L.J. 826, 826-29 & n.8 (1978) (recounting retreat of some commentators from support for deconcentration policies); Panel Discussion, 54 ANTITRUST L.J. 31, 31-33 (1985) (discussing changes in the views of William Baxter, a supporter of the original Neal Task Force deconcentration proposals).

209. *See* 1 NCRALP REPORT, *supra* note 4, at viii-ix.

210. *Id.* at vi-vii.

211. *See, e.g.*, Bork, *Statement of Robert H. Bork*, 48 ANTITRUST L.J. 891, 893-95 (1979) (disputing benefits of a no-fault monopolization cause of action and identifying costs of a program of dissolution suits); Decker, *Do the Proposals Make Any Sense From a Litigation*

coming amid the collapse of many divestiture initiatives begun in the late 1960s and early 1970s, demonstrated the continuing intellectual pull of deconcentration in the third period of activism.

II. The Future of Deconcentration: Prospects for Revival

Deconcentration now stands in one of its historical periods of decline. In view of recent experience, one cannot be faulted for concluding that the current dearth of activity is hardly temporary. Sobering enforcement failures such as the *IBM* case,[212] the ambiguous welfare effects of the AT&T divestiture,[213] and the broad acceptance of Chicago School perspectives toward dominant firms all seem to signal the end of the section two government divestiture suit. Frederick Rowe, an experienced antitrust practitioner and student of deconcentration battles past, has said "the antitrust crusade against the concentration of economic power has foundered."[214]

As a matter of positive historical analysis, I believe the burial of deconcentration as a central antitrust concern is wholly premature. Previous deconcentration cycles strongly suggest that the eclipse of the monopolization divestiture case is not lasting. Periods of relative inactivity lasting seventeen and thirteen years, respectively, followed this century's first two deconcentration eras. It has been nearly eight years since the settlement of the government's monopolization suit against AT&T[215] and the dismissal of the *IBM* case.[216] Notwithstanding its lowly status today as an antitrust concern, can a resurrection of deconcentration be expected toward the middle or end of the 1990s? I believe the underlying conditions that fueled the three previous eras of deconcentration activity could evoke a fourth— albeit probably a limited—round of government Sherman Act ·divestiture cases by the end of this century.

Standpoint? Con, 49 ANTITRUST L.J. 1245, 1251 (1980) (concluding adoption of a no-fault cause of action would not streamline monopolization litigation); Leary, *Do the Proposals Make Any Sense From a Business Standpoint? Con*, 49 ANTITRUST L.J. 1281, 1282-85 (1980) (questioning soundness of structural tests used to trigger liability in no-fault proposals).

212. United States v. IBM Corp., [1961-1970 Transfer Binder] Trade Reg. Rep. (CCH) ¶ 45,069 (S.D.N.Y. filed Jan. 17, 1969) (complaint alleging monopolization and attempted monopolization). The Justice Department filed a stipulation of dismissal in 1982. *See In re* International Business Machs. Corp., 687 F.2d 591, 593 (2d Cir. 1982).

213. *See* P. TEMIN, *supra* note 6, at 353-66. Public perceptions about the net effects of the Bell System divestiture promise to be significant in determining public receptivity to future deconcentration lawsuits. *See* Baker, *supra* note 20, at 926 (stating AT&T divestiture "has 'antitrust' written all over it. If the public (however wrongly) comes away with the feeling that the whole thing was a major disaster, the resulting political reaction may exact political barriers to future section 2 cases requesting divestiture remedies.").

214. Rowe, *supra* note 3, at 1539 (footnote omitted). Rowe similarly observed that "[o]nce hailed as a Charter of Freedom and an American 'national religion,' antitrust is sinking into decline. Its grandiose crusades against concentration of economic power are over, and a regime of retreat and revision is taking shape." *Id.* at 1512 (footnotes omitted).

215. United States v. AT&T Co., 552 F. Supp. 131 (D.D.C. 1982), *aff'd sub nom.* Maryland v. United States, 460 U.S. 1001 (1983).

216. *In re* International Business Machs. Corp., 687 F.2d 591 (2d Cir. 1982).

A.   *Enforcement and Doctrinal Permissiveness*

The first historical precondition for a deconcentration revival already has been satisfied. With exceptions, the period since 1981 has featured enforcement policies and doctrines that take a comparatively permissive approach toward evaluating single-firm conduct and horizontal mergers. During past lulls in deconcentration activity, the unwillingness or inability of public enforcement agencies and courts to curb dominant firm behavior, or to impose substantial limits upon horizontal mergers, facilitated the creation of market positions that later became the focus of Sherman Act section two scrutiny.

Tolerance for single-firm conduct and horizontal consolidation characterized federal antitrust enforcement policy during the Reagan Administration. Since 1981, the FTC and the Antitrust Division have disavowed past government enforcement philosophies due to their claimed tendencies to assume that "bigness is bad."[217] Reagan antitrust officials argued that, among other specific failures, a foolish preoccupation with concentration ratios and a pervasive suspicion toward fundamentally benign or procompetitive business conduct yielded unduly restrictive merger policies and a substantial collection of misconceived monopolization suits.[218]

To reverse these enforcement trends, the Reagan antitrust agencies pledged themselves to apply more permissive merger standards and, with few exceptions, to withdraw the government from the section two enforcement arena.[219] Measured against this agenda, the Reagan Administration succeeded almost completely.[220] From 1981 through 1988, federal section two enforcement efforts consisted of initiating three new actions[221] and settling the *AT&T* case.[222] Placed in historical context, this trio of new cases constituted the smallest number of monopolization and attempted monopolization prosecutions the federal agencies have initiated in any eight-year period since 1900.[223] In addition to this dramatic retreat in the section two area, the Reagan antitrust agencies substantially loosened horizontal merger enforcement standards.[224]

In important respects, the rightward shift of federal enforcement practice has mirrored and reinforced the increasingly conservative tendencies of federal courts since the mid-1970s in deciding cases that deal with

217. *See, e.g.*, Report of the FTC Transition Team, *reprinted in* 127 Cong. Rec. 21,349, 21,350 (1981) (report of Reagan transition team for the FTC).
218. *See* Kovacic, *Built to Last? The Antitrust Legacy of the Reagan Administration*, 35 Fed. B. News & J. 244, 245-46 (1988) [hereinafter *Legacy*]; Kovacic, *Public Choice and the Public Interest: Federal Trade Commission Antitrust Enforcement During the Reagan Administration*, 33 Antitrust Bull. 467, 477-78 (1988) [hereinafter *Public Choice*].
219. *See* Kovacic, *Legacy, supra* note 218, at 245-46.
220. *Id.*; *see also* Kovacic, *Public Choice, supra* note 218, at 480-81.
221. *See* United States v. American Airlines, Inc., 743 F.2d 1114 (5th Cir. 1984); United States v. Kentucky Utils. Co., [1980-1988 Transfer Binder] Trade Reg. Rep. (CCH) ¶ 45,081 (D. Ky. filed Feb. 26, 1981); AMERCO, 109 F.T.C. 135 (1987) (consent order). In all of these matters, the government exclusively sought conduct remedies.
222. United States v. AT&T Co., 552 F. Supp. 131 (D.D.C. 1982), *aff'd sub nom.* Maryland v. United States, 460 U.S. 1001 (1983).
223. *See* Posner, *supra* note 27, at 405.
224. *See* Krattenmaker & Pitofsky, *Antitrust Merger Policy and the Reagan Administration*, 33 Antitrust Bull. 211, 225-28 (1988).

single-firm conduct. With rare, noteworthy exceptions such as *Aspen Skiing Co. v. Aspen Highlands Skiing Corp.*,[225] the federal judiciary has given dominant firms increasingly broad discretion to choose pricing, product development, promotion, and distribution strategies.[226] This narrowing of section two liability reflects heightened judicial solicitude for efficiency concerns, particularly dynamic efficiency attributable to innovation.[227] These tendencies have been reinforced since 1981 by Reagan Administration judicial appointments that have accounted for three current members of the Supreme Court and over fifty percent of all federal district and appellate court judges.[228]

From all indications, it is reasonable to assume that the Bush Administration will pursue an antitrust agenda similar to President Reagan's.[229] The federal agencies probably will continue to de-emphasize most theories of monopolization and attempted monopolization and will maintain a comparatively tolerant view in reviewing mergers. Moreover, if past patterns repeat themselves, by 1992 President Bush probably will appoint as much as one quarter of the federal judiciary. Most of these appointees are likely to reflect the comparatively conservative antitrust preferences of the Bush Administration. In sum, by 1992, this country will have experienced a twelve-year experiment with enforcement agency policies—and witnessed a somewhat longer trend in conservative judicial analysis—that favor dominant firm discretion and accept substantial increases in concentration by means of horizontal merger.

Past deconcentration experience suggests that these and other Reagan-Bush regulatory policies have planted, or will sow, the seeds for the section two enforcement targets of the late 1990s and beyond. One readily can imagine, for example, future administrations turning the deconcentration lens toward the commercial airline industry—a sector shaped by Reagan Department of Transportation policies that allowed mergers to proceed on the basis of robust assumptions that ease of entry would frustrate output restriction schemes.[230] Dislocations in the international trade arena—for example, the establishment of draconian tariffs or strin-

---

225. 472 U.S. 585 (1985); *see also* McGahee v. Northern Propane Gas Co., 858 F.2d 1487 (11th Cir. 1988) (departing from recent trend in Sherman Act predatory pricing decisions by emphasizing importance of defendant's subjective intent in evaluating liability under § 2).

226. *See* Hurwitz & Kovacic, *supra* note 29, at 139-50; *see also* Liebeler, *Whither Predatory Pricing? From Areeda and Turner to Matsushita*, 61 Notre Dame L. Rev. 1052, 1054-68 (1986) (recounting defendants' success since 1975 in defeating predatory pricing claims).

227. *See* Kovacic, *Federal Antitrust Enforcement in the Reagan Administration: Two Cheers for the Disappearance of the Large Firm Defendant in Nonmerger Cases*, 12 Res. L. & Econ. 173, 180-81 (forthcoming 1989).

228. *See* Kovacic, The Reagan Judiciary Examined: A Comparison of Antitrust Voting Records of Carter and Reagan Appointees to the Federal Courts of Appeals (Washington Legal Foundation Working Paper Series No. 34, Apr. 1989).

229. *See, e.g., Looking Forward: Antitrust in the Bush Administration—Interview with Timothy J. Muris*, Antitrust, Spring 1989, at 6, 6 (predicting continuity between Reagan and Bush antitrust policies); Kovacic, *Steady Reliever at Antitrust*, Wall St. J., Oct. 10, 1989, at A18, col. 4 (noting that core elements of Reagan antitrust program probably will be conserved and consolidated).

230. This possibility is suggested in Baker, *supra* note 20, at 925-26; *see also* Valente & Rose, *Concern Heightens About the Airline Industry's March Toward Near Domination by Only a Few Major Carriers*, Wall St. J., Mar. 10, 1989, at A10, col. 1.

gent import quotas—also could boost the antitrust visibility and perceived market power of large domestic companies whose market significance has been discounted by analytical approaches that define markets in global terms to account for the competitive significance of foreign suppliers.[231]

B.   *The Political Environment and the*
Stature of the Business Community

Of the three formative conditions identified in Section I,[232] the future political environment is the least predictable, yet perhaps the most important. A major resurgence of popular sentiment against large corporations is only as far away as the next business scandal or economic crisis. The specific identity or timing of the triggering events may be unforeseeable, but their recurrence is not a matter of serious doubt. The requisite destabilizing events have occurred often enough in the past to allow confident predictions that they will happen again.[233]

Political upheaval can take at least two basic forms. One is a serious, general economic downturn, occasioned by either a slow decline in growth rates or a sudden shock along the lines of the October 1987 stock market plunge.[234] A second source is highly focused public backlash against a pronounced increase in prices or deterioration in service within a specific industry.[235] In either case, the comparatively permissive regulatory policies of the 1980s will supply an easily grasped collection of perceived causes, and large companies believed to have benefitted from lax government oversight predictably will draw close and hostile attention. One can expect critics of Reagan antitrust enforcement to recommend the realignment of dominant firms or highly concentrated industries to curb the abuses and cure the economic ills associated with policies that welcomed the assemblage and maintenance of substantial market power. Whatever form their

---

231. Modern analytical trends in accounting for foreign competition in defining relevant markets and measuring market power are discussed in ABA Antitrust Section, Monograph No. 12, Horizontal Mergers: Law and Policy 247-54 (1986).

232. *See supra* notes 103-211 and accompanying text.

233. For example, the 1929 stock market crash severely damaged the status of the business community and helped set the foundation for the second deconcentration era. *See supra* notes 69-93 and accompanying text. Though less dramatic, the energy price increases of the early 1970s aroused political pressure that inspired the FTC's shared monopoly suit against the petroleum industry. *See* Kovacic, *supra* note 108, at 637-39 (describing political forces that shaped the FTC's decision to prosecute the *Exxon* case).

234. From Oct. 13-19, 1987, the stock market fell by 31%, representing a loss of approximately $1 trillion in the value of all outstanding stocks in the United States. Report of the Presidential Task Force on Market Mechanisms 1 (Jan. 1988). A presidential commission later concluded that the October 1987 crash "brought the financial system near to a breakdown." *Id.* at 59.

235. Possible candidates for public wrath could include the airline and cable television industries, both of which are experiencing significant consolidation in the aftermath of statutory and policy changes that relaxed public control of their activities. *See* Emshwiller, *Prying Open the Cable-TV Monopolies*, Wall St. J., Aug. 10, 1989, at B1, col. 3 (describing growing dissatisfaction with cable television companies); McGinley, *Republicans Grit Their Teeth and Call for Airline Regulation, Citing Higher Fares and Reduced Competition at Big Airports*, Wall St. J., Sept. 21, 1989, at A24, col. 1 (noting dissatisfaction with prices and service in domestic airline industry).

response takes, elected officials and heads of antitrust enforcement agencies are unlikely to ignore the political pressures a grave economic crisis or business scandal would generate.

C. *Intellectual Foundation*

Since the mid-1970s, the center of gravity in antitrust thinking has moved substantially to the right of the ideological spectrum.[236] Propelling this shift has been a body of scholarship that, among other features, promotes the primacy of allocative efficiency as a decisionmaking criterion and rejects nonefficiency concerns as bases for establishing or applying antitrust rules;[237] accords great weight to the "comparative advantage" of market forces, vis-à-vis government enforcement agencies and federal judges, in eroding market power and ensuring acceptable economic outcomes;[238] and attributes the persistence of concentrated market structures chiefly to superior performance.[239] Today these views frequently supply the point of departure for antitrust discourse and find little or no useful role for the Sherman Act as a tool for attacking single-firm exclusionary conduct or "shared" monopolization.[240]

The strength and direction of a future round of deconcentration initiatives will depend partly on the availability of a competing intellectual vision that commands support for monopolization suits to restructure dominant firms. To rebut the prevailing conservative intellectual orthodoxy in antitrust, proponents of more aggressive section two enforcement are likely to proceed along two lines of attack.[241] The first will be to look beyond allocative efficiency consequences and build enforcement programs that give heavy emphasis to wealth transfer effects and other nonefficiency concerns.[242] In its most expansive form, such an approach would assert that

---

236. I have traced this development in Kovacic, The Antitrust Paradox Revisited: Robert Bork and the Transformation of Modern Antitrust Policy (Washington Legal Foundation Working Paper Series No. 32, Feb. 1989).

237. The preeminent statement of this view appears in R. Bork, *supra* note 199, at 50-115 (examining goals of antitrust in light of argument that "responsibility of the federal courts for the integrity and virtue of law requires that they take consumer welfare as the sole value that guides antitrust decisions").

238. This concept has been developed most extensively and cogently in the writing of Judge Easterbrook. *See* Easterbrook, *Allocating Antitrust Decisionmaking Tasks*, 76 Geo. L.J. 305, 306-07 (1987); Easterbrook, *The Limits of Antitrust*, 63 Tex. L. Rev. 1, 14-17 (1984); Easterbrook, *Workable Antitrust Policy*, 84 Mich. L. Rev. 1696, 1703-05 (1986).

239. This perspective has drawn support from recent historical studies that explain the emergence of some oligopolistic market structures as a natural consequence of efficiency-enhancing efforts to devise superior managerial systems. *See, e.g.*, A. Chandler Jr., *supra* note 41, at 484-90; Chandler Jr., *The Coming of Oligopoly and its Meaning for Antitrust*, in National Competition Policy: Historians Perspectives on Antitrust and Government-Business Relationships in the United States 61 (Federal Trade Commission 1981).

240. *See, e.g.*, R. Posner, *supra* note 4, at 94-95 (criticizing deconcentration as a Sherman Act policy goal); Easterbrook, *supra* note 7, at 30 (same).

241. The intellectual basis for a liberal or moderate redirection of antitrust policy is suggested in the published proceedings of the Airlie House Conference on the Antitrust Alternative held in 1987. The papers from the conference are collected in 76 Geo. L.J. 237-346 (1987) and 62 N.Y.U. L. Rev. 931-1171 (1987).

242. *See, e.g.*, Lande, *supra* note 133, at 69-70 (concluding Congress' central aim in enacting antitrust laws was to prevent unfair transfers of wealth from consumers to producers); Lande,

the political and social benefits of dispersing economic power deserve substantial weight in framing antitrust policy for concentrated industries.[243]

The second intellectual foundation for new deconcentration measures will come from recent literature that accepts the centrality of efficiency concerns but argues that efficiency considerations, properly analyzed, dictate greater efforts to address dominant firm strategic behavior and nonprice predation strategies.[244] An efficiency-oriented approach or a philosophy that embraces nonefficiency values also could employ the no-fault monopolization theories developed by commentators such as Phillip Areeda, Donald Turner, and Oliver Williamson and given prominence in the NCRALP recommendations.[245] The development of proenforcement theories also will draw upon recent empirical studies suggesting that substantial market power exists in some concentrated industries.[246]

III.   LESSONS FOR THE FUTURE

The history of deconcentration initiatives suggests that this country has not seen the end of the section two divestiture suit. To anticipate some recurrence of deconcentration activism, however, is not to predict results that exceed the limited success of earlier trustbusting campaigns. A survey of past experience, particularly the outcomes from the 1969-1982 era, necessarily leads one to ask whether the section two divestiture suit should remain a component of the government's inventory of antitrust tools into the Sherman Act's second century.

As a matter of antitrust theory, the answer is yes. The availability of a monopolization or an attempted monopolization divestiture suit provides valuable symmetry in the modern enforcement landscape for two reasons.

The Rise and (Coming) Fall of Efficiency as the Ruler of Antitrust, 33 ANTITRUST BULL. 429, 464-65 (1988) (predicting demise of a singleminded efficiency approach to antitrust policymaking).

243. *See, e.g.,* Curran, *Beyond Economic Concepts and Categories: A Democratic Refiguration of Antitrust Law,* 28 ST. LOUIS U.L.J. 349, 361 (1987) ("Current antitrust theories destroy democratic values and subvert justice to render the current social order politically illegitimate."); Flynn, *The Reagan Administration's Antitrust Policy, 'Original Intent' and the Legislative History of the Sherman Act,* 33 ANTITRUST BULL. 259, 306 (1988) ("the Sherman Act is an expression of basic social and political values to be followed in the private economic sphere").

244. *See* Encaoua, Geroski & Jacquemin, *Strategic Competition and the Persistence of Dominant Firms: A Survey,* in NEW DEVELOPMENTS IN THE ANALYSIS OF MARKET STRUCTURE 55 (J. Stiglitz & G. Mathewson eds. 1986) (describing effect of strategic investments on market structure); Hilke & Nelson, *Diversification and Predation,* 37 J. INDUS. ECON. 107, 110 (1988) (applying to predatory price analysis notion that sunk costs must be considered in entry decisions); Krattenmaker, Lande & Salop, *Monopoly Power and Market Power in Antitrust Law,* 76 GEO. L.J. 241, 253-64 (1987) (proposing framework for evaluating strategies designed to raise costs of rival firms); Krattenmaker & Salop, *Anticompetitive Exclusion: Raising Rivals' Costs to Achieve Power Over Price,* 96 YALE L.J. 209, 249-53 (1986) (describing use of anticompetitive, exclusionary rights agreement); Smiley, *Empirical Evidence on Strategic Entry Deterrence,* 6 INT'L J. INDUS. ORG. 167, 172-74 (1988) (detailing survey results concerning relative frequency of strategies employed by firms to limit entry into marketplace); Williamson, *Delimiting Antitrust,* 76 GEO. L.J. 271, 289-93 (1987) (identifying objectionable strategic behavior used to eliminate competition).

245. *See supra* notes 202, 209-11 and accompanying text.

246. *See* Bresnahan, *Empirical Studies of Industries with Market Power,* in 2 HANDBOOK OF INDUSTRIAL ORGANIZATION 1011, 1051-53 (1989).

First, for nearly fifteen years, many commentators across the political spectrum have advocated liability standards that give single firms broad discretion in choosing business strategies, including the choice of pricing, promotion, and product development tactics. This trend primarily originated as a result of an influential article by Phillip Areeda and Donald Turner that proposed the use of an average variable cost test to screen out welfare-reducing predatory pricing claims.[247] Widespread judicial and executive acceptance of this and other cost-based predation standards reflects a decision to ensure consumers the benefits of low prices in the short-term at some risk that permissive conduct standards might yield or protect market power over the longer run. The section two divestiture suit supplies a useful form of antitrust insurance if the prevailing wisdom about the extreme unlikelihood of successful predation, whether by price or nonprice strategies, proves incorrect, if only in rare but important instances.[248]

A second reason to retain the monopolization divestiture suit stems from recent merger enforcement policy. The Reagan Administration loosened the government's standards for reviewing horizontal mergers.[249] Not only did the Reagan merger guidelines raise the nominal enforcement thresholds, but the Antitrust Division and the FTC also applied the guidelines' criteria in ways that created even broader zones of discretion for the business community.[250] In a number of instances, parties undertaking horizontal transactions benefitted from extremely favorable enforcement agency assessments about the nature of entry conditions.[251] If recent enforcement policies erred in allowing transactions that ultimately yield genuine market power, the section two divestiture suit affords a valuable means for correction.[252]

In principle, there are sensible bases for keeping the section two divestiture suit in the government's antitrust arsenal. In practice, the case

---

247. Areeda & Turner, *Predatory Pricing and Related Practices Under Section 2 of the Sherman Act*, 88 Harv. L. Rev. 697, 716-18 (1975). The significance of the Areeda and Turner article is discussed in Hurwitz & Kovacic, *supra* note 29, at 77-79; Liebeler, *supra* note 226, at 1052-57.

248. Areeda and Turner have constructed a single-firm monopolization framework that provides a backstop should their predatory pricing test prove to be excessively permissive. As mentioned above, the two scholars have proposed a no-fault monopolization cause of action that would allow the government to seek the dissipation of substantial, persistent monopoly power without demonstrating that the monopolist engaged in "exclusionary conduct." *See* 3 P. Areeda & D. Turner, Antitrust Law ¶¶ 614-23 (1978).

249. *See supra* note 224 and accompanying text.

250. *See* Leddy, *Recent Merger Cases Reflect Revolution in Antitrust Policy*, Legal Times, Nov. 3, 1986, at 17, col. 1 (showing how Antitrust Division, in practice, has established horizontal merger enforcement thresholds that substantially exceed nominal limits set out in government's guidelines).

251. *See, e.g.*, Echlin Mfg. Co., 105 F.T.C. 410, 487-92 (1985) (relying on ease of entry to dismiss challenge to merger involving postacquisition market share of 46%).

252. Donald Baker has observed the Reagan Administration took "many more chances on horizontal mergers than its predecessors did." Baker, *supra* note 20, at 926. He predicts that "[t]aking *some* of those chances will likely prove to be clearly wrong, with distasteful monopoly consequences being paraded across the media in at least a few cases." *Id.* It would also be possible to rely on cases such as United States v. E.I. du Pont de Nemours & Co., 353 U.S. 586 (1957) to use the Clayton Act's antimerger provisions to strike down a merger whose anticompetitive consequences become apparent some years after the transaction occurs.

for retention is relatively weak. Past deconcentration initiatives repeatedly have fallen victim to one or more of three well-chronicled problems: (1) the government chose the wrong cases or used an ultimately unsupportable theory;[253] (2) the lawsuits took so long that ongoing changes in industry conditions undercut the government's suggested remedial plan;[254] and (3) judges declined to order divestiture to remedy adjudicated violations of section two of the Sherman Act.[255] Even when the government gains the relief it originally sought, doubts typically surround the divestiture plan's effects. The government's defeats are unmistakable, and its victories partial at best.[256]

Can one reasonably expect the federal enforcement agencies to do better in the future? Past deconcentration episodes indicate that the future success of federal section two divestiture enforcement will depend chiefly on the capabilities of the enforcement agencies responsible for selecting and adjudicating monopolization cases. If the government's pursuit of monopolization divestiture suits is to improve and serve useful public ends, two institutional prerequisites must be satisfied.

First, the government must recruit and retain skilled professionals, both in management and staff-related positions. Particularly in the third deconcentration era, public enforcement agencies suffered gravely from their inability to acquire and retain the human capital necessary to accomplish tasks vital to a successful deconcentration endeavor. These tasks include developing a theory of liability that is legally and economically sound, choosing appropriate industries and firms for application of the theory, litigating the lawsuit, and presenting a feasible plan for structural relief. Capable professionals who join and remain with the agencies supply the foundations of competence, judgment, and continuity on which a successful section two case is built.

Today there is little evidence that the antitrust agencies can fulfill this requirement.[257] At all levels of the FTC and the Antitrust Division, the opportunity costs confronting skilled attorneys are enormous and growing steadily. The GS-11 entry level attorney today receives $30,000 to $45,000 less than his counterpart in a private law firm, and the highest antitrust agency official earns about $81,000—less than the starting wage for a new associate in some major metropolitan areas.[258] These massive salary differentials have two consequences: (1) they severely impede the recruitment of top quality attorneys at all levels, and (2) they guarantee a breathtaking

---

253. *See, e.g.*, Exxon Corp., 98 F.T.C. 453, 460-61 (1981) (complaint dismissed following eight years of pretrial discovery and motions practice).

254. *See, e.g.*, United States v. Aluminum Co. of Am., 91 F. Supp. 333, 416-19 (S.D.N.Y. 1950) (denying government request for divestiture in action brought in 1937).

255. *See, e.g.*, United States v. American Can Co., 230 F. 859, 903 (D. Md. 1916) ("I am frankly reluctant to destroy so finely adjusted an industrial machine as the record shows defendant to be.").

256. For illustrations of unmistakable defeats, see *supra* notes 18, 20, 65 and accompanying text. For examples of victories whose net effects are disputed, see *supra* notes 5-7, 93 and accompanying text.

257. I develop this point in Kovacic, *supra* note 227, at 186-92; Kovacic, *Public Choice, supra* note 218, at 497-500.

258. *See* Kerlow, *Keeping a Lid on Associate Salaries*, LEGAL TIMES, Aug. 21, 1989, at 9, col. 1.

turnover rate, as attorneys join the agencies with the sole aim of gaining the experience that will launch a more elegant private sector career.

The second institutional prerequisite is to make long-term investments in the development of an analytical infrastructure that ensures good theory development, case selection, and evaluation. This infrastructure requires several ingredients. One of the agency's most valuable assets should be its institutional memory. The Antitrust Division and the FTC need to build new monopolization cases on lessons learned from past experience. For example, the government's inattentiveness to remedial issues has accounted significantly for the dissatisfying results attained in section two cases in which the government prevailed on liability questions.[259] In the ideal development of a monopolization suit, Professor Sullivan writes, "[t]he remedy would be neither an afterthought, nor a reward allowed to the trial attorney for winning the lawsuit, but a public policy goal integral to the entire proceeding."[260] The accumulated experience from past remedial contests must guide the agencies' development of new proposals for structural relief.

A second necessary infrastructure element consists of ongoing economic analysis of industry conditions necessary to choose candidates for monopolization challenge. The enforcement agencies' economists should perform industry studies that assess the empirical validity of recent economic literature that proposes closer antitrust scrutiny of large firm conduct,[261] suggest appropriate targets for new cases, and evaluate the effects of completed section two litigation. In the past decade, resource constraints and changes in enforcement ideology have led the agencies —most notably, the FTC's Bureau of Economics—to de-emphasize long-range industry analysis and data collection.[262] These developments also appear to have discouraged the agencies from investing in the preparation of ex post evaluations of the effects of completed lawsuits.[263] Programs that take stock of past enforcement episodes and monitor current industry developments are crucial to the intelligent selection of section two targets.

The issue of analytical resources suggests an important paradox that helps to explain the government's weak performance in the section two area. Investments in middle and long-term analytical capabilities tend to generate returns that fall largely beyond the relatively brief tenures of high

259. *See* L. SULLIVAN, *supra* note 4, at 141-47 (discussing remedies for monopolization and limitations on their effectiveness).
260. *Id.* at 146.
261. *See supra* note 244 and accompanying text.
262. *See* REPORT OF THE AMERICAN BAR ASSOCIATION SECTION OF ANTITRUST LAW SPECIAL COMMITTEE TO STUDY THE ROLE OF THE FEDERAL TRADE COMMISSION, *reprinted in* 58 ANTITRUST L.J. 43, 101-04 (1989). Despite the many criticisms made of the overall purpose and specific features of the FTC's discontinued line of business program, I share the view of commentators such as Professor Baxter that the Commission has an important part to play in collecting line of business or similar data as a tool for assessing appropriate policy toward dominant firms. *See* Baxter, *How Government Cases Get Selected—Comments from Academe*, 46 ANTITRUST L.J. 586, 590-91 (1977).
263. For two examples of this type of analysis, see P. HUBER, *supra* note 19; FEDERAL TRADE COMMISSION, IMPACT EVALUATIONS OF FEDERAL TRADE COMMISSION VERTICAL RESTRAINTS CASES (Aug. 1984).

level agency officials, who would prefer to invest in projects they can more readily appropriate. The initiation of a major section two case, on the other hand, presents the agency's leadership with an accomplishment for which credit can be claimed when the political environment rewards such action. Thus, the incentives that influence enforcement agency leadership elicit section two cases when the political climate is right, but they fail to generate investments in the institutional infrastructure necessary to ensure that these initiatives will succeed.[264]

Today, the federal enforcement agencies suffer fundamental, growing weaknesses in both their human capital and their analytical infrastructure. These conditions have several important implications for the prosecution of structural cases. They diminish one's confidence that the enforcement agencies will avoid excessive false positives in case selection. They also raise serious doubts about the government's ability to bring structural lawsuits to a timely conclusion.[265] In short, until the necessary institutional conditions are established, the government is unlikely to improve upon the weak results of past deconcentration endeavors. Unless the institutional preconditions for success are satisfied, there is no useful social purpose to be served by greater recourse to the section two divestiture suit.

IV. CONCLUSION

Gilbert Montague was one of the first members of the private bar to gain wide renown for his mastery of antitrust law. Montague wrote extensively on antitrust topics, and in 1932 he commented on proposals to revise the Sherman Act. Antitrust enforcement at the time was moribund, but Montague focused on what he believed to be its unusual recuperative powers. He wrote that

> [o]ne of the peculiarities of the Sherman Act is the frequency with which, under expanding interpretations of the Supreme Court, the Act has successively been found to be amply effective to accomplish one after another of most of the things that economists, publicists, and even several Presidents of the United States at one time or another have assumed were quite beyond the scope of the Act.[266]

He added that the statute's most remarkable attribute was perhaps that "its periods of greatest growth have always immediately followed the periods when its critics have been most firmly convinced that the Act is hopelessly inadequate."[267]

In the 1980s government enforcement of the Sherman Act's ban on monopolization fell below levels that prevailed in the early 1930s, when the

---

264. *See* Kovacic, *supra* note 227, at 186-92.

265. The long duration of most § 2 litigation (often eight to ten years) routinely exposes government cases to industry change that undercuts both the theory of liability and the underlying premises for the proposed relief. *See* R. POSNER, *supra* note 4, at 232-36; Baker, *supra* note 20, at 899.

266. Montague, *Proposals for the Revision of the Anti-trust Laws*, in THE FEDERAL ANTI-TRUST LAWS 23, 62 (M. Handler ed. 1932).

267. *Id.*

future vitality of the Sherman Act seemed doubtful. Fresh memories of the deconcentration experiences of the 1970s have convinced many that the divestiture suit is a hopelessly flawed instrument of antitrust policy. In many respects it is harder today than it was in the early 1930s to imagine a revival of the section two divestiture action as an important antitrust weapon.

Yet Montague knew some history, and his assessment in 1932 has meaning a half-century later. Three basic features of the country's past deconcentration experiences explain the resilience Montague identified. First, deconcentration constitutes antitrust's cyclical response to eras of permissiveness in the treatment of market power, whether gained through single-firm conduct or through consolidation. Federal antitrust enforcement policy and judicial decisionmaking today confer substantial discretion on dominant firms in their choice of business strategies. Since 1981, the federal enforcement agencies have given firms significantly greater freedom to acquire horizontal rivals. These are the types of policies in which the targets of future deconcentration initiatives have taken root.

Second, deconcentration ebbs and flows with the tides of politics. Ronald Reagan's ideological predecessor in the White House was Calvin Coolidge, whose administration disdained attacks on corporate size and viewed mergers tolerantly.[268] "The Coolidge era is usually viewed as a period of extreme conservatism," writes historian William Leuchtenburg, "but it was thought of at the time as representing a great stride forward in social policy, a New Era in American life."[269] Less than a year after Coolidge left office, the Depression engulfed this country and destroyed the aura of respect and deference large corporations had enjoyed in the 1920s. The unpredictable, recurring forces of crisis and scandal at any time can unleash the political floods that press public officials to harness large firms. Deconcentration has proven a favored device toward this end.

Third, deconcentration periodically surfaces in an upswelling of ideas that justify policies to redress private monopoly and disperse economic power. Conservative trends in antitrust analysis over the past decade have weakened, but not destroyed, the intellectual base for deconcentration. When the political environment changes, there will be an inventory of theories that policymakers can use to pursue new monopolization initiatives.

The persuasive impact of these intellectual tools likely will be enhanced, because many advocates of the existing conservative orthodoxy reduce them to caricatures and thus fail to address their underlying logic seriously. In 1985 the Deputy Assistant Attorney General for Antitrust told a conference that antitrust analysis "need not be very sophisticated, of course, to determine that such antitrust notions as 'no fault monopolization' have little economic merit and can be explained as merely a knee-jerk reaction to economic success and a suspicion of capitalism."[270] Whatever

---

268. Coolidge, who saw probusiness ideals as a secular creed that inspired the nation's greatest achievements, stated that " '[t]he man who builds a factory builds a temple. The man who works there worships there.' " A. SCHLESINGER, *supra* note 69, at 57.

269. W. LEUCHTENBURG, *supra* note 67, at 201.

270. C. Rule, Deregulating Antitrust: The Quiet Revolution, Speech before the 19th New

comfort or appeal one finds in this assessment, it is hardly a satisfying or accurate critique of the no-fault proposals of commentators such as Phillip Areeda, Donald Turner, and Oliver Williamson—scholars not ordinarily associated with a knee-jerk reaction to economic success or a suspicion of capitalism. If the existing orthodoxy eventually gives way to a more activist vision of antitrust policy, complacency and self-congratulation will deserve much credit for the change.

These formative influences yielded three major periods of deconcentration activity and they are likely to converge again in the future to produce a fourth. Past experience supplies scant basis for predicting that the next round of initiatives will improve upon the disappointing results of former deconcentration eras. Why, then, will a new collection of enforcement officials set off to climb a mountain that routinely has conquered its challengers? The answer may be that the durability of the deconcentration impulse ultimately has little to do with realistic expectations that a broad-based program of Sherman Act divestiture suits will dissolve existing aggregations of market power. Its recurring hold on public policy instead derives from its attractiveness as a symbolic outlet for public antipathy toward large corporate size.

One year before he assumed the position that made him history's most famous antitrust enforcer, Thurman Arnold acidly called the antitrust laws a charade that let the country harmlessly express its indignation at the discomforting but necessary process of economic concentration.[271] Arnold noted the apparent futility of the dissolution of the Standard Oil Trust in 1911 and observed that "a crusade against the Aluminum Company of America is in the first stages of its long struggle through the courts."[272] He explained that "[t]he reason why these attacks always ended up with a ceremony of atonement, but few practical results, lay in the fact that there were no new organizations growing up to take over the functions of those under attack."[273] Arnold added that "the antitrust laws, instead of breaking up great organizations, served only to make them respectable and well thought of by providing them with the clothes of rugged individualism."[274]

In sum, Arnold concluded that the antitrust laws were "a great moral gesture" and "a most important symbol."[275] Their symbolic value inhered in their power to deflect calls for more comprehensive regulatory schemes of lesser utility. Arnold said that some had "founded political careers on the continuance of such crusades, which were entirely futile but enormously picturesque . . . ."[276] One year later, Arnold launched a grand crusade of his own. Future crusades may prove largely futile, as well, but the powerful symbolic value inherent in the deconcentration vision ensures that other antitrust policymakers will embrace it in the Sherman Act's second century.

England Antitrust Conference 10 (Nov. 8, 1985).
271. T. Arnold, The Folklore of Capitalism 207-29 (1937).
272. *Id.* at 220.
273. *Id.*
274. *Id.* at 227.
275. *Id.* at 217.
276. *Id.*

THE ANTITRUST PARADOX REVISITED: ROBERT BORK AND THE TRANSFORMATION OF MODERN ANTITRUST POLICY

William E. Kovacic†

I. INTRODUCTION

Since the passage of the Sherman Act in 1890,[1] antitrust's periodic upheavals in judicial analysis, public enforcement, and legislation have derived crucial force from the outcome of well-defined episodes in a continuing contest of ideas.[2] Amid a vast expanse of commentary, the prescriptive works that have decisively influenced the intellectual debate over federal antitrust policy constitute a modest collection at best. To understand antitrust's past and to predict the future direction of what Thurman Arnold once called a "preaching device,"[3] one must study the formative works of antitrust's leading theologians.

† Associate Professor, George Mason University School of Law. This Article is based in part upon a working paper titled "The Antitrust Paradox Revisited: Robert Bork and the Transformation of Modern Antitrust Policy" (Washington Legal Foundation, Feb. 1989). The author thanks the Smith-Richardson Foundation for its support in preparing the Article and gratefully acknowledges the research assistance of Sean J. Coleman and Steve C. Taylor. The author also is indebted to Kathryn M. Fenton, Michael S. Greve, Robert H. Lande, Michael P. McDonald, Shannon O'Chester, and E. Thomas Sullivan for many useful suggestions and discussions.

1. 26 Stat. 209 (1890) (codified as amended at 15 U.S.C. §§ 1-7 (1982)).
2. *See, e.g.*, Kovacic, *Failed Expectations: The Troubled Past and Uncertain Future of the Sherman Act as a Tool for Deconcentration*, 74 IOWA L. REV. 1105, 1128-39 (1989) (describing the influence of intellectual debate on the use of the Sherman Act to restructure concentrated industries); Rowe, *The Decline of Antitrust and the Delusions of Models: The Faustian Pact of Law and Economics*, 72 GEO. L.J. 1511 (1984) (analyzing impact of changes in industrial organization economic theory upon antitrust doctrine and policy); *see also*, Bork, *Judicial Precedent and the New Economics*, in ANTITRUST POLICY IN TRANSITION: THE CONVERGENCE OF LAW AND ECONOMICS 5, 7 (E. Fox & J. Halverson eds. 1984) (comments describing modern Chicago School scholarship that generated "a kind of 30-year intellectual war in antitrust").
3. T. ARNOLD, THE FOLKLORE OF CAPITALISM 211-12 (1937).

Modern antitrust experience demonstrates the power of intellectual visions in shaping doctrine and public enforcement practice. The evolution of antitrust policy over the past three decades is evinced by two books. In the 1960s and the 1970s, every serious antitrust practitioner and scholar owned a well-thumbed copy of Carl Kaysen's and Donald Turner's *Antitrust Policy*.[4] Following its publication in 1959, this single-volume prescriptive analysis gained recognition as the leading antitrust work of its time.[5] Reflecting the professional backgrounds and accomplishments of its authors, the book presented an unmatched synthesis of economic and legal learning in antitrust.[6] The Kaysen-Turner volume profoundly influenced the development of antitrust policy. Among other contributions, it supplied an indispensable basis for renewed efforts in the 1960s and 1970s to redress perceived instances of single and multi-firm monopoly power by restructuring concentrated industries.[7]

---

4. C. KAYSEN & D. TURNER, ANTITRUST POLICY: AN ECONOMIC AND LEGAL ANALYSIS (1959).

5. *See* M. HANDLER, H. BLAKE, R. PITOFSKY & H. GOLDSCHMID, CASES AND MATERIALS ON TRADE REGULATION 92 (1st ed. 1975) ("Every student and practitioner of antitrust law should be familiar with the [Kaysen-Turner] book."); L. SULLIVAN, ANTITRUST 15 (1977) (calling the Kaysen-Turner volume "a towering statement"); *see also* Rowe, *supra* note 2 (describing the influence of Kaysen, Turner, and other commentators upon modern antitrust thinking).

6. Kaysen and Turner brought rich backgrounds and professional accomplishments to the task of writing their book. Carl Kaysen was a distinguished industrial organization economist and a professor of economics at Harvard University. By 1959, his extensive list of major publications in the antitrust field included a widely-cited analysis of his experiences as a neutral expert selected to assist the trial court in United States v. United Shoe Machinery Corp., 110 F. Supp. 295 (D. Mass. 1953), *aff'd*, 347 U.S. 521 (1954) (per curiam). *See* C. KAYSEN, UNITED STATES V. UNITED SHOE MACHINERY: AN ECONOMIC ANALYSIS OF AN ANTITRUST CASE (1956). Among other professional distinctions, Kaysen later served for ten years as the director of the Institute for Advanced Studies in Princeton.

Donald Turner, who held both a law degree and a doctorate in economics, was a professor at Harvard Law School. Like his coauthor, Turner's writing had established him as one of the country's leading antitrust scholars. *See, e.g.*, Turner, *Antitrust Policy and the Cellophane Case*, 70 HARV. L. REV. 281 (1956). The influence of the Kaysen-Turner book on antitrust thinking derived partly from Turner's subsequent appointment to head the Antitrust Division of the Department of Justice during the Johnson administration. Turner's two-year tenure as Assistant Attorney General for Antitrust is treated in part in S. WEAVER, DECISION TO PROSECUTE: ORGANIZATION AND PUBLIC POLICY IN THE ANTITRUST DIVISION 128-36 (1977).

7. Kaysen and Turner warned that "[T]he principal defect of present

As the impact of Kaysen's and Turner's work grew in the 1960s, so too did the prominence of Robert Bork as the leading intellectual counterweight to the deconcentration-orientation of the two Harvard scholars. Both in public discussion and in his writing, Bork disputed the analytical and empirical underpinnings of antitrust policies that Kaysen, Turner, and others had proposed to decrease industrial concentration.[8] More broadly, Bork became the foremost advocate for a redirection of antitrust toward policies, often referred to as the "Chicago School" vision of antitrust, whose exclusive aim was to proscribe conduct (such as horizontal

---

antitrust law is its inability to cope with market power created by jointly acting oligopolists." C. Kaysen & D. Turner, *supra* note 4, at 110. They proposed new legislation that mandated the restructuring of concentrated industries. *Id.* at 110-19, 261-66. The Kaysen-Turner study was particularly influential in shaping the thinking of President Johnson's White House Task Force on Antitrust Policy. Chaired by Phil Neal, dean of the University of Chicago Law School, the White House Task Force recommended legislation to restructure concentrated industries. Prominent task force members who supported the deconcentration proposal included such noted antitrust authorities as William Baxter, William Jones, and Paul MacAvoy. In a dissent that foreshadowed important themes of *The Antitrust Paradox*, Robert Bork opposed the deconcentration measure. *See* WHITE HOUSE TASK FORCE REPORT ON ANTITRUST POLICY, *reprinted in* 411 Antitrust & Trade Reg. Rep. (BNA) at 411 (May 27, 1969) (Special Supplement: Part II).

The Kaysen-Turner book also guided the Senate Antitrust and Monopoly Subcommittee's development in the early 1970s of "The Industrial Reorganization Act," a bill that would have mandated the restructuring of various concentrated industries. *See The Industrial Reorganization Act: Hearings on S. 1167 Before the Subcomm. on Antitrust and Monopoly of the Senate Comm. on the Judiciary*, 93d Cong., 1st Sess., pt. 1, at 3-34 (1973) (reprinting S. 1167). Senator Philip Hart, the chief sponsor of the Subcommittee's deconcentration proposal, told Donald Turner that he and Carl Kaysen "really were the first" in their effort in *Antitrust Policy* to "put something together on paper in the way of an attempted solution at the concentration problem." *Id.* at 293. "I won't speak for what the Neal Commission may have drawn from it," Senator Hart explained to Turner, "but I can confess that we, obviously, have drawn heavily from your proposal in developing S. 1167, so I am particularly in your debt." *Id.* at 294. The Antitrust Subcommittee's bill triggered an extensive debate over the desirability of deconcentration legislation. *See Industrial Concentration: The New Learning* 339-426 (H. Goldschmid, H. Mann & J. Weston eds. 1974) (discussing legislative deconcentration proposals).

8. *See, e.g., An Interview with the Honorable Donald F. Turner, Assistant Attorney General in Charge of the Antitrust Division*, 30 A.B.A. SEC. ANTITRUST REP. 100, 106-08 (1966) (question and answer session involving Assistant Attorney General Turner and, among others, Robert Bork); Bork & Bowman, *The Crisis in Antitrust*, FORTUNE, Dec. 1963, at 138; Bork, *The Supreme Court Versus Corporate Efficiency*, FORTUNE, Aug. 1967, at 92; Bork, *Antitrust in Dubious Battle*, FORTUNE, Sept. 1969, at 103.

price fixing) that injured consumers by reducing economic efficiency.[9]

In 1978, Bork reinforced his stature as the nation's leading conservative antitrust scholar with the publication of *The Antitrust Paradox*.[10] Just as Kaysen and Turner had done twenty years earlier in *Antitrust Policy*, Bork's *Antitrust Paradox* defined the agenda for antitrust discourse in its time. Bork's powerful mixture of history, law, and economics catalyzed many important doctrinal and policy developments that have become fixtures in modern antitrust law. As one distinguished group of antitrust practitioners correctly observed in 1987 during the pendency of his failed nomination to the Supreme Court, Robert Bork's writing in the antitrust field "has been among the most influential scholarship ever produced"; his *Antitrust Paradox* "is among the most important works written in this field in the past 25 years."[11]

If the Senate had approved his nomination to the Court,[12] Bork probably would have reinforced the Court's conservative

---

9. *See The Goals of Antitrust: A Dialogue on Policy*, 65 COLUM. L. REV. 363 (1965) (symposium of four articles dealing with the proper goals of and bases for antitrust enforcement; two articles authored by Bork and Ward Bowman, and two articles authored by William K. Jones and Harlan Blake); Bork, *Legislative Intent and the Policy of the Sherman Act*, 9 J. L. & ECON. 7 (1966). For useful discussions of the emergence of a Chicago School perspective in antitrust, *see* G. E. GARVEY & G. J. GARVEY, ECONOMIC LAW AND ECONOMIC GROWTH 103-20 (1990); Posner, *The Chicago School of Antitrust Analysis*, 127 U. PA. L. REV. 925 (1979); Nelson, *Comments on a Paper by Posner*, 127 U. PA. L. REV. 949 (1979); *see also* Fox & Sullivan, *Antitrust Retrospective and Prospective: Where Are We Coming From? Where Are We Going?*, 62 N.Y.U. L. REV. 936, 969-88 (1987).

10. R. BORK, THE ANTITRUST PARADOX: A POLICY AT WAR WITH ITSELF (1978). Bork, of course, was not the sole conservative luminary in the antitrust field at this time. Others whose writing had established themselves as influential proponents of a conservative reorientation of antitrust policy included Armen Alchian, Yale Brozen, Harold Demsetz, John McGee, Richard Posner, and George Stigler. In 1976, for example, Posner had published a widely-cited single volume prescriptive analysis of antitrust policy. *See* R. POSNER, ANTITRUST LAW: AN ECONOMIC PERSPECTIVE (1976).

11. Letter from James T. Halverson, Immediate Past Chairman of the Section of Antitrust Law of the American Bar Association, to Benjamin C. Bradlee, Executive Editor, The Washington Post (Aug. 7, 1987), *reprinted in Nomination of Robert H. Bork to be an Associate Justice of the United States Supreme Court: Report of the Senate Comm. on the Judiciary*, 100th Cong., 1st Sess. 331 (1988) (letter of fifteen past chairmen of ABA's Section of Antitrust Law submitted at hearings on Bork's nomination to the Supreme Court).

12. Bork's nomination to the Court and his rejection by the Senate are examined in E. BRONNER, BATTLE FOR JUSTICE: HOW THE BORK NOMINATION

tendencies in deciding antitrust cases. Nonetheless, his defeat in the Senate had considerably less significance for the future direction of antitrust doctrine than his detractors claimed during the confirmation process.[13] The rejection of Bork's nomination obscured the substantial extent to which the federal judiciary, including the Supreme Court, already had embraced his antitrust views. From an antitrust perspective, Bork's nomination would have been far more important had it occurred twenty years earlier. His antitrust preferences would have placed him at the distant right on a spectrum dominated by a comparatively liberal and interventionist orthodoxy. In one sense, Bork's antitrust writings, especially *The Antitrust Paradox*, effectively put him on the Court well before the Senate refused his nomination in 1987.

This Article measures the depth and durability of Robert Bork's imprint on modern antitrust policy by focusing on Bork's *Antitrust Paradox*. This Article has two basic goals. The first is to analyze Bork's contribution to an important development in the intellectual history of antitrust. Since 1890, no single scholarly work has exerted a greater influence than *The Antitrust Paradox* on the direction of antitrust policy. The dramatic shift in antitrust orthodoxy from the expansionism of the 1960s and early 1970s to the permissiveness of the 1980s is one of the most striking developments in post-World War II economic regulation. Many forces have influenced this reorientation, but the contest of ideas in intellectual circles has played a particularly central role in this adjustment. Publication of *The Antitrust Paradox* was a pivotal event in the reformation of antitrust doctrine and policy.

The Article's second objective is to evaluate the permanence of the comparatively conservative antitrust consensus that Bork's

---

SHOOK AMERICA (1989); P. McGUIGAN & D. WEYRICH, NINTH JUSTICE: THE FIGHT FOR BORK (1990); M. PERTSCHUK & W. SCHAETZEL, THE PEOPLE RISING: THE CAMPAIGN AGAINST THE BORK NOMINATION (1989). For Bork's own account of these events, see R. BORK, THE TEMPTING OF AMERICA (1989).

13. The views of those who opposed Bork's nomination on the basis of his antitrust preferences are collected in *Nomination of Robert H. Bork to be Associate Justice of the Supreme Court of the United States: Hearings Before the Comm. on the Judiciary*, 100th Cong., 1st Sess., pt. 3, at 3413-3536 (1989); *see also Foreward: Antitrust, the Supreme Court, and the Bork Factor*, 19 ANTITRUST L. & ECON. REV. 1, 11 (1987) (editorial predicting that, without successful effort to block the Bork nomination, "antitrust may well be entering its 'twilight' on the eve of the 100th anniversary of the Sherman Act"); Orland, *The Parodox in Bork's Antitrust Paradox*, 9 CARDOZO L. REV. 115, 127 (1987) ("Professor Bork's views bespeak intellectual arrogance and lack of jurisprudential integrity.").

book has been instrumental in building. It also considers the likelihood that rival visions of antitrust policy will succeed in displacing the underlying basis of the antitrust agenda proposed in *The Antitrust Paradox*. In particular, the Article discusses the durability of *The Antitrust Paradox*'s perspective in the face of emerging scholarship that challenges fundamental assumptions upon which Bork's conception of appropriate antitrust doctrine and enforcement policy rests.

II. CONTEXT AND CONTENT

In fundamental respects, the roots of *The Antitrust Paradox* extend back to Bork's experiences as a law student at the University of Chicago in the early 1950s. Among other important influences, Bork's analytical perspective in antitrust was shaped by Aaron Director, who published little but whose seminars and tutelage of students such as Bork, Henry Manne, and Richard Posner played a vital part in establishing the modern law and economics movement.[14] Even had its policy impact been minimal, *The Antitrust Paradox* still would have been noteworthy as a distillation and extension of the oral tradition that Director and colleagues such as Ronald Coase and Edward Levi had created at Chicago.[15] The book, however, proved to be considerably more than an interesting contribution to the intellectual history of antitrust.

---

14. *See* R. BORK, *supra* note 10, at ix (recounting Bork's intellectual debt to Aaron Director); Bork, *supra* note 2, at 6-7; *see also* Rusakoff & Kamen, *A Trip Across the Political Spectrum*, Washington Post, July 26, 1987, at A1, col. 1 (discussing Director's influence on Bork's thinking). Director's contributions to modern law and economics scholarship and to the emergence of a Chicago School perspective in antitrust are treated in *The Fire of Truth: A Remembrance of Law and Economics at Chicago, 1932-1970*, 26 J. L. & ECON. 163 (1983); *see also* Kitch, *The Intellectual Foundations of Law and Economics*, 33 J. LEGAL EDUC. 184 (1983). The writings of Director's prominent former students and colleagues are replete with acknowledgments of his formative influence. *See, e.g.*, R. POSNER, *supra* note 10, at x; G. STIGLER, MEMORIES OF AN UNREGULATED ECONOMIST 166-70 (1988).

15. *The Antitrust Paradox* also built extensively upon Bork's later professional work, including several influential articles he completed as a member of the Yale Law School faculty in the 1960s. *See, e.g.*, Bork, *Legislative Intent and the Policy of the Sherman Act*, 9 J. L. & ECON. 7 (1966); Bork, *The Rule of Reason and the Per Se Concept: Price Fixing and Market Division*, 74 YALE L.J. 775 (1965); Bork, *The Rule of Reason and the Per Se Concept: Price Fixing and Market Division—Part II*, 75 YALE L.J. 373 (1966).

A. Context: "The Crisis in Antitrust"[16]

In assessing the future of antitrust, *The Antitrust Paradox* offered heavy doses of alarm and gloom. Bork concluded, "[t]he thesis of this book has been that modern antitrust has so decayed that the policy is no longer intellectually respectable. Some of it is not respectable as law; more of it is not respectable as economics; and . . . a great deal of antitrust is not even respectable as politics."[17] Bork viewed most institutions playing major roles in shaping antitrust doctrine—Congress, the courts, the public enforcement agencies, the academic community, and the business community (and its agent, the private bar)—as either sustaining or acquiescing in increasingly interventionist policies that routinely trampled efficiency considerations in order to shelter weaker firms from the rigors of rivalry. Each ominous force, as Bork perceived it, is described below.

1. Congress and the Prospect of New Legislation

The Antitrust Paradox displayed an abiding concern with the possibility that Congress might enact one of several suggested measures to restructure large segments of American industry.[18] "A new era of antitrust expansion seems likely to begin in Congress, which is influenced by popular moods,"[19] Bork warned. A disturbing indication of the prevailing popular mood was an apparent congressional receptivity to what Bork labelled "increasingly serious proposals for new antitrust legislation."[20] As evidence of this trend, Bork pointed to recent legislative consideration of measures that, respectively, would adopt a general ban on industrial concentration exceeding certain levels,[21] require the vertical divestiture of the petroleum industry,[22] and permit the restructuring of individual dominant firms without regard to fault.[23]

---

16. Bork titled the introduction of his book "The Crisis in Antitrust." R. BORK, *supra* note 10, at 3.

17. *Id.* at 418.

18. *Id.* at 3-7, 175-78.

19. *Id.* at 5.

20. *Id.* at 163.

21. *Id.* at 164 (referring to the legislative proposals that were based upon Kaysen's and Turner's *Antitrust Policy* and President Johnson's White House Task Force on Antitrust Policy).

22. *Id.* at 6 (discussing the Senate's consideration of the Petroleum Industry Competition Act of 1976).

23. *Id.* (discussing "no-fault" monopolization legislation introduced by Senator Philip Hart).

By summoning these measures, Bork unquestionably gave rhetorical force to his argument that Congress was careening toward a senseless dismantling of fundamentally efficient corporations. Whether he correctly apprehended the mood and inclination of Congress in 1978, however, is doubtful. One hesitates to use the superior vantage point of hindsight to question the analysis of an observer contending with the cluttered field of vision of the moment. Nonetheless, Bork neglected an important qualifying consideration in interpreting the legislative activity he described as evidence of a dangerous, steady movement toward the enactment of expansive deconcentration legislation.

The Congress, in the early to mid-1970s that developed and debated the proposals Bork mentioned in *The Antitrust Paradox*, began a substantial shift to the right in 1976.[24] This trend was

---

24. In the 1970s, the high water mark of liberal antitrust influence in Congress was the enactment of the Hart-Scott-Rodino Antitrust Improvements Act of 1976, 90 Stat. 1390 (1976) (codified as amended in scattered sections of 15 U.S.C. § 1311 (1982)). Bork cited this statute as evidence of antitrust expansionism in Congress. R. BORK, *supra* note 10, at 6. In drawing this conclusion, Bork overstated the new statute's significance. The Hart-Scott-Rodino measure's most controversial provision gave state governments parens patriae authority to challenge Sherman Act violations by recovering three times the damages suffered by persons living within the state. 15 U.S.C. § 15b (Supp. 1990). *The Antitrust Paradox* did not mention that in 1977 the Supreme Court substantially reduced the reach of the parens patriae power. The Court ruled that consumers who purchase goods from an innocent middleman may not recover treble damages from a manufacturer engaged in a price-fixing conspiracy with other manufacturers. *See* Illinois Brick Co. v. Illinois, 431 U.S. 720 (1977).

The second most noteworthy provision of the 1976 statute required companies to notify the federal antitrust enforcement agencies before making acquisitions and, in certain instances, to refrain from consummating such transactions until a mandatory waiting period had expired. 15 U.S.C. § 18a (Supp. 1990). Bork wrote that the measure "made mergers more difficult." R. BORK, *supra* note 10, at 6. Few decisions under the statute had been rendered when *The Antitrust Paradox* appeared in 1978, but subsequent events suggest that the statute has not exerted a uniformly discouraging influence on merger and acquisition activity. Rather, the statute's premerger notification requirements have introduced a degree of certainty and predictability into the government's antitrust review process that business managers seem to regard favorably. In particular, the review process has substantially reduced the possibility that firms might face antitrust attack for a merger long after the transaction takes place. In his discussion of merger policy in *The Antitrust Paradox*, Bork stated: "There should be a time limit within which a merger must be challenged. . . . [I]t is desirable that enforcement authorities not have a club they can hold over a firm forever. They can at present control or influence a company's market behavior by threatening a merger suit . . . ." *Id.* at 223. In practice, the 1976 statute has supplied the time limit Bork

especially evident in the Senate, the origin of the most serious legislative deconcentration measures.[25] In the fall of 1976, Philip Hart, Mike Mansfield, and John Pastore retired from the Senate. Vance Hartke, Gale McGee, Frank Moss, and John Tunney were defeated in the general election. Several of these legislators held influential posts in the Senate hierarchy,[26] and most of their seats

---

recommended. *But see* California v. American Stores Co., 110 S. Ct. 1853 (1990) (establishing ability of state governments and private parties to obtain divestiture to remedy violations of Clayton Act's antimerger provision; divestiture deemed available notwithstanding merged entity's compliance with Hart-Scott-Rodino premerger notification requirements and implementation of partial divestiture to satisfy federal enforcement agency's concerns).

25. The Senate was the source of four major deconcentration proposals. The first and most sweeping was Senator Philip Hart's Industrial Reorganization Act. *See Hearings on S. 1167 Before the Subcomm. on Antitrust and Monopoly of the Senate Comm. on the Judiciary*, 93d Cong., 1st Sess., pt. 1, at 3 (1973). This bill created a rebuttable presumption of monopoly power for selected industries (chemicals and drugs, electrical machinery and equipment, electronic computing and communication equipment, energy, iron and steel, motor vehicles, and non-ferous metals) in which rates of return and four-firm concentration ratios exceeded specified levels. The Industrial Reorganization Act was the subject of extensive hearings before the Antitrust and Monopoly Subcommittee, but it never came up for a formal vote within the Subcommittee or the full Judiciary Committee.

A second proposal was Senator Birch Bayh's Petroleum Industry Competition Act of 1976. *See The Petroleum Industry Competition Act of 1976*, S. REP. No. 1005, 94th Cong., 2d Sess., pt. 1, at 161 (1976). This bill required the country's twenty largest petroleum companies to participate in one of three major lines of business (production, transmission, or refining/marketing) to the exclusion of the others and mandated the divorcement by integrated oil companies of petroleum pipelines. Both the Antitrust and Monopoly Subcommittee and the full Judiciary Committee approved the Petroleum Industry Competition Act, but the measure did not reach the Senate floor.

The third measure was Senator James Abourezk's Interfuel Competition Act of 1975. *See Hearings on S. 489 Before the Subcomm. on Antitrust and Monopoly of the Senate Comm. on the Judiciary*, 94th Cong., 1st Sess. 6 (1975). The Interfuel Competition Act compelled producers or refiners of petroleum or natural gas to divest their interests in other energy sources, including coal, nuclear power, geothermal steam, and solar power. This measure was the subject of limited hearings and never received a vote within either the Antitrust and Monopoly Subcommittee or the full Judiciary Committee.

The fourth proposal was Senator Philip Hart's Monopolization Reform Act of 1976, S. 3429, 94th Cong., 2d Sess., 122 CONG. REC. 13,872 (1976). This "no fault" monopolization bill would have eliminated the consideration of a defendant's conduct as a legal requirement in monopolization cases. There were no hearings held or votes taken on this measure.

26. Senator Mansfield, for example, had served as the Senate Majority Leader since 1964. Senators McGee and Moss held important positions on the

were filled by individuals with much narrower antitrust preferences.[27] While it is questionable whether Congress would have
enacted deconcentration legislation later in the 1970s even if Hart,
Mansfield, McGee, Moss, and other liberal legislators had not left
the Senate,[28] their departure marked a change in congressional

---

Senate Appropriations Committee and Senate Commerce Committee, respectively,
and had used these posts to advocate dramatic expansions, by legislation and
through federal enforcement activity, of the reach of antitrust in dealing with
large corporations. *See* Kovacic, *The Federal Trade Commission and Congressional Oversight of Antitrust Enforcement: A Historical Perspective*, in PUBLIC
CHOICE AND REGULATION: A VIEW FROM INSIDE THE FEDERAL TRADE COMMISSION
63, 82-83 (R. MacKay, J. Miller III & B. Yandle eds. 1986); Kovacic, *The Federal
Trade Commission and Congressional Oversight of Antitrust Enforcement*, 17
TULSA L.J. 587, 632-34 (1982).

The most significant event was the retirement of Philip Hart. From 1963
until his departure from Congress, Hart chaired the Antitrust and Monopoly
Subcommittee of the Senate Judiciary Committee. Hart and his subcommittee
staff presided over an extraordinary collection of hearings involving economic
concentration and the significance of corporate size in the American economy.
In this capacity, Hart became the intellectual and spiritual leader of congressional
advocates of various proposals to restructure concentrated industries. His retirement not only deprived the deconcentration enthusiasts of his intellect and
knowledge, but it also denied them the force of his character. Hart's personal
qualities gained him enormous respect in the Senate, and his strongest admirers
included many who believed his antitrust policy preferences to be utterly wrongheaded.

27. For example, Hartke, McGee, Moss, and Tunney were defeated for reelection in 1976 by Richard Lugar, Malcolm Wallop, Orrin Hatch, and S. I.
Hayakawa, respectively.

28. In addition to giving too little weight to the membership changes of
1976, Bork's analysis of the congressional mood miscalculated the degree and
durability of support for the deconcentration measures he cited as evidence of
growing momentum for new legislation. For example, he noted that the Petroleum
Industry Competition Act of 1976, *supra* note 25, "won astonishingly wide
support in the Senate in 1976." R. BORK, *supra* note 10, at 6. The Senate
Judiciary Committee approved this vertical divestiture measure by an 8 to 7 vote,
but one member of the majority, Senator Robert Byrd, stated that he would
oppose the measure if it reached the Senate floor. *See* Petroleum Industry
Competition Act of 1976, S. REP. No. 1005, 94th Cong., 2d Sess., pt. 1, at 179
(1976). Byrd's willingness to vote the bill out of committee and his declaration
that he would oppose the bill before the Senate belied a fundamental weakness
in congressional support for a final, binding measure to restructure the petroleum
industry. Many legislators appear to have been willing to cast symbolic votes in
1976 against the petroleum industry but were not inclined to adhere to such
positions when a dispositive vote on the merits approached. Subsequent commentary has analyzed such behavior as a species of rent-seeking in which
legislators signal their support for, or ambivalence toward, new regulatory legislation to elicit campaign contributions and other electoral resources from

preferences that virtually foreclosed favorable consideration of the types of bills to which *The Antitrust Paradox* referred. In short, the deconcentration measures that Bork described with alarm in 1978 had no realistic prospects for legislative success after 1976.

2. Judicial Hostility to Efficiency Concerns

A key ingredient of Bork's case for antitrust reform was a devastating chronicle of Supreme Court decisions that had slighted, or explictly subordinated, efficiency concerns in framing liability rules. Although several important targets of Bork's criticism date back throughout the one-hundred year history of the federal antitrust laws,[29] the chief focus of his attack was a remarkable decade-long stretch of antitrust jurisprudence that began with the *Brown Shoe v. United States*[30] merger case in 1962 and ended with *United States v. Topco Associates, Inc.*[31] in 1972. As Bork skillfully recounted, this period featured the Court's adoption or extension of restrictive standards involving horizontal mergers,[32] vertical mergers,[33] conglomerate mergers,[34] resale price maintenance,[35] exclusive dealing agreements,[36] tying arrangements ,[37] price discrimination,[38] vertical territorial restrictions,[39] and horizontal restraints.[40]

Throughout this parade of expansive antitrust prohibitions, Bork identified two basic destructive trends. First, the Court

---

companies that would be affected by the proposed initiative. *See* McChesney, *Rent Extraction and Rent Creation in the Economic Theory of Regulation*, 16 J. LEGAL STUD. 101 (1987).

29. *See, e.g.*, Dr. Miles Medical Co. v. John D. Park & Sons Co., 220 U.S. 373, 408 (1911) (establishing a rule of per se illegality for resale price maintenance). *Dr. Miles* is discussed in R. BORK, *supra* note 10, at 32-33, 280-81, 288-89.

30. 370 U.S. 294 (1962).

31. 405 U.S. 596 (1972).

32. *See, e.g.*, United States v. Von's Grocery Co., 384 U.S. 270 (1966); United States v. Pabst Brewing Co., 384 U.S. 546 (1966).

33. *See Brown Shoe Co.*, 370 U.S. at 294.

34. *See* Federal Trade Comm'n v. Procter & Gamble Co., 386 U.S. 568 (1967).

35. *See* Albrecht v. Herald Co., 390 U.S. 145 (1968) (holding per se ban upon resale price maintenance applicable to setting maximum resale prices).

36. *See* Federal Trade Comm'n v. Brown Shoe Co., 384 U.S. 316, 319-22 (1966).

37. *See* Fortner Enters., Inc. v. United States Steel Corp., 394 U.S. 495 (1969).

38. *See* Utah Pie Co. v. Continental Baking Co., 386 U.S. 685 (1967).

39. *See* United States v. Arnold, Schwinn & Co., 388 U.S. 365 (1967).

40. *See Topco*, 405 U.S. at 596.

willingly relied heavily upon non-efficiency values to establish the scope of the antitrust statutes. As the singular modern example of this trend, Bork offered the *Brown Shoe* merger opinion, which he viewed as having "considerable claim to the title" of being "the worst antitrust essay ever written."[41] In a schizophrenic passage dealing with the vertical effects of Brown Shoe's acquisition of Kinney, the Court rejected the view that antitrust doctrine should favor rules of rivalry that enhanced efficiency.[42] On one hand, the Court acknowledged that consumers might profit from the unification of Brown's shoe manufacturing operations with Kinney's retailing network. The Court observed that "[o]f course, some of the results of large integrated or chain operations are beneficial to consumers. Their expansion is not rendered unlawful by the mere fact that small independent stores may be adversely affected. It is competition, not competitors, which the [Clayton] Act protects."[43]

On the other hand, the Court dismissed the view that solicitude for the fate of individual firms should play no role—or even merely a minor role—in antitrust decisionmaking. After stating that antitrust protects "competition, not competitors,"[44] the Court concluded that "[w]e cannot fail to recognize Congress' desire to promote competition through the protection of viable, small, locally owned businesses."[45] In considering the aims that motivated enactment of the Clayton Act's antimerger provision, the Court concluded that "Congress appreciated that occasional higher costs and prices might result from the maintenance of fragmented industries and markets. It resolved these competing considerations in favor of decentralization."[46]

Although *Brown Shoe* ultimately gave primacy to non-efficiency values, the Court's opinion at least recognized that some efficiencies were at stake. The second unsettling trend underscored in *The Antitrust Paradox* was the Court's tendency during this period to completely disregard or dismiss the possibility that stringent liability rules might sacrifice valuable efficiencies. Nowhere

---

41. R. BORK, *supra* note 10, at 210. In another passage, Bork said the Supreme Court had used *Brown Shoe* to convert the Clayton Act's antimerger provision "to a virulently anticompetitive regulation." *Id.* at 198.
42. *Brown Shoe*, 370 U.S. at 344.
43. *Id.*
44. *Id.*
45. *Id.*
46. *Id.*

was this more evident than in the Court's harsh treatment of vertical contractual restrictions. As Bork documented, the Court's hostility toward vertical restraints stemmed from the mistaken conviction that such restrictions seldom, if ever, served to increase efficiency.[47] The Court's embrace of stringent liability standards for vertical contractual agreements, coupled with its then-prevailing skepticism toward vertical mergers, severely constrained manufacturers in devising strategies for distributing their goods.

While painting a bleak picture of Supreme Court antitrust jurisprudence, Bork acknowledged that the flow of ill-conceived doctrine had subsided since *Topco* in 1972.[48] Moreover, in post-*Topco* decisions such as *United States v. General Dynamics Corp.*,[49] *Continental T.V., Inc. v. GTE Sylvania, Inc.*,[50] and *United States Steel Corp. v. Fortner Enterprises, Inc.* (*Fortner II*),[51] Bork rec-

---

47. R. BORK, *supra* note 10, at 280-309, 365-81. Perhaps the most striking example of the Court's failure to account for the efficiency benefits of vertical restraints was its application of a per se ban on vertical market division agreements in United States v. Arnold, Schwinn & Co., 388 U.S. 365 (1967). "Under the Sherman Act," Justice Fortas' majority opinion explained, "it is unreasonable without more for a manufacturer to seek to restrict and confine areas or persons with whom an article may be traded after the manufacturer has parted with dominion over it. . . . Such restraints are so obviously destructive of competition that their mere existence is enough." *Id.* at 379 (citations omitted).

48. For an analysis identifying *Topco* as the endpoint of the expansive Supreme Court antitrust jurisprudence associated with the Warren Court, *see* Kovacic, *Federal Regulation of Business: Antitrust and Environmental Law*, in SIGNIFICANT BUSINESS DECISIONS OF THE SUPREME COURT, 1986-1987 TERM 57 (1988).

49. 415 U.S. 486 (1974). If *Topco* concluded the era of Warren Court populism, *General Dynamics* tentatively began a more sophisticated application of economic analysis (and a greater sensitivity to efficiency concerns) in Supreme Court antitrust cases. *See Horizontal Mergers: Law and Policy* 1986 ABA SEC. ANTITRUST REP. 12, at 41-43, 55-57. *General Dynamics* also marked the federal government's first defeat in a horizontal merger case since 1950, when Congress enacted the Celler-Kefauver Amendment to the Clayton Act. *See* Note, *Horizontal Mergers After United States v. General Dynamics Corp.*, 92 HARV. L. REV. 491, 492 (1978).

50. 433 U.S. 36 (1977). In probably the most important antitrust decision of the past twenty-five years, *Sylvania* overruled *Schwinn*'s per se prohibition upon vertical market division agreements and adopted the rule of reason as the basis for evaluating non-price vertical restraints.

51. 429 U.S. 610 (1977). In *Fortner II*, the Court retreated from the expansive liability potential inherent in the predecessor case of United States Steel Corp. v. Fortner Enters., Inc., 394 U.S. 495 (1969) by finding that the tying product lacked "uniqueness."

ognized the possibility that the Court was changing its course.[52] He noted that "[a] majority of the current Supreme Court has recently taken a significant step toward reforming a part of anti- trust, and prospects for an intelligible, proconsumer law may now be brighter than they have been for several decades."[53] Not only had the post-*Topco* Court begun to reshape liability standards in a manner Bork found encouraging, but its decisions in *Brunswick Corp. v. Pueblo Bowl-O-Mat Inc.*,[54] and *Illinois Brick Co. v. Illinois*[55] also had started to place formidable procedural obstacles in the path of private parties seeking to pursue antitrust claims.[56]

---

52. These decisions and their favorable possibilities are discussed in R. BORK, *supra* note 10, at 218, 285-88, 298, 368-70, 419. Bork regarded *Sylvania* as the sole unambiguous signal that the Court might be ready to take efficiency concerns to heart. "The tendencies described [toward perverse treatment of efficiency concerns] are not, of course, inexorable, and any assessment must at least pause to note hopeful developments." Bork concluded that:

> The *Sylvania* decision . . . is important not only because it reached a correct result by giving favorable consideration and dispositive weight to business efficiency and consumer welfare for the first time in decades. It is also a hopeful development because the majority eschewed political and social argument, and ignored the themes of dealer 'bondage' and business egalitarianism that were so prominent in the jurisprudence of preceding Courts.

Id. at 419.

53. R. BORK, *supra* note 10, at 5.

54. 429 U.S. 477 (1977).

55. 431 U.S. 720 (1977).

56. In Brunswick Corp. v. Pueblo Bowl-O-Mat, Inc., 429 U.S. 477 (1977), the Court established the requirement that private plaintiffs demonstrate "antitrust injury"to pursue treble damage actions. In Illinois Brick Co. v. Illinois, 431 U.S. 720 (1977), the Court barred treble damage recovery by indirect purchasers. *The Antitrust Paradox* did not mention *Brunswick* or *Illinois Brick* and their impli- cations for private antitrust litigation. These omissions are somewhat curious as *Brunswick* appeared in 1977 before *Fortner II* (which Bork did discuss), and *Illinois Brick* appeared soon after. *Illinois Brick* severely limited the reach of the Hart-Scott-Rodino Antitrust Improvements Act of 1976 that Bork mentioned disapprovingly. *See supra* note 24.

With regard to *Brunswick*, it is possible that Bork considered the case to be unusual and applicable to a narrow set of cases. Certainly, few observers at the time predicted the substantial breadth and importance that subsequent antitrust decisions would give *Brunswick* as a basis for denying standing to private parties. *See* Susman, *Standing in Private Antitrust Cases: Where is the Supreme Court Going?*, 52 ANTITRUST L.J. 465 (1983); *See also*, Page, *The Scope of Antitrust Violations*, 37 STAN. L. REV. 1445, 1459-60 (1985) (Discussing subsequent judicial interpretation of *Brunswick*). Nonetheless, given the path of pre-*Brunswick* an- titrust analysis, the decision was interesting for its author (Justice Marshall), its result (rejection of a private plaintiff's suit for damages), its margin (a unanimous

Indeed, with the decisions of *Sylvania*, *Fortner II*, *Brunswick*, and *Illinois Brick*, 1977 had been an exceedingly good year for those who wanted the Supreme Court to take a conservative tack in antitrust.

Bork viewed the post-*Topco* developments in the Court's thinking with an abundance of caution, despite their promise of important adjustments in antitrust doctrine. The Court's latest decisions were best interpreted as a pause "between cycles of antitrust expansion,"[57] rather than evidence of a fundamental shift in direction. Bork warned that, "[e]xtensions of old doctrine to new fields have been relatively infrequent in the last half dozen years or so, but there is scant comfort in that"[58] since "[t]he situation will not last."[59] An "accidental equilibrium" rather than "settled ideology" had accounted for the mild retreat from expansionism. Therefore, the durability of recent departures from liberal orthodoxy was doubtful.[60] Bork stated that "[u]nless the

---

court), and some of its language. On the latter point, the *Brunswick* Court said: "The antitrust laws . . . were enacted for the 'protection of *competition*, not *competitors*.'" *Brunswick*, 429 U.S. at 488 (quoting Brown Shoe Co. v. United States, 370 U.S. 320 (1962)). *Id.* at 488 (emphasis in the original). It was intriguing that the Court invoked *Brown Shoe* for the "competition, not competitors" proposition. The *Brunswick* opinion omitted a later passage in *Brown Shoe* where the Court repeated its "competition, not competitors" admonition while announcing that it would vindicate Congress' desire to protect small firms as an end in itself, despite the possible efficiency losses such an approach might entail. *See supra* notes 41-47 and accompanying text. The *Brunswick* Court implicitly read out of *Brown Shoe* the "business egalitarianism" that Bork deplored in *The Antitrust Paradox*. This was an additional piece of evidence that change was at hand.

57. R. BORK, *supra* note 10, at 4. In another passage of *The Antitrust Paradox* Bork stated: "Whether we are witnessing the birth of a countertrend in the intellectual development of the law it is far too early to say. For the moment, we must deal with the main trends as they have unfolded for most of the history of the policy." *Id.* at 419.

58. *Id.* at 4.

59. *Id.*

60. *Id.* at 4-5. Here Bork exaggerated the extent to which the more conservative equilibrium in judicial antitrust analysis was merely "accidental." For example, he overlooked the role that a 1975 article by Phillip Areeda and Donald Turner had begun to play in reformulating the lower courts' treatment of predatory pricing claims. *See* Areeda & Turner, *Predatory Pricing and Related Practices Under Section 2 of the Sherman Act*, 88 HARV. L. REV. 697 (1975). In their article, Areeda and Turner proposed a liability standard that created a conclusive presumption of legality for pricing above average variable cost. Bork was aware of their proposal and criticized it in *The Antitrust Paradox* as being excessively restrictive of business conduct and unduly prone to misapplication by

theory of antitrust is understood and the law brought more into
line with it, the law will surely move on again, becoming even
more unnecessarily restrictive of business freedom."[61] Accordingly,
a major goal of his book was to provide an ideological structure
to solidify and extend the tentative gains achieved in the recent
Supreme Court decisions.

3. The Misguided Antitrust Enforcement Agencies

Bork felt that much of the responsibility for the wayward path
of antitrust rested at the doorstep of the federal enforcement
agencies, the Department of Justice Antitrust Division (Antitrust
Division) and the Federal Trade Commission (FTC). To Bork the
government enforcement agencies' contribution to the development
of antitrust doctrine had not always been counterproductive. In
the early history of the Sherman Act, the Justice Department
"succeeded in establishing as law most of what can be regarded
as sound policy: the per se rule against price fixing and similar
naked eliminations of competition, the rule against large horizontal
mergers, and the rule against predation."[62] Thus, *The Antitrust
Paradox* gave the Justice Department good marks for its role in
prosecuting early formative cases such as *United States v. Joint
Traffic Association*[63] and *Standard Oil Co. of New Jersey v. United
States.*[64]

The government's subsequent enforcement record received a
dismal evaluation. Amid a handful of positive accomplishments,
the government agencies had spawned many "bizarre theories,"
regularly promoted "anticompetitive" extensions of the law, and
"represented the anti-free market position" in antitrust litigation.[65]

---

private plaintiffs, government enforcement bodies, and federal judges. R. BORK,
supra note 10, at 154. Bork failed to mention, however, that three existing court
of appeals decisions had invoked the Areeda-Turner rule to dispose of predatory
pricing claims. *See* Janich Bros., Inc. v. American Distilling Co., 570 F.2d 848
(9th Cir. 1977), *cert. denied*, 439 U.S. 829 (1978); Hanson v. Shell Oil Co., 541
F.2d 1352 (9th Cir. 1976), *cert. denied*, 429 U.S. 1074 (1976); International Air
Indus., Inc. v. American Excelsior Co., 517 F.2d 714 (5th Cir. 1975), *cert.
denied*, 424 U.S. 943 (1976). These cases were significant not only for their results
(defendants' victories), but also because they gave decisive effect to a comparatively permissive cost-based, economically-oriented rule in reviewing the challenged
pricing conduct.
  61. R. BORK, *supra* note 10, at 5.
  62. *Id.* at 415.
  63. 171 U.S. 505 (1898) (prohibiting horizontal price fixing).
  64. 221 U.S. 1 (1911) (dismembering the Standard Oil trust).
  65. R. BORK, *supra* note 10, at 415.

Among their specific policy failures, the agencies had spearheaded the adoption of draconian standards governing mergers,[66] vertical restraints,[67] and price discrimination.[68] Moreover, both the Antitrust Division and the FTC were said to be engaged in harmful efforts to disassemble major elements of American business enterprise.[69] Of the two agencies, the worst villain was the FTC, which had "proved less expert about economics and business realities, and more hostile to competition, than any other group connected with the operation of the antitrust system."[70]

The explanation for the government's propensity to develop bad policy resided largely in the institutional incentives that guided the agencies' choice of enforcement theories. The Antitrust Division and the FTC, Bork wrote, "are organized to advance a single principle, and it is observable throughout government, as elsewhere, that men and women in organizations whose existence and success is defined by a single principle tend to push that principle well past the point at which a more balanced judgment would conclude, not merely that the returns were diminishing, but that

---

66. *Id.* at 198-218. Bork's list of governmental blunders included: FTC v. Proctor & Gamble Co., 386 U.S. 568 (1967) (conglomerate merger); United States v. Pabst Brewing Co., 384 U.S. 546 (1966) (horizontal merger); United States v. Von's Grocery Co., 384 U.S. 270 (1966) (horizontal merger); Brown Shoe Co. v. United States, 370 U.S. 294 (1962) (merger with horizontal and vertical features).

67. R. BORK, *supra* note 10, at 280-309. Bork's disfavored government cases involving vertical restraints included United States v. Arnold, Schwinn & Co., 388 U.S. 365 (1967); FTC v. Brown Shoe Co., 384 U.S. 316 (1966).

68. R. BORK, *supra* note 10, at 382-401. Among other causes, Bork blamed the misapplication of the Robinson-Patman Act upon the FTC's "hostility" to the statute's cost justification defense. *Id.* at 391-93.

69. *Id.* at 163. As examples, Bork mentioned the Antitrust Division's monopolization cases against IBM and AT&T and the FTC's shared monopolization suits against the country's leading petroleum refiners and breakfast cereal manufacturers. *See* United States v. IBM Corp., [1961-1970 Transfer Binder] Trade Reg. Rep. (CCH) (P) 45,069 (S.D.N.Y. filed Jan. 17, 1969) (complaint charging IBM with monopolization and attempted monopolization); United States v. AT&T Co., [1970-1979 Transfer Binder] Trade Reg. Rep. (CCH) (P) 45, 074 (D.D.C. filed Nov. 20, 1974) (complaint charging AT&T with monopolization, attempted monopolization, and conspiracy to monopolize); In re Exxon Corp., 98 F.T.C. 453, 456-59 (1981) (complaint charging eight domestic petroleum refiners with agreement to monopolize and maintenance of noncompetitive market structure); In re Kellogg Co., 99 F.T.C. 8, 11-16 (1982) (complaint charging four breakfast cereal manufacturers with maintenance of highly concentrated, noncompetitive market structure and shared monopolization).

70. R. BORK, *supra* note 10, at 48. In another passage, Bork said, "[t]he Federal Trade Commission is notoriously hostile to efficiency." *Id.* at 252.

the principle itself had become deformed through the pressure required to extend it ever farther against equally valid competing principles."[71] Not satisfied with their valuable accomplishments in generating rules against horizontal price-fixing and large horizontal mergers, the agencies had sought to "continually press on to fresh territory, seeking theories that broaden the application of the law and make violations easier to establish."[72]

4. The Frailty of Business Resistance

Bork believed that a fundamental source of the enforcement agencies' success in extending the frontiers of antitrust liability emerged from a comparison between the government agencies and the chief target of their enforcement work—the business community. The Antitrust Division and the FTC brought several distinctive, powerful weapons to their antitrust struggles with private firms. These weapons included a virtually permanent institutional status, long-range perspective, careful focus upon the importance of doctrinal development, and substantial prestige in the eyes of federal judges.[73] Strengthened by these traits, the government agencies waited patiently to bring cases that would facilitate a deterministic march toward more expansive liability standards whose adoption would increase the agencies' power and importance.

Bork argued that this strategy frequently succeeded because the government's adversaries were comparatively feeble. Most businesses cared little about the long-term development of the antitrust doctrine and, consequently, expended little energy to blunt its expansionist tendencies. Moreover, the prospect of making investments whose returns would accrue largely to free-riding companies that cheered for, but would not fund, the success of the defense discouraged those who might have contested a proposed rule on broad policy grounds. The private bar shared its clients' nearsightedness. It likewise declined to devote resources to waging a protracted, broad-based policy war.[74] Bork concluded that these characteristics of private companies and their lawyers tended "to press in one direction and to deny the courts the full assistance they should obtain from counsel."[75] Because corporate defendants

---

71. *Id.* at 415.
72. *Id.*
73. *Id.* at 415-16.
74. *Id.* at 414-16.
75. *Id.* at 416.

lacked incentives to present an effective defense, Bork concluded that "[c]oncepts of extremely dubious merit or even of undoubted pernicious tendency pass into law and become conventional wisdom without ever having been subjected to the rigorous testing that informed adversary debate provides."[76]

While Bork's assessment of the balance of power between the government agencies and their business counterparts contained some persuasive points, it exaggerated the asymmetry of the contest. Bork failed to discuss several significant contemporaneous developments that foreshadowed what, in Bork's model, was emerging as an uncharacteristically potent business response to the expansionist impulses of the federal enforcement agencies, the judiciary, and Congress in the 1970s. One noteworthy trend that Bork overlooked was that the major government monopolization suits of the late 1960s and early 1970s galvanized the affected companies to mount powerful, broad-based defenses. No litigation demonstrated this more clearly than IBM's response to the monopolization suit filed by the Antitrust Division in 1969, on the final day of the Johnson Administration.[77] The government's suit accused IBM of using a collection of unlawful pricing, product development, and marketing strategies to monopolize the digital computer industry.[78] The Antitrust Division proposed to redress IBM's monopoly by breaking the company up into four or more computer companies.[79] This suit, in turn, inspired a host of computer companies to file private antitrust claims against IBM.[80] According to one estimate, by 1976, IBM faced a potential liability of $4 billion in private treble damage suits alone.[81]

IBM did not take these developments lying down. With its financial well-being and very existence at stake, IBM unleashed a

---

76. Id.
77. United States v. IBM Corp., [1961-1970 Transfer Binder] Trade Reg. Rep. (CCH) (P) 45,069 (S.D.N.Y. Jan. 17, 1969).
78. See F. FISHER, J. McGOWAN & J. GREENWOOD, FOLDED, SPINDLED, AND MUTILATED—ECONOMIC ANALYSIS AND U.S. v. IBM 353-68 (1983) (reprinting the Justice Department's original complaint and amended complaint against IBM).
79. See id.
80. See, e.g., Symbolic Control, Inc. v. IBM Corp., 643 F.2d 1339 (9th Cir. 1980) (challenging IBM's pricing and product promotion conduct); California Computer Prods., Inc. v. IBM Corp., 613 F.2d 727 (9th Cir. 1979) (challenging IBM's product development and pricing conduct); Greyhound Computer Corp. v. IBM Corp., 559 F.2d 488 (9th Cir. 1977) (challenging IBM's pricing conduct), cert. denied, 434 U.S. 1040 (1978).
81. See J. GOULDEN, THE MILLION DOLLAR LAWYERS 191 (1978).

withering, sophisticated attack upon the legal and economic propositions its adversaries were seeking to sustain.[82] By the mid-1970s, it was apparent that the government's case was in serious trouble.[83] Among other difficulties, the inexorable forward motion and institutional stability that *The Antitrust Paradox* had identified as major advantages of the government enforcement agencies were nowhere to be seen in the Antitrust Division's handling of the case. Instead, IBM's teams of experienced, highly skilled lawyers and economists had gained the advantage against a prosecution team beset by disorganization and whirlwind turnover in personnel. In 1982, after the case had "spanned the terms of five Presidents, nine Attorney Generals, and seven Assistant Attorney Generals,"[84] the government relented and dropped the case.[85] Moreover, despite some initial setbacks early in the 1970s, the IBM litigation juggernaut ultimately crushed most of the company's private adversaries.[86]

Other companies facing government monopolization cases copied IBM's strategy and mounted effective defenses of their own. In monopolization suits in which the government sought sweeping structural relief, the country's leading breakfast cereal manufacturers and petroleum refiners routed the FTC.[87] Industry also

---

82. IBM's litigation stategy is recounted in J. STEWART, THE PARTNERS 53-113 (1983). The company's efforts to challenge the economic analysis underpinning the Antitrust Division's case are described by IBM's principal outside economic experts in F. FISHER, J. MCGOWAN & J. GREENWOOD, *supra* note 78.

83. Donald Baker, who headed the Antitrust Division from 1976 to 1977, wrote that "[b]y even the mid-1970s, it was clear that the [IBM] case was a relic." Baker, *Government Enforcement of Section Two*, 61 NOTRE DAME L. REV. 898, 910 (1986). Baker quotes Bork as calling the IBM case "the Antitrust Division's Vietnam." *Id.* at 899 n.13.

84. *Id.* at 899 n.13.

85. *See In re IBM Corp.*, 687 F.2d 591, 593 (2d Cir. 1982) (affirming dismissal of IBM case). By the time the government moved to dismiss its suit against IBM, the trial had consumed 700 calendar days, the transcript exceeded 104,000 pages, and the parties had introduced approximately 17,000 exhibits. *See Post-Mortem on IBM Case Provides Forum for Conflicting Perspectives*, 42 ANTITRUST & TRADE REG. REP. (BNA) 310-11 (1982).

86. *See, e.g.*, Transamerica Computer Co. v. IBM Corp., 698 F.2d 1377 (9th Cir. 1983), *cert. denied*, 464 U.S. 955 (1983) (affirming judgment for IBM); Memorex Corp. v. IBM Corp., 636 F.2d 1188 (9th Cir. 1980), *cert. denied*, 452 U.S. 972 (1981) (affirming grant of directed verdict for IBM); California Computer Prods., Inc. v. IBM Corp., 613 F.2d 727 (9th Cir. 1979) (affirming grant of directed verdict for IBM); Telex Corp. v. IBM Corp., 510 F.2d 894 (10th Cir. 1975), *cert. denied*, 423 U.S. 802 (1975) (reversing judgment for plaintiff).

87. *See In re Kellogg Co.*, 99 F.T.C. 8 (1982) (dismissing shared monop-

prevailed over the government in monopolization and attempted monopolization cases against major producers of chemicals,[88] replacement tires,[89] coffee,[90] and bread.[91] Although the government prevailed in monopolization cases against AT&T[92] and Xerox,[93] the regularity with which private firms defeated the Antitrust Division and FTC in deconcentration suits filed during the late 1960s and 1970s discredited the notion that highly focused, aggressive public enforcement agencies invariably would prevail against large, but quiescent business adversaries.[94]

In addition to a robust litigation counterattack, many companies targeted by congressional deconcentration proposals during the 1970s began substantial efforts to contest the intellectual foundations of deconcentration and vigorously campaigned for fuller inclusion of efficiency considerations in policy formation concern-

---

olization complaint); In re Exxon Corp., 98 F.T.C. 453 (1981) (dismissing shared monopolization complaint). The *Exxon* litigation best illustrates the magnitude of the defendants' success in opposing FTC monopolization initiatives begun in the 1970s. At the time of its dismissal in 1981, the *Exxon* case had consumed eight years in discovery and other pretrial proceedings, and it was clear that the beginning of the trial was nowhere in sight. See *Exxon*, 98 F.T.C. at 460 (Commission dismissal order stating that "both complaint counsel and respondents agree that completion of discovery is at least several years away."). By one estimate, the *Exxon* respondents and the FTC spent a total of nearly $100 million on the litigation before the case was dismissed. Porter, "The Federal Trade Commission v. The Oil Industry: An Autopsy on the Commission's Shared Monopoly Case Against the Nation's Eight Largest Oil Companies," 27 ANTITRUST BULL. 753, 756 (1982).

88. *See* In re E.I. DuPont de Nemours & Co., 96 F.T.C. 653, 751 (1980) (dismissing attempted monopolization complaint).

89. *See* United States v. Goodyear Tire & Rubber Co. and United States v. Firestone Tire & Rubber Co., [1970-1979 Transfer Binder] Trade Reg. Rep. (CCH) (P) 45,073, at 53,539 (N.D. Ohio Mar. 2, 1976) (dismissing complaints alleging attempted monopolization).

90. *See* In re General Foods Corp., 103 F.T.C. 204, 364-68 (1984) (dismissing attempted monopolization complaint).

91. *See* In re ITT Corp., 104 F.T.C. 280, 451 (1984) (dismissing attempted monopolization complaint).

92. *See* United States v. AT&T Corp., [1970-1979 Transfer Binder] Trade Reg. Rep. (CCH) (P) 45,074 at 53,589-3 (D.D.C. Nov. 20, 1974) (complaint alleging monopolization, attempted monopolization, and conspiracy to monopolize), *consent decree entered*, 552 F. Supp. 131, 178-79, 225 (D.D.C. 1982), *aff'd sub nom. Maryland v. United States*, 460 U.S. 1001 (1983).

93. *See* In re Xerox Corp., 86 F.T.C. 364, 367-68 (1975) (consent agreement settling suit charging monopolization and attempted monopolization).

94. *See* Kovacic, *supra* note 2, at 1106-09, 1119-20 (discussing limited success of government deconcentration suits from 1969-1982).

ing concentrated industries. Individual corporations and trade associations funded academic seminars and research projects to
reexamine the economic bases for assaults upon corporate size.[95]
The business community also assumed an active role in shaping
the judiciary's analysis of antitrust issues. Business organizations
frequently filed amicus briefs in important antitrust matters coming
before the Supreme Court.[96] Firms also supported new programs
designed to instruct federal judges in the rudiments of microeconomic theory relevant to antitrust policy.[97]

---

95. Two examples illustrate the importance of this development. First,
corporate donors provided most of the funding for the Columbia Law School
Conference on Industrial Concentration held at Airlie House on March 1-2, 1974.
The "Airlie House" conference brought together a broad spectrum of practitioners, government officials, and academics to hear and debate papers concerning
market concentration and proposals to restructure major segments of American
industry. The conference featured presentations by Yale Brozen, Harold Demsetz,
John McGee, Richard Posner, and Fred Weston, all of whom attacked the
existing structuralist orthodoxy. The "New Learning" of the Chicago School
questioned the logical bases of the structuralist assumptions upon which deconcentration proposals rested. The conference papers and proceedings were published
in a popular volume, the title of which demonstrated the shift in focus away
from the structuralists and toward the Chicago School. *See* INDUSTRIAL CONCEN-
TRATION: THE NEW LEARNING (H. GOLDSCHMID, H. MANN & J. WESTON eds.
1974). More than any other event in the 1970s, the Airlie House Conference
turned the intellectual tide against deconcentration.
    Second, attempts to restructure the petroleum industry, either through vertical
divestiture or through prohibitions upon oil company ownership of competing
energy sources, were actively opposed by corporations and trade associations.
Acting individually or through trade associations, such as the American Petroleum
Institute, firms targeted for divestiture funded research by academics who, in
testimony and in scholarly publications, attacked the reasoning behind the energy
industry deconcentration proposals. *See, e.g., The Petroleum Industry: Hearings
on S. 2387 and Related Bills Before the Subcomm. on Antitrust and Monopoly
of the Senate Comm. on the Judiciary*, 94th Cong., 1st Sess., pt. 3, at 1849,
1891 (1976) (testimony, respectively, of Edward Mitchell and Richard Mancke).
By the end of the decade, industry funding had generated a substantial body of
literature opposing divestiture of the country's leading energy firms.
    96. For example, the Motor Vehicle Manufacturers Association filed an
amicus brief authored by Donald Turner when the *Sylvania* case was on appeal
to the Supreme Court. *Sylvania*, 433 U.S. at 37 & *. The Association's brief
made a strong case for the abandonment of *Schwinn*'s rule of per se illegality
for vertical market divisions. In important respects, Justice Powell's majority
opinion in *Sylvania* adopted arguments the Association had advanced.
    97. In 1976, for example, Henry Manne's Law and Economics Center held
its first economics institute for federal judges. A substantial part of the funding
for the institute came from corporate donors. By 1980, nearly 15% of the federal
judiciary had participated in the annual program. *See* Barbash, *Big Corporations*

The major corporations reactions to government deconcentration initiatives was apparent when *The Antitrust Paradox* was published in 1978. In attempting to describe the balance of power between the public and private sectors in 1978, Bork overestimated both the institutional weaknesses of the business community and the private bar and the institutional strengths of the antitrust enforcement agencies. Target corporations took careful measure of the cascade of legislative proposals and lawsuits that sought in the late 1960s and early 1970s to restructure substantial sectors of the American economy. It was one thing for executives to accommodate themselves (as they had) to annoying, efficiency-reducing limits on mergers and the choice of distribution strategies. It was entirely another matter to shrug-off challenges to the continued existence of their companies. Businesses perceived the deconcentration orientation of antitrust as a grave threat to their survival. By 1978, major corporations had joined the battle with a vengeance.

5. An Intervention-Minded Intellectual Community

A final, possible explanation for antitrust's tendency toward manifest destiny was what Bork described as an "intellectual class" motivated by an "apparent affinity . . . for expansions of the public sector at the expense of the private sector."[98] At the core of this group were academics, whose work had supplied the intellectual structure for important elements of what Bork regarded as destructive antitrust policy. If the preferences of academics and other intellectuals including "journalists, lawyers, government officials, and others whose jobs center on ideas and words" could not be reshaped, their work would continue to generate public acceptance for antitrust policies which entail ever more intrusive

---

Bankroll Seminars For U.S. Judges, Washington Post, Jan. 20, 1980, at A1; *See also* Guzzardi, Jr., *Judges Discover the World of Economics,* FORTUNE, May 21, 1979, at 58. Critics of the economics seminars have argued that corporate sponsors are engaged in a transparent effort to imbue participating judges with pro-defendant biases. *See* Mueller, *The Anti-Antitrust Movement and the Case of Lester Thurow,* 13 ANTITRUST L. & ECON. REV., No. 3, at 59, 71 (1981); *cf.* Scherer, *Making the Rule of Reason Analysis More Manageable,* 56 ANTITRUST L.J. 229, 231 (1987) (observing that the Manne seminars "have done a rather good job" of "bringing judges up to a level of economic understanding at which they can handle cases," but noting that "the economics [that the seminars] present has been quite limited and one-sided ideologically.").

98. R. BORK, *supra* note 10, at 424.

government intervention in the affairs of business.[99] Thus, to win the contest for the future of antitrust, it would first be necessary to prevail in the battle of ideas.

Bork recognized that some reorientation of academic thinking was already underway. He stated: "[r]ecently there have been signs of a new stirring in the intellectual community, a new distrust of statist solutions, a new willingness to reconsider old economic policies and pieties."[100] At an earlier time, the policy views of *The Antitrust Paradox* might have been deemed "merely idiosyncratic," but in 1978 "its position might be agreed to, at least in its general outlines, by a not altogether insignificant number—albeit a minority—of economists and academic lawyers."[101] The purpose of Bork's book was to build a majority.

6. Summary

The preface to *The Antitrust Paradox* mentioned that a collection of personal and professional circumstances had delayed the completion of the book well beyond the author's original timetable. After writing a first draft in 1969, Bork twice set the manuscript aside for extended periods before finishing it in 1977, while a resident scholar at the American Enterprise Institute.[102] In important respects, the antitrust environment Bork described in *The Antitrust Paradox* fit 1969 more closely than it did 1978. The stark portrayals of a deconcentration-minded Congress, an economically backward Supreme Court, unconstrained government enforcement agencies, and a lethargic, overmatched business community would have been more convincing had the book appeared five years earlier. Measured against Bork's ideal vision of antitrust policy, the world was less dismal, and its outlook less discouraging, than *The Antitrust Paradox* indicated.[103] For this reason, the book was not as revolutionary in 1978 as it might have been if earlier publication had been achieved.

This assessment does not materially detract from the influence of Bork's work. As Bork pointed out, the less expansive equilib-

99. *Id.* at 424-25.
100. *Id.* at 425.
101. *Id.*
102. *Id.* at ix-x; *see also Paradox Revisited: Interview with Judge Robert H. Bork*, 3 ANTITRUST 16 (Summer 1989) (recounting circumstances that delayed completion of *The Antitrust Paradox*).
103. It is possible that Bork portrayed the antitrust world in unduly pessimistic terms simply to make the content of his argument clear and to highlight his policy recommendations.

rium of antitrust in 1978 was unstable, and its duration was unpredictable.[104] Bork correctly questioned whether recent steps toward moderation would easily be reversed by an immediate reinvigoration of the antitrust jurisprudence of the Warren Court.[105] Against this uncertain backdrop, the purpose of *The Antitrust Paradox* was to see that the pendulum continued its tentative movement to the right and that its future equilibrium was both conservative and lasting.

B. Content: Policy Prescriptions

The Antitrust Paradox proposed a major reorientation of antitrust policy. The book made its case for reform in essentially two parts. The first focused on the appropriate goals of antitrust enforcement. The second derived specific, recommended enforcement approaches. The interrelated issues of goals and means are treated separately below.

1. Efficiency as the Exclusive Goal of Antitrust

"Antitrust policy cannot be made rational until we are able to give a firm answer to one question: What is the point of the law— what are its goals?"[106] So began the introduction to the foundation for Bork's substantive prescriptions for antitrust policy. "Everything else follows from the answer we give,"[107] he continued. "Is the antitrust judge to be guided by one value or by several? If by several, how is he to decide cases where a conflict in values arises? Only when the issue of goals has been settled is it possible to frame a coherent body of substantive rules."[108]

In Bork's view, a fatal misstep of antitrust jurisprudence was the tendency of courts to answer this fundamental inquiry by giving decisive effect to a "cornucopia of social values" that judges mistakenly had attributed to Congress in passing the antitrust statutes.[109] Bork argued that the sole appropriate basis for antitrust enforcement is the enhancement of "consumer wel-

---

104. R. BORK, *supra* note 10, at 419.
105. It was not unreasonable to suggest that *Continental T.V., Inc. v. GTE Sylvania, Inc.*, 433 U.S. 36 (1977), might prove merely to be an outlier from an assembly line designed mainly to produce *Brown Shoe v. United States*, 370 U.S. 294 (1962).
106. R. BORK, *supra* note 10, at 50.
107. *Id.*
108. *Id.*
109. *Id.*

fare."[110] Bork argued that the legislature's "consumer welfare" mandate could only be interpreted as a command to create rules that promoted economic efficiency.[111] Thus, in Bork's view, all other suggested goals, such as achieving a politically attractive distribution of economic power, ensuring the survival of small businesses, or preventing the transfer of consumer surplus from consumers to producers, must be ignored.[112]

The basis for Bork's call for an unbending efficiency orientation was twofold. First, his reading of the legislative histories of the Sherman, Clayton, and Federal Trade Commission Acts convinced him that Congress had sought to achieve no other goals in these statutes because of their overriding concern with consumer welfare.[113] Bork acknowledged that the legislative debates contained occasional mention of various political and social aims, but he dismissed these expressions as idiosyncratic and inapplicable to Congress as a whole.[114] Bork's treatment of wealth transfer effects was characteristic of his assessment of the role played by non-efficiency concerns. He recognized that the appropriate scope of antitrust liability rules would change if one attached antitrust significance to distortions in the distribution of wealth that arise

---

110. *Id.* at 66. "The legislative histories of the antitrust statutes . . . do not support any claim that Congress intended the courts to sacrifice consumer welfare to any other goal. The Sherman Act was clearly presented and debated as a consumer welfare prescription." *Id. See also* Bork, ECONOMICS AND ANTITRUST: RESPONSE, 3 CONTEMP. POL'Y ISSUES 35, 37 (Winter 1984-85):

In the legislative history of the Sherman Act, there is much concern for consumers and for small business. However, there is not one word suggesting that the interests of small producers or any other value is to be preferred to consumer welfare. . . . Other antitrust enactments have different histories, and all sorts of fears and social values can be found in the debates. But never once, so far as I know, did any congressman suggest that the purpose of the laws was not to protect consumers or that the consumer interest was over to be sacrificed to other values.

111. R. BORK, *supra* note 10, at 91. Bork stated that "[t]he whole task of antitrust can be summed up as the effort to improve allocative efficiency without impairing productive efficiency so greatly as to produce either no gain or a net loss in consumer welfare." *Id.*

112. *Id.* at 56-66.

113. *Id.* at 66.

114. In an earlier article from which some material for *The Antitrust Paradox* was drawn, Bork wrote that there was "not a scintilla of support" in the legislative history of the Sherman Act for "broad social, political and ethical mandates." Bork, *Legislative Intent and the Policy of the Sherman Act*, 9 J. L. & ECON. 7, 10 (1966).

from monopoly overcharges.[115] Nonetheless, from his reading of the legislative histories, Bork stated that "it seems clear [that] the income distribution effects of economic activity should be completely excluded from the determination of the antitrust legality of the activity."[116]

Second, Bork argued that anything other than a single-minded focus upon efficiency would prove unadministrable in the routine decision of cases.[117] Since the critical provisions of the antitrust statutes are comparatively broad, allowing individual federal judges to interpret terms such as "competition" or "restraint of trade" by reference to vaguely defined political and social values would result in a chaotic scheme of antitrust standards. Each judge's effort to determine what the political and social values mean in an individual case would be impressionistic, and courts would have no guidance for balancing gains in political or social decentralization against losses in efficiency.[118] Ultimately, Bork concluded that giving effect to non-efficiency values would enmesh the courts in a constitutionally suspect effort to perform fundamentally legislative policy-making functions.[119]

2. An Efficiency-Oriented Antitrust Policy

Bork argued that the search for sensible antitrust rules began and ended with economic learning and the insights it afforded

---

115. R. BORK, *supra* note 10, at 110. Bork explained: "Those who continue to buy after a monopoly is formed pay more for the same output, and that shifts income from them to the monopoly and its owners, who are also consumers. This is not dead-weight loss due to restriction of output but merely a shift in income between two classes of consumers. The consumer welfare model, which views consumers as a collectivity, does not take this income effect into account. If it did, the results of trade-off calculations would be significantly altered." *Id.*

116. *Id.* at 111. Bork added that "[i]t may be sufficient to note that the shift in income distribution does not lessen total wealth, and a decision about it requires a choice between two groups of consumers that should be made by the legislature rather than by the judiciary." *Id.* As this passage shows, Bork was convinced that Congress had made no such choice in passing the existing antitrust statutes.

117. *Id.* at 72-89, 107-115.

118. *Id.* at 79-80; *see also id.* at 20 ("The [Sherman Act] was intended to strike at cartels, horizontal mergers of monopolistic proportions, and predatory business tactics. Wide discretion was delegated to the courts to frame subsidiary rules, but it was also clear . . . that the delegation was confined by the policy of advancing consumer welfare.").

119. *Id.* at 72-79, 82-84, 88-89. Bork elaborated and sharpened the constitutional element of his administrability argument in later presentations. *See* Bork, *The Role of the Courts in Applying Economics*, 54 ANTITRUST L.J. 21, 24 (1985); Bork, *supra* note 110, at 37-38.

about efficiency. "There is no body of knowledge other than conventional price theory that can serve as a guide to the effects of business behavior upon consumer welfare,"[120] Bork stated. "To abandon economic theory is to abandon the possibility of a rational antitrust law."[121] An antitrust policy faithful to efficiency concerns would adhere to four basic guidelines.[122]

First, antitrust doctrine should ban "[t]he suppression of competition by horizontal agreement, such as the nonancillary agreements of rivals or potential rivals to fix prices or divide markets."[123] Bork applauded the longstanding per se rule against classic cartel behavior such as price fixing and market division, stating that "[i]ts contributions to consumer welfare over the decades have been enormous."[124] As an important corollary to this precept, however, Bork asserted that antitrust law should "permit agreements on prices, territories, refusals to deal, and other suppressions of rivalry that are ancillary . . . to an integration of productive economic activity."[125]

Second, merger enforcement policy should be limited to the prohibition of "[h]orizontal mergers creating very large market shares (those that leave fewer than three significant rivals in any market)."[126] Setting the enforcement thresholds at these levels, Bork argued, would permit firms to capture virtually all efficiencies to be gained by merger and would obviate the need for the case-by-case application of an efficiencies defense to rebut inferences drawn from concentration data alone.[127] In addition, Bork proposed that antitrust policy embrace a rule of per se legality for all other transactions, including vertical and conglomerate mergers.[128]

Third, doctrines designed to control exclusionary conduct should focus solely upon "[d]eliberate predation engaged in to drive rivals from a market, prevent or delay the entry of rivals, or discipline

---

120. R. BORK, *supra* note 10, at 117.
121. *Id.*
122. *Id.* at 405-07.
123. *Id.* at 406; *see also id.* at 263-68.
124. *Id.* at 263.
125. *Id.* at 406.
126. *Id.*
127. *Id.* at 124-29.
128. *Id.* at 406. Bork stated that "[i]t seems quite clear that antitrust should never interfere with any conglomerate merger." *Id.* at 248. His conclusion about vertical transactions was only slightly less sweeping. "[I]n the absence of a most unlikely proved predatory power and purpose, antitrust should never object to the verticality of any merger." *Id.* at 245.

existing rivals."[129] In particular, additional attention should be paid to the misuse of the government and quasi-governmental institutions to exclude or discipline rivals.[130] At the same time, antitrust should abandon its concern with numerous types of single-firm behavior, including predatory price cutting and price discrimination.[131]

Fourth, a standard of per se legality should be applied to vertical contractual restraints: tying arrangements, resale price maintenance, vertical market division, exclusive dealing, and requirements contracts.[132] Coupled with his proposal for a hands-off approach to vertical mergers, Bork's recommendation for vertical contractual restrictions would remove vertical problems from the scope of antitrust analysis.

In applying the general guidlines outlined above, Bork urged that courts and enforcement agencies follow a policy of "nonintervention" in instances in which "chances seem roughly equal that the activity is beneficial or harmful."[133] Bork offered the following rationales for withholding intervention in ambiguous cases:

> First, antitrust enforcement is a very costly procedure, and it makes no economic sense to spend resources to do as much harm as good. There is then a net economic loss. Second, private restriction of output may be less harmful to consumers than mistaken rules of law that inhibit efficiency. Efficiency that may not be gained in one way may be blocked because other ways are too expensive, but a market position that creates output restriction and higher prices will always be eroded if it is not based upon superior efficiency. Finally, when no affirmative case for intervention is shown, the general preference for freedom should bar legal coercion.[134]

Thus, Bork concluded, antitrust should attack only demonstrably harmful episodes of business conduct. A presumption favoring

---

129. *Id.* at 406; *see also id.* at 136-60.
130. *Id.* at 347-64, 406-07.
131. *Id.* at 149-59, 382-401, 406. In particular, Bork stated that "[t]he attempt to counter the supposed threat to competition posed by price discrimination constitutes what is surely antitrust's least glorious hour." *Id.* at 382.
132. *Id.* at 406. *See also id.* at 280-309, 365-81.
133. R. BORK, *supra* note 10, at 133.
134. *Id.*

forbearance should apply to behavior presenting a balance of anticompetitive and procompetitive traits.

The adoption of a public enforcement program consistent with the foregoing guidelines would entail a major reallocation of the government's antitrust resources. Specifically, Bork suggested that the Antitrust Division increase the proportion of its enforcement resources flowing to the detection and prosecution of horizontal price-fixing.[135] Bork also recommended that the government reform antitrust policy by means other than filing lawsuits.[136] The enforcement agencies should take a more active role in appearing before other antitrust policymaking institutions—courts, legislatures, and regulatory agencies—"to extend the competitive ethic as broadly as possible."[137]

III. INFLUENCE UPON DOCTRINE AND ENFORCEMENT POLICY

Following its publication, *The Antitrust Paradox* quickly became, and remains today, a prominent reference point for judicial discourse and government policymaking.[138] This section assesses how Bork's analysis has influenced antitrust doctrine and government enforcement policy over the past ten years. As a framework for treating relevant adjustments in doctrine and policy since 1978, the discussion below uses Bork's antitrust agenda. Before beginning this review, a major qualification is in order. In discussing the "influence" of *The Antitrust Paradox*, I do not intend to minimize the importance of other factors that have shaped the developments treated below. Two examples illustrate the caution necessary in evaluating the impact of *The Antitrust Paradox* or any other scholarly work in this period.

---

135. "Price-fixing cases deliver more consumer welfare for the enforcement dollar than any other kind of prosecution," Bork stated. *Id.* at 406. Bork attached great significance to improving the Antitrust Division's network of field offices. "Experience with antitrust suggests that there is far more price fixing in the economy than the enforcement authorities detect," he wrote. "The major reason for the poor detection record is the paucity of Antitrust Division field offices." Bork proposed that the Antitrust Division create more field offices "by dispersing the personnel now concentrated in Washington." *Id.*

136. *Id.* at 406-07.

137. *Id.* at 407.

138. For example, a recent LEXIS search revealed that 107 federal court opinions and 11 FTC opinions have cited *The Antitrust Paradox*. Within the federal judiciary, the book has been cited in ten Supreme Court cases, sixty-three court of appeals cases, and thirty-four district court cases.

The publication of *The Antitrust Paradox* coincided with economic changes that created witnin the United States a political environment hostile to some antitrust policies of the post-World War II era.[139] The late 1970s featured the commencement of a serious national debate about the competitiveness of American industry. In particular, the success of Japanese and European companies in capturing market share from American companies had raised concerns that the United States was on the verge of losing its position as the world's foremost source of innovation and technological progress.[140] The ascent of America's foreign economic rivals unquestionably affected the institutions responsible for antitrust policy. The "dominant firms" whose "predatory" conduct once elicited calls for divestiture had either lost their market leadership or were now seen as valuable sources of innovation. Consideration of deconcentration legislation soon ceased, and Congress instead encouraged horizontal competitors to pool their research and development work to achieve scale economies.[141]

By the end of the 1970s, technologically progressive firms, such as Kodak, IBM, and Xerox, had defeated a number of private monopolization challenges to their product development activities.[142] Judges in these cases ceased mentioning the social benefits

139. The importance of the political climate as a determinant of antitrust policy is discussed in Baker & Blumenthal, *Ideological Cycles and Unstable Antitrust Rules*, 31 ANTITRUST BULL. 323, 337-38 (1986); Gellhorn, *Climbing the Antitrust Staircase*, 31 ANTITRUST BULL. 341, 347-48 (1986); Kaplow, *Antitrust, Law & Economics and the Courts*, 50 LAW & CONTEMP. PROBS. 181, 182 (1987); Kovacic, *supra* note 2, at 1123-28.

140. *See, e.g.*, U. S. DEP'T OF COMMERCE, FINAL REPORT OF THE ADVISORY COMMITTEE ON INDUSTRIAL INNOVATION (1979).

141. For example, in the National Cooperative Research and Development Act of 1984, Congress provided that certain research and development joint ventures are to be evaluated under the rule of reason and the corporations may be held liable for actual damages, rather than treble damages, for antitrust violations. 15 U.S.C. §§ 4302-03 (1986). For a discussion of the 1984 statute's background and requirements, see Foster, Curtner & Dell, *The National Cooperative Research Act of 1984 as a Shield from the Antitrust Laws*, 5 J. L. & COM. 347 (1985); Wright, *The National Cooperative Research Act of 1984: A New Antitrust Regime for Joint Research and Development Ventures*, 1 HIGH TECH. L.J. 133 (1986).

142. *See, e.g.*, Berkey Photo, Inc. v. Eastman Kodak Co., 603 F.2d 263 (2d Cir. 1979), *cert. denied*, 444 U.S. 1093 (1980); California Computer Prods., Inc. v. IBM Corp., 613 F.2d 727 (9th Cir. 1979); ILC Peripherals Leasing Corp. v. IBM Corp., 458 F. Supp. 423 (N.D. Cal. 1978), *aff'd sub nom.* Memorex Corp. v. IBM Corp., 636 F.2d 1188 (9th Cir. 1980) (per curiam), *cert. denied*, 452 U.S. 972 (1981); In re IBM Peripheral EDP Devices Antitrust Litigation, 481 F. Supp.

of curbing dominant firm discretion and instead expressed concern about adopting liability rules that might reduce incentives to innovate.[143] In 1962, *Brown Shoe* gave primacy to non-efficiency goals when American firms were preeminent and faced few threats from abroad. By 1980, it was far more difficult for courts to discount efficiency and vindicate social aims as American companies struggled to stay abreast of their potent foreign counterparts.

A second complication in attributing policy changes to *The Antitrust Paradox* arises from the existence of important contemporaneous works that advocated similar doctrinal adjustments. In the middle to late-1970s, a number of eminent commentators recommended, as Bork did in *The Antitrust Paradox*, that courts give dominant firms substantially greater discretion in their choice of pricing strategies.[144] Among the advocates of a more permissive pricing standard were Phillip Areeda and Donald Turner, who, in 1975, proposed an average variable cost pricing test.[145] They suggested a more restrictive rule than Bork's standard of per se legality for all single firm pricing decisions. Nonetheless, the Areeda-Turner proposal made courts and enforcement agencies far more skeptical of predatory pricing allegations.[146] Similarly, Oliver Williamson's writings in the 1970s prescribed, as did Bork, a far more permissive approach toward vertical contractual restraints and contributed a significant analytical basis for enforcement policy changes in the 1980s.[147]

Thus, it is important to keep in mind that Bork did not write in a vacuum. The rightward shift of antitrust policy during the past fifteen years stemmed from a variety of economic, political, social, and intellectual forces. Nevertheless, *The Antitrust Paradox* played a singularly influential role in transforming antitrust doc-

---

965 (N.D. Cal. 1979), *aff'd*, 698 F.2d 1377 (9th Cir. 1983), *cert. denied*, 464 U.S. 955 (1983); SCM Corp. v. Xerox Corp., 463 F. Supp. 983 (D. Conn. 1978), *aff'd*, 645 F.2d 1195 (2d Cir. 1981), *cert. denied*, 455 U.S. 1016 (1982).

143. *See* Hurwitz & Kovacic, *Judicial Analysis of Predation: The Emerging Trends*, 35 VAND. L. REV. 63, 113-28 (1982).

144. These proposals are discussed in Hay, *A Confused Lawyer's Guide to the Predatory Pricing Literature*, in STRATEGY, PREDATION, AND ANTITRUST ANALYSIS 155 (S. Salop ed. 1981); Hurwitz & Kovacic, *supra* note 143, at 66-83.

145. *See* Areeda & Turner, *supra* note 60.

146. *See* Hurwitz & Kovacic, *supra* note 143, at 139-50; Liebeler, *Whither Predatory Pricing? From Areeda and Turner to Matsushita*, 61 NOTRE DAME L. REV. 1052 (1986).

147. *See, e.g.,* O. WILLIAMSON, MARKETS AND HIERARCHIES: ANALYSIS AND ANTITRUST IMPLICATIONS 82-131 (1975).

trine and policy. Although he was not the sole cause of change, Bork gave major impetus to the redirection of antitrust doctrine and policy. By providing a compelling intellectual vision and a specific agenda for change, Bork channelled existing political and economic currents toward an assault upon many foundations of the post-World War II antitrust orthodoxy. The major contributions of his book are discussed below.

A. *The Goals of Antitrust*

Since Ronald Reagan's election in 1980, the federal enforcement agencies have largely embraced Bork's vision of antitrust policy. Reagan appointees to the Antitrust Division and the FTC routinely emphasized that the enhancement of productive and allocative efficiency would be the antitrust agencies' exclusive aim, although recent statements by Bush Administration officials have suggested a concern for wealth transfer effects.[148] These attitudes created a substantial redirection of federal enforcement policy

---

148. Reagan antitrust officials repeatedly embraced a single minded efficiency orientation. For example, in 1987, Charles F. Rule, the Assistant Attorney General for Antitrust, explained the Reagan Justice Department's views in terms that evoke Bork's work. Speaking at an antitrust conference, Rule said "'[c]onsumer welfare' is the guiding principle of this Administration's antitrust enforcement policy." Rule explained that "[a]n interpretation of the antitrust laws that is not founded on the objective criterion of consumer welfare embodied in the statutory language, but that calls for government intervention in the market to achieve ill-defined subjective 'values,' is a prescription for tyranny. It is nothing more than central planning by lawyers." Rule's presentation also echoed Bork's argument in *The Antitrust Paradox* concerning the constitutional implications of doctrines that give effect to social and political concerns. "Nowhere in the language of the antitrust laws," Rule said, "is there a mandate to keep businesses small or industries atomistic, to redistribute wealth to select classes of citizens, or to achieve any other identifiable social or political goals. . . . Advocating an enforcement agenda based on vague populist concerns and which yields results that reduce consumer welfare is fundamentally at odds with the principle of separation of powers." C. Rule, "Antitrust, Consumers and Small Business" 3, 8-9 (Nov. 13, 1987) (speech before the 21st New England Antitrust Conference); *see also* Rule & Meyer, *An Antitrust Enforcement Policy to Maximize the Economic Wealth of All Consumers*, 33 ANTITRUST BULL. 677 (1988). For similar views from Reagan antitrust officials, *see* Oliver, *The Role of the Federal Trade Commission in Formulating and Implementing Competition Policy*, 34 FED. B. NEWS & J. 200 (June 1987); Calvani, *Consumer Welfare Is Prime Objective of Antitrust*, Legal Times 14 (Dec. 24-31, 1984); Taylor, *A Talk With Antitrust Chief William Baxter*, Wall St. J., Mar. 4, 1982, at 28, col. 3 (quoting Assistant Attorney General Baxter: "The sole goal of antitrust is economic efficiency").

THE WAYNE LAW REVIEW [Vol. 36:1413

during the Reagan administration.[149] Since 1981 the Antitrust Division and FTC have channelled their enforcement resources almost entirely toward prohibiting horizontal contractual restraints and large horizontal mergers and to acting as competition advocates before other government bodies.[150]

Within the federal courts, *The Antitrust Paradox* has triggered a renewed debate about the goals of antitrust and the appropriate bases for establishing standards of business conduct.[151] At first

---

149. This redirection is described in Langenfeld & Walton, *Regulatory Reform Under Reagan—The Right Way and the Wrong Way*, in REGULATION AND THE REAGAN ERA: POLITICS, BUREAUCRACY, AND THE PUBLIC INTEREST 41 (B. Yandle & R. Meiners eds. 1989); Kovacic, *Federal Antitrust Enforcement in the Reagan Administration: Two Cheers for the Disappearance of the Large Firm Defendant in Nonmerger Cases*, 12 RES. IN L. & ECON. 173 (1989) [hereinafter *Federal Antitrust Enforcement*]; Kovacic, *Built to Last? The Antitrust Legacy of the Reagan Administration*, 35 FED. B. NEWS & J. 244 (June 1988) [hereinafter *Legacy*]. Terry Eastland, who served as Director of Public Affairs at the Justice Department during the Reagan Administration, has summarized the Reagan Antitrust policy as follows:

In antitrust policy, the Reagan Administration took the stand that the size of companies should not be the dominating concern; instead, economic efficiency and the consumer welfare it produced became the touchstone. The Antitrust Division sent the message that business could undertake economically beneficial initiatives that might once have been regulated or outlawed. At the same time, the division focused its enforcement efforts on, and gained record numbers of convictions for, price fixing and bid rigging—the heart of antitrust violations.

Eastland, *What Next for Justice Department?*, Legal Times, Oct. 31, 1988, at 18.

150. *See* Kovacic, *Federal Antitrust Enforcement*, supra note 149, at 177-78; Kovacic, *Legacy*, supra note 149, at 244-45; *see also* Kovacic, *Public Choice and the Public Interest: Federal Trade Commission Antitrust Enforcement During the Reagan Administration*, 33 ANTITRUST BULL. 467 (1988) [hereinafter *Public Choice*]. Notwithstanding a general consistency with Reagan administration enforcement approaches, the Bush antitrust agencies have expanded the focus of federal enforcement. *See infra* text accompanying notes 178, 207, 209; *see also* Mufson, *supra* note 148 (discussing expansion of FTC and Antitrust Division enforcement by Bush appointees).

151. The intellectual contest over goals has surfaced in several court of appeals decisions in which the choice of goals has been a central, and sometimes disputed, basis for determining liability. *See* USA Petroleum Co. v. Atlantic Richfield Co., 859 F.2d 687 (9th Cir. 1985), *rev'd*, 110 S. Ct. 1884 (1990); McGahee v. Northern Propane Gas Co., 858 F.2d 1487 (11th Cir. 1988), *cert. denied*, 109 S. Ct. 2110 (1989); Rothery Storage & Van Co. v. Atlas Van Lines, Inc., 792 F.2d 210 (D.C. Cir. 1986), *cert. denied*, 479 U.S. 1033 (1987); Paschall v. The Kansas City Star Co., 727 F.2d 692 (8th Cir. 1984) (en banc), *cert. denied*, 469 U.S. 872 (1984); MCI Communications Corp. v. AT&T Co., 708 F.2d 1081 (7th Cir. 1983), *cert. denied*, 464 U.S. 891 (1983).

glance, a reading of antitrust cases since 1978 would seem to suggest that Bork's efficiency view has gained substantial judicial support. Most significantly, in 1979, the Supreme Court cited *The Antitrust Paradox* with approval in *Reiter v. Sonotone Corp.*,[152] for the proposition that the legislative debates "suggest that Congress designed the Sherman Act as a 'consumer welfare prescription.'"[153] Five years later, in *NCAA v. Board of Regents*,[154] the Court quoted *Reiter* for the proposition that Congress crafted the Sherman Act as a "consumer welfare prescription."[155] *Reiter* and *The Antitrust Paradox* have led several lower courts to embrace the view that the antitrust laws are designed to promote "consumer welfare."[156]

Some observers have interpreted *Reiter* and later cases as an endorsement of Bork's efficiency thesis. In an Interstate Commerce Commission matter in 1983, Judge Posner stated that "[t]he allocative-efficiency or consumer welfare concept of competition dominates current thinking, judicial and academic, in the antitrust field,"[157] citing *Reiter* and *The Antitrust Paradox* as supporting

---

152. 442 U.S. 330, 343 (1979).
153. *Id.* at 343 (citing R. Bork, *The Antitrust Paradox* 66 (1978)).
154. 468 U.S. 85 (1984).
155. *Id.* at 107.
156. *See* Consolidated Metal Prod., Inc. v. American Petroleum Inst., 846 F.2d 284, 292-293 (5th Cir. 1988) ("the rule of reason requires plaintiffs to show that the defendants' actions amounted to a conspiracy against the market—a concerted attempt to reduce output and drive up prices or otherwise reduce consumer welfare" [footnote omitted]); Marrese v. Interqual, Inc., 748 F.2d 373, 387 (7th Cir. 1984), *cert. denied*, 472 U.S. 1027 (1985) ("We add that in the instant case, a further concern of this court is to promote the intended purpose of the Sherman Act as a 'consumer welfare prescription'" [citing *NCAA's* quotation of *Reiter*]); Satellite Fin. Planning Corp. v. First Nat'l Bank of Wilmington, 633 F. Supp. 386, 394 (D. Del. 1986) ("Antitrust laws restrict anticompetitive conduct in order to advance consumer welfare. *See generally* R. BORK, THE ANTITRUST PARADOX (1978). They are not meant to redress personal wrongs that do not impact on competition or adversely affect consumers. The primary purpose of the antitrust statutes, to benefit consumers through competition, must guide the Court in deciding antitrust issues before it."); *See also* Central Florida Enters, Inc. v. FCC, 683 F.2d 503, 507 n.20 (D.C. Cir. 1982) ("Our antitrust laws similarly dictate that competition—and, thereby, *consumers*—are to be protected rather than competitors. *See generally* R. BORK, *The Antitrust Paradox* (1978)" [emphasis in the original]) (dictum).
157. C. & O. Ry. Co. v. ICC, 704 F.2d 373, 376 (7th Cir. 1983) (dictum). Like Judge Posner, Bork regards judicial endorsement of a "consumer welfare" approach as acceptance of an allocative efficiency standard. *See* Bork, *supra* note 2, at 15 ("These are a variety of cases, like *Brown Shoe*, in which non economic

authority. Judge Posner unquestionably understands and accepts Bork's view that consumer welfare means nothing more than economic efficiency. It is hardly clear, however, whether other jurists who have written about the "consumer welfare" aims of the antitrust laws comprehend or endorse Bork's logic.

Chief Justice Burger's majority opinion in *Reiter* illustrated the ambiguity in question. *Reiter* concluded that Congress designed the Sherman Act as a "consumer welfare prescription," but the Court stopped short of explicitly equating "consumer welfare" with the pursuit of economic efficiency. Nothing in the opinion indicated that the Court considered and rejected alternative meanings, such as the prevention of wealth transfers from consumers to producers. Rather, shortly before its description of congressional intent, the Court suggested that "consumer welfare" might mean more than allocative efficiency. "The essence of the antitrust laws is to ensure fair price competition in an open market,"[158] the Court explained. "Here, where petitioner alleges a wrongful deprivation of her money because the price of the hearing aid she bought was artificially inflated by reason of respondents' anticompetitive conduct, she has alleged an injury in her 'property' . . . ."[159] The Court then added that Congress had made private treble damage suits available "as a means of protecting consumers from overcharges resulting from price fixing."[160]

These comments in *Reiter* suggest that the Court might be receptive to a definition of consumer welfare that encompasses such non-efficiency concerns as wealth transfer effects. The Court's later decision in *NCAA* quoted *Reiter*'s "consumer welfare prescription" language in a discussion that could be interpreted as primarily involving allocative efficiency effects of the challenged practice.[161] Nonetheless, *NCAA* did not confront the wealth trans-

---

concepts were said by the Supreme Court to play an important role. The Supreme Court has since said that only economic concepts and consumer welfare, or economic efficiency, are the activating principles of the law.") *Id.* (footnote omitted).

158. 442 U.S. at 342.

159. *Id.*

160. *Id.* at 343.

161. 468 U.S. at 107. After quoting *Reiter*, Justice Stevens' majority opinion stated: "A restraint that has the effect of reducing the importance of consumer preference in setting price and output is not consistent with this fundamental goal of antitrust law. Restrictions on price and output are the paradigmatic examples of restraints of trade that the Sherman Act was intended to prohibit." *Id.* More recently, however, in Atlantic Richfield Co. v. USA Petroleum Co.,

fer issue, and nothing in the decision indicated that the Court regarded efficiency as the sole content of "consumer welfare." Indeed, the Court's intriguing, but cryptic, recent discussions of goals lead one to seriously doubt whether the Court, if confronted with the issue, would conclude that Congress' concern with "consumer welfare" did not extend to the wealth transfer consequences of a horizontal price-fixing cartel.

The lower courts' characterizations of the Sherman Act as a "consumer welfare" prescription, likewise, have not answered the question of precisely what Congress' perceived solicitude for consumer welfare entails. Most courts that have stated that Congress intended the antitrust laws as "consumer welfare prescriptions" have done so without defining consumer welfare or have implied that it encompasses more than efficiency.[162] Courts that have recognized the definitional issue that *Reiter*'s language raised have tended to qualify their acceptance of a consumer welfare standard by indicating that economic efficiency is not its sole ingredient.[163]

---

110 S. Ct. 1884 (1990), Justice Stevens has stated that he regards the goals of antitrust to encompass more than efficiency. In a dissent joined by Justice White, Justice Stevens stated: "The Court, in its haste to excuse illegal behaviour in the name of efficiency has cast aside a century of understanding that our antitrust laws are designed to safeguard more than efficiency and consumer welfare, and that private actions not only compensate the injured, but also deter wrongdoers." *USA Petroleum*, 110 S. Ct. at 1903 (Justice Stevens, dissenting).

162. Satellite Fin. Planning Corp. v. First Nat'l Bank of Wilmington, 633 F. Supp. 386 (D. Del. 1986) provides a representative illustration of how imperfectly some courts have comprehended Bork's conception of consumer welfare as an efficiency precept. In *Satellite Financial*, the court observed: "Antitrust laws restrict anticompetitive conduct in order to advance consumer welfare. See generally R. BORK, THE ANTITRUST PARADOX (1978). They are not meant to redress personal wrongs that do not impact on competition or adversely affect consumers. The primary purpose of the antitrust statutes, to benefit consumers through competition, must guide the court in deciding antitrust issues before it." *Id*. at 394. This quotation is interesting in two basic respects. First, after mentioning "consumer welfare," the court does not go on to state that consumer welfare means economic efficiency alone. It is doubtful that the court understood how Bork reasoned that Congress' desire to promote consumer welfare could only be interpreted as a single-minded concern with economic efficiency. Second, the court's elaboration of the meaning of "consumer welfare" is consistent with the attainment of values other than economic efficiency. For example, wealth transfers from consumers to monopolists can be said to "adversely affect consumers." One could argue that one way competition "benefit[s] consumers" is to proscribe conduct that yields such transfers.

163. See Consolidated Metal Prod., Inc. v. American Petroleum Inst., 846 F.2d 284 (5th Cir. 1988). In *Consolidated*, the court stated that "the rule of reason requires plaintiffs to show that the defendants' actions amounted to a

In addition, other recent cases have explicitly rejected analytical approaches that exclude consideration of social and political values in framing antitrust liability standards.[164]

On the whole, judicial discussion of Bork's argument on goals has been intriguing but inconclusive. No decision to date, including *Reiter* and *NCAA*, has retraced the logic of Bork's position and endorsed a concept of "consumer welfare" that includes only economic efficiency. Moreover, the courts' limited attempts to elaborate on the consumer welfare standard indicate that many tribunals would be receptive to including concerns, such as wealth transfer effects, in the consumer welfare calculus, if a case squarely posed the issue. Thus, while *The Antitrust Paradox* has established an impressive beachhead in the contest over antitrust's goals, Bork's vision of consumer welfare as economic efficiency has yet to triumph within the judiciary.

Although Bork's efficiency interpretation has not won the battle for the minds of federal judges, it is worth underscoring the extent of his gains to date. Perhaps most important, *The Antitrust Paradox* has attracted considerable judicial attention to what Bork properly characterized as a fundamental aspect of antitrust policy. By leading courts, as well as the parties before them, to reconsider the underlying purposes of the antitrust statutes, Bork has discouraged a rote acceptance of the proposition in *Brown Shoe* that social and political values are paramount, or coequal with efficiency, in the antitrust decisionmaking calculus.

In offering his efficiency vision of goals, Bork also has gained an advantage in the intellectual debate. The frequency with which judges have cited *The Antitrust Paradox* favorably on the issue of goals has shifted the burden of persuasion to his opponents to indicate how non-efficiency values are to be considered. In her concurrance to Judge Bork's opinion in *Rothery Storage & Van. Co. v. Atlas Van Lines, Inc.*,[165] Judge Wald observed that "[u]ntil

---

conspiracy against the market—a concerted attempt to reduce output and drive up prices or otherwise reduce consumer welfare." *Id.* at 292-93. To this passage the court appended a footnote that cited three articles that encourage consideration of values other than economic efficiency in defining consumer welfare. *See also* Rothery Storage & Van Co. v. Atlas Van Lines, Inc., 792 F.2d 210, 231 (D.C. Cir. 1986) (Wald, J., concurring), *cert. denied*, 479 U.S. 1033 (1987).

164. *See, e.g.*, McGahee v. Northern Propane Gas Co., 858 F.2d 1487, 1497-98 (11th Cir. 1988) ("In passing antitrust legislation, Congress's purpose was not only an economic one, but was also a political one, a purpose of curbing the power some individuals and corporations had over the economy" [citations omitted]), *cert. denied*, 109 S.Ct. 2110 (1989).

165. 792 F.2d 210 (D.C. Cir. 1986), *cert. denied*, 479 U.S. 1033 (1987).

the Supreme Court indicates that the *only* goal of antitrust law is to promote efficiency, as the panel uses that term, I think it more prudent to proceed with a pragmatic, albeit nonarithmetic and even untidy rule of reason analysis, than to adopt a market power test as the exclusive filtering-out device for all potential violators who do not command a significant market share."[166] Judge Wald did not indicate what "pragmatic" factors the consideration of non-efficiency goals might entail, much less suggest how much weight each factor, and its corresponding goal, would receive in an "untidy rule of reason analysis." In general, judges who have quarrelled with Bork's assessment of goals have yet to devise an administrable, alternative framework in which conflicting efficiency and non-efficiency concerns are to be applied.

B. Horizontal Restraints

The federal government's horizontal restraints enforcement policy since 1978 reads as though *The Antitrust Paradox* largely served as its blueprint. Several major characteristics of the government's enforcement program parallel Bork's recommendations. Since 1978, and particularly since Ronald Reagan's election in 1980, the Antitrust Division has significantly expanded its criminal price-fixing enforcement activities.[167] In addition, the FTC has substantially increased the proportion of horizontal restraints matters in its antitrust enforcement mix.[168] Both federal agencies have devoted more resources toward competition advocacy before federal, state, and local government bodies.[169] Finally, the Antitrust

---

166. *Id.* at 231-32 (emphasis in the original).

167. *See Report of the American Bar Association Section of Antitrust Law Task Force on the Antitrust Division of the U.S. Department of Justice, reprinted in* 58 ANTITRUST L.J. 747, 755, 763-64 (1990) [hereinafter *ABA Antitrust Division Task Force*]; *60 Minutes with Charles F. Rule, Acting Assistant Attorney General, Antitrust Division*, 56 ANTITRUST L.J. 261 (1987); Marcus, *Rule Defends Antitrust Enforcement*, Washington Post, Sept. 4, 1987, at F1, col. 6; *see also 60 Minutes with the Honorable James F. Rill, Assistant Attorney General, Antitrust Division, U.S. Department of Justice*, 59 ANTITRUST L.J. 45, 60 (1990) (Assistant Attorney General Rill: "We do have a war against economic crime and we are going to try and use every legitimate constitutional means to win that war.").

168. *See* Oliver, *supra* note 148, at 203; Kovacic, *Public Choice, supra* note 150, at 480-82.

169. This trend has been most pronounced at the FTC. *See Report of The American Bar Association Section of Antitrust Law Special Committee to Study the Role of the Federal Trade Commission, reprinted in* 58 ANTITRUST L.J. 43, 93-96 (1989).

Division and the FTC have adopted analytical approaches similar to Bork's for distinguishing "naked" horizontal restrictions upon output from ancillary restraints designed to make an integration of economic functions more efficient.[170]

Bork's distinction between "naked" and "ancillary" restrictions also has influenced judicial analysis of horizontal restraints. Most notably, the Supreme Court relied upon *The Antitrust Paradox* in *NCAA* where it decided to apply a modified rule of reason to horizontal output restrictions adopted as part of a joint venture among direct rivals.[171] Here, as well as in other cases, Bork's analysis has shaped the emergence of a horizontal restraints framework that gives greater attention to efficiency arguments.[172] During his tenure on the D.C. Circuit, Bork participated directly in this development in his majority opinion in *Rothery*. In *Rothery*, Bork concluded that Supreme Court decisions over the past fifteen years effectively overruled *Topco*.[173] Although Bork's *Rothery* opinion did not cite *The Antitrust Paradox*, it essentially replicated the approach he had presented in his book, and used it as the foundation for analyzing the challenged conduct.

C. Mergers

Federal merger enforcement policy since 1978 has reflected major elements of Bork's recommendations. Antitrust Division and FTC evaluation of horizontal transactions has moved substantially in the direction Bork proposed. The 1982 Justice Department Merger Guidelines raised the threshold of illegality for horizontal mergers significantly above levels contained in the Department's 1968 Guidelines, but stopped short of Bork's more permissive

---

170. *See, e.g.*, U.S. Department of Justice, *Antitrust Guidelines for International Operations*, 4 Trade Reg. Rep. (CCH) 13,109 (Nov. 10, 1988); In re Massachusetts Board of Registration in Optometry, 110 F.T.C. 549 (1988); In re General Motors Corp., 103 F.T.C. 374 (1984) (consent order).

171. NCAA v. Board of Regents, 468 U.S. 101 (1984).

172. *See, e.g.*, Polk Bros., Inc. v. Forest City Enters., Inc., 776 F.2d 185, 189 (7th Cir. 1985); Mid-South Grizzlies v. National Football League, 550 F. Supp. 558, 566 (E.D. Pa. 1982), *aff'd*, 720 F.2d 772 (3d Cir. 1983), *cert. denied*, 467 U.S. 1215 (1984); *see also* Business Elecs. Corp. v. Sharp Elecs. Corp., 485 U.S. 717, 729 n.3 (1988) (applying Bork's distinction between naked and ancillary contractual restraints in a vertical restraints context).

173. Rothery Storage & Van Co. v. Atlas Van Lines, Inc., 792 F.2d 210, 226-29 (D.C. Cir. 1986), *cert. denied*, 479 U.S. 1033 (1987). *See also* Kovacic, *The Rule of Reason: D.C. Circuit Adopts Judge Bork's Analysis*, Legal Times, Oct. 6, 1986, at 20.

standards.[174] Consistent with *The Antitrust Paradox*, the 1982 Guidelines rejected an efficiencies defense, but the 1984 Guidelines reversed this position.[175] The FTC's 1982 Statement on Horizontal Mergers contained no numerical criteria but endorsed an analytical framework similar to Bork's.[176] As with the Justice Department's 1982 Guidelines, the FTC statement rejected an efficiencies defense. Although the federal agencies' enforcement thresholds are less generous than Bork had proposed, in practice both the Antitrust Division and the FTC during the Reagan administration tended to allow transactions yielding combined market shares that substantially exceed their guidelines' stated limits.[177] Since 1989, however, Bush Administration enforcement officials have stated their intention to apply the government's merger guidelines more strictly than their Reagan counterparts did.[178]

Federal enforcement decisions have closely tracked Bork's prescriptions for vertical and conglomerate transactions. Although Bork proposed a rule of per se legality for vertical mergers, the 1982 and 1984 Justice Guidelines contain limited prohibitions upon such transactions.[179] In practice, these nominate restrictions have proven to be virtually meaningless, as the federal enforcement agencies have not brought a merger case challenging a vertical

---

174. The 1982 Justice Guidelines are reprinted at 4 Trade Reg. Rep. (CCH) (P) 13,102. The 1968 Merger Guidelines are reprinted at 4 Trade Reg. Rep. (CCH) (P) 13,101. In an interview in 1989, Bork observed that the enforcement thresholds in the Reagan Administration's merger guidelines "áre probably too low. But there is such an improvement over what went before." *Paradox Revisited: Interview with Judge Robert H. Bork*, 3 ANTITRUST 16, 17 (Summer 1989).

175. 4 Trade Reg. Rep. (CCH) (P) 13,103, 20,564.

176. 4 Trade Reg. Rep. (CCH) (P) 13,200.

177. *See* Krattenmaker & Pitofsky, *Antitrust Merger Policy and the Reagan Administration*, 33 ANTITRUST BULL. 211, 226-28 (1988); *see also ABA Antitrust Division Task Force, supra* note 167, at 758-61.

178. *See* Bell & Herfort, *Justice, FTC Signal Tougher Merger Enforcement Standards*, 4 ANTITRUST 5 (Summer 1990); *see also 60 Minutes with the Honorable Janet D. Steiger, Chairman, Federal Trade Commission*, 59 ANTITRUST L.J. 3, 13 (1990) (describing commitment to "increased vigilance in merger review"); James F. Rill, Assistant Attorney General, Antitrust Division, "Antitrust Enforcement: An Agenda for the 1990's" (Nov. 3, 1989) (speech before the 23rd Annual New England Antitrust Conference), *reprinted in* 7 Trade Reg. Rep. (CCH) (P) 50,026, at 48,216 (acknowledging a "generalized perception" that federal merger enforcement had been "overly lenient" and had not always followed the government's guidelines) [hereinafter Rill *Antitrust Enforcement*].

179. *See* 4 Trade Reg. Rep. (CCH) (P) 13,103, at 20,565-67 (1984 guidelines); 4 Trade Reg. Rep. (CCH) (P) 13,102, at 20,540-42 (1982 guidelines).

transaction since 1981. The Justice Guidelines also have retained a partial ban upon conglomerate transactions when such transactions have horizontal effects.[180] The agencies have not challenged a conglomerate transaction since President Reagan took office in 1981.

In applying substantive merger standards, several antitrust tribunals have used Bork's analysis to assess the height and significance of barriers to entry.[181] Two of these decisions, *United States v. Waste Management, Inc.*[182] and *In re Echlin Manufacturing Co.*,[183] gave decisive effect to Bork's view that ease of entry should dictate a finding of legality, and thus, the courts dismissed merger challenges involving market shares substantially above the federal enforcement agencies' guidelines.[184] Although it did not apply Bork's merger recommendations, the Supreme Court has also cited *The Antitrust Paradox*'s treatment of predation claims in the course of denying private plaintiffs standing to attack a merger.[185] However, one court of appeals decision has reversed a district court ruling that invoked Bork's discussion of vertical merger policy to reject a private challenge to the termination of a consent agreement.[186] The Second Circuit stated, "[w]e believe it was an error to apply 'contemporary economic theory' to the extent it may be distinct from precedent."[187]

---

180. 4 Trade Reg. Rep (CCH) (P) 13,103 at 20,564-65 (1984 guidelines); 4 Trade Reg. Rep (CCH) (P) 13,102 at 20,539-40 (1982 guidelines).
181. *See* United States v. Waste Management, Inc., 743 F.2d 976, 983 (2d Cir. 1984); Hospital Corp. of America v. FTC, 106 F.T.C. 361, 491 (1985), *aff'd*, 807 F.2d 1381 (7th Cir. 1986), *cert. denied*, 481 U.S. 1038 (1987); In re Echlin Mfg. Co., 105 F.T.C. 410, 486-87 (1985).
182. 743 F.2d 976, 983 (2d Cir. 1984).
183. 105 F.T.C. 410, 486-87 (1985).
184. *Waste Management*, 743 F.2d at 981-84 (ease of entry deemed sufficient to rebut presumption of illegality arising from post-acquisition market share of 48.8%); *Echlin*, 105 F.T.C. (ease of entry warrants dismissal of antimerger complaint against firms with combined market share of 46%).
185. Cargill, Inc. v. Monfort of Colo., Inc., 479 U.S. 104, 121-22 & n.17 (1986).
186. *See* United States v. American Cyanamid Co., 719 F.2d 558 (2d Cir. 1983), *cert. denied*, 465 U.S. 1101 (1984).
187. *Id.* at 567. Other appellate panels occasionally have resisted Bork's suggestion that principles of economic analysis should govern the content of antitrust standards. In discussing the meaning of "competitive injury" in a primary line Robinson-Patman Act case, the Eleventh Circuit recently stated: "For the time being, we are satisfied merely to make it clear that when confronted with contemporary economic argument on the one hand and judicial precedent on the other, we feel, unlike those of a more activist bent, *see, e.g.*, R. BORK,

D. *Predation*

Since 1981, federal enforcement policy has paralleled Bork's prescriptions for analyzing claims of unlawful exclusion. The Antitrust Division and the FTC have initiated no predatory pricing, product development, or promotion suits since 1981.[188] At the same time, the agencies have given greater attention to the misuse of government processes to exclude rivals.[189] The FTC's sole monopolization or attempted monopolization suit since 1981 involved the misuse of judicial proceedings to disadvantage a rival.[190] The federal enforcement agencies' rejection of traditional theories of unlawful exclusion has produced a striking departure from previous government enforcement practice. From 1981 through 1988, the federal government filed fewer monopolization and attempted monopolization cases than in any other eight-year period since 1900.[191] Although some observers have called for an expansion of government monopolization and attempted monopolization enforcement,[192] significant growth in resources dedicated to developing such cases is unlikely in the foreseeable future.[193]

Modern judicial analysis of exclusionary conduct also has drawn extensively upon *The Antitrust Paradox*. The Supreme Court's decisions in *Matsushita Electric Industrial Co. v. Zenith Radio Corp.*[194] and *Cargill, Inc. v. Monfort of Colorado, Inc.*[195]

THE ANTITRUST PARADOX, at 36, that economic argument is not ultimately controlling, judicial precedent is." Alan's of Atlanta, Inc. v. Minolta Corp., 903 F.2d 1414, 1418 n.6 (11th Cir. 1990).

188. *See* Kovacic, *Legacy, supra* note 149, at 245.

189. *See, e.g., 60 Minutes with Daniel Oliver, Chairman, Federal Trade Commission*, 56 ANTITRUST L.J. 239, 242 (1987); Averitt & Calvani, *The Role of the FTC in American Society*, 39 OKLA. L. REV. 39, 50 (1986).

190. *See AMERCO*, 109 F.T.C. 135 (1987) (consent order); *see also Federal Trade Commission 75th Anniversary Symposium*, 58 ANTITRUST L.J. 797, 809-10 (1990) [hereinafter *FTC Symposium*] (FTC Bureau of Competition Director Kevin J. Arquit: "[O]n the issue of non-price predation, we have put a lot of resources into that and a very unhappy fact is that we have not come up with very much. . . . There are also very serious constitutional hurdles, but we will continue to look for non-price predation cases.").

191. *See* Kovacic, *supra* note 2, at 1140.

192. *See ABA Antitrust Division Task Force, supra* note 167, at 766-67.

193. *See FTC Symposium, supra* note 190, at 809-11 (discussing FTC interest in pursuing nonprice predation and predatory pricing cases, but noting limited availability of resources for such matters).

194. 475 U.S. 574 (1985).

195. 479 U.S. 104 (1986).

both cited Bork's view that successful predation is rare.[196] *Matsushita* began its evaluation of the plaintiff's predatory pricing theory with a long quotation from Bork's book.[197] Referring to *The Antitrust Paradox*, the *Matsushita* Court stated: "As this explanation shows, the success of [predatory pricing] schemes is inherently uncertain: the short-run loss is definite, but the long-run gain depends on successfully neutralizing the competition."[198] In its tone and content, *Matsushita* is a robust endorsement of the economically-oriented jurisprudence Bork espouses, as well as an embodiment of Bork's view that antitrust should intervene only to correct clearly harmful conduct.[199] Although neither *Matsushita* nor *Monfort* adopted Bork's suggestion that predatory pricing claims invariably be dismissed, the Court in both cases indicated that such allegations should be regarded skeptically. Other tribunals have drawn upon *The Antitrust Paradox*'s assessment of the competitive significance of predatory pricing strategies in dismissing monopolization and attempted monopolization suits based upon challenges to single firm pricing behavior.[200]

Judicial treatment of non-price exclusionary behavior often shows Bork's imprint, as well. The emphasis Bork placed upon considering efficiency rationales for questioned behavior has become an important component in the courts' evaluation of single-firm conduct. Although many commentators have criticized its result and reasoning, the Supreme Court's decision in *Aspen Skiing v. Aspen Highlands Skiing Corp.*[201] drew upon *The Antitrust Paradox* to define "improper exclusion" and to assess the possible efficiency rationales for the defendant's decision to withdraw from a joint marketing and operating venture.[202] Other tribunals have

---

196. Matsushita Elec. Indus. Co. v. Zenith Radio Corp., 475 U.S. 574, 589 (1985); Cargill, Inc. v. Monfort of Colo., Inc., 479 U.S. 104, 121 (1986).
197. *Matsushita*, 475 U.S. at 589.
198. *Id.*
199. Among other features, *Matsushita* invites courts to grant defendants summary judgment against antitrust conspiracy claims where the evidence before the court is as consistent with a procompetitve or competitively neutral explanation as with an anticompetive explanation. 475 U.S. at 588. *Matsushita* also encourages trial judges to dismiss any claim that "makes no economic sense." *Id.* at 587. For a discussion of *Matsushita's* significance, *see* DeSanti & Kovacic, *Matsushita: Its Construction and Application by the Lower Courts*, 59 ANTITRUST L.J. (1990).
200. *See ITT Corp.*, 104 F.T.C. 280, 402 n.30 (1984); *General Foods Corp.*, 103 F.T.C. 204, 343 n.19 (1984).
201. 472 U.S. 585 (1984).
202. Aspen Skiing Co. v. Aspen Highlands Skiing Corp., 472 U.S. 585, 602-03, 608-09 n.39 (1984).

embraced Bork's view that antitrust should intervene to sanction only those types of conduct whose efficiency-reducing traits are unmistakeable.[203] Finally, it is unusual to find reported opinions that address allegations of sham litigation or other misuses of government processes that do not cite Bork's treatment of these species of exclusionary conduct.[204] Bork's call for closer scrutiny of efforts to manipulate the levers of the regulatory, administrative, and judicial processes—either to raise the costs of rival firms or to exclude them from markets outright—has provided a central point of departure for analysis of such conduct within antitrust tribunals and academic circles.[205]

E. Vertical Restraints

Consistent with Bork's recommendations, the Reagan antitrust enforcement agencies essentially abandoned serious efforts to enforce prohibitions against vertical restraints and other distribution practices, such as price discrimination.[206] Since 1981, after Reagan appointees assumed the leadership of the Antitrust Division and the FTC, these agencies have initiated three matters dealing with vertical restraints, tying, or price discrimination.[207] In 1985, the

---

203. *See* Consolidated Metal Prod., Inc. v. American Petroleum Inst., 846 F.2d 284, 297 (5th Cir. 1988) ("An individual business decision that is negligent or based on insufficient facts or illogical conclusions is not a sound basis for antitrust policy" [citing *The Antitrust Paradox*]).

204. Examples of cases that have relied on Bork's insights in this area include: Szabo Food Serv., Inc. v. Canteen Corp., 823 F.2d 1073, 1082-83 (7th Cir. 1987), *cert. dismissed*, 485 U.S. 901 (1988); Handgards, Inc. v. Ethicon, Inc., 743 F.2d 1282, 1294-95 (9th Cir. 1984), *cert. denied*, 469 U.S. 1190 (1985); Litton Sys., Inc. v. AT&T Co., 700 F.2d 785, 812 n.39 (2d Cir. 1983), *aff'd*, 746 F.2d 168 (2d Cir. 1984), *cert. denied*, 464 U.S. 1073 (1984); MCI Communications Corp. v. AT&T Co., 708 F.2d 1081, 1158 (7th Cir. 1983), *cert. denied*, 464 U.S. 891 (1983); Clipper Exxpress v. Rocky Mountain Motor Tariff Bureau, Inc., 674 F.2d 1252, 1269 n.28 (9th Cir. 1982), *cert. denied*, 459 U.S. 1227 (1983); Landmarks Holding Corp. v. Bermant, 664 F.2d 891, 896 (2d Cir. 1981).

205. *See, e.g.*, Hurwitz, *Abuse of Governmental Processes, the First Amendment, and the Boundaries of Noerr*, 74 GEO. L.J. 65 (1985).

206. *See* Kovacic, *Federal Antitrust Enforcement, supra* note 149, at 177.

207. The first initiative is a price discrimination prosecution challenging the granting of volume discounts by book publishers to book retailing chains. *See Harper & Row*, FTC Docket Nos. 9217-22 (Dec. 28, 1988), *reported in* 5 Trade Reg. Rep. (CCH) (P) 22,634. The second is a consent order that bars a tying arrangement involving the use of out-patient and in-patient dialysis services. *See In re Gerald S. Friedman*, Dkt C-3290 (FTC consent order, June 18, 1990), *reported in* 5 Trade Reg. Rep. (CCH) (P) 22,811 (1990). The third is a proposed

Justice Department issued Vertical Restraints Guidelines that identified limited circumstances in which the Antitrust Division could challenge nonprice distribution restraints.[208] Following the practice of the Reagan administration, the Bush administration is unlikely to apply these Guidelines to prosecute nonprice vertical restraints. However, recent actions by Bush administration enforcement officials have suggested a greater willingness to use a rule of per se illegality to challenge episodes of resale price maintenance[209] —a practice that the Reagan antitrust lendership often described as benign or procompetitive.[210]

Judicial treatment of vertical restraints issues in the past ten years also has often mirrored Bork's preferences. Many decisions have relied explicitly upon *The Antitrust Paradox*. Most important, the Supreme Court's decision in *Business Electronics Corp. v. Sharp Electronics Corp.*,[211] drew upon Bork's analysis when it increased the burden of proof plaintiffs must bear to establish that a manufacturer and its retailers agreed to set resale prices.[212] The Court retained the rule of per se illegality for resale price maintenance, but this doctrinal continuity has given little comfort to

---

consent order that prohibits a swimming pool equipment firm from using resale price maintenance in the distribution of automatic pool cleaning devices. *See* In re Kreepy Krauly USA, Inc., F.T.C. File No. 901-0089 (proposed consent order, Jan. 10, 1991), *reported in* 60 Antitrust & Trade Reg. Rep. (BNA), No. 1499 at 70 (Jan. 17, 1991).

208. U.S. Department of Justice, *Vertical Practices Guidelines*, 4 Trade Reg. Rep. (CCH) (P) 13,105 (1985).

209. *See* Barrett, *FTC's Hard Line on Price Fixing May Foster Discounting*, Wall St. J., Jan. 11, 1991, at B1, col. 3 (discussing implications of FTC decision to enter proposed consent agreement banning use of resale price maintenance by swimming pool cleaning equipment firm); *See also* Rill, *Antitrust Enforcement*, *supra* note 178, at 48,219. ("The [Antitrust] Division will not advocate changes to the *per se* rule [against resale price maintenance] . . . . we will not hesitate to bring a resale price maintenance case, contingent only on evidence sufficient to establish a genuine resale price maintenance conspiracy and facts showing a significant regional impact.)"; *60 Minutes with the Honorable Janet D. Steiger, Chairman, Federal Trade Commission*, 59 ANTITRUST L.J. 3, 20 (1990) (Chairman Steiger: "Vertical price-fixing is per se illegal. We're going to enforce the law.").

210. *See, e.g.*, *Panel discussion: Interview with William F. Baxter, Assistant Attorney General, Antitrust Division*, 50 ANTITRUST L.J. 151, 154 (1981) (resale price maintenance sometimes "is a positively useful, pro-competitive tool"); *Interview with James C. Miller, III, Chairman, Federal Trade Commission*, 57 ANTITRUST L.J. 3, 8 (1982) ("RPM can be procompetitive").

211. 485 U.S. 717 (1988).

212. Business Elecs. Corp. v. Sharp Elecs. Corp., 485 U.S. 717, 729-30 n.3 (1988). The dissent in *Sharp* also used *The Antitrust Paradox* to evaluate the challenged restriction. *See id.* at 745-50 & n.10.

plaintiffs contemplating challenges to vertical pricing restrictions. *Sharp* continued the trend of recent Court decisions that indirectly erode the per se ban against resale price maintenance by making it more difficult to prove the fact of an agreement.[213]

However, Bork's greatest impact in the vertical restraints field has been in the area of tying arrangements. In *Jefferson Parish Hospital District No. 2 v. Hyde*,[214] Justice O'Connor's concurring opinion cited *The Antitrust Paradox* when she argued that the Court should abandon all remnants of per se analysis in evaluating tying arrangements.[215] Although *Jefferson Parish* stopped short of adopting the rule of per se legality that Bork would apply to all vertical restraints, the Court majority substantially eroded the existing per se ban against tying. Moreover, Bork's analysis has led to the acceptance of a more permissive approach in evaluating such agreements in the lower courts.[216]

IV. DURABILITY OF BORK'S INFLUENCE

Current antitrust analysis bears the deep imprint of the central policy propositions of *The Antitrust Paradox*. In the federal enforcement arena, many of Bork's enforcement preferences were enshrined as the policies of the Reagan administration. Despite some apparent departures from the Reagan antitrust agenda,[217] the Bush antitrust agencies are likely to pursue enforcement approaches that focus upon prosecution of horizontal output restrictions and comparatively large horizontal mergers.[218] However, the dramatic

---

213. *See* Monsanto Co. v. Spray-Rite Serv. Corp., 465 U.S. 752 (1984).

214. 466 U.S. 2 (1984).

215. Jefferson Parish Hosp. Dist. No. 2 v. Hyde, 466 U.S. 2, 36 & n.4 (1984).

216. *See, e.g.*, Grappone, Inc. v. Subaru of New England, Inc., 858 F.2d 792, 795-97 (1st Cir. 1988); Will v. Comprehensive Accounting Corp., 776 F.2d 665, 672 n.2 (7th Cir. 1985), *cert. denied*, 475 U.S. 1129 (1986); Kenworth of Boston, Inc. v. Paccar Fin. Corp., 735 F.2d 622 (1st Cir. 1984); Hirsh v. Martindale-Hubbell, Inc., 674 F.2d 1343, (9th Cir. 1982), *cert. denied*, 459 U.S. 973 (1982); Shop & Save Food Mkts., Inc. v. Pneumo Corp., 683 F.2d 27, 31 (2d Cir. 1982) (Feinberg, J., concurring), *cert. denied*, 459 U.S. 1038 (1982).

217. *See supra* notes and accompanying text; *see also* Smart, *Psst! The Trustbusters Are Back in Town*, BUS. WEEK, June 25, 1990, at 64; Mufson, *Return of the Trustbusters?*, Washington Post, June 17, 1990, at H1, col. 1.

218. *See* Interview with Timothy J. Muris, *reprinted in* 3 ANTITRUST 6 (1989); Kovacic, "Steady Reliever at Antitrust," Wall St. J., Oct. 10, 1989, at A18, col. 4; *see also 60 Minutes with the Honorable James F. Rill, Assistant Attorney General, Antitrust Division, U.S. Department of Justice*, 59 ANTITRUST

change in federal enforcement preferences in the 1980s elicited expanded efforts by state governments to bring cases to challenge mergers and distribution practices that the federal agencies regarded as benign or procompetitve.[219] The influence of Bork's work is also evident in the decisions of the federal judiciary, particularly the Supreme Court and the federal courts of appeals.[220] Much of Bork's antitrust agenda—once regarded as exceedingly extreme— has entered and redefined the mainstream of contemporary antitrust analysis.

Although many of its precepts are ingrained in public enforcement practice, judicial decisionmaking, and academic discourse, *The Antitrust Paradox* has not commanded universal assent. Rather, Bork's treatise has inspired a vast body of commentary that criticizes major elements of the book's analysis and proposes significantly different paths for the future of antitrust.[221] This section of the Article assesses the durability of Bork's perspectives in the face of a new body of literature that proposes major departures from the existing conservative orthodoxy. It first discusses the principal lines of attack that Bork's opponents have taken in challenging the policy agenda of *The Antitrust Paradox*. It then considers the likelihood that the competing visions of antitrust will displace *The Antitrust Paradox* as a central basis for framing antitrust rules.

A. The New Contest of Ideas

Bork's own experiences underscore the foundational role that intellectual inquiry has played in stimulating antitrust revolutions.

L.J. 45 (1990) (Assistant Attorney General Riff: "Merger enforcement and criminal antitrust enforcement are the two top priorities of the [Justice] Department's Antitrust Division."); *60 Minutes with the Honorable Janet D. Steiger, Chairman, Federal Trade Commission*, 59 ANTITRUST L.J. 3, 9 (1990) (Chairman Steiger: "[W]e will continue to focus the majority of our nonmerger resources on horizontal activity, because that is the area in which we are most likely to find anticompetitive behavior.").

219. *See* Brockmeyer, *Report on the NAAG Multi-state Task Force*, 58 ANTITRUST L.J. 215, 216 (1989)(discussing state resale price maintenance enforcement initiatives; Constantine, *The States' Role in Challenging National Mergers Is Vital*, 3 ANTITRUST 37 (Spring 1989) (discussing state antimerger enforcement initiatives).

220. *See* Kovacic, *Reagan's Judicial Appointees and Antitrust in the 1990s*, 59 FORDHAM L. REV. (forthcoming).

221. Several representative critiques appear in *Papers Presented at the Airlie House Conference on The Antitrust Alternative*, 62 N.Y.U. L. REV. 931 (1987); *Airlie House Conference on The Antitrust Alternative*, 76 GEO. L.J. 237 (1987).

Dramatic shifts in economic conditions and political preferences provide the environment in which antitrust change flourishes, but it is the availability of ideas justifying adjustments in enforcement policy and analysis that determine the extent of departures from the status quo.[222] The emergence of an increasingly competitive global economy and a more conservative social order probably would have dictated a retreat from expansive antitrust rules in the late 1970s and early 1980s, regardless of the state of academic learning. However, Bork's scholarship provided an attractive intellectual basis upon which advocates of regulatory retrenchment could take the fullest possible advantage of economic and political circumstances favoring change. To assess the likely direction of future policy change, three focal points of analysis in the modern literature that contests the perspectives of *The Antitrust Paradox* must be considered.

1. Is Efficiency All That Counts?

Evaluations of Bork's work have focused most extensively on his argument that economic efficiency is the exclusive proper concern of antitrust policy. The bulk of subsequent, goals-oriented commentary has been historical in nature. The emphasis upon historical interpretation reflects the considerable weight Bork's policy prescriptions placed upon his assessment of the legislative debates preceeding the enactment of the antitrust statutes. Indeed, Bork introduced the body of *The Antitrust Paradox* by observing that "[o]ne of the uses of history is to free us of a falsely imagined past."[223]

A broad consensus of scholars who have examined Bork's history has rejected his conception of orginal congressional intent, particulary his view that efficiency concerns were the dominant impulses in the legislative process.[224] Numerous commentators have argued that Congress intended non-efficiency aims to be para-

---

222. *See* Kovacic, *supra* note 2, at 1128-39; *cf.* Crew & Rowley, *Feasibility of Deregulation: A Public Choice Analysis*, in DEREGULATION AND DIVERSIFICATION OF UTILITIES 5, 17 (M. Crew ed. 1989) ("We must never underestimate the power of ideas. . . . The role of the political economist as entrepreneurial provider of hypotheses concerning institutional reform . . . is not to be underestimated.").

223. R. Bork, *supra* note 10, at 15.

224. For a representative assessment, *see* Hovenkamp, *Antitrust Policy After Chicago*, 84 MICH. L. REV. 213, 249 (1985)("the legislative histories of the various antitrust laws fail to exhibit anything resembling a dominant concern for economic efficiency").

mount, or at least co-equal with efficiency considerations, in antitrust enforcement.[225] Such critiques have rested upon a reexamination of the legislative history of the antitrust statutes[226] and extensive analysis of the economic, political, and jurisprudential environment that shaped the thinking of Congress in the formative era of the feredal antitrust system.[227] Collectively, these works demonstrate that Congress conceived the antitrust system to embrace objectives reaching well beyond attainment of productive and allocative efficiency.

Although orginal intent is important to Bork's view of statutory interpretation,[228] it did not provide the sole foundation for his efficiency thesis. A second, equally important basis for rejecting all goals other than efficiency was the lack of an administrable mechanism for judges to apply non-efficiency values in deciding antitrust cases.[229] This aspect of Bork's goals analysis has attracted far less scholarly attention, and decidedly fewer convincing rebuttals, than his original intent justification. A noteworthy exception is Robert Lande's two-level assault on Bork's efficiency view.[230] Like many other scholars, Lande persuasively challenges Bork's original intent interpretation.[231] In reviewing the legislative histories

---

225. These authorities are collected in Flynn, *The Reagan Administration's Antitrust Policy, 'Original Intent' and the Legislative History of the Sherman Act*, 33 ANTITRUST BULL. 259 (1988); May, *The Role of the States in the First Century of the Sherman Act and the Larger Picture of Antitrust History*, 59 ANTITRUST L.J. 93, 94-95 (1990).

226. *See, e.g.*, Flynn, *supra* note 225 (emphasizing analysis of Sherman Act's legislative history); Lande, *Wealth Transfers as the Original and Primary Concern of Antitrust: The Efficiency Interpretation Challenged*, 34 HASTING L.J. 65 (1982) [hereinafter Lande *Wealth Transfers*] (emphasizing analysis of legislative histories of Sherman, Clayton, and Federal Trade Commission Acts).

227. Major studies that have challenged Bork's original intent efficiency thesis in the context of examining comtemporary economic, legal, and political theory in the late nineteenth and early twentieth centuries include May, *Antitrust Practice and Procedure in the Formative Era: The Constitutional and Conceptual Reach of State Antitrust Law, 1880-1918*, 135 U. PA. L. REV. 495 (1987); Millon, *The Sherman Act and the Balance of Power*, 61 S. CAL. L. REV. 1219 (1989); Peritz, *The 'Rule of Reason' in Antitrust Law: Property Logic in Restraint of Competition*, 40 HASTINGS L.J. 285 (1989).

228. *See* R. BORK, *supra* note 12, at 5 ("[T]he judge is bound to apply the law as those who made the law wanted him to.").

229. *See supra* notes 117-119 and accompanying text.

230. *See* Lande, *The Rise and (Coming) Fall of Efficiency as a Rule of Antitrust*, 33 ANTITRUST BULL. 429 (1988) [hereinafter *Fall of Efficiency*]; Lande, *supra* note 226; *see also* Lande, *An Anti-Antitrust Activist?*, 9 NAT'L. L.J. 13, 128 (Sept. 7, 1987).

231. *See* Lande, *Wealth Transfers supra* note 226.

of the antitrust statutes, Lande shows that preventing the transfer of wealth from consumers to monopolists and members of cartels was one of Congress' foremost concerns.

Lande also mounts an effective challenge to Bork's position on administrability.[232] His work demonstrates that the application of a wealth transfer standard would be no more analytically complex than using an allocative efficiency criterion for identifying conduct worthy of condemnation.[233] Acceptance of Lande's view would supply a basis for several adjustments in the enforcement of prevailing antitrust policy. One adjustment would be the use of less generous horizontal merger thresholds. Perhaps more important, a focus on transfer effects would dictate more aggressive efforts to challenge some forms of conduct that involve price discrimination (such as tying arrangements), where the wealth transfer effects can be substantial.[234]

Administrability considerations promise to become more significant in the future as scholars continue to debate the goals of antitrust. Such a development is likely in large part because modern historical scholarship has begun to question the feasibility of giving effect to original legislative intent.[235] For example, James May's examination of antitrust's formative era finds that the early antitrust statutes took root in "a powerful, widely shared vision of a natural, rights-based political and economic order that simultaneously tended to ensure opportunity, efficiency, prosperity, justice, harmony, and freedom."[236] May rejects goal interpretations that

232. See Lande, Fall of Efficiency, supra note 230, at 452-54; see also Fisher, Johnson & Lande, Price Effects of Horizontal Mergers, 77 CALIF. L. REV. 777 (1989); Fisher & Lande, Efficiency Considerations in Merger Enforcement, 71 CALIF. L. REV. 1580 (1983).
233. See Fisher, Johnson & Lande, supra note 231; Fisher & Lande, supra note 231. For an effort to address administrability concerns in applying a multi-goal standard, see Foy, The Modernization of Antitrust: A New Equilibrium, 66 CORNELL L. REV. 1140, 1179-90 (1981).
234. See Lande, Chicago's False Foundation: Wealth Transfers (Not Just Efficiency) Should Guide Antitrust, 58 ANTITRUST L.J. 631, 643-44 (1989). It is conceivable that the evaluation of distribution practices would be influenced more deeply than merger enforcement if a wealth transfer standard gained acceptance. See Calvani, Rectangles & Triangles: A Response to Mr. Lande, 58 ANTITRUST L.J. 657 (1989) (finding little effect in shifting to a wealth transfer approach to evaluate mergers).
235. See Kovacic, Comments and Observations, 59 ANTITRUST L.J. 119, 121-23 (1990).
236. May, Antitrust in the Formative Era: Political and Economic Theory in Constitutional and Antitrust Analysis, 1880-1918, 50 OHIO ST. L.J. 257, 391 (1989).

discern a single, overriding legislative purpose. Rather, if original intent is to govern current antitrust policy, May concludes that commentators and antitrust policymakers must attain "the formulation and application of an approach reasonably faithful to the animating economic, moral, and political concerns of [the] initial period of antitrust legislation and adjudication."[237]

May's analysis raises serious doubts about efforts to rely upon original intent interpretations that identify a dominant goal. Commentators today often perceive the multiplicity of aims recited in the legislative debates as disjointed and internally inconsistent.[238] Where Congress once saw a mutually reinforcing unity among a diversity of aims, commentators now identify disharmony and a need for tradeoffs among conflicting objectives. The challenge posed by Professor May's analysis — to conceive a modern policy model that gives full harmonious effect to multiple original goals now believed to be inconsistent — may prove unmanageable. If this turns out to be the case, modern views of correct policy, rather than goal interpretations based on original intent, will provide the basis for shaping antitrust doctrine.[239] Such a development would place a premium upon devising an administrable framework for applying one's preferred antitrust value system. Proposals by commentators such as Bork and Lande, who have dealt with the administrability issue most directly and rigorously, are likely to command the closest attention among judges and enforcement officials.

2. Does Efficiency Dictate a Broader Enforcement Net?

Critics of Bork's evaluation of goals seek to offer an alternative model for shaping doctrine and enforcement policy. A second group of commentators accepts the efficiency model of analysis but contends that an efficiency-based approach warrants a fuller menu of enforcement efforts than Bork proposed.[240] Critiques

---

237. *Id.* at 395.

238. *Id.* at 394 ("In the later twentieth century, none of the differing 'schools' of antitrust analysis can accept even implicitly the full formative era vision of a natural, harmonious, rights-based economic order simultaneously tending to maximize opportunity, efficiency, wealth, fairness, and political freedom through the aid of 'nondiscretionary' judicial elaboration.").

239. *Cf.* Dewey, *Economists and Antitrust: The Circular Road*, 35 ANTITRUST BULL. 349, 355 (1990) ("What Congress intended by [the Sherman Act] in 1890 is of antiquarian interest only.").

240. *See* Baker, *Recent Developments in Economics that Challenge Chicago School Views*, 58 ANTITRUST L.J. 645 (1989).

operating within an efficiency framework have argued for more robust enforcement along essentially three lines.

First, a number of commentators argue that *The Antitrust Paradox* underestimated the welfare-reducing implications of various types of single-firm conduct. In particular, these commentators assert that Bork relied excessively upon static price theory and slighted strategy considerations that enable firms to deter entry, raise the costs of rival firms, and thereby impose net welfare losses upon society.[241] The foundation for modern proposals to expand antitrust scrutiny of single-firm behavior has been an outpouring of economic scholarship applying game theory.[242] Among other contributions, this literature has suggested how incumbent dominant firms can deter entry by adopting pricing strategies that exploit the incumbent's superior information about its costs and market conditions.[243]

A second body of commentary contends that Bork erred by assuming that antitrust's concern with vertical contractual restraints and vertical foreclosure are entirely misplaced. Some contributions to the recent economic literature advocate the continued scrutiny of resale price maintenance using a rule of reason standard.[244] The

---

241. *See, e.g.,* Encaoua, Geroski & Jacquemin, *Strategic Competition and the Persistence of Dominant Firms: A Survey,* in NEW DEVELOPMENTS IN THE ANALYSIS OF MARKET STRUCTURE 55 (J. Stiglitz & G. Mathewson eds. 1986); Williamson, *Delimiting Antitrust,* 76 GEO. L.J. 271 (1987); Krattenmaker & Salop, *Anticompetitive Exclusion: Raising Rivals' Costs to Achieve Power Over Price,* 96 YALE L.J. 209 (1986).

242. One scholar has described this literature as "the primary post-Chicago development in theoretical industrial organization economics." Baker, *supra* note 240, at 646 n.8. For summaries of modern game theory scholarship and its application to single-firm conduct, *see* J. TIROLE, THE THEORY OF INDUSTRIAL ORGANIZATION 361-88 (1988); Holt & Scheffman, *Strategic Business Behavior and Antitrust,* in ECONOMICS & ANTITRUST POLICY 39 (R. Larner & J. Meeham, Jr. eds. 1989); Ordover & Saloner, *Predation, Monopolization, and Antitrust,* in 1 HANDBOOK OF INDUSTRIAL ORGANIZATION 537 (R. Schmalensee & R. Willig eds. 1989); Salop, *Strategy, Predation, and Antitrust Analysis: An Introduction,* in STRATEGY, PREDATION, AND ANTITRUST ANALYSIS 1 (S. Salop ed. 1981); Shapiro, *The Theory of Business Strategy,* 20 RAND J. ECON. 125 (1989).

243. *See* Kreps & Wilson, *Reputation and Imperfect Information,* 27 J. ECON. THEORY 253 (1982); Milgrom & Roberts, *Information Asymmetries, Strategic Behavior, and Industrial Organization,* 77 AM. ECON. REV. 184 (1987).

244. *See, e.g.,* Comanor, *Vertical Price Fixing, Vertical Market Restrictions, and the New Antitrust Policy,* 98 HARV. L. REV. 983 (1985); Comanor & Kirkwood, *Resale Price Maintenance and Antitrust Policy,* 3 CONTEMP. POL'Y ISSUES 9 (1985); Scherer, *The Economics of Vertical Restraints,* 52 ANTITRUST L.J. 687 (1983).

new economic literature on raising rivals' costs also offers anti-competitive hypotheses for certain efforts by firms to deny their rivals access to suppliers or distribution networks.[245]

Finally, many of the same commentators argue that Bork's preferred approach to evaluating mergers is too permissive and cannot be justified on efficiency grounds. They argue for more restrictive policies toward horizontal transactions,[246] particularly in industries characterized by significant product differentiation.[247] Consistent with the new economics' emphasis on vertical exclusion, other commentators have provided anticompetitive explanations for some vertical mergers that would dictate continuing antitrust attention to foreclosure effects.[248] The inclination of legal and economic scholars to examine specific mergers and other forms of conduct that Bork would ignore is based partly upon the development of new empirical techniques for evaluating entry conditions and measuring market power.[249]

3. Are Bork's Prescriptions Too Interventionist?

Criticism of *The Antitrust Paradox* has not come exclusively from the left. Though decidedly a minority among attorneys and economists, a growing number of observers have argued that Bork embraced too expansive a view of antitrust's proper role. In particular, Bork is said to have miscalculated the usefulness of rules banning horizontal price fixing.[250] These commentators assert that cartels typically disintegrate on their own, making enforcement

---

245. *See* Baker, *Vertical Restraints Among Hospitals, Physicians and Health Insurers that Raise Rivals' Costs*, 14 AM. J.J. & MED. 147 (1988); Krattenmaker & Salop, *supra* note 241; Krattenmaker & Salop, *Analyzing Anticompetitive Exclusion*, 56 ANTITRUST L.J. 71 (1987); Salop & Scheffman, *Cost-Raising Strategies*, 36 J. INDUS. ECON. 19 (1987).

246. *See* Krattenmaker & Pitofsky, *supra* note 177.

247. *See* Baker & Bresnahan, *The Gains from Merger or Collusion in Product-Differentiated Industries*, 33 J. INDUS. ECON. 427 (1985).

248. *See* Salinger, *The Meaning of 'Upstream' and 'Downstream' and Implications for Modelling Vertical Mergers*, 37 J. INDUS. ECON. 373 (1989).

249. *See* Bresnahan, *Empirical Studies of Industries with Market Power*, in 2 HANDBOOK OF INDUSTRIAL ORGANIZATION 1011 (R. Schmalensee & R. Willig eds. 1989); Bresnahan & Schmalensee, *The Empirical Renaissance in Industrial Economics: An Overview*, 35 J. INDUS. ECON. 371 (1987).

250. *See, e.g.*, Dewey, *supra* note 239, at 363-64; Dewey, *What Price Theory Can—and Cannot—Do for Antitrust*, 3 CONTEMP. POL. ISSUES 3, 5 (1984-85).

against them unnecessary or have valuable efficiency properties.[251] Short of endorsing a hands-off policy toward all horizontal agreements, a number of commentators on both sides of the political spectrum argue that antitrust doctrine should take a more permissive view toward horizontal agreements formed for the purpose of facilitating research and development.[252] Finally, the most extreme attack on Bork's positive enforcement agenda has consisted of proposals that Congress repeal the antitrust statutes.[253]

B. Institutional Impediments to Change

A century of experience has seen the rise and fall of numerous views concerning the proper role of antitrust in ordering the country's economic affairs.[254] The history of antitrust policy has featured reoccurring cycles of activism triggered by social, political, and economic change. There is every reason to expect that pressures similar to those that generated earlier periods of antitrust expansion will arise again to press against the structures of Chicago School thinking. Will the analytical pillars of *The Antitrust Paradox* yield to demands for a broader enforcement agenda? At least two institutional factors will retard the rate of change.

1. The Crumbling Public Enforcement Infrastructure

Even if the Democrats had regained the White House in the 1988 election, federal antitrust agencies would have been poorly positioned to drastically adjust the government's mix of new antitrust cases and depart significantly from a Borkian agenda.[255] To make its own regulatory reform preferences endure, the Reagan administration nearly halved the size of the federal antitrust enforcement institutions. Over the past decade, the public enforcement infrastructure has weakened qualitatively, as well. Growing

---

251. *See, e.g.*, Bittlingmayer, *Decreasing Cost and Competition: A New Look at the Addyston Pipe Case*, 25 J.L. Econ. 201 (1982); Dewey, *Information, Entry, and Welfare: The Case for Collusion*, 69 Am. Econ. Rev. 587 (1979); High, *Bork's Paradox: Static vs. Dynamic Efficiency in Antitrust Analysis*, 3 Contemp. Pol. Issues 21, 30-31 (1984-85).

252. *See, e.g.*, Jorde & Teece, *Competition and Cooperation: Striking the Right Balance*, Calif. Mgmt. Rev. 25 (Spring 1989).

253. *See* Armentano, *Time to Repeal Antitrust Regulation?*, 35 Antitrust Bull. 311 (1990).

254. *See* Kovacic, *supra* note 2; Rowe, *supra* note 5.

255. *See* Kovacic, *Federal Antitrust Enforcement, supra* note 149, at 186-92; Kovacic, *Public Choice, supra* note 150, at 497-500.

differentials between private and public compensation rates have made it increasingly difficult for the Antitrust Division and the FTC to recruit and retain skilled attorneys. At the present time, the federal antitrust agencies will adhere largely to a Borkian agenda—focusing on horizontal price-fixing and horizontal mergers—because they lack the institutional means to do otherwise.

2. Conservative Judicial Antitrust Preferences

The federal judiciary is likely to act as a substantial counterweight to a major leftward shift in antitrust policy because the prescriptions of *The Antitrust Paradox* have gained considerable favor among federal judges.[256] Judicial appointments since 1980 have reinforced the conservatism that began to emerge in appellate decisions in the 1970s. President Reagan appointed three Justices to the Supreme Court as well as approximately half of the judges currently sitting on the lower federal courts.[257] President Bush has appointed one Justice to the Supreme Court and, if history holds true, he will select between 20 and 25 percent of the federal bench by the end of 1992. In making his appointments, President Bush probably will continue the pattern of conservatism that characterized his predecessor's choices.[258] Like Ronald Reagan, President Bush may continue the pattern of nominating conservative academics such as Antonin Scalia, Robert Bork, Frank Easterbrook, Douglas Ginsburg, Richard Posner, and Ralph Winter, individuals whose academic experience positions them to imbue antitrust with conservative rules of decision. These and other judges with similar

---

256. *See* Kovacic, *Reagan's Judicial Appointees and Antitrust in the 1990s*, 59 FORDHAM L. REV. (forthcoming) (analyzing voting behavior of Carter and Reagan appointees).

257. *See* Kamen & Marcus, *A Chance to Deepen Stamp on the Courts*, Washington Post, Jan. 29, 1989, at A1, col. 4.

258. *See* Johnston, *Bush Appears Set to Follow Reagan by Putting Conservatives on Bench*, N.Y. Times, May 31, 1989, at B5, col. 1; Moran, *In His Own Image*, Legal Times, Dec. 31, 1990 at 1, col. 3. The District of Columbia Circuit's decision in United States v. Baker Hughes, Inc., 908 F.2d 981 (D.C. Cir. 1990) may provide a telling glimpse of the future. In an opinion by Judge Clarence Thomas, a Bush appointee, the court of appeals rejected a Justice Department challenge to a merger of two manufacturers of drilling rigs. The court acidly criticizes the Department's theory, noting that "[T]he government hardly maximizes its scarce resources when it allows statistics alone to trigger its ponderous enforcement machinery." *Id.* at 63,981 n.13. A Reagan appointee (Judge David Sentelle) and a Carter appointee (Judge Ruth Ginsburg) joined Judge Thomas' opinion.

antitrust preferences will exert considerable control over how successfully public or private litigants pursue theories of liability that entail major extensions of antitrust doctrine beyond the comparatively conservative boundaries of the 1980s.

V. Conclusion: An Overall Assessment

Determining cause and effect in the contest of antitrust policy views is an uncertain process. The publication of *The Antitrust Paradox* was not the sole event of its time. Rather, the appearance of this volume coincided with a gradual rightward shift in the nation's political preferences, a decline in the relative position of American firms in the world economy, and intellectual ferment in the law and economics of antitrust policy. The transformation of antitrust policy over the past decade had many sources, and it would be rash to suggest that it flowed from a single book.

It is equally clear that the transformation would have proceeded much differently had Robert Bork not sequestered himself at the American Enterprise Institute in the Spring of 1977 and completed the scholarly journey he began at Yale in the late 1960s. Bork and others had made many of its principal points before, but *The Antitrust Paradox* provided a single, powerful synthesis of a conservative vision whose essential foundations were built in Chicago in the early 1950s. Notwithstanding the contributions of other individuals and social forces, this compelling vision has served to shape the antitrust world in several significant ways.

Bork's book has inspired a valuable ongoing debate about the goals of the antitrust laws. His scholarship is the dominant cause of the revival of efforts since 1978 by historians and others to examine the historical origins of the American antitrust system. Regardless of whether his original intent efficiency thesis is correct (I believe his intent-based interpretation of the legislative debates is ultimately unsupportable), he has clarified and improved the content of policy discourse through his insistence that careful attention to goals is an essential predicate to sensible public enforcement choices and judicial decisionmaking. In addition, he has forced his opponents to propose how non-efficiency objectives—social and political aims—are to be administered in the decision to prosecute and in the adjudication of individual cases. Bork's efficiency prescription will retain its power and influence because his adversaries, with rare exceptions, have failed to formulate administrable alternative goal structures. The burden of proof today rests with those who would sacrifice efficiency for other goals, and few have born the burden successfully.

Even among those who reject Bork's single-minded focus on efficiency, Bork's analysis has elicited an increasingly broad recognition that efficiency concerns deserve greater weight in antitrust policymaking. Today most commentators agree that the hostility (or indifference) of many Warren-era decisions to efficiency was inappropriate. Even those who have criticized Reagan antitrust policies as unduly permissive have routinely disavowed any desire to return to the restrictive approaches of the 1960s.[259] *The Antitrust Paradox* unmistakeably shifted the center of the debate and mainstream policy views to the right.[260] Just as Bork exaggerated the disarray of antitrust in 1978, so too, opponents to his nomination to Supreme Court refused to acknowledge how extensively his views had gained acceptance.

In addition to fostering a greater solicitude for efficiency as a broad policymaking criterion, Bork's book has influenced the reconstruction of specific antitrust doctrine. Bork's analysis has played an important part in guiding enforcement agencies and courts to recast enforcement policy and doctrine concerning horizontal restraints, vertical restraints, and single-firm conduct.[261] For at least the short term, this trend is likely to continue. Within the judiciary, Bork's influence is evident in the opinions of court of appeals judges such as Frank Easterbrook, Douglas Ginsburg, Richard Posner, and Ralph Winter. Even though the Senate rejected Bork's nomination to the Supreme Court, his thinking is nonetheless evident in the writings of the Court.[262]

This is not to say that we are witnessing a relentless, irreversible march toward full adoption of Bork's precepts. The debate on goals is hardly over. *The Antitrust Paradox*'s greatest rhetorical strength—its insistence that Congress intended no goal other than

---

259. *See, e.g.*, Fox & Sullivan, *Antitrust—Retrospective and Prospective: Where Are We Coming From? Where Are We Going?*, 62 N.Y.U. L. Rev. 936, 944 (1987); Pitofsky, *Does Antitrust Have a Future?*, 76 Geo. L.J. 321, 323-24 (1987).

260. *See Bork Confirmation Hearings*, *supra* note 11, at 291-92 (quoting, among others, Philip Areeda, Donald Baker, James Halverson, and Thomas Kauper).

261. Jonathan Baker makes the point as follows: "Over the past fifteen years, the courts and enforcement agencies have created Robert Bork's antitrust paradise." Baker, *supra* note 240, at 655.

262. Every current member of the Court except Justice Souter has joined in an opinion that cites *The Antitrust Paradox* favorably. Justice Scalia probably is most familiar with the content of *The Antitrust Paradox*. In the preface of the volume, Bork thanked him for reading the final chapter of the book. R. Bork, *supra* note 10, at x.

the attainment of economic efficiency—is also a great weakness. Bork's conclusion that efficiency guided the enactment of the antitrust laws rested substantially upon the type of "falsely imagined past" that he said was a major source of undue antitrust expansionism.[263] Whether opponents of Bork's view can exploit his historical overstatement and convince courts and policymakers to apply rival models of antitrust goals remains to be seen. Even if the efficiency model prevails, one can expect economists and lawyers to develop impressive arguments for extending the reach of antitrust within the efficiency model.

That *The Antitrust Paradox* will figure prominently in the tension over future policy development is a powerful testament to its influence. Perhaps the best assessment of the impact of *The Antitrust Paradox* was written within a year of the book's publication. In a 1979 book review, Oliver Williamson wrote:

[t]he core issues with which antitrust must come to terms are the ones that Bork addresses in this book, and his tendency to define antitrust issues narrowly ensures that the dialogue will continue. Whether efficiency is the only legitimate antitrust goal is certain to be disputed by many thoughtful students of antitrust, and even within an efficiency framework, static economic analysis must sometimes give way to intertemporal and process analysis if dominant firm issues are to be addressed in relevant terms.[264]

Concluding his review, Williamson predicted that "antitrust can look forward to a lively future, in which Professor Bork and this book will doubtlessly play influential parts. The Antitrust Paradox is essential reading for antitrust scholars and practitioners alike."[265] So it is today.

---

263. R. Bork, *supra* note 10, at 15.
264. Williamson, Book Review, 46 U. CHI. L. REV. 526, 530 (1979).
265. *Id.* at 530-31.

Does Collusion Pay . . . Does Antitrust Work?*

DAVID F. LEAN
JONATHAN D. OGUR
ROBERT P. ROGERS
Federal Trade Commission
Washington, D. C.

I. Introduction [1]

While the per se illegality of price fixing has been relatively uncontroversial compared to other aspects of antitrust policy, some argue that market forces can break down collusion, even without intervention by the authorities [20]. This argument raises the possibility that collusion is not profitable, and that antitrust policy is unnecessary and ineffective.

Relatively few studies have examined either the impact of conspiracy on profitability, or the effectiveness of antitrust intervention [18, 276–77]. In one of these studies, Asch and Seneca [1] looked at a sample of 51 firms that were found guilty of, or that pleaded *nolo contendere* to, Sherman Act conspiracy charges during 1958–67. When these companies were compared to a random sample of 50 other firms, the authors found (to their surprise) that the conspiring firms were less profitable than those in the control group, other things equal. In another study, Sultan [20] observed a positive but insignificant relationship between price fixing meetings and turbine generator prices. In a subsequent simulation analysis, however, he found a significant impact of conspiracy: predicted turbine generator prices for a model including conspiracy effects were about nine percent higher than those for a model without conspiracy [20, 348]. In sum, the questions of conspiracy's impact and antitrust's effectiveness remain uncertain.

The present study examines the impacts of collusion and antitrust conduct remedies on profitability in electrical equipment markets. We inquire whether conspiracy raised equipment manufacturers' returns and whether antitrust conduct remedies were an effective policy response. We also examine whether market signaling increased turbine generator makers' profitability after antitrust ended the conspiratorial meetings. [2]

In the next section, we provide a short history of collusion in electrical equipment markets between 1950 and 1970. Then, we describe the structure-conduct-performance

*The authors are staff members in the Federal Trade Commission's Bureau of Economics. The views expressed in this paper are the authors' and therefore do not necessarily reflect the position of the Federal Trade Commission.

1. The analysis of this paper has benefited from critical comments by Keith Anderson, John Kwoka, James Langenfeld, William Long, John Peterman, David Ravenscraft, Donald Sant, F. M. Scherer, and Robert Tollison. However, any remaining errors are the authors'.

2. Market signaling can be thought of as the attempt by rival sellers to increase prices, using public communication (e.g. in the media or in published price books) and facilitating practices such as "most favored buyer" contractual arrangements. Signaling is thus an alternative form of conduct to conspiratorial meetings. To the best of our knowledge, no previous studies have tried to estimate the effect of market signaling on rates of return.

model that we use to estimate the impacts of collusion and antitrust on profitability. Following that, we discuss the data used for estimation of the model. And finally, we present the results of that estimation.

II. Collusion in Electrical Equipment Markets

During the 1950s, more than 30 electrical equipment manufacturers engaged in elaborate conspiracies to fix the prices they charged utilities [7; 24]. The conspirators' illegal meetings covered 20 product lines with annual sales approaching $2 billion in the late 1950s. The meetings ended in 1959 at about the same time that a Department of Justice investigation was beginning. Following successful prosecution under Section 1 of the Sherman Act, conspiring companies and individual officers were fined more than $1 million, and some executives received jail sentences. Subsequent damage suits by privately-owned utilities and by state and local governments obtained refunds from the manufacturers, lowering their after-tax incomes in the early 1960s by more than $150 million. Consent agreements with the manufacturers forbade further price fixing activities, and the available evidence indicates that the meetings were not resumed [14, 925; 22, 3].

In 1963, however, The General Electric Company announced major changes in its turbine generator pricing policies [5, 27] which were interpreted by the Department of Justice as an attempt to engage in price signaling. These changes included a revised price book that greatly simplified price calculation for the complex, custom-built product and a published multiplier that facilitated price change computation. Another important change was the initiation of a "price protection" (or most favored buyer) policy in which any discount given to one buyer would be granted retroactively to all buyers who had ordered in the previous six months. Through this policy, GE raised the cost to itself of discounting. In early 1964 GE's major rival, Westinghouse Electric Corporation, responded with similar price policy changes. These policies continued in effect at least until the end of the decade.

A Department of Justice investigation of the revised turbine generator pricing policies found no evidence of conspiracy between GE and Westinghouse. However, interpreting the two companies' new policies as devices to achieve adherence, via public communication and facilitating practices, to the same quoted price, Justice obtained modifications in the consent agreements with the companies to forbid the objectionable activities.

Despite the passage of more than 20 years since the equipment manufacturers' conspiracies were exposed, their impact remains in question. In numerous damage suits, utilities argued, and the courts generally agreed, that the meetings raised equipment prices [2]. Manufacturers and others asserted, however, that uncontrollable cheating on agreements prevented price elevation [23; 20]. Similarly, the impact of price signaling is uncertain.

In addition to being unsettled questions, the impacts of conspiracy, signaling, and conduct remedies on electrical equipment markets are important ones. Proper implementation of antitrust policy in the future requires information on the successes and failures of past applications. The electrical equipment conspiracies were one of the most widespread, dramatic violations of the Sherman Act's Section 1. The conduct remedies imposed were among the strongest ever. The investigation of market signaling involved a novel extension of the antitrust laws to a form of conduct alleged to fix prices without conspiracy. In addition to banning certain facilitating practices, the remedies required sellers to reduce the amount of information on prices and pricing policy that they make public about their product. This implies that, in a highly concentrated industry such as turbine generators, too much such information can be disseminated, from a public welfare point of view.

III. The Model

To estimate the effects of collusion and antitrust on profitability, we use a structure-conduct-performance model. The performance variable to be explained is the ratio of product line operating income to net sales $(OPSALE)$.[3] The explanators include conduct variables to capture the effects of conspiracy and signaling, as well as industry structure variables, product line characteristics, and company characteristics that might influence product line profitability.[4]

In general, our model can be written as follows:

Profitability $= f$(seller conduct, industry structure, company size,
market share, capital / sales ratio),

where all variables are defined on an annual basis for product lines. While profitability is assumed to be endogenous, industry structure, seller conduct, and all other explanatory variables are assumed to be determined exogenously.[5]

Our model differs from most previous structure-conduct-performance models in its treatment of conduct. First, conduct variables appear explicitly in our model — in fact they are the main focus of our study. Due perhaps to a paucity of data, most previous studies have examined only structure-performance links.[6] Second, we assume that, between 1950 and 1970, the electrical equipment manufacturers' decision whether or not to conspire on prices was determined largely by public policy. In other words, the choice between clearly illegal price fixing meetings and other (possibly legal) forms of pricing, such as market signaling, is assumed to have depended primarily on the probabilities of detection and punishment and on the cost of any resulting penalties [3]. These probabilities and penalties are assumed to have depended, in turn, on antitrust policy.

The historical relationship between antitrust and conspiracy in the electrical equip-

---

3. In this paper, we will use the following terminology: "company" will refer to data for an entire firm, which may include operations in several industries; "industry" data will consist of the sum of all companies' data pertaining to a particular product market; and "product line" will mean the data of a single company that relate to its operations in a single industry. For example, data for General Electric Company are company data, turbine generator data for all companies that make turbine generators are industry data, and General Electric's turbine generator data are product line data.

4. See Table III for brief definitions of these variables, and Lean, Ogur, and Rogers [11] for more detailed definitions and further discussion of them.

5. An alternative would be to attempt to construct and estimate a simultaneous equation model in which profitability, collusion, and, perhaps, concentration were endogenous. However, in previous studies [19;13] which estimated three-equation models, the authors noted that simultaneous equation bias appears not to be important in structure-performance models [19, 1109], or seems no more important than the bias due to the omission of relevant explanatory variables [13, 646]. With regard to the latter bias, Maddala [12, 231] suggests that OLS estimation is more robust in the presence of specification errors than many simultaneous-equation estimation methods. Hence, single equation estimation of structure-conduct-performance models may be the preferred method and certainly provides useful results.

6. Some previous studies that included conduct variables are discussed in Lean, Ogur, and Rogers [11, 14–17].

ment industries is consistent with Becker's [3] theory of crime. The electrical equipment cases significantly reduced the expected net returns to conspiracy relative to the returns to other forms of pricing. Prior to those cases, criminal penalties were generally too small, relative to the expected gains, to deter price fixing [16, 388–95]. Fines were insignificant, and jail sentences were almost never imposed. By contrast as a result of criminal prosecutions some electrical equipment executives were jailed, and several were fired or demoted. In addition, a large number of damage suits obtained refunds for equipment buyers that cost the conspiring manufacturers more than $150 million after taxes [11, 28]. As described above in section II, the evidence indicates that the meetings ended when antitrust investigations began, and were not resumed.

The importance of the link between antitrust policy and conspiracy is also suggested by the industrial organization paradigm. Although that paradigm emphasizes links from structure to conduct to performance, Scherer [18, 5–6] refers to ". . . public policy measures [an element of 'basic conditions'] designed to improve performance by manipulating structure *or* conduct" (emphasis added). Antitrust's "conduct remedies", the focus of our study, are a familiar example of measures designed to affect performance by changing conduct, but not structure.[7]

The conduct variables in our model represent periods of price fixing conspiracy during the 1950s and a period of price signaling during the 1960s. Three of these variables, $CON5054$, $CON5659$, and $CON5759$, capture the impacts of conspiratorial meetings during the periods 1950–54, 1956–59, and 1957–59, respectively. A fourth conduct variable, $CON55$, represents the "white sale", a period of sharp price reductions starting in January 1955, accompanied by a cessation of meetings in at least some markets [20, 40, 46, and 63]. And $CON5059$ permits an appraisal of conspiracy's impact over the entire decade of the 1950s. Finally, $SIG6470$ captures the effect of price signaling between 1964, when GE and Westinghouse made major revisions in their pricing policies, and 1970, the end of our study period. We expect these conduct variables to have positive regression coefficients, with that of $CON55$ smaller than the others.

The conduct variables discussed thus far capture the average effect of conspiracy across the eight product markets in our sample. In some regressions, we instead use eight product-specific conspiracy variables to permit variation in the impact of conspiracy across markets. We expect these conspiracy variables to have positive coefficients.[8]

Data on the organization of conspiracies in the eight electrical equipment industries in our sample consist primarily of the number of participants in each conspiracy. As indicated in the indictments [11, 57–59] this number varied from three in the meter industry to nine in the insulator industry. Findings by Comanor and Schankerman [4] suggest that such variation is associated with differences in the organization of price fixing activities. Those authors observed that in a sample of sealed bid markets,[9] the collusive pricing scheme varied with the number of conspirators. In industries with a relatively large number of firms, conspirators tended to set identical prices without attempting to allocate market shares. By contrast, in industries with few sellers, conspirators were more likely to allocate market shares by rotating low bid status and charging different prices. Given the existence

7. Examination of data obtained from electrical equipment manufacturers indicates that the structure of the electrical equipment industries was essentially unchanged from 1950 to 1970. For example, these industries remained highly concentrated throughout that period [11, 77].
8. The names of these variables are listed in Table III.
9. The government-utility portion of electrical equipment markets uses sealed bidding.

of at least this difference in conspiracy organization, it is of interest to test whether the effectiveness of conspiracy varies across the industries in our sample.

Following Kwoka [10], we use two variables to capture the effect of industry concentration on sellers' profitability: $CONC2$, the two-firm concentration ratio, and $SELLER3$, the third largest seller's market share. Based on the numerous industry-level structure-performance studies in the literature, we would expect $CONC2$ to have a positive coefficient. However, studies by Ravenscraft [17] and by others at the line of business or company level [17, 26] have observed negative concentration-profitability relationships when the positive impact of market share is taken into account. $SELLER3$'s coefficient allows us to test for electrical equipment markets the hypothesis that the third leading firm tends to undermine industry pricing agreements [10]. Under the assumption that the impact of these firms' pricing policy varies positively with their market share, $SELLER3$ will have a negative coefficient if third leading firms are price cutters.

Also included in our model are other industry structure variables that affect the ability of sellers to raise prices and profitability. $GROWDEV$ is a measure of excess demand, which we expect to have a positive coefficient. Unlike the demand growth variables in most structure-performance studies, $GROWDEV$ is designed to reflect the part of total demand growth that sellers do not anticipate in their capacity expansion decisions, i.e., the deviations from the growth trend [11, 34]. It is these deviations, positive and negative, that should increase or decrease seller profitability.[10] The industry asset/sales ratio, $ASALIND$, is designed to capture the allegedly disruptive effect of a high fixed/variable cost ratio on the ability of sellers to maintain price agreements in the face of cyclical demand fluctuations [18, 205–12]. According to this hypothesis, $ASALIND$'s coefficient is negative. On the other hand, Telser [21, 199] argues that, in these circumstances, sellers will be particularly careful to avoid such breakdowns, and to the extent they succeed, profit/sales ratios will be higher. The custom building of some electrical equipment may facilitate quality competition and make price agreements more difficult to police. The variable $CUSTOM$ is included in our model to capture this effect. We expect it to have a negative coefficient. Finally, competition from foreign producers of electrical equipment is represented by $IMPORTS$. We expect this variable to have a negative coefficient.[11]

Given industry structure, profitability has been observed to vary with the magnitude of seller operations [11, 37–39]. Our model includes two variables to express the effects of size: $COMSIZE$, absolute company size, and $SHARE$, market share or product line size in relation to industry size. We expect both of these variables to have positive coefficients. $COMSIZE$ is intended to reflect any advantages of large companies over smaller ones. For example, previous studies have found that large firms borrow at lower interest rates than small firms [18]. $SHARE$ is included to express the sum of any large suppliers' advantages over their smaller rivals, such as cost advantages or advantages in producing high-quality products.

Finally, Weiss [25] has observed that the use of accounting data in a structure-conduct-performance model requires the inclusion of a capital/sales variable to correct for the presence of normal returns in observed profits. In our model, the capital/sales variable is $ASALPRLN$, product line assets/sales, and is expected to have a positive coefficient.

10. The assumption that electrical equipment manufacturers projected demand growth at a constant exponential rate is reasonable in the light of the extremely stable growth of demand for electricity during the time period under study.

11. Using Census and trade publication information, we identified the year for each industry in which import sales first became important. These judgments were necessarily crude, but in the absence of sufficiently disaggregated import data, the best we could make.

IV. The Data

Of the 20 industries in which conspiracy was uncovered, this study examines eight.[12] The chosen markets account for just over 60 percent of total sales affected by the electrical equipment conspiracies. The industries included in our sample are: insulators, steam turbine generators, steam surface condensers, demand and watt-hour meters, power transformers, distribution transformers, power circuit breakers, and power capacitors.

Data on these eight industries were collected by a Federal Trade Commission survey of 35 firms, many of which had access to the records of other companies in addition to their own, due to mergers and acquisitions. As a result, the survey obtained data for about 70 firms that made one or more of the eight products during the 1950–70 period. The resulting sample is unique in that it contains annual data on sales, assets, and profits at the product line level.[13] Thus, our observations more closely approximate true economic markets than those usually available for economic analysis.

Using the survey data, we were able to develop 553 annual observations for product lines during the 1950–70 period. Due to company organizational changes and differing data retention policies across companies, many more observations are available per year from 1957 on than for earlier years. The changing composition of companies and industries could bias our results, for example if the profitability of the firms whose data are available for 1950–70 differs systematically from that of the firms whose data become available in 1957.

To control for this possible bias, we carried out our analysis using two data samples, one for 1957–70, and one for the entire 1950–70 period. We assumed that the 1957–70 sample would be free of bias because change in the composition of firms and industries was minimal during that period. When we used the 1950–70 sample, we included in our model dummy variables that reflect the year of initial data availability for each firm. These variables ($DATA50$, $DATA53$, $DATA55$, and $DATA56$) are designed to capture systematic differences in profitability that could bias our results.

Another possible source of bias is the accounting treatment of antitrust damage payments by some electrical equipment manufacturers.[14] Some firms subtracted damages from net sales and/or added them to cost of operations. If these adjustments were allocated to the product line level, bias could result because post-conspiracy profits would be reduced even if the conspiracy had not been successful. Because we did not know whether such allocation was done, we deleted from our sample, for the years in which damage payments were made, all 23 product line observations of the firms that followed this accounting convention.[15] After adjustments, the resulting data samples consisted of 527 observations for 1950–70 and 446 observations for 1957–70.[16]

12. Our selection was made primarily on the basis of industry size. However, we omitted such large product groups as industrial controls and low-voltage distribution equipment which contain several industries.

13. The electrical equipment data are in some ways similar to the Federal Trade Commission's Line of Business (LB) data in that both permit estimation of structure-performance relationships at a lower level of aggregation than the industry [17, 22–24]. The electrical equipment data are however, less aggregated than the LB data [11, 103–105].

14. Following the American Institute of Certified Public Accountants' recommendations at that time, most companies in our sample subtracted damage payments (net of taxes) from retained earnings. As a result, income statement items such as sales and operating income were not affected.

15. 1977 — over a decade after the payments in question — Financial Accounting Standards Board Standard #16 required any legal damage payments to be shown on the income statement in the year paid (telephone interview with technical standards staff of the American Institute of Certified Public Accountants).

16. Three product line observations were deleted to eliminate the impact on our analysis of the disequilibrium associated with either entry or exit. For the same reason, Ravenscraft [17] eliminated "births and deaths" from his sample.

Table I. OLS Regression Results

Independent Variables	Equations			
	(1)	(2)	(3)	(4)
Intercept	−5.00	−6.02	14.90	14.26
	(−0.83)	(−0.86)	(2.07)	(1.98)
GROWDEV	4.72*	5.00*	4.92*	4.98*
	(6.03)	(5.32)	(8.53)	(5.91)
CONC2	8.00	9.75	−16.56	−15.91
	(1.07)	(1.13)	(−2.18)	(−2.06)
SELLER3	116.02*	114.46*	20.36	22.50
	(7.16)	(6.42)	(0.99)	(1.09)
COMSIZE	0.45	0.05	0.02	−0.01
	(1.03)	(1.05)	(0.05)	(−0.03)
SHARE	30.34*	30.31*	28.09*	28.31*
	(6.47)	(6.42)	(6.06)	(6.10)
ASALIND	−23.60*	−23.24*	−13.76*	−14.22*
	(−4.70)	(−4.00)	(−3.84)	(−3.98)
ASALPRLN	−1.03	−1.03	−1.26	−1.29
	(−1.29)	(−1.27)	(−1.62)	(−1.65)
IMPORTS	−0.17	0.06	0.35	0.10
	(−0.13)	(0.05)	(0.25)	(0.07)
CUSTOM	−8.50*	−9.23*	−3.95*	−3.87*
	(−5.36)	(−5.01)	(−2.47)	(−2.42)
CON5059				4.46*
				(3.41)
CON5054			6.77*	
			(3.45)	
CON55			2.78	
			(0.88)	
CON5659			3.98*	
			(2.89)	
CON5759	2.65*			
	(1.91)			
INSULCON		3.08		
		(1.24)		
CDSRCON		3.31		
		(0.67)		
TURBNCON		0.56		
		(0.13)		
METERCON		4.57		
		(0.88)		
DISTCON		1.21		
		(0.43)		

Table I. (continued)

Independent Variables	Equations			
	(1)	(2)	(3)	(4)
PTRANCON		2.59 (0.77)		
BREAKCON		8.62* (1.86)		
CAPCON		1.22 (0.29)		
SIG6470	10.64* (3.15)	9.83* (2.69)	3.03 (0.91)	3.05 (0.92)
DATA50			4.02* (3.15)	4.46* (3.64)
DATA53			14.75* (4.78)	14.74* (4.77)
DATA55			12.54* (3.26)	12.26* (3.19)
DATA56			1.23 (0.35)	1.18 (0.34)
R^2	0.39	0.39	0.39	0.39
F	27.13	16.56	20.64	23.17
Sample Size	446	446	527	527
Years	57-70	57-70	50-70	50-70

* Coefficient has the predicted sign and is significantly different from zero at the 5-percent level or higher. t-statistics are in parentheses.

V. The Results

Tables I and II present, respectively, ordinary least squares (OLS) and generalized least squares (GLS) regression results for our structure-conduct-performance model.[17] Most of the independent variables have coefficients of the expected sign, and the overall explanatory power of the equations is similar to that in other recent structure-conduct-performance studies.[18]

Equations (1) and (5) pertain to the 1957-70 period and embody the maintained

17. Because structure-conduct-performance models often have heteroskedastic errors, the OLS t-statistics may be misleading. Lacking theory to guide us in choosing variables and a functional form to explain heteroskedasticity, we used a testing and correction procedure described in Maddala [12, 263-64]. First, application of a likelihood-ratio test to the OLS residuals (grouped according to the predicted value of OPSALE) indicated that heteroskedasticity was probably present. Next, dividing the standard deviation of the residuals for each group by the standard deviation for the entire sample, we constructed weights for the data and reestimated the model. This resulted in a substantial reduction in the variation of residual standard deviations across groups. It did not, however, totally eliminate this variation. The results obtained through use of this procedure are presented in the GLS equations.

18. Several goodness-of-fit measures exist for GLS regressions [9, 251-57]. In this study we use the R^2 calculated from the F-statistic that tests the hypothesis that all coefficients (except the weighted constant term) are equal to zero. This R^2 is bounded by zero and one, and it gives the percentage of dependent-variable variation that is explained by the independent variables.

Table II. GLS Regression Results

Independent Variables	Equations			
	(5)	(6)	(7)	(8)
Intercept	−12.09	−17.39	13.00	12.25
	(−3.04)	(−3.62)	(1.89)	(1.78)
GROWDEV	5.42*	6.21*	4.47*	4.56*
	(9.26)	(8.53)	(5.56)	(5.67)
CONC2	13.09*	22.44*	−11.88	−10.83
	(2.33)	(3.33)	(−1.64)	(−1.50)
SELLER3	127.99*	136.67*	13.53	15.93
	(12.51)	(12.06)	(0.68)	(0.80)
COMSIZE	0.20	0.02	0.02	−0.02
	(0.81)	(0.61)	(0.06)	(−0.05)
SHARE	32.59*	34.24*	26.30*	26.60*
	(9.07)	(9.66)	(6.06)	(6.11)
ASALIND	−18.59*	−21.70*	−11.96*	−12.44*
	(−4.51)	(−4.68)	(−3.64)	(−3.79)
ASALPRLN	−1.96	−1.99	−1.55	−1.58
	(−1.67)	(−1.69)	(−1.91)	(−1.96)
IMPORTS	0.47	0.26	1.00	0.66
	(0.50)	(0.26)	(0.74)	(0.49)
CUSTOM	−8.74*	−9.83*	−3.92*	−3.81*
	(−6.47)	(−6.02)	(−2.60)	(−2.52)
CON5059				4.23*
				(3.35)
CON5054			6.71*	
			(3.72)	
CON55			2.84	
			(0.98)	
CON5659			3.66*	
			(2.77)	
CON5759	2.02*			
	(2.28)			
INSULCON		3.78*		
		(2.54)		
CDSRCON		0.70		
		(0.16)		
TRUBNCON		−4.39		
		(−1.72)		
METERCON		0.28		
		(0.11)		
DISTCON		0.10		
		(0.06)		

Table II. (continued)

Independent Variables	Equations			
	(5)	(6)	(7)	(8)
PTRANCON		2.44 (1.13)		
BREAKCON		10.49* (3.45)		
CAPCON		2.28 (0.54)		
SIG6470	7.00* (2.69)	4.73 (1.62)	0.41 (0.13)	0.41 (0.13)
DATA50			3.15* (2.58)	3.77* (3.23)
DATA53			13.84* (4.77)	13.94* (4.80)
DATA 55			11.48* (3.11)	11.22* (3.03)
DATA56			−0.54 (−0.16)	−0.59 (−0.17)
R^2	0.32	0.32	0.26	0.26
F	20.45	12.58	11.78	13.26
Sample Size	446	446	527	527
Years	57-70	57-70	50-70	50-70

* Coefficient has the predicted sign and is significantly different from zero at the 5-percent level or higher. *t*-statistics are in parentheses.

hypothesis that conspiracy had the same impact in each of the eight product markets. The results are consistent with the existence of a successful conspiracy during the latter part of the 1950s. Profit/sales ratios are about two percentage points higher during 1957–59 than otherwise.

Equations (2) and (6) also pertain to the 1957–70 period, but relax the hypothesis of an equal conspiracy impact across electrical equipment markets. According to the results, some conspiracies appear to have been successful in raising product line returns, while others appear to have failed. During 1957–59, profit/sales ratios were over three percentage points higher in insulators and over 10 percentage points higher in circuit breakers (according to the GLS results in Table II). With the exception of turbine generators, all other product lines have higher returns during 1957–59, but none is significantly higher. Contrary to expectations, turbine generator returns are lower during 1957–59.[19]

Equations (3) and (7) examine the longer 1950–70 period and divide the conspiracy into two parts: 1950–54, when meetings may have been relatively infrequent and unor-

19. An F-test comparing the unrestricted model in equation (6) with the restricted model of equation (5) obtained a value of $F = 2.06$ which indicates an approximately significant difference at the 0.05 level [$F(0.05,7,120) = 2.09$; F (0.05, 7, infinity) = 2.01].

ganized, and 1956–59, when organized meetings may have been held relatively frequently.[20] This division allows us to test whether the conspiracy was more effective in the latter part of the 1950s than earlier in that decade. The intervening year, 1955, was the time of the "white sale" when meetings were discontinued and prices fell sharply [20, 40, 46, and 63]. The results again suggest that meetings raised profitability. Profit/sales ratios were over six percentage points higher in 1950–54 and over three percentage points higher in 1956–59. By contrast, profit/sales ratios were not significantly higher in 1955. No support is given, however, to the notion that the meetings were more effective after the white sale than before. To the contrary, the coefficient of *CON5054* is larger than that of *CON5659*.

In equations (4) and (8), we replace the three conspiracy variables with a variable equal to one for the entire 1950s (*CON5059*). With this regression, we estimated that profit/sales ratios were over four percentage points higher over that decade. Thus, even when we include the white sale year, the conspiracy appears to have raised average returns for sellers in the eight product markets in our sample.[21]

These findings suggest that, in general, electrical equipment sellers were not able to maintain prices as much above costs by non-conspiratorial pricing methods during the white sale and after antitrust investigation ended the conspiracy. The possible exception to this conclusion is turbine generators. The results in equations (1), (2), and (5) suggest that turbine generator price signaling succeeded in raising prices relative to costs. These equations provide estimates indicating that signaling caused an increase in turbine generator profitability ranging from 4 to 11 percentage points. In the remaining equations, however, we observe no significant increase in turbine generator profit/sales ratios during 1964–70.

CONC2's coefficients provide only partial support for the hypothesis that seller concentration facilitates collusion. *CONC2* is positively related to profitability in four of the eight equations in Tables I and II. Although not significant in the OLS regressions, *CONC2*'s coefficient becomes significant after we correct for heteroskedasticity. In the other four equations, however, *CONC2* is negatively related to profitability. While inconsistent with the findings of most industry-level concentration-profitability studies, this result is consistent with the results recently obtained by Ravenscraft [17] using line of business data and by others [17, 26] using LB or company data.

Contrary to Kwoka's findings [10, 33], the third largest firms' shares are positively related to profit/sales ratios. Moreover, this relationship is highly significant in four of the eight equations. Rather than playing a price cutting role, the third largest seller in electrical equipment markets may have assisted its larger rivals in maintaining price above cost.

Of the four other variables expected to affect the ability of sellers to achieve higher prices, three have significant coefficients with the predicted sign. The excess demand variable's coefficient is positive, while those of custom-building and the asset/sales ratio are negative. In other words, strong demand relative to capacity raises returns, while an increased opportunity for quality competition and a high fixed/variable cost ratio make price coordination more difficult.

Market share also has a significant positive relationship with the profit/sales ratio. In other words, sellers who are large in relation to the market appear to have cost or price

20. Sultan asserts that the frequency and organization of the meetings increased after the white sale [20, 54, 64 and 65]. For an opposing view, see Judge Feinberg [14, 923–6].
21. An F-test comparing the unrestricted model in equation (7) to the restricted model of equation (8) obtained a value of $F = 1.92$ which indicates no significant difference at the 0.05 level [$F(0.05, 2, \text{infinity}) = 3.00$].

advantages over their smaller rivals. The extent of these advantages is an important issue that we address elsewhere.[22]

By contrast with the coefficients of relative size, the absolute company size variable's coefficients are not significant. Earlier studies [6; 8] obtained similar results with these two variables. The capital/sales and import competition variables had insignificant coefficients that may reflect specification errors. For example, our model assumes that the normal return to capital is constant across electrical equipment industries and over time, thus ignoring possible risk differences. The *IMPORTS* variable is simply a crude proxy due to a paucity of disaggregated data; more precise measurement might change the results.

VI. Summary and Conclusions

By contrast with the findings of some earlier studies, our analysis suggests that collusion can raise rates of return. On average for eight electrical equipment markets during the 1950s, we observe significant effects on profitability of conspiratorial meetings by sellers. Further analysis suggests, however, that higher returns may have been limited to the insulator and circuit breaker markets. While conspiratorial meetings seem not to have raised turbine generator profit/sales ratios, price signaling appears to have done so. Because the public communication aspect of signaling is probably less effective than face to face communication in meetings, it may be that the facilitating practices element of signaling was the key to its apparent success.[23]

Our analysis suggests that, where collusion has raised sellers' returns, antitrust prosecution can lower them and reduce any social losses that were occurring. However, our analysis also suggests that, if antitrust intervention is limited to traditional forms of conspiracy (e.g., meetings in hotel rooms or other private communications), it may leave other forms of effective collusion untouched. In other words by devoting some attention to public communication and facilitating practices, the antitrust authorities may increase the benefits of their activities to society.

---

22. In Lean, Ogur, and Rogers [11, 63–73], we divided electrical equipment sellers into two strategic groups, leaders and nonleaders, along lines suggested in Porter [15, 215]. Our results are consistent with the hypothesis that cost or price advantages of large relative size do not extend beyond that of smallest leading seller.

23. An alternative explanation for this result is that while turbine generator meetings covered only a small fraction of the machines sold, signaling activities covered every sale.

Table III. Definition of Variables

$OPSALE$ = operating income/net sales
$CONC2$ = the two firm concentration ratio
$GROWDEV$ = the deviation of real industry sales about trend
$ASALIND$ = industry assets/sales
$ASALPRLN$ = product line assets/sales
$CUSTOM$ = 1 if industry's product is made to order
$IMPORTS$ = 1 if import competition is present
$CON5054$ = 1 in conspiracy years 1950-54
$CON55$ = 1 in white sale year 1955
$CON5659$ = 1 in conspiracy years 1956-59
$CON5759$ = 1 in conspiracy years 1957-59
$CON5059$ = 1 in conspiracy years 1950-59
$SIG6470$ = 1 in turbine generator market signaling years 1964-70
$COMSIZE$ = real company net sales
$SHARE$ = company market share
$SELLER3$ = third-largest seller's market share
$DATA50$ = 1 if 1950 is the year of initial data availability
$DATA53$ = 1 if 1953 is the year of initial data availability
$DATA55$ = 1 if 1955 is the year of initial data availability
$DATA56$ = 1 if 1956 is the year of initial data availability
$INSULCON$ = 1 in insulator conspiracy years 1957-59
$CDSRCON$ = 1 in condenser conspiracy years 1957-59
$TURBNCON$ = 1 in turbine generator conspiracy years 1957-59
$METERCON$ = 1 in meter conspiracy years 1957-59
$DISTCON$ = 1 in distribution transformer conspiracy years 1957-59
$PTRANCON$ = 1 in power transformer conspiracy years 1957-59
$BREAKCON$ = 1 in circuit breaker conspiracy years 1957-59
$CAPCON$ = 1 in power capacitor conspiracy years 1957-59

References

1. Asch P. and J. J. Seneca, "Is Collusion Profitable?" *Review of Economics and Statistics*, February 1976, 1-10. Reprinted in *Journal of Reprints for Antitrust Law and Economics: Predatory Conduct and Empirical Studies in Collusion*. New York: Federal Legal Publications, 1980.
2. Bane, C. A. *The Electrical Equipment Conspiracies: The Treble-Damage Actions*. New York: Federal Legal Publications, 1973.
3. Becker, G. S., "Crime and Punishment: An Economic Approach." *Journal of Political Economy*, March/April 1968, 169-217.
4. Comanor, W. S. and M. A. Schankerman, "Identical Bids and Cartel Behavior." *Bell Journal*, Spring 1976, 281-86.
5. *Electrical World*, May 27, 1963, 27.
6. Federal Trade Commission. *Economic Report on the Influence of Market Structure on the Profit Performance of Food Manufacturing Industries*. Washington, D.C.: Government Printing Office, 1969.
7. Herling, J. *The Great Price Conspiracy*. Washington, D.C.: Luce, 1962.
8. Imel, B. and P. Helmberger, "Estimation of Structure-Profits Relationships with Application to the Food Processing Sector." *American Economic Review*, September 1971, 617-27.
9. Judge, G. G., W. E. Griffiths, R. C. Hill, H. Lutkepohl, and T. C. Lee. *Introduction to the Theory and Practice of Econometrics*. New York: Wiley, 1980.
10. Kwoka, J. *Market Share, Concentration, and Competition in Manufacturing Industries*. Washington, D.C.: Federal Trade Commission, 1978.
11. Lean, D. F., J. D. Ogur, and R. P. Rogers. *Competition and Collusion in Electrical Equipment Markets: An Economic Assessment*. Washington, D.C.: Federal Trade Commission, 1982.
12. Maddala, G. S. *Econometrics*. New York: McGraw-Hill, 1977.

13. Martin, S., "Advertising, Concentration, and Profitability: The Simultaneity Problem." *Bell Journal*, Autumn 1979, 639–47.

14. *Ohio Valley Electric et al. v. General Electric et al.* 244 F. Supp. 914, 1965.

15. Porter, M. E., "The Structure Within Industries and Companies' Performance." *Review of Economics and Statistics*, May 1979, 214–27.

16. Posner, R. A., "A Statistical Study of Antitrust Enforcement." *Journal of Law and Economics*, October 1970, 365–419.

17. Ravenscraft, D. J., "Structure-Profit Relationships at the Line of Business and Industry Level." *Review of Economics and Statistics*, February 1983, 22–31.

18. Scherer, F. M. *Industrial Market Structure and Economic Performance.* 2nd edition. Chicago: Rand McNally, 1980.

19. Strickland, A. D. and L. W. Weiss, "Advertising, Concentration, and Price/Cost Margins." *Journal of Political Economy*, October 1976, 1109–21.

20. Sultan, R. G. M. *Pricing in the Electrical Oligopoly*, Vols. I and II. Cambridge, Mass.: Harvard University Press, 1975.

21. Telser, L. *Competition, Collusion, and Game Theory*. Chicago: Aldine, 1972.

22. *U.S. v. General Electric and Westinghouse.* Plaintiff's Memorandum, Civil No. 28228, 1965.

23. U.S. Senate Subcommittee on Antitrust and Monopoly. *Administered Prices.* Washington, D.C.: Government Printing Office, 1961.

24. Walton, C. and F. Cleveland. *Corporations on Trial: The Electric Cases.* California: Wadsworth, 1964.

25. Weiss, L. W. "The Concentration-Profit Relationship and Antitrust," in *Industrial Concentration: The New Learning*, edited by H. J. Goldschmid, H. M. Mann, and J. F. Weston. Boston: Little, Brown Company, 1974.

Maintaining Economic Competition: The Causes and Consequences of Antitrust

MICHAEL S. LEWIS-BECK

Economic competition is part of the American creed. When it apppeared seriously threatened by the growth of the "trusts" at the end of the nineteenth century, the Sherman Act was passed. Since then, Congress has enacted further antitrust legislation to preserve economic competition. Moreover, the platforms of the major political parties have regularly contained an antitrust plank. While Richard Hofstader could once write that the antitrust movement was "one of the faded passions of American reform," this no longer seems true.[1] Current surveys suggest that the public is again aroused over big business abuse, and increasingly favors the breakup of large corporations.[2] Checking corporate excesses and heightening competition are primary goals of consumer advocates.[3] In the

* I would like to thank anonymous reviewers for their contributions to the development of this paper. Also, I wish to acknowledge the invaluable research assistance of Greg Brunk, Paul Gough, and Richard Hardy.

[1] *The Paranoid Style in American Politics and other Essays*, (New York: Knopf, 1965), 188.

[2] Robert Lekachman, "Giving Big Business the Business," *The New York Times Book Review*, December 26, 1976, 5.

[3] Mark J. Green with Beverly C. Moore, Jr. and Bruce Wasserstein, *The Closed Enterprise System* (New York: Grossman, 1972); Ralph Nader, Mark Green, and Joel Seligman, *Taming the Giant Corporation* (New York: W. W. Norton, 1976).

1976 presidential campaign, both candidates came out strongly for strict antitrust enforcement.[4] Despite this contemporary interest, and the prominence of antitrust as an abiding value in American politics, it has received remarkably little systematic, quantitative study. Of course, a number of works on antitrust are available, but they tend to be legalistic or speculative.[5] As economists Clair Wilcox and William Shepherd observe, "There exists no recent, full, analytical appraisal of antitrust's effects."[6] A leading scholar of antitrust law, Richard Posner argues that this lack of statistical investigation is a major reason for inefficient enforcement.[7] His own impressive examination is essentially an accounting of the number and types of cases over time. My analysis takes the next step, focusing on the causes and consequences of these enforcement patterns. After considering the purposes and measurement of antitrust efforts, I evaluate leading hypotheses on the political and economic determinants of antitrust enforcement. Then, I analyze the impact of antitrust policy, to see whether it actually helps or hinders economic competition.

ANTITRUST ENFORCEMENT

There are a number of laws whose ostensible purpose is the preservation of economic competition. Major legislation in this area includes the Sherman Antitrust Act (1890), which outlawed combinations in "restraint of trade" and "monopolization;" the Clayton Act (1914), which specifically made illegal price discrimination, exclusive and tying contracts, intercorporate stockholdings, and interlocking directorates, when they "substantially lessen competition;" and the Celler-Kefauver Antimerger Act (1950), which strengthened the prohibitions of the Clayton Act against acquisition

[4] New York Times, August 1, 1976, Sec. E, 14.
[5] Donald J. Dewey, Monopoly in Economics and Law (Chicago: Rand McNally, 1959); Carl Kaysen and Donald F. Turner, Antitrust Policy (Cambridge: Harvard University Press, 1959); William Letwin, Law and Economic Policy in America (New York: Random House, 1965); A. D. Neale, The Antitrust Laws of the United States (rev. ed.; Cambridge: Cambridge University Press, 1970); S. N. Whitney, Antitrust Policies (2 vols.; New York: Twentieth Century Fund, 1958).
[6] Public Policies toward Business (5th ed.; Homewood, Illinois: Irwin, 1975), 285n.
[7] "A Statistical Study of Antitrust Enforcement," The Journal of Law and Economics, 13 (October 1970), 418-419.

of stock or assets of a competing corporation.[6] The Antitrust Division of the Justice Department and the Federal Trade Commission (FTC) are the organizations chiefly responsible for enforcement of the antitrust laws. While I ultimately examine the role of both, I focus on the Antitrust Division because it is older, has more prestige, has more money for antitrust efforts, and is generally considered more effective.[9]

As Mark Green and his colleagues remark, "filing cases is the Division's main business."[10] Therefore, I take the annual number of antitrust cases initiated as the primary measure of enforcement activity, as did Posner.[11] Data were gathered on the number of antitrust cases instituted each year by the Justice Department, from 1890 to 1974 (the mean number of cases brought annually $= 21.22$, the standard deviation $= 18.68$).[12]

THE INFLUENCE OF ECONOMIC COMPETITION ON ANTITRUST
ENFORCEMENT

Given that the prime goal of the Antitrust Division is maintaining economic competition, a reasonable expectation is that enforcement would increase in response to diminished competition. A difficulty with testing this hypothesis stems from the lack, among economists, of a generally accepted definition of competition.[13] However, a number of measures have served as proxies for economic competition, and clearly appear relevant to the Division's mission. I look at two such measures: mergers and aggregate concentration. My emphasis will be on mergers because, in addition to offering a better data base, they are conceptually more satisfactory.

[8] For a useful summary of the antitrust laws, see Clair Wilcox, *Public Policies toward Business* (4th ed.; Homewood, Illinois: Irwin, 1971), Ch. 3.

[9] Green, et al., *Closed Enterprise*, 321-322; Posner, "A Statistical Study," 419; Wilcox, *Public Policies*, Ch. 5, 262.

[10] Green, et al., *Closed Enterprise*, 119.

[11] Posner, "A Statistical Study."

[12] The number of cases instituted annually by the Department of Justice from 1890-1969 is reported in Posner, "A Statistical Study," 366. I updated the series to 1974, drawing on relevant issues of U.S. Department of Justice, *Annual Report of the Attorney General of the United States* (Washington, D.C.: Government Printing Office), and adjusting for the redundant reporting of cases, as does Posner, "A Statistical Study," 366-367.

[13] See George J. Stigler, "Perfect Competition, Historically Contemplated," *Journal of Political Economy*, 65(1:1957), for a review of its various meanings.

The leading student of American merger movements, Ralph Nelson, defines a merger as "'the combination into a single economic enterprise of two or more previously independent enterprises."[14] Willard Mueller, former Director of Economics at the FTC, argues that mergers, more than any other economic factor, explain the structure of United States industry.[15] Political scientists have used merger figures as a principle indicator of competitiveness in the economy.[16] For economists, however, the conceptual overlap between mergers and (reduced) competition is not as complete. The dispute centers on the type of merger which occurs. A horizontal merger, which joins direct competitors, clearly reduces competition. But some contend that a vertical merger (the union of buyer and seller) or a conglomerate merger (combination of firms which neither directly compete nor are in a buyer-seller relationship), may have a neutral, rather than a negative, impact on competition.[17] The great bulk of industrial combinations have been horizontal, but conglomerate mergers have recently assumed more importance. Unfortunately, these discriminations as to kind of combination cannot be made over the span of merger observations. This limitation is not particularly troublesome here, because the government has regarded conglomerate mergers as harmful to competition.[18] However, in the consideration of antitrust effects, where this is an important issue, an attempt will be made to separate out conglomerate mergers.

Drawing on various sources, a lengthy series of annual observations on mergers in manufacturing and mining was assembled, extending from 1895-1973 (the mean $= 604.32$, the standard deviation $= 597.11$).[19] The central hypothesis is that as mergers, X_t, in-

[14] *Merger Movements in American History, 1895-1956* (Princeton: Princeton University Press, 1959), 3.
[15] *A Primer on Monopoly and Competition* (New York: Random House, 1970), 65.
[16] For current examples, see Ira Katznelson and Mark Kesselman, *The Politics of Power* (New York: Harcourt Brace Jovanovich, 1975), 112-114; Mark V. Nadel, *Coporations and Political Accountability* (Lexington, Massachusetts: D. C. Heath, 1976), 121-128.
[17] Wilcox and Shepherd, *Public Policies*, 227-231.
[18] Lawrence G. Goldberg, "The Effect of Conglomerate Mergers on Competition," *The Journal of Law and Economics*, 16 (April 1973), 139-141.
[19] The observations for 1895-1918 are from Nelson, *Merger Movements*, 37, Table 14, corrected for underreporting (Nelson, *Merger Movements*, 25-28) by multiplying each observation by 3.2, the ratio derived from the overlapping

crease, the Antitrust Division will increase its enforcement activity, indicated by a rise in cases filed, Y_t. Ordinary least squares (OLS) regression of Y_t on X_t yields,

$$Y_t = 19.976 + .003X_t + e_t \qquad (1.1)$$
$$(6.75) \quad (1.00)$$
$$R^2 = .013 \qquad d = .36 \qquad N = 79$$

where R^2 = the coefficient of determination, d = Durbin-Watson statistic, N = number of observations, e = error, and the values in parentheses below the parameter estimates are the t ratios.

The coefficient for X_t is not significant at the .05 level. (When $|t| > 2.0$, the parameter estimate is considered significant at the .05 level, with a two-tailed test. This is the level and test of significance that will be used throughout the paper).[20] A protest might be registered against this negative conclusion. A legitimate expectation is that the antitrust response is delayed, rather than immediate. The enforcement role of the Antitrust Division is largely passive. It is spurred to action when a complaint is received, often from members of the business community who are in competition with the supposed lawbreaker. On the average, it takes about one year of investigating the complaint before a case would actually be filed.[21] Therefore, it could be a few years before the less competitive environment translated itself into antitrust cases instituted. More formally, the suggestion is that a realistic model would lag the merger variable n number of years, i.e.,

$$Y_t = a + bX_{t-n} + e_t \qquad (1.2)$$

This model was estimated, first lagging mergers one year, X_{t-1}, and

---

years (1919 and 1920) of the full Nelson series with the Thorp series; the observations for 1919-1939 are from Willard L. Thorp, "The Merger Movement," in *The Structure of Industry*, U.S., Temporary National Economic Committee, Monograph No. 27 (Washington, D.C.: Government Printing Office, 1941), 233; the observations for 1940-1968 are from U.S. Congress, Senate, *Economic Report on Corporate Mergers*, Staff Report of the Federal Trade Commission, Economic concentration hearings before the Subcommittee on Antitrust and Monopoly of the Committee on the Judiciary, 91st Cong., 1st sess., pursuant to S. Res. 40, Part 8A, appendix to Part 8 (Washington, D.C.: Government Printing Office, 1969), 665, Table 1-1; the observations for 1969-1973 are from U.S. Bureau of the Census, *Statistical Abstract of the United States* (Washington, D.C.: Government Printing Office, 1975), 506, No. 834.
[20] See Harry H. Kelejian and Wallace E. Oates, *Introduction to Econometrics: Principles and Applications* (New York: Harper and Row, 1974), 90-92.
[21] Green et al., *Closed Enterprise*, 118-119, 136.

then lagging it t-2, t-3, t-4, and t-5. The slope estimate becomes even less significant than in Eq. 1. In enforcing the antitrust statutes, the Division apparently fails to react to the general level of merger activity.

Lack of attention to mergers does not necessarily mean that the Justice Department is unresponsive to all signs of competitive conditions. Economic concentration measures are currently popular devices for assessing competition. There are two basic types of concentration: market and aggregate. Market concentration refers to the degree of control of an industry by its major firms. As an industry becomes dominated by its leading firms, it tends to lose its competitive structure. For example, some argue that when the top four firms have 50 percent of the market (a "four-firm concentration ratio of 50 percent"), monopolistic conditions prevail. While the use of a market concentration ratio has great appeal, it does not appear feasible in the context of this time-series analysis. F. M. Scherer, in his excellent treatment of the economic concentration issue, explicitly warns that "long run analyses [of market concentration] plunge us into the realm of incommensurables."[22] Part of the problem is that the industry definitions, which are used to develop the concentration ratios, have not remained constant over time; also, observations exist on relatively few years.[23] (see Barber, 1969; Blair, 1972; Marfels, 1975) Nevertheless, while the impact of market concentration cannot be directly assessed, there is evidence that it is related to aggregate concentration, which is measured here.[24]

Aggregate concentration refers to the extent to which manufacturing assets or sales in the entire economy are controlled by a few corporations. Students of American politics have been especially sensitive to the apparent rise in aggregate concentration, in part because of the implication that reduced economic competition means

[22] *Industrial Market Structure and Economic Performance* (Chicago: Rand McNally, 1971), 61.

[23] See Richard J. Barber, *The American Corporation* (New York: Dutton, 1970); John M. Blair, *Economic Concentration: Structure, Behavior, and Public Policy* (New York: Harcourt Brace Jovanovich, 1972); Christian Marfels, "A Bird's Eye View to Measures of Concentration," *The Antitrust Bulletin*, 20 (Fall 1975); Scherer, *Industrial Market Structure*, 49-63; William G. Shepherd, *Market Power and Economic Welfare* (New York: Random House, 1970).

[24] Mueller, *A Primer*, 37-38.

reduced political competition.[25] The measure I use is the common one of the percentage of total manufacturing assets held by the nation's 200 largest corporations, 1929-1973.[26] According to this indicator, aggregate concentration has risen rather steadily over time, measuring 45.8 percent in 1929 and 56.9 percent in 1973. Has antitrust enforcement intensified in order to combat this heightened economic concentration? Apparently not.

Regressing (OLS) enforcement activity, Y_t, on aggregate concentration, X_t, initially suggests there is a significant positive impact, which increases as X_t is lagged to three years, $b_{Y_t X_{t-3}} = 1.94$, ($t=3.76$). But before adopting this finding, it is necessary to recall that the data compose a time-series. Hence, the t ratios from OLS are generally biased in the direction of showing statistical significance, because of the usual correlation of the error terms. In this particular instance, the bias could lead to accepting, incorrectly, the hypothesis that aggregate concentration significantly influences antitrust enforcement. The Durbin-Watson statistic for the regression, $d = .95$, does suggest an autocorrelation problem. To adjust for it, I reestimate using the Cochrane-Orcutt (CORC) iterative procedure, which assumes a first-order autoregressive model of the error terms. This revised, correct estimate of the slope indicates that, in fact, aggregate concentration has *no* significant effect on antitrust cases filed, $b_{Y_t X_{t-3}} = .89$, ($t = 1.15$). (This example illustrates the misleading results that ordinary least squares estimation can

[25] Kenneth M. Dolbeare and Murray J. Edelman, *American Politics: Policies, Power, and Change* (2nd ed.; Lexington, Massachusetts: D. C. Heath, 1974), 191-193; Thomas R. Dye and L. Harmon Zeigler, *The Irony of Democracy: An Uncommon Introduction to American Politics* (North Scituate, Massachusetts: Duxbury Press, 1975), 109-110; Edwin M. Epstein, *The Corporation in American Politics* (Englewood Cliffs, New Jersey: Prentice-Hall, 1969), Ch. 8; Edward S. Greenberg, *Serving the Few: Corporate Capitalism and the Bias of Government Policy* (New York: Wiley, 1974), 36-42; Nadel, *Corporations*, 120-121.

[26] The observations for 1929-1941, 1947-1968 are from FTC, *Economic Report*, 173, Table 3-3. The observations from 1969-1973 are from Census, *Statistical Abstract 1975*, 502, No. 825. Data from 1942-1946 were not available; therefore, the mean of the series was substituted for each of these years. This procedure yields least squares estimators known as "zero order regression estimators." One advantage of these estimators is that when the correlation between X and Y is low, as it appears here, the mean square error of these estimators is smaller than that of OLS estimators calculated strictly from the cases with no missing values; see Jan Kmenta, *Elements of Econometrics* (New York: Macmillan, 1971), 341-345.

generate with time-series data. Therefore, my general analytic strategy will be to correct for autocorrelation with the CORC procedure before drawing any final conclusions about the presence of an effect. Further, a word about lagged values is in order. Throughout the paper, whenever it seems theoretically plausible that an effect might be delayed, the hypothesis is examined by lagging the independent variable up to three years, at least. The slope coefficient finally reported comes from the lag, t-n, or nonlag, t, which allowed the variable its maximum possible impact. In this way, more opportunity was given for a relationship to emerge, if one existed.)[27]

In evaluating this negative result on the effect of aggregate concentration, a caution must be entered. Even though "percentage of assets held by the top 200 corporations" is one of the better avail-

---

[27] The statistical package used to obtain the OLS estimates and these Cochrane-Orcutt (CORC) estimates was the Econometric Software Package (ESP), developed by J. Phillip Cooper, Graduate School of Business, University of Chicago. For discussion of CORC, see Kmenta, *Elements*, 269-292, from which the following description of the procedure is drawn. Assume we apply the CORC adjustment to this simple bivariate regression model.

$Y_t = a + bX_t + e_t$.

Step 1. Estimate the equation with OLS.

Step 2. Calculate the residuals, $\hat{e}_1, \hat{e}_2, \ldots \hat{e}_n$.

Step 3. Obtain an autocorrelation estimate, $\hat{\rho}$, by correlating $\hat{e}_t$ with $\hat{e}_{t-1}$.

Step 4. Construct the adjusted variables, $(Y_t - \hat{\rho}Y_{t-1})$ and $(X_t - \hat{\rho}X_{t-1})$.

Step 5. Obtain parameter estimates adjusted for autocorrelation by securing OLS estimates of $(Y_t - \hat{\rho}Y_{t-1}) = a^* + b(X_t - \hat{\rho}X_{t-1}) + u_t$.

Step 6. Repeat the above process (i.e., estimating autocorrelation, constructing new variables, and estimating the parameters) until the parameter values stabilize.

While this iterative procedure may appear quite lengthy, my experience is that convergence is achieved after a few rounds (1-5), and that the initial autocorrelation estimate is quite close to the final one. The practical implication is that, in general, it is fairly safe to stop with the parameter estimates obtained after the first autocorrelation adjustment. In fact, Kmenta, *Elements*, 288 notes that the estimators from this "two-stage" procedure have the same asytmptotic properties as the maximum likelihood estimators.

Hopefully, it is obvious that if the OLS estimates are not significant, the CORC estimates will likewise not be significant, given the positive autocorrelation which infects almost all time-series data. Thus, if Eq. 1, which aims to estimate the impact of mergers on antitrust enforcement, is reestimated using CORC, the nonsignificance reported with the OLS equation holds. The CORC estimate indicates that the effect of mergers is even less significant, as would be expected, $b_{y_t x_t} = .001$, $(t = .42)$.

able measures of aggregate concentration, it poses serious analysis difficulties. Scherer, who himself relies on this type of measure, admits that the problems with using the aggregate concentration indicators over time are acute.[28] For example, the limited variation of aggregate concentration values (here the range is only 15.8 percent) makes these parameter estimates rather unreliable.[29] Thus, because the null finding on aggregate concentration may very well be in error, I report it with some tentativeness. However, outside support comes from the view, held by some economists, that mergers are a major cause of aggregate concentration.[30] (The data at hand do show that mergers are correlated .729 with aggregate concentration.) Given the two are highly related, the expectation would be that aggregate concentration, like mergers, has no effect on antitrust enforcement, which is indeed my finding.[31]

The foregoing linear regression analyses of the merger and aggregate concentration variables suggest, surprisingly, that antitrust activity is independent of changing levels of economic competition. Notwithstanding legislative intent, the Division's enforcement of the antitrust laws does not appear stimulated by indications of intensified anticompetitive behavior. This finding compliments John Siegfried, who concludes that consideration of economic benefits, "in the

[28] Scherer, *Industrial Market Structure*, 41.

[29] On this difficulty, see Kmenta, *Elements*, 297.

[30] Phillip I. Blumberg, *The Megacorporation in American Society: The Scope of Corporate Power* (Englewood Cliffs, New Jersey: Prentice-Hall, 1975), 47-52; Ronald S. Bond, "Mergers and Mobility among the Largest Corporations, 1948-1968," *The Antitrust Bulletin*, 20, (fall 1975), 505-520; FTC, *Economic Report;* Mueller, *A Primer*, 81.

[31] This high correlation between mergers and aggregate concentration also suggests the rationale for the bivariate hypothesis testing strategy which I employ. The independent variables of this study generally exhibit extreme multicollinearity, which means their effects often cannot be reliably separated in multiple regression analysis. Suppose the equation $Y = a + b_1 X_1 + b_2 X_2 + e$. A high positive correlation of X_1 with X_2 could produce an estimate of b_2 that is statistically insignificant, even if X_2 were actually a cause of Y (see Kmenta, *Elements*, 405). Determining whether this insignificant result is valid, or simply a product of multicollinearity, can be difficult. One approach is to analyze the effect of X_2 in a separate equation, $Y = a + b_2 X_2 + e$. This allows X_2 to maximize its apparent effect on Y, for it does not have to "share" the explanation with X_1. Of course, the estimate for b_2 will be biased, exaggerating the effect of X_2 (see Kelejian and Oates, *Introduction*, 217-219). Under these unduly favorable conditions of the bivariate regression model, if statistical significance is not uncovered, then its emergence in a multiple regression context would neither be expected nor reliable.

form of efficiency gains and income redistributions," does not influence antitrust case work.[32] Such results prompt the further question of whether antitrust activity is at all responsive to the economic environment. Posner offers the hypothesis that enforcement varies with the general state of the economy.[33] Periods of economic expansion, for example, might be accompanied by a greater incidence of antitrust violations, causing more cases to be brought. This possibility was tested by regressing antitrust cases filed, Y_t, on the GNP growth rate, X_t, and, then, on the unemployment rate, Z_t.[34] Estimation (CORC) indicates the GNP growth rate is not significantly related to antitrust enforcement, $b_{y_t x_t} = .03$, ($t = .20$). Similarly, significance is not approached when the GNP variable is lagged (t-1, t-2, t-3). Also, the supposed significant effect of unemployment also fails to emerge (CORC), $b_{y_t x_{t-1}} = .46$, ($t = 1.16$).

Thus, the overall level of economic activity does not seem to influence the level of antitrust enforcement. Nor is it more specifically affected by the degree of competitiveness in the economy. Contrary to expectatoins, antitrust enforcement is quite unrelated to presumably relevant conditions of the economic system.

THE INFLUENCE OF PARTISAN POLITICS ON ANTITRUST ENFORCEMENT

Upon reflection, the absence of an antitrust response to diminished economic competition appears less surprising. A rationalistic view of law enforcement, which supposes increased crime produces more crime-fighting, is perhaps naive. The traditional notion that an agency mechanically administers the law as need be, in the form handed to it by the "political" branches of government, is no longer widely held.[35] Instead, it is recognized that politics pervades ad-

[32] "The Determinants of Antitrust Activity," *The Journal of Law and Economics*, 18 (October 1975), 568.

[33] Posner, "A Statistical Study," 367.

[34] Data on the GNP growth rate, to 1970, were obtained from U.S. Bureau of Economic Analysis, *Long Term Economic Growth 1860-1970* (Washington, D.C.: Government Printing Office, 1973), 105, Chart 17; data for 1971-1974 are from Census, *Statistical Abstract 1975*, 382, No. 618. The annual percentage unemployed, to 1970, was taken from Economic Analysis, *Long Term Economic*, 212, Series B1 and B2; the figures for 1971 to 1975 were taken from Census, *Statistical Abstract 1975*, 349, No. 571.

[35] Frank J. Goodnow, *Politics and Administration* (New York: Russell and Russell, 1900).

ministration. The Antitrust Division provides no exception to this rule. In addition to formal political influences (e.g., the President appoints the head, the Congress sets the budget), the Division is often subject to informal political pressures. The President sometimes pushes for a case to be initiated or dropped. Members of Congress do likewise.[36] For example, it was claimed Senator Pastore ". . . preached anti-poverty to the Justice Department and has all but undone the Government's assault on Kaiser Aluminum Chemical Corp.'s (sic) acquisition from the U.S. Rubber of a wire and cable plant in Bristol, Rhode Island."[37]

It is reasonable to assume that these instances of political influence are motivated in part by partisan considerations.[38] A common belief is that Republicans, because of their allegedly greater attachment to the free enterprise system, pursue antitrust enforcement more earnestly than Democrats.[39] Others content that support for antitrust is bipartisan.[40] Below, I examine the effect of partisanship on antitrust enforcement, looking first at the Presidency and then at the Congress.

Since the Sherman Act, both Democratic and Republican presidents have occasionally asserted themselves on the antitrust issue. Although Theodore Roosevelt cultivated his reputation as a serious trustbuster, his immediate successors actually started more cases than he did. Democrat Woodrow Wilson, for example, initiated over twice as many suits as TR. In his 1912 campaign against Roosevelt, Wilson spoke out forcefully against big business combinations: "The masters of the government of the United States are the combined capitalists and manufacturers of the United States. . . . [the laws should] pull apart, and gently, but firmly and persistently dissect."[41] But after Wilson, antitrust languished under the Republican presidencies of Harding, Coolidge, and Hoover. In the eyes of one critic, during these Republican administrations, "in-

---

[36] For a superb discussion of the "politics" of antitrust, see Green et al., *Closed Enterprise*, Ch. 2.

[37] Quoted in Kenneth G. Elzinga, "The Antimerger Law: Pyrrhic Victories?," *The Journal of Law and Economics*, 12 (April 1969), 73.

[38] Nadel, *Corporations*, 236, explicitly endorses this view.

[39] See Green et al., *Closed Enterprise*, 113.

[40] Dolbeare and Edelman, *American Politics*, 193; Mueller, *A Primer*, 158; Wilcox, *Public Policies*, 52-53, 91-92.

[41] Quoted in Hofstadter, *The Paranoid Style*, 208.

dustry enjoyed, to all intents and purposes, a moratorium from the Sherman Act. . . ."[42]

Such patterns hint that, in fact, Democratic presidents are more vigorous enforcers of antitrust. But these examples are confined to a few administrations. To discover if a general partisan impact exists, I regress annual number of cases filed, Y_t, on the President's party label, X_t.[43] However, it is perhaps unrealistic to expect that the presidential impact would make itself felt immediately; after taking office, some time will pass before the President presses for a suit and finally gets it instituted. Indeed, OLS estimates suggest this is the pattern, for apparently significant effects do not emerge until X_{t-3}. But, when the CORC adjustment is made this relationship does not hold up, $b_{Y_t X_{t-3}} = -.88$, ($t = -.23$). The conclusion is that the President does not exert a significant partisan influence on antitrust enforcement. This result parallels that of Posner.[44] Still, one may charge that this analysis fails to incorporate the more qualitative impact of presidential partisanship. To investigate this possibility, Posner related the initiation of "landmark" cases to presidential party, and again found a negligible relationship.[45] Clearly, at least at the presidential level, antitrust enforcement is a bipartisan affair.

Congressional influence in antitrust is extensive. In addition to deciding on the Division's budget, Congress may actually grant special treatment to certain corporations, as with the Lockheed "bail-out" bill. Louis Kohlmeier estimates that about one-fourth of the nation's businesses have been specifically exempted from the strictures of antitrust.[46] Also, even the mildest inquiries from Congress receive immediate attention from the Division. All congressional correspondence is answered within 48 hours. In explaining this practice, a Policy Planning Director remarked, "They can de-

[42] Quoted in Wilcox, *Public Policies*, 91.

[43] Republican was scored "1" and Democrat was scored "0." Observations, to 1900, were taken from U.S. Bureau of the Census, *Historical Statistics of the United States, Colonial Times to 1957* (Washington, D.C.: Government Printing Office, 1960), 682-683, Series Y 27-31; observations for 1901-1975 were taken from Census, *Statistical Abstract 1975*, 435, No. 705.

[44] Posner, "A Statistical Study," 411-412.

[45] *Ibid.*, 412-413.

[46] *The Regulators: Watchdog Agencies and the Public Interest* (New York: Harper and Row, 1969), 104.

stroy us with the stroke of a pen."[47] The Senate Antitrust and
Monopoly Subcommittee, which was chaired by Phillip Hart, has
the second largest subcommittee budget in Congress. It is regarded
as more productive than the House Antitrust Subcommittee, which
has a much smaller budget. This hints that partisanship might have
greater opportunity for influence in the Senate than in the House.
More generally, the direction (although not the significance) of the
presidential findings suggests that as Republicanism in Congress
increases, antitrust enforcement would diminish.

To examine the impact of Senate partisanship, the annual percentage of Republican seats, X_t, was used to predict antitrust cases instituted, Y_t. A similar equation was estimated for the House.[48]
Does antitrust enforcement vary with the changing partisan composition of the Congress? The answer is negative, for both houses.
While the strength of the slope coefficient increases as X_t is lagged,
as one might expect, significance (.05 level) is never attained. For
the Senate, the CORC estimate is $b_{Y_t X_{t-8}} = -.36$, ($t = -1.59$). This
implies that, for every three additional Republican Senators, only
one less antitrust case is pursued. However, even this apparent
effect, trivial as it would be, is not statistically significant according
to the t ratio. The impact of House Republicanism appears still
weaker; the comparable estimate is $b_{Y_t X_{t-8}} = -.09$, ($t = -.62$).

Political party cleavages, while they may be quite important for
other public outcomes, appear irrelevant for antitrust policy. Neither the party preference of the President, nor party differences in
Congress exhibit a meaningful impact on the number of cases the
Division files. This bipartisan hypothesis of antitrust enforcement
receives further endorsement when the dependent variable is the
Division's budget, rather than its cases.[49] In his work on the politics

---

[47] Green, et al., Closed Enterprise, 119.

[48] The annual percentage of Senate and House seats, respectively, that were
Republican was calculated from Census, Historical Statistics, 691, Series Y139-
145, for 1868-1958; and from Census, Statistical Abstract 1975, 444, No. 715,
for 1959-1975.

[49] The annual Antitrust Division budget figures (in thousands of current
dollars) for 1921-1975 were taken from the actual outlays reported in the
appropriate issues of U.S., The Budget of the United States Government
(Washington, D.C.: Government Printing Office). To adjust the budget figure
from current dollars to constant dollars, it was divided by the year's Consumer
Price Index (1967 = 100), given in Economic Analysis, Long Term Economic,

of congressional appropriations, Richard Fenno found that party control of the Congress can influence agency funding.[50] However, the data at hand indicate that the Antitrust Division budget is *not* affected by variations in congressional partisanship (CORC estimates showed that percentage of Republican seats for the Senate, X_t, and House, Z_t, in turn, were not significantly related at the .05 level to the Antitrust Division budget, Y_t, even lagging the partisanship measures up to three years: $b_{Y_t X_{t-3}} = -.18$, $t = -1.35$; $b_{Y_t Z_{t-3}} = -.07$, $t = -.67$. This null finding was repeated when President's party, P_t, was used as the independent variable, $b_{Y_t P_{t-3}} = 1.11$, $t = .42$).

While these results may be interpreted as bipartisan support, it is certainly not eager support. Neither Democrats nor Republicans seem firmly committed to maintaining economic competition. Of course the Antitrust Division budget has grown, but at a slower pace than that of most other agencies.[51] What backing it has seems due largely to its law enforcement role, which members of Congress tend to view as "essential."[52] However, unlike the FBI, the Division is not granted virtually whatever it requests.[53] The congressional goal for antitrust is not one of "stamping out anticompetitive crime." Rather the aim appears to be maintaining minimal, perhaps merely symbolic, protection for the business community and the public-at-large. This implication is bolstered when the effects of antitrust enforcement are analyzed.

THE EFFECTS OF ANTITRUST ENFORCEMENT

Although antitrust has occupied a prominent place in American political lore, there is little quantitative knowledge of its competitive impact. Georgge Stigler suggests scholars have shied away from a quantitative assessment because "The task is formidable."[54] That is has remained so is apparent from the current evaluation by Wilcox and Shepherd, who conclude "nobody really knows what

---

222-223, Series B69, and in Census, *Statistical Abstract 1975*, 422, No. 687, for 1971-1975.

[50] *The Power of the Purse* (Boston: Little, Brown, 1966), 382-384.
[51] Green, et al., *Closed Enterprise*, 122-124.
[52] Fenno, *The Power*, 370.
[53] Green, et al., *Closed Enterprise*, 124.
[54] George J. Stigler, "The Economic Effects of the Antitrust Laws," *The Journal of Law and Economics*, 9 (October 1966), 225.

effects it has."[55] Below I examine the influence of antitrust on merges. First, I regress the annual merger level, Y_t, on the number of antitrust cases filed, X_t. OLS analysis implies that X_t has a positive effect, which is not even in the expected direction, $b_{Y_t X_t} = 3.67$, ($t = 1.00$). Further, as X_t is lagged, this positive relation actually increases. Antitrust activity, as measured by cases brought, does not appear to enhance economic competition.

But, a critic might object that these findings mask the true competitive effects of antitrust, because the merger variable includes conglomerate mergers, which became especially important in the 1960s. While the government has challenged conglomerate mergers, there is controversy over their impact. Some economists argue they can be quite anticompetitive, but others disagree.[56] Ideally, then, the effects of antitrust should be assessed with conglomerate mergers excluded. However, as Stigler observes, "it seems incredible but it is true that all forms of merger are combined in the standard merger series."[57] Nevertheless, it is possible to adjust the series for the presence of conglomerate mergers, using the merger by type data available since 1948. Therefore, I reduce total merger scores for these years, to the extent their conglomerate merger percentage exceeds the conglomerate merger percentage of the base period, 1948-51. (The computation of these adjusted scores is fully detailed in the footnote).[58] This procedure tends to smooth out the

[55] Wilcox and Shepherd, Public Policies, 111.

[56] U.S., Congress, Senate, Testimony, John M. Blair, Economic concentration hearings before the Subcommittee on Antitrust and Monopoly of the Committee on the Judiciary, 91st Cong. 1st sess; pursuant to S. Res. 40, Part 8 (Washington, D.C.: Government Printing Office, 1969-1970), 4890; Goldberg, "The Effects of Conglomerate,"; Mueller, A Primer, Ch. 6.

[57] Stigler, "The Economic Effects," 232.

[58] "Assets" and "number" data on all mergers by type are available back to 1948, for "large" mergers. The absence of these data on all mergers is not an obstacle. The number of large mergers, defined as the number of concerns with assets of 10,000,000 dollars or more acquired, correlates almost perfectly with the total number of mergers, $r = .955$, for 1948-1973; data on the number of large mergers were obtained from U.S. Federal Trade Commission, Bureau of Economics, Statistical Report on Mergers and Acquisitions, (Washington, D.C.: Government Printing Office, October, 1973, 61-62). The proportion of merger activity which is conglomerate is virtually identical, regardless of whether the determination is by number of concerns acquired, or assets acquired. (For 1948-1973, conglomerate mergers were 73.1 percent of the large mergers, representing 74.1 percent of the assets acquired; see U.S. Federal Trade Commission, Bureau of Economics, Statistical Report on Mergers and

potentially confounding conglomerate merger wave, and leave a series with variations attributable largely to horizontal mergers, which are unambiguously anticompetitive.[59] If I regress (OLS) this adjusted merger series, labelled here and elsewhere as M_t, on anitrust cases, X_t, the following results are obtained:

$$M_t = 552.16 - 1.65X_t + e_t \qquad\qquad (1.3)$$
$$(6.20)\ (-.53)$$
$$R^2 = .004 \qquad d = 1.02 \qquad N = 79$$

While the slope is now in the expected direction, it is not close to being statistically significant. Even adjusting for conglomerate mergers, the antitrust enforcement of the Division does not appear to foster economic competition.

However, a further protest might be raised. When the residuals from Eq. 3 are plotted against time, a serious deviation occurs at 1899, where the observed score is more than five standard errors of estimate above the predicted score. The presence of such an extreme outlier, which represents the peak of the first merger wave, may be distorting the overall estimate of effect. If the 1899 observation is excluded by simply taking 1900 as the beginning year of the series, rather than 1895, OLS yields $b_{m_t x_t} = .77$, $(t = .36)$. Still antitrust manifests no effect. Another approach is to log M_t

---

Acquisitions, (Washington, D.C.: Government Printing Office, October, 1975, 117).

I employ the "assets acquired" measure because the series is more complete, with data available for individual years, or smaller groups of years; for 1948-1959, see FTC, Economic Report, 673, Table 1-9; for 1961-1964, Census, Statistical Abstract 1969, 485, No. 712; for 1960, 1965-1973, Census, Statistical Abstract 1977, 569, No. 932. The years at the beginning of the series, 1948-1951, with 37.5 percent of the assets acquired in conglomerate mergers, serve as a base period. (In order to analyze the entire series, 1895-1973, establishment of some allowable, base proportion of conglomerate mergers was necessary. If all the conglomerate mergers were simply removed from the merger scores for each year from 1948, then overadjustment would result. That is, one would be left with a series where the observations before 1948 contained conglomerate mergers, but the observations for 1948 and after counted no conglomerate mergers at all.)

[59] The number of vertical mergers has been few and essentially constant over time; as a source of constant error, they do not threaten the validity of the ensuing estimates; see Herbert L. Costner, "Theory, Deduction, and Rules of Correspondence," in Causal Models in the Social Sciences, ed. H. M. Blalock, Jr. (Chicago: Aldine, 1971), 299-305.

which, in addition to pulling in outliners, preserves the sample size. Using OLS,

$$\log e \ M_t = 5.88 + .0024X_t + e_t \qquad (1.4)$$
$$(42.04) \qquad (.49)$$
$$R^2 = .003 \qquad d = .42 \qquad N = 79$$

Once again, enforcement shows no impact on mergers.

Because the Antitrust Division is the prime enforcer of the antitrust laws, its failure is most critical. However, there are other institutions with antitrust responsibilities which must shoulder part of the blame for an ineffective policy. The antitrust tasks of the FTC are quite similar to the Division's. Despite possible advantages as an independent administrative agency, the FTC has tended to concentrate on minutiae. In the 1960s, its reputation fell so low that its dismemberment was even called for.[60] Some contend that it has undergone revitalization, beginning with the leadership of Miles Kirkpatrick in 1969. However, other observers are skeptical about any real change in FTC performance. As Wilcox and Shepherd recently commented, "Frequently being 'revitalized,' it is rarely vital."[61] Clearly, the FTC has had no effect on anticompetitive behavior, according to my analysis. When the merger variable, M_t, is regressed (OLS) on FTC antitrust enforcement, X_t, as measured by the number of "restraint-of-trade" cases instituted each year, 1915-1974, (mean = 18.72, standard deviation = 18.17), then $b_{m_t x_t} = -2.69$, ($t = -1.22$).[62] Antitrust enforcement at the FTC has not resulted in significant reductions in anticompetitive activity.

Thus far, the focus has been on antitrust actions of the FTC or the Division. However, a great number of private cases have been brought as well. In the period 1965-1969, for example, 2,822 were initiated (excluding electrical equipment cases). Data problems stand in the way of a profound analysis of the impact of these private suits. A record of private antitrust cases filed before 1938 does not exist. Further, many private cases result from a Department of

---

[60] Edward F. Cox, Robert C. Fellmeth, and John E. Schulz, *The Nader Report on the Federal Trade Commission* (New York: Richard W. Baron, 1969).
[61] Wilcox and Shepherd, *Public Policies*, 143.
[62] The annual number of these cases brought from 1915 to 1969 is reported in Posner, "A Statistical Study," 369. I updated the series to 1974, utilizing U.S., Congress, House, *Agricultural-Environmental and Consumer Protection Appropriations for 1975*, 93d Cong., 2d sess. (Washington, D.C.: Government Printing Office, 1975), 926.

Justice judgement. Also, a large number of private suits may follow from one antitrust violation. For these reasons, Posner asserts that in "no event would it be proper" to combine these private cases with the public ones in order to form an aggregate measure of antitrust activity.[63] However, he does provide some rough estimates for the pre-1938 period, along with more reliable estimates for subsequent years, which allow construction of a crude private cases variable, X_t.[64] Regressing (OLS) mergers, M_t, on X_t yields $b_{m_t x_t} =$ .51, ($t = 1.31$). This finding implies the bringing of private antitrust cases does not influence merger activity significantly.

A possible criticism of "number of cases brought" as a measure of antitrust activity is that it does not capture the qualitative dimension. For example, perhaps the Division has begun to bring fewer, but more important, cases. Posner doubts this contention, arguing that in such a situation average case length would increase, which it has not.[65] However, it would be useful to have a more direct indicator of the qualitative side of enforcement. While there are many characteristics that distinguish a case as important, an overriding one is cost. For a major suit, the Division can easily spend 500,000 dollars.[66] Hence, one global measure of enforcement quality is the size of the Division budget. The expectation, then, is that increased expenditures reduce anticompetitive behavior, other things being equal. But, regressing (OLS) mergers, M_t, on the Division budget (in constant dollars), X_t, yields $b_{m_t x_t} = 3.54$, ($t = 2.37$). Heightened Division expenditures do not appear to lower the merger level. The finding is repeated when the equation is estimated (OLS) to assess the effect of FTC budget increases (in constant dollars), $b_{m_t x_t} = 2.56$, ($t = 3.21$).[67] Clearly, greater spending

---

[63] Posner, "A Statistical Study," 372.

[64] *Ibid.*, 371, provides figures for 1895-1969, for five-year periods. To obtain a rough estimate of the private cases for each year, it was necessary to divide the total for the relevant five-year period by five. For example, the total for the 1945-1949 period = 399; thus, the estimate for, say, 1946 = 399 ÷ 5 = 79.8.

[65] Posner, "A Statistical Study," 367.

[66] Wilcox, *Public Policies*, 90.

[67] The Federal Trade Commission budget figures (in thousands of current dollars) for 1921-1975 were taken from the actual outlays reported in the appropriate issues of U.S., *The Budget of the United States Government* (Washington, D.C.: Government Printing Office). To adjust the budget figure from current dollars to constant dollars, it was divided by the year's Consumer

by the enforcement agencies has not at all dampened anticompetitive merger activity.

Thus far, the important role of the courts has been neglected. Under the first fifty years of the Sherman Act, the Supreme Court was hesitant to act against manufacturing combinations. After the landmark U. S. Steel case of 1920, monopolistic combinations appeared virtually legal. However, more rigorous interpretations of the law have been reinforced by passage of the Celler-Kefauver Antimerger Act in 1950, which strengthened Section 7 of the Clayton Act. In fact, the courts have upheld the Antitrust Division and and the FTC in every major case brought under Celler-Kefauver.[68] While conglomerate mergers are covered, it is generally acknowledged that the Celler-Kefauver Act has been most effective against horizontal mergers.[69] Further, according to some, this antimerger statute has exercised an anticompetitive deterrent beyond that coming from the formal sanctions. In this view, firms have actually decided not to merge because the law has become so "strong."[70] Thus, one might expect Celler-Kefauver to have an impact on merger activity greater than the actual number of antitrust cases would imply. An estimate of the courts' effect, and the Celler-Kefauver Act in general, comes from analysis of the time-series of the adjusted merger variable, M_t. The hypothesis is that post-1950 anticompetitive merger activity would be significantly lower than pre-1950 anticompetitive merger activity. To test this hypothesis, I regressed M_t on a dichotomous dummy variable for time, X_t, scored "0" if the observation occurred in 1950 or before, and "1" if the observations occurred after 1950. Estimating (OLS) the equation yields a slope of $b_{m_t x_t} = 151.70$, ($t = 1.22$). These findings indicate that the recent, sterner antitrust opinions of the courts, and the Celler-Kefauver Act more generally, have not managed to reduce anticompetitive mergers below the earlier level. While this assessment departs from the prevailing view, support comes from

---

Price Index (1967 = 100), given in Economic Analysis, *Long Term Economic*, 222-223, Series B69, and in Census, *Statistical Abstract 1975*, 422, No. 687, for the years after 1970.

[68] See Wilcox, *Public Policies*, Ch. 7, for a good discussion of antitrust in the courts.

[69] Goldberg, "The Effects of Conglomerate," 138-139; Stigler, "The Economic Effects," 232.

[70] Elzinga, "The Antimerger Law," 43-44.

Kenneth Elzinga, who finds that government victories under this antimerger statute have been overwhelmingly "Pyrrhic," for they do not provide "effective relief."[71] Without "effective relief," i.e., the undoing of the illegal aspects of the merger, there is no real cost to breaking the law, and it will be broken.

In the preceding paragraphs, I have looked at the effects of various antitrust activities, in turn, on merger activity. The results of this analysis are conveniently summarized in the CORC estimates of the following multiple regression equation:

$$(1.5)$$

$$M_t = 690.8 + 2.6X_{1t} - 2.4X_{2t} - 6.6X_{3t} + 2.4X_{4t} + 6.64X_{5t} - 27.9X_{6t} + e_t$$

$$(3.6) \quad (1.2) \quad (-.8) \quad (-1.3) \quad (.8) \quad (.4) \quad (-3.0)$$

$$R^2 = .76 \qquad d = 1.64 \qquad N = 52$$

where M_t = annual mergers (adjusted for conglomerates); X_{1t} = annual number of antitrust cases initiated by the Division; X_{2t} = annual number of restraint-of-trade cases instituted by the FTC; X_{3t} = the annual Antitrust Division budget (constant dollars); X_{4t} = the annual FTC budget (constant dollars); X_{5t} = a dummy variable for the Celler-Kefauver Act, scored "0" for 1950 or before, and "1" after 1950, X_{6t} = annual unemployment rate; the N covers years 1922 to 1973 (one observation of the initial 53 was necessarily lost with CORC); the values in parentheses are the t ratios. Anticompetitive mergers are influenced by general economic conditions, as the significant coefficient for the unemployment rate indicates.[72] But, they have not been significantly depressed by the presence of the Celler-Kefauver Act, or the enforcement efforts of the Antitrust Division and the FTC, either in terms of cases brought or money spent.

What accounts for the failure of antitrust? Probably, the most important reason is the extremely limited resources at the disposal of the agencies. A corporation under attack may doubt that resources are so scarce. William E. LaMothe, president of the Kellogg Company, in responding to the FTC assault on concentration in the breakfast cereal business, lamented "its enormous power and enormous budget and its enormous staff."[73] However, perhaps

[71] Ibid., 43-53, 74-76.
[72] See Nelson, Merger Movements; Goldberg, "The Effects of Conglomerate," 141-142.
[73] New York Times, August 8, 1976, Sec. F, 12.

Ralph Nader's summary is more generally accurate: "The posture of two agencies [the Division and the FTC] with a combined budget of $20 million and 550 lawyers and economists trying to deal with anticompetitive abuses in a trillion-dollar economy, not to mention an economy where the 200 largest corporations control two-thirds of all manufacturing assets, is truly a charade."[74] When the Antitrust Division, for example, takes up a case, it is routinely outgunned. By comparison to the industry under challenge, which can generally muster whatever resources are needed for its defense, the efforts of the Division are meager. On the average, only two or three lawyers attend to each of the nation's five or so largest industries. For a major case, maybe four or five lawyers, with a couple of economists, will be involved.[75] Further, while major suits are especially costly, the total Antitrust Division budget, in 1975 for example, was only 16,700,000 (current) dollars.

To attribute ineffectual antitrust enforcement to limited resources, even though the budget variables examined in Eq. 5 manifest no impact on mergers, implies there is a threshold effect. For instance, the Antitrust Division budget level has not yet influenced mergers, because the upper bound on expenditures has been so low. If the budget could be meaningfully increased beyond the values observed thus far, it would significantly curtail merger activity. Some economists argue that, optimally, this increase should be five-fold.[76] But it is by no means certain that this robust increment would be sufficient. As critic Edward Mason remarked, "Even if the Antitrust Division and the Federal Trade Commission enjoyed appropriations five times as large as they now have, they could not conceivably bring a tenth of the cases it would be possible to bring."[77] A rather pessimistic inference is that the budget increases needed for effective antitrust enforcement are of a magnitude which bars their acceptance in the congressional political arena.

CONCLUSIONS

Antitrust has not worked to protect the competitive structure of the American economy. More precisely, the efforts of the Antitrust Division, the FTC, and the courts have exerted no significant nega-

[74] Green, et al., Closed Enterprise, xii.
[75] Wilcox and Shepherd, Public Policies, 122.
[76] Ibid., 122.
[77] Quoted in Green, et al., Closed Enterprise, 115.

tive effect on anticompetitive mergers, according to the regression models estimated here. The American public continues to bear the costs of lessened competition, such as higher prices, greater corporate profits, reduced technological innovation, more economic inequality. At most, antitrust actions have symbolic value.[78] The knowledge that the antitrust division and the FTC are at work, coupled with the observance of an occasional court ruling against a major company, act to convince people that a competitive economy is being preserved. They are further reassured with favorable antitrust utterances by political figures of both parties. In fact, antitrust endorsement, not antitrust enforcement, is part of the ritual behavior of American politicians.

The lack of antitrust impact becomes more understandable when the linkages of government and the corporations are recalled. Effective law enforcement implies an antagonistic, watchful relationship between "police" and possible "lawbreaker." The idea of government as a *regulator* of business stresses this conflictual image. However, government normally aims to help corporations rather than constrain them. According to some investigators, the national economic regulatory bodies were originally created at the urging of big business.[79] In the view of Daniel Elazer, the business community still appears, by and large, to support federal regulation.[80] The formal assistance of government to corporate enterprise, which includes special subsidies, services, tax benefits, and contracts, is extensive and growing.[81] Informally, high level officials can be persuaded to bend in favor of corporate interests. In the Senate, for example, liberals as well as conservatives quickly sacrifice antitrust principles: "Senator Hartke is for steel quotas, Senator McCarthy supported the oil and drug industries, Senator Muskie favors shoe quotas, and Senator Javits . . . wants to disembowel our foreign antitrust efforts."[82] The pervasive lack of real commitment to a policy of competition is summed up by the minuscule Antitrust

[78] Murray J. Edelman, *The Symbolic Uses of Politics* (Champaign-Urbana: University of Illinois Press, 1964).

[79] Greenberg, *Serving the Few*, 96-99; Gabriel, Kolko, *The Triumph of Conservatism: A Reinterpretation of American History, 1900-1916* (New York: Free Press, 1963), 3, 57-58.

[80] *American Federalism: A View from the States* (New York: Crowell, 1972), 215-216.

[81] See Wilcox and Shepherd, *Public Policies*, Ch. 25, for a review of this aid.

[82] Green, *et al.*, *Closed Enterprise*, 59-60.

Division budget, which virtually *guarantees* antitrust activity will be no more than symbolic.

The prospects for meaningful antitrust reform appear rather dim. Any serious effort would require the allocation of much more money than is likely to be forthcoming. Both Democrats and Republicans, whether in the White House or in the Congress, seem satisfied with the Antitrust Division budget, small as it is. Among those who make policy, maintaining economic competition is in reality a very low priority. In such a circumstance, recent possibilities, such as the Industrial Reorganization Act and the federal chartering of corporations, cannot be expected to alter significantly American economic patterns.

The Antitrust Bulletin/Summer 1986   409

The evolution of Clayton section 7 enforcement and the beginnings of U.S. industrial policy

BY BRUCE M. OWEN*

The ascendancy of Chicago school philosophy[1] in the enforcement of merger policy has had and continues to have unforeseen and ironic effects. It is the purpose of this article to review recent trends in merger enforcement policy and to speculate about the

---

* Economists Incorporated, Washington, D.C.; former Director of the Antitrust Division's Economic Policy Office.

AUTHOR'S NOTE: *Useful suggestions from my colleagues and from Hugh P. Morrison, Jr., George A. Hay, Steven C. Salop, and Lawrence J. White are gratefully acknowledged.*

[1]   The term "Chicago school," of course has many meanings. As used herein, "Chicago school economics" refers principally to the following ideas: that the competitive market model is an appropriate and useful basis for the analysis of proposed policies or changes in market structure; that the central goal of government in economic affairs is, or ought to be, to maximize the efficiency with which resources are allocated, or equivalently to maximize consumer welfare; and that, in general, governmental intervention in the marketplace should be minimized because it is less likely in practice to lead to efficient resource allocation than private markets, even somewhat imperfect ones. There is also a tendency for unsophisticated proponents of this view to focus on equilibrium states, and to minimize the disequilibrium process. Most economists and antitrust practitioners have adopted significant elements of the Chicago view, marking its success as

likely future directions of that policy. This article reviews the history of economists and economic analysis in Department of Justice and Federal Trade Commission merger investigations, discusses the role and style of economic analysis in current decisions, and projects current trends into the future. The article points out that, because of the efficiency defense in merger investigations and for other reasons, the antitrust enforcement agencies are already engaged in making industrial policy. This development is the natural outcome of a long-term historical trend in the intellectual basis for antitrust enforcement policy. Moreover, it is argued that, because the skills presently employed to make antitrust enforcement decisions are of more general applicability, and because of the underlying evolution of confidence in the reliability of microeconomic analysis in policy making, it would be logical to expect a movement toward an integration of antitrust, trade, tax, and other policies affecting U.S. industrial structure.

A. The reform movement

There has been a 25-year trend toward increased use of microeconomic analysis in government policy making. Leaving aside a brief period of interest in microeconomics by analysts during World War II,[2] the governmental fascination with this discipline dates from the Pentagon "whiz kids" of Robert McNamara. The whiz kids were interested primarily in improving

---

an intellectual revolution. Just as President Nixon announced that "We are all Keynesians now," so is it true that we are all, to some extent, Chicagoans. As a result, the reader would not go far wrong in substituting the term "economic analysis" for "Chicago school" in characterizing current enforcement policy.

2 The wartime analysts were academic economists and mathematicians who were interested in what is today called operations research. *See Operations Research*, 13 NEW ENCYCLOPAEDIA BRITANNICA 594 (1982), for a brief history.

the efficiency of defense operations, especially weapons procure-ment.[3]

Throughout the 1960s there was a waxing flow of academic research aimed at analyzing from an economic perspective the nature and effects of government regulatory intervention. Both the planning, programming, and budgeting system (PPBS) whiz kids and the early academic students of regulatory institutions were interested originally in perfecting the efficiency and effec-tiveness of the federal machinery. Increasingly, however, the analysis became critical and even cynical, perhaps in response to what appeared to the analysts as massive resistance by the bureaucracy to the adoption of proposed improvements. Just as Pentagon bureaucrats resisted the PPBS paradigm, regulatory officials at the Interstate Commerce Commission and elsewhere tended to ignore the academic literature on regulatory economics. It became difficult for the "academic scribblers"[4] to believe that there were not ulterior motives behind this disinterest in self-improvement.

One result of the perceived resistance to reform was that the analysts, returning to their academic roosts in the post-Kennedy era, began to seek explanations of the behavior of the govern-ment itself. It did not take long before models of self-interested bureaucrats and institutions began to emerge, along with models of the regulatory mechanism as extensions of industry interests in protectionism and cartelization.[5] One implication that grew out

---

3   RAND Corporation economists Charles Hitch and Roland McKean were the leaders of the whiz kids. For a discussion of the planning, programming, and budgeting system (PPBS) they advocated, *see* Korb, *The Budget Process in the Department of Defense, 1947-77: The Strengths and Weaknesses of Three Systems*, 37 PUBLIC ADMIN. REV. 334 (1977).

4   J. M. KEYNES, THE GENERAL THEORY OF EMPLOYMENT, INTEREST, AND MONEY 383 (1936).

5   For surveys of the academic literature on regulation, *see* Noll & Joskow, *Regulation in Theory and Practice: An Overview*, in STUDIES IN PUBLIC REGULATION 1 (G. Fromm ed. 1981); B. M. OWEN & R. BRAEUTI-

of this fresh perception of self-interested regulators and bureaucrats was the notion that outside forces would have to be marshaled in order to initiate reform; endogenous reform seemed inconsistent with the model of bureaucratic behavior. Regulatory "reform"[6] began to appear on the agendas of various political interests, partly in response to the climate of opinion beginning to prevail in academic circles.[7]

Simple models of the competitive process of the sort associated with Chicago school teachings were already becoming a popular focus of attention in the legal literature. It became increasingly respectable to turn to economic models to explain and predict the effects of alternative regulatory policies. By the 1970s, newly minted lawyers were likely to have been taught, either as undergraduates or in law school or both, that economics

GAM, THE REGULATION GAME (1978); Peltzman, *Toward a More General Theory of Regulation*, 19 J.L. & ECON. 211 (1976); R. G. NOLL & B. M. OWEN, THE POLITICAL ECONOMY OF DEREGULATION (1983); and REGULATORY REFORM: WHAT ACTUALLY HAPPENED (L. Weiss & M. Klass eds. 1986).

6   Reform, at first, meant tinkering with the forms and procedures of administrative law to make the agencies more responsive to consumer interests; quite soon, however, reform came to mean wholesale deregulation.

7   While Republican platforms have generally called for less government intervention, it seems to have been the Democrats who first explicitly took up the banner of regulatory reform. Thus, the 1972 Democratic party platform called for adjustments to ". . . rate-making and regulatory activities, with particular attention to regulations which increase prices for food, transportation, and other necessities. . . ." 2 NATIONAL PARTY PLATFORMS 786 (D. G. Johnson comp. 1978). This recognition that regulation could adversely affect consumers had, by 1976, turned to acceptance of the Chicago school view that the regulators might be the handmaidens of the regulated. Thus, the 1976 Democratic party platform called for "Public calendars of scheduled meetings between regulators and regulated, and freedom of information policies . . . ," along with the creation of ". . . an independent consumer agency with the staff and power to intervene in regulatory matters on behalf of the . . . public." *Id.* at 922. By 1980, both parties were calling for deregulation in general and in specific industries.

was a useful approach to the analysis of regulatory problems, and that regulators and existing regulatory institutions were often more responsive to the narrow industrial interests of those regulated than to the interests of consumers. They were also by the 1970s likely to have been taught the basic message that competition, even if imperfect, was likely to be less distorting than regulation, and to have acquired a certain trust in market outcomes. Regulatory institutions had achieved legitimacy at the expense of free markets in the Great Depression; this legitimacy was now, among important groups of opinion leaders, reversed. Finally, a focus on competitive models carried with it a focus on consumer economic welfare as the natural policy touchstone. The earlier, much vaguer, public interest standard could readily encompass such objectives as "stability" or "orderly markets" conducive to producer interests. A narrower economic consumer-interest standard would have had the effect of making much of the older regulatory machinery obsolete or misdirected in any event, even if its motives and effectiveness were not suspect.

Antitrust enforcement was, in one sense, simply part of the regulatory process that came under the sway of the reform movement. Antitrust enforcement differed from other regulatory institutions in the sense that it was not regarded by most academics as generally protective of business interests; it was, however, often protective of the interests of some businesses—especially small, inefficient ones. For many years enforcement agencies sometimes tried to protect competitors rather than the competitive process, a problem that persists today in the context of private actions under the Sherman Act. Antitrust also differed from most other regulatory institutions in having a stronger tradition of intellectual ties to the academic world; partly for this reason, reform came to antitrust enforcement somewhat earlier than to other regulatory agencies. While not in itself reform of antitrust policy, one of the earliest manifestations of the trend toward reform was the Antitrust Division's regulatory intervention program.[8]

---

[8] *See generally* Baker, *The Role of Competition in Regulated Industries*, 11 BOSTON C. IND. & COMM. L. REV. 571 (1970); Antitrust and Regulated Industries—*Charles River Bridge* Re-Crossed, Address by

The intervention program, styled "competition advocacy," was begun in the late 1960s and early 1970s. As a result of this early experience, the Division was well equipped to lead the deregulation movement that arose in the mid-1970s.[9] One factor in the decision to engage in competition advocacy may have been the *Philadelphia National Bank* case, extending the reach of the antitrust laws into the regulated banking sector, and adopting a contemporary economic analysis of the merger issues.[10] After some early success in the stockbroker industry, the Division undertook to advocate the elimination of regulatory barriers to entry and the use of antitrust analysis and antitrust principles to gauge the desirability of regulatory policies such as encouragement of rate bureaus or minimum rate regulation. There was substantial activity of this sort in the communications and transportation areas. For several years the Antitrust Division probably spent somewhat more resources and energy intervening at other agencies than in reforming its own use of economic analysis. Nevertheless, in antitrust enforcement as in other regulatory programs, key decision makers came increasingly to believe that economics—rather than "law"—was the most appropriate framework for deciding policy issues, and with increasing regularity decision makers were trained in economics or prepared to listen to those who were. That cases make economic sense gradually became a necessary condition of enforcement, though there were occasional lapses.[11]

Donald I. Baker before the Third Annual New England Antitrust Conference, Boston (Oct. 3, 1969), published under the same title at 60 CORNELL L. REV. 159 (1975); Zimmerman, *The Legal Framework of Competitive Policies Toward Regulated Industries*, in PROMOTING COMPETITION IN REGULATED MARKETS (A. Phillips ed. 1975); Kauper, *The Role of Economic Analysis in the Antitrust Division Before and After the Establishment of the Economic Policy Office*, 29 ANTITRUST BULL. 111 (1984).

[9]   *See* Kauper, *supra* note 8, at 124-25.

[10]   United States v. Philadelphia National Bank, 374 U.S. 321 (1963).

[11]   United States v. Cuisinarts, 516 F. Supp. 1008, 1022 (D. Conn. 1981).

The strengthening of economic analysis in the Department of Justice has a 20-year history, beginning with the appointment of the academic lawyer/economist, Donald Turner, as head of the Antitrust Division in 1966. Turner and each of his successors appointed an academic economist as a special assistant. In 1973 the incumbent special assistant, George Hay, was made director of a new Economic Policy Office (EPO) which, by the end of the Carter administration, employed about 50 economists. The word "economist" in earlier years had meant no more than "gatherer and compiler of numerical data." But as EPO grew in size, its composition of Ph.D.-level analytical economists also increased. Finally, in September 1985, the director of the Economic Policy Office was elevated to the rank of deputy assistant attorney general and the EPO was split into two sections of economists at the same time that the number of litigating legal sections, composed of lawyers, was reduced from nine to five.

The establishment of economists at the Department of Justice was more or less paralleled by events at the Federal Trade Commission, where the process culminated in the appointment of James C. Miller III, a microeconomist with substantial credentials in the deregulation movement, as chairman.

B. The style of current merger analysis

The historical evolution in merger enforcement that has brought us to the current ascendancy of economic analysis is unlikely to end suddenly. But before we speculate as to its future development, it is worthwhile briefly to consider the current style of merger analysis. While in many respects a retrenchment from the excesses of highly motivated but undisciplined enforcement in the past, the current agency style is in its own way quite radical, and even in certain dimensions undisciplined.[12]

Modern Clayton section 7 enforcement starts with the economic premise that merger activity is motivated by expecta-

---

[12] While this section is to some degree critical of current enforcement policy, it is not my intention to suggest that the current approach is not a substantial improvement on what has gone before.

tions of economic gain. Such gain can arise from various sources: tax savings, economies of scale or scope, risk reduction, and so on. One potential source of gain is a reduction in competition leading to higher profits, generally through tacit or explicit cooperation among rivals in pricing, but sometimes through the creation of monopoly power in the combined firm. The goals of section 7 enforcement are, somewhat controversially, limited by the terms of the new 1982 and 1984 Merger Guidelines to opposing those mergers that enhance the probability of collusion.[13] In practice, however, the agencies do in fact take account of a much less limited set of criteria.

There are two reasons for examining efficiency effects other than those affecting the probability of collusion. The first reason for conducting a broader inquiry is the need to explain, within the context of the economic model described above, why the merger is taking place. Although present to some extent in every case, this tendency is especially strong in cases involving a failing firm or division. Hence, the agencies will (at least) listen to any argument having to do with the efficiency effects of a proposed merger. The second reason for the inquiry is to see whether there is any prospect that, even if the risk of collusion is enhanced, there might be offsetting cost reductions; this is the so-called "efficiency defense."[14] If there is no cost-reducing or other efficiency gain, economic analysts are often willing to infer that the

---

[13]   Less commonly, of course, the merger may create monopoly power directly. A major element of the new guidelines was the enunciation of the "hypothetical monopolist" paradigm for market definition. *See* U.S. Department of Justice Merger Guidelines § 2.1 (June 14, 1984) [hereinafter cited as 1984 Guidelines]. This paradigm had been in use by Department of Justice economists since the mid-1970s, but was generally inaccessible to practitioners. Not only practitioners but many analysts continued throughout the 1970s to use Standard Industrial Classification (SIC) categories as "markets." The hypothetical monopolist paradigm in the guidelines, of course, defines markets entirely in terms of the demand-side factors affecting the risk of collusion.

[14]   *See* Fisher & Lande, *Efficiency Considerations in Merger Enforcement*, 71 CALIF. L. REV. 1582 (1983).

primary motivation[15] of the merger partners is anticompetitive, simply because that is seen as the only remaining motivation or intent.[16] Put another way, if the potential anticompetitive effects, however doubtful, are not offset by some efficiency gain, there is no reason to permit the merger.[17] The scope of this broader efficiency goal will be discussed more fully below. But let us first examine the basis for the goal that is embodied explicitly in the guidelines.

There is theoretical support for the proposition that fewer competing sellers are more likely to be able to reach, and enforce, a collusive agreement than a greater number. The idea dates at least to Stigler's seminal article,[18] but it has not been significantly advanced since, at least on a theoretical level. There is no generally accepted theoretical basis for any quantification of the notion. That is, we do not have any way to know, in general, *how much* the probability of collusion increases as the number or concentration of sellers declines. So far as the theory goes, it could be a lot or a little. Thus, there is no basis in oligopoly theory for the adoption of any particular change in concentration

---

15 Even if efficiencies are the primary motivation for the merger in the sense that the merger partners expect greater gains from that source than from any enhancement in the probability of collusion, the expected social costs of collusion, the effects of which reach firms other than the merger partners, may outweigh the private gains from increased efficiency.

16 It is unclear whether sufficient attention is paid to errors, taxes, and other possible motivations.

17 There has sometimes, in recent merger investigations, been a hint that a demonstration of efficiencies is a necessary (some would even say, sufficient) element of a successful defense of the transaction before the agencies. For a view rationalizing this practice, *see* Muris, *The Efficiency Defense Under Section 7 of the Clayton Act*, 30 Case W. Res. L. Rev. 381 (1980).

18 G. J. Stigler, *A Theory of Oligopoly*, 72 J. Pol. Econ. 44 (1964). Some would trace these insights to the Harvard economist Edward Chamberlin, others to the nineteenth-century French economist A. Cournot.

as significantly, much less unacceptably, enhancing the likelihood of collusion, even if all the other factors affecting that probability were held constant.[19] The empirical literature is equally bereft of any generally accepted basis for the conclusion that increases in concentration in the range identified by the guidelines as dangerous are in fact associated with a significantly higher incidence of *collusion*, as opposed to the more ambiguous connection with higher *profits*.[20]

Thus, the threshold levels of concentration and changes in concentration embodied in the new Merger Guidelines, for all their apparent conservative grounding in a highly focused and research-based enforcement goal, are in the end based on no firmer theoretical ground than that underlying the rest of civil antitrust enforcement policy; they are only somewhat more explicit and precise. And the ground that underlies the rest of civil enforcement policy is in turn really nothing more than a consensus growing out of experience and tradition that is only constrained by the need to rationalize policy in academically respectable terms, a standard subject to change over time. The high priests who can confer this respectability are the law professors and commentators, and they are, for the moment at least, fascinated with the Chicago school model of the competitive process. The result is that enforcement decisions and policies that cannot be rationalized in terms of the standard competitive

---

[19]   *See* G. J. STIGLER, THE ECONOMIST AS PREACHER 49 (1982); Baxter, *Responding to the Reaction: The Draftsman's View*, 71 CALIF. L. REV. 618, 626 (1983).

[20]   *But see* Baxter, *supra* note 19, at 626-27. For surveys of the relevant literature, *see* Pautler, *A Review of the Economic Basis for Broad-Based Horizontal Merger Policy*, 28 ANTITRUST BULL. 571 (1983); Weiss, *The Concentration–Profits Relationship and Antitrust*, in INDUSTRIAL CONCENTRATION: THE NEW LEARNING (H. Goldschmid et al. eds. 1974). Some useful empirical evidence is provided by Hay & Kelley, *An Empirical Survey of Price Fixing Conspiracies*, 17 J.L. & ECON. 13 (1974). Finally, Plott, *Industrial Organization Theory and Experimental Economics*, 20 J. ECON. LIT. 1485 (1982), summarizes the recent experimental oligopoly research.

economic model have fallen into disrepute. It has not been very long since it was regarded on campus and in Washington as acceptable to say, in support of a proposed Clayton section 7 action, that the firms involved, or their executives, were "too powerful." The last echoes of Warren Court antitrust populism have now died away at the agencies, even if not in court. Similarly, no matter the theoretical economic merit of certain vertical restraint cases,[21] it is as a practical matter virtually unthinkable that either agency would today bring a vertical case, so closely associated are they with the "errors" of the older enforcement philosophy.[22]

In spite of the fact that enforcement policy is to some substantial extent subject to the breezes of fashionable thinking, those in charge of making enforcement decisions have their own traditions and vision of what makes sense. The career civil servants at the top of the decision-making process have imposed a sense of order and consistency, and they have resisted what seem to them to be excesses of the Right and the Left in case management.

Nevertheless, the notion now preeminent that economic efficiency is the underlying goal of antitrust enforcement policy has permeated the thinking of agency staffs, and has acquired a significance that takes merger policy far beyond the narrow focus

---

[21] U.S. Department of Justice, Vertical Restraints Guidelines § 3.2 (Jan. 23, 1985); for a more general treatment, *see* R. Caves, Vertical Restraints as Integration by Contract: Evidence and Policy Implications (Harvard Institute of Economic Research Discussion Paper 754, 1980).

[22] The only exception, presumably, would be a case where the vertical restraint was secondary to a regulatory distortion such as that which underlay the economic theory of *United States v. AT&T*; this possibility is noted in the 1984 Guidelines, *supra* note 13, § 4.23. Lawrence White claims that the proposed enforcement action announced against the Showtime–The Movie Channel joint venture was a vertical case brought by the Baxter regime. *See* White, *Antitrust and Video Markets: The Merger of Showtime and The Movie Channel as a Case Study*, in VIDEO MEDIA COMPETITION (E. Noam ed. 1985), especially at 355-60.

of the guidelines on collusion. In day-to-day practice both the economists and the lawyers making enforcement decisions feel at liberty to make arguments and to indulge in judgments that far exceed the bounds of the guidelines, primarily in order to understand and make sense of the proposed transaction and to identify its welfare effects. These judgments, while certainly articulated in terms of the traditional antitrust pigeonholes, are in fact often based primarily on intuitive and somewhat superficial understandings of the facts pertaining to the particular case. However careful the staff investigation has been, the press of time means that decision making at the review level is necessarily based in each case on somewhat stylized "facts." Stylized facts are simply those made to fit some economic or legal pigeonhole.[23] Few cases fit any pigeonhole exactly or precisely. The violence done to the facts in characterizing them for reviewing authorities is under the control of the investigating staff. The staff does not always take full advantage of this situation, and often forwards an incoherent picture to reviewing authorities, who are then (as with appellate courts) forced more or less to invent the facts necessary to support some intellectually acceptable theory of the case.

All this is and probably always has been a commonplace of the enforcement process. What is changed is the range of theories or paradigms regarded as acceptable in pigeonholing particular cases. Relatively novel economic theories are now regarded as acceptable pigeonholes.[24] I do not suggest that any economic theory employed to analyze particular cases has been unsound, or that novelty is exceptionable. The point, rather, is that these theories are far less focused on collusion than the guidelines

---

[23] *See* Hay, *Pigeonholes in Antitrust*, 29 ANTITRUST BULL. 133 (1984).

[24] For example, the "raising costs to rivals" model associated with the writings of Professor Salop and various coauthors has been frequently at least a corroborating theory in agency antitrust analysis. *See, e.g.*, Salop & Scheffman, *Raising Rivals' Costs*, 73 AM. ECON. REV. PAPERS & PROC. 267 (1983). Professor Salop himself regards this theory as not so novel, having its roots in such behavior as that which gave rise to the essential facilities doctrine. (Personal communication.)

would lead one to expect, and that there is an increasing tendency to conduct a general welfare analysis of proposed transactions. But because merger enforcement decisions are seldom memorialized, and because economic analysis at this level includes both art and science, there is little discipline in this process other than that arising from the oral traditions and experience of the staffs themselves.[25] In this period of relatively low government salaries and consequently high turnover, oral traditions cannot be a strong source of discipline. The existence of the guidelines is evidence of the recognition that predictability and consistency are important, yet merger enforcement decisions are not regularly accompanied by opinions rationalizing them. In view of the changing enforcement policies of the agencies, it may well be useful to insist on published reasoning in future decisions. Although written opinions are surely not without risks and drawbacks,[26] the need to rationalize any inconsistency with prior practice may introduce some useful consistency into a process which, if I am correct about the scope of the analysis actually employed, is much needed.

A second theme of current merger enforcement is a marked willingness not merely to evaluate but to participate in the design of "fixes." Both the FTC and the Antitrust Division today are prepared to engage in, or approve of, structural fixes in the hothouse atmosphere of merger investigations that would formerly have been regarded as appropriate only in rarer and more leisurely Sherman section 2 proceedings. One problem with this is that business reorganizations of significant dimension are carried out, approved, or initiated at the suggestion of enforcement officials whose picture of the industry is composed of stylized facts.

---

25 The statements by commissioners in G.M./Toyota were exceptional at the FTC, and Tunney Act proceedings do not arise from most DOJ enforcement decisions. Many proposed transactions are withdrawn entirely if enforcement action is threatened.

26 The principal drawback is the danger of revealing unnecessarily proprietary information, and thus perhaps deterring some socially desirable transactions.

In *United States v. AT&T,* a Sherman section 2 case, the Department of Justice did engage in an elaborate restructuring, and continues to engage in ongoing regulation of a major industry. But in the case of LTV's roughly contemporaneous proposed acquisition of Republic Steel,[27] the Department also felt competent[28] to evaluate the claimed efficiencies from rationalization of the facilities, to take account of U.S. international trade policy, to insist that particular plants be spun off to buyers approved by itself, and to permit or not permit other detailed structural changes in the industry. Much of the analysis was conducted under the pressure of Hart–Scott–Rodino deadlines. Previous, less "conservative," administrations would have taken the view that the original proposed merger should either be approved or not, and that any fixes take place before that approval would be granted. In Arco/Alcan the Department went further and participated actively in the design of an elaborate joint venture to manage a major aluminum rolling facility, creating a set of artificial structural conditions that it believed would produce incentives to expand capacity and output.[29]

In G.M./Toyota the FTC approved an equally elaborate joint venture between two leading car makers to manufacture Japanese-designed cars in California.[30] One rationale for approval was

---

[27] As Judge Pratt notes in his memorandum opinion approving the consent order in the Tunney Act proceeding in United States v. The LTV Corporation, 1984 Trade Cas. (CCH) ¶ 16,133 (D.D.C. 1984), the course of the prosecutorial process involved vigorous attempts on the part of other executive branch agencies to intervene in support of the parties to the transaction.

[28] Actually, the DOJ in this case hired an outside firm of technical experts to assist its in-house economists to evaluate the transaction in its various forms.

[29] *See* 47 ATRR 651-53 (1984). Criticism of this plan would probably center on its enforceability and on the opportunity provided by joint venture operations to exchange information and to achieve greater cooperation.

[30] *See* Statement of James C. Miller III Concerning G.M./Toyota Joint Venture, April 11, 1984; Statement of James C. Miller III, George

the likelihood that the scheme would permit the Japanese to circumvent the restrictive auto import policies of other agencies.[31] As in the case of Arco/Alcan, the agency analysis seems to have focused entirely on the economic incentive structure being created. Earlier analysts would have emphasized the suspicion that any form of cooperation among competitors would ultimately serve as a veil for collusion.

The FTC's willingness to pass on the intricacies of structural fixes is further illustrated by the Whirlpool/KitchenAid transaction.[32] Whirlpool wished to acquire KitchenAid despite a substantial apparent product overlap in dishwashers and other products. Whirlpool sought to solve its antitrust problem by arranging to sell KitchenAid's *manufacturing* assets to Emerson under rather complicated conditions that were alleged to give Emerson substantial incentives to enter the dishwasher business. Whirlpool retained the KitchenAid *brand* name. Whatever the merits of the divestiture of manufacturing assets, earlier analysts would probably have focused on the brand name itself, in a consumer product, as a substantial marketing asset serving as a barrier to entry. The FTC, however, apparently concluded that the brand market was broader than dishwasher brands. Meanwhile, in various private third-party competitor lawsuits, the focus was entirely on the adequacy of the manufacturing fix.

Finally, the trade press reports an incident in which FTC staffers are alleged to have delayed an investigation of an apparent concerted policy of rental car companies to ignore National Highway Transportation Safety Board (NHTSB) safety

---

W. Douglas, and Terry Calvani Concerning Proposed General Motors/ Toyota Joint Venture (same date); and dissenting statements of Commissioners Bailey and Pertschuk (same date); *reprinted at* 46 ANTITRUST & TRADE REG. REP. (BNA) 726-27 (1984).

31 Both here and in LTV/Republic the antitrust agencies were in effect gaming other agencies of government in an apparent effort to counteract actual or potential protectionist U.S. trade policy.

32 *See* 49 ATRR 63-65 (1985).

recalls, because of an unwillingness on the part of the staff to assume that such recalls were efficiency-enhancing.[33]

The pro- or antibusiness philosophy of passing administrations thus finds its counterpart in the changing perspectives of enforcement staffs. The traditional, somewhat inchoate distrust of businessmen's motives, found in jaded prosecutors who have read, perhaps, too much business correspondence intended to be private, has been succeeded for the moment at least by the economists' detached, clinical concern with structure/incentive relationships.

Nothing in my discussion of the preceding enforcement decisions, or those that follow, is intended to be critical of the results achieved by the agencies. The point is simply that structural fixes are now thought feasible and even natural in circumstances where they would not previously. One contributory factor in this trend, aside from the rise of economic analysis, has been the availability of a richer information environment. The Antitrust Division's expanded civil investigative demand authority, and the expedited discovery procedures of the Hart–Scott–Rodino Antitrust Improvements Act, have each contributed to greatly improved enforcement data.

The notion that it is within the capability of economic analysis to design or even recognize suitable fixes for industrial pathologies is not limited to merger investigations. One hallmark of the ascendancy of economists at the Department of Justice was an increasing attention to relief issues in civil cases of all kinds. Relief had often in the past been an ad hoc, last-minute affair, like ordering champagne for the victory party. But by the late 1970s it had actually become acceptable to decide not to bring "winnable" civil cases because of the absence of any effective relief. It was principally the newly acquired ability to engage in systematic economic analysis of the effects of alternative forms of relief that caused this change. Such analysis generally concerned itself with whatever welfare effects could be discerned,

---

[33]   179 FTC Watch 3 (Dec. 16, 1983).

and was by no means limited to the impact on collusion possibilities.

Thus, it was only in about 1980, over 10 years after the complaint was filed, that relief issues were first addressed seriously in the *IBM* Sherman section 2 case.[34] And, while relief in the Sherman section 2 case against AT&T may have received more precomplaint attention than other cases of its time, relief in that case did not receive further attention until 1980.[35] Whatever may have been the merit of the government's liability case in *IBM*, it became clear that there was no sensible structural relief. In contrast, the opportunity to remedy structural deficiencies *thought to be traceable to the inefficient incentives created by utility regulation* made AT&T an attractive target for the new enforcement philosophy.[36] To design relief in monopoly cases such as *AT&T* requires substantial faith in our understanding of the effects of industrial structure on economic performance.[37] A

[34]   This claim is literally untrue in the sense that earlier trial staffs and economists at the Division did consider and analyze relief issues. However, this early analysis did not survive changing staffs and the passage of time, and by 1980 the Division felt the need to visit the issues ab novo.

[35]   The same caveat may apply as in note 34, *supra*.

[36]   At least ex post. The 1974 complaint was preceded by a C.I.D. (Civil Investigative Demand) investigation aimed at AT&T's exclusionary behavior with respect to the specialized common carriers.

[37]   Indeed, the AT&T experience can be characterized even more strongly. In seeking to eliminate public and private entry barriers in an industry (long-distance communications) long assumed to be a natural monopoly, reformers at the Federal Communications Commission and DOJ were prepared to conduct a natural experiment. If entry resulted in a competitive market structure, consumers would benefit; if not, the natural monopoly claim would have been verified, albeit at substantial expense. In order to pursue this experiment, the reformers are now advocating abandonment of price regulation of AT&T, a move naturally viewed with great alarm by AT&T's smaller competitors. *See* J. HARING, THE FCC, THE OCCs AND THE EXPLOITATION OF AFFECTION (FCC Office of Plans and Policy 1985).

similar conviction must underlie the willingness to advocate regulatory reform, and to guide the regulatory agencies toward a more competition-oriented policy. Given the trust that is being placed on it, one hopes this faith is warranted.

C. The evolution of industrial policy *qua* antitrust enforcement

Regulatory reform has succeeded. Rearguard actions are under way at various agencies, but the mainstream view, left and right, is clearly pro-deregulation. Similarly, despite pockets of resistance, economic analysis is ascendant at both antitrust enforcement agencies. Judicial developments are necessarily more glacial, but the appointment to influential appellate courts of such strong-minded jurists as former professors Bork, Breyer, Easterbrook, Posner, Scalia, and Winter signals the changing picture there as well.

Enforcement staffs are likely to feel increasingly comfortable with the idea that they can analyze the likely consumer welfare effects of any given proposed change in industrial market structure. They will be called upon to do so not only in connection with mergers, as they have been doing, but also in connection with several certification programs recently established to grant limited antitrust immunity to certain export associations[38] and R&D activities.[39] Such analysis will also continue in the context of regulatory intervention in the health sector, the professions, and other industries.

But from a modern perspective it is anomalous that the powerful remedial tools of antitrust enforcement and trade sanctions should only be applied negatively—that is, only in situations where someone is thought to have violated the law. There is no particular reason to suppose that the greatest potential gains from the application of economic analysis to industry structure should be found in industries where some colorable case of law violation

---

[38] Export Trading Company Act of 1982.

[39] National Cooperative Research Act of 1984.

can be found.[40] Instead, the most important opportunities for beneficial intervention may be found in industries that are not themselves litigious, or characterized by a degree of, or change in, concentration likely to trigger Clayton section 7 scrutiny. Indeed, it may be precisely in relatively unconcentrated industries subject to experience or learning curve effects that the competitive process bringing about eventual equilibrium might be regarded as most in need of intervention. As Michael Spence and others have noted, there are significant interactions among the various tax, trade, R&D, and antitrust policies employed by the government, and it makes little sense to try to wield them independently.[41] The fact that they have been isolated in the past simply reflects the fact that the policies have served different and often irreconcilable purposes. The growing consensus that economic welfare analysis is the most appropriate framework for such intervention, and the reforms leading to its adoption, may provide for the first time a basis for integrating these policy instruments.

Only in the regulated industries, such as banking, airlines, and communications, where structural change has sometimes been within the scope of the regulatory agency's jurisdiction on the path to deregulation, has it been possible in principle at least to apply economic analysis operationally to the problem of optimizing industry structure. But outside of the regulated industries, there is little reason to wait until some antitrust violation has occurred, or a merger is proposed, to consider whether the structure of the industry is best suited to optimize consumer welfare. The structural pathologies that the agency staffs are

---

40   Of course, the Chicago school tradition might point to the endogeneity of legal rules, and perhaps suggest that the laws themselves tend to be those most likely to lead to efficiency gains as a result of enforcement activity.

41   For a brief but insightful summary of some of the ways in which structural, trade, tax, and other policies interact, and the circumstances that might (for example) justify increased concentration or a blockage of foreign access to domestic markets, *see* Spence, *Industrial Organization and Competitive Advantage in Multinational Industries*, 74 AM. ECON. REV. PAPERS & PROC. 356 (1984).

willing to cure in the course of regulatory intervention or merger fix-ups are surely more widespread. And it seems undeniable that, if the state of economic knowledge will support approval of such fixes as those in Arco/Alcan, Whirlpool, and G.M./ Toyota, then it will support far less restricted structural intervention.

The creation of an analytic machine that is divorced from the earlier "law enforcement" ethic, and the trend toward microeconomic rationality as a reform theme at other agencies, including even those concerned with trade policy,[42] certainly suggest the likelihood that agency staffs will seek new worlds to conquer. The antitrust agencies are too limited in their purposes to contain these skills and ideas; it is a matter of complete indifference to an economic analyst whether some correctable structural pathology does or does not lead to provable violations of law. The result, logically, of acting on this realization and of taking up the challenge, posed by such theorists as Spence, to integrate policy, would be an economic regulatory agency modeled in some respects on the Ministry of Trade and Industry (MITI), or the related proposals that have come from the advocates of a new industrial policy for America.[43] The latter idea, while clearly growing out of liberal interventionist roots, can be seen also to meet the capabilities that current conservative analysts and policy makers are apparently prepared to employ in merger investigations.

The future of Clayton section 7 enforcement, then, seems very likely to lie in the direction of a general expansion of its

---

[42]   The reference is to the administration's recent Internation Trade Commission appointments, rather than to any significant changes in policy. Regulatory reform at, for example, the Civil Aeronautics Board was preceded by the appointment of commissioners whose views were substantially at odds with the legislation they were supposed to implement.

[43]   *See, e.g.*, R. B. REICH, THE NEXT AMERICAN FRONTIER (1983). For two contrasting perspectives on industrial policy, *compare* Miller et al., *Industrial Policy: Reindustrialization Through Competition or Coordinated Action?*, 2 YALE J. REG. 1 (1984) *with* Eizenstat, *Reindustrialization Through Coordination or Chaos?*, 2 YALE J. REG. 39 (1984). *See generally*, TOWARD A NEW U.S. INDUSTRIAL POLICY? (M. Wachter & S. Wachter eds. 1983).

fundamental methodology toward an integrated national industrial policy. Such a policy would combine in one place responsibility for implementation of trade and antitrust policy, along perhaps with tax policy, and a new authority designed to deal with structural problems in particular industries in situations intermediate between the rather extreme circumstances now treated by the incipiency of Clayton section 7 and the apocalypse of Sherman section 2.

D. Evaluation

What is ironic about the developments at the antitrust agencies is that a reform aimed at reducing the scope of undisciplined intervention motivated in the past primarily by populist idealism has led to the introduction of what may be a far more interventionist policy. Whereas the old populist mentality was often content with symbolic acts—typified by bringing lawsuits without regard to the existence of suitable relief, as in *IBM*—the new style is far more interested in the effectiveness of intervention and in the relationship between structure and incentives, than in the symbolism of punishment or of populist constraints on business latitude.

Let us suppose this vision of the future of the role of economic analysis in Clayton section 7 enforcement is accurate. It makes sense, undeniably, to broaden the scope of industrial policy and to integrate or at least coordinate trade, tax, and other government programs that affect the performance of U.S. industry. One basis for such a judgment lies in the demonstrated usefulness of microeconomic analysis. But it is surely inevitable that any broadening of the scope of that analysis outside of the antitrust area will lead to its thorough politicization. Can economists and sound economic analysis survive in such an environment? One doubts that the same institutional and traditional safeguards that have to some extent protected the independence and integrity of the law enforcement process will continue to be operative. One must then ask whether the resulting policies will not culminate in the ultimate irony: detailed regulatory supervision of the economy conducted by free-market enthusiasts.

Economic Perspectives— Volume 1, Number 2— Fall 1987— Pages 3–12

Symposium on Mergers and Antitrust

Steven C. Salop

Mergers and acquisitions spark ongoing controversy in the económics profession and in society at large. This is not surprising. Billion dollar deals not only involve a great deal of money, but they often raise economic issues implicating capital and labor markets as well as the markets for the products sold by the merger partners. Because of this, merger enforcement is probably the most widely known area of antitrust. However, economists who do not specialize in industrial organization generally have little understanding of the type of competitive analysis that forms the basis for merger enforcement by the antitrust authorities and the courts. This is unfortunate. Not only does this analysis have important social implications, but when formulated rigorously, the analytic model used in antitrust represents a simple, yet quite sophisticated, microeconomic model of competition.

In the past ten years, economics and economists have become far more important in antitrust. The so-called "Chicago school" of antitrust has provided the intellectual rationale for a considerable loosening of antitrust law. Its intellectual leaders, for example, Robert Bork, Richard Posner, and Frank Easterbrook, have become judges and soon may ascend to (or already have joined) the Supreme Court. Economists like James Miller and George Douglas have become Federal Trade Commissioners, and the staff economists at the Commission and the Department of Justice have gained considerable influence.

■ *Steven C. Salop is Professor of Economics at the Georgetown University Law Center, Washington, D.C.*

The *Journal of Economic Perspectives* organized this symposium to provide economists who do not specialize in industrial organization and policy makers now considering reform proposals with a better sense of the type of competitive analysis carried out in evaluating mergers and the controversies involved in proposals to reform merger law. The *Journal* asked three mainstream industrial organization economists to comment on both current merger enforcement and merger reform proposals: Lawrence White, Franklin Fisher, and Richard Schmalensee.

Lawrence White was one of the authors of the 1982 Department of Justice Merger Guidelines that now provide the basic analytic framework for mergers, if not all of antitrust regulation. White was the Federal Trade Commission's expert economist in the recent litigation that blocked the proposed acquisition of Dr Pepper by Coca-Cola. He is currently a board member of the Federal Home Loan Bank Board. Franklin Fisher is a former Clark Award recipient in econometrics who now specializes in industrial organization. In antitrust, he is probably best known for his spirited defense of IBM in the various antitrust cases brought against it. Richard Schmalensee has written extensively about industrial organization and antitrust, including important papers on advertising, brand reputation and market power. He has been an expert economist in a number of cases, including the Federal Trade Commission's case against Kellogg and other major cereal companies.

U.S. Merger Policy

United States merger policy is mainly carried out by the Department of Justice (DOJ) and Federal Trade Commission (FTC). Under the Hart-Scott-Rodino Pre-Merger Notification Act, an acquiring firm with assets or sales in excess of $100 million must report all proposed acquisitions of assets valued in excess of $15 million to these agencies. A merger cannot be consummated until one of the agencies has evaluated its likely effects on competition. If a problem is found, the merging parties can either withdraw the proposal, negotiate a method of alleviating the agency's concern (for example, by selling off a plant or an entire division), or litigate the acquisition's legality. Very few cases are litigated. Between 1982 and 1986, the FTC and DOJ brought enforcement actions against only 56 mergers out of the more than 7700 reported.[1]

Mergers are evaluated under Section 7 of the Clayton Act. A merger is considered illegal if it "substantially decreases competition or tends to create a monopoly." Thus, Section 7 is concerned with market power in its incipiency. This "incipiency standard" is controversial because it could be, and in the past was, interpreted very broadly. For example, in the 1962 *Brown Shoe* case, the government blocked a merger

[1]See *Antitrust & Trade Regulation Reporter*, March 5, 1987, vol. 52, page 452. Private parties (customers, suppliers or competitors) and states also can sue to block a proposed merger. Because of the federal government's primary role in the process, however, private and state litigation generally has little significance. However, more cases are being brought by private parties, often successfully, since the government has so relaxed its merger enforcement.

between Brown Shoe and Kinney Shoe. Brown and Kinney were ranked third and eighth in the industry. Although the firms' market shares were low, the Supreme Court was concerned that, "if a merger achieving 5% control were now approved, we might be required to approve future merger efforts by Brown's competitors seeking similar market shares. The oligopoly Congress sought to avoid would then be furthered and it would be difficult to dissolve the combinations previously approved." Both Brown and Kinney were retailers as well as manufacturers. The Court also was concerned about the trend to both horizontal consolidation and vertical integration and treated the potential efficiency benefits of the merger as a rationale for blocking it.

Four years later in the *Von's Grocery* case, the Supreme Court held illegal the merger of Von's Grocery and Shopping Bag, the third and sixth largest supermarket chains in the Los Angeles area. The firms had a combined market share of only 7.5 percent. Yet the Court was concerned with the "trend towards concentration" in the market, as indicated by the fact that the number of owners of single ("mom and pop") stores fell from approximately 5300 in 1950 to 3600 in 1963. In Justice Stewart's dissent, in which he concluded that there were no substantial entry barriers into grocery retailing, he wrote: "The sole consistency that I can find is that in litigation under Section 7, the Government always wins."

Reflecting this concern about incipient market power, the 1968 Merger Guidelines stated the intention of the Department of Justice to attack mergers in concentrated markets where the combined share of the parties was as low as 8 percent. These market share standards were controversial even then.

The trend cited by Justice Stewart was reversed beginning with the 1974 *General Dynamics* case.[2] In that decision, in permitting the merger, the Court opened the door to detailed analysis of variables other than concentration and market shares. In 1982, the Department of Justice issued new Merger Guidelines to reflect the current state of the law. However, the 1982 Guidelines made a more fundamental contribution than simply updating the market share standards.[3] They also set out a unified conceptual framework for analyzing the competitive effects of horizontal mergers, a framework that reflects industrial organization economics more closely. While important aspects of the Guidelines are quite controversial among economists, most economists agree that the basic framework is an exceedingly useful analytical tool, not just for merger policy, but for much of industrial organization economics.[4]

---

[2] This case involved the merger of two coal companies, one of which had already contractually committed itself to sell the bulk of its reserves. The coal companies argued that calculating market shares and concentration without taking into account the fact that most of the reserves already were committed gave a misleading impression of the power of the two firms. The Supreme Court agreed, holding that market share and concentration statistics may be rebutted with other evidence.

[3] The Guidelines were revised again in 1984, although not dramatically. Some of the most significant revisions are discussed later in this introduction.

[4] The Department of Justice's far more controversial Vertical Merger Guidelines, issued at the same time, are not discussed in the Symposium. For a recent critique of these standards, see Krattenmaker, Thomas, and Steven C. Salop, "Anticompetitive Exclusion: Raising Rivals' Costs to Gain Power over Price," *Yale Law Journal*, December 1986, *96*, 209–294.

The Merger Guidelines only reflect Department of Justice enforcement policy, not the law itself. They do not represent legal precedent, even though they do influence courts. The Reagan Administration has proposed amending the Clayton Act to alter substantive merger law. The amendment would have two main effects. First, it would require analysis of variables other than concentration, notably entry barriers and efficiency benefits. This change is intended to mandate by statute the basic approach taken in the Merger Guidelines. Second, the amendment would eliminate the "incipiency standard" of illegality by deleting the "tend to create a monopoly" language of Section 7 of the Clayton Act. This change would raise the evidentiary standard for proving market power above the levels of *Von's Grocery* and *Brown Shoe*. The amendment is apparently also intended to mandate enforcement at the current or at a somewhat more permissive level. Perhaps most significantly, it is intended to permit potential cost savings to justify increases in market power.

The purpose of this symposium is to evaluate current merger policy and reform proposals and to set out economists' "best practice" of merger evaluation. To this end, the symposium participants analyze the Department of Justice Guidelines and the proposals for reforming them. The symposium also highlights the issues on which policy makers should focus in judging reform proposals.

Basic Merger Analysis

The Department of Justice Horizontal Merger Guidelines are not concerned with aggregate industrial concentration as measured, for example, by the share of the economy's assets owned by the largest 500 corporations. They focus only on the likelihood that a merger may create or increase market power: that is, the ability to set price above the competitive level. The Guidelines are built on the premise that collusion, either in the form of a "hotel room" conspiracy or tacit coordination, is less likely to succeed in less concentrated markets, in markets where few entry barriers exist, and in markets where competitive price cuts are more difficult for rivals to detect rapidly. The Guidelines are premised on the recognition that significant cost savings can flow from mergers and acquisitions, and enforcement standards governing concentration and ease of entry should be set accordingly. The degree to which potential cost savings should count as an offset and therefore permit mergers that create or increase market power is more controversial.

To evaluate the possible competitive impact of a horizontal merger, the Guidelines set out a five-part protocol. First, a relevant market is determined for evaluating competitive effects. Second, concentration in the market is calculated, using the Herfindahl-Hirshman Index (HHI). The HHI is defined as the sum of squared market shares of the firms in the market, where market shares are treated as whole numbers, not fractions. The possible values for the HHI range from zero for an industry with an infinite number of tiny firms to 10,000 for a single firm monopoly market.[5] Third, the likelihood of entry into the market is evaluated. Fourth, other competitive factors that might affect the likelihood of successful collusion are evaluated, including producer information exchanges and contracting practices. Fifth, any efficiency benefits, primarily cost savings, are analyzed. These five elements then are balanced. Most economists agree that this five-part protocol is a reasonable way, in the words of Franklin Fisher, to organize the data. It is the weights the Guidelines place on these factors in this balancing, and the methodology by which to measure the factors, that are disputed.

The Guidelines measure market concentration and ease of entry in the context of a "relevant antitrust market," defined on the basis of the own-price elasticity for a set of products (and geographic area). In particular, a relevant antitrust market is defined as a set of products and geographic area, such that if all the production capacity in the set were owned by a single firm (a "hypothetical monopolist"), that firm profitably could raise price by at least some percentage (for example, 5 percent or 10 percent) above the *current* (not necessarily competitive) level for a "significant non-transitory" time period. This methodology is referred to as the "5 percent (or 10 percent) test" and is the key concept of the Guidelines.

In evaluating the profitability of a price rise, the Guidelines evaluate the potential for substitution by buyers to other products ("demand substitution") and capacity switchovers by sellers of other products ("supply substitution"), as well as substitution to producers whose plants are located in other places ("geographic diversion") that would occur within 12 months in response to the price increase.

The Guidelines evaluate "ease of entry" in a similar way. Entry is considered "easy" if, in response to the hypothetical price increase, enough new capacity would be brought on line within 24 months to render the price rise unprofitable. By defining market power as the ability to raise prices, the administration reform proposal would support this approach to market definition and ease of entry.

According to the Guidelines, ease of entry and market concentration are given the most weight. Indeed, in the 1982 Guidelines, efficiencies and other factors were treated as "tiebreakers" that only came into play in otherwise "close" cases.

Ease of entry could be considered the primary variable, in that "easy entry" can justify even merger to an apparent monopoly, where the "monopolist" is actually constrained by many potential entrants; consider a merger between the only two taxicab companies in a town where no medallion or reputation is required to compete.

If entry is not "easy," primary focus then is placed on market concentration. Once markets are defined, concentration is relatively easy to measure, and according to many economists, higher concentration raises the likelihood of successful (tacit or

[5] For example, if an industry is comprised of one firm with 80 percent and two firms with 10 percent each, the HHI would equal 6600 (that is, $(80)^2 + (10)^2 + (10)^2$). For an industry comprised of N equal-sized firms, the HHI = $10,000 \div N$. The Herfindahl-Hirshman Index replaced the Four- and Eight-Firm Concentration Ratios (that is, the aggregate market share held by the top four or eight firms) used in the 1968 Guidelines and major court decisions. In practice, these concentration indices are highly correlated.

express) collusion. According to the DOJ Guidelines, if the post-merger HHI remains below 1000, the DOJ threshold for an "unconcentrated" market, all mergers are permitted, despite entry barriers or other factors. In the parlance of enforcers, the HHI of 1000 is a "safe harbor." A post-merger HHI of 1800 defines the threshold of a "highly concentrated" market. If the post-merger HHI exceeds 1800 and entry is not "easy," the DOJ "generally" will attempt to block mergers that increase the HHI by at least 50 points, and will attempt to block mergers that increase the HHI by more than 100 points, except in "extraordinary cases."[6] Mergers with HHI's in the "gray area" between 1000 and 1800 will only be blocked if they would raise the HHI by at least 100 points. In this gray area, ease of entry and other factors are given the most weight.

Even if concentration and entry barriers both are high, noncompetitive pricing is not a certainty. Sophisticated buyers may utilize long term contracts to destabilize collusive agreements, and product heterogeneity and the potential for secret price cuts may reduce the likelihood of successful collusion. On the other hand, information exchanges among producers and (ironically named) "buyer protection" clauses such as most-favored-customer and meeting competition provisions may increase the likelihood that oligopolistic pricing coordination will succeed. In the Guidelines, these "plus" and "minus" factors are taken into account in "close" cases. Some observers claim that, in recent practice, merger policy has been made some what more permissive by giving more weight to those "minus" factors that reduce the likelihood of successful coordination. The administration bill, by eliminating the "incipiency standard," would tend to increase further the weight placed on the "minus" factors.

Finally, under the 1984 revisions of the Guidelines, mergers likely to raise prices will be permitted nonetheless if the parties can demonstrate by "clear and convincing evidence" that the merger is "reasonably necessary" to create significant cost savings or other efficiency benefits. These benefits include achieving economies of scale as well as direct technological improvements. By the "reasonably necessary" standard, the Guidelines will not consider efficiencies achievable by means short of merger. In that case, a competitively troublesome merger need not be permitted because the cost savings will be achieved anyway. Where a merger is reasonably necessary for achieving efficiencies, the Guidelines do not state how cost savings and monopoly price increases should be balanced.

This balancing issue is important and quite controversial. Even modest cost decreases would swamp any short run deadweight losses from monopoly pricing, if the Department of Justice were indifferent to the distribution of the gains between consumers and stockholders and cared only about total social welfare. In the parlance of antitrust, the issue is a matter of interpreting "consumer welfare" (and "competition") either to mean the welfare of *purchasers* of the products or to mean aggregate

---

[6]The Guidelines also contain a "leading firm proviso." No acquisition of a firm with a market share exceeding 1 percent is permitted for the leading firm in the industry, if the market share of the leading firm exceeds 35 percent.

400

economic efficiency.[7] The controversy has become sharper because the administration leans to the latter interpretation, while most courts seem generally to favor the former.

Issues for Analysis

This conceptual framework raises two difficult questions. How should these variables be measured and, once measured, how should they be weighted? In practice, what might appear initially to be purely a measurement issue also may imply an enforcement standard, which creates a significant problem for the policy maker. For example, by defining a relevant antitrust market according to the degree of substitution within twelve months rather than six months, markets will be defined more broadly and this expansion of the market definition will, as a general matter, tend to permit more mergers.[8] That permissiveness can be offset, of course, by tightening either the concentration or entry standards. This choice raises a difficult balancing issue. What is the correct mix: to define markets tightly and set high concentration thresholds or vice versa?

These basic issues are the ones that face economists and policy makers in evaluating merger enforcement and merger reform. These are the controversies the participants were asked to address. To focus their analysis, we also posed a number of specific questions. These questions provide a framework for analysis. They may well be useful to readers in forming their own opinions and organizing their own thoughts.[9]

Market Definition

1. How should relevant antitrust markets be defined? What initial price should be used as the benchmark in the test? The Guidelines' use of the current price as the benchmark has been criticized as preventing deterioration of the competitive environment, but placing no weight at all on the potential for increased competition in the future.[10] This issue also forms part of the question of the appropriate legal standard for evaluating the likelihood of anticompetitive effects.

---

[7]By training, economists might lean to the aggregate efficiency standard, at least initially. After all, economics purports to have little insight into the "proper" distribution of wealth. But simply because economic theory has little to contribute does not mean that society should be indifferent to the distribution, where losers are not compensated for their losses by winners. For example, consider a worker who steals $100 from a capitalist and invests the proceeds at a higher return than the capitalist earned. Would the higher social return justify the involuntary transfer?

[8]Lawrence White stresses the exceptions to this generalization in his article.

[9]Also, teachers may wish to use these questions to organize class discussion or formulate examination questions.

[10]In this regard, the Guidelines are accused of committing the "cellophane fallacy." In the 1956 case against Du Pont, the Supreme Court held that cellophane was not a relevant market, and Du Pont had no market power, because *at current prices*, any further cellophane price rises would be constrained by competition from other flexible wrappings. This conclusion was fallacious, of course. The fact that no further price rises were possible does not mean that the market was competitive. Rather, perhaps Du Pont could raise price no further because it already was charging the monopoly price. The DOJ's use of the current price as the benchmark arises from a policy judgment that merger policy only should prevent

2. Some commentators claim that while the "5 percent test" approach looks good on paper, it has failed in practice for two reasons. First, it is so hypothetical (hypothetical buyers and competitors with perfect information responding to a price rise by a hypothetical monopolist) that the result generally will be entirely subjective. As a result, it gives the agency enormous discretion. This is, of course, in striking contrast to the concreteness of the HHI levels. Put another way, the apparent concreteness of the HHIs is dissolved by the mushiness of the 5 percent test. Second, and based on the first point, critics have claimed that the agencies have administered the test in practice to broaden markets far beyond practical boundaries by accepting weak subjective evidence of potential substitution instead of insisting on "hard evidence" of actual substitution. Have the DOJ and the FTC been defining markets too narrowly or too broadly? Has the evidentiary standard been too low? Should the agencies be constrained to use only "hard evidence" of actual or very likely substitution?

3. The 1982 Guidelines specified a 5 percent price test. The 1984 Guidelines contemplate larger price increases as well. It has been suggested that, in practice, the Department of Justice has now increased the price percentage to 10 percent, instead of 5 percent. In general, this change would broaden markets and lead to less enforcement. Which is the better test, 10 percent or 5 percent?

4. How should foreign competition be included in the merger analysis? At one extreme, some commentators would ignore foreign capacity altogether on the grounds that the potential for exogenous exchange rate changes and the chance of tariffs and quotas make the prospects for increased foreign competition too risky. At the other extreme, some argue that if the domestic market has any imports at all, then the entire foreign capacity could be diverted to the United States if prices rose to noncompetitive levels. Should imports be treated identically with domestic capacity, if no quotas exist? If quotas do exist, how should foreign capacity be included in the analysis?

Market Concentration

5. Some economists conclude that the "new industrial organization learning" demonstrates that although market concentration may be easy to calculate, it has no predictive value. They say that absolutely no weight should be placed on concentration, that it should be ignored in evaluating mergers. How should concentration enter the analysis?

6. Market definition and concentration are related, of course. As a practical matter, the broader the market definition, the lower market concentration will tend to be. What threshold concentration levels for enforcement guidelines are implied by the optimal market definition?

7. Some evidence suggests that the enforcement agencies in the current administration have brought almost no cases where the HHI is below 1800, the threshold defining "highly concentrated" markets. Is this a beneficial policy change?

additional market power and not serve also to preserve the possibility of dissipating already exercised market power.

Ease of Entry

8. The DOJ Guidelines do not discuss the determinants of ease of entry in any detail. How should ease of entry be measured in merger analysis? George Stigler defined an entry barrier as limited to costs that entrants (but not incumbents) must bear, while Joe Bain's definition includes the potential entry-deterring effects of "post-entry" price competition. In particular, should the presence of significant scale economies and sunk costs that are identical for all firms be treated as impediments or barriers to entry? What about advertising and reputation?

9. Similarly, despite the weight placed on ease of entry in the Guidelines, the Justice Department did not attempt to devise a method for grading ease of entry into categories (such as low, moderate and high barriers), comparable to the current grading system for market concentration. Should such a grading system be designed to facilitate quantitative analysis of this crucial variable?

10. In evaluating the likelihood of unilateral output reductions and tacit collusion, how much weight should be placed on ease of entry? Should merger to monopoly be permitted in those situations where entry is "very" easy?

"Plus" and "Minus" Factors

11. Should evidence about competitive factors relating to contracting practices and information be used as "tiebreakers," or should these factors be weighted more or less heavily? In the extreme, could it be argued that the use of long term contracts by industrial buyers should make any merger short of a true single firm monopoly permissible, regardless of concentration or even ease of entry, on the grounds that sophisticated buyers can devise means of maintaining competition even if only two firms are bidding?

Efficiencies

12. How should cost savings and other efficiency benefits be reckoned into merger analysis, if at all? Should cost savings be evaluated in each case or should likely cost savings (on average) be used only in setting overall enforcement thresholds? Can sufficiently credible cost savings information be generated during the short pre-merger screening period to make case-by-case evaluation useful? What should be the evidentiary standard on the merger partners? What should be the benchmark for defining when a merger is "reasonably necessary" to achieve cost efficiencies—a comparison with the unmerged status quo or some less restrictive hypothetical alternative like licensing, alternative merger partners, or a joint venture?

13. In specifying the general standard for evaluating claims of cost savings, should the criterion be indifferent to wealth transfers from purchasers to stockholders? That is, should a merger likely to produce cost savings be permitted even if it also leads to market power and higher prices, if the cost savings exceed the deadweight loss triangle? How should considerations of dynamic rent-seeking and innovation incentives be included in the analysis?

Balancing

14. In summary, do the DOJ Guidelines place the correct relative weights on the five factors? Should more or less weight be placed on some of the variables? What are the appropriate enforcement thresholds? Stated another way, what are optimal Merger Guidelines? Should the "incipiency standard" be eliminated altogether or simply interpreted less expansively than in *Brown Shoe* and *Von's Grocery*?

15. Current merger policy clearly is more permissive than in previous administrations. As a general matter, has the current administration gone too far or not far enough in loosening merger enforcement?

Using these questions as a basic framework, each participant was asked to set out his own analysis. The drafts then were circulated among the participants so they could sharpen their disagreements or achieve consensus in their revisions.

Note

Many economists may be unfamiliar with the court cases and legal citations that recur throughout this introduction and symposium. Probably the easiest way to collect the relevant material is by using an antitrust casebook. One good example is Handler, *et al.*, *Trade Regulation: Cases and Materials*. 2nd ed. Mineola, NY: Foundation Press, 1983. This book (like other such casebooks), contains the text of the Clayton Act, the Department of Justice Merger Guidelines, and key court cases like *Brown Shoe*, *Von's Grocery*, *General Dynamics*, and *Du Pont*.

■ *Thomas Krattenmaker and the symposium participants provided helpful comments.*

International Review of Law and Economics (1985), 5 (39–57)

THE POSITIVE ECONOMICS OF ANTITRUST POLICY: A SURVEY ARTICLE

WILLIAM F. SHUGHART II

AND

ROBERT D. TOLLISON

George Mason University, Fairfax VA 22030, USA

I. INTRODUCTION

Most discussions of antitrust assume that policy is formulated by a benign government. The conventional wisdom seems to be that the basic legislative framework of antitrust in the USA—the Sherman, Clayton and Federal Trade Commission (FTC) Acts—as well as the relevant actors—the Congress, judiciary, antitrust bar, and enforcement agencies—serve the public interest, where by 'public interest' is meant some normative standard such as maximizing consumer welfare. Thus, whenever antitrust policy fails (and it does so quite often by many accounts), the failures are attributed to one or more of a number of correctable errors. Those criticizing antitrust policy accordingly lecture to government, calling upon the agencies to do a better job, for lawyers and judges to learn economic principles, or for incumbent policy-makers to be replaced with people better able to serve the public interest.

This conception of antitrust stands in sharp contrast to the by now widely known interest-group model of regulation. Modern scholarship in law and economics has shown in case after case that when government intervenes to correct market 'failures,' it ends up doing so to the benefit of some groups at the expense of others. The interest-group model stresses that the ultimate level and pattern of government action results from the interplay between self-interested demanders of wealth transfers and self-interested suppliers of regulation who seek political survival. Deadweight costs are imposed on the economy as a by-product of this process.

In this paper we attempt to pierce the rhetorical veil of the conventional wisdom by suggesting that antitrust bureaucracy operates much like regulatory bureaucracy in general. To do so we trace the development of the small body of literature that takes a positive approach to the study of antitrust policy. Our review begins in Section II with a summary of the conventional wisdom. The review presented there is not intended to be exhaustive. Rather, we have selected literature that we believe to be illustrative of the dominant thinking. Our critique suggests that the standard approach to antitrust treats anticompetitive business practices as arising from the activities of private individuals seeking only their own gain on the one hand, and necessary corrective actions taken by individuals seeking only the public good on the other. In Buchanan's terms this is not a closed behavioral system.[1] In one setting individuals are assumed to be selfish; in another they are selfless. The analyst cannot have it both ways. A decision about how individuals behave in general must be made.

0144-8188/85/01 0039-19 $03.00 © 1985 Butterworth & Co (Publishers) Ltd

Some of the steps along the way toward the positive approach are reviewed in Section III. We treat this segment of the literature as falling into three broad categories. First are studies that focus on the left-hand side of the antitrust equation, case output. This purely empirical work sorts historical enforcement efforts into a variety of compartments such as the number and types of cases, charges brought, firms and products involved, recidivism rates, and so forth. Second, we review the literature that addresses the benefits and costs of antitrust enforcement. These studies seek to identify, primarily by reference to welfare-loss models, appropriate targets for antitrust intervention. Our third category consists of analyses of agency organizational behavior—in particular, those presenting evidence on the private incentives faced by enforcement personnel.

In Section IV we summarize the papers that constitute the beginnings of a positive approach to the analysis of antitrust policy. In one way or another, this small body of literature seeks to answer the question, which public and whose interest does antitrust serve? Among the topics covered are the extent to which Congress influences case-bringing activities, who wins and who loses from enforcement efforts, and the origins of the antitrust statutes.

A concrete example of the positive approach is given in Section V. There we sketch a model of dual antitrust enforcement that contrasts the effects on antitrust output and its cost of alternative institutional arrangements. In both cases, two budget-maximizing agencies having similar mandates serve a sponsor, the US Congress. In the first setting, the bureaus compete. In the second setting, the agencies collude by dividing up their areas of enforcement responsibility. This chronology approximates the historical development of US antitrust since in 1948 the FTC and Antitrust Division concluded a liaison agreement for the purposes of allocating cases and sharing information. Section VI contains some concluding remarks.

There are some important omissions from our review. Because economic theory has more to say about the effects of governmental policies than why particular laws are enacted, we do not have much to say about the origins of the major pieces of antitrust legislation. Furthermore, in discussing antitrust, the literature often fails to differentiate among the legislature, the judiciary, the antitrust bar, and the enforcement agencies. Of necessity, our discussion tends to blur this distinction as well, focusing mostly on enforcement. Finally, we confine our review to studies of US antitrust policy.

The current state of the debate on antitrust has moved away from proposals for marginal changes in law or enforcement. The whole purpose of a procompetitive policy has come under attack from the ideological extremes. The left sees antitrust as interfering with the development of an 'industrial policy' that would increase the ability of US firms to compete in the world market. The right equates firm size with efficiency, and wants government to stop its antitrust attack on big business. We suggest that both sides of the debate would benefit from understanding the positive issues associated with antitrust. Reform, after all, does not take place in a vacuum, and knowledge of how antitrust institutions function can only be helpful to the process of antitrust reform.

II. THE CONVENTIONAL WISDOM

The conventional wisdom on antitrust is based on a benign view of government. Most discussions of policy are clothed in the garb of the public interest, and those enforcing the law are pictured as individuals somehow able to transcend the self-interested motivations normally attributed to behavior in the market-place. In this section we illustrate the popular thinking to make a basic point: The conventional wisdom leaves the discussion of antitrust on a normative plane. Both supporters and critics have recourse only to assertions about 'good' and 'bad' law, or 'good' and 'bad' enforcement. Such an approach is not very helpful in understanding how antitrust works.

Except for subsequent passage of a half-dozen important amendments, the body of US antitrust law was laid out in three statutes enacted around the turn of the century. In brief, the Sherman Act (1890) prohibits 'every contract, combination in the form of trust or otherwise, or conspiracy, in restraint of trade or commerce among the several States . . .' (Section 1), and declares guilty of a misdemeanor 'every person who shall monopolize, or attempt to monopolize . . .' (Section 2). The Clayton Act (1914) prohibits price discrimination, exclusive dealing and tying contracts, acquisitions of competing companies, and interlocking directorates where the effect of the practice 'may be to substantially lessen competition or tend to create a monopoly', and the substantive section (5) of the FTC Act (1914) bans 'unfair methods of competition'.

The standard history argues that the political pressure for passage of the Sherman Act arose among small businessmen and farmers who complained of the 'rough methods of the trust builders'.[2] The latter group was particularly vocal, believing itself to have been squeezed between rising monopoly prices for machinery and other finished goods on the one hand, and falling agricultural prices on the other.[3] Similarly, the Clayton and FTC Acts are supposed to have grown out of dissatisfaction with enforcement efforts under, and judicial interpretations of, the Sherman Act.[4] The Clayton Act therefore prohibited certain specific practices through which it was thought monopoly could be attained (i.e., mergers, price discrimination), and the FTC Act established an agency that combined broad investigative, prosecutorial, and adjudicative functions.

In evaluating the purposes of these statutes, the traditional approach has been to treat them as innocent of economic motivation. The intent of Congress in enacting the laws was a public-spirited concern with consumer welfare,[5] and the role of the antitrust officials charged with enforcement is explicitly or implicitly assumed to be the maintenance of competition 'by prohibiting private restrictions of it, and by preventing the development of monopoly'.[6]

The normative approach to antitrust is not limited to commentators of any one political persuasion. For example, Scherer views antitrust as 'one of the more important weapons wielded by government in its effort to harmonize the profit-seeking behavior of private enterprises with the public interest'. A benevolent government is able to achieve this harmony 'by inhibiting or prohibiting certain undesirable kinds of *business conduct*, and by channelling and sharpening *market structure* along competitive lines so as to increase the likelihood that desirable conduct and performance will emerge more or less automatically'.[7] Similarly, Posner suggests that the importance of economic efficiency as a social value 'establishes a *prima facie* case for having an antitrust policy'.[8] Elzinga and Breit see antitrust as a public good designed to correct the 'market failure' due to monopoly. They, in fact, argue that 'the importance of antitrust enforcement is one of those rare issues that cuts across even the most formidable of ideological barriers'.[9]

In the main, then, 'it is tempting (and common) to regard the antitrust policy simply as a kind of economic engineering project'.[10] Competition leads to efficiency, and antitrust is the means by which competition is maintained. Moreover, danger lies in a policy of *laissez faire* because of the abuses of monopoly.[11] Unchecked monopoly forecloses markets, restricts output, and stifles innovation.[12] As such, 'a much more widespread pattern of growth by merger, an efflorescence of collusive agreements of all sorts, and the use of various exclusionary and otherwise anticompetitive practices now forbidden would all follow on the abandonment of a procompetitive public policy'.[13] Thus, the centerpiece of antitrust legislation, the Sherman Act, 'remains above partisan controversy as a "charter of freedom", a constitution governing the economy of the United States'.[14]

Given that the purposes of antitrust lie outside economic analysis in the conventional view, policy failures are ascribed to a variety of correctable errors. The most prominent of these is the 'neglect of economic principles [by] the judges, lawyers, and enforcement personnel who are responsible for giving meaning to the vague language of the antitrust statutes . . .'.[15] Accordingly, a literature has grown up which attempts to instruct the antitrust bar in economic theory by offering critiques of specific cases. These case studies examine the evidence before the court, evaluate the economic merits of the charges, and then confer approval or disapproval on the ultimate decision.

It is fair to say that many more 'bad' than 'good' cases have been made example of in the literature. In recent memory, only the *Sylvania* decision has received widespread support from economists.[16] The more usual case study finds that the evidence presented was 'weak and at times bordered on fiction', that 'neither the government nor the Courts seemed able to distinguish competition from monopolizing',[17] and that at best 'nothing was accomplished by bringing this case'.[18] Other critiques suggest alternative explanations for the behavior of the defendants,[19] contend that the economic theory underlying the case was 'erroneous',[20] or focus on the effectiveness of the remedy.[21] There are a great many examples of each of these approaches.[22]

When errors in the case law are uncovered, the common recommendation is for closer adherence to economic principles in the future. Some commentators, however, go so far as to call for wholesale changes in the antitrust statutes. Bork prescribes legal reforms so as to ban only horizontal agreements and 'deliberate predation',[23] while Posner suggests scrapping all but Section 1 of the Sherman Act.[24] Kaysen and Turner offer a detailed list of proposals to limit more effectively 'undue market power',[25] and Williamson hopes that his own theoretical contributions will close a glaring loophole in the law: 'Antitrust policy has long been plagued by the problem of continued dominance of an industry by a single firm which has obtained its position by lawful means'.[26] Others call for more careful analysis,[27] or merely express faith in the 'modest promise of antitrust'.[28]

Another segment of the critical literature on antitrust examines empirically the assumptions underlying the theoretical basis for antitrust, the structure–conduct–performance paradigm. As Demsetz has argued, there are two systems of belief about monopoly.[29] One sees monopoly in the private sector as the primary threat; the other sees monopoly sponsored by government as the most worrisome source of market power. Those taking the latter view have attacked the former by attempting to show that there is no necessary link between industry structure and market performance, in particular, that relatively high levels of concentration in certain industries may be the result of survival by a small number of efficient firms. Examples of this approach are the studies by Brozen, Demsetz and Peltzman.[30] As such, these papers call the conventional wisdom into question, and perhaps can be seen as attempts to improve antitrust by providing better information to enforcers.

While in no way attempting to diminish the importance of these contributions, it is clear that the conventional wisdom on antitrust is based on a benign view of government. One cannot support antitrust intervention to correct markets which have failed to provide some standard of competition, without admitting that comparable failures can exist in the proposed corrective measures. It is disingenuous to explain policy failures, the granting of exemptions to antitrust law, and the existence of 'a body of substantive doctrine and a system of sanctions and procedures that are poorly suited to carrying out the fundamental objectives of antitrust policy . . .'[31] within a model where the behavior of individuals shifts from that of self-interested maximizers when making private choices to that of public benefactors when confronted with policy choices.

In few other places in economics does this benign view of government exist any longer. Modern scholarship in the areas of public finance and regulation has moved the discussion of policy away from normative issues by suggesting that the individuals who enact legislation and enforce the law are the same people who behave in their own interest when making market decisions. Our basic point is that antitrust can be fruitfully analyzed from the same perspective.

III. STEPS ALONG THE WAY

Early attempts to understand the workings of antitrust consisted of purely empirical studies of enforcement efforts, analyses of the operations and incentives of the antitrust bureaucracy, and comparisons of actual case-bringing activities with the standards suggested by economic theory. We summarize each of these steps in turn.

Pure empiricism

An important segment of the literature on antitrust approaches the topic by sorting the time series of cases brought into a variety of categories. The leading paper here is by Posner,[32] but an early effort by Stigler is noteworthy.[33] Subsequent contributions have focused on the historical activities of one agency or the other, on certain types of violations, or on particular phases of the enforcement process.

Stigler assessed the general effects of the antitrust laws on aggregate concentration, on the frequency of merger, and on the prevalence of collusion. Using data covering roughly 1890 to 1960 and contrasting US concentration levels in selected industries with corresponding UK statistics, Stigler found that the Sherman Act had had only modest effects on the market shares of leading firms. Similar conclusions were reached for the antimerger laws, but the Sherman Act did seem to have eliminated the most efficient methods of collusion.

Posner investigated seven broad dimensions of antitrust case output with data covering the period from passage of the Sherman Act through 1969. These were number of cases filed annually, the length of antitrust proceedings, agency won–lost records, remedy choices, violations alleged, and industries involved. Whenever possible, he reported data for the Antitrust Division, the FTC, and for private antitrust litigation.

Posner's menu of results provides interesting insights into the activities of the antitrust establishment. A representative sample includes the observations that the variation in the level of Justice Department antitrust activity was roughly correlated with changes in GNP through 1940, but not thereafter; that although most antitrust cases were settled either by a consent judgment or by a *nolo contendere* plea, when the respondent exercised his right to judicial review in matters before the

Commission, the average length of FTC cases was far greater than the average length of litigated Antitrust Division matters; and that both the FTC and Justice Department have enjoyed a high level of success on appeal in restraint of trade and other traditional antitrust cases. In addition, Posner found that a significant proportion of civil antitrust decrees are regulatory in nature, that imprisonment is a rarely used solution in Justice Department criminal cases, and that a large percentage of Antitrust Division and FTC cases are brought in industries not normally regarded as concentrated. Overall, Posner concluded that 'antitrust enforcement is inefficient, and the first step toward improvement must be . . . a greater interest in the dry subject of . . . antitrust statistics'.[34]

Clabault and Block offer a compendium of Antitrust Division cases brought under the Sherman Act, organizing the data in a variety of formats.[35] Similarly, Shughart and Tollison focus on a subset of FTC cases—those involving firms that repeatedly violated the laws enforced by the Commission.[36] They found that recidivists accounted for about 23 per cent of the agency's overall workload, and presented evidence on recidivism rates over time, the violations most likely to have been involved in repeat offenses, the products most often sold by multiple violators, and elapsed time between offenses. Repeat offenders before the Commission were much more often charged with unfair or deceptive advertising infractions than with traditional antitrust violations. The largest component of the latter were infractions of Sections 2 and 3 of the Clayton Act, as amended by the Robinson–Patman Act, which prohibited price discrimination.

Empirical antitrust studies also include work that analyzes certain types of violations. For example, Hay and Kelley limited their research to horizontal price-fixing cases brought by the Antitrust Division. They examined 'all Section 1 criminal cases which were filed *and* won in trial or settled by *nolo contendere* pleas from January 1963 to December 1972 . . .',[37] comparing the facts in each case with the factors economic theory suggests facilitate collusion. Their findings indicated that 'industries colluding at one point in time often can be found to be colluding at later points in time, in spite of Antitrust action in the interim'. The results led Hay and Kelley to conclude that 'applying dissolution to habitual offenders may provide the publicity necessary to raise further the perceived cost of violating the antitrust laws and thus force compliance by firms in industries prone to conspiracy'.[38]

Among US manufacturing firms during 1958 to 1967, colluding producers were found by Asch and Seneca to be 'consistently less profitable' than non-colluders.[39] They interpreted this evidence as suggesting either that low profits motivate firms to enter into collusive agreements, or that the antitrust authorities more often prosecute unsuccessful cartels. Similarly, Palmer found that firms having below-average growth rates during 1966–70 were disproportionately represented in antitrust suits charging horizontal restraint of trade.[40]

The effectiveness of relief measures in merger cases has been examined by Elzinga.[41] His data consisted of a sample of 39 Clayton Act Section 7 cases filed by 1960, and settled by the end of 1964. By Elzinga's reckoning, the remedial measures were 'unsuccessful' in 21 of the cases and 'deficient' in eight others. When he expanded his evaluative criteria to include the time span between acquisition and relief order, 35 out of 39 cases ended in less than 'sufficient' relief.

With few exceptions, the statistical studies on antitrust represent data manipulation without a theory. This segment of the literature nevertheless sheds light on the output of the antitrust agencies, presenting a record that is largely one of policy failure. Although the Antitrust Division and the FTC can be judged 'successful' on their own terms, i.e., having brought cases that more often than not end in consent orders or no-contest pleas, these cases involve respondents that operate in unconcentrated industries, and impose penalties having less than substantial deterrent effects. At best, antitrust enforcement appears empirically inefficient.

Organizational behavior

Another early step toward positive analysis was taken by Weaver in her study of decision-making within the Antitrust Division.[42] Based on the results of interviews during 1971 with about 100 staff members, private attorneys, and other observers of the Division, she sought to answer the question, 'Why does the division choose to bring any particular case'?[43] Weaver's main contribution was to elicit information on the private incentives motivating public prosecutors. According to Weaver, events during the early 1950s, such as passage of the Celler–Kefauver Act and the indictment of electrical equipment manufacturers for price-fixing, made 'antitrust expertise a more valuable commodity to the business community and to law firms serving it'. Because of this increased demand, 'experience in the Antitrust Division became newly valuable to a young lawyer who wanted eventually to work in private practice . . .'. And, the experience wanted was trial experience in the federal courts.[44]

Weaver's work thus suggests that, at the margin, getting to trial may win over the merits of a particular case in the decision to prosecute. Unfortunately, her study suffers from the faults common to interview evidence, i.e., that what people say often diverges from what they do, and from her inability to examine internal Antitrust Division documents. Weaver nevertheless helps to pierce the veil of the public-interest assumption.

The incentive structure faced by Federal Trade Commission attorneys has been examined by Katzman, who also notes that the ultimate career goal of most legal staff members is a job with a prestigious law firm.[45] Such goals mean that managers will find that 'structural matters and industrywide cases threaten the morale of the staff because they often involve years of tedious investigation before they reach the trial stage'. In consequence, upper-level Commission executives may support 'the opening of a number of easily prosecuted matters, which may have little value to the consumer . . . in an effort to satisfy the staff's perceived needs'.[46]

Katzman's main point is that one cannot explain the Commission's case selection process on the basis of industry economic characteristics. Rather, the decision to prosecute is dominated by factors internal to the FTC—staff career objectives, the availability of enforcement resources, Congressional influence, and so on. Katzman's study thus reaches conclusions similar to those of Weaver, and is also subject to the same methodological criticism of reliance on interviews for evidence.

The attack assembled by Clarkson and Muris on the FTC focuses on internal organizational conflicts, staff incentives, and external constraints.[47] For example, they suggest that the Commission substituted cases employing the market concentration doctrine for Robinson–Patman matters to resolve internal conflicts between lawyers and economists, and because the increased complexity of the caseload provided human capital benefits to the attorney staff. In addition, Clarkson and Muris attribute the FTC's failure to bring many price-fixing cases to the desire of Commission attorneys to differentiate themselves in the private job market from their Justice Department counterparts.[48] The value of their study lies in the insights into the functioning of the Commission offered by Clarkson and Muris and the other contributors to their book. It is in this sense that we classify their book under the heading of organizational behavior.

Several attempts have been made to compare the actual distribution of antitrust cases across industries with the pattern that would emerge if the agencies chose cases so as to maximize consumer welfare. In a sense these studies represent a positive effort to ascertain whether the economic model of the public interest has actually been followed or has any chance of being followed by antitrust bureaucrats.

The benefit–cost approach to antitrust is based on the concept of Pareto optimality. Under this standard, monopoly is inferior to perfect competition because monopoly lowers consumer welfare. The welfare loss comes about in two ways. These are a pure transfer from producers to consumers that materializes in the form of monopoly profits, and a deadweight cost to society arising because the monopolist restricts output below the competitive level. The assumption, then, is that de-monopolization through antitrust will reduce the size of such welfare losses by moving price and output toward the competitive norm. Such a gain will be realized if the public costs of removing monopoly are less than the benefit to society in terms of improved welfare. The empirical basis of this approach was the work by Harberger and others which offered estimates of the economy-wide welfare loss due to monopoly.[49]

Triangles

The basic welfare-loss model is illustrate in Figure 1, where D is a linear, long-run demand schedule for some product, and C is long-run average and marginal cost, assumed to be constant and identical for all firms. In equilibrium, a competitive industry produces Q_c units per time period and charges price $P_c = C$. With monopoly, output is restricted to Q_m and price rises to P_m. Given the same costs, the monopolist

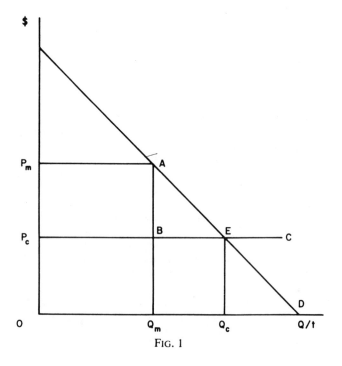

Fig. 1

earns profits equal to the area of the rectangle $P_m ABP_c$, a sum which formerly was part of consumer surplus (the area under the demand schedule above P_c).

Although the monopolist's profit is a pure redistribution, the area of the triangle ABE is a deadweight loss to society. It is neither retained by consumers nor captured by the producer. As such, the welfare-loss triangle provides a measure of the benefit to society of de-monopolization. Ideally, then, antitrust enforcement would proceed by, first, rank-ordering industries on the basis of the relative magnitudes of their welfare-loss triangles, and then by bringing action against firms in those industries serially until the year's enforcement budget was exhausted. In practice, however, estimating the size of the triangle presents difficulties. One approach requires information on the price elasticity of demand; another is based on the Lerner index, price minus marginal cost all over price.[50] Accordingly, various empirical surrogates for the size of the welfare loss have been employed, including profit-to-sales ratios, industry concentration measures, and sales alone.

Trapezoids[51]

Estimates by Harberger and others placed the economy-wide welfare loss due to monopoly at less than 1 per cent of GNP. This relatively low figure led Mundell to observe that 'unless there is a thorough reexamination of the validity of the tools upon which these studies are founded . . . someone will inevitably draw the conclusion that economics has ceased to be important'.[52] The profession was rescued by Tullock when he suggested that the social cost of monopoly exceeded that given by the simple deadweight loss triangle.[53] In particular, Tullock argued that any resources spent to capture the profit rectangle, $P_m ABP_c$ in Figure 1, also represented a reduction in social welfare.

Under what can be termed competitive rent-seeking, the monopoly rents in Figure 1 will be fully transformed into a social cost. Consider Posner's example.[54] Suppose that ten risk-neutral bidders seek a monopoly right worth $100 000. If they cannot collude and if bids are non-refundable, then each person will bid $10 000 for the right. At the social level, the monopoly rents are exactly dissipated—$100 000 is spent to capture $100 000.

Such rent-seeking activities are normally associated with artificial scarcities created by government. Moreover, depending on the institutional framework within which rent-seeking takes place, and on other factors such as whether or not the supply curve of bidders is upward sloping, all monopoly rents in the economy need not be dissipated. The important insight of rent-seeking theory, however, is that the welfare loss due to monopoly in an industry may be as large as the area of the trapezoid, $P_m AEP_c$, in Figure 1. Indeed, Posner has estimated that rent-seeking costs constitute about 3 per cent of GNP.

In sum, the benefit–cost approach suggests that antitrust can improve social welfare by reducing the costs of monopoly. The question is, then, does actual enforcement activity follow such a model?

Welfare loss and antitrust

Long, Schramm and Tollison compared the actual distribution of cases brought by the Justice Department's Antitrust Division with the pattern that would obtain if the agency selected cases on the basis of net benefit to society, i.e., prosecuted first those matters where the value of the reduction in welfare loss net of the cost of bringing the cases was greatest.[55] Their basic technique was to regress the number of cases instituted by industry on various industry-specific welfare-loss measures. (They assumed that the cost of bringing cases was constant across industries.) The model performed best in predicting case-bringing activities when industry size, as measured by sales, was used as a proxy for welfare loss, but overall, the evidence cut against the hypothesis that Antitrust Division behavior was grounded on a benefit–cost calculus. Specifically, the results suggested that 'the composite measures of the potential benefits from antitrust action . . . tested—the welfare-loss triangle alone or together with excess profits—appear to play a minor role in explaining antitrust activity'.[56]

In subsequent comments on Long, Schramm and Tollison, Asch and Siegfried presented additional evidence that enforcement efforts by the antitrust bureaucracy do not follow the welfare-loss model. Asch regressed the number of cases brought per year by industry on average annual industry sales, the number of firms as of 1967, and average annual sales per firm.[57] On the basis of separate results for both the FTC and the Antitrust Division, he suggested that 'case-bringing activity cannot be characterized as predominantly "rational" or predominantly "random" . . .'.[58] Similarly, using a sample of industries significantly less aggregated than that employed by Long, Schramm and Tollison, Siegfried found that 'the conclusions of Long *et al.* remain unchanged. It appears that greater levels of excess profits and lower levels of welfare losses are associated with more antitrust cases'.[59] Moreover, when he refined his reduced-form equation to include a better measure of the benchmark rate of return, and to control for the possible number of cases in each industry, coefficient signs were reversed and the explanatory power of the regressions plummeted. Siegfried concluded that 'economic variables have little influence on the Antitrust Division'.[60]

In sum, the available evidence suggests that the antitrust bureaucracy does not select cases to prosecute on the basis of potential net benefit to society.[61]

IV. POSITIVE BEGINNINGS

In this section, we summarize the small body of literature that takes a positive approach to antitrust policy analysis. The papers we review cover topics that are largely unconnected. If there is a central theme, however, it is that most of the studies apply the interest-group model of government to antitrust.

The interest-group model was formalized in the work of Stigler and Peltzman.[62] Although the theory is usually put in terms of producer interests versus consumer interests, it is in reality much more general. Once it is realized that certain groups within the polity can use the political apparatus of the state to their own benefit, the theory generates a rich set of predictions about regulatory outcomes in which, generally, groups having concentrated interests in the regulatory process gain at the expense of groups having more diffuse interests. As examples, large firms may gain at the expense of small firms, coalitions of high-income consumers and some producers may gain at the expense of low-income consumers, residents of certain states may gain at the expense of other states' residents, and so forth.

The central theme of this paper is that antitrust policy can be fruitfully analyzed from the same perspective. At this point we hold no brief as to the nature of the specific wealth transfers involved in antitrust enforcement. In fact, the broad language of the laws suggests that there is no single redistribution at work, for example, from business as a whole to consumers, but that there may be a whole range of political margins to be cleared by the antitrust bureaucracy. To illustrate, Baxter considered several hypotheses in his 'attempt to identify the political constituency for the passage and enforcement of the antitrust laws in the United States'.[63] These included the conventional wisdom, i.e., that 'public-spirited legislators pass these laws and the public-spirited judiciary enforces them because they profit all consumers . . .', the hypothesis that the private antitrust bar is the most direct beneficiary of antitrust activity, the idea that the laws give public officials 'a relatively low cost vehicle for the expansion of their own power and their own budgets', and the hypothesis that antitrust enforcement benefits small firms at the expense of their larger rivals.[64] Although Baxter is only able to bring sketchy evidence to bear on each of these hypotheses, he asks the question that the positive approach seeks to answer: which public and whose interest does antitrust serve?

Faith, Leavens and Tollison suggest that the interests served by antitrust are those of the congressmen sitting on committees having budgetary or oversight mandates with respect to the enforcement agencies.[65] Specifically, they consider whether there is a geographic bias in the case-bringing activities of the FTC such that enforcement favors firms operating in the jurisdictions of the relevant committee members. Using data on Commission case-bringing activity for the period 1961–79, Faith, Leavens and Tollison find that matters brought against companies located in the jurisdictions of important committee members—especially cases involving firms in the districts represented by the members of key House subcommittees—are more likely to be dismissed than matters involving firms located in other jurisdictions. Overall, their results 'lend support to a private-interest theory of FTC behavior . . .' in which 'representation on certain committees is apparently valuable in antitrust proceedings'.[66]

Similarly, using a median-voter model, Weingast and Moran explained the significant policy reversals by the FTC during the late 1970s as a function of membership turnover on the congressional committees overseeing the Commission.[67] Their purpose was to test 'two opposing approaches about regulatory agency behavior. The first assumes agencies operate independently of the legislature and hence exercise discretion; the second assumes that Congress controls agency decisions'.[68] Weingast and Moran presented evidence favoring the latter hypothesis. That is, the FTC drew back from its activist posture in 1979 because key committee members in Congress were replaced by individuals opposed to such activism. The authors concluded that their 'results show that FTC activity is remarkably sensitive to changes in the subcommittee composition'.[69]

Another important segment of the positivist literature seeks to identify winners and losers from ongoing enforcement efforts. In a study of 772 mergers using data from the capital market, Ellert found that firms against which complaints were brought generated larger abnormal returns for stockholders prior to the challenged acquisitions than acquiring firms not indicted.[70] In both cases, however, most of the abnormal returns had been earned far enough in advance of the mergers that Ellert doubted them to have been due to capitalizations of anticipated monopoly rents. Ellert also found that firms ordered to divest acquired assets had provided larger abnormal returns to stockholders than acquirers permitted to retain assets, and that the issuance of a complaint reduced stockholder wealth by about 2 per cent regardless of the eventual outcome of the case. Ellert's study thus provides evidence that enforcement of the antimerger law penalizes efficient management.

Burns examined the effects on stockholder wealth of the dissolutions in 1911 of Standard Oil, American Tobacco, and American Snuff.[71] His data indicated that 'the performance of the snuff, tobacco, and petroleum industries was not significantly altered by the replacement of each trust with independent rivals',[72] i.e., that investors evaluated the dissolutions 'as "better than expected" and ultimately "benign" in their competitive effects'.[73] Burns was unable to resolve whether his results implied 'no successor competition' or 'no monopoly in the first place', but the inference in either case appears to be that trust-busting is ineffective.[74]

In studying the origins of the Robinson–Patman Act, Tom Ross found evidence that grocery chains suffered wealth reductions, that food brokers benefitted, and that there were no significant effects on the market values of grocery manufacturers or other chains.[75] Moreover, the wealth effects of Robinson–Patman enforcement were found to be substantial and largely associated with issuance of a complaint, not the ultimate outcome of the case. The Ross results suggest a transfer of wealth from large to small firms.

A wealth transfer in the opposite direction has been found by Altrogge and Shughart with respect to enforcement of consumer protection laws by the FTC.[76] They test an implication of Peltzman's model that in maximizing their political majority, regulators may choose to 'exploit differences within the group that, taken as a whole, either wins or loses'.[77] Using data derived from 57 civil penalty cases before the Commission between 1979 and 1981, Altrogge and Shughart discover that the majority of the variation in fines is explained by variations in firm size, where size is measured by sales. Moreover, an increase in firm size results in a less than proportional increase in penalty, *ceteris paribus*, suggesting that the fines assessed by the Commission operate as a regressive tax on law violators, transferring wealth from small firms to large.

In a recent paper, Stigler examined the conventional view that the main support for passage of the Sherman Act can be traced to the Granger Movement.[78] He found no empirical evidence favoring the proposition that agricultural interests had reason to be distressed by railroad market power or by monopoly in general. To the contrary, 'for the farmers to combat the railroads—who were major benefactors of western agriculture—was in fact perverse behavior'.[79] In a separate test, Stigler analyzed the congressional vote on the Capper–Volstead Act (1922), which exempted agricultural cooperatives from the antitrust laws' reach. He regressed the per cent of each state's House delegation voting yes on Capper–Volstead on two variables measuring the importance of agriculture to the state economy. Representatives from states having larger percentages of their populations on farms tended to support the exemption.[80]

In another test of the interest-group model, Amacher, Higgins, Shughart and Tollison examined FTC enforcement activities under the Clayton Act.[81] They found a countercyclical and statistically significant relationship between cases alleging price discrimination violations and several alternative measures of general business conditions, lending support to the proposition that 'regulation will tend to be more heavily weighted towards "producer protection" in depressions and toward "consumer protection" in expansions'.[82] The authors conclude that their result 'can be rationalized under the view that the FTC is in the business of transferring wealth from consumers either to protect small business or to shore up cartels'.[83]

Distributional gains and losses from the FTC's advertising substantiation program have been noted by Higgins and McChesney.[84] Although advertising substantiation is a consumer protection rather than a traditional antitrust issue, the workings of the program shed light on the effects of government intervention by an antitrust enforcement bureau. Higgins and McChesney showed that FTC case selection under advertising substantiation, which requires advertisers to possess a 'reasonable basis' for their claims prior to making them, does not follow a 'public interest' model. In particular, the Commission appeared to focus its enforcement activities under this program on industries having the greatest wealth redistribution potential, i.e., industries populated by firms with disparate market shares and reputations. Moreover, Higgins and McChesney found that the introduction of the advertising substantiation program had positive and significant effects on the market values of large advertising agencies. Their results 'are consistent with the observed resistance by advertisers and ad agencies to any relaxation of substantiation requirements'.[85]

These few largely unconnected studies which take a positive approach to the analysis of antitrust suggest that enforcement activities benefit some groups at the expense of others, and that what the conventional wisdom attributes to policy 'failure' is in reality the understandable behavior of self-interested enforcers operating under given constraints. In any case, this small body of literature suggests that antitrust bureaucracy operates much like regulatory bureaucracy in general.

V. THE POSITIVE APPROACH ILLUSTRATED: DUAL ENFORCEMENT

An important issue in antitrust policy concerns the desirability of having the laws enforced by two separate agencies with somewhat overlapping jurisdictions. Much of the discussion on both sides of the debate has been normative in nature. For example, the quality of antitrust output under dual enforcement is often discussed, where quality refers to the relative number of 'good' and 'bad' cases under the current bureaucratic structure compared with some idealized benchmark that might exist with a single antitrust agency. Much weight is placed on the fact that the FTC's mandate under Section 5 is broad, and that the Commission is both prosecutor and judge. Importance is also given to the FTC's status as an independent agency in contrast to the Justice Department's position as a line item in the executive branch budget. In short, the standard critique does not focus on the economic implications of dual enforcement, as such, but on the nature of the FTC's authority versus that of the Antitrust Division.

In this section, we abstract from the quality issue mentioned above to summarize a model developed by Higgins, Shughart and Tollison that examines aggregate antitrust law enforcement activity as a function of the degree of competition between the two agencies.[86] The historical development of US antitrust institutions supplies the conditions for a unique natural experiment. Between 1890 and 1914 the Justice Department was the sole antitrust agency, having responsibility for enforcing the Sherman Act. Dual enforcement began in 1914 when the FTC Act was passed. During the next 34 years the Commission and Antitrust Division respectively and independently enforced the FTC and Sherman Acts, and had joint responsibility for seeing that the provisions of the Clayton Act were obeyed. In 1948 the *Cement Institute* decision and a formal liaison agreement between the agencies began a period of information exchange and case allocation which effectively turned the antitrust law institutions into a system of collusive dual enforcement.[87]

Basing their model on Niskanen's seminal treatment of government bureaus as budget maximizers and assuming that the agencies behave according to Cournot output conjectures, Higgins, Shughart and Tollison compare aggregate antitrust output and its cost under single agency, independent dual, and collusive dual enforcement.[88] In particular, they show that independent dual enforcement leads to more aggregate output than single-agency enforcement, that output per budget dollar is greater under independent dual enforcement than under single-agency enforcement, and that independent dual enforcement leads to more output (and more output per budget dollar) than collusive dual enforcement.

Specifically, assume that both agencies have identical cost functions, $C(X_1)$ and $C(X_2)$, and that the production cost for each agency is functionally independent of the other's output. Further assume that average cost is constant and that the agencies share a linear 'demand' curve $R(X)/X$, where $X = X_1 + X_2$, i.e., each agency receives appropriations in proportion to its output share. For the simple case where the cost constraint is not binding, each agency maximizes

$$X_i R(X)/X \tag{1}$$

If $R(X)X = a - bX$, then equilibrium is defined by

$$a - 2bX_1 - bX_2 = 0 \text{ and} \tag{2}$$

$$a - bX_1 - 2bX_2 = 0$$

With competition, then, each agency supplies $a/3b$ units of output for a total of $2a/3b$.

In contrast, suppose the two agencies collude in order to maximize joint revenue. Equilibrium is then defined by

$$a - 2bX = 0 \tag{3}$$

and each agency produces some portion of $a/2b$ units of output. Total output under independent dual enforcement, $2a/3b$, exceeds total output under collusion, $a/2b$, by $a/6b$.

In testing this prediction as well as others concerning the budgetary costs of enforcement under competition and collusion, Higgins, Shughart and Tollison employed the annual number of antitrust cases instituted as a surrogate for agency output. Output and budget data for both agencies were available for the years 1932 through 1981, and they compared mean annual case output, real budgets, and real output per budget dollar for the independent dual enforcement subperiod, 1932–48, with the years during which the two agencies colluded, 1949–81. Higgins, Shughart and Tollison found that total antitrust activity remained roughly the same (239 cases per year in 1932–48 and 249 cases per year in 1949–81), but that average cases per dollar fell substantially. That is, the mutually agreed to division of enforcement responsibility according to industry and, to a lesser extent, according to type of violation established by the FTC-Justice liaison agreement appeared to cut each agency's output per dollar in half. This suggests that following the 1948 agreement, the two agencies employed relatively more attorneys, economists, and other bureaucratic inputs per case than would have been used in the absence of collusion.

The important point about this example is that a positive analysis of antitrust policy is capable of generating testable implications concerning the behavior of the antitrust agencies. Higgins, Shughart and Tollison developed a theory that predicted that antitrust output, however measured, would be larger and produced at a lower unit cost under independent dual enforcement than under single agency or collusive dual enforcement. Empirical tests using historical agency budgets and case production figures failed to refute the model's main predictions. It is from such efforts that the activities of the antitrust bureaucracy become understandable.

VI. CONCLUDING REMARKS

Antitrust is one of the few remaining areas in which it is commonly assumed that government operates in the public interest. The conventional wisdom views the purposes of antitrust as beyond controversy, and treats the enforcement agencies, despite their tendency to error, as well-intentioned guardians of the market-place. This makes the standard critique normative, consisting of efforts to identify good and bad laws, good and bad cases, and ending with suggestions for change—better laws, better judges, better bureaucrats. Moreover, such critiques have by and large been ineffective: 'Economists have their glories but I do not believe that the body of American antitrust law is one of them'.[89]

In this paper we have taken a positive approach by asking whose public and whose interest does antitrust serve. We argue that antitrust policy can fruitfully be analyzed from this interest-group perspective. To illustrate the positive approach, we have reviewed the small body of literature that approaches antitrust policy by suggesting that the individuals who enforce antitrust law are the same people who act in their own interest when making market decisions. We have provided one concrete example of our recommended approach—the effects on antitrust output of dual enforcement with competition or collusion—but there are obviously many more aspects of anti-trust policy to be explored. We leave these as areas for future research.

REFERENCES AND NOTES

1. J. M. Buchanan, 'Toward Analysis of Closed Behavioral Systems,' in J. M. Buchanan and R. D. Tollison (eds.), *Theory of Public Choice*, University of Michigan Press (1972), pp. 11–23.
2. A. D. Neale and D. G. Goyder, *The Antitrust Laws of the U.S.A.: A Study of Competition Enforced by Law*, Cambridge University Press (3rd ed.—1980), p. 15. A detailed account of the origins of the Sherman Act is given by W. Letwin, *Law and Economic Policy in America: The Evolution of the Sherman Antitrust Act*, Random House (1965).
3. F. M. Scherer, *Industrial Market Structure and Economic Performance*, Rand McNally (2nd ed.—1980), p. 493.
4. *Ibid.*, p. 494.
5. R. H. Bork, *The Antitrust Paradox*, Basic Books (1978), p. 7.
6. J. Bain, *Industrial Organization*, John Wiley (2nd ed.—1968), p. 515. But, *see* R. H. Lande, 'Wealth Transfers as the Original and Primary Concern of Antitrust: The Efficiency Interpretation Challenged,' (1982) 34 Hastings L. J. 65, who suggests that allocative efficiency is of secondary importance in explaining the origins of antitrust law. In his view, Congress intended to forestall wealth transfers from consumers to firms having market power.
7. Scherer, *supra*, note 3, p. 491. Emphasis in original.
8. R. A. Posner, *Antitrust Law, An Economic Perspective*, University of Chicago Press (1976), p. 4.
9. K. Elzinga and W. Breit, *The Antitrust Penalties: A Study in Law and Economics*, Yale University Press (1976), p. ix.
10. Neale and Goyder, *supra*, note 2, p. 441.
11. C. Wilcox, *Public Policies Towards Business*, Irwin (3rd ed.—1966), p. 49.
12. *Ibid.*
13. C. Kaysen and D. F. Turner, *Antitrust Policy*, Harvard University Press (1959), p. 5.
14. Neale and Goyder, *supra*, note 2, p. 440, quoting the 1955 Report of the Attorney General's National Committee to Study the Antitrust Laws.
15. Posner, *supra*, note 8, p. 236.
16. For example, *see* Bork, *supra*, note 5, pp. 285–288. In *Continental T.V. Inc. v GTE*

Sylvania Inc., 433 U.S. 36 (1977), the Supreme Court broke with precedent to consider business efficiency in holding that Sylvania's retailer franchise system was not *per se* illegal. In the face of a declining market share in retail television sales, Sylvania had in 1962 phased out its wholesale distributor network, and instituted a plan of selling directly to a smaller and more select group of franchised retailers. In the process, Sylvania franchised a new San Francisco retailer, Young Brothers, at a location in close proximity to one of its previously most successful franchisees, Continental T.V. Inc. Continental sued, alleging that Sylvania's new territorial restrictions constituted a *per se* violation of Section 1 of the Sherman Act. The Court held, however, that Sylvania's actions had no 'pernicious effect on competition.' Indeed, such 'vertical restrictions promote interbrand competition by allowing the manufacturer to achieve certain efficiencies in the distribution of his products.' For details, *see* P. Areeda, *Antitrust Analysis: Problems, Text, Cases*, Little Brown (3rd ed.—1981), pp. 685–699. A somewhat less approving view of the case is given by S. Altschuler, '*Sylvania*, Vertical Restraints, and Dual Distribution,' (1980) 25 Antitrust Bull. 1.

17. J. L. Peterman, 'The Brown Shoe Case,' (1975) 18 J. Law and Econ. 81, p. 143.
18. J. L. Peterman, '*The Federal Trade Commission v Brown Shoe Company*,' (1975) 18 J. Law and Econ. 361, p. 393.
19. J. L. Peterman, 'The International Salt Case,' (1979) 22 J. Law and Econ. 351, and F. J. Cummings and W. E. Ruhter, 'The Northern Pacific Case,' (1979) 22 J. Law and Econ. 329 are examples.
20. D. Flath, 'The American Can Case,' (1980) 25 Antitrust Bull. 169, p. 193.
21. A. Zelenitz, 'The Attempted Promotion of Competition in Related Goods Markets: The Ford-Autolite Divestiture Case,' (1980) 25 Antitrust Bull. 103.
22. Representative studies are M. Adelman, *A&P: A Study in Price-Cost Behavior and Public Policy*, Harvard University Press (1966); K. Elzinga, 'Predatory Pricing: The Case of the Gunpowder Trust,' (1970) 13 J. Law and Econ. 233; D. F. Lean, J. D. Ogur, and R. P. Rogers, *Competition and Collusion in Electrical Equipment Markets: An Economic Assessment*, Federal Trade Commission (1982); and J. S. McGee, 'Predatory Price Cutting: The Standard Oil (N.J.) Case,' (1958) 1 J. Law and Econ. 137.
23. Bork, *supra*, note 5, pp. 405–407.
24. Posner, *supra*, note 8, p. 212.
25. Kaysen and Turner, *supra*, note 13, pp. 44–49.
26. O. Williamson, *Markets and Hierarchies: Analysis and Antitrust Implications*, The Free Press (1975), p. 209.
27. F. M. Fisher, 'Diagnosing Monopoly,' (1979) 19 Quarterly Rev. Econ. and Bus. 7, p. 33.
28. D. Dewey, 'Mergers and Cartels: Some Reservations About Policy,' (1969) 51 Am. Econ. Rev. 255.
29. H. Demsetz, 'Two Systems of Belief About Monopoly,' in H. J. Goldschmid, H. M. Mann, and J. F. Weston (eds.), *Industrial Concentration: The New Learning*, Little Brown (1974), pp. 164–184.
30. Y. Brozen, 'Bain's Concentration and Rates of Return Revisited,' (1971) 14 J. Law and Econ. 351; H. Demsetz, *supra*, note 29; H. Demsetz, 'Economics As a Guide to Antitrust Regulation,' (1976) 19 J. Law and Econ. 371; and S. Peltzman, 'The Gains and Losses from Industrial Concentration,' (1979) 22 J. Law and Econ. 229.
31. Posner, *supra*, note 8, p. 236.
32. R. A. Posner, 'A Statistical Study of Antitrust Law Enforcement,' (1970) 13 J. Law and Econ. 365.
33. G. J. Stigler, 'The Economic Effects of the Antitrust Laws,' (1966) 9 J. Law and Econ. 225.
34. Posner, *supra*, note 32, p. 419. A recent update of Posner's study by Gallo and Bush extends the data through 1981. As far as possible, they cover the same territory in the same format. Among other results, Gallo and Bush note an attenuation in the duration of both Justice Department and FTC cases as well as a greater willingness to impose fines and imprisonment as remedial measures. (They attribute both of these changes to an

increase in the number of bid-rigging cases brought by the Antitrust Division.) Furthermore, the two agencies were able to improve considerably their already high success rate in antitrust proceedings, but the Justice Department remained hesitant to apply dissolution or significant divestiture as a remedy in monopolization cases. *See* J. C. Gallo and S. Bush, 'The Anatomy of Antitrust Enforcement for the Period 1963–1981,' (1983) unpublished manuscript.

35. J. M. Clabault and M. Block, *Sherman Act Indictments, 1955–1980*, Federal Legal Publications (1981).
36. W. F. Shughart II and R. D. Tollison, 'Antitrust Recidivism in Federal Trade Commission Data: 1914–1982,' (1983) unpublished manuscript.
37. G. A. Hay and D. Kelley, 'An Empirical Survey of Price-Fixing Conspiracies,' (1974) 17 J. Law and Econ. 13, p. 18.
38. *Ibid.*, p. 28.
39. P. Asch and J. J. Seneca, 'Is Collusion Profitable?' (1976) 58 Rev. Econ. and Stat. 1.
40. J. Palmer, 'Some Economic Conditions Conducive to Collusion,' (1972) 6 J. Econ. Issues 29.
41. K. Elzinga, 'The Antimerger Law: Pyrrhic Victories,' (1969) 12 J. Law and Econ. 43.
42. S. Weaver, *Decision to Prosecute: Organization and Public Policy in the Antitrust Division*, MIT Press (1977).
43. *Ibid.*, p. 66.
44. *Ibid.*, pp. 38–40.
45. R. A. Katzman, *Regulatory Bureaucracy: The Federal Trade Commission and Antitrust Policy*, MIT Press (1980).
46. *Ibid.*, p. 83.
47. K. W. Clarkson and T. J. Muris (eds.), *The Federal Trade Commission Since 1970: Economic Regulation and Bureaucratic Behavior*, Cambridge University Press (1981).
48. *Ibid.*, pp. 303–304.
49. A. Harberger, 'Monopoly and Resource Allocation,' (1954) 44 Am. Econ. Rev. 77.
50. For example, *see* D. Kamerschen, 'An Estimation of the "Welfare Losses" from Monopoly in the American Economy,' (1966) 4 Western Econ. J. 221.
51. This section draws heavily on the discussion in R. D. Tollison, 'Rent Seeking: A Survey,' (1982) 35 Kyklos 575.
52. R. A. Mundell, 'Review of Jansenn's *Free Trade, Protection and Customs Union*,' (1982) 52 Am. Econ. Rev. 621, p. 622.
53. G. Tullock, 'The Welfare Costs of Tariffs, Monopolies, and Theft,' (1967) 5 Western Econ. J. 224.
54. R. A. Posner, 'The Social Costs of Monopoly and Regulation,' (1975) 83 J. Pol. Econ. 807.
55. W. F. Long, R. Schramm, and R. D. Tollison, 'The Determinants of Antitrust Activity,' (1973) 16 J. Law and Econ. 351.
56. *Ibid.*, p. 361.
57. P. Asch, 'The Determinants and Effects of Antitrust Policy,' (1975) 17 J. Law and Econ. 578.
58. *Ibid.*, pp. 580–581.
59. J. J. Siegfried, 'The Determinants of Antitrust Activity,' (1975) 17 J. Law and Econ. 559, p. 563.
60. *Ibid.*, p. 573.
61. For a recent attempt to apply benefit–cost analysis to antitrust case selection, *see* W. F. Long, D. F. Lean, D. J. Ravenscraft, and C. L. Wagner III, *Benefits and Costs of the Federal Trade Commission's Line of Business Program, Vol. I: Staff Analysis*, Federal Trade Commission (1983), and the rebuttal by R. D. Tollison, R. S. Higgins and W. F. Shughart II, *Benefits and Costs of the FTC's Line of Business Program: Recommendations*, Federal Trade Commission (1983). There is also an extensive literature that applies the welfare-loss model to the analysis of merger cases. The important work here is by O. Williamson, 'Economies as an Antitrust Defence: The Welfare Tradeoffs,' (1968) 58 Am.

Econ. Rev. 18; O. Williamson, 'Economies as an Antitrust Defense: Corruption and Reply,' (1968) 58 Am. Econ. Rev. 1372; O. Williamson, 'Economies as an Antitrust Defense: Reply,' (1969) 59 Am. Econ. Rev. 954; O. Williamson, 'Economies as an Antitrust Defense Revisited,' (1977) 125 U. Penn. L. R. 699; M. E. DePrano and J. B. Nugent, 'Economies as an Antitrust Defense: Comment,' (1969) 59 Am. Econ. Rev. 947; R. Jackson, 'The Consideration of Economies in Merger Cases,' (1970) 43 J. Bus. 439: and P. Ross, 'Economies as an Antitrust Defense: Comment,' (1968) 58 Am. Econ. Rev. 1371.

62. G. J. Stigler, 'The Theory of Economic Regulation,' (1971) 3 Bell J. Econ. 7, and S. Peltzman, 'Toward a More General Theory of Regulation,' (1976) 19 J. Law and Econ. 211.

63. W. Baxter, 'The Political Economy of Antitrust,' in R. D. Tollison (ed.), *The Political Economy of Antitrust: Principal Paper by William Baxter*, D. C. Heath (1980), pp. 3–49.

64. *Ibid.*, pp. 3–8.

65. R. Faith, D. Leavens, and R. D. Tollison, 'Antitrust Pork Barrel,' (1982) 25 J. Law and Econ. 329.

66. *Ibid.*, p. 342.

67. B. R. Weingast and M. J. Moran, 'Bureaucratic Discretion or Congressional Control? Regulatory Policymaking by the Federal Trade Commission,' (1983) 91 J. Pol. Econ. 765.

68. *Ibid.*, p. 765.

69. *Ibid.*, p. 793.

70. J. Ellert, 'Mergers, Antitrust Law Enforcement and Stockholder Returns,' (1976) 31 J. Fin. 715.

71. M. R. Burns, 'The Competitive Effects of Trust-Busting: A Portfolio Analysis,' (1977) 85 J. Pol. Econ. 717.

72. *Ibid.*, p. 718.

73. *Ibid.*, p. 732.

74. *Ibid.*, p. 719.

75. T. W. Ross, 'Winners and Losers Under the Robinson–Patman Act,' (1984) 27 J. Law and Econ. 243.

76. P. Altrogge and W. F. Shughart II, 'The Regressive Nature of Civil Penalties,' (1984) 4 Int. Rev. Law and Econ. 55.

77. Peltzman, *supra*, note 62, p. 219.

78. G. J. Stigler, 'The Origin of the Sherman Act,' (1985) 14 J. Legal Stud. 1.

79. *Ibid.*, p. 4.

80. The existence of exemptions to antitrust law raises some interesting questions. For example, how do they affect the overall level of enforcement activity? On the one hand, placing certain industries and market transactions beyond the law reduces the number of enforcement opportunities. On the other hand, the agencies may have responded to the exemptions by increasing their enforcement activities in the areas remaining within their reach.

81. R. C. Amacher, R. S. Higgins, W. F. Shughart II, and R. D. Tollison, 'The Behavior of Regulatory Activity Over the Business Cycle,' Econ. Inquiry, forthcoming.

82. Peltzman, *supra*, note 62, p. 227.

83. Amacher, Higgins, Shughart, and Tollison, *supra*, note 81, p. 12.

84. R. S. Higgins and F. McChesney, 'Truth and Consequences: The Federal Trade Commission's Ad Substantiation Program,' (1983) unpublished manuscript.

85. *Ibid.*, p. 44.

86. R. S. Higgins, W. F. Shughart II, and R. D. Tollison, 'Dual Enforcement of the Antitrust Laws,' (1983) unpublished manuscript.

87. *FTC* v *Cement Institute et al.*, 333 U.S. 683 (1948). The US Supreme Court held that the Commission could condemn conduct that offends the Sherman Act under Section 5 of the FTC Act, and that filing of a Justice Department suit did not require termination of FTC proceedings.

88. W. A. Niskanen, *Bureaucracy and Representative Government*, Aldine (1971). Niskanen's assumption that bureaus make all-or-none offers to their sponsors is not retained,

however. For a description of an equilibrium with all-or-none offers, *see* R. J. Mackay and C. L. Weaver, 'Agenda Control by Budget Maximizers in a Multi-Bureau Setting,' (1981) 37 Public Choice 447. In such models, budget 'fat' (rents) accrues to the sponsor, usually the congressional oversight committee, while in the Higgins, Shughart, and Tollison framework rents are imputed in the payments to bureaucratic inputs.

89. G. J. Stigler, 'The Economists and the Problem of Monopoly,' (1982) 72 Am. Econ. Rev. 1, p. 7.

Economic Perspectives— Volume 1, Number 2— Fall 1987— Pages 13–22

Antitrust and Merger Policy: A Review and Critique

Lawrence J. White

Any antitrust policy that tries to put some restrictions on mergers must have a conceptual basis. One such framework might be a populist approach in which only absolute or relative size of the merger partners and/or the resulting entity would be the criterion. Political rhetoric often embodies this approach.

An alternative approach—the one that underlies the 1982 Department of Justice Merger Guidelines—concerns itself with the possible exercise of market power.[1] I believe this second approach is more consistent with the language of Section 7 of the Clayton Act itself, which instructs the Department of Justice and the Federal Trade Commission to prevent those mergers the effects of which "may be substantially to lessen competition, or to tend to create a monopoly." This market power approach also places merger policy in a realm that is susceptible to economic analysis; for this reason as well, this approach appeals to me.

The Merger Guidelines are firmly rooted in the standard oligopoly theory developed by Chamberlin (1933), Fellner (1949), and Stigler (1964), and strengthened

---

[1]The 1982 Guidelines were modified modestly in 1984. Unless otherwise indicated, my references to the Guidelines will encompass both versions.

■ *Lawrence J. White is a Board Member, Federal Home Loan Bank Board, and Professor of Economics, New York University. During 1982–83 he was Director of the Economic Policy Office of the Antitrust Division of the U.S. Department of Justice and one of the authors of the 1982 Merger Guidelines.*

by the insights of game theory's "prisoners' dilemma:" The more easily a group of sellers (who collectively might have market power) can coordinate and police their mutual actions, the more likely are they to approximate a monopoly outcome. From this basic insight flow subsidiary propositions concerning the number and size distribution of sellers, entry conditions, product characteristics, the nature of buyers, and so on.

The Chamberlin-Fellner-Stigler proposition is just that: a hypothesis that should be tested against reality. An alternative hypothesis—for example, "it only takes two to make a horse race"—might better approximate companies' actual behavior in markets. Or the empirical conditions that would allow the joint exercise of market power along the Chamberlin-Fellner-Stigler lines might never appear in the real world.

By now, hundreds of articles have been written that offer tests of and commentary on these basic tenets of oligopoly theory. As is well known, two major schools interpret the collective wisdom of those tests differently. One believes that the tests generally support the proposition that oligopoly behavior and the joint exercise of market power are real phenomena with significant consequences for prices and profits; the other believes that any effects attributed to market concentration are simply indications that more efficient companies are better able to expand market share and earn higher profits.

This article is not the place to review or assess that literature. (Reviews are provided in Scherer (1980) and Goldschmid, *et al.* (1974).) Instead, the reader should simply be warned that I reside in the former camp. And the philosophy of the Guidelines of which I am a co-author rests on this foundation as well.

Market Definition

The most important conceptual contribution of the 1982 Guidelines to merger analysis is their approach to market definition. Merger law had long appreciated that market definition is crucial, since market shares and concentration are meaningful indications of the likelihood that firms will exercise market power only if market boundaries are defined properly. But the 1968 Department of Justice Guidelines offered little help, and the economics literature prior to 1982 offered few useful theoretical or empirical guidelines.[2]

The 1982 Guidelines take a straightforward approach. Since merger policy is concerned with the possible exercise of market power, enforcement analysis should seek a market definition that focuses on where that behavior is possible. (Other structural indicators, discussed below, then indicate whether the merger increases the likelihood of that behavior.) The Guidelines take a 5 percent price increase sustained for one year as the threshold for defining significant market power. They define a market as the smallest group of firms (spread across product and geographic space)

---

[2] For earlier efforts, see Hogarty and Elzinga (1973) and Horowitz (1981). For a later effort, see Stigler and Sherwin (1985).

that could, if they acted in concert (that is, acted jointly as a monopolist), raise prices from their current (or otherwise expected) levels by 5 percent and sustain that increase profitably for a year.

The 5 percent is an arbitrary number, reflecting tradeoffs among concerns about the welfare losses from the possible exercise of market power, the incentives for coordinated behavior among oligopolists, and noise in any data that might be used to make a determination. The economists at the Department of Justice had favored a 10 percent, two-year test (which would still be my preference); the lawyers generally favored the 5 percent, one-year test that eventually prevailed. These smaller figures, which tend to define narrower markets, may seem to imply greater sensitivity to market power and hence more potential antitrust violations. If markets are defined too narrowly, however, the analysis may improperly indicate that the merger partners are in different markets and hence do not compete. For example, in both *U.S. v. Continental Can*, 378 U.S. 441 (1964) and *U.S. v. Virginia National Bancshares Inc.*, 1982–2 Trade Cases (CCH) at 871 (1982), the Department of Justice urged the court to define markets more broadly (so as to include both merger partners), while the defendants argued for narrower market boundaries.

The Guidelines deliberately chose *actual* (or likely future) prices as the starting point for the 5 percent test. The Guidelines' concern over mergers is whether enhanced market power will raise prices from where they would otherwise be. Thus, enforcement officials need not try to hypothesize at what levels competitive prices might be. In addition to the philosophical argument against trying to identify the competitive level of prices, the practical problems of identifying and defending that level could easily overwhelm any merger enforcement effort. One only need ask, "From where the market is today (or is likely to be tomorrow), could this merger possibly make things worse?" As a consequence, in theory, if one believed that the sellers in a market were already colluding perfectly and pricing at monopoly levels, a merger among them should not be opposed. In practice, no such circumstance is ever likely to present itself. Enforcement agencies are unlikely to conclude that even a small rival does not provide some check on the current or prospective market power of the dominant firm in a duopoly.

This use of actual prices has sometimes led to claims that the Guidelines have fallen victim to the "cellophane fallacy" and that competitive prices instead should be used. In *U.S. v. E.I. Du Pont de Nemours and Co.*, 351 U.S. 377 (1956), the Supreme Court decided that Du Pont did not have a monopoly over cellophane, because, the Court found, there were many substitutes for cellophane that customers could and did use. The problem, as a number of commentators have correctly pointed out, is that any profit-maximizing monopolist would raise its price until some (but not most) of its customers have been driven to the use of substitutes; thus, the presence of substitutes was not necessarily an indication of the absence of market power (Stocking and Mueller, 1955; Posner, 1976).

To the contrary, however, the Guidelines avoid a "cellophane fallacy." Again, the concern of the Guidelines is, "Might this merger make things worse?" To continue the cellophane example, if Du Pont really had a monopoly of cellophane and subsequently wanted to merge with an aluminum foil producer, the monopoly-level price of cellophane should be the one (along with the price of aluminum foil and possibly of other wrapping materials as well) from which the 5 percent test of some version of a "flexible wrapping materials" market should be based. At a competitive price of cellophane, it might have few substitutes, and cellophane and aluminum foil would falsely be found to be in different markets.

The Guidelines do leave one market definition problem unresolved: Against what product base should the 5 percent price increase be calculated? If two otherwise similar industries have sharply different levels of value added relative to their final prices, because of different production relationships or different contractual arrangements as to what is included in "the price," the 5 percent test would have different consequences for market boundaries. For example, the natural gas pipelines industry has the tradition of taking ownership of the gas it transports, so the "product" it sells at a city gate is "transported gas." By contrast, the oil pipeline industry has a tradition of being a common carrier, so its product is only "transportation services." A 5 percent test applied to the former would indicate a much larger price increase relative to the value added in that industry, and hence wider market boundaries, than would a 5 percent test applied to the latter industry.

This problem seems to have no good solution. Applying a price increase test only to value added would quickly run afoul of differences in relative levels of value added among firms in the same industry. The Guidelines' procedure taking the specific pricing practices of the industry under consideration as a given seems to be the best practical answer.

Market Share Concentration and Entry Conditions

With the market boundaries defined, the enforcement agencies must then try to determine whether the merger is likely to create or heighten the exercise of market power among the firms in that market. The Guidelines focus on market share concentration as the primary quantitative indicator of possible enforcement action. Then, they ask about conditions of entry.

The Guidelines use the Herfindahl-Hirschman Index (HHI) as their primary market concentration guide, with concentration levels of 1000 and 1800 as the two key levels. Any merger in a market with a post-merger HHI below 1000 is unlikely to be challenged; a merger in a market with a post-merger HHI above 1800 is likely to be challenged (if the merger partners have market shares that cause the HHI to increase by more than 100), unless other mitigating circumstances exist, like easy entry. Mergers in markets with post-concentration HHI levels between 1000 and 1800 require further analysis before a decision is made whether to challenge.

If entry conditions are easy, virtually any merger would be allowed; with high entry barriers, mergers in the middle and upper HHI bands receive closer scrutiny and factors discussed below become important to the analysis. Little quantitative guidance is provided for measuring the height of entry barriers.

Since economic theory indicates that market concentration is unlikely to influence the exercise of market power very much if entry is easy, the Guidelines might justly be accused of reversing the order of importance of and the quantitative attention paid to those two structural features. However, this ordering decision was largely a pragmatic reaction to the fact that market shares are easily measured and quantified (after market boundaries have been delineated), while entry barriers are not. As Richard Schmalensee points out in this journal, the use of the HHI does provide a readily computable "safe harbor" that allows a large number of mergers to be easily dismissed as highly unlikely to create market power problems. But, to some extent, the Guidelines may be likened to the drunk who, though he thinks he probably lost his keys in the middle of the road, spends most of his time looking for them on the sidewalk "because the light is better there."

It is worth noting that HHI levels of 1000 and 1800 translate empirically into four-firm concentration (CR4) levels of 50 percent and 70 percent, respectively.[3] A few of the profits-concentration studies have asked whether some "critical concentration ratio" appears to mark a change in an industry's behavior—like higher prices or profits—and most of them have found that significant changes do seem to take place when the CR4 passes beyond the 50 percent to 60 percent range (White, 1976; Geithman, *et al.*, 1981; Bradburd and Over, 1982). A draft version of the 1982 Guidelines had an HHI of 1600 as its upper decision point, which would translate to a CR4 of 65 percent. Thus, a set of 1000 and 1600 HHI decision points might be argued to be roughly bounding the critical concentration ratio range. The 1800 upper point represents a less defensible standard on these grounds, and I favored at the time (and still do) a 1600 decision point.

Consideration of Other Market Characteristics

The Guidelines suggest that other market characteristics may also influence enforcement decisions. Drawing again on oligopoly theory (Stigler, 1964), the Guidelines suggest that product characteristics, the structure of the buyers' side of the market, and the antitrust history of the merging firms and their rivals will also be examined. Product homogeneity may make coordinated behavior among oligopolists easier, since there are fewer product quality dimensions for a "cheater" to use as a cover for surreptitious price cutting. (Conversely, product heterogeneity should imply, ceteris paribus, that markets are smaller and concentration higher. See, for example, Schwartz and Wilde (1982).) Large, knowledgeable buyers may be able to "shop around," induce price cuts, and undermine efforts at coordinated behavior. A history of antitrust violations may indicate structural (or sociological) conditions that are conducive to coordinated behavior.

[3] This simple translation is based on ordinary least squares regressions that have been run on industry market share data where both the HHI and the CR4 have been computed. The four-firm concentration ratio represents the percentage of an industry's sales that are accounted for by the largest four sellers.

As in the case of entry conditions, the Guidelines are silent as to any suggestions for quantifying these considerations, nor are their weights in the overall enforcement decision indicated.

Cost Efficiencies

The 1982 Guidelines indicated an unwillingness to consider increased efficiency of production as a reason to allow an otherwise questionable merger; the 1984 Guidelines are more sympathetic to cost efficiencies. It is difficult for an economist to argue that such efficiencies should be ignored. Williamson (1968) provides a clear analysis of the potential trade-offs between enhanced market power and efficiencies consequent to a merger. Nonetheless, I am more sympathetic with the earlier approach.

Efficiencies are easy to promise, yet may be difficult to deliver. All merger proposals will promise theoretical savings in overhead expense, inventory costs, and so on; they will tout "synergies." On the other hand, diseconomies of large scale caused by managerial limitations may also be present. Further, particular mergers may create unexpected corporate culture clashes and difficulties in melding two managerial and production systems. The mergers of the Pennsylvania Railroad and the New York Central, of Pan Am and National Airlines, and of LTV and Republic Steel come readily to mind. Also, if a merger between two firms is likely to enhance oligopolistic coordination in the market generally, it is the social loss from the market-wide coordination—not just the merged entity—that has to be offset by the efficiency gains of the merger. On balance, this author is more comfortable with the skeptical approach of the 1982 Guidelines. Not incidentally, this approach appears to be consistent with the Supreme Court's interpretation of the Clayton Act, as expressed in *Brown Shoe Co. v. U.S.*, 370 U.S. 294 (1962).

Application of the Guidelines

The 1982 Guidelines were promulgated in June of that year, but the approach that they embody was influencing Department of Justice enforcement prior to their appearance. In addition, the Federal Trade Commission appears to have absorbed the learning of the Guidelines for its enforcement efforts as well. In effect, the Guidelines have shaped enforcement experience for five years.

At the beginning, it should be made clear that enforcement efforts cannot be assessed from simple counts of the number of enforcement actions filed in U.S. District Courts. This holds true for at least two reasons. (For further discussion, see Salop and White, 1986.) First, suits are filed and cases litigated only when the parties are each relatively optimistic as to their chances of receiving a favorable judgment at trial (and the perceived stakes are large relative to the costs of litigation). The simple existence of an enforcement standard will deter many potential mergers (for example, between

General Motors and Ford) because the parties know they have no chance of withstanding an enforcement challenge. Second, the enforcement agencies can often arrange settlements with merger applicants, in which potentially offending product lines or branch locations of the parties in an otherwise acceptable merger can be sold to third parties. Whether these settlements are reached before or after a suit is filed can greatly affect the apparent number of suits without affecting the substance of the enforcement effort itself.

Consequently, assessments of merger enforcement must undertake the much harder and less easily quantified task of evaluating the mergers that are permitted and making comparisons across enforcement regimes. Clearly, merger enforcement has been less stringent during the past six years than during the previous three decades. How much of this is due to the influence of the Guidelines themselves, to the political and economic inclinations of the Reagan administration (which surely would have asserted themselves regardless of the presence or absence of this particular set of Guidelines), and how much to the general "new learning" in industrial organization and antitrust is unclear.

Having left the Department of Justice in August 1983, my impressions and assessment of enforcement since then must necessarily be those of an outsider. My general impression is that the application of the Guidelines has largely been sensible. My personal preference would probably be for somewhat more stringent enforcement. But it should immediately be acknowledged, enforcement has not been wholly dormant. The Federal Trade Commission and Department of Justice have brought enforcement actions and/or insisted on structural settlements in important cases, such as Warner-Polygram, Coca-Cola–Dr Pepper, and LTV-Republic. (Indeed, if the enforcement agencies had not brought these actions, one might have concluded Section 7 had been effectively repealed.[4]) And, at the same time, I surely would not want to go back to the world of *Brown Shoe* or *Von's Grocery*, in which mergers were halted in markets with relatively low levels of seller concentration and little consideration was given to conditions of entry.

The Department of Transportation seems to have been especially lax in its enforcement actions with respect to airlines, approving some mergers like Northwest-Republic and TWA-Ozark for which the Antitrust Division had recommended rejection. In a world of airport slot constraints (and in which those slots are non-tradable and unpriced), entry may not be easy in all airline markets. Greater caution appears to be warranted.

A few other aspects of enforcement are worth noting: First, the Guidelines have addressed the way in which foreign production should be introduced into the analysis. Under the 1982 Guidelines, if foreign producers could effectively thwart an effort by domestic producers to raise prices by 5 percent, the former should be included in the market with, perhaps, a caveat that Congress can far more easily restrain competition

---

[4] It should be noted that the author was a consultant to and expert witness for the Federal Trade Commission in its successful suit to halt the Coca-Cola–Dr Pepper merger.

from a selected group of foreign producers than from a comparable group of domestic producers. The caveat would be useful as a "tiebreaker" in close cases. But if import quotas already constrain foreign producers, they would not be able to expand their shipments so as to take advantage of (and thereby thwart) a 5 percent price rise. In this latter case, they should not be included in the market. But the 1984 Guidelines allow foreign producers who are restricted by quotas to be included nevertheless in the relevant market. (A footnote in the 1984 Guidelines' section on "Significance of Market Shares" states, however, that where quotas place a limit on the imports from all foreign sources, the market share of foreign sources would be given "little, if any, weight.")

Second, the approach that enforcement has taken with respect to barriers to entry has largely been sensible. Since I have argued that the primary concern is whether this merger will make things worse, the focus should be primarily on the costs and other factors that entrants have to bear, regardless of whether incumbents have borne equal costs. Thus, for example, significant economies of scale and the necessity of investment in specialized resources that may have limited alternative uses should be considered as barriers, as suggested by Bain (1956). Similarly, relatively heavy advertising and other promotional costs should be counted as a barrier to entry, since they represent sunk costs that cannot be retrieved if the entry effort is unsuccessful; again, this approach should be true irrespective of whether incumbents engage in similar expenses.

It appears that enforcement has largely followed this approach. In the Federal Trade Commission's challenge to the proposed merger between Coca-Cola and Dr Pepper, for example, the Commission argued that entry into the carbonated soft drink market was quite difficult; among the reasons cited were the exceptionally large sums necessary for advertising and promoting new soft drink products and the apparent economies of scale among bottlers in their distribution and promotion function.

Third, the 5 percent price test apparently has not been used as a rigid guideline. Indeed, it probably could not be, since in most instances the data are insufficient (especially within the time pressures of a Hart-Scott-Rodino pre-merger review) to allow this degree of precision. Instead, it is valuable for the focus it puts on the exercise of market power and the general magnitude of effects that would be of concern.

Fourth, Leddy (1986) has alleged that the Department of Justice has not brought any enforcement actions against mergers where the market HHI was less than 2000. If this accusation is true, then current enforcement practice represents a significant loosening of the original enforcement intent of the Guidelines: Mergers in markets with HHI between 1000 and 1800 require further examination rather than an automatic clearance. It seems highly improbable that *all* such mergers were in markets with easy enough entry or other characteristics that would make the enhanced exercise of market power unlikely. This new enforcement standard (if the allegation is correct) may reflect a revised view of the likelihood of coordinated behavior in oligopolistic industries. In any event, if it is true, the Department of Justice should (at a minimum) acknowledge this change in enforcement intent and revise the Guidelines accordingly.[5] As I have indicated, however, my preference would be for more stringent enforcement, which means a reversion to the intent of the Guidelines to stop mergers that are in markets in the 1000 to 1800 HHI range when other market characteristics make this appropriate.

An Advance in Merger Policy

The Department of Justice Merger Guidelines of the 1980s are certainly not perfect, nor have they been applied perfectly. But they represent an important advance over that which preceded them, and they represent an exceedingly sensible way to think about merger enforcement and especially about market definition in a merger context. Merger policy has surely improved as a consequence of their development and application.

Should the language of Section 7 be changed? I think not. Its language has proved adequately flexible to encompass new interpretations. I believe that it should remain flexible.

Similarly, I do not believe that the Merger Guidelines should be put into law. Though the Guidelines do represent a modern microeconomics approach to merger, the learning and understanding of microeconomics may well change in future years. The Guidelines, as an enforcement guide, are relatively easy to change in response to that new learning; laws are much harder to change. Public policy is better served with broad guidelines set into law, as represented by the current language of Section 7, and sensible enforcement.

■ *I would like to thank Steven Salop, Carl Shapiro, and Timothy Taylor for helpful comments on an earlier draft.*

---

[5]Similarly, if (as has been alleged), the Department of Justice is now regularly using a 10 percent price test for market definition, this change too should be formally acknowledged. In the light of data limitations, the practical difference between a 5 percent and 10 percent test may not be great. Also, as discussed in the text, I favor a 10 percent standard.

References

Bain, J., *Barriers to New Competition*. Cambridge, MA: Harvard University Press, 1956.

Bradburd, Ralph C., and A. Mead Over, Jr., "Sticky Equilibria and Critical Levels of Concentration," *Review of Economics and Statistics*, February 1982, *64*, 50–58.

Chamberlin, Edward H., *The Theory of Monopolistic Competition*. Cambridge, MA: Harvard University Press, 1933.

Fellner, William J., *Competition Among the Few*. New York: Knopf, 1949.

Geithman, Frederick, Howard P. Marvel, and Leonard W. Weiss, "Concentration, Price, and Critical Concentration Ratios," *Review of Economics and Statistics*, August 1981, *63*, 346–353.

Goldschmid, Harvey, H. Michael Mann, and J. Fred Weston, eds., *Industrial Concentration: The New Learning*, Boston: Little, Brown, 1974.

Hogarty, Thomas, and Kenneth G. Elzinga, "The Problem of Geographic Market Delineation in Antimerger Suits," *Antitrust Bulletin*, 1973, *28*, 45–81.

Horowitz, Ira, "Market Definition in Antitrust Analysis: A Regression-Based Approach," *Southern Economic Journal*, July 1981, *44*, 1–16.

Leddy, Mark, "Recent Merger Cases Reflect Revolution in Antitrust Policy," *Legal Times*, November 3, 1986, 2.

Posner, Richard A., *Antitrust Law: An Economic Perspective*. Chicago: University of Chicago Press, 1976.

Salop, Steven C., and Lawrence J. White, "Private Antitrust Litigation: An Economic Analysis," *Georgetown Law Journal*, April 1986, *74*, 201–263.

Scherer, F. M., *Industrial Market Structure and Economic Performance*. 2nd ed. Chicago: Rand-McNally, 1980.

Schwartz, Alan, and Louis L. Wilde, "Competitive Equilibria in Markets for Heterogeneous Goods Under Imperfect Information: A Theoretical Analysis with Policy Implications," *Bell Journal of Economics*, Spring 1982, *13*, 181–193.

Stigler, George J., "A Theory of Oligopoly," *Journal of Political Economy*, February 1964, *72*, 55–69.

Stigler, George J., and Robert A. Sherwin, "The Extent of the Market," *Journal of Law and Economics*, October 1985, *28*, 555–585.

Stocking, George W., and Willard F. Mueller, "The Cellophane Case and the New Competition," *American Economic Review*, March 1955, *45*, 29–63.

White, Lawrence, J., Is There a Critical Concentration Ratio?" In Goldfeld, Stephen, and Richard E. Quandt, eds., *Studies in Non-Linear Estimation*. Cambridge, MA: Ballinger, 1976, ch. 5.

Williamson, Oliver E., "Economies as an Antitrust Defense: The Welfare Tradeoffs," *American Economic Review*, March 1968, *58*, 18–36.

ACKNOWLEDGMENTS

Barnett, Stephen R. "The FCC's Nonbattle against Media Monopoly." *Columbia Journalism Review* 11 (1973): 43–50. Reprinted with the permission of the Columbia University Graduate School of Journalism. Courtesy of *Columbia Journalism Review*.

Baumol, William J. and Janusz A. Ordover. "Use of Antitrust to Subvert Competition." *Journal of Law and Economics* 28 (1985): 247–65. Courtesy of Yale University Law Library.

Benson, Bruce L., M.L. Greenhut, and Randall G. Holcome. "Interest Groups and the Antitrust Paradox." *Cato Journal* 6 (1987): 801–17. Reprinted with the permission of the Cato Institute. Courtesy of the Cato Institute.

Coate, Malcolm B. and Fred S. McChesney. "Empirical Evidence on FTC Enforcement of the Merger Guidelines." *Economic Inquiry* 30 (1992): 277–93. Reprinted with the permission of Western Economic Association International. Courtesy of Western Economic Association International.

Demsetz, Harold. "Industry Structure, Market Rivalry, and Public Policy." *Journal of Law and Economics* 16 (1973): 1–9. Reprinted with the permission of the University of Chicago Press. Courtesy of Yale University Law Library.

Eisner, Marc Allen and Kenneth J. Meier. "Presidential Control Versus Bureaucratic Power: Explaining the Reagan Revolution in Antitrust." *American Journal of Political Science* 34 (1990): 269–87. Reprinted from *American Journal of Political Science*, by permission of the authors and the University of Texas Press. Courtesy of the University of Texas Press.

Gallo, Joseph C., Joseph L. Craycraft, and Steven C. Bush. "Guess Who Came to Dinner: An Empirical Study of Federal Antitrust Enforcement for the Period 1963–1984." *Review of Industrial Organization* 2 (1985): 106–30. Courtesy of the author.

Gellhorn, Ernest. "Climbing the Antitrust Staircase." *Antitrust Bulletin* 31 (1986): 341–57. Reprinted with the permission of

Federal Legal Publications, Inc. Courtesy of Yale University Law Library.

Heaton, Jr., George R. "Government Structural Policies and the Automobile Industry." *Policy Studies Review* 2 (1983): 762–81. Reprinted with the permission of Transaction Publishers. Courtesy of Yale University Social Science Library.

Hovenkamp, Herbert. "Antitrust Policy after Chicago." *Michigan Law Review* 84 (1985): 213–84. Reprinted with the permission of the Michigan Law Review Association. Courtesy of the Michigan Law Review Association.

Kovacic, William E. "Failed Expectations: The Troubled Past and Uncertain Future of the Sherman Act as a Tool for Deconcentration." *Iowa Law Review* 74 (1989): 1105–150. Reprinted with the permission of the *Iowa Law Review*. Courtesy of the *Iowa Law Review*.

Kovacic, William E. "*The Antitrust Paradox* Revisited: Robert Bork and the Transformation of Modern Antitrust Policy." *Wayne Law Review* 36 (1990): 1413–71. Reprinted with the permission of the *Wayne Law Review*. Courtesy of Yale University Law Library.

Lean, David F., Jonathan D. Ogur, and Robert P. Rogers. "Does Collusion Pay . . . Does Antitrust Work?" *Southern Economic Journal* 51 (1985): 828–41. Reprinted with the permission of the University of North Carolina at Chapel Hill, Southern Economic Association. Courtesy of Yale University Sterling Memorial Library.

Lewis-Beck, Michael S. "Maintaining Economic Competition: The Causes and Consequences of Antitrust." *Journal of Politics* 41 (1979): 169–91. Reprinted from the *Journal of Politics*, by permission of the author and the University of Texas Press. Courtesy of the University of Texas Press.

Owen, Bruce M. "The Evolution of Clayton Section 7 Enforcement and the Beginnings of U.S. Industrial Policy." *Antitrust Bulletin* 31 (1986): 409–29. Reprinted with the permission of Federal Legal Publications, Inc. Courtesy of Yale University Law Library.

Salop, Steven C. "Symposium on Mergers and Antitrust." *Journal of Economic Perspectives* 1 (1987): 3–12. Reprinted with the permission of the American Economic Association. Courtesy of Yale University Social Science Library.

Shughart II, William F. and Robert D. Tollison. "The Positive Economics of Antitrust Policy: A Survey Article." *International Review of Law and Economics* 5 (1985): 39–57. Reprinted with the permission of Butterworth-Heinemann Ltd. Courtesy of Yale University Law Library.

White, Lawrence J. "Antitrust and Merger Policy: A Review and Critique." *Journal of Economic Perspectives* 1 (1987): 13–22. Reprinted with the permission of the American Economic Association. Courtesy of Yale University Law Library.